MEET THE TEAM BEHIND
THE BEST TEST PREP FOR THE PSAT/NMSQT

The best minds to help you get the best PSAT/NMSQT scores

In this book, you'll find our commitment to excellence, an enthusiasm for the subject matter, and an unrivaled ability to help you master the PSAT/NMSQT. REA's dedication to excellence and our passion for education make this book the very best test prep for the PSAT/NMSQT.

Drew D. Johnson, a graduate of Rice University, has written and contributed to a number of books on test preparation for grades K-12. Formerly a secondary English teacher, he has wide-ranging experience as an educational writer, editor, and consultant.

Brian Higginbotham, a graduate of Trinity University, San Antonio, Texas, has provided extensive educational consulting and instruction for college and graduate test preparation, and various high school subjects. As a remedial reading instructor at Northwest Vista College, San Antonio, he also helped guide students through the fine details of the college application process.

Michael Snow graduated from Rice University with degrees in English, economics, and art history. A former English teacher, Michael has been a freelance educational writer and test-preparation specialist for more than twelve years.

We also gratefully acknowledge the following for their editorial contributions:

Robert A. Bell, Ph.D., Suzanne Coffield, M.A., Anita Price Davis, Ed.D., George DeLuca, J.D., Christopher Dreisbach, Ph.D., Joseph D. Fili, M.A.T., Marilyn B. Gilbert, M.A., Bernice E. Goldberg, Ph.D., Leonard A. Kenner, Gary Lemco, Ph.D., Maxine Morrin, Ph.D., Marcia Mungenast, Sandra B. Newman, M.A., Richard C. Schmidt, Ph.D., and Archibald Sia, Ph.D.

Research & Education Association

The Very Best Coaching & Study Course for

PSAT
NMSQT

Research & Education Association
61 Ethel Road West
Piscataway, New Jersey 08854
E-mail: info@rea.com

**The Very Best Coaching and Study Course
for the PSAT /NMSQT**

Printed in the United States of America

Library of Congress Control Number 2005931759

International Standard Book Number 0-7386-0075-X

REA® is a registered trademark of
Research & Education Association, Inc.

CONTENTS

ABOUT RESEARCH & EDUCATION ASSOCIATION

Founded in 1959, Research & Education Association is dedicated to publishing the finest and most effective educational materials—including software, study guides, and test preps—for students in middle school, high school, college, graduate school, and beyond.

REA's Test Preparation series includes books and software for all academic levels in almost all disciplines. Research & Education Association publishes test preps for students who have not yet completed high school, as well as high school students preparing to enter college. Students from countries around the world seeking to attend college in the United States will find the assistance they need in REA's publications. For college students seeking advanced degrees, REA publishes test preps for many major graduate school admission examinations in a wide variety of disciplines, including engineering, law, and medicine. Students at every level, in every field, with every ambition can find what they are looking for among REA's publications.

REA's practice tests are always based upon the most recently administered exams, and include every type of question that you can expect on the actual exams.

REA's publications and educational materials are highly regarded and continually receive an unprecedented amount of praise from professionals, instructors, librarians, parents, and students. Our authors are as diverse as the fields represented in the books we publish. They are well-known in their respective disciplines and serve on the faculties of prestigious high schools, colleges, and universities throughout the United States and Canada.

Today, REA's wide-ranging catalog is a leading resource for teachers, students, and professionals.

We invite you to visit us at *www.rea.com* to find out how "REA is making the world smarter."

STAFF ACKNOWLEDGMENTS

We would like to thank REA's Larry B. Kling, Vice President, Editorial, for supervising development; Pam Weston, Vice President, Publishing, for setting the quality standards for production integrity and managing the publication to completion; Christine Reilley, Senior Editor, and Diane Goldschmidt, Associate Editor, for editorial quality assurance; Jeremy Rech, Graphic Artist, for interior page design; and Christine Saul, Senior Graphic Artist, for cover design.

We also gratefully acknowledge the team at Publication Services for editing, proofreading, page composition, and post-production file mapping.

PSAT/NMSQT INDEPENDENT STUDY SCHEDULE

The following study schedule allows for thorough preparation for the PSAT/NMSQT. Although it is designed for eight weeks, it can be condensed to about half that long by collapsing two weeks into one. If you are not enrolled in a structured course, be sure to set aside enough time, at least two hours each day, to study. But no matter which study schedule works best for you, the more time you spend studying, the more prepared and relaxed you will feel on the day of the exam.

Week	Activities
1	Read and study Chapter 1, which will introduce you to the PSAT/NMSQT. Take the Diagnostic Test to determine your strengths and weaknesses. Score each section by using the score chart found in Chapter 1. You can then determine the subjects in which you need to strengthen your skills by using the cross-referencing chart provided at the end of the Diagnostic Test.
2	Study the Basic Verbal Skills Review. Be sure to thoroughly work through the Vocabulary Enhancer and complete all the drills. If you have particular trouble with any of the drill questions, go back and study the corresponding section of the review.
3	Study the reviews on Sentence Completion Questions and Critical Reading Questions. Complete all drills using the tips and techniques you have learned.
4	Study the Basic Math Skills Review, and be sure to complete all drill questions. If any particular type of question gives you trouble, review that section again.
5	Study the separate reviews on Regular Math and Student-Produced Response questions. Answer each drill using the methods you have learned in the review.
6	Study the Writing Skills Review in Chapter 9. Be sure to complete all the drills. If you have trouble with a particular type of question, be sure to revisit the corresponding section in the review.
7	Take the Practice Test, and after scoring your exam, review carefully all incorrect answer explanations. If there are any types of questions that are particularly difficult for you, review those subjects by studying again the appropriate section.
8	Review any problem areas and retake Practice Test.

CHAPTER 1

MASTERING THE PSAT/NMSQT

MASTERING THE PSAT/NMSQT

You hold in your hands REA's fully updated test preparation for the PSAT. Inside, our street-smart, PSAT-savvy test experts will equip you with critical insight into the PSAT's content and format.

ABOUT THIS BOOK

All the study and preparation you will need to master the PSAT/NMSQT (Preliminary Scholastic Assessment Test/National Merit Scholarship Qualifying Test) is right here. This book presents in-depth comprehensive reviews designed with the crucial test information, proven strategies, and test information. A full-length diagnostic exam and a full-length practice exam carefully derived from the latest version of the PSAT/NMSQT will hone your test-taking skills and build your understanding of this all-important rehearsal for the SAT. Both exams cover every type of question you can expect to encounter on the PSAT/NMSQT. Following each test are answer keys with thoroughly detailed explanations. All of this is in the name of smarter study to put you in the best possible position to score high!

ABOUT THE TEST

Who Takes the Test and What Is It Used for?

The PSAT/NMSQT is nearly always taken by high school sophomores and juniors for three main reasons:

(1) It is good practice for the SAT.

(2) Taking the PSAT/NMSQT allows you to compete for scholarships offered through the National Merit Scholarship Corporation and other programs. National Merit Scholarships are given to outstanding college-bound students. Qualifying criteria include performance on the PSAT. Top scorers on the PSAT in each state become semifinalists and compete for college scholarships. It goes without saying that scholarships can make your college expenses (and thus your college *life*) much easier to bear.

(3) You also get to participate in the Student Search Service. Nearly 1.5 million students take the PSAT/NMSQT each year. This means there is a great deal of competition for scholarship money and the opportunity to be considered by colleges. The Student Search Service is a program that matches your academic background and interests to appropriate colleges and scholarship services. Once your data is processed, you will receive information from the schools and scholarship services you have chosen.

How Important Are My PSAT/NMSQT Scores?

Always keep in mind that if you don't do well on the PSAT/NMSQT, you can probably take the test again. This is easiest to do if you are a sophomore. The PSAT is not a requirement for entering college, so if you do not score well, it in no way means you will not get into college. A poor score also is not an absolute indicator that you will not do well on the SAT. Colleges you apply to need never know your PSAT scores. And don't let your score on the PSAT change your plans about attending college. Remember, after all, that the PSAT is still a *preliminary* test.

Who Administers the Test?

Educational Testing Service (ETS), which is under contract to the College Board, develops and administers the PSAT/NMSQT. The process involves the assistance of ETS-approved educators throughout the country. Test development is designed and implemented to ensure that the content and difficulty level of the test are appropriate.

When Should the PSAT/NMSQT Be Taken?

You should take the PSAT/NMSQT optimally during your sophomore year of high school. You can also take it in your junior year.

Why Should I Take the PSAT/NMSQT?

Taking the PSAT/NMSQT helps familiarizes you with the types of questions and format of the actual SAT. If you are thinking of attending college, you should take the PSAT/NMSQT because it will give you practice for the SAT, provide an opportunity to obtain scholarships to help pay for college, and give colleges a chance to see your potential for success as a college student.

The test provides you with the opportunity to register for scholarship competition as well as entering you in the Student Search Service. You will also get in some good practice for the SAT.

When and Where Is the Test Given?

The PSAT/NMSQT is administered once a year in October at many locations, including high schools, throughout the United States. A school may choose one of two days on which to administer the test.

To receive information on upcoming administrations of the PSAT/NMSQT, consult the *PSAT/NMSQT Student Bulletin*, which can be obtained from your guidance counselor or by contacting the following:

PSAT/NMSQT Office   *National Merit Scholarship Corp.*
P.O. Box 6720   *1560 Sherman Ave., Suite 200*
Princeton, NJ 08541-6720   *or*   *Evanston, IL 60201-4897*
Telephone: (609) 771-7070   *Telephone: (847) 866-5100*
Website: www.collegeboard.com   *Website: www.nationalmerit.org*

Is there a Registration Fee?

You must pay a PSAT registration fee. Financial assistance is granted in certain situations. Contact your academic advisor for more information on financial assistance.

HOW TO USE THIS BOOK

What Should I Study First?

Remember that the PSAT/NMSQT tests knowledge acquired throughout your education. Taking the sample exams in this book will familiarize you with the types of questions, directions, and format of the actual exam. Our diagnostic and practice exams will also help you establish a good sense of timing for which to pace yourself when practicing each section.

The best place to start is with the subject reviews. Note the suggestions for test-taking, and then take the Diagnostic Test, which will pinpoint your weak areas. Go back and focus on those problem areas. The reviews include information you need to know for the exam. Make sure to follow up your diagnostic work by taking the practice exam, which will expose you to the format and procedures of the actual PSAT/NMSQT.

One final point: Brushing up on areas you did *well* on is a great way to stay on top of a subject and build confidence for test day.

I Started Too Late. What Do I Do Now?

You know that last-minute studying and cramming the night before is not the best way to prepare for the PSAT but for whatever reason, you're just starting now and the test is right around the corner. Maybe you simply forgot . . . maybe you just procrastinate when it comes to these things. This book can *still* help you pass.

You won't master the PSAT this way but you may still get a good enough score. First, take the diagnostic test to pinpoint your strengths and weaknesses. Review the areas where you show weakness. If you have time after this, also review those areas you are strong in. Review the test-taking tips in this chapter and then take a practice exam. Grade yourself and see where you did well and where you did poorly. Review your weak areas again. Then take another practice exam. Repeat if time permits. With skill and effort (and a little luck), this crash course may help. We find this last method to be the least desirable, but we realize that not everyone can give themselves enough time to do it the right way. Of course, if you score poorly, you can always register for the next exam. Just remember to plan and do that one right.

FORMAT OF THE PSAT/NMSQT

Section	Number of Questions	Skills/Areas Covered
Critical Reading	*13 multiple-choice* *35 multiple-choice*	*Sentence Completions* *Critical Reading*
Mathematics	*28 Regular Math multiple-choice* *10 Student-Produced Response*	*Arithmetic* *Algebra* *Geometry*
Writing Skills	*14 multiple-choice* *20 multiple-choice* *5 multiple-choice*	*Identifying Sentence Errors* *Improving Sentences* *Improving Paragraphs*

Total Testing Time: 130 minutes (plus instructions and break period)

All of the questions on the PSAT/NMSQT are in multiple-choice format except for the Student-Produced Response mathematics questions. No answer choices will be provided for these questions. You must enter your answer in a special grid. All of the multiple-choice questions will have five options lettered (A) through (E). Be aware that there is a time limit for each section, so you should keep track of how long you have left in each section. Using the practice exam will help you prepare for this task.

SECTIONS OF THE PSAT/NMSQT

Critical Reading Sections

There are two separate critical reading sections on the PSAT/NMSQT which contain a mix of two different question types: Sentence Completion and Critical Reading.

- Sentence Completion: A sentence is given with one or two words omitted. You choose the word or words that best complete the sentence.

- Critical Reading: There are 5–7 reading passages on the PSAT/NMSQT, including one double passage consisting of two related selections. The questions test your critical reading skills—that is, how well you analyze material rather than simply recall factual information.

Section 1:   7 Sentence Completion questions
(25 minutes)   3–4 reading passages with 18 Critical Reading questions

Section 3:   6 Sentence Completion questions
(25 minutes)   2–3 reading passages with 17 Critical Reading questions

Mathematics Sections

You will encounter three different types of math questions on the PSAT/NMSQT; they will test your arithmetic, algebra, and geometry skills.

- Regular Math: These are questions of the usual multiple-choice format which will ask you to perform basic mathematics.

- Student-Produced Response (Grid-In): These questions require you to solve a problem and enter the solution into a grid, instead of choosing the correct answer from among the provided answer choices.

The 38 math questions may be arranged as follows:

Section 2:   20 Regular Math questions
(25 minutes)

Section 4:   10 Student-Produced Response questions
(25 minutes)   8 Regular Math questions

Writing Skills Section

There are three different types of Writing Skills questions on the PSAT/NMSQT: Identifying Sentence Errors, Improving Sentences, and Improving Paragraphs.

Identifying Sentence Errors: These questions test your ability to find errors of structure and usage in sentences. Several words and phrases in the sentence will be underlined; you must choose the incorrect word or phrase or, if the sentence is correct as is, choose "No error."

Improving Sentences: These questions ask you to revise the part of a sentence that is underlined. The question gives you five choices—answer (A) is the same as the underlined part, which is to say the sentence needs no revision. Choices (B–E) are alternate phrasings of the underlined section. You should choose the phrase that most clearly communicates the original idea of the sentence.

Improving Paragraphs: Some of these questions are essentially the same as the Sentence Improvement questions except that they ask you to ensure that the revised sentence makes sense in the context of the entire passage. Some questions ask you about the structure and meaning of the reading as a whole.

The breakdown of the 39 writing skills questions is as follows:

Section 5:   14 Error Identification questions
(30 minutes)   20 Sentence Improvement questions
                             5 Paragraph Improvement questions

ABOUT THE REVIEW SECTIONS

The reviews in this book not only teach you the skills needed to approach PSAT/NMSQT questions, but also provide strategies for attacking each type of question. We also provide drills to help reinforce what you learn. By using the reviews in conjunction with the practice exams, you will sharpen your test-taking skills for the PSAT/NMSQT.

Verbal Reviews

In the Basic Verbal Skills Review, you will find advice for refining your verbal skills, as well as an extensive vocabulary enhancer containing a list of words commonly found on the PSAT/ NMSQT. There are also separate reviews for both types of critical reading questions: Sentence Completions and Critical Reading. In these reviews, the types of questions you will encounter on the PSAT/NMSQT will be presented, along with step-by-step strategies for answering them.

Mathematics Reviews

The Basic Math Skills Review will help to reinforce the arithmetic, algebra, and geometry concepts you need to know in order to succeed on the PSAT/NMSQT. Included are drills with questions that will help reinforce these skills. Next, you will find separate reviews for Regular Math and Student-Produced Response questions. These reviews will present every possible question type that you will find on the math test, and will also provide step-by-step strategies and tips for solving the problems.

Writing Skills Review

The Writing Skills review will hone your English Language skills. It reviews and drills many grammar points that you will find useful for the writing skills questions on the exam.

SCORING THE PSAT/NMSQT

How Do I Score My Practice Exam?

Critical Reading Sections

Count the number of correct responses in the critical reading sections (Section 1 and Section 3). Next, count up the number of incorrect responses. Enter these numbers into the corresponding blanks on the provided scoring worksheet. Next, multiply the number of incorrect answers by one-fourth (this is the penalty for answering incorrectly). Subtract this product from the total number of correct answers. Fractions should be rounded off: round up for one-half or more and round down for less than one-half. Add the subtotals for Sections 1 and 3 together; this will yield your total number of points for the verbal section.

Mathematics Sections

Count the number of correct responses in the math sections (Section 2 and Section 4). Count up the number of incorrect responses for the regular math questions (Section 2 and Section 4, Nos. 11–18). Enter this number in the worksheet, multiply by one-fourth, and subtract the product from the total number of correct answers in that section. You do not need to count the number of incorrect answers for the Student-Produced questions (Section 4, Nos. 1–10) because there is no penalty for incorrect answers to this question type. Once again, fractions should be rounded off. Add all of the subtotals together to yield the total of mathematics points.

Writing Skills Section

Count the number of correct responses in the writing section. Next, count the number of incorrect responses. Enter these numbers into the corresponding blanks on the provided scoring worksheet. Then multiply the number of incorrect answers by one fourth and subtract this product from the total number of correct answers. If the number is a fraction, round it off—this is your number of points for the writing section.

SCORING WORKSHEET

How Do I Calculate My Scaled Score?

Scores on the PSAT/NMSQT range from 20 to 80. Take the total number of points for each section, your Raw Score, and check the following chart for its corresponding Scaled Score. To convert your PSAT/NMSQT score to an SAT score, just add a zero to the end of your score.

This will give you a general idea of where your score would fall in terms of the SAT scores. Remember, the questions on the PSAT/NMSQT are taken from a pool of SAT questions, but the more difficult questions are excluded from the PSAT/NMSQT. Therefore, your estimated SAT score is not completely accurate. If your performance is not as good as you had expected, don't worry. With each practice exam you are building skills to do well on the PSAT/NMSQT and the SAT. (See the Conversion Table for Total Scores on page 13.)

Verbal Sections

Section 1   _____ – 1/4 (_____) = _____
correct   incorrect   subtotal

+

Section 3   _____ – 1/4 (_____) = _____
correct   incorrect   subtotal

Total Verbal Raw Score   _____
(add Sections 2, 5, and 7)   total

Mathematics Sections

Section 2   _____ – 1/4 (_____) = _____
correct   incorrect   subtotal

+

Section 4   _____ – 1/4 (_____) = _____
Regular Math   correct   incorrect   subtotal

+

Section 4   _____ – 1/4 (_____) = _____
Grid-ins   correct   incorrect   subtotal

Total Mathematics Raw Score   _____
total

Writing Skills Section

Section 5   _____ – 1/4 (_____) = _____
correct   incorrect   total

STUDYING FOR THE PSAT/NMSQT

It is critical for you to choose the time and place for studying that work best for you. Some students may set aside a certain number of hours every morning to study, while others may choose to study at night before going to sleep. Other students may study during the day, on the bus, waiting on a line, or even while eating lunch. Only you can determine when and where your study time will be most effective. But be consistent and use your time wisely. Work out a study routine and stick to it!

When you take the practice exams, try to make your testing conditions as much like the actual test as possible. Turn your television and radio off. Sit down at a quiet table that is free from noises and distractions. And time yourself.

After completing the practice exam, score your test and thoroughly review the answer explanations for questions you answered incorrectly. Do not review too much at any one time. Concentrate on one problem area at a time by reviewing the questions and explanations, and by studying our review until you are confident you completely understand the material.

Keep track of your scores and mark them on the Scoring Worksheet. By doing so, you will be able to gauge your progress and discover any outstanding weaknesses in particular sections. You should carefully study the reviews in your areas of difficulty.

PSAT/NMSQT TEST-TAKING TIPS

Although you may be unfamiliar with standardized tests such as the PSAT/NMSQT, there are many ways to acquaint yourself with this type of examination. Remember, familiarization by itself is a great way to alleviate test-taking anxieties. Here are some ways to help you become accustomed to the PSAT/NMSQT:

Become comfortable with the overall format and flow of the PSAT/NMSQT. When you are practicing to take the PSAT/NMSQT, simulate the conditions under which you will be taking the actual test. Stay calm and pace yourself. After simulating the test only a couple of times, you will boost your chances of doing well, and you will be able to sit down for the actual PSAT/NMSQT much more confidently.

Know the directions and format for each section of the test. Familiarizing yourself with the directions and format of the different test sections will not only save you time, but will also ensure that you are familiar enough with the PSAT/NMSQT to avoid nervousness (and the mistakes caused by being nervous).

Work on easier questions first. If you find yourself working too long on one question, make a mark next to it in your test booklet and continue. After you have answered all of the questions that you can, go back to the ones you have skipped.

If you are unsure of an answer, *guess*. But if you do guess, guess wisely. Use the process of elimination by going through each answer to a question and eliminating as many of the answer choices as possible. By eliminating three answer choices, you give yourself a fifty-fifty chance of getting the item correct since there will only be two choices left from which to make your guess.

Be sure that you are making your answer in the oval that corresponds to the number of the question in the test booklet. Since your test is graded by machine, marking one answer in the wrong space will throw off the rest of your test. Do your scratch work in the test booklet only.

Read all of the possible answers. Just because you think you have found the correct response, do not automatically assume that it is the best answer. You should read through each choice before marking your answer on the sheet to be sure that you are not making a mistake by jumping to conclusions.

You don't have to answer every question. You are not penalized if you do not answer every question. The only penalty you receive is if you answer a question incorrectly. Try to use the guessing strategy, but if you are truly stumped by a question, do not answer it.

Work quickly and steadily. You will have only twenty-five minutes to work on each verbal and math section and only thirty minutes for the writing skills questions, so you will need to work as quickly as possible and work steadily to avoid focusing on one problem too long. Taking the practice exams in this book will help you to budget your precious time.

THE DAY OF THE TEST

Before the Test

On the day of the test, you should wake up early (it is hoped after a decent night's rest) and have a good breakfast. Make sure to dress comfortably so that you are not distracted by being too hot or too cold while taking the test. Also, plan to arrive at the test center early. This will allow you to collect your thoughts and relax before the test, and will also spare you the anguish that comes with being late. If you arrive after the test begins, you will not be admitted, and will not receive a refund.

If you would like, you may wear a watch to the test center, but do not wear one that makes noise; this may disturb other test-takers. You are also permitted to use a calculator on the test. You can use any programmable or non-programmable four-function, scientific, or graphing calculator. No pocket organizers, hand-held or laptop computers, paper tape, or noisy (or "talking") calculators may be used. In addition, no calculator requiring an external power source will be allowed. Finally, no sharing of calculators will be permitted; you must bring your own. Consult the official registration bulletin for details.

YOUR TEST DAY CHECKLIST:

✓ Get a good night's sleep. Tired test takers consistently perform poorly.

✓ Wake up early.

✓ Dress comfortably. Keep your clothing temperature appropriate. You'll be sitting in your test clothes for hours. Clothes that are itchy, tight, too warm, or too cold take away from your comfort level.

✓ Eat a good breakfast.

✓ Take these items with you to the test center:

- Several sharpened No. 2 pencils. Pencils are not provided at the test center.

- Admission ticket

- A valid photo ID which contains your name and signature. Good examples of these are a driver's license, student ID card or a current alien registration card.

✓ Arrive at your test center early. Remember, no one is allowed into a test session after the test has begun.

✓ Compose your thoughts and try to relax before the test.

During the Test

When you arrive at the test center, try to find a seat where you feel you will be comfortable. Once you enter the test center, follow all of the rules and instructions given by the test supervisor. If you do not, you risk being dismissed from the test and having your scores canceled.

When all of the test materials have been passed out, the test instructor will give you directions for filling out your answer sheet. You must fill this sheet out carefully since this information will be printed on your score report.

Remember that you can write in your test booklet, as no scratch paper will be provided. Mark your answers in the appropriate spaces on the answer sheet. Each numbered row will contain five ovals corresponding to each answer choice for that question. Fill in the oval that corresponds to your answer darkly, completely, and neatly. You can change your answer, but remember to completely erase your old one. Only one answer should be marked; accurate scoring is riding on this, as your answer sheet will be machine-scored—stray lines or extraneous marks may cause the machine to score your answer incorrectly. When you have finished working on a section, you may wish to go back and check your answers.

After the Test

When you have completed the PSAT/NMSQT, you may hand in your test materials and leave. Then, go home and relax!

When Will I Receive My Score Report and What Will It Look Like?

You may not receive your score for several weeks because your school gets them first to allow for compilation of data about students' performances. Aside from your school, you and the National Merit Scholarship Corporation (co-sponsors of the test) are the only other people to see your score, unless you sign up for entrance into the scholarship competitions. You can do this simply by indicating on your PSAT/NMSQT answer form that you would like to be entered into the competition and by answering a few additional questions.

When you do receive your scores, a test book and a PSAT/NMSQT score report will be included. This is so you can review the questions you answered incorrectly and figure out why you chose the wrong answer. Included on the PSAT/NMSQT score report are:

- your scores for the verbal, math, and writing skills sections
- a percentile of where your score falls in relation to others taking the PSAT/NMSQT
- the answers you gave on the exam
- the correct answers to the exam
- the difficulty level of each question on the exam
- a summary of your performance on the varying levels of question difficulty
- information about your grade average and future plans
- recommendations for high school courses in your field of interest
- typical courses in your indicated college major
- alternative majors to consider
- careers associated with your indicated major
- skills associated with doing well in the major
- an estimated SAT score
- selection index number
- eligibility for NMSC programs

From among those candidates who choose to participate in the scholarship programs, the top-scoring students are assigned a selection index number. This number is then used, along with other information, to screen out potential scholarship recipients. To determine the selection index number, add together your verbal, math, and writing skills scores. The pool of eligible students is reduced to about 14,000 individuals who compete for 6,500 monetary awards. These awards may be given out by colleges, corporations, or the government. Students must individually pursue the scholarships sponsored by corporations and colleges, but all finalists are automatically enrolled for the National Merit Scholarship competition. Special scholarships are also available for minority students. For more information about these scholarships, see your advisor.

The Student Selection Service provides information to colleges about PSAT/NMSQT test takers and gives the schools a first look at potential students. Colleges can enroll in this service and receive information about students, especially those who express an interest in a certain school.

CONVERSION TABLE FOR TOTAL SCORES

Verbal

P	S	P	S	P	S	P	S
52	80	39	68	26	56	13	44
51	80	38	67	25	55	12	43
50	79	37	66	24	54	11	42
49	78	36	65	23	53	10	41
48	77	35	64	22	53	9	40
47	76	34	64	21	52	8	38
46	75	33	63	20	51	7	36
45	74	32	62	19	50	6	34
44	73	31	61	18	49	5	33
43	72	30	60	17	48	4	32
42	71	29	59	16	47	3	31
41	70	28	58	15	46	2	30
40	68	27	57	14	45	1	29

Mathematics

P	S	P	S	P	S	P	S
40	80	30	66	20	54	10	42
39	80	29	65	19	53	9	41
38	79	28	64	18	52	8	40
37	77	27	62	17	51	7	38
36	75	26	60	16	50	6	37
35	73	25	59	15	48	5	36
34	71	24	58	14	47	4	35
33	70	23	57	13	46	3	34
32	68	22	56	12	45	2	33
31	67	21	55	11	44	1	32

Writing skills

P	S	P	S	P	S	P	S
39	80	29	67	19	55	9	45
38	79	28	66	18	54	8	44
37	78	27	64	17	53	7	43
36	77	26	63	16	52	6	42
35	76	25	62	15	50	5	40
34	75	24	61	14	49	4	39
33	73	23	60	13	48	3	38
32	71	22	58	12	48	2	37
31	70	21	57	11	47	1	36
30	68	20	56	10	46		

CHAPTER 2

A DIAGNOSTIC TEST

CHAPTER 2

A DIAGNOSTIC TEST

Now that you have some background information concerning the PSAT/NMSQT, you are ready to take the diagnostic test. This test is designed to help you identify where your strengths and weaknesses lie. You will want to use this information to help you study for the PSAT/NMSQT. It is a complete test, so take this diagnostic test in the same way you would take the actual PSAT/NMSQT. Situate yourself in a quiet room so that there will be no interruptions and keep track of the time allotted for each section. When you are finished with the test, refer to the charts that follow to evaluate your performance. The entries in the chart refer to the questions you answered incorrectly and where to look in the book for a discussion of material covered in that type of problem.

SECTION 1

TIME: 25 Minutes
24 Questions

For each question in this section, select the best answer from among the given choices and fill in the corresponding oval on the answer sheet.

DIRECTIONS: Each sentence below has one or two blanks, each blank indicating that something has been omitted. Beneath the sentence are five lettered words or sets of words. Choose the word or set of words that BEST fits the meaning of the sentence as a whole.

EXAMPLE

Although the critics found the book _____, many of the readers found it rather _____.

(A) obnoxious . . . perfect   (D) comical . . . persuasive

(B) spectacular . . . interesting   (E) popular . . . rare

(C) boring . . . intriguing   Ⓐ Ⓑ ● Ⓓ Ⓔ

1. The teacher told the class to pay close attention to the lecture because it was _____ , and they would be tested on the information it contained.

   (A) significant   (D) expedited
   (B) unseemly   (E) superfluous
   (C) highlighted

2. Max Planck, a physicist, discovered a constant by which to measure the amount of energy _____ by light particles.

   (A) extracted   (D) collapsing
   (B) implanted   (E) aligned
   (C) radiated

3. Many religions use _____ as an expression of faith and _____ .

   (A) prayer . . . blasphemy
   (B) atonement . . . heresy
   (C) animism . . . monotheism
   (D) belief . . . asceticism
   (E) fasting . . . discipline

4. The _____ attitude of the administrator was worsened by her _____ questions.

   (A) contemptuous . . . compassionate
   (B) condescending . . . superficial
   (C) punitive . . . fascinating
   (D) refreshing . . . haranguing
   (E) culpable . . . humbling

5. Although the diplomat was a wily negotiator, she had difficulty convincing people of that because of her _____ manner of relating to them.

   (A) devious   (D) mutinous
   (B) Machiavellian (E) titular
   (C) ingenuous

6. When the company is ready to hold interviews for new employees, the personnel office _____ hiring notices to the local newspapers.

   (A) terminates   (D) directs
   (B) seeks   (E) decreases
   (C) overlooks

7. Tile manufacturers need high-quality clay; this is why brickyards are invariably located in places where high-quality clay is _____ and can be readily _____ .

   (A) present . . . verified
   (B) evident . . . procured
   (C) nearby . . . obtained
   (D) abundant . . . accessed
   (E) visible . . . utilized

DIRECTIONS: Read each passage and answer the questions that follow. Each question will be based on the information stated or implied in the passage or its introduction.

Questions 8–12 are based on the following passage.

The following passage discusses the development and early study of Roman archaeology.

1   The emergence of archaeology as a subject worthy in its own right was to come . . . in the late seventeenth and eighteenth centuries. The origins of modern archaeology are . . .
5   to be seen in [the] shift away from . . . texts alone to the physical remains as well. Mercati in the sixteenth century was the first to write a treatise on what we would regard today as archaeology. At the same time, academic
10   societies were being founded to promote the investigation of natural phenomena, including archaeology. The next stage in the emergence of Roman archaeology was the development of an aesthetic appreciation of ancient art and
15   architecture. Artists such as Palladio, Piranesi, and Winkelmann drew and recorded surviving buildings and sculptures. Out of Palladio's architectural work came much of the inspiration for the neoclassical revival of the eighteenth
20   century. Winkelmann is best known as an art historian, whose judgments on ancient art were to color opinions about the Greeks and Romans for most of the neoclassical period. He maintained that Roman art was inferior to
25   Greek as it slavishly copied the Greek originals. . . . This may be true up to a point, but at the time it prejudiced many people against Roman art, and Roman archaeology became less popular as a result. Excavations of ancient
30   sites started in the eighteenth century with the ransacking of Herculaneum and Pompeii for statues and other works of art. At the same time, expeditions were being organized by such groups as the Society of Dilettanti for the
35   purpose of carrying off sculpture and ancient

art objects for private and public collections in northern Europe. Museums such as the British Museum were founded and soon filled to bursting with material of all kinds, including Roman finds. The accumulation of artifacts, 40 and the increasingly enthusiastic appreciation of the ancient world by the leisured classes, led to a more rigorous historical approach on the part of scholars, exemplified by Edward Gibbon's *Decline and Fall of the Roman Em-* 45 *pire* (1788). More scientific excavations started with the planned program of King Murat to uncover all of Pompeii in the 1810s, which he decided to do not only to recover works of art, but also to discover the ancient town plan. 50 Upstanding monuments elsewhere started to be conserved and treasured as part of Europe's heritage.

After the early years of the nineteenth century, public interest in the ancient world 55 changed. No longer were the Greeks and Romans used as the inspiration of contemporary writings, architecture, and art, for fashions were changing from the neoclassical to the romantic and the Gothic revival. Roman history 60 and archaeology became a more academic discipline, with such great scholars as Theodor Mommsen laying the foundations of the modern study of the subject. The archaeological contribution to Roman history began to realize 65 its true potential, especially in the provinces outside Italy, where large-scale excavations at the end of the nineteenth century led to a much clearer understanding of the great differences between the various regions of the Empire. A 70 good example is the complete excavation of the Roman town of Calleva (Silchester, Hampshire, England) by the Society of Antiquaries.

2 1 1 1 1 1 1 1 1 1 1

8. The original inspiration to excavate Pompeii arose from

(A) a spirit of piracy and looting.

(B) the admiration for Palladio's work.

(C) the influence of Winkelmann on a generation of scholars.

(D) Gibbon's work on the history of Rome.

(E) the neoclassical concern with methods of preservation.

9. The author treats Winkelmann as an art historian

(A) whose authority still resists criticism or question.

(B) who single-handedly altered tastes toward the Gothic.

(C) whose prejudices tended to devalue the Roman contributions.

(D) responsible for the Society of Dilettanti.

(E) directly influential on the work of Theodor Mommsen.

10. The "more rigorous historical approach" (line 43) of scholars was brought about

(A) in the middle of the nineteenth century.

(B) by the excavations at Calleva.

(C) by the definitive work by Mercati.

(D) partly by the influence of collectors, such as the British Museum.

(E) by the repeated efforts of King Murat.

11. The author indicates that archaeology can provide

(A) few clues as to the sources of ancient civilizations.

(B) no real relationship between the Roman and Greek cultures.

(C) little insight beyond which Winkelmann has already given us.

(D) an explanation for the disasters at Pompeii and Herculaneum.

(E) a distinct cultural character in a national and a regional sense.

12. The author interprets King Murat's efforts at Pompeii

(A) as part of a continued line of plundering ancient sites.

(B) in the tradition of personal aggrandizement and greed.

(C) as expanding the role of archaeology in European life.

(D) as limiting the involvement of science to mere theory.

(E) as an expression of resistance to Gibbons' theories.

20 *PSAT/NMSQT*

Questions 13–16 are based on the following passage.

This passage discusses the rise of the study of humanities and the classics in Italy and those responsible for its development.

1   The Italian cultivation of classical literature had attained its highest point, and was already verging toward decline. More than a century had passed since Petrarch had kindled
5   the first enthusiasm. It requires some effort of the imagination for us to realise what that movement meant. The men of the fourteenth century lived under a Church that claimed the surrender of the reason, not only in matters of
10   faith, but in all knowledge: philosophy and science could speak only by the doctors whom she sanctioned. When the fourteenth century began to study the classics, the first feeling was one of joy in the newly revealed dignity
15   of the human mind; it was a strange and delightful thing, as they gradually came to know the great writers of ancient Greece and Rome, to see the reason moving freely, exploring, speculating, discussing, without restraint. And
20   then those children of the Middle Age were surprised and charmed by the forms of classical expression,—so different from anything that had been familiar to them. Borrowing an old Latin word, they called this new learning
25   *humanity*; for them, however, the phrase had a depth of meaning undreamt of by Cicero. Now, for the first time, they felt that they had entered into full possession of themselves; nothing is more characteristic of the Italian
30   renaissance than the self-asserting individuality of the chief actors; each strives to throw the work of his own spirit into relief; the common life falls into the background; the history of that age is the history of men rather than of
35   communities.

13. In line 1, the word "cultivation" most nearly means

  (A) growth.   (D) study.
  (B) refinement. (E) enrichment.
  (C) support.

14. In the sentence "philosophy and science could speak . . . sanctioned" (lines 10–12), the author stresses the Church's

  (A) commitment to education.
  (B) absolute control of thought.
  (C) growing sensitivity to new ideas.
  (D) dependence upon Greek thought.
  (E) freedom from political influence.

15. When the author states that "nothing is more characteristic . . . chief actors" (lines 29–31), he implies that

  (A) self-assertion is a sign of progress.
  (B) the Middle Ages valued self-assertion.
  (C) the Renaissance developed a clear sense of community.
  (D) the Middle Ages valued community over the individual.
  (E) the Church supported the growth of self-assertion.

16. In the sentence "each strives to throw" (lines 31–32), the author creates an analogy to

  (A) sculpture.   (D) film.
  (B) painting.   (E) music.
  (C) architecture.

Questions 17–24 are based on the following passage.

The following passage addresses individual rights and the justification for government to abridge those rights.

1   Although democratic nations are founded on the principle of individual liberties and rights, there clearly must be a balance between the scope of individual freedom and the needs
5   of government. Theoretically, individual rights must be curtailed where their exercise constitutes a threat to the very preservation of the nation or of the states and local communities within it. Whether a nation, a state, or a local-
10 ity, the community at large does have a public interest that it can and should pursue with diligence. In the broadest sense, the decisions made by legislative majorities reflect community interests, although such interests are also
15 represented by the executive and the judiciary. Only at the federal level is the judiciary independent of direct political control, under the system of separation of powers and checks and balances. At the state and local levels, judges
20 are still mostly elected, making them directly accountable to the people. An elected judiciary is less likely to stand apart from the political process in making its decisions on the scope of individual liberties and rights. Such rights
25 therefore are more likely to be limited if there is a public clamor for their restriction (as, for example, where the elected officials of localities respond to local public opinion by demanding controls over "obscene" magazines, movies,
30 and books). While there may be political excesses that threaten to limit civil liberties and rights, there are also legitimate governmental needs that may call for a modification of individual freedoms. This occurs when these civil
35 freedoms are used, or misused, to attack the very foundations of the system itself. This problem becomes most acute during times of war or civil unrest. During such times the Supreme Court has given the government wide powers to
40 curb individual freedom. Perhaps the most extraordinary abridgment of the rights of citizens occurred in 1941, when a Japanese attack was considered by large numbers of people within and outside the government, including military
45 leaders, to be an imminent possibility on the West Coast. An even more likely probability considered was sabotage and subversion by Japanese infiltrators. These fears eventually led to the establishment of concentration camps for
50 Japanese-Americans, largely based upon an executive order by President Roosevelt, a decision that was upheld by the Supreme Court, against constitutional challenges in *Korematsu v. United States* in 1944. Writing for the majority of
55 the Court, Justice Hugo Black said that during wartime, military necessity justified the order, which excluded Japanese-Americans from the West Coast. Did the exclusionary order constitute racial discrimination? No. The Court said
60 that although only the Japanese-Americans were excluded, the reason was not of race but of military necessity. *Korematsu* was an extreme case, but it illustrates the degree to which civil rights have been denied on the basis of the
65 public interest.

In drawing the line between public interest and individual freedom, the Supreme Court has relied upon the "balancing test," which attempts to weigh the needs of government against the
70 rights of individuals to determine the proper balance between permissible government restraints and individual freedom. One of the most important spheres of civil liberties, where the balancing test has been applied, regards the
75 civil liberties and rights enumerated in the First Amendment, particularly the liberties of speech, press, and the right of assembly. In addition to the balancing test, the "clear and present danger" test is used in determining the permissible scope
80 of political speech, press, and assembly. In this political sphere the clear and present danger test is used to judge the extent to which Congress or the state legislatures may regulate and control the expression of political ideas.
85

From Peter Woll and Robert H. Binstock, America's Political System, 4th edition. Reprinted by permission of McGraw-Hill, Inc. ©1991.

17. Based on the passage, with which of the following statements would the authors be most likely to agree?

    (A) Individual rights are superior to governmental needs.

    (B) Governmental needs are superior to individual rights.

    (C) A balance must be struck between individual rights and governmental needs.

    (D) Political excesses can never limit civil liberties.

    (E) The balance of individual rights and governmental needs is irrelevant to democracy.

18. Based on the passage, we can reasonably infer which of the following?

    (A) Local judges are mostly elected.

    (B) Federal judges are mostly elected.

    (C) State judges are not accountable to the people.

    (D) Federal judges are not elected.

    (E) State judges are not elected.

19. According to the authors, which of the following are in a better position to protect individual liberties?

    (A) Members of Congress

    (B) Federal judges

    (C) State judges

    (D) The President

    (E) The Supreme Court

20. Based on the passage, what type of governmental needs can justify limitations on individual liberties?

    (A) Any type of governmental needs

    (B) Those needs that restrict civil rights

    (C) Those that threaten the nation

    (D) No governmental need justifies limitations on individual liberties.

    (E) Those that threaten individuals of other nations

21. According to the authors, what was the justification for the abridgment of rights in *Korematsu*?

    (A) Fear of Japanese invasion

    (B) Racial discrimination

    (C) Public opinion

    (D) Electoral pressures

    (E) Legal precedent

22. Based on the passage, the establishment of concentration camps for Japanese-Americans was found to be which of the following?

    (A) Justified   (D) Unnecessary

    (B) Illegal   (E) Unjustified

    (C) Unconstitutional

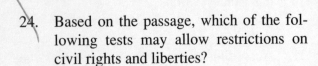

23. Which of the following liberties is not specifically mentioned in the passage as a First Amendment liberty?

(A) Speech
(B) Press
(C) Religion
(D) Assembly
(E) Right to bear arms

24. Based on the passage, which of the following tests may allow restrictions on civil rights and liberties?

   I. Balancing test
  II. Rational basis test
 III. Clear and present danger test

(A) I and II
(B) I and III
(C) II and III
(D) I, II, and III
(E) None of the Above

SECTION 2

TIME: 25 Minutes
20 Questions

"I'm working this section in red pen and at night its 3:30am Friday I should finish this up "God is real" sleep deprived 15 year old Boy

:P

<u>**DIRECTIONS**</u>: **Solve each problem, using any available space on the page for scratch work. Then decide which answer choice is the best and fill in the corresponding oval on the answer sheet.**

NOTES

The extra comments are for fun I wrote them in while working on it

(1) The use of a calculator is permitted. All numbers used are real numbers.

(2) Figures that accompany problems in this test are intended to provide information useful in solving the problems. They are drawn as accurately as possible EXCEPT when it is stated in a specific problem that the figure is not drawn to scale. All figures lie in a plane unless otherwise indicated.

REFERENCE INFORMATION

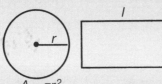

My Score test.

$A = \pi r^2$
$C = 2\pi r$

$A = lw$

$A = \frac{1}{2}bh$

$V = lwh$

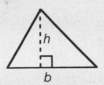
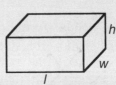

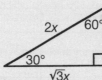

$V = \pi r^2 h$

$c^2 = a^2 + b^2$

Special Right Triangles

Interesting Fact! This Section was originally skipped due to me not feeling like doing any math.

The number of degrees of arc in a circle is 360.
The measure in degrees of a straight angle is 180.
The sum of the measures in degrees of the angles of a triangle is 180.

1. A solid block 1' × 2' × 3' weighs 6 kg. What is the weight (in kg) of a solid block of the same material 4' × 5' × 6'?

   (A) 36 kg   (D) 90 kg
   (B) 120 kg   (E) 720 kg
   (C) 20 kg

   Not sure

2. The first of <u>five</u> morning classes begins at 8 a.m. The last class ends at 11:40 a.m. Allowing 5 minutes between classes, how many minutes are there in each class period?

   (A) 40   (D) 55
   (B) 45   (E) 60
   (C) 50

   not sure

3. How many one-cm cubes can be put in a box 10 cm wide, 10 cm long, and 10 cm deep?

   (A) 30   (D) 10,000
   (B) 100   (E) 100,000
   (C) 1,000

   sure

4. A group of girl scouts forms a solid square with g girl scouts on a side. If 72 girl scouts are released, the remaining girl scouts form a square with $(g-2)$ girl scouts on a side. What is the value of g?

   (A) 15   (D) 30
   (B) 19   (E) 36
   (C) 24

   not sure

5. How many 10-gallon cans of milk will be needed to fill 160 pint containers?

   (A) 1   (D) 16
   (B) 2   (E) 20
   (C) 3

   Not sure

6. The area of a circle is 298. What is the diameter of the circle? (Use $\pi = \frac{22}{7}$.)

   (A) 3.14   (D) 25
   (B) 7   (E) 49
   (C) 19.47

7. If $x + y = \frac{1}{k}$ and $x - y = k$, what is the value of $x^2 - y^2$?

   (A) 4   (D) k^2
   (B) 1   (E) $\frac{1}{k^2}$
   (C) 0

   Not sure

8. If $3^{a-b} = \frac{1}{9}$ and $3^{a+b} = 9$, then $a =$

   (A) −2.   (D) 2.
   (B) 0.   (E) 3.
   (C) 1.

   not sure

9. If $2X + Y = 2$ and $X + 3Y > 6$, then

   (A) $Y \geq 2.$ (D) $Y < 2.$
   (B) $Y > 2.$ (E) $Y = 2.$
   (C) $Y < 2.$

   Not Sure

10. A man paid $3,500 for a used car. At the end of five years he was given $500 for it toward the purchase of a new car. What was the average yearly amount of depreciation?

    (A) $250   (D) $650
    (B) $500   (E) $3,000
    (C) $600

    Sure

11. $\overline{KL}$ is parallel to $\overline{MN}$. $\overline{OPQR}$ is a straight line. If $\angle KPO$ is 4 times $\angle MQR$, what is the measure of $\angle RQN$?

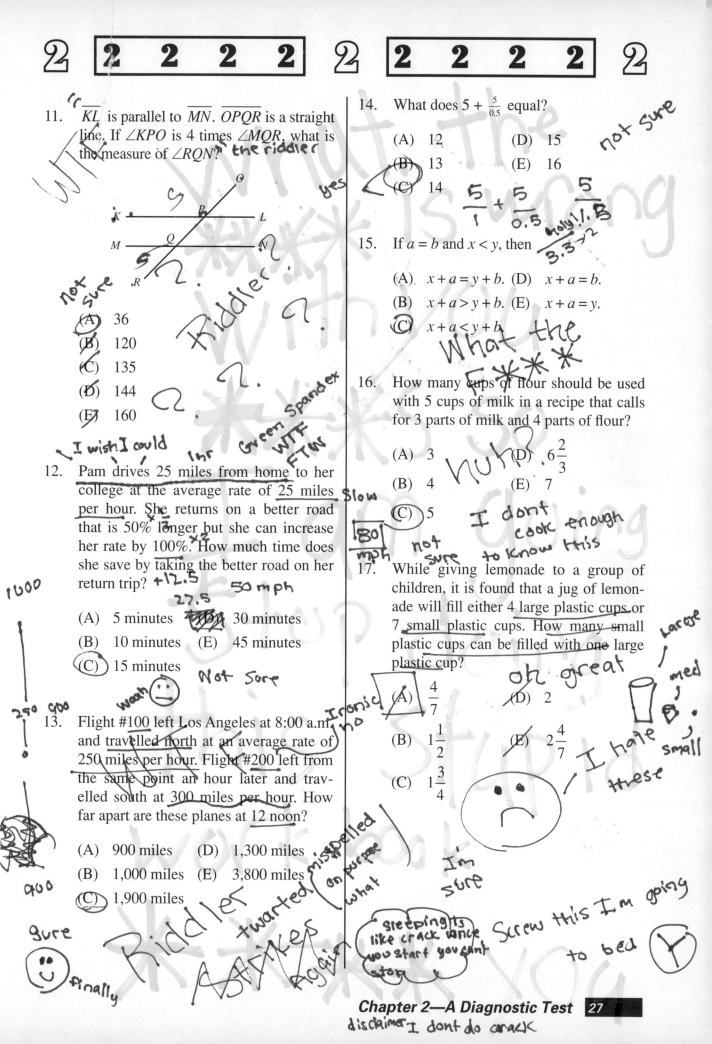

(A) 36
(B) 120
(C) 135
(D) 144
(E) 160

12. Pam drives 25 miles from home to her college at the average rate of 25 miles per hour. She returns on a better road that is 50% longer but she can increase her rate by 100%. How much time does she save by taking the better road on her return trip?

(A) 5 minutes (D) 30 minutes
(B) 10 minutes (E) 45 minutes
(C) 15 minutes

13. Flight #100 left Los Angeles at 8:00 a.m. and travelled north at an average rate of 250 miles per hour. Flight #200 left from the same point an hour later and travelled south at 300 miles per hour. How far apart are these planes at 12 noon?

(A) 900 miles (D) 1,300 miles
(B) 1,000 miles (E) 3,800 miles
(C) 1,900 miles

14. What does $5 + \frac{5}{0.5}$ equal?

(A) 12 (D) 15
(B) 13 (E) 16
(C) 14

15. If $a = b$ and $x < y$, then

(A) $x + a = y + b.$ (D) $x + a = b.$
(B) $x + a > y + b.$ (E) $x + a = y.$
(C) $x + a < y + b.$

16. How many cups of flour should be used with 5 cups of milk in a recipe that calls for 3 parts of milk and 4 parts of flour?

(A) 3 (D) $6\frac{2}{3}$
(B) 4 (E) 7
(C) 5

17. While giving lemonade to a group of children, it is found that a jug of lemonade will fill either 4 large plastic cups or 7 small plastic cups. How many small plastic cups can be filled with one large plastic cup?

(A) $\frac{4}{7}$ (D) 2
(B) $1\frac{1}{2}$ (E) $2\frac{4}{7}$
(C) $1\frac{3}{4}$

18. During what period did the sharpest increase in profits occur?

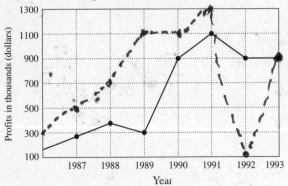

(A) 1987–1988

(B) 1988–1989

(C) 1989–1990

(D) 1990–1991

(E) 1992–1993

really

Sure I thought it was supposed to get harder as we work along

19. Four associates own a business establishment in the ratio of 8:5:3:1. Approximately what part of the total business does the person with the smallest interest control?

(A) 2%   (D) 29%

(B) 6%   (E) 47%

(C) 8%

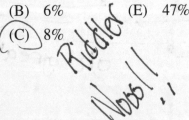

Not sure

20. A prime number is an integer greater than 1 that is evenly divisible only by itself and 1. Which of the following represents a prime number when $n = 4$?

(A) $n^2 + 2 = 18$ (D) $5n$ 20

(B) $n^2 + 2n$ 24   (E) $n^2 - 4$ 12

(C) $3n + 1$ 13

Sure

SECTION 3

TIME: 25 Minutes
24 Questions

For each question in this section, select the best answer from among the given choices and fill in the corresponding oval on the answer sheet.

DIRECTIONS: Each sentence below has one or two blanks, each blank indicating that something has been omitted. Beneath the sentence are five lettered words or sets of words. Choose the word or set of words that BEST fits the meaning of the sentence as a whole.

EXAMPLE

Although the critics found the book _____, many of the readers found it rather _____.

(A) obnoxious . . . perfect

(B) spectacular . . . interesting

(C) boring . . . intriguing

(D) comical . . . persuasive

(E) popular . . . rare

Ⓐ Ⓑ ● Ⓓ Ⓔ

1. It was difficult to approach the author and congratulate him because his attitude was so _____ .

   (A) gaudy   (D) retaliatory
   (B) swaggering (E) indirect
   (C) courteous

2. Herodotus and Thucydides were both ancient Greek _____ , but their styles of recording and analyzing events differed greatly.

   (A) dramatists   (D) scientists
   (B) historians   (E) politicians
   (C) psychoanalysts

3. Everyone has had the experience of hearing a line of reasoning that sounds _____, but that one still wants to _____ .

   (A) logical . . . dispute
   (B) topical . . . believe
   (C) recent . . . fabricate
   (D) murky . . . classify
   (E) rational . . . apprehend

4. The class was _____ with the mathematical theorems, but had not yet been taught how to _____ the proofs.

   (A) ecstatic . . . right
   (B) enlightened . . . discount
   (C) cautious . . . dismiss
   (D) familiar . . . demonstrate
   (E) satisfied . . . circumvent

5. When the class went to the zoo on a trip, they learned that cats are more _____ related to lions than dogs are to each other.

   (A) intrinsically
   (B) intimidatingly
   (C) intimately
   (D) imminently
   (E) immanently

6. The theory of evolution, among other things, _____ that human beings are descended from a line of animals that originally belonged to the biological classification of apes.

   (A) teaches   (D) hovers
   (B) believes   (E) ponders
   (C) posits

DIRECTIONS: Read the passage and answer the questions that follow. Each question will be based on the information stated or implied in the passage or its introduction.

Questions 7–10 are based on the following passage.

In the following passage, written in 1849, Henry David Thoreau discusses his philosophy of government.

1 I heartily accept the motto,—"That government is best which governs least"; and I should like to see it acted up to more rapidly and systematically. Carried out, it finally amounts to
5 this, which also I believe,—"That government is best which governs not at all"; and when men are prepared for it, that will be the kind of government which they will have. Government is at best but an expedient; but most governments
10 are usually, and all governments are sometimes, inexpedient. The objections which have been brought against a standing army, and they are many and weighty, and deserve to prevail, may also at last be brought against a standing
15 government. The government itself, which is only the mode which the people have chosen to execute their will, is equally liable to be abused and perverted before the people can act through it. Witness the present Mexican war, the work
20 of comparatively a few individuals using the standing government as their tool; for, in the outset, the people would not have consented to this measure.

This American government,—what is it
25 but a tradition, though a recent one, endeavoring to transmit itself unimpaired to posterity, but each instant losing some of its integrity? It has not the vitality and force of a single living man; for a single man can bend it to his
30 will. It is a sort of wooden gun to the people themselves. But it is not the less necessary for this; for the people must have that idea of government which they have. Governments show thus how successfully men can be imposed

on, even impose on themselves, for their own 35 advantage. It is excellent, we must all allow. Yet this government never of itself furthered any enterprise, but by the alacrity with which it got out of its way. It does not keep the country free. It does not settle the West. It does not 40 educate. The character inherent in the American people has done all that has been accomplished; and it would have done somewhat more, if the government had not sometimes got in its way. For government is an expedient 45 by which man would fain succeed in letting one another alone; and, as has been said, when it is most expedient, the governed are most let alone by it. Trade and commerce, if they were not made of India rubber, would never manage 50 to bounce over the obstacles which legislators are continually putting in their way; and, if one were to judge these men wholly by the effects of their action and not partly by their intentions, they would deserve to be classed and 55 punished with those mischievous persons who put obstructions on the railroads.

But to speak practically and as a citizen, unlike those who call theselves no-government men, I ask for, not at once no government, but 60 at once a better government. Let every man make known what kind of government would command his respect, and that will be one step toward obtaining it.

7. Generally speaking, Thoreau believes that

   (A) individual men assert more real force in the world than governments.

   (B) only governments make the contributions of individual men possible.

   (C) the future of America lies in its corporations.

   (D) governments are resistant to change and rarely improve.

   (E) individual men impede the progress of government too often.

8. The term "alacrity" (line 38) means

   (A) determination. (D) quickness.
   (B) sensitivity. (E) ruthlessness.
   (C) secrecy.

9. The fact that Thoreau sees government as a "wooden gun" (line 30)

   (A) reduces the notion of government to a mere "toy," something useless.
   (B) suggests that government is a relatively new institution.
   (C) is his way of mocking the inexperience of the legislators.
   (D) does not veil his rather sinister perception of government.
   (E) does not negate the force that government exerts on its citizens.

10. Thoreau's objections to a standing government

   (A) derive from his clear call to abolish government.
   (B) are motivated by his fear of anarchy.
   (C) find representation in his example of the Mexican war.
   (D) are in direct contrast to his views on standing armies.
   (E) are based on the impractical uses that business makes of established parties.

Questions 11–15 are based on the following passage.

The following passage is excerpted from a book of letters and memories of the life of Charlotte Cushman.

In the old, historic part of Boston, close by 1
the chime of bells given to the American colonists by King George, under the vigilant eye of the old cockerel, there stood, in 1816, a "rough cast" house. Here amid the summer heats, was 5
born, of stern Puritan stock, a blue-eyed girl who afterwards, single-handed, fought her way to an eminence where she stood a queen, her royal right unchallenged! Boston proudly boasts that her day and generation had not 10
Charlotte Cushman's equal. In 1867 the old house was torn down, and in its place was built a handsome brick school-house. For five years it had no name; then—happy thought!—a member of the school board proposed it 15
should be called the "Cushman School," in honor of the celebrated actress. Some of the old conservatives were startled into a mild remonstrance. A public building named, forsooth, for a woman! What matter that it was 20
a girls' school, and women only for teachers! Fortunately there was no mayor who must be flattered with an educational namesake; so the vote was carried, and today a woman's name is graven in letters of granite upon its facade. 25
On the fifth of January, 1872, Miss Cushman made a tour of the building, gracing each room with her presence. Then all were assembled in the hall for a dedicatory service. On the floor were seated the pupils, a thousand girls; on 30
the platform, teachers and visitors; and in the centre, Miss Cushman. Here she made her "maiden speech," as she smilingly said. Those upturned girlish faces were all the inspiration she needed, and a flush of enthusiasm 35
gathered on her pale face. For their encouragement she told them she walked those very streets, a school-girl as poor as the poorest among them. With rapid gestures of her large, shapely hands, her eyes glowing with the fire 40
of her own peculiar genius and her habitual

intensity, she told them that whatever she had attained had been by giving herself to her work. A patience that tired not, an energy that
45 faltered not, a persistence that knew no flagging, principles that swerved not, and the victory was hers, after long years of hard work. Higher than her intellectual strength, higher than her culture or genius or graces of charac-
50 ter, she ranked her ability for work. This was the secret of her success, and the legacy she bequeathed the girls of the Cushman School. They knew something of her history; that she had educated herself; that she had stoutly re-
55 sisted the shafts of disease; that the great men of the age delighted to do her honor; that she was an earnest, religious woman, upon whose fair name rested no shadow of suspicion.

11. The primary focus of the passage is on the

(A) numerous appearances made by the celebrated actress Charlotte Cushman.

(B) richness and complexity of Boston.

(C) events leading to and including the dedication of the Cushman School.

(D) fact that many opposed the dedication.

(E) opening of a school for girls.

12. When referring to dedicating the school to a woman, the author

(A) is very much opposed since there were many who needed to be recognized.

(B) expresses intense interest in the exact source of the choice.

(C) expresses enthusiastic approval.

(D) expresses appreciation to the mayor who made it all possible.

(E) concludes that there was no other choice since there was no mayor who needed recognition.

13. In lines 3–4 the words "vigilant eyes of the old cockerel" mean most nearly

(A) the watchful eye of the one in charge—the mayor.

(B) the eye full of revenge belonging to the one in charge—the mayor.

(C) the eye full of revenge of the town dowager or cockerel or older woman.

(D) the constant eye of the weather cock.

(E) the constant eye of the storm or the hurricane.

14. Based on this passage, the author's reaction to suffrage for women would be

(A) enthusiastic approval of the right.

(B) objective assessment of suffrage.

(C) disdain for the entire idea.

(D) a careful study of the effect on male counterparts.

(E) appreciation for those opposing the idea.

15. The tone of the author is

(A) irony.   (D) enthusiasm.

(B) hostility.   (E) disdain.

(C) sarcasm.

DIRECTIONS: Read the passages and answer the questions that follow. Each question will be based on the information stated or implied in the selections or the introduction, and may be based on the relationship between the passages.

Questions 16–24 are based on the following passages.

Each passage considers the proposition that dreams can be immoral. Passage 2 offers a critique of the arguments offered in Passage 1.

Passage 1

1   If in a dream I commit a murder, have I acted immorally? Many answer "no" since the dreamer has no control over the contents of the dream and since those contents are imaginary,
5 not real. Yet the question persists as to whether dreams can have moral significance, so further discussion of these answers seems worthwhile.

The kind of control a dreamer would have to exercise in order to give the dream moral
10 significance would have to involve free will, otherwise it would be unfair to punish him for something which was not his fault. But two facts demonstrate the unlikelihood that dreamers have free will. First, the source of
15 the dream clearly acts independent of our control. If the source is external to us—such as God or demons, as monotheistic scriptures suggest—then it is obvious that we receive the dream without having the freedom not to.
20 If the source is within us, which is the prevailing view, it appears to act spontaneously: neurophysiologist Alan Hobson argues, for example, that the dream begins with random neurochemical firings of the brain, followed
25 by the brain's retrieval of certain images stored in memory in an attempt to define the neurochemical event.

Second, whatever the source of the dream, it is evident from our own experiences that
30 dreams take twists and turns, jump from one scene to another, without our being able to predict these events or control them once they are under way. It's almost as if the dreamer were a passive member of the audience, even
35 when he is one of the characters of the dream.

The other argument against the belief that actions in dreams can be immoral centers on the fact that dream contents are imaginary, not real. As philosopher Margaret Macdon-
40 ald points out, it would be absurd to regard an imaginary murder as a real murder. And dreams are imaginary events. What's more, the moralistic position leads to greater absurdity when we switch the example from an
45 "immoral" one to a "moral" one. Suppose in my dream I commit an act of heroism? Ought I to be commended for doing a morally good deed? Of course not. The imaginary act of heroism has no more moral force in a positive
50 way, than the imaginary act of murder has in a negative way.

It is clear, then, that dream acts have no moral significance either positively or negatively.

Passage 2

On the face of it, the argument that dream
55 acts can have no moral significance is a good argument. Dreamers appear to have no control over their dreams and almost certainly dreams are imaginary events. But there are weaknesses in these claims sufficient to leave open the
60 possibility that dreamers are capable of acting morally or immorally in their dreams.

The argument from lack of control rests on the claim that dreamers lack the free will to choose either a right or wrong action and thus
65 are immune to charges of immorality. One objection to this is that control over our dreams may not be the morally significant point. As Freud points out, "unless the dream is inspired by alien spirits, it is part of my own being."
70 For this reason, he argues, we must assume full responsibility for our dream content—good or bad—since there is no one else to blame.

The second argument against the claim that dream acts can have moral significance is
75 that dreams are imaginary and just as an imaginary act of murder, for example, is not a real murder, any action in a dream must not be the real action which we might regard as immoral. This is morally inconclusive since, as Augus-
80 tine points out, the immorality of an action lies not in the possibility or reality of that action, but in the intent to carry it out. Now it appears that some dreams confront us with a choice of Actions which we can intend to do or not do.
85 The intent in a dream to commit murder, e.g., already indicates a morally significant character flaw—even if the intent is not carried out. So it may be true that I cannot commit a real murder in my dream and thus ought not to be
90 punished for having committed a real murder, but I nevertheless can behave morally or immorally by intending to act morally or immorally. Whether or not morality really lies in the intent or on the carrying out of that intent re-
95 mains a question for another time. But we now see that the question whether dream acts can be immoral is not settled simply by appealing to the imaginary character of dreams. Given these possible objections to two of the stron-
100 ger arguments against the claim that dreams have moral significance, we must conclude that many of them probably do have moral significance after all.

16. Which of the following statements best sums up the argument in Passage 2?

   (A) No argument against the possibility of moral dreams is a good argument, so there are moral and immoral dreams.

   (B) Two of the stronger arguments against the possibility of morally significant dreams are weak and thus it is probable that dreams can be moral or immoral.

   (C) Given Freud's authority, it is clear that we have control over our dreams and, therefore, arguments to the contrary fail.

   (D) Given the imaginary nature of dreams and the fact that we have no control over them, there is no moral significance to dreams.

   (E) We do have control over our dreams and they are not imaginary, so the argument in Passage 1 is invalid.

17. Which of the following, if true, would weaken the position of Passage 2?

   (A) Dreams are imaginary.

   (B) Freud believed that dreamers do have control over their dreams.

   (C) The morality of an action does not lie in the intent to carry it out.

   (D) Hobson is not a physiologist.

   (E) Dreams are neurochemical.

18. According to lines 6 through 8, what is the relationship between the moral significance of an act and the free will of the person acting?

    (A) An action has no moral significance unless it is done from free will.

    (B) All actions done from free will are morally significant actions.

    (C) If God and demons are the source of our dreams, then we have no free will.

    (D) If dreams occur in us spontaneously, then we have no free will.

    (E) All acts that are in our control are acts done from free will.

19. How does Passage 2 regard the position attributed to Margaret Macdonald in lines 39–41?

    (A) As wrong

    (B) As irrelevant to the question whether dreams can be morally significant

    (C) As consistent with Freud's position

    (D) As support for the claim that dreamers have no control over their dreams

    (E) As support for the claim that dreams are not imaginary

20. Which of the following is not a reason given in Passage 2 for the claim that dreams may have moral significance?

    (A) Dreams may confront us with a choice of actions.

    (B) Intention is more important to the morality or immorality of an action than the possibility of that action.

    (C) Intention is more important to the morality or immorality of an act than the reality of that action.

    (D) Dreams may not be imaginary.

    (E) Given a choice of actions in dreams, we can intend or not intend to do them.

21. Which of the following statements best characterizes the underlying assumption in lines 43–45 concerning moralistic positions?

    (A) If it is possible to act immorally in a dream, it must also be possible to act morally.

    (B) It is possible to commit an act of heroism in a dream.

    (C) It is possible to commit an act of murder in a dream.

    (D) An imaginary act of murder is immoral not moral.

    (E) Dream contents are imaginary, not real.

22. What is Passage 2's position on the imaginary character of dreams?

   (A) It is possible that dreams are imaginary, which makes the argument that dream acts can have no moral significance a good argument.

   (B) It is possible that dreams are imaginary, but even if they are, this is inconclusive as an answer to the question about a dream's moral significance.

   (C) Dreams are not imaginary, since it is possible to have choices in dreams.

   (D) Dreams are not imaginary, since dreams are actions and an imaginary action is not an action.

   (E) Dreams are not imaginary, since they are random neurochemical events.

23. If what is said in lines 22–27 about Alan Hobson is true, which of the following must be true?

   (A) Hobson believes that imagery in dreams precedes random neurochemical firings.

   (B) Hobson would disagree with Freud's claim that we are morally responsible for the content of our dreams.

   (C) Hobson would agree with Macdonald's statement that an imaginary murder is no murder.

   (D) Hobson believes that unless dreamers have control over their dreams, the dreams are not morally significant.

   (E) Hobson believes that random neurochemical firings of the brain precede imagery in a dream.

24. Which statement below best characterizes the position of Passage 1 and of Passage 2 concerning the "lack of control" argument?

   (A) They disagree on whether we may have control over our dreams.

   (B) They agree that we may have control over our dreams.

   (C) They consider the imaginative character of dreams to be more important.

   (D) Passage 2 considers this argument to be more significant than Passage 1.

   (E) Passage 2 argues that Augustine's position weakens Passage 1's support of the argument.

SECTION 4

TIME: 25 Minutes
  18 Questions

DIRECTIONS: Solve each problem, using any available space on the page for scratch work. Then decide which answer choice is the best and fill in the corresponding oval on the answer sheet.

NOTES

(1) The use of a calculator is permitted. All numbers used are real numbers.

(2) Figures that accompany problems in this test are intended to provide information useful in solving the problems. They are drawn as accurately as possible EXCEPT when it is stated in a specific problem that the figure is not drawn to scale. All figures lie in a plane unless otherwise indicated.

REFERENCE INFORMATION

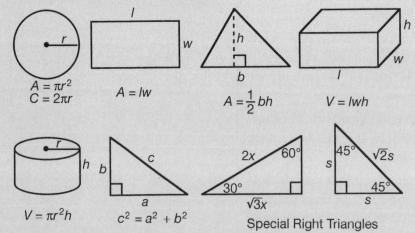

$A = \pi r^2$
$C = 2\pi r$

$A = lw$

$A = \frac{1}{2}bh$

$V = lwh$

$V = \pi r^2 h$

$c^2 = a^2 + b^2$

Special Right Triangles

The number of degrees of arc in a circle is 360.
The measure in degrees of a straight angle is 180.
The sum of the measures in degrees of the angles of a triangle is 180.

DIRECTIONS FOR STUDENT-PRODUCED RESPONSE QUESTIONS

For each of the questions below (1–10), solve the problem and indicate your answer by marking the ovals in the special grid, as shown in the examples below.

Answer: $\frac{9}{5}$ or 9/5 or 1.8

Either position is correct.

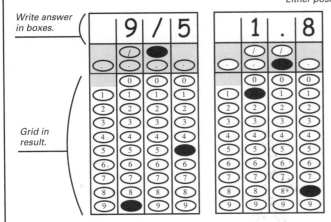
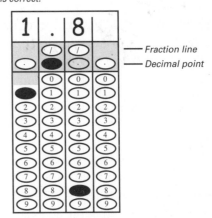

— Fraction line
— Decimal point

NOTE: You may start your anwers in any column, space permitting. Columns not needed should be left blank.

- Mark no more than one oval in any column.

- Because the answer sheet will be machine scored, you will receive credit only if the ovals are filled in correctly.

- Although not required, it is suggested that you write your answer in the boxes at the top of the columns to help you fill in the ovals accurately.

- Some problems may have more than one correct answer. In such cases, grid only one answer.

- No question has a negative answer.

- Mixed numbers such as $3\frac{1}{2}$ must be gridded as 3.5 or 7/2.

(If [3|1|/|2] is gridded, it will be interpreted as $\frac{31}{2}$, not $3\frac{1}{2}$.)

- **Decimal Accuracy:** If you obtain a decimal answer, enter the most accurate value the grid will accommodate. For example, if you obtain an answer such as 0.6666 ..., you should record the result as .666 or .667. Less accurate values such as .66 or .67 are not acceptable.

Acceptable ways to grid $\frac{2}{3}$ = .6666...

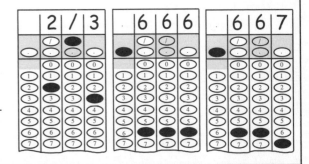

1. Simplify the fraction below.

$$\frac{2}{3} \times \frac{9}{4} \times \frac{16}{12} \times \frac{3}{8}$$

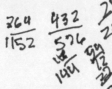

2. A class of 24 students contains 16 males. What is the ratio of females to males?

$16:8$

3. Let $2^x = 64$ and $2^y = 256$. Solve for 2^{y-x}.

16,384

4. Suppose x equals 10% of zy and y equals 20% of w. What fraction of wz equals x?

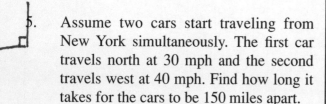

5. Assume two cars start traveling from New York simultaneously. The first car travels north at 30 mph and the second travels west at 40 mph. Find how long it takes for the cars to be 150 miles apart.

6. Find a natural number x with the following properties:

   a) x is a multiple of 21.
   b) x is a multiple of 15.
   c) x is a multiple of 35.
   d) x is less than 225.

7. Let $f(x) = x^2 - 1$ and $g(x) = 3x + 2$. Find the value of $g(f(3))$.

8. Consider the figure given below. What is the value of $x + 2y$?

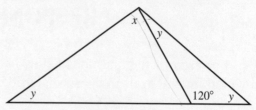

Note: Figure not drawn to scale.

9. Final exam scores on a science exam are given below.

Score	Percentage of Students
50 – 59	9%
60 – 69	5%
70 – 79	25%
80 – 89	40%
90 – 100	21%

If there were 80 students in the class, how many students scored between 60 and 89?

10. Find a solution to the equation below.

$$\frac{1}{r^2} - 7\frac{1}{r} + 10 = 0$$

11. A rectangular wall has the dimensions F and G. A rectangular window in the wall has the dimensions K and L. Represent the shaded area of the wall.

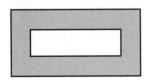

(A) $FG + KL$

(B) $FG - KL$

(C) $KL - FG$

(D) $(FG)^2 - (KL)^2$

(E) None of these

12. Simplify: $\sqrt{\dfrac{B^2}{16} - \dfrac{B^2}{25}}$ $\quad \dfrac{B}{4} - \dfrac{B}{5}$

(A) $\dfrac{B}{20}$ (D) $\dfrac{3B}{40}$

(B) $\dfrac{3B}{20}$ (E) $\dfrac{4B}{9}$

(C) $\dfrac{B}{20}$

13. To obtain a final average of 85% in a certain subject, what grade must a student earn in a test after having an average of 83% in four examinations?

(A) 87 (D) 93

(B) 89 (E) 95

(C) 91

14. A rectangular solid is 10 cm long and 5 cm wide. How high must it be to have a volume of 200 cu cm?

(A) 1 (D) 4

(B) 2 (E) 5

(C) 3

15. If a garage can wash 5 cars in 30 minutes, how long would it take to wash 30 cars?

(A) 3 hours

(B) 3 hours 5 minutes

(C) 5 hours

(D) 6 hours

(E) 30 hours

16. Mr. Baker is 30 years old when his son is 4 years old. In how many years will Mr. Baker be five times as old as his son?

(A) 2 (D) $3\dfrac{1}{2}$

(B) $2\dfrac{1}{2}$ (E) 4

(C) 3

17. A suede jacket was purchased at a cost of $96, after a 60% discount. What was the original price of the purchase?

(A) $134.40 (D) $250

(B) $153.60 (E) $144

(C) $240

18. The area of a right triangle whose legs are in the ratio of 3:4 is 96. The length of the hypotenuse is

(A) 12. (D) 96.

(B) 16. (E) 400.

(C) 20.

SECTION 5

TIME: 30 Minutes
39 Questions

DIRECTIONS: Each of the following sentences may contain an error in diction, usage, idiom, or grammar. Some sentences are correct. Some sentences contain one error. No sentence contains more than one error.

If there is an error, it will appear in one of the underlined portions labeled A, B, C, or D. If there is no error, choose the portion labeled E. If there is an error, select the letter of the portion that must be changed in order to correct the sentence.

EXAMPLE

He drove <u>slowly</u> and <u>cautiously</u> in order to <u>hopefully</u> avoid having an <u>accident</u>.
        A   B   C   D
<u>No error.</u>
  E   Ⓐ Ⓑ ● Ⓓ Ⓔ

1. Each campus appointed their own commit-
        A
   tee to apply the findings of the city-wide
                     B
   survey concerning ways in which the
                          C
   school district can save money. No error.
                     D   E

2. When I asked Gary and John what would
           A
   be good for dinner, the boys said they
      B
   could care less about eating liver for the
      C   D
   main dish with spinach for a vegetable.

   No error.
   E

3. John will be liable for damages to Mrs.
                A
   Simon's car because he was fascinated by
                              B
   his new red truck and driving so fast
                                     C
   that he failed to conform to a law limit-
                     D
   ing the speed of any vehicle within the

   city limits. No error.
              E

4. I have seen, more than anything else, that
   A   B   C
   self-esteem is a problem in many people
                   D
   of all ages and nationalities. No error.
                                 E

5. Mr. Burgess made sure the ten-year-olds

   were accommodated with quarters for
        A
   a video games party; afterwards, he de-

   clined to say how much the event cost
          B
   him but allowed as how it was more than
               C
   he had expected. No error.
      D   E

6. This afternoon's boating accident having
                                       A
   turned out differently through the efforts
             B
   of Jack Williams, a fellow vacationer

   who knows CPR, so the little girl has
   C   D
   survived. No error.
            E

7. Three hundred years ago John Milton
                 A
   protested against laws which required a
   B
   government official to approve of any
                          C   D
   manuscript before it was published.

   No error.
   E

8. Often <u>called</u> members of the "Fourth Es-
   A
   tate," journalists have <u>rapidly developed into</u>
   B **C**
   powerful people, influencing public opinion
   and government policy that <u>has</u> a bearing
   D
   on the course of history. <u>No error.</u>
   E

9. Totaling <u>more than expected</u>, the groom's
   A
   wedding expenses <u>included</u> hiring a lim-
   B
   ousine for the trip to the airport after the
   wedding, <u>buying gifts</u> for his groomsmen,
   C
   and <u>a tuxedo</u> for the ceremony. <u>No error.</u>
   D **E**

10. <u>Our viewing</u> these photographs of Dad
    A
    standing in front of the throne at Macchu
    Pichu <u>brings</u> back pleasant memories for
    B
    <u>we</u> children, reminding us <u>of the need for</u>
    C **D**
    more family get-togethers. <u>No error.</u>
    E

11. Finally confessing to the <u>theft of</u> money
    A
    collected for a class movie, Jules said
    <u>he only</u> stole money once in his life and
    B
    <u>his</u> conscience would not allow <u>him</u> to
    C **D**
    enjoy spending it. <u>No error.</u>
    E

12. If <u>a person</u> is a criminal, <u>he</u> should be
    A **B**
    punished for <u>it;</u> unfortunately, many
    C
    criminals are <u>never</u> caught. <u>No error.</u>
    D **E**

13. An intriguing habit many hawks have
    <u>is bringing</u> a fresh green branch <u>daily</u> to
    A **B**
    line the nest <u>during the season</u> in which
    C
    <u>they</u> are mating and rearing their young.
    D
    <u>No error.</u>
    E

14. Hawks and owls can be seen <u>more frequent</u>
    A
    in populated areas than <u>most people</u>
    B
    <u>suppose</u>, and it is <u>possible</u> to hear screech
    C **D**
    owls at night when the adult birds
    feed their chicks. <u>No error.</u>
    E

DIRECTIONS: In each of the following sentences, some portion of the sentence is underlined. Under each sentence are five choices. The first choice has the same wording as the original. The other four choices are reworded. Sometimes the first choice containing the original wording is the best; sometimes one of the other choices is the best. Choose the letter of the best choice. Your choice should produce a sentence which is not ambiguous or awkward and which is correct, clear, and precise.

This is a test of correct and effective English expression. Keep in mind the standards of English usage, punctuation, grammar, word choice, and construction.

EXAMPLE

When you listen to opera, <u>a person may not appreciate it</u>.

- (A)   a person may not appreciate it.
- (B)   it may not be appreciated by a person.
- (C)   which may not be appreciated by one.
- (D)   you may not appreciate it.
- (E)   appreciating it may be a problem for you.

15. The new secretary proved herself <u>to be not only capable and efficient but also a woman who was adept</u> at working under pressure and handling irate customers.

- (A)   to be not only capable and efficient but also a woman who was adept
- (B)   not only to be capable or efficient but also a woman who was adept
- (C)   not only to be capable and efficient but also a woman who was adept
- (D)   to be not only capable and efficient but also adept
- (E)   to be not only capable and efficient but also an adept woman

16. <u>Hunting, if properly managed and carefully controlled</u>, can cull excess animals, thereby producing a healthier population of wild game.

- (A)   Hunting, if properly managed and carefully controlled
- (B)   Managing it wisely, carefully controlled hunting
- (C)   Managed properly hunting that is carefully controlled
- (D)   Properly and wisely controlled, careful hunting
- (E)   If properly managed, hunting, carefully controlled

17. In spite of my reservations, <u>I agreed on the next day to help her put up new wallpaper</u>.

    (A) I agreed on the next day to help her put up new wallpaper.

    (B) I agreed on the next day to help put up her new wallpaper.

    (C) I agreed to help her put up new wallpaper on the next day.

    (D) I, on the next day, agreed to help her put up new wallpaper.

    (E) I agreed to, on the next day, help her put up new wallpaper.

18. <u>We saw many of, though not nearly all, the existing Roman ruins</u> along the Mediterranean coastline of Africa.

    (A) We saw many of, though not nearly all, the existing Roman ruins

    (B) We saw many, though not nearly all, of the existing Roman ruins

    (C) Seeing many, though not nearly all, of the existing Roman ruins

    (D) Having seen many of, though not nearly all, the existing Roman ruins

    (E) Many of, though not nearly all, the existing Roman ruins we saw

19. <u>The horned owl is a carnivore who hunts a diversity of creatures, like</u> hares, grouse, and ground squirrels.

    (A) The horned owl is a carnivore who hunts a diversity of creatures, like

    (B) The horned owl, a carnivore who hunts a diversity of creatures like

    (C) A hunting carnivore, the horned owl likes a diversity of creatures

    (D) The horned owl likes a diversity of carnivorous creatures, such as

    (E) The horned owl is a carnivore that hunts a diversity of creatures, such as

20. In many of his works Tennessee Williams, <u>of whom much has been written</u>, has as main characters drifters, dreamers, and those who are crushed by having to deal with reality.

    (A) of whom much has been written

    (B) of who much has been written

    (C) of whom much has been written about

    (D) about him much having been written

    (E) much having been written about him

21. The world history students wanted to know <u>where the Dead Sea was at and what it was famous for</u>.

    (A) where the Dead Sea was at and what it was famous for.

    (B) where the Dead Sea is at and for what it is famous.

    (C) where the Dead Sea is located and why it is famous.

    (D) at where the Dead Sea was located and what it was famous for.

    (E) the location of the Dead Sea and what it is famous for.

22. Literary historians <u>cannot help but admit that they do not know</u> whether poetry or drama is the oldest form of literature.

    (A) cannot help but admit that they do not know

    (B) cannot admit that they do not admit to knowing

    (C) cannot help admitting that they do not know

    (D) cannot help but to admit that they do not know

    (E) cannot know but admit that they do not

23. Getting to know a person's parents <u>will often provide an insight to</u> his personality and behavior.

   (A)   will often provide an insight to
   (B)   will often provide an insight into
   (C)   will often provide an insight for
   (D)   will provide often an insight for
   (E)   often will provide an insight with

24. Upon leaving the nursery, Mr. Greene, together with his wife, <u>put the plants in the trunk of the car they had just bought.</u>

   (A)   put the plants in the trunk of the car they had just bought.
   (B)   put in the plants to the trunk of the car they had just bought.
   (C)   put into the trunk of the car they had just bought the plants.
   (D)   put the plants they had just bought in the trunk of the car.
   (E)   put the plants into the trunk of the car.

25. The way tensions are increasing in the Middle East, some experts <u>are afraid we may end up with a nuclear war.</u>

   (A)   are afraid we may end up with a nuclear war.
   (B)   being afraid we may end up with a nuclear war.
   (C)   afraid that a nuclear war may end up over there.
   (D)   are afraid a nuclear war may end there.
   (E)   are afraid a nuclear war may occur.

26. <u>Whether Leif Erickson was the first to discover America or not</u> is still a debatable issue, but there is general agreement that there probably were a number of "discoveries" through the years.

   (A)   Whether Leif Erickson was the first to discover America or not
   (B)   That Leif Erickson was the first to discover America
   (C)   That Leif Erickson may have been the first to have discovered America
   (D)   Whether Leif Erickson is the first to discover America or he is not
   (E)   Whether or not Leif Erickson was or was not the first discoverer of America

27. <u>People who charge too much are likely to develop</u> a bad credit rating.

   (A)   People who charge too much are likely to develop
   (B)   People's charging too much are likely to develop
   (C)   When people charge too much, likely to develop
   (D)   That people charge too much is likely to develop
   (E)   Charging too much is likely to develop for people

28. The museum of natural science has a special exhibit of gems and minerals, <u>and the fifth graders went to see it on a field trip</u>.

   (A) and the fifth graders went to see it on a field trip.

   (B) and seeing it were the fifth graders on a field trip.

   (C) when the fifth graders took a field trip to see it.

   (D) which the fifth graders took a field trip to see.

   (E) where the fifth graders took their field trip to see it.

29. <u>Having studied theology, music, along with medicine</u>, Albert Schweitzer became a medical missionary in Africa.

   (A) Having studied theology, music, along with medicine

   (B) Having studied theology, music, as well as medicine

   (C) Having studied theology and music, and, also, medicine

   (D) With a study of theology, music, and medicine

   (E) After he had studied theology, music, and medicine

30. When the Mississippi River threatens to flood, sandbags are piled along its banks, <u>and they do this to keep its waters from overflowing</u>.

   (A) and they do this to keep its waters from overflowing.

   (B) to keep its waters from overflowing.

   (C) and then its waters won't overflow.

   (D) and, therefore, keeping its waters from overflowing.

   (E) and they keep its waters from overflowing.

31. <u>Because of the popularity of his light verse</u>, Edward Lear is seldom recognized today for his travel books and detailed illustrations of birds.

   (A) Because of the popularity of his light verse

   (B) Owing to the fact that his light verse was popular

   (C) Because of his light verse, that was very popular

   (D) Having written light verse that was popular

   (E) Being the author of popular light verse

32. Lincoln's Gettysburg Address, <u>despite its having been very short and delivered after a two-hour oration by Edward Everett</u>, is one of the greatest speeches ever delivered.

   (A) despite its having been very short and delivered after a two-hour oration by Edward Everett

   (B) which was very short and delivered after a two-hour oration by Edward Everett

   (C) although it was very short and delivered after a two-hour oration by Edward Everett

   (D) despite the fact that it was very short and delivered after a two-hour oration by Edward Everett

   (E) was very short and delivered after a two-hour oration by Edward Everett

33. China, <u>which ranks third in area and first in population among the world's countries</u> also has one of the longest histories.

(A) which ranks third in area and first in population among the world's countries

(B) which ranks third in area and has the largest population among the world's countries

(C) which is the third largest in area and ranks first in population among the world's countries

(D) in area ranking third and in population ranking first among the world's countries

(E) third in area and first in the number of people among the world's countries

34. <u>Leonardo da Vinci was a man who</u> was a scientist, an architect, an engineer, and a sculptor.

(A) Leonardo da Vinci was a man who

(B) The man Leonardo da Vinci

(C) Being a man, Leonardo da Vinci

(D) Leonardo da Vinci

(E) Leonardo da Vinci, a man who

DIRECTIONS: The following passages are considered early draft efforts of a student. Some sentences need to be rewritten to make the ideas clearer and more precise.

Read each passage carefully and answer the questions that follow. Some of the questions are about particular sentences or parts of sentences and ask you to make decisions about sentence structure, diction, and usage. Some of the questions refer to the entire essay or parts of the essay and ask you to make decisions about organization, development, appropriateness of language, audience, and logic. Choose the answer that most effectively makes the intended meaning clear and follows the requirements of standard written English. After you have chosen your answer, fill in the corresponding oval on your answer sheet.

EXAMPLE

(1) On the one hand, I think television is bad, But it also does some good things for all of us. (2) For instance, my little sister thought she wanted to be a policemen until she saw police shows on television.

Which of the following is the best revision of the underlined portion of sentence 1 below?

On the one hand, I think television <u>is bad, But it also</u> does some good things for all of us.

(A) is bad; But it also

(B) is bad. but is also

(C) is bad, and it also

(D) is bad, but it also

(E) is bad because it also

Ⓐ Ⓑ Ⓒ ● Ⓔ

Questions 35–39 are based on the following passage.

(1) Actually, the term "Native Americans" is incorrect. (2) Indians migrated to this continent from other areas, just earlier then Europeans did. (3) The ancestors of the Anasazi—Indians of the four-state area of Colorado, New Mexico, Utah, and Arizona—probably crossed from Asia into Alaska. (4) About 25,000 years ago while the continental land bridge still existed. (5) This land bridge arched across the Bering Strait in the last Ice Age. (6) About A.D. 500 the ancestors of the Anasazi moved onto the Mesa Verde a high plateau in the desert country of Colorado. (7) The Wetherills, five brothers who ranched the area, is generally given credit for the first exploration of the ruins in the 1870s and 1880s. (8) There were some 50,000 Anasazi thriving in the four-corners area by the 1200s. (9) At their zenith A.D. 700 to 1300, the Anasazi had established wide-spread communities and built thousands of sophisticated structures—cliff dwellings, pueblos, and kivas. (10) They even engaged in trade with Indians in surrounding regions by exporting pottery and other goods.

35. Which of the following best corrects the grammatical error in sentence 7?

(A) The Wetherills, a group of five brothers who ranched in the area, is generally given credit for the first exploration of the ruins in the 1870s and 1880s.

(B) The Wetherills, five brothers who ranched in the area, are generally given credit for the first exploration of the ruins in the 1870s and 1880s.

(C) The Wetherills are generally given credit for the first exploration of the ruins in the 1870s and 1880s, five brothers who ranched in the area.

(D) The Wetherills, generally given credit for the first exploration of the area, is five brothers who ranched in the area.

(E) Best as it is.

36. Which of the following sentences would best fit between sentences 9 and 10 of the passage?

(A) Artifacts recovered from the area suggest that the Anasazi were artistic, religious, agricultural, classless, and peaceful.

(B) By 12,000 to 10,000 B.C., some Indians had established their unique cultures in the southwest.

(C) The Navaho called their ancestors the Anasazi, the Ancient Ones.

(D) I think it is unfortunate that such a unique and innovative culture should have disappeared from the country.

(E) Before Columbus reached the New World, the Anasazi had virtually disappeared.

37. Which of the following is an incomplete sentence?

    (A) 4   (D) 7
    (B) 5   (E) 10
    (C) 6

38. Which of the following best corrects the underlined portion of sentence 9?

    At their zenith A.D. 700 to 1300, the Anasazi had established widespread communities and built thousands of sophisticated structures—cliff dwellings, pueblos, and kivas.

    (A) At their zenith which was from A.D. 700 to 1300
    (B) At their zenith B.C. 700 to 1300
    (C) At their zenith, from A.D. 700 to 1300,
    (D) At their zenith, being A.D. 700 to 1300,
    (E) At their zenith, of A.D. 700 to 1300,

39. Which of the following would be the best way to punctuate sentence 6?

    (A) About A.D. 500, the ancestors of the Anasazi moved onto the Mesa Verde a high plateau, in the desert country of Colorado.
    (B) About A.D. 500 the ancestors of the Anasazi moved, onto the Mesa Verde: a high plateau in the desert country of Colorado
    (C) About A.D. 500 the ancestors of the Anasazi moved onto the Mesa Verde: a high plateau, in the desert country of Colorado.
    (D) About A.D. 500, the ancestors of the Anasazi moved onto the Mesa Verde, a high plateau in the desert country of Colorado.
    (E) Best as it is.

Begin with number 1 for each section. If a section has fewer questions than answer spaces, leave the extra answer spaces blank. Be sure to erase any errors or stray marks completely.

SECTION 1

1 Ⓐ Ⓑ Ⓒ Ⓓ Ⓔ	11 Ⓐ Ⓑ Ⓒ Ⓓ Ⓔ	21 Ⓐ Ⓑ Ⓒ Ⓓ Ⓔ	31 Ⓐ Ⓑ Ⓒ Ⓓ Ⓔ
2 Ⓐ Ⓑ Ⓒ Ⓓ Ⓔ	12 Ⓐ Ⓑ Ⓒ Ⓓ Ⓔ	22 Ⓐ Ⓑ Ⓒ Ⓓ Ⓔ	32 Ⓐ Ⓑ Ⓒ Ⓓ Ⓔ
3 Ⓐ Ⓑ Ⓒ Ⓓ Ⓔ	13 Ⓐ Ⓑ Ⓒ Ⓓ Ⓔ	23 Ⓐ Ⓑ Ⓒ Ⓓ Ⓔ	33 Ⓐ Ⓑ Ⓒ Ⓓ Ⓔ
4 Ⓐ Ⓑ Ⓒ Ⓓ Ⓔ	14 Ⓐ Ⓑ Ⓒ Ⓓ Ⓔ	24 Ⓐ Ⓑ Ⓒ Ⓓ Ⓔ	34 Ⓐ Ⓑ Ⓒ Ⓓ Ⓔ
5 Ⓐ Ⓑ Ⓒ Ⓓ Ⓔ	15 Ⓐ Ⓑ Ⓒ Ⓓ Ⓔ	25 Ⓐ Ⓑ Ⓒ Ⓓ Ⓔ	35 Ⓐ Ⓑ Ⓒ Ⓓ Ⓔ
6 Ⓐ Ⓑ Ⓒ Ⓓ Ⓔ	16 Ⓐ Ⓑ Ⓒ Ⓓ Ⓔ	26 Ⓐ Ⓑ Ⓒ Ⓓ Ⓔ	36 Ⓐ Ⓑ Ⓒ Ⓓ Ⓔ
7 Ⓐ Ⓑ Ⓒ Ⓓ Ⓔ	17 Ⓐ Ⓑ Ⓒ Ⓓ Ⓔ	27 Ⓐ Ⓑ Ⓒ Ⓓ Ⓔ	37 Ⓐ Ⓑ Ⓒ Ⓓ Ⓔ
8 Ⓐ Ⓑ Ⓒ Ⓓ Ⓔ	18 Ⓐ Ⓑ Ⓒ Ⓓ Ⓔ	28 Ⓐ Ⓑ Ⓒ Ⓓ Ⓔ	38 Ⓐ Ⓑ Ⓒ Ⓓ Ⓔ
9 Ⓐ Ⓑ Ⓒ Ⓓ Ⓔ	19 Ⓐ Ⓑ Ⓒ Ⓓ Ⓔ	29 Ⓐ Ⓑ Ⓒ Ⓓ Ⓔ	39 Ⓐ Ⓑ Ⓒ Ⓓ Ⓔ
10 Ⓐ Ⓑ Ⓒ Ⓓ Ⓔ	20 Ⓐ Ⓑ Ⓒ Ⓓ Ⓔ	30 Ⓐ Ⓑ Ⓒ Ⓓ Ⓔ	40 Ⓐ Ⓑ Ⓒ Ⓓ Ⓔ

SECTION 2

1 Ⓐ Ⓑ Ⓒ Ⓓ Ⓔ	11 Ⓐ Ⓑ Ⓒ Ⓓ Ⓔ	21 Ⓐ Ⓑ Ⓒ Ⓓ Ⓔ	31 Ⓐ Ⓑ Ⓒ Ⓓ Ⓔ
2 Ⓐ Ⓑ Ⓒ Ⓓ Ⓔ	12 Ⓐ Ⓑ Ⓒ Ⓓ Ⓔ	22 Ⓐ Ⓑ Ⓒ Ⓓ Ⓔ	32 Ⓐ Ⓑ Ⓒ Ⓓ Ⓔ
3 Ⓐ Ⓑ Ⓒ Ⓓ Ⓔ	13 Ⓐ Ⓑ Ⓒ Ⓓ Ⓔ	23 Ⓐ Ⓑ Ⓒ Ⓓ Ⓔ	33 Ⓐ Ⓑ Ⓒ Ⓓ Ⓔ
4 Ⓐ Ⓑ Ⓒ Ⓓ Ⓔ	14 Ⓐ Ⓑ Ⓒ Ⓓ Ⓔ	24 Ⓐ Ⓑ Ⓒ Ⓓ Ⓔ	34 Ⓐ Ⓑ Ⓒ Ⓓ Ⓔ
5 Ⓐ Ⓑ Ⓒ Ⓓ Ⓔ	15 Ⓐ Ⓑ Ⓒ Ⓓ Ⓔ	25 Ⓐ Ⓑ Ⓒ Ⓓ Ⓔ	35 Ⓐ Ⓑ Ⓒ Ⓓ Ⓔ
6 Ⓐ Ⓑ Ⓒ Ⓓ Ⓔ	16 Ⓐ Ⓑ Ⓒ Ⓓ Ⓔ	26 Ⓐ Ⓑ Ⓒ Ⓓ Ⓔ	36 Ⓐ Ⓑ Ⓒ Ⓓ Ⓔ
7 Ⓐ Ⓑ Ⓒ Ⓓ Ⓔ	17 Ⓐ Ⓑ Ⓒ Ⓓ Ⓔ	27 Ⓐ Ⓑ Ⓒ Ⓓ Ⓔ	37 Ⓐ Ⓑ Ⓒ Ⓓ Ⓔ
8 Ⓐ Ⓑ Ⓒ Ⓓ Ⓔ	18 Ⓐ Ⓑ Ⓒ Ⓓ Ⓔ	28 Ⓐ Ⓑ Ⓒ Ⓓ Ⓔ	38 Ⓐ Ⓑ Ⓒ Ⓓ Ⓔ
9 Ⓐ Ⓑ Ⓒ Ⓓ Ⓔ	19 Ⓐ Ⓑ Ⓒ Ⓓ Ⓔ	29 Ⓐ Ⓑ Ⓒ Ⓓ Ⓔ	39 Ⓐ Ⓑ Ⓒ Ⓓ Ⓔ
10 Ⓐ Ⓑ Ⓒ Ⓓ Ⓔ	20 Ⓐ Ⓑ Ⓒ Ⓓ Ⓔ	30 Ⓐ Ⓑ Ⓒ Ⓓ Ⓔ	40 Ⓐ Ⓑ Ⓒ Ⓓ Ⓔ

SECTION 3

1 Ⓐ Ⓑ Ⓒ Ⓓ Ⓔ	11 Ⓐ Ⓑ Ⓒ Ⓓ Ⓔ	21 Ⓐ Ⓑ Ⓒ Ⓓ Ⓔ	31 Ⓐ Ⓑ Ⓒ Ⓓ Ⓔ
2 Ⓐ Ⓑ Ⓒ Ⓓ Ⓔ	12 Ⓐ Ⓑ Ⓒ Ⓓ Ⓔ	22 Ⓐ Ⓑ Ⓒ Ⓓ Ⓔ	32 Ⓐ Ⓑ Ⓒ Ⓓ Ⓔ
3 Ⓐ Ⓑ Ⓒ Ⓓ Ⓔ	13 Ⓐ Ⓑ Ⓒ Ⓓ Ⓔ	23 Ⓐ Ⓑ Ⓒ Ⓓ Ⓔ	33 Ⓐ Ⓑ Ⓒ Ⓓ Ⓔ
4 Ⓐ Ⓑ Ⓒ Ⓓ Ⓔ	14 Ⓐ Ⓑ Ⓒ Ⓓ Ⓔ	24 Ⓐ Ⓑ Ⓒ Ⓓ Ⓔ	34 Ⓐ Ⓑ Ⓒ Ⓓ Ⓔ
5 Ⓐ Ⓑ Ⓒ Ⓓ Ⓔ	15 Ⓐ Ⓑ Ⓒ Ⓓ Ⓔ	25 Ⓐ Ⓑ Ⓒ Ⓓ Ⓔ	35 Ⓐ Ⓑ Ⓒ Ⓓ Ⓔ
6 Ⓐ Ⓑ Ⓒ Ⓓ Ⓔ	16 Ⓐ Ⓑ Ⓒ Ⓓ Ⓔ	26 Ⓐ Ⓑ Ⓒ Ⓓ Ⓔ	36 Ⓐ Ⓑ Ⓒ Ⓓ Ⓔ
7 Ⓐ Ⓑ Ⓒ Ⓓ Ⓔ	17 Ⓐ Ⓑ Ⓒ Ⓓ Ⓔ	27 Ⓐ Ⓑ Ⓒ Ⓓ Ⓔ	37 Ⓐ Ⓑ Ⓒ Ⓓ Ⓔ
8 Ⓐ Ⓑ Ⓒ Ⓓ Ⓔ	18 Ⓐ Ⓑ Ⓒ Ⓓ Ⓔ	28 Ⓐ Ⓑ Ⓒ Ⓓ Ⓔ	38 Ⓐ Ⓑ Ⓒ Ⓓ Ⓔ
9 Ⓐ Ⓑ Ⓒ Ⓓ Ⓔ	19 Ⓐ Ⓑ Ⓒ Ⓓ Ⓔ	29 Ⓐ Ⓑ Ⓒ Ⓓ Ⓔ	39 Ⓐ Ⓑ Ⓒ Ⓓ Ⓔ
10 Ⓐ Ⓑ Ⓒ Ⓓ Ⓔ	20 Ⓐ Ⓑ Ⓒ Ⓓ Ⓔ	30 Ⓐ Ⓑ Ⓒ Ⓓ Ⓔ	40 Ⓐ Ⓑ Ⓒ Ⓓ Ⓔ

SECTION 4

1 Ⓐ Ⓑ Ⓒ Ⓓ Ⓔ	11 Ⓐ Ⓑ Ⓒ Ⓓ Ⓔ	21 Ⓐ Ⓑ Ⓒ Ⓓ Ⓔ	31 Ⓐ Ⓑ Ⓒ Ⓓ Ⓔ
2 Ⓐ Ⓑ Ⓒ Ⓓ Ⓔ	12 Ⓐ Ⓑ Ⓒ Ⓓ Ⓔ	22 Ⓐ Ⓑ Ⓒ Ⓓ Ⓔ	32 Ⓐ Ⓑ Ⓒ Ⓓ Ⓔ
3 Ⓐ Ⓑ Ⓒ Ⓓ Ⓔ	13 Ⓐ Ⓑ Ⓒ Ⓓ Ⓔ	23 Ⓐ Ⓑ Ⓒ Ⓓ Ⓔ	33 Ⓐ Ⓑ Ⓒ Ⓓ Ⓔ
4 Ⓐ Ⓑ Ⓒ Ⓓ Ⓔ	14 Ⓐ Ⓑ Ⓒ Ⓓ Ⓔ	24 Ⓐ Ⓑ Ⓒ Ⓓ Ⓔ	34 Ⓐ Ⓑ Ⓒ Ⓓ Ⓔ
5 Ⓐ Ⓑ Ⓒ Ⓓ Ⓔ	15 Ⓐ Ⓑ Ⓒ Ⓓ Ⓔ	25 Ⓐ Ⓑ Ⓒ Ⓓ Ⓔ	35 Ⓐ Ⓑ Ⓒ Ⓓ Ⓔ
6 Ⓐ Ⓑ Ⓒ Ⓓ Ⓔ	16 Ⓐ Ⓑ Ⓒ Ⓓ Ⓔ	26 Ⓐ Ⓑ Ⓒ Ⓓ Ⓔ	36 Ⓐ Ⓑ Ⓒ Ⓓ Ⓔ
7 Ⓐ Ⓑ Ⓒ Ⓓ Ⓔ	17 Ⓐ Ⓑ Ⓒ Ⓓ Ⓔ	27 Ⓐ Ⓑ Ⓒ Ⓓ Ⓔ	37 Ⓐ Ⓑ Ⓒ Ⓓ Ⓔ
8 Ⓐ Ⓑ Ⓒ Ⓓ Ⓔ	18 Ⓐ Ⓑ Ⓒ Ⓓ Ⓔ	28 Ⓐ Ⓑ Ⓒ Ⓓ Ⓔ	38 Ⓐ Ⓑ Ⓒ Ⓓ Ⓔ
9 Ⓐ Ⓑ Ⓒ Ⓓ Ⓔ	19 Ⓐ Ⓑ Ⓒ Ⓓ Ⓔ	29 Ⓐ Ⓑ Ⓒ Ⓓ Ⓔ	39 Ⓐ Ⓑ Ⓒ Ⓓ Ⓔ
10 Ⓐ Ⓑ Ⓒ Ⓓ Ⓔ	20 Ⓐ Ⓑ Ⓒ Ⓓ Ⓔ	30 Ⓐ Ⓑ Ⓒ Ⓓ Ⓔ	40 Ⓐ Ⓑ Ⓒ Ⓓ Ⓔ

SECTION 5

1 Ⓐ Ⓑ Ⓒ Ⓓ Ⓔ	11 Ⓐ Ⓑ Ⓒ Ⓓ Ⓔ	21 Ⓐ Ⓑ Ⓒ Ⓓ Ⓔ	31 Ⓐ Ⓑ Ⓒ Ⓓ Ⓔ
2 Ⓐ Ⓑ Ⓒ Ⓓ Ⓔ	12 Ⓐ Ⓑ Ⓒ Ⓓ Ⓔ	22 Ⓐ Ⓑ Ⓒ Ⓓ Ⓔ	32 Ⓐ Ⓑ Ⓒ Ⓓ Ⓔ
3 Ⓐ Ⓑ Ⓒ Ⓓ Ⓔ	13 Ⓐ Ⓑ Ⓒ Ⓓ Ⓔ	23 Ⓐ Ⓑ Ⓒ Ⓓ Ⓔ	33 Ⓐ Ⓑ Ⓒ Ⓓ Ⓔ
4 Ⓐ Ⓑ Ⓒ Ⓓ Ⓔ	14 Ⓐ Ⓑ Ⓒ Ⓓ Ⓔ	24 Ⓐ Ⓑ Ⓒ Ⓓ Ⓔ	34 Ⓐ Ⓑ Ⓒ Ⓓ Ⓔ
5 Ⓐ Ⓑ Ⓒ Ⓓ Ⓔ	15 Ⓐ Ⓑ Ⓒ Ⓓ Ⓔ	25 Ⓐ Ⓑ Ⓒ Ⓓ Ⓔ	35 Ⓐ Ⓑ Ⓒ Ⓓ Ⓔ
6 Ⓐ Ⓑ Ⓒ Ⓓ Ⓔ	16 Ⓐ Ⓑ Ⓒ Ⓓ Ⓔ	26 Ⓐ Ⓑ Ⓒ Ⓓ Ⓔ	36 Ⓐ Ⓑ Ⓒ Ⓓ Ⓔ
7 Ⓐ Ⓑ Ⓒ Ⓓ Ⓔ	17 Ⓐ Ⓑ Ⓒ Ⓓ Ⓔ	27 Ⓐ Ⓑ Ⓒ Ⓓ Ⓔ	37 Ⓐ Ⓑ Ⓒ Ⓓ Ⓔ
8 Ⓐ Ⓑ Ⓒ Ⓓ Ⓔ	18 Ⓐ Ⓑ Ⓒ Ⓓ Ⓔ	28 Ⓐ Ⓑ Ⓒ Ⓓ Ⓔ	38 Ⓐ Ⓑ Ⓒ Ⓓ Ⓔ
9 Ⓐ Ⓑ Ⓒ Ⓓ Ⓔ	19 Ⓐ Ⓑ Ⓒ Ⓓ Ⓔ	29 Ⓐ Ⓑ Ⓒ Ⓓ Ⓔ	39 Ⓐ Ⓑ Ⓒ Ⓓ Ⓔ
10 Ⓐ Ⓑ Ⓒ Ⓓ Ⓔ	20 Ⓐ Ⓑ Ⓒ Ⓓ Ⓔ	30 Ⓐ Ⓑ Ⓒ Ⓓ Ⓔ	40 Ⓐ Ⓑ Ⓒ Ⓓ Ⓔ

Only answers entered in the ovals in each grid area will be scored.

SECTION 4 STUDENT-PRODUCED RESPONSES

DIAGNOSTIC TEST

ANSWER KEY

Section 1 Critical Reading	Section 2 Math	Section 3 Critical Reading	Section 4 Math	Section 5 Writing Skills	
1. A	1. B	1. B	1. .75 or 3/4	1. A	25. E
2. C	2. A	2. B	2. 1/2	2. C	26. B
3. E	3. C	3. A	3. 4	3. D	27. A
4. B	4. B	4. D	4. 1/50	4. E	28. D
5. C	5. B	5. E	5. 3	5. C	29. E
6. D	6. C	6. C	6. 105 or 210	6. A	30. B
7. D	7. B	7. A	7. 26	7. B	31. A
8. A	8. B	8. D	8. 150	8. D	32. C
9. C	9. B	9. E	9. 56	9. D	33. A
10. D	10. C	10. C	10. 1/5 or 1/2	10. C	34. D
11. E	11. D	11. C	11. B	11. B	35. B
12. C	12. C	12. C	12. B	12. C	36. A
13. C	13. C	13. D	13. D	13. B	37. A
14. B	14. D	14. A	14. D	14. A	38. C
15. D	15. C	15. D	15. A	15. D	39. D
16. B	16. D	16. B	16. B	16. A	
17. C	17. C	17. C	17. C	17. C	
18. D	18. C	18. A	18. C	18. B	
19. B	19. B	19. B		19. E	
20. C	20. C	20. D		20. A	
21. A		21. A		21. C	
22. A		22. B		22. C	
23. C		23. E		23. B	
24. B		24. B		24. D	

DETAILED EXPLANATIONS

SECTION 1—VERBAL

1. (A) "Significant" (A) is the answer because it means important. If something is "unseemly" (B), it is disadvantageous, and a teacher would not tell a class to take notes on material that would not be to their advantage. "Highlighted" (C) is not an adjective, and therefore not a type of lesson, which this sentence calls for, and "expedited" (D) means improvised, which would have no meaning in the context of this sentence. "Superfluous" (E) means not crucial, or extra, and again, the teacher would not tell the class to take notes if the material were not crucial.

2. (C) The answer is "radiated" (C) because that means emitted, or given out. For something to be "extracted" (A), it must be pulled out, and this cannot be the answer because it would imply that something pulls energy out of light instead of light emitting energy, which is the case. "Implanted" (B) means put in, which, for similar reasons, would be faulty reasoning. For something to be "collapsing" (D) it would be falling in on itself, which is indicated nowhere else in the sentence. For something to be "aligned" (E) with something else, it must be parallel to it, which is extraneous to any meaning in this sentence.

3. (E) Many religions in the world use "fasting" (E), going without food and/or liquids for certain periods of time, to express their faith in that religion and submit to religious "discipline." Since "blasphemy" (A) means speaking in opposition to a deity, "prayer" would not be an expression of this, but its opposite. "Atonement" is repenting for one's transgressions, and while many world religions urge people to do this, that would not amount to "heresy" (B), which is maintaining a doctrine or belief which is designed to thwart the basic tenets of a religion. "Animism" (C) is the belief that objects have souls, and no monotheistic (belief in one God) religion holds this belief. "Asceticism" (D) is self-denial in the interests of religion, but "belief" would not be an expression of self-denial.

4. (B) If a person has a "condescending" (B) attitude, meaning haughty and putting others down, then one would expect "superficial" (not authentic or genuine) questions to be the ones asked by such a person. If someone has a "contemptuous" (A) attitude, the questions he or she asks will not be "compassionate," which means the ability to put oneself in another's place. Contempt is looking down on someone, the opposite of feeling compassion. If an attitude is "punitive" (C), it is punishing, and questions coming from a person with this attitude would not be "fascinating," but frightening. A "refreshing" (D) attitude is one that is delightful to the people around, which would indicate no "haranguing" (critical) questioning. If an attitude is "culpable" (E), it is deserving of blame, which would indicate that no "humbling" (embarrassing) questions would be asked, so this cannot be the correct answer either.

5. (C) The answer is "ingenuous" (C), because that means open and sincere, both are qualities that would get people to trust her, and assist her in her roles as diplomat and negotiator. "Devious" (A) and "Machiavellian" (B) both refer to dishonest, deceitful styles. Neither would enable a diplomat to be a wily (shrewd) negotiator, where people must make constant compromises. "Mutinous" (D) means uncontrolled, which would also work against effective negotiating. "Titular" (E) means honorary, which, although she might have honorary achievements, makes no sense in the context of this sentence.

6. (D) "Directs" (D) means sends, or forwards, so this is the correct answer. "Terminates" (A) means ends, so this would be the opposite of what the company would do if seeking new employees. The verb "seeks" (B) cannot be used to describe what the company does with hiring notices, as it means what the company does in terms of new employees (seeks them). To "overlook" (C) is to ignore or pass over, and to "decrease" (E) is to limit and pare down in number, so these, again, would not be what a company would do if it wanted to hire new employees.

7. (D) The correct answer is "abundant . . . accessed" (gain access to). The makers require a large quantity (abundant) of high-quality clay, and, once found, the clay must be accessed, or easily gotten to, in order to be of use. All of the first words in the other choices are possible answers; (A) "present," (B) "evident," (C) "nearby," and (E) "visible." However, they do not address the key words "large quantities," and are incorrect as the best answers for this question. Since we have chosen "abundant" as the correct answer, it is not necessary to address the secondary choices.

8. (A) Archaeology has ignoble roots in plunder, not in admiration of Palladio (B), nor in academic response to Gibbon (D) and Winkelmann (C). (E) is a distractor.

9. (C) Winkelmann belittled Roman art as merely imitative (line 16), but his opinions have not prevailed (A), as the work of Mommsen (E) attests. A neoclassicist, Winkelmann did not recommend the Gothic (C). There is no stated connection between Winkelmann and the Dilettanti (D).

10. (D) Collectors, including museums, upgraded archaeology in order to provide authenticity of findings, this well before the nineteenth century (A). Calleva (B) far exceeds in time this rigor; King Murat (E), while possibly influential, is cited not for repeated efforts, but only for one, at Pompeii (line 30). Mercati (C), while a pioneer, is not credited with sixteenth century definitive "rigor."

11. (E) Archaeology embraces local and national traits (lines 40–44) with many clues, not few (A), and is not limited by Winkelmann's influences (C). It has reassessed the relation of Greece and Rome, negating (B). (D) is a distractor, more in the province of geology than archaeology.

12. (C) Whatever Murat's personal motives, which are not clearly identified as greedy (B) nor marauding (A), his excavations extended beyond loot into physical anthropology (line 32). Murat's efforts were practical, not theoretical (D). (E) is a distractor not based on the text.

13. (C) The active support or patronage is usually tied up in the metaphorical usage. The growth or fruition is encouraged (A). Such encouragement may lead to a refined product or strain (B). The study itself is subject to support (D). The ground may be enriched through such nourishment (E).

14. (B) These subjects can be examined only by approved authorities. The Church's commitment to broad education (A) is dubious. The "surrender of reason" hardly fastens new ideas (C). Greek thought enters the discussion only several lines later (D). The Church's connection with civil authority does not arise in this passage (E).

15. (D) The Middle Ages, by implied contrast to the Renaissance, valued community over the individual. The author here (A) attaches no explicit value to this shift. Quite the opposite of self-assertion, the Middle Ages, according to the author, valued denial of the individual (B). The Renaissance sense of community is not central to this analogy (C). Although its role goes unnoticed here, the Church would not be viewed as friendly to the growth of individuality (E).

16. (B) The analogy is to painting, evident in the terms "relief" and "background." It is not three-dimensional (A). The author stresses depiction of human beings (C). The art form is visual, not based in sound (E). It does predate the development of film (D), although a modern reader may neglect that fact.

17. (C) The authors tell us this in the first sentence of the passage when they say, "there clearly must be a balance between the scope of individual freedom and the needs of government." The authors note there may be instances when either individual rights or governmental needs dominate, but these are extreme cases (e.g., *Korematsu*) and the usual case is to strike a balance between the two. Thus, both (A) and (B) are incorrect. (D) is incorrect because the authors admit in the first sentence of the second paragraph that "there may be political excesses that threaten to limit civil liberties and rights. . . ." Although it is true that a threatened limitation is not necessarily a limitation, if it did not sometimes occur the author would have been remiss in mentioning the possibility without indicating it hasn't happened. (E) is clearly negated by the focus of the passage on these issues.

18. (D) In the fourth sentence of the first paragraph the authors tell us that federal judges are independent of direct political control. In the next sentence the authors contrast this by telling us most state and local judges are elected "making them directly accountable to the people." We can thus infer that federal judges are not elected (which is true). Thus, (B) is incorrect. This same statement also makes (C) incorrect. Although (A) is true, we do not have to infer that local judges are mostly elected. We are directly told this is the case in the fifth sentence of the first paragraph. (E) Nowhere in the passage is it mentioned that state judges are not elected.

19. (B) In the first sentence of the second paragraph the authors mention the concern of political excesses. In the sixth sentence of the first paragraph, the authors suggest elected judges might be influenced by the political process in making its decisions. In the fourth sentence of the first paragraph we are told federal judges are not subject to direct political control. Thus, federal judges are better able to make decisions protecting individual liberties even though such decisions may run counter to public preferences. (A), (C), and (D) are all incorrect because each of these groups is elected and therefore subject to political influences. The Supreme Court (E), according to the authors, actually facilitated "the most extraordinary abridgment of the rights of citizens."

20. (C) The authors address this question in the second paragraph when they tell us, "there are also legitimate governmental needs that may call for a modification of individual freedoms. This occurs when these civil freedoms are used or misused, to attack the very

foundations of the system itself." In the third paragraph the authors discuss how World War II concentration camps for Japanese-Americans were justified on the basis of the fear the Japanese would attack the West Coast. Thus, when the nation is threatened, individual liberties may be limited. It is clear, then, that (D) is incorrect. It should be equally clear that (A) is incorrect. The third paragraph illustrates that the governmental need must be great to justify the magnitude of the restrictions placed on Japanese-Americans. In addition, in the first sentence of the second paragraph the authors note the limitation that the governmental need must be *legitimate*. (B) is incorrect because it suggests that the government may restrict civil rights when it needs to restrict civil rights. This merely restates the question and does not answer it. The rights of other nations' individuals (E) are not addressed here.

21. (A) This point is made in the first sentence of the third paragraph. The fear of the Japanese invading the West Coast, along with the fear of subversive activities, justified the extraordinary limitation of the rights of the Japanese-Americans relocated to concentration camps. (B) is incorrect because we are told the Supreme Court specifically rejected the possibility that the exclusion of Japanese-Americans was racially motivated. Rather, it was based on military necessity (sixth sentence of the third paragraph). (C) and (D) are incorrect because there is no mention of electoral pressures of public opinion in the discussion of the exclusion and *Korematsu*. According to the passage there was no legal precedent (E) for the detention of Japanese-Americans.

22. (A) In the third sentence of the third paragraph we are told the order excluding Japanese-Americans from the West Coast was upheld by the Supreme Court against constitutional challenges (making (C) incorrect). In the following sentences we are told the exclusion was justified by military necessity. If the exclusion was upheld and justified, it cannot be considered either unnecessary or illegal, making (B), (D), and (E) incorrect.

23. (C) The second sentence of the fourth paragraph indicates, "One of the most important spheres of civil liberties where the balancing test has been applied regards the civil liberties and rights enumerated in the First Amendment, particularly the liberties of *speech*, *press*, and *the right of assembly* (emphasis added)." Although the free exercise of religion is a First Amendment liberty, it is *not* specifically mentioned in the passage. Since (A), (B), and (D) are all mentioned, they are all incorrect. The passage does not address the right to bear arms (E).

24. (B) The fourth paragraph of the passage introduces the balancing and clear and present danger tests. Since the authors have previously indicated in both discussion and by example that restrictions on civil rights and liberties may sometimes be allowed, the purpose of these tests is to aid in the determination of when restrictions are justified. Thus, application of both the balancing test (I) and the clear and present danger test (III) may allow restrictions on civil rights and liberties. The rational basis test (II) is not mentioned in the passage, so we cannot make any judgments as to what it allows.

DETAILED EXPLANATIONS

SECTION 2—MATH

1. **(B)** Use ratio and proportion.

$$1' \times 2' \times 3' = 6 \text{ kg}$$
$$4' \times 5' \times 6' = x$$
$$\frac{6}{120} = \frac{6}{x}$$
$$6x = 720$$
$$x = \frac{720}{6}$$
$$x = 120$$

2. **(A)** Time from 8:00 a.m. to 11:40 a.m. equals 220 minutes. Time allowed between the first and second class, second and third class, third and fourth class, fourth and last class equals 20 minutes. Time for instruction in all five classes is

$$220 - 20 = 200 \text{ minutes.}$$

Time for each class period is

$$200 \div 5 = 40 \text{ minutes.}$$

3. **(C)**

$$V = LWH$$
$$= 10 \times 10 \times 10 = 1,000$$

Choice (A) just added the three dimensions, (B) only considered the two dimensions, and (D) and (E) considered the fourth and fifth power, respectively.

4. **(B)**

$$g^2 - 72 = (g - 2)^2$$
$$g^2 - 72 = g^2 - 4g + 4$$
$$4g = 76$$
$$g = 19$$

5. (B)

$$4 \text{ quarts} = 1 \text{ gallon}$$
$$2 \text{ pints} = 1 \text{ quart}$$
$$8 \text{ pints} = 1 \text{ gallon}$$
$$80 \text{ pints} = 10 \text{ gallons}$$
$$160 \text{ pints} = (2) \text{ 10-gallon cans}$$

6. (C)

Area of circle $= \pi r^2$

$$\pi r^2 = 298$$
$$\frac{22}{7} r^2 = 298\left(\frac{7}{22}\right)$$
$$r^2 = 94.8181$$
$$r = 9.73$$

Diameter $= 19.47$

7. (B) A very easy solution is: $x + y = \frac{1}{k}$, now substitute for k its given value:

$$x + y = \frac{1}{x - y}$$

cross multiplying gives $x^2 - y^2 = 1$.

8. (B)

$$(3^{a+b})(3^{a-b}) = 9 \times \frac{1}{9}$$
$$3^{2a} = 1$$
$$3^{2a} = 30 \quad (\text{since } 3^0 = 1)$$
$$2a = 0$$
$$a = 0$$

9. (B) If $2X + Y = 2$, then

$$2X = 2 - Y, \text{ or } X = 1 - \frac{Y}{2}$$

Substituting in $X + 3Y > 6$, we get

$$1 - \frac{Y}{2} + 3Y > 6.$$

Thus, $\frac{5Y}{2} > 5$, or $Y > 2$.

10. (C) $\$3,500 - \$500 = \$3,000$ (total depreciation)

$\$3,000 \div 5 =$ average yearly depreciation $= \$600$

11. (D) Let $x = \angle MQR$. Then

$$4x(\angle KPO) + x(\angle MQR) = 180$$
$$5x = 180$$

$$x = 36$$

Then $4x(\angle RQN) = 144$.

12. (C) Distance ÷ rate = time

Trip to college: 25 miles ÷ 25 mph = 1 hr

Trip from college: 37.5 miles ÷ 50 mph = 0.75 hr or 45 min

Saving = 0.25 hr = 15 min

13. (C) Time for flight #100 = 4 hrs

$$250 \times 4 = 1{,}000 \text{ miles}$$

Time for flight #200 = 3 hrs

$$300 \times 3 = 900 \text{ miles}$$

Let x = distance between planes at 12:00 noon

$$= 1{,}000 + 900 = 1{,}900 \text{ miles}.$$

14. (D) $5 + \left(\dfrac{5}{0.5}\right) = 5 + 10 = 15$

15. (C) If equal quantities are added to unequal quantities, the resulting sums are unequal in the same order. Therefore,

$$x + a < y + b.$$

16. (D) Let x = number of cups of flour to be used with 5 cups of milk.

$$\frac{\text{milk}}{\text{flour}} = \frac{3}{4} = \frac{5}{x}$$

$$\frac{3}{x} = 20$$

$$x = \frac{20}{3} = 6\frac{2}{3} \text{ cups of flour}$$

17. (C) Four large cups will fill seven large cups, therefore you can set up a proportion

$$\frac{\text{small cup}}{\text{large cup}} = \frac{7}{4}$$

Let x = number of small plastic cups that can be filled with one large cup.

$$\frac{7}{4} = \frac{x}{1}$$

$$4x = 7$$

$$x = \frac{7}{4}$$

$$x = 1\frac{3}{4}$$

18. (C) Choice (C) shows a sharp rise. Choices (A) and (D) show rise. Choice (B) shows a drop. Choice (E) shows neither a drop nor a rise.

19. (B)

Total = 34

$$\frac{2}{34} = \frac{1}{17} = 6\%$$

20. (C)

$3n + 1 = 3\,(4) + 1 = 13$ (prime number)

(A) $n^2 + 2 = 4^2 + 2 = 1$

(B) $n^2 + 2n = 4^2 + 2(4) = 16 + 8 = 2$

(D) $5n = 5\,(4) = 2$

(E) $n^2 - 4 = 4^2 - 4 = 16 - 4 = 1$

DETAILED EXPLANATIONS

SECTION 3—VERBAL

1. **(B)** The answer is "swaggering" (B) because that is a boastful attitude, and if a person is boastful, it is difficult to congratulate him or her. It is much easier to give praise to someone who demonstrates humility, which is the opposite of a swaggering attitude. "Gaudy" (A) means glaringly colorful, which would not describe an attitude. If someone is "courteous" (C), he or she is polite, and such a person would not be difficult to approach to congratulate. If someone is "retaliatory" (D), he or she wants to get revenge for something, and this sentence does not supply enough information for this to be the choice. While it may be difficult to talk to someone who has an "indirect" (E) manner, it is hard to say what an indirect attitude (what the sentence states) would be.

2. **(B)** These men were "historians" (B) because recording and analyzing events is what historians do. "Dramatists" (A) are playwrights, who do not record events, but create fictional works about them, expressed in plays. There could be no "psychoanalysts" (C) in ancient Greece because this method of treatment was developed in the nineteenth century A.D. These men were not "scientists" (D) either, because what scientists do is not record and analyze events, but discover the natural laws underlying them. They were also not "politicians" (E), because politicians govern people, which is not what the sentence states.

3. **(A)** Hearing an argument that sounds "logical," but that one still does not like or agree with, and that one still wants to disagree with, or "dispute" (A) is the best choice. If an argument is "topical" (B) it is based on timely events. The sentence provides no reason that one would want to dispute such a line of reasoning, so the context of this sentence does not indicate that this is the answer. To "fabricate" (C) is to make something up, or lie. Again, the sentence provides no context for coming to this conclusion. If something is "murky" (D), it is difficult to decipher, which would not prompt a listener to try to "classify" the line of reasoning; in fact, it would make that very difficult. If a line of reasoning is "rational" (E), that means it is sensible, which would offer little resistance to understanding, or apprehension, so this choice makes no sense either.

4. **(D)** The answer is (D), because students "familiar" with theorems would also need to be taught how to "demonstrate" the proofs for them. It is not likely that a class would be "ecstatic" (A) about mathematics, as the heightened emotion would be expected if they won the lottery, not if they were working on mathematics problems. Too, "right" here does not mean "write," so it is difficult to decide what this might mean. If the class is "enlightened" (B), they are taught something, but that would not lead to them discounting proofs; just the opposite would be expected. Similar reasons are those that account for rejecting (C) as the answer, since even if they were "cautious," the sentence

says nothing about why they would want to "dismiss" the proofs for the theorems. In addition, a class can be "satisfied" (E) with what they are learning, but that would not account for their wanting to "circumvent" (get around) the proofs instead of learning to do them.

5. (E) The answer is "immanently" (E), because spelled with an "a," "immanently" means genetically, and cats are more closely genetically related to lions than different breeds of dogs are to each other. "Intrinsically" (A) means characteristically, and while this might be considered as an answer here, it is not the most precise one, so should not be chosen. "Intimidatingly" (B) means in a threatening manner, which bears no relation to the rest of the sentence. "Intimately" (C) means closely but, for reasons similar to those stated for (A), should not be chosen (it is not the most precise answer). "Imminently" (D) means approaching, which has no meaning in this context.

6. (C) The answer is "posits" (C), as that means states. A theory doesn't teach (A) anything: people do. Similarly, a theory, in itself, can't believe (B), because it is not a person. To hover (D) is to float in the air, which makes no sense in this context. To ponder (E) is to wonder about, and again, it is impossible for a theory to ponder anything, because a theory is not a living thing.

7. (A) Lines 38–39 and 48–49 tell us that men thrive when government gets out of the way, denying (B) and (E). Thoreau has no words for corporations (C); and a "better government" (line 61) is possible, negating (D).

8. (D) Alacrity means speed, celerity.

9. (E) Government is not "the less necessary" (line 31) for being an ineffective weapon, denying the literal reading of (A). Line 25's "tradition" of government denies (B), and by extension, (C). Thoreau has mitigating remarks for government (lines 45–47, 61–64), denying (D).

10. (C) The Mexican war (lines 19–21) provides Thoreau with an example of government acting beyond the people. He does not espouse anarchy (see line 60), denying (A). Mexico confirms his view of standing armies, negating (D). Thoreau does not see anarchy as imminent (B). Business surmounts government in Thoreau's experience (line 49), denying (E).

11. (C) The primary focus of the passage is on the events leading to and including the dedication of the Cushman School. (C) is the best answer. The article *mentions in passing* the richness and complexity of Boston (B) and the fact that the conservatives opposed the dedication (D); neither (B) nor (D) are the primary focus of the passage. The passage mentions that Charlotte was a celebrated actress (A), but that is not the primary focus. The passage is more than just about the opening of a school. Some of the events leading to that opening are given. (E) should not be chosen.

12. (C) When referring to dedicating the school to a woman, the author expresses enthusiastic approval. (C) is the best choice. The conservatives—not the writer—were opposed; (A) should not be selected. The author does not seem to be concerned with who made the choice; she is just pleased with the choice itself. (B) is not the best choice. The writer does not actually "express appreciation to the mayor who made it all possible"; she merely mentions in passing that had there been a mayor who needed recognition, Cushman School might not be in existence. (D) is not the correct choice. She does not indicate that there was really no other choice; she merely mentions that no mayor needed recognition. (E) should not be chosen.

13. **(D)** In lines 3–4 the words "vigilant eyes of the cockerel" mean most nearly the constant eye of the weather cock. (D) is the best choice. Since the cockerel is a bird—not a mayor—neither (A) nor (B) should be chosen. A cockerel is not an older woman; (C) is not a good selection. A hurricane or storm does often have an eye, but the words cockerel are in direct reference to the weather vane with the rooster; (E) is not a good choice.

14. **(A)** Based on this passage, the author's reaction to suffrage for women would be enthusiastic approval of the right. (A) is the best selection. The writer would probably show enthusiasm for—not total objectivity—to suffrage for women; (B) is not a good choice. The writer seems to value women and would likely not show complete disdain for the entire idea. (C) is not the best choice. It is not likely that the author would engage in a careful study of the effect on male counterparts. (D) is not the most likely choice for her. It is not likely that the writer would show appreciation for those opposing the idea—just as she did not show appreciation for those who opposed a school with a woman's name.

15. **(D)** The tone of the author is enthusiasm. In fact, the writer is very open about her enthusiasm. (D) is the best choice. The writer does not use irony—a happening contrary to the expected. (A) is not the best choice. The author does not employ hostility (B) or animosity; neither does she use sarcasm (C) or disdain (E).

16. **(B)** The opening and closing paragraphs of Passage 2 state that the weakness of the stronger arguments against the moral significance of dreams makes it probable that dreams can be moral or immoral. Passage 2 addresses only two arguments against the possibility of moral dreams, it does not claim that no such argument is good (A). It acknowledges that we may have no control over our dreams (lines 56 and 57), but cites Freud (C) to show that this point might be irrelevant. Choice (D) sums up the argument of Passage 1, not of Passage 2. Passage 2 does not say that we have control over our dreams or that dreams are not imaginary (E).

17. **(C)** One of the premises in support of Passage 2 is Augustine's claim that the morality of an action lies in the intent to carry it out, thus if it is false, Passage 2's position weakens. Passage 2 accepts the possibility that dreams are imaginary (A), but regards this as morally inconclusive. It never tells us what Freud thinks about a dreamer's control over dreams (B). Since Passage 2 rests on Freud's and Augustine's positions, and since these positions might be true whether or not dreams are neurochemical, it is irrelevant whether Hobson is a neurophysiologist (D) and whether dreams are neurochemical (E).

18. **(A)** Lines 8 through 10 state explicitly that an action must be done from free will in order to have moral significance. They do not say that all actions done from free will are morally significant (B). They do not deny that we have free will altogether even if God or demons are the source of dreams (C), and even if dreams occur spontaneously (D). They talk about a certain kind of controlled act, not about all acts in our control (E).

19. **(B)** Passage 2 concedes the possibility that, as Macdonald states, imaginary acts are not real acts, but it dismisses this point as being morally inconclusive. It does not label her view as wrong (A). It says nothing about the relationship between Freud's position (C) and Macdonald's. Macdonald's position has to do with the imaginary character of dreams, not the dreamer's control (D). It makes no reference to the claim that dreams are not imaginary (E).

20. (D)   The passage says nothing about whether dreams are imaginary. It does say dreams may confront us with choices of actions (A); intention is morally more significant to an action than the possibility (B) or the reality (C) of that action; and that given a choice of actions in dreams, we can intend or not intend to do them (E).

21. (A)   The assumption is that if dreams can be immoral then they can also be moral. From this assumption it would be consistent to conclude that it is possible to commit an action of heroism (B) or an act of murder (C) in a dream, and that an act of murder in the dream, even if imaginary, would be immoral (D). The moralistic position, as stated in Passage 1, says nothing about the reality of dream contents (E), only about the morality of those contents.

22. (B)   Passage 2 accepts that dreams may be imaginary (line 58) but argues that Augustine's position shows the imaginary nature of dreams to be inconclusive as an answer to the moral question. Passage 2 denies the argument that dream acts can have no moral significance (A). Because Passage 2 accepts the possibility that dreams can be imaginary, choices (C), (D), and (E) are incorrect.

23. (E)   Lines 22 through 24 state that, for Hobson, random neurochemical firings precede the dream images. This is contrary to choice (A). The passage says nothing about Hobson's position on the morality of dreams, so it is unclear whether he would agree with Freud (B) or with Macdonald (C), or with the position that dreamers must have control of their dreams in order for the dreams to be morally significant (D).

24. (B)   Both passages do agree that we may have no control over our dreams, even though they may disagree about the significance of this point. Thus, it is incorrect to say they disagree about whether we can control our dreams (A). There is no indication that either passage considers the "imaginary character of dreams" argument to be more important than the "lack of control" argument (C). Passage 2 does not regard this argument as having the significance that Passage 1 thinks it has (D). Passage 2 uses Augustine's position against the "imaginary character of dreams" argument, not the "lack of control" argument (E).

DETAILED EXPLANATIONS

SECTION 4—MATH

1. Canceling factors common to both the numerator and denominator we get

$$\frac{2}{3} \times \frac{9}{4} \times \frac{16}{12} \times \frac{3}{8} = \frac{12}{16} = \frac{3}{4}$$

The answer can be entered as either $\frac{3}{4}$ or .75.

2. It is given that there are 24 students in all and 16 are male. By subtracting 16 from 24, we find that there are 8 females in the class. Setting up a ratio of females to males we get 8 to 16. Simplifying this we get 1 to 2, or written differently, $\frac{1}{2}$.

Note: Because this is a ratio, there is no other way to grid this response besides the one shown. Gridding .5 would not be acceptable in this case.

3. $$2^{y-x} = \frac{2^y}{2^x} = \frac{265}{64} = 4$$

4. (1) 10% of $zy = x =$ and   (2) $20\%w = y =$

$$\left(\frac{1}{10}\right)zy = x \qquad\qquad \left(\frac{2}{10}\right)w = y$$

Plug the second equation into the first and you get

$$\left(\frac{1}{10}\right)z\left(\left(\frac{2}{10}\right)w\right) = x = \left(\frac{2}{100}\right)zw = x$$

Therefore, zw is $\frac{2}{100}$, or $\frac{1}{50}$ of x.

5. The distance the first car travels in time t is given by $d_1(t) = 30t$ and the distance the second car travels is given by $d_2(t) = 40t$. Since the cars are traveling in perpendicular directions, we use the Pythagorean Theorem via the diagram below.

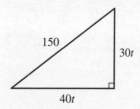

We have

$$d^2(t) = d_1{}^2(t) + d_2{}^2(t)$$

hence $(150)^2 = (30t)^2 + (40t)^2$

$$22{,}500 = 900t^2 + 1{,}600t^2$$

$$22{,}500 = 2{,}500t^2$$

$$\sqrt{\frac{22{,}500}{2{,}500}} = t$$

$$\frac{150}{50} = t$$

$$3 \text{ hours} = t$$

6.   If x is a multiple of 21, 15, and 35 it will be a multiple of the least common multiple of 21, 15, and 35. In order to calculate the least common multiple, we look at the prime decomposition of these numbers. We have

$$21 = 3 \times 7$$

$$15 = 3 \times 5$$

$$35 = 5 \times 7$$

The least common multiple is obtained as follows;

1)   For each prime, consider the highest power h to which the prime occurs in any of the factorizations. This yields a factor of the form p^h.

2)   The least common multiple is the product of the above factors.

In our case, each of the primes that occur (i.e., 3, 5, and 7) only occur to the first power; hence, we obtain least common multiple = $3 \times 5 \times 7 = 105$.

In order to satisfy condition d) x must be less than 225; thus, the two possible solutions are 105 and 210.

7.   First we find the value of $f(3)$. This is given by $f(3) = 3^2 - 1 = 8$; thus $g(f(3)) = g(8) = 3(8) + 2 = 26$.

8.   From the large triangle we have

$y + (x + y) + y = 180$

From the left inner triangle we have

$x + y + 60 = 180$

These equations simplify to

$$x + 3y = 180 \qquad (1)$$

$$x + y = 120 \qquad (2)$$

Subtracting (2) from (1) you get

$$2y = 60$$

$$y = 30$$

Plugging back into (2) you get

$$x + 30 = 120$$

$$x = 90$$

Therefore you can get

$$x + 2y = 90 + 60 = 150$$

9.   The percentage of students who scored between 60 and 89 is equal to 5% + 25% + 40% = 70%; hence, the number of students who scored between 60 and 89 is

$$70\%(80) = \frac{7}{10}(80) = 56.$$

10.   Letting $\frac{1}{r} = x$ we obtain the quadratic equation

$$x^2 - 7x + 10 = 0$$

Upon factoring we obtain

$$(x - 2)(x - 5) = 0.$$

This yields $x = 2$ and $x = 5$ and thus the solutions $r = \frac{1}{2}$ and $r = \frac{1}{5}$.

11. (B)   The shaded area is the outside rectangle minus the inside rectangle.

$$(F)(G) - (K)(L)$$

12. (B)   Since 16 and 25 are perfect squares, use their product as your common denominator.

$$\sqrt{\frac{25B^2 - 16B^2}{16 \times 25}} = \sqrt{\frac{9B^2}{16 \times 25}}$$

Now take the square root of the top and the square root of the bottom.

$$\frac{3B}{4 \times 5} = \frac{3B}{20}$$

13. (D)   Sum of four exams = (83) × (4) = 332. Sum required for average of 85% after five exams = (85) × (5) = 425. Difference (grade required on fifth exam) = 93.

14. (D)

$$V = LWH$$

$$200 = 10 \times 5 \times H$$

$$200 = 50H$$

$$\frac{200}{50} = H$$

$$4 = H$$

15. (A)   It takes 6 minutes to wash one car. 30 ÷ 5 = 6. Therefore, 30 × 6 = 180 minutes = 3 hours.

16. (B)   Let x = time needed to reach the desired age ratio. At that time the son will be $4 + x$ years old and Mr. Baker will be $30 + x$ years old.

$$5(4 + x) = 30 + x$$

$$20 + 5x = 30 + x$$

$$5x - x = 30 - 20$$

$$4x = 10$$

$$x = 2\frac{1}{2}$$

17. (C) Let x = original price of purchase.

$$x - .60x = \$96$$

$$.40x = \$96$$

$$x = \frac{\$96}{.40}$$

$$x = \$240$$

18. (C) Let legs = $3x$ and $4x$.

$$\text{Area} = \frac{(3x)(4x)}{2} = 96$$

$$\frac{12x^2}{2} = 96$$

$$6x^2 = 96$$

$$x^2 = \frac{96}{6}$$

$$x^2 = 16$$

$$x = 4$$

Let legs = 12 and 16. Apply the Pythagorean theorem.

$$h^2 = (12)^2 + (16)^2$$

$$h^2 = 144 + 256$$

$$h^2 = 400$$

$$h = \sqrt{400}$$

$$h = 20$$

DETAILED EXPLANATIONS

SECTION 5—WRITING SKILLS

1. **(A)** "Campus" is a singular noun; therefore, the pronoun referring to "campus" should be "its" so that the pronoun will agree with its antecedent. Choices (B), "findings of," and (C), "in which," both have prepositions appropriately used. Choice (D), "can," is a helping verb in the correct tense.

2. **(C)** Choice (C) should read, "could not care less." A person using this expression is indicating his or her total lack of interest in something; to say, "I could care less" indicates some interest, so the correct expression is "I could not care less." Choice (A) is the correct subject pronoun; choice (B), "good," is the adjective form used to follow the linking verb "be" and choice (D) is a gerund used as the object of a preposition.

3. **(D)** The idiom is "conform with" a law; something or someone will "conform to" an environment. Choices (A) and (B) are correctly used idioms. Choice (C) is the proper form of the adjective.

4. **(E)** Choice (A), "have seen," is the present perfect tense, which is used to make a statement about something occurring in the past but continuing into the present. The speaker has observed the problem of lack of self-esteem, but this problem has not stopped in the present time. Choice (B) is a comparative form, and "else" of choice (C) is necessary when comparing one thing with the group of which it is a member or part. (The observation about self-esteem is but one of several observations the speaker has made.) Choice (D) has a preposition to indicate relationship between "problem" and "people."

5. **(C)** "Allowed as how" is used sometimes in speaking, but the proper expression should be "allowed that." "Accommodated with," choice (A), is an idiom used to indicate "to supply with." Choice (B) is an infinitive phrase followed by a subordinate clause as the direct object. Choice (D), "had expected," is the past perfect tense to indicate previous past action: Mr. Burgess's estimate of the cost was made before the actual event.

6. **(A)** As this sentence reads, it is a fragment. "Having" should be eliminated, leaving "turned out" as the main verb in the proper tense. Choice (D), "so," is a coordinating conjunction relating two events of cause-and-effect; therefore, both main clauses should be independent. Choice (B) is the adverb form modifying the verb "turned out," and choice (C), "who," is the nominative form serving as the subject of "knows."

7. **(B)** "Protested against" is redundant; "protested" is sufficient. "Ago" in choice (A) is an adjective used following the noun "years" or as an adverb following "long." Choice (C) is a correct idiom. Choice (D), "any," is an adjective.

8. (D) Two subjects joined by "and" require a plural verb; "public opinion and government policy" should be completed by "have." Choice (A), "called," is a participle modifying "journalists." Choice (B), "rapidly," is an adverb modifying choice (C), which is a correct idiom.

9. (D) The expression should read, "renting (or buying) a tuxedo," in order to complete the parallelism following choice (B) "included": "hiring a limousine" and "buying gifts," choice (C). Choice (A) is a correct expression that can also be phrased, "more than he expected," if greater clarity is desired.

10. (C) The object pronoun "us" should follow the preposition "for." In choice (A), "viewing" is a gerund used as the subject and therefore requires the possessive adjective "our." Choice (B) is the verb. Choice (D) is a correct idiom.

11. (B) The modifier "only" is misplaced. To place this word before "stole" indicates that stealing is a minor problem; also, the meaning of the sentence clearly indicates Jules has stolen money one time, so the sentence should read, "stole money only once." Choice (A) is a correct preposition; choice (C) is a possessive pronoun modifying "conscience"; and choice (D) is an object pronoun as the object of "allow."

12. (C) There is no antecedent for "it." Choice (A), "a person," is the subject to which "he" in choice (B) refers. "Never" in choice (D) is a correctly placed adverb. The sentence should include a phrase such as "a crime" to serve as the antecedent of "it," or the phrase "for it" could be deleted.

13. (B) The adverb "daily" is misplaced and should be placed with "is bringing," choice (A), or with "habit." Choice (C) is a prepositional phrase, and choice (D) is a subject pronoun for the subordinate clause.

14. (A) The adverb form, "frequently," should be used to modify the verb. Choices (B) and (C) are a correct subject-verb combination. The adjective form, "possible," of choice (D) follows the linking verb "is."

15. (D) The conjunction "not only . . . but also" must be properly placed to indicate which qualities are being discussed and to maintain proper parallelism. Choice (D) contains three adjectives to follow the verb "to be": "capable and efficient" and "adept." Choices (A), (B), (C), and (E) are not parallel. In addition, choices (B) and (C) have "to be" after the conjunction, and this construction would require another verb after the second conjunction, "but also."

16. (A) This sentence contains two concepts, proper management and careful control. In choice (A) these two concepts are concisely worded and appear in parallel form. Choice (B) has no noun for "Managing" to modify. Choice (C) would be acceptable with the addition of commas to set off the introductory phrase. Choice (D) mangles the concepts, and the wording in choice (E) is poor.

17. (C) Choice (A) is a "squinting" modifier: it is unclear if "on the next day" tells when "I agreed" or when "to put up." Choice (B) does not clarify this problem. Choice (D) unnecessarily splits the subject and the verb, and choice (E) unnecessarily splits an infinitive.

18. (B) The interrupter, "though not nearly all," should be placed so as not to split important parts of the sentence. Choices (A), (D), and (E) are incorrect because the interrupter splits a preposition and its object. Choices (C) and (D) will produce a fragment because the subject "we" is missing.

19. (E) To mean "for example," the expression "like" is incorrect; the correct usage is "such as." Moreover, only a person can be referred to as "who." Therefore, choices (A) and (B) are incorrect. Choices (C) and (D) incorrectly use "likes" as a verb, thereby changing the intent of the sentence.

20. (A) Choice (A) correctly uses the object pronoun "whom" to follow the preposition "of." Choice (B) uses the wrong pronoun. Choice (C) inserts an extraneous preposition "about" that has no object. Choice (D) is awkward wording; choice (E) is also poor wording, especially with the pronoun "him" so far away from its antecedent.

21. (C) Choice (C) clearly and simply deals with the location and the fame of the Dead Sea. It is incorrect to use a preposition with no object in order to end a sentence. Choices (A), (D), and (E) are incorrect because they end with "famous for." Also, in the phrase, "where the Dead Sea is at," the word *at* is redundant; it is sufficient to write "where the Dead Sea is." Therefore, choices (A) and (B) are incorrect. Finally, since the Dead Sea still exists, the verbs must be in the present tense.

22. (C) The phrase "cannot help" should be followed by a gerund, not by "but." Choice (C) follows "cannot help" with the gerund "admitting." Choices (A) and (E) are incorrect because they follow "cannot help" with "but." The wording of choice (B), "cannot admit," and choice (E), "cannot know," twists the meaning of the sentence.

23. (B) The correct idiom is to have an insight into a situation or person. While "to" in choice (A) is close in meaning, it is not exact; "for" and "with" of choices (C), (D), and (E) are unacceptable. The location of "often" in choice (D) is poor, and the location of "often" in choice (E) makes no significant change in the meaning.

24. (D) It is obvious that the Greenes have just purchased plants: "Upon leaving the nursery." The location of the modifying phrase, "they had just bought," should be carefully placed in the sentence so it clearly modifies "plants" and not "car." Choice (D) has the modifying phrase immediately following "plants," and the meaning is clear. The wording of choices (A), (B), and (C) makes the reader think the car has just been purchased. Choice (E) omits the concept "they had just bought."

25. (E) Choice (E) retains the central idea while eliminating the wording problems of the other choices. There is no antecedent for "we" in choices (A) and (B). Also, the phrase "end up" is redundant; "up" should be eliminated. Therefore, choice (C) is incorrect. Choice (D) introduces a new concept of "war may end over there," an idea clearly not intended by the original.

26. (B) Choice (B) clearly and precisely states the issue of debate. Choice (C) is eliminated because it is too wordy and not the precise issue under debate. The correlative conjunctions, "whether . . . or," should be followed by parallel structures. Choice (A) follows "Whether" with a subject-verb combination not seen after "not." Choice (D) is parallel but in the wrong tense. Choice (E) has "Whether or not" run together and uses poor wording in the rest of the sentence.

27. (A) Choice (A) has both correct agreement and clear reference. Choice (B) has a subject-verb agreement problem, "charging . . . are." Choice (C) produces a fragment. It is unclear in choice (D) who will have the bad credit rating, and the wording of choice (E) has the obvious subject, "people," in a prepositional phrase.

28. (D) Choice (D) correctly presents the fifth grade field trip in a subordinate clause modifying "exhibit." Choices (A) and (B) have the coordinating conjunction "and," but the first part of the sentence is not equal in meaning or importance to the second part of the sentence. Choice (C) introduces "when" with no antecedent. Choice (E) uses "where" as the subordinating conjunction, but it is too far from its antecedent and is not the important idea of the sentence.

29. (E) This sentence presents two problems, namely use of a preposition instead of a coordinating conjunction to join the objects of the participle "having studied" and failure to show a time relationship. Choice (E) corrects both problems. Choice (B) simply replaces the preposition "along with" by "as well as"; choice (C) unnecessarily repeats the conjunction "and" rather than using the quite appropriate series construction. None of the choices (A), (B), (C), or (D) correctly shows the time relationship.

30. (B) This sentence contains the ambiguous pronoun "they," for which there is no antecedent and fails to show the relationship of the ideas expressed. Choice (B) eliminates the clause with the ambiguous pronoun and correctly expresses the reason for the sandbag placement. Choice (C) suggests that the two clauses joined by "and" are equal and does not show the subordinate relationship of the second to the first. Choice (D) introduces a dangling phrase with a coordinating conjunction, "and," that suggests the joining of equals, and choice (E) retains both errors from the original sentence.

31. (A) This sentence is correct in standard written English. Choices (B) and (C) introduce unnecessary words that add nothing to the meaning and make the sentence awkward and wordy; choices (D) and (E) do not correctly show relationship.

32. (C) Choice (C) shows the relationship accurately and eliminates the awkward gerund construction as the object of the preposition "despite." The adjective clause in choice (B) fails to show the relationship of the original sentence; choice (D) introduces the superfluous words "the fact that." Choice (E) inappropriately places the qualifying information in equal and parallel construction to the main idea of the sentence.

33. (A) This sentence is correct in standard written English. Choices (B) and (C) lose the strength of the parallelism in choice (A). Choice (D), although containing parallel construction, is idiomatically awkward with its participial phrases. Choices (B), (C), and (E) all exhibit wordiness.

34. (D) The original sentence, choice (A), contains the obvious and redundant words "was a man who." Choices (B), (C), and (E) are also unnecessarily verbose. Choice (D) makes the statement in the most direct way possible and represents correct standard usage.

35. (B) "The Wetherills" is plural, and the verb must agree. Choice (B) correctly changes "is" to "are"; the rest of the sentence is fine. (A) adds the singular "a group" which may make the verb "is" seem right, though it still modifies "The Wetherills" and must agree accordingly. (C) corrects the verb problem, but misplaces the clause "five brothers who ranched in the area" at the end of the sentence where it is unclear. (D) fails to correct the verb disagreement and places the clause at the end of the sentence, which alters the sense.

36. (A) Choice (A) best continues the topic of sentence 9, which concerns the cultural achievements of the Anasazi, and provides a nice transition toward the final sentence. (B) concerns an entirely different historical epoch, and is clearly irrelevant. (C) may fit somewhere in this essay, but not between sentences 9 and 10, where this new fact would seem obtrusive. (D) introduces the personal voice of the author, which is contrary to the expository tone in the passage thus far, and which would not fit between the factual content of sentences 9 and 10. (E) would be a good topic sentence for a new paragraph, but would not be good here.

37. (A) Sentence 4 is a dependent prepositional clause and would be best added onto sentence 3.

38. (C) The years of the Anasazi's zenith are best set off by commas and turned into a prepositional phrase, and of the two choices that do this, (C) uses "from," which is more appropriate than (D) "being." Without the punctuation, choice (A) is awkward; if the phrase were set off by commas, it would be acceptable, though (C) is more concise. (B) is just wrong; from the context of the passage it is clear that the Anasazi thrived in the years A.D. and not B.C.

39. (D) Choice (D) best utilizes commas that clarify the sense of the sentence. Choice (A) places the second comma incorrectly. (B) and (C) both utilize a colon, and each has an unnecessary comma. Choice (E) is correct as written.

CHAPTER 3

BASIC VERBAL SKILLS REVIEW

CHAPTER 3

BASIC VERBAL SKILLS REVIEW

I.   THE VOCABULARY ENHANCER

II. KNOWING YOUR WORD PARTS
(The most common prefixes, roots, and suffixes)

In order to perform successfully on the PSAT, you must be as familiar as possible with the different aspects of the test. One particular characteristic that becomes obvious when practicing the PSAT verbal questions is that without a strong, college-level vocabulary, it is virtually impossible to do well on the Sentence Completion section or the Critical Reading section.

But don't give up! Not all students have strong vocabularies, and if you don't, there are still ways to build on it before taking the PSAT. A game of Scrabble® will help build your vocabulary. But surely the most effective way to build your vocabulary is to read as much as you can. Reading increases your familiarity with words and their uses in different contexts. By reading every day, you can increase your chances of recognizing a word and its meaning in a question.

As you read books, newspapers, and magazines, ask yourself these questions:

*   What was the main idea of this material?

*   What was the author's purpose in writing this material?

*   How did the author make his arguments?

*   What tone did the author use? Doing so will enhance your understanding of what you are reading. This ultimately leads to a stronger vocabulary and an increase in your reading abilities.

Unfortunately, you may not remember all the words that you read. This is why we have provided you with a necessary tool to building your vocabulary. We know that learning new words requires much time and concentration. Therefore, rather than giving you an extensive list of thousands of words, we have narrowed down our vocabulary list so that you will be able to study all the words without becoming overwhelmed. Our list consists of 600 words. The first 300 are essential vocabulary, covering the most frequently tested words on the PSAT. These words have appeared over and over again on the PSAT. In addition, we have provided a second list of 300 words that are commonly tested on the PSAT. It is very important to study all 600 words because any of them could appear on the test. Although these are not the only words you may encounter, they will give you a strong indication as to the appropriate level of vocabulary that is present on the PSAT and prevent you from wasting time studying words that will never appear on the test.

OUR VOCABULARY ENHANCER

The Vocabulary Enhancer is a list of the most frequently tested words on the PSAT. The most effective way to study these words is one section at a time. Identify the words you don't know or that are defined in unusual ways, and write them on index cards with the word on one side and the definition on the other. Test yourself on these words by completing the drills that follow each section. Doing the same for the list of additional words will also help you. In addition, studying our table of prefixes, roots, and suffixes will allow you to dissect words in order to determine the meaning of any unfamiliar words.

I. THE VOCABULARY ENHANCER (THE MOST FREQUENTLY TESTED WORDS ON THE PSAT)

GROUP 1

abstract – *adj.* – not easy to understand; theoretical

acclaim – *n.* – loud approval; applause

acquiesce – *v.* – to agree or consent to an opinion

adamant – *adj.* – not yielding; firm

adversary – *n.* – an enemy; foe

advocate – 1. *v.* – to plead in favor of; 2. *n.* – supporter; defender

aesthetic – *adj.* – showing good taste; artistic

alleviate – *v.* – to lessen or make easier

aloof – *adj.* – distant in interest; reserved; cool

altercation – *n.* – controversy; dispute

altruistic – *adj.* – unselfish

amass – *v.* – to collect together; accumulate

ambiguous – *adj.* – not clear; uncertain; vague

ambivalent – *adj.* – undecided

ameliorate – *v.* – to make better; to improve

amiable – *adj.* – friendly

amorphous – *adj.* – having no determinate form

anarchist – *n.* – one who believes that a formal government is unnecessary

antagonism – *n.* – hostility; opposition

apathy – *n.* – lack of emotion or interest

appease – *v.* – to make quiet; to calm

apprehensive – *adj.* – fearful; aware; conscious

arbitrary – *adj.* – based on one's preference or judgment

arrogant – *adj.* – acting superior to others; conceited

articulate – 1. *v.* – to speak distinctly; 2. *adj.* – eloquent; fluent; 3. *adj.* – capable of speech; 4. *v.* – to hinge; to connect; 5. *v.* – to convey; to express effectively

---

DRILL: GROUP 1

DIRECTIONS: Match each word in the left column with the word in the right column that is most opposite in meaning.

Word				Match			
1. ___articulate	6. ___abstract	A.	hostile	F.	disperse
2. ___apathy	7. ___acquiesce	B.	concrete	G.	enthusiasm
3. ___amiable	8. ___arbitrary	C.	selfish	H.	certain
4. ___altruistic	9. ___amass	D.	reasoned	I.	resist
5. ___ambivalent	10. ___adversary	E.	ally	J.	incoherent

DIRECTIONS: Match each word in the left column with the word in the right column that is most similar in meaning.

Word				Match			
11. ___adamant	14. ___antagonism	A.	afraid	D.	insistent
12. ___aesthetic	15. ___altercation	B.	disagreement	E.	hostility
13. ___apprehensive		C.	tasteful		

GROUP 2

assess – *v.* – to estimate the value of

astute – *adj.* – cunning; sly; crafty

atrophy – *v.* – to waste away through lack of nutrition

audacious – *adj.* – fearless; bold

augment – *v.* – to increase or add to; to make larger

austere – *adj.* – harsh; severe; strict

authentic – *adj.* – real; genuine; trustworthy

authoritarian – *n.* – acting as a dictator; demanding obedience

banal – *adj.* – common; petty; ordinary

belittle – *v.* – to make small; to think lightly of

benefactor – *n.* – one who helps others; a donor

benevolent – *adj.* – kind; generous

benign – *adj.* – mild; harmless

biased – *adj.* – prejudiced; influenced; not neutral

blasphemous – *adj.* – irreligious; away from acceptable standards

blithe – *adj.* – happy; cheery; merry

brevity – *n.* – briefness; shortness

candid – *adj.* – honest; truthful; sincere

capricious – *adj.* – changeable; fickle

caustic – *adj.* – burning; sarcastic; harsh

censor – *v.* – to examine and delete objectionable material

censure – *v.* – to criticize or disapprove of

charlatan – *n.* – an imposter; fake

coalesce – *v.* – to combine; come together

collaborate – *v.* – to work together; cooperate

DRILL: GROUP 2

DIRECTIONS: Match each word in the left column with the word in the right column that is most opposite in meaning.

	Word				Match		
1.	___augment	6.	___authentic	A.	permit	F.	malicious
2.	___biased	7.	___candid	B.	heroine	G.	neutral
3.	___banal	8.	___belittle	C.	praise	H.	mournful
4.	___benevolent	9.	___charlatan	D.	diminish	I.	unusual
5.	___censor	10.	___blithe	E.	dishonest	J.	fake

Word		Match	
11. ___collaborate	14. ___censure	A. harmless	D. cooperate
12. ___benign	15. ___capricious	B. cunning	E. criticize
13. ___astute		C. changeable	

GROUP 3

compatible – *adj.* – in agreement with; harmonious

complacent – *adj.* – content; self-satisfied; smug

compliant – *adj.* – yielding; obedient

comprehensive – *adj.* – all-inclusive; complete; thorough

compromise – *v.* – to settle by mutual adjustment

concede – *v.* – 1. to acknowledge; admit; 2. to surrender; to abandon one's position

concise – *adj.* – in few words; brief; condensed

condescend – *v.* – to come down from one's position or dignity

condone – *v.* – to overlook; to forgive

conspicuous – *adj.* – easy to see; noticeable

consternation – *n.* – amazement or terror that causes confusion

consummation – *n.* – the completion; finish

contemporary – *adj.* – living or happening at the same time; modern

contempt – *n.* – scorn; disrespect

contrite – *adj.* – regretful; sorrowful

conventional – *adj.* – traditional; common; routine

cower – *v.* – to crouch down in fear or shame

defamation – *n.* – harming a name or reputation; slandering

deference – *adj.* – yielding to the opinion of another

deliberate – 1. *v.* – to consider carefully; to weigh in the mind; 2. *adj.* – intentional

denounce – *v.* – to speak out against; condemn

depict – *v.* – to portray in words; to present a visual image deplete – v. – to reduce; to empty

depravity – n. – moral corruption; badness

deride – v. – to ridicule; to laugh at with scorn

DRILL: GROUP 3

DIRECTIONS: Match each word in the left column with the word in the right column that is most opposite in meaning.

	Word				Match		
1.	___deplete	6.	___condone	A.	unintentional	F.	support
2.	___contemporary	7.	___conspicuous	B.	disapprove	G.	beginning
3.	___concise	8.	___consummation	C.	invisible	H.	ancient
4.	___deliberate	9.	___denounce	D.	respect	I.	virtue
5.	___depravity	10.	___contempt	E.	fill	J.	verbose

DIRECTIONS: Match each word in the left column with the word in the right column that is most similar in meaning.

	Word				Match		
11.	___compatible	14.	___comprehensive	A.	portray	D.	thorough
12.	___depict	15.	___complacent	B.	content	E.	common
13.	___conventional			C.	harmonious		

GROUP 4

desecrate – v. – to violate a holy place or sanctuary

detached – adj. – separated; not interested; standing alone

deter – v. – to prevent; to discourage; to hinder

didactic – adj. – 1. instructive; 2. dogmatic; preachy

digress – v. – to stray from the subject; to wander from topic

diligence – n. – hard work

discerning – adj. – distinguishing one thing from another

discord – n. – disagreement; lack of harmony

discriminating – 1. v. to distinguish one thing from another; 2. v. – to demonstrate bias; 3. adj. – able to distingush

disdain – 1. n. – intense dislike; 2. v. – to look down upon; scorn

disparage – v. – to belittle; to undervalue

disparity – *n.* – difference in form, character, or degree

dispassionate – *adj.* – lack of feeling; impartial

disperse – *v.* – to scatter; to separate

disseminate – *v.* – to circulate; to scatter

dissent – *v.* – to disagree; to differ in opinion

dissonance – *n.* – harsh contradiction

diverse – *adj.* – different; dissimilar

document – 1. *n.* – official paper containing information; 2. *v.* – to support; to substantiate; to verify

dogmatic – *adj.* – stubborn; biased; opinionated

dubious – *adj.* – doubtful; uncertain; skeptical; suspicious

eccentric – *adj.* – odd; peculiar; strange

efface – *v.* – to wipe out; to erase

effervescence – *n.* – 1. liveliness; spirit; enthusiasm; 2. bubbliness

egocentric – *adj.* – self-centered

DRILL: GROUP 4

DIRECTIONS: Match each word in the left column with the word in the right column that is most opposite in meaning.

	Word			Match		
1.	D detached	6.	B dubious	A. agree	F.	respect
2.	E deter	7.	___diligence	B. certain	G.	compliment
3.	___dissent	8.	___disdain	C. lethargy	H.	sanctify
4.	I discord	9.	J desecrate	D. connected	I.	harmony
5.	J efface	10.	F disparage	E. assist	J.	restore

DIRECTIONS: Match each word in the left column with the word in the right column that is most similar in meaning.

	Word			Match		
11.	___effervescence	14.	___document	A. stubborn	D.	liveliness
12.	___dogmatic	15.	___eccentric	B. distribute	E.	odd
13.	___disseminate			C. substantiate		

GROUP 5

elaboration – *n.* – act of clarifying; adding details

eloquence – *n.* – the ability to speak well

elusive – *adj.* – hard to catch; difficult to understand

emulate – *v.* – to imitate; to copy; to mimic

endorse – *v.* – to support; to approve of; to recommend

engender – *v.* – to create; to bring about

enhance – *v.* – to improve; to compliment; to make more attractive

enigma – *n.* – mystery; secret; perplexity

ephemeral – *adj.* – temporary; brief; short-lived

equivocal – *adj.* – doubtful; uncertain

erratic – *adj.* – unpredictable; strange

erroneous – *adj.* – untrue; inaccurate; not correct

esoteric – *adj.* – incomprehensible; obscure

euphony – *n.* – pleasant sound

execute – *v.* – 1. to put to death; to kill; 2. to carry out; to fulfill

exemplary – *adj.* – serving as an example; outstanding

exhaustive – *adj.* – thorough; complete

expedient – *adj.* – helpful; practical; worthwhile

expedite – *v.* – to speed up

explicit – *adj.* – specific; definite

extol – *v.* – to praise; to commend

extraneous – *adj.* – irrelevant; not related; not essential

facilitate – *v.* – to make easier; to simplify

fallacious – *adj.* – misleading

fanatic – *n.* – enthusiast; extremist

DRILL: GROUP 5

DIRECTIONS: Match each word in the left column with the word in the right column that is most opposite in meaning.

Word				Match			
1. ___extraneous	6.	___erratic	A.	incomplete	F.	eternal
2. ___ephemeral	7.	___explicit	B.	delay	G.	condemn
3. ___exhaustive	8.	___euphony	C.	dependable	H.	relevant
4. ___expedite	9.	___elusive	D.	comprehensible	I.	indefinite
5. ___erroneous	10.	___extol	E.	dissonance	J.	accurate

DIRECTIONS: Match each word in the left column with the word in the right column that is most similar in meaning.

Word			Match		
11. ___endorse	14. ___fallacious	A.	enable	D.	worthwhile
12. ___expedient	15. ___engender	B.	recommend	E.	deceptive
13. ___facilitate		C.	create		

GROUP 6

fastidious – *adj.* – fussy; hard to please

fervent – *adj.* – passionate; intense

fickle – *adj.* – changeable; unpredictable

fortuitous – *adj.* – accidental; happening by chance; lucky

frivolity – *adj.* – giddiness; lack of seriousness

fundamental – *adj.* – basic; necessary

furtive – *adj.* – secretive; sly

futile – *adj.* – worthless; unprofitable

glutton – *n.* – overeater

grandiose – *adj.* – extravagant; flamboyant

gravity – *n.* – seriousness

guile – *n.* – slyness; deceit

gullible – *adj.* – easily fooled

hackneyed – *adj.* – commonplace; trite

hamper – *v.* – to interfere with; to hinder

haphazard – *adj.* – disorganized; random

hedonistic – *adj.* – pleasure seeking

heed – *v.* – to obey; to yield to

heresy – *n.* – opinion contrary to popular belief

hindrance – *n.* – blockage; obstacle

humility – *n.* – lack of pride; modesty

hypocritical – *adj.* – two-faced; deceptive

hypothetical – *adj.* – assumed; uncertain

illuminate – *v.* – to make understandable

illusory – *adj.* – unreal; false; deceptive

DRILL: GROUP 6

DIRECTIONS: Match each word in the left column with the word in the right column that is most opposite in meaning.

	Word				Match		
1.	___heresy	6.	___fervent	A.	predictable	F.	beneficial
2.	___fickle	7.	___fundamental	B.	dispassionate	G.	orthodoxy
3.	___illusory	8.	___furtive	C.	simple	H.	organized
4.	___frivolity	9.	___futile	D.	extraneous	I.	candid
5.	___grandiose	10.	___haphazard	E.	real	J.	seriousness

DIRECTIONS: Match each word in the left column with the word in the right column that is most similar in meaning.

	Word				Match		
11.	___glutton	14.	___hackneyed	A.	hinder	D.	overeater
12.	___heed	15.	___hindrance	B.	obstacle	E.	obey
13.	___hamper			C.	trite		

GROUP 7

immune – *adj.* – protected; unthreatened by

immutable – *adj.* – unchangeable; permanent

impartial – *adj.* – unbiased; fair

impetuous – *adj.* – 1. rash; impulsive; 2. forcible; violent implication – *n.* – suggestion; inference

inadvertent – *adj.* – not on purpose; unintentional

incessant – *adj.* – constant; continual

incidental – *adj.* – extraneous; unexpected

inclined – *adj.* – 1. apt to; likely to; 2. angled

incoherent – *adj.* – illogical; rambling

incompatible – *adj.* – disagreeing; disharmonious

incredulous – *adj.* – unwilling to believe; skeptical

indifferent – *adj.* – unconcerned

indolent – *adj.* – lazy; inactive

indulgent – *adj.* – lenient; patient

inevitable – *adj.* – sure to happen; unavoidable

infamous – *adj.* – having a bad reputation; notorious

infer – *v.* – to form an opinion; to conclude

initiate – 1. *v.* – to begin; to admit into a group; 2. *n.* – a person who is in the process of being admitted into a group

innate – *adj.* – natural; inborn

innocuous – *adj.* – harmless; innocent

innovate – *v.* – to introduce a change; to depart from the old

insipid – *adj.* – uninteresting; bland

instigate – *v.* – to start; to provoke

intangible – *adj.* – incapable of being touched; immaterial

DRILL: GROUP 7

DIRECTIONS: Match each word in the left column with the word in the right column that is most opposite in meaning.

Word				Match			
1. ___immutable	6. ___innate	A.	intentional	F.	changeable
2. ___impartial	7. ___incredulous	B.	articulate	G.	avoidable
3. ___inadvertent	8. ___inevitable	C.	gullible	H.	harmonious
4. ___incoherent	9. ___intangible	D.	material	I.	learned
5. ___incompatible	10. ___indolent	E.	biased	J.	energetic

DIRECTIONS: Match each word in the left column with the word in the right column that is most similar in meaning.

Word			Match		
11. ___impetuous	14. ___instigate	A. lenient	D. conclude
12. ___incidental	15. ___indulgent	B. impulsive	E. extraneous
13. ___infer		C. provoke	

GROUP 8

ironic – *adj.* – contradictory; inconsistent; sarcastic

irrational – *adj.* – not logical

jeopardy – *n.* – danger

kindle – *v.* – to ignite; to arouse

languid – *adj.* – weak; fatigued

laud – *v.* – to praise

lax – *adj.* – careless; irresponsible

lethargic – *adj.* – lazy; passive

levity – *n.* – silliness; lack of seriousness

lucid – *adj.* – 1. shining; 2. easily understood

magnanimous – *adj.* – forgiving; unselfish

malicious – *adj.* – spiteful; vindictive

marred – *adj.* – damaged

meander – *v.* – to wind on a course; to go aimlessly

melancholy – *n.* – depression; gloom

meticulous – *adj.* – exacting; precise

minute – *adj.* – extremely small; tiny

miser – *n.* – penny pincher; stingy person

mitigate – *v.* – to alleviate; to lessen; to soothe

morose – *adj.* – moody; despondent

negligence – *n.* – carelessness

neutral – *adj.* – impartial; unbiased

nostalgic – *adj.* – longing for the past; filled with bittersweet memories

novel – *adj.* – new

DRILL: GROUP 8

DIRECTIONS: Match each word in the left column with the word in the right column that is most opposite in meaning.

	Word				Match		
1.	___irrational	6.	___magnanimous	A.	extinguish	F.	ridicule
2.	___kindle	7.	___levity	B.	jovial	G.	kindly
3.	___meticulous	8.	___minute	C.	selfish	H.	sloppy
4.	___malicious	9.	___laud	D.	logical	I.	huge
5.	___morose	10.	___novel	E.	seriousness	J.	stale

DIRECTIONS: Match each word in the left column with the word in the right column that is most similar in meaning.

	Word				Match		
11.	___ironic	14.	___jeopardy	A.	lessen	D.	carelessness
12.	___marred	15.	___negligence	B.	damaged	E.	danger
13.	___mitigate			C.	sarcastic		

GROUP 9

nullify – *v.* – to cancel; to invalidate

objective – 1. *adj.* – open-minded; impartial; 2. *n.* – goal

obscure – *adj.* – not easily understood; dark

obsolete – *adj.* – out of date; passe

ominous – *adj.* – threatening

optimist – *n.* – person who hopes for the best; person who sees the good side

orthodox – *adj.* – traditional; accepted

pagan – 1. *n.* – polytheist; 2. *adj.* – polytheistic

partisan – 1. *n.* – supporter; follower; 2. *adj.* – biased; one-sided

perceptive – *adj.* – full of insight; aware

peripheral – *adj.* – marginal; outer

pernicious – *adj.* – dangerous; harmful

pessimism – *n.* – seeing only the gloomy side; hopelessness

phenomenon – *n.* – 1. miracle; 2. occurrence

philanthropy – *n.* – charity; unselfishness

pious – *adj.* – religious; devout; dedicated

placate – *v.* – to pacify

plausible – *adj.* – probable; feasible

pragmatic – *adj.* – matter-of-fact; practical

preclude – *v.* – to inhibit; to make impossible

predecessor – *n.* – one who has occupied an office before another

prodigal – *adj.* – wasteful; lavish

prodigious – *adj.* – exceptional; tremendous

profound – *adj.* – deep; knowledgeable; thorough

profusion – *n.* – great amount; abundance

DRILL: GROUP 9

DIRECTIONS: Match each word in the left column with the word in the right column that is most opposite in meaning.

	Word				Match		
1.	___objective	6.	___plausible	A.	scanty	F.	minute
2.	___obsolete	7.	___preclude	B.	assist	G.	anger
3.	___placate	8.	___prodigious	C.	superficial	H.	pessimism
4.	___profusion	9.	___profound	D.	biased	I.	modern
5.	___peripheral	10.	___optimism	E.	improbable	J.	central

DIRECTIONS: Match each word in the left column with the word in the right column that is most similar in meaning.

	Word				Match		
11.	___nullify	14.	___pernicious	A.	invalidate	D.	threatening
12.	___ominous	15.	___prodigal	B.	follower	E.	harmful
13.	___partisan			C.	lavish		

GROUP 10

prosaic – *adj.* – tiresome; ordinary

provincial – *adj.* – regional; unsophisticated

provocative – *adj.* – 1. tempting; 2. irritating

prudent – *adj.* – wise; careful; prepared

qualified – *adj.* – experienced; indefinite

rectify – *v.* – to correct

redundant – *adj.* – repetitious; unnecessary

refute – *v.* – to challenge; to disprove

relegate – *v.* – to banish; to put to a lower position

relevant – *adj.* – of concern; significant

remorse – *n.* – guilt; sorrow

reprehensible – *adj.* – wicked; disgraceful

repudiate – *v.* – to reject; to cancel

rescind – *v.* – to retract; to discard

resignation – *n.* – 1. quitting; 2. submission

resolution – *n.* – proposal; promise; determination

respite – *n.* – recess; rest period

reticent – *adj.* – silent; reserved; shy

reverent – *adj.* – respectful

rhetorical – *adj.* – having to do with verbal communication

rigor – *n.* – severity

sagacious – *adj.* – wise; cunning

sanguine – *adj.* – 1. optimistic; cheerful; 2. red

saturate – *v.* – to soak thoroughly; to drench

scanty – *adj.* – inadequate; sparse

DRILL: GROUP 10

DIRECTIONS: Match each word in the left column with the word in the right column that is most opposite in meaning.

	Word				Match		
1.	___provincial	6.	___remorse	A.	inexperienced	F.	affirm
2.	___reticent	7.	___repudiate	B.	joy	G.	extraordinary
3.	___prudent	8.	___sanguine	C.	pessimistic	H.	sophisticated
4.	___qualified	9.	___relevant	D.	unrelated	I.	forward
5.	___relegate	10.	___prosaic	E.	careless	J.	promote

DIRECTIONS: Match each word in the left column with the word in the right column that is most similar in meaning.

Word			Match		
11. ___provocative	14. ___rescind	A. drench	D. severity		
12. ___rigor	15. ___reprehensible	B. tempting	E. disgraceful		
13. ___saturate		C. retract			

GROUP 11

scrupulous – *adj.* – honorable; exact

scrutinize – *v.* – to examine closely; to study

servile – *adj.* – slavish; groveling

skeptic – *n.* – doubter

slander – *v.* – to defame; to maliciously misrepresent

solemnity – *n.* – seriousness

solicit – *v.* – to ask; to seek

stagnant – *adj.* – motionless; uncirculating

stanza – *n.* – group of lines in a poem having a definite pattern

static – *adj.* – inactive; changeless

stoic – *adj.* – detached; unruffled; calm

subtlety – *n.* – 1. understatement; 2. propensity for understatement; 3. sophistication; 4. cunning

superficial – *adj.* – on the surface; narrow-minded; lacking depth

superfluous – *adj.* – unnecessary; extra

surpass – *v.* – to go beyond; to outdo

sycophant – *adj.* – flatterer

symmetry – *n.* – correspondence of parts; harmony

taciturn – *adj.* – reserved; quiet; secretive

tedious – *adj.* – time-consuming; burdensome; uninteresting

temper – *v.* – to soften; to pacify; to compose

tentative – *adj.* – not confirmed; indefinite

thrifty – *adj.* – economical; pennywise

tranquility – *n.* – peace; stillness; harmony

trepidation – *n.* – apprehension; uneasiness

trivial – *adj.* – unimportant; small; worthless

DRILL: GROUP 11

DIRECTIONS: Match each word in the left column with the word in the right column that is most opposite in meaning.

Word				Match			
1. ___scrutinize	6. ___tentative	A.	frivolity	F.	skim
2. ___skeptic	7. ___thrifty	B.	enjoyable	G.	turbulent
3. ___solemnity	8. ___tranquility	C.	prodigal	H.	active
4. ___static	9. ___solicit	D.	chaos	I.	believer
5. ___tedious	10. ___stagnant	E.	give	J.	confirmed

DIRECTIONS: Match each word in the left column with the word in the right column that is most similar in meaning.

Word				Match			
11. ___symmetry	14. ___subtle	A.	understated	D.	fear
12. ___superfluous	15. ___trepidation	B.	unnecessary	E.	flatterer
13. ___sycophant		C.	balance		

GROUP 12

tumid – *adj.* – swollen; inflated

undermine – *v.* – to weaken; to ruin

uniform – *adj.* – consistent; unvaried; unchanging

universal – *adj.* – concerning everyone; existing everywhere

unobtrusive – *adj.* – inconspicuous; reserved

unprecedented – *adj.* – unheard of; exceptional

unpretentious – *adj.* – simple; plain; modest

vacillation – *n.* – fluctuation

valid – *adj.* – acceptable; legal

vehement – *adj.* – intense; excited; enthusiastic

venerate – *v.* – to revere

verbose – *adj.* – wordy; talkative

viable – *adj.* – 1. capable of maintaining life; 2. possible; attainable

vigor – *n.* – energy; forcefulness

vilify – v . – to slander

virtuoso – *n.* – highly skilled artist

virulent – *adj.* – deadly; harmful; malicious

vital – *adj.* – important; spirited

volatile – *adj.* – changeable; undependable

vulnerable – *adj.* – open to attack; unprotected

wane – *v.* – to grow gradually smaller

whimsical – *adj.* – fanciful; amusing

wither – *v.* – to wilt; to shrivel; to humiliate; to cut down

zealot – *n.* – believer; enthusiast; fan

zenith – *n.* – point directly overhead in the sky

DRILL: GROUP 12

DIRECTIONS: Match each word in the left column with the word in the right column that is most opposite in meaning.

	Word				Match			
1.	___uniform	6.	___vigor	A.	amateur	F.	support
2.	___virtuoso	7.	___volatile	B.	trivial	G.	constancy
3.	___vital	8.	___vacillation	C.	visible	H.	lethargy
4.	___wane	9.	___undermine	D.	placid	I.	wax
5.	___unobtrusive	10.	___valid	E.	unacceptable	J.	varied

DIRECTIONS: Match each word in the left column with the word in the right column that is most similar in meaning.

	Word				Match			
11.	___wither	14.	___vehement	A.	intense	D.	possible
12.	___whimsical	15.	___virulent	B.	deadly	E.	shrivel
13.	___viable			C.	amusing		

ADDITIONAL VOCABULARY

The following words are among the terms most commonly found on the PSAT.

abandon – 1. *v.* – to leave behind; 2. *v.* – to give something up; 3. *n.* – freedom; enthusiasm; impetuosity

abase – *v.* – to degrade; to humiliate; to disgrace

abbreviate – *v.* – to shorten; to compress; to diminish

aberrant – *adj.* – abnormal

abhor – *v.* – to hate

abominate – *v.* – to loathe; to hate

abridge – *v.* – 1. to shorten; 2. to limit; to take away

absolve – *v.* – to forgive; to acquit

abstinence – *n.* – self-control; abstention; chastity

accede – *v.* – to comply with; to consent to

accomplice – *n.* – co-conspirator; partner; partner-in-crime

accrue – *v.* – to collect; to build up

acrid – *adj.* – sharp; bitter; foul-smelling

adept – *adj.* – skilled; practiced

adverse – *adj.* – negative; hostile; antagonistic; inimical

affable – *adj.* – friendly; amiable; good-natured

aghast – *adj.* – 1. astonished; amazed; 2. horrified; terrified; appalled

alacrity – *n.* – 1. enthusiasm; fervor; 2. liveliness; sprightliness

allocate – *v.* – set aside; designate; assign

allure – 1. *v.* – to attract; to entice; 2. *n.* – attraction; temptation; glamour

amiss – 1. *adj.* – wrong; awry; 2. *adv.* – wrongly; mistakenly

analogy – *n.* – similarity; correlation; parallelism; simile; metaphor

anoint – *v.* – 1. to crown; to ordain; 2. to smear with oil

anonymous – *adj.* – nameless; unidentified

arduous – *adj.* – difficult; burdensome

awry – 1. *adv.* – crooked(ly); uneven(ly); 2. *adj.* wrong; askew

baleful – *adj.* – sinister; threatening; evil; deadly

baroque – *adj.* – extravagant; ornate

behoove – *v.* – to be advantageous; to be necessary

berate – *v.* – to scold; to reprove; to reproach; to criticize

bereft – *adj.* – hurt by someone's death

biennial – 1. *adj.* – happening every two years; 2. *n.* – a plant which blooms every two years

blatant – *adj.* – 1. obvious; unmistakable; 2. crude; vulgar

bombastic – *adj.* – pompous; wordy; turgid

burly – *adj.* – strong; bulky; stocky

cache – *n.* – 1. stockpile; store; heap; 2. hiding place for goods

calamity – *n.* – disaster

cascade – 1. *n.* – waterfall; 2. *v.* – to pour; to rush; to fall

catalyst – *n.* – anything that creates a situation in which change can occur

chagrin – *n.* – distress; shame

charisma – *n.* – appeal; magnetism; presence

chastise – *v.* – to punish; to discipline; to admonish; to rebuke

choleric – *adj.* – cranky; cantankerous

cohesion – *n.* – the act of holding together

colloquial – *adj.*– casual; common; conversational; idiomatic

conglomeration – *n.* – mixture; collection

connoisseur – *n.* – expert; authority (usually refers to a wine or food expert)

consecrate – *n.* – sanctify; make sacred; immortalize

craven – *adj.* – cowardly; fearful

dearth – *n.* – scarcity; shortage

debilitate – *v.* – to deprive of strength

deign – *v.* – to condescend; to stoop

delineate – *v.* – to outline; to describe

demur – 1. *v.* – to object; 2. *n.* – objection; misgiving

derision – *n.* – ridicule; mockery

derogatory – *adj.* – belittling; uncomplimentary

destitute – *adj.* – poor; poverty-stricken

devoid – *adj.* – lacking; empty

dichotomy – *n.* – branching into two parts

disheartened – *adj.* – discouraged; depressed

diverge – *v.* – to separate; to split

docile – *adj.* – manageable; obedient

duress – *n.* – force; constraint

ebullient – *adj.* – showing excitement

educe – *v.* – to draw forth

effervescence – *n.* – bubbliness; enthusiasm; animation

emulate – *v.* – to follow the example of

ennui – *n.* – boredom; apathy

epitome – *n.* – model; typification; representation

errant – *adj.* – wandering

ethnic – *adj.* – native; racial; cultural

evoke – *v.* – to call forth; to provoke

exotic – *adj.* – unusual; striking

facade – *n.* – front view; false appearance

facsimile – *n.* – copy; reproduction; replica

fathom – *v.* – to comprehend; to uncover

ferret – *v.* – to drive or hunt out of hiding

figment – *n.* – product; creation

finite – *adj.* – measurable; limited; not everlasting

fledgling – *n.* – 1. inexperienced person; beginner; 2. young bird

flinch – *v.* – to wince; to draw back; to retreat

fluency – *n.* – smoothness of speech

flux – *n.* – current; continuous change

forbearance – *n.* – patience; self-restraint

foster – *v.* – to encourage; to nurture; to support

frivolity – *n.* – lightness; folly; fun

frugality – *n.* – thrift

garbled – *adj.* – mixed up

generic – *adj.* – common; general; universal

germane – *adj.* – pertinent; related; to the point

gibber – *v.* – to speak foolishly

gloat – *v.* – to brag; to glory over

guile – *n.* – slyness; fraud

haggard – *adj.* – tired-looking; fatigued

hiatus – *n.* – interval; break; period of rest

hierarchy – *n.* – body of people, things, or concepts divided into ranks

homage – *n.* – honor; respect

hubris – *n.* – arrogance

ideology – *n.* – set of beliefs; principles

ignoble – *adj.* – shameful; dishonorable

imbue – *v.* – to inspire; to arouse

impale – *v.* – to fix on a stake; to stick; to pierce

implement – *v.* – to begin; to enact

impromptu – *adj.* – without preparation

inarticulate – *adj.* – speechless; unable to speak clearly

incessant – *adj.* – uninterrupted

incognito – *adj.* – unidentified; disguised; concealed

indict – *v.* – to charge with a crime

inept – *adj.* – incompetent; unskilled

innuendo – *n.* – hint; insinuation

intermittent – *adj.* – periodic; occasional

invoke – *v.* – to ask for; to call upon

itinerary – *n.* – travel plan; schedule; course

jovial – *adj.* – cheery; jolly; playful

juncture – *n.* – critical point; meeting

juxtapose – *v.* – to place side-by-side

knavery – n – rascality; trickery

knead – *v.* – mix; massage

labyrinth – *n.* – maze

laggard – *n.* – a lazy person; one who lags behind

larceny – *n.* – theft; stealing

lascivious – *adj.* – indecent; immoral

lecherous – *adj.* – impure in thought and act

lethal – *adj.* – deadly

liaison – *n.* – connection; link

limber – *adj.* – flexible; pliant

livid – *adj.* – 1. black-and-blue; discolored; 2. enraged; irate

lucrative – *adj.* – profitable; gainful

lustrous – *adj.* – bright; radiant

malediction – *n.* – curse; evil spell

mandate – *n.* – order; charge

manifest – *adj.* – obvious; clear

mentor – *n.* – teacher

mesmerize – *v.* – to hypnotize

metamorphosis – *n.* – change of form

mimicry – *n.* – imitation

molten – *adj.* – melted

motif – *n.* – theme

mundane – *adj.* – ordinary; commonplace

myriad – *adj.* – innumerable; countless

narcissistic – *adj.* – egotistical; self-centered

nautical – *adj.* – of the sea

neophyte – *n.* – beginner; newcomer

nettle – *v.* – to annoy; irritate

notorious – *adj.*– infamous; renowned

obdurate – *adj.* – stubborn; inflexible

obligatory – *adj.* – mandatory; necessary

obliterate – *v.* – to destroy completely

obsequious – *adj.* – slavishly attentive; servile

obstinate – *adj.* – stubborn

occult – *adj.* – mystical; mysterious

opaque – *adj.* – dull; cloudy; nontransparent

opulence – *n.* – wealth; fortune

ornate – *adj.* – elaborate; lavish; decorated

oust – *v.* – to drive out; to eject

painstaking – *adj.* – thorough; careful; precise

pallid – *adj.* – sallow; colorless

palpable – *adj.* – tangible; apparent

paradigm – *n.* – model; example

paraphernalia – *n.* – equipment; accessories

parochial – *adj.* – religious; narrow-minded

passive – *adj.* – submissive; unassertive

pedestrian – *adj.* – mediocre; ordinary

pensive – *adj.* – reflective; contemplative

percussion – *adj.* – striking one object against another

perjury – *n.* – the practice of lying

permeable – *adj.* – porous; allowing to pass through

perpetual – *adj.* – enduring for all time

pertinent – *adj.* – related to the matter at hand

pervade – *v.* – to occupy the whole of

petty – *adj.* – unimportant; of subordinate standing

phlegmatic – *adj.* – without emotion or interest

phobia – *n.* – morbid fear

pittance – *n.* – small allowance

plethora – *n.* – condition of going beyond what is needed; excess; overabundance

potent – *adj.* – having great power or physical strength

privy – *adj.* – private; confidential

progeny – *n.* – children; offspring

provoke – *v.* – to stir action or feeling; arouse

pungent – *adj.* – sharp; stinging

quaint – *adj.* – old-fashioned; unusual; odd

quandary – *n.* – dilemma

quarantine – *n.* – isolation of a person to prevent spread of disease

quiescent – *adj.* – inactive; at rest

quirk – *n.* – peculiar behavior; startling twist

rabid – *adj.* – furious; with extreme anger

rancid – *adj.* – having a bad odor

rant – *v.* – to speak in a loud, pompous manner; to rave

ratify – *v.* – to make valid; to confirm

rationalize – *v.* – to offer reasons for; to account for

raucous – *adj.* – disagreeable to the sense of hearing; harsh

realm – *n.* – an area; sphere of activity

rebuttal – *n.* – refutation

recession – *n.* – withdrawal; depression

reciprocal – *n.* – mutual; having the same relationship to each other

recluse – *n.* – solitary and shut off from society

refurbish – *v.* – to make new

regal – *adj.* – royal; grand

reiterate – *v.* – to repeat; to state again

relinquish – *v.* – to let go; to abandon

render – *v.* – to deliver; to provide; to give up a possession

replica – *n.* – copy; representation

resilient – *adj.* – flexible; capable of withstanding stress

retroaction – *n.* – an action elicited by a stimulus

reverie – *n.* – the condition of being unaware of one's surroundings; trance

rummage – *v.* – to search thoroughly

rustic – *adj.* – plain and unsophisticated; homely

saga – *n.* – a legend; story

salient – *adj.* – noticeable; prominent

salvage – *v.* – to rescue from loss

sarcasm – *n.* – ironic; bitter humor designed to wound

satire – *n.* – a novel or play that uses humor or irony to expose folly

saunter – *v.* – to walk at a leisurely pace; to stroll

savor – *v.* – to receive pleasure from; to enjoy

seethe – *v.* – to be in a state of emotional turmoil; to become angry

serrated – *adj.* – having a sawtoothed edge

shoddy – *adj.* – of inferior quality; cheap

skulk – *v.* – to move secretly

sojourn – *n.* – temporary stay; visit

solace – *n.* – hope; comfort during a time of grief

soliloquy – *n.* – a talk one has with oneself (esp. on stage)

somber – *adj.* – dark and depressing; gloomy

sordid – *adj.* – filthy; base; vile

sporadic – *adj.* – rarely occurring or appearing; intermittent

stamina – *n.* – endurance

steadfast – *adj.* – loyal

stigma – *n.* – a mark of disgrace

stipend – *n.* – payment for work done

stupor – *n.* – a stunned or bewildered condition

suave – *adj.* – effortlessly gracious

subsidiary – *adj.* – subordinate

succinct – *adj.* – consisting of few words; concise

succumb – *v.* – to give in; to yield; to collapse

sunder – *v.* – to break; to split in two

suppress – *v.* – to bring to an end; to hold back

surmise – *v.* – to draw an inference; to guess

susceptible – *adj.* – easily imposed; inclined

tacit – *adj.* – not voiced or expressed

tantalize – *v.* – to tempt; to torment

tarry – *v.* – to go or move slowly; to delay

taut – *adj.* – stretched tightly

tenacious – *adj.* – persistently holding to something

tepid – *adj.* – lacking warmth, interest, enthusiasm; lukewarm

terse – *adj.* – concise; abrupt

thwart – *v.* – to prevent from accomplishing a purpose; to frustrate

timorous – *adj.* – fearful

torpid – *adj.* – lacking alertness and activity; lethargic

toxic – *adj.* – poisonous

transpire – *v.* – to take place; to come about

traumatic – *adj.* – causing a violent injury

trek – *v.* – to make a journey

tribute – *n.* – expression of admiration

trite – *adj.* – commonplace; overused

truculent – *adj.* – aggressive; eager to fight

turbulence – *n.* – condition of being physically agitated; disturbance

turmoil – *n.* – unrest; agitation

tycoon – *n.* – wealthy leader

tyranny – *n.* – absolute power; autocracy

ubiquitous – *adj.* – ever present in all places; universal

ulterior – *adj.* – buried; concealed

uncanny – *adj.* – of a strange nature; weird

unequivocal – *adj.* – clear; definite

unique – *adj.* – without equal; incomparable

unruly – *adj.* – not submitting to discipline; disobedient

unwonted – *adj.* – not ordinary; unusual

urbane – *adj.* – cultured; suave

usurpation – *n.* – act of taking something for oneself; seizure

usury – *n.* – the act of lending money at illegal rates of interest

utopia – *n.* – imaginary land with perfect social and political systems

vacuous – *adj.* – containing nothing; empty

vagabond – *n.* – wanderer; one without a fixed place

vagrant – 1. *n.* – homeless person; 2. *adj.* – rambling; wandering; transient

valance – *n.* – short drapery hanging over the window frame

valor – *n.* – bravery

vantage – *n.* – position giving an advantage

vaunted – *adj.* – boasted of

velocity – *n.* – speed

vendetta – *n.* – feud

venue – *n.* – location

veracious – *adj.* – conforming to fact; accurate

verbatim – *adj.* – employing the same words as another; literal

versatile – *adj.* – having many uses; multifaceted

vertigo – *n.* – dizziness

vex – *v.* – to trouble the nerves; to annoy

vindicate – *v.* – to free from charge; to clear

vivacious – *adj.* – animated; gay

vogue – *n.* – modern fashion

voluble – *adj.* – fluent

waft – *v.* – to move gently by wind or breeze

waive – *v.* – to give up possession or right

wanton – *adj.* – unruly; excessive

warrant – *v.* – to justify; to authorize

wheedle – *v.* – to try to persuade; to coax

whet – *v.* – to sharpen

wrath – *n.* – violent or unrestrained anger; fury

wry – *adj.* – mocking; cynical

xenophobia – *n.* – fear of foreigners

yoke – *n.* – harness; collar; bond

yore – *n.* – former period of time

zephyr – *n.* – a gentle wind; breeze

II. KNOWING YOUR WORD PARTS

While taking the PSAT, you will have nothing but your own knowledge to rely on when you come into contact with unfamiliar words. Even though we have provided you with the 600 most commonly tested PSAT words, there is a very good chance that you will come across words that you still do not know. Therefore, you will need to review our list of the most common prefixes, roots, and suffixes in order to be prepared.

Learn the meanings of the prefixes, roots, and suffixes in the same way that you learned the vocabulary words and their meanings. Be sure to use index cards for the items you don't know or find unusual. Look over the examples given and then try to think of your own. Testing yourself in this way will allow you to see if you really do know the meaning of each item. Knowledge of prefixes, roots, and suffixes is essential to a strong vocabulary and, therefore, to a high score on the verbal PSAT.

PREFIXES

Prefix	Meaning	Example
ab –, a –, abs –	away, without, from	absent – away, not present apathy – without interest abstain – keep from doing, refrain
ad –	to, toward	adjacent – next to address – to direct toward
ante –	before	antecedent – going before in time anterior – occurring before
anti –	against	antidote – remedy to act against an evil antibiotic – substance that fights against bacteria
be –	over, thoroughly	bemoan – to mourn over belabor – to exert much labor upon
bi –	two	bisect – to divide biennial – happening every two years
cata –, cat –, cath –	down	catacombs – underground passageways catalogue – descriptive list catheter – tubular medical device
circum –	around	circumscribe – to draw a circle around circumspect – watchful on all sides
com –	with	combine – to join together communication – to have dealings with
contra –	against	contrary – opposed contrast – to stand in opposition
de –	down, from	decline – to bend downward decontrol – to release from government control
di –	two	dichotomy – cutting in two diarchy – system of government with two authorities
dis –, di–	apart, away	discern – to distinguish as separate dismiss – to send away digress – to turn aside
epi –, ep –, eph –	upon, among	epidemic – happening among many people epicycle – circle whose center moves around in the circumference of a greater circle epaulet – decoration worn to ornament or protect the shoulder ephedra – any of a large genus of desert shrubs
ex –, e –	from, out	exceed – go beyond the limit emit – to send forth
extra –	outside, beyond	extraordinary – beyond or out of the common method extrasensory – beyond the senses

Prefix	Meaning	Example
hyper –	beyond, over	hyperactive – over the normal activity level hypercritic – one who is critical beyond measure
hypo –	beneath, lower	hypodermic – parts beneath the skin hypocrisy – to be under a pretense of goodness
in –, *il* –, *im* –, *ir* –	not	inactive – not active illogical – not logical imperfect – not perfect irreversible – not reversible
in –, *il* –, *im* –, *ir* –	in, on, into	instill – to put in slowly illation – action of bringing in impose – to lay on irrupt – to break in
inter –	among, between	intercom – to exchange conversations between people interlude – performance given between parts in a play
intra –	within	intravenous – within a vein intramural – within a single college or its students
meta –	beyond, over, along with	metamorphosis – change over in form or nature metatarsus – part of foot beyond the flat of the foot
mis –	badly, wrongly	misconstrue – to interpret wrongly misappropriate – to use wrongly
mono –	one	monogamy – to be married to one person at a time monotone – a single, unvaried tone
multi –	many	multiple – of many parts multitude – a great number
non –	no, not	nonsense – lack of sense nonentity – not existing
ob –	against	obscene – offensive to modesty obstruct – to hinder the passage of
para –, *par* –	beside	parallel – continuously at equal distance apart parenthesis – sentence inserted within a passage
per –	through	persevere – to maintain an effort permeate – to pass through
poly –	many	polygon – a plane figure with many sides or angles polytheism – belief in the existence of many gods
post –	after	posterior – coming after postpone – to put off until a future time
pre –	before	premature – ready before the proper time premonition – a previous warning
pro –	in favor of, forward	prolific – bringing forth offspring project – throw or cast forward

Prefix	Meaning	Example
re –	back, against	reimburse – to pay back retract – to draw back
semi –	half	semicircle – half a circle semiannual – half-yearly
sub –	under	subdue – to bring under one's power submarine – to travel under the surface of the sea
super –	above	supersonic – above the speed of sound superior – higher in place or position
tele –, tel –	across	telecast – transmit across a distance telepathy – communication between mind and mind at a distance
trans –	across	transpose – to change the position of two things transmit – to send from one person to another
ultra –	beyond	ultraviolet – beyond the limit of visibility ultramarine – beyond the sea
un –	not	undeclared – not declared unbelievable – not believable
uni –	one	unity – state of oneness unison – sounding together
with –	away, against	withhold – to hold back withdraw – to take away

DRILL: PREFIXES

DIRECTIONS: Provide a definition for each prefix.

1. pro– _____

2. com– _____

3. epi– _____

4. ob– _____

5. ad– _____

DIRECTIONS: Identify the prefix in each word.

6. efface _____

7. hypothetical _____

8. permeate _____

9. contrast _____

10. inevitable _____

ROOTS

Root	Meaning	Example
act, ag	do, act, drive	activate – to make active agile – having quick motion
alt	high	altitude – height alto – high singing voice
alter, altr	other, change	alternative – choice between two things altruism – living for the good of others
am, ami	love, friend	amiable – worthy of affection amity – friendship
anim	mind, spirit	animated – spirited animosity – violent hatred
annu, enni	year	annual – every year centennial – every hundred years
aqua	water	aquarium – tank for water animals and plants aquamarine – semiprecious stone of sea-green color
arch	first, ruler	archenemy – chief enemy archetype – original pattern from which things are copied
aud, audit	hear	audible – capable of being heard audience – assembly of hearers audition – the power or act of hearing
auto	self	automatic – self-acting autobiography – story about a person who also wrote it
bell	war	belligerent – a party taking part in a war bellicose – warlike
ben, bene	good	benign – kindly disposition beneficial – advantageous
bio	life	biotic – relating to life biology – the science of life
brev	short	abbreviate – make shorter brevity – shortness
cad, cas	fall	cadence – fall in voice casualty – loss caused by death
capit, cap	head	captain – the head or chief decapitate – to cut off the head
cede, ceed, cess	to go, to yield	recede – to move or fall back proceed – to move onward recessive – tending to go back

Root	Meaning	Example
cent	hundred	century – hundred years centipede – insect with a hundred legs
chron	time	chronology – science dealing with historical dates chronicle – register of events in order of time
cide, cis	to kill, to cut	homicide – one who kills; planned killing of a person incision – a cut
clam, claim	to shout	acclaim – receive with applause proclamation – announce publicly
cogn	to know	recognize – to know again cognition – awareness
corp	body	incorporate – combine into one body corpse – dead body
cred	to trust, to believe	incredible – unbelievable credulous – too prone to believe
cur, curr, curs	to run	current – flowing body of air or water excursion – short trip
dem	people	democracy – government formed for the people epidemic – affecting all people
dic, dict	to say	dictate – to read aloud for another to transcribe verdict – decision of a jury
doc, doct	to teach	docile – easily instructed indoctrinate – to instruct
domin	to rule	dominate – to rule dominion – territory of rule
duc, duct	to lead	conduct – act of guiding induce – to overcome by persuasion
eu	well, good	eulogy – speech or writing in praise euphony – pleasantness or smoothness of sound
fac, fact, fect, fic	to do, to make	facilitate – to make easier factory – location of production confect – to put together fiction – something invented or imagined
fer	to bear, to carry	transfer – to move from one place to another refer – to direct to
fin	end, limit	infinity – unlimited finite – limited in quantity
flect, flex	to bend	flexible – easily bent reflect – to throw back
fort	luck	fortunate – lucky fortuitous – happening by chance

Root	Meaning	Example
fort	strong	fortify – strengthen fortress – stronghold
frag, fract	break	fragile – easily broken fracture – break
fug	flee	fugitive – fleeing refugee – one who flees to a place of safety
gen	class, race	engender – to breed generic – of a general nature in regard to all members
grad, gress	to go, to step	regress – to go back graduate – to divide into regular steps
graph	writing	telegraph – message sent by telegraph autograph – person's own handwriting or signature
ject	to throw	projectile – capable of being thrown reject – to throw away
leg	law	legitimate – lawful legal – defined by law
leg, lig, lect	to choose, gather, read	illegible – incapable of being read ligature – something that binds election – the act of choosing
liber	free	liberal – favoring freedom of ideals liberty – freedom from restraint
log	study, speech	archaeology – study of human antiquities prologue – address spoken before a performance
luc, lum	light	translucent – slightly transparent illuminate – to light up
magn	large, great	magnify – to make larger magnificcnt – great
mal, male	bad, wrong	malfunction – to operate incorrectly malevolent – evil
mar	sea	marine – pertaining to the sea submarine – below the surface of the sea
mater, matr	mother	maternal – motherly matriarchy – government by mothers or women
mit, miss	to send	transmit – to send from one person or place to another mission – the act of sending
morph	shape	metamorphosis – a changing in shape anthropomorphic – having a human shape
mut	change	mutable – subject to change mutate – to change a

Root	Meaning	Example
nat	born	innate – inborn native – a person born in a place
neg	deny	negative – expressing denial renege – to deny
nom	name	nominate – to put forward a name nomenclature – process of naming
nov	new	novel – new renovate – to make as good as new
omni	all	omnipotent – all powerful omnipresent – all present
oper	to work	operate – to work on something cooperate – to work with others
pass, path	to feel	pathetic – affecting the tender emotions passionate – moved by strong emotion
pater, patr	father	paternal – fatherly patriarchy – government by fathers or men
ped, pod	foot	pedestrian – one who travels on foot podiatrist – foot doctor
pel, puls	to drive, to push	impel – to drive forward compulsion – irresistible force
phil	love	philharmonic – loving harmony or music philanthropist – one who loves and seeks to do good for others
port	carry	export – to carry out of the country portable – able to be carried
psych	mind	psychology – study of the mind psychiatrist – specialist in mental disorders
quer, ques, quir, quis	to ask	querist – one who inquires inquiry – to ask about question – that which is asked inquisitive – inclined to ask questions
rid, ris	to laugh	ridiculous – laughable derision – to mock
rupt	to break	interrupt – to break in upon erupt – to break through
sci	to know	science – systematic knowledge of physical or natural phenomena conscious – having inward knowledge
scrib, script	to write	transcribe – to write over again script – text of words
sent, sens	to feel, to think	sentimental – feel great emotion sensitive – easily affected by changes

Root	Meaning	Example
sequ, secut	to follow	sequence – connected series consecutive – following one another in unbroken order
solv, solu, solut	to loosen	dissolve – to break up absolute – without restraint
spect	to look at	spectator – one who watches inspect – to look at closely
spir	to breathe	inspire – to breathe in respiration – process of breathing
string, strict	to bind	stringent – binding strongly restrict – to restrain within bounds
stru, struct	to build	strut – a structural piece designed to resist pressure construct – to build
tang, ting, tact, tig	to touch	tactile – perceptible by touching tangent – touching, but not intersecting contact – touching contiguous – to touch along a boundary
ten, tent, tain	to hold	tenure – holding of office contain – to hold
term	to end	terminate – to end terminal – having an end
terr	earth	terrain – tract of land terrestrial – existing on earth
therm	heat	thermal – pertaining to heat thermometer – instrument for measuring temperature
tort, tors	to twist	contortionist – one who twists violently torsion – act of turning or twisting
tract	to pull, to draw	attract – draw toward distract – to draw away
vac	empty	vacant – empty evacuate – to empty out
ven, vent	to come	prevent – to stop from coming intervene – to come between
ver	true	verify – to prove to be true veracious – truthful
verb	word	verbose – use of excess words verbatim – word for word
vid, vis	to see	video – picture phase of television vision – act of seeing external objects

Root	Meaning	Example
vinc, vict, vanq	to conquer	invincible – unconquerable victory – defeat of enemy vanquish – to defeat
viv, vit	life	vital – necessary to life vivacious – lively
voc	to call	vocation – a summons to a course of action vocal – uttered by voice
vol	to wish, to will	involuntary – outside the control of will volition – the act of willing or choosing

DRILL: ROOTS

DIRECTIONS: Provide a definition for each root.

1. cede _____
2. fact _____
3. path _____
4. ject _____
5. ver _____

DIRECTIONS: Identify the root in each word.

6. acclaim _____
7. verbatim _____
8. benefactor _____
9. relegate _____
10. tension _____

SUFFIXES

Suffix	Meaning	Example
–able, –ble	capable of	believable – capable of believing legible – capable of being read vivacious – full of life
–acious, –icious, *–ous*	full of	delicious – full of pleasurable smell or taste wondrous – full of wonder
–ant, –ent	full of	eloquent – full of eloquence expectant – full of expectation

Suffix	Meaning	Example
–ary	connected with	honorary – for the sake of honor disciplinary – relating to a field of study
–ate	to make	ventilate – to make public consecrate – to dedicate
–fy	to make	magnify – to make larger testify – to make witness
–ile	pertaining to, capable of	docile – capable of being managed easily infantile – pertaining to infancy
–ism	belief, ideal	conservationism – ideal of keeping safe sensationalism – matter, language designed to excite
–ist	doer	artist – one who creates art pianist – one who plays the piano
–ose	full of	verbose – full of words grandiose – striking, imposing
–osis	condition	neurosis – nervous condition psychosis – psychological condition
–tude	state	magnitude – state of greatness multitude – state of quantity

DRILL: SUFFIXES

DIRECTIONS: Provide a definition for each suffix.

1. –ant, –ent _____

2. –tude _____

3. –ile _____

4. –fy _____

5. –ary _____

DIRECTIONS: Identify the suffix in each word.

6. audacious _____

7. expedient _____

8. gullible _____

9. grandiose _____

10. antagonism _____

DETAILED EXPLANATIONS

VERBAL DRILLS

Drill: Group 1

1. (J) *Articulate* means to speak distinctly and to express ideas clearly and effectively. Therefore the opposite would be unclear and ineffective speech. Answer (J), *incoherent*, is the best response.

2. (G) Since *apathy* is the lack of emotion or interest, its opposite would mean to be full of emotion and interest. Answer (G), *enthusiasm*, best reflects this opposite meaning.

3. (A) The opposite of *amiable* is not friendly, or unfriendly. Answer (A), *hostile* means to be aggressive and wanting to fight—a very unfriendly way to be.

4. (C) Since *altruistic* means unselfish, then its opposite must mean selfish. Answer (C), *selfish*, is the best response.

5. (H) Since *ambivalent* means undecided, then its opposite must mean decided, or having made a decision. Answer (H), *certain*, is the best response.

6. (B) The definition of *abstract*—not easily understood; theoretical—refers to intangible issues and ideas. Therefore its opposite would be something that is physical, tangible, or *concrete* (B).

7. (I) Since *acquiesce* means to agree to an opinion, its opposite would be to not agree. Answer (I), *resist*, is the best response.

8. (D) *Arbitrary* refers to something that is based on one's personal preference or judgement. There is no rationality or reasoning involved, therefore the opposite of *arbitrary* would be *reasoned* (D).

9. (F) Since *amass* means to collect or accumulate, its opposite would be to get rid of, or *disperse* (F).

10. (E) Since an *adversary* is an enemy or a foe, then its opposite would be a friend, or an *ally* (E).

11. (D) *Adamant* describes someone or something that is unyielding and firm. *Insistent* (D) is similar in meaning because it means to not give up; not surrender.

12. (C) *Aesthetic* describes something that is artistic; visually pleasing to the eye; or reflecting good taste, and therefore *tasteful* (C) is the best response.

13. (A) *Apprehensive* refers to someone who is fearfully aware, and therefore is considered *afraid* (A).

14. (E) *Antagonism* refers to any opposition or *hostility* (E).

15. (B) An *altercation* is a dispute or minor conflict between two or more people and can therefore be considered a *disagreement* (B).

Drill: Group 2

1. (D) The definition of *augment* is to make larger or add to. Therefore its opposite would be to make smaller, or take away from. *Diminish* (D) is the best answer.

2. (G) Since the meaning of *biased* is to be prejudicial or not neutral, then its opposite would be *neutral* (G).

3. (I) Since *banal* means common and ordinary, its opposite meaning is not ordinary or common. *Unusual* (I) is the best response

4. (F) The opposite of *benevolent*—kind and generous—would be something destructive and evil. Therefore *malicious* (F) is the best response.

5. (A) *Censor* is to prohibit objectionable material from being printed, aired, or heard. So the opposite would be to *permit* (A), or allow.

6. (J) If something is real or genuine, or someone is trustworthy, they can be considered *authentic*. The opposite would describe something unreal, not genuine, and untrustworthy. *Fake* (J) is the best response

7. (E) Since *candid* describes anything that is honest, truthful, and sincere, the opposite would be anything insincere or *dishonest* (E).

8. (C) To *belittle* someone is to make them feel small, worthless, and unimportant. Therefore the opposite would be to praise (C) them, which would make them feel big, worthy, and very important.

9. (B) A *charlatan* is an imposter or phony; someone who is fake. Therefore the opposite would be anyone who is true to themselves and others. *Heroine* (B) is the best response.

10. (H) Since *blithe* describes anything that is happy, cheerful, or merry, its opposite must be anything that is sad, depressing or *mournful* (H).

11. (D) The definition of collaborate is to work together; to cooperate. Therefore *cooperate* (D) is the best response.

12. (A) *Benign* means something that is *harmless* (A).

13. (B) Someone who is *astute* is very perceptive, tricky, and *cunning* (B).

14. (E) To *censure* someone means to publicly disapprove and *criticize* (E) his speech or actions.

15. (C) *Capricious* is used to describe someone or something that has unpredictable or *changing* (C) habits.

Drill: Group 3

1. (E) Since *deplete* means to fill or empty something, such as a bank account or resource, its opposite would be to make full or fill. *Fill* (E) is the best response.

2. (H) *Contemporary* is used to describe any persons or things that exist, or are happening, at the same time or current. So the opposite would mean something that is out of date, or not current. *Ancient* (H) is the best response.

3. (J) Something is considered concise when it can be summed up or expressed in very few words. Therefore the opposite would mean wordy, or extended out to unnecessary length. *Verbose* (J) is the best response.

4. (A) *Deliberate* refers to something that is done on purpose. It is thought through with intended results. *Unintentional* (A) refers to something that was not done on purpose, the results were accidental and not thought through and is therefore the best response.

5. (I) *Depravity* refers to a lack of any and all types of morality, a badness that is really bad. The opposite would refer to any one or thing that is morally upright above and good, such as *virtue* (I).

6. (B) To *condone* an action means to overlook it, or understand the reasons for it in such a way as to approve of it. Therefore the opposite would be *disapprove* (B).

7. (C) Since *conspicuous* means noticeable, or easy to see, then its opposite would be something that is unnoticeable, or *invisible* (C).

8. (G) *Consummation* refers to anything that has reached an end, or the highest degree possible. Therefore its opposite would be something that is *beginning* (G).

9. (F) When someone *denounces* something, they speak out against it and try to suppress or get rid of it. The opposite would be to help, or *support* (F) someone or something.

10. (D) To have scorn, anger, and absolutely no respect for someone is to have *contempt* for them. The opposite would be to have cordiality or *respect* (D).

11. (C) When something is *compatible* it is thought to work, or interact, well with something else, causing no conflicts. *Harmonious* (C) is the best response.

12. (A) *Depict* means to express something in words, or portray in an image. Therefore *portray*, (A) is the best response.

13. (E) *Conventional* is used to describe anything that is routine, ordinary, or everyday. *Common* (E) is the best response.

14. (D) If a student is to have a *comprehensive* math exam at the end of a semester, it is expected that everything taught throughout the semester will appear on the exam. In other words, it would be a *thorough* (D) exam.

15. (B) *Complacent* describes someone who is self-satisfied, or happy with the way things are. They are *content* (B) with their lives.

Drill: Group 4

1. (D) *Detached* refers to things that are unconnected, either in a physical or mental capacity. Therefore the opposite would be *connected* (D).

2. (E) Since *deter* means to prevent or stop something from happening, its opposite would be to help or encourage. *Assist* is the best response.

3. (A) *Dissent* means to disagree, or differ in opinion, therefore its opposite would mean to consent, or *agree* (A).

4. (I) *Discord* is the official term given to any disagreement or lack of compatibility. Therefore its opposite would mean something that is in agreement, or *harmonious* (I).

5. (J) *Efface* is the action of wiping out or erasing someone or something. Therefore its opposite would be to build up, or *restore* (J) someone or something.

6. (B) If something is *dubious*, its origins or authenticity are doubtful or suspicious, uncertain. The opposite would be something of *certain* (B) origin or authenticity.

7. (C) *Diligence* refers to persistent, unrelenting, hard work. Its opposite would be inconsistent, perfunctory, or lazy work. The best answer is *lethargy* (C).

8. (F) To have intense dislike, hatred, or contempt for someone is to hold him in *disdain*. The opposite would then be to have a liking, or *respect* (F) for someone.

9. (H) To *desecrate* means to vandalize, or violate a holy place, to take away its sacredness. Therefore the opposite would mean to restore, or make sacred. *Sanctify* (H) is the best response.

10. (G) *Disparage* refers to the action of belittling, or breaking down someone's self-esteem. The opposite, *compliment* (G) refers to the action of building up someone's self-esteem.

11. (D) According to the definition, *effervescence* means to be full of spirit, enthusiasm, and *liveliness* (D).

12. (A) *Dogmatic* describes someone who strictly adheres to certain opinions, or personal biases. Therefore they are considered *stubborn* (A).

13. (B) *Disseminate* refers to the action of scattering or circulating among many people or things. It means to *distribute* (B) out into the world.

14. (C) *Document* refers to the act of supporting or verifying. The answer most similar in meaning is *substantiate* (C), which means to prove, or provide support for.

15. (E) *Eccentric* describes anything that is out of the ordinary, not existing within standard rules or customs. *Odd* (E) is the best response.

Drill: Group 5

1. (H) *Extraneous* describes anything that is not essential, or not relevant to a particular issue or topic. The opposite would be *relevant* (H).

2. (F) *Ephemeral* describes anything that is temporary, or short-lived. Its opposite would therefore be anything that is long-lived, or not temporary. *Eternal* (F) is the best response.

3. (A) To search for something thoroughly or completely is to have searched for it *exhaustively*. The opposite would be not thorough or *incomplete* (A).

4. (B) To hasten, or speed up a process is to *expedite* a process. The opposite would be to slow down, or *delay* a process (B).

5. (J) *Erroneous* describes any type of information that is untrue, incorrect, or false. There-fore the opposite describes anything that is true, correct, or *accurate* (J).

6. (C) Something that is unpredictable, strange, or not following any set patterns is said to be *erratic*. The opposite is something that is predictable and follows a set pattern, and can therefore be *dependable* (C).

7. (I) *Explicit* describes something that is clearly expressed, specific, and definite. The oppo-site would be muddled, unspecific, and *indefinite* (I).

8. (E) Since *euphony* is any kind of pleasant sound, its opposite must be an unpleasant or dis-cordant sound. *Dissonance* (E) is the best response.

9. (D) Something that is difficult to understand, or *elusive*, is the same as incomprehensible. Therefore its opposite is *comprehensible* (D).

10. (G) *Extol* is to praise or commend an individual or action, so its opposite would be to criti-cize, or *condemn* an individual or action (G).

11. (B) When a person or group of people *endorses* a presidential candidate, they are support-ing, approving, and *recommending* (B) him for office.

12. (D) *Expedient*, similar to expedite, describes anything that is helpful or advantageous, and therefore, *worthwhile* (D).

13. (A) To help in a way that both speeds up and makes easier is to *facilitate*. *Enables* (A), which means to make happen, is the best response.

14. (E) *Fallacious* describes anything that is misleading or *deceptive* (E).

15. (C) *Engender* is the act of making or creating something, bringing it into existence. *Create* (C) is the best response.

Drill: Group 6

1. (G) Since *heresy* is an opinion or belief that offends the status quo, it is considered un-orthodox. The opposite would be *orthodox* (G), which means established beliefs or opinions.

2. (A) *Fickle* describes someone that changes his mind often and erratically, a characteristic that is unpredictable. The opposite would be *predictable* (A).

3. (E) Since *illusory* describes anything that is false or unreal, its opposite must be something that is true or *real* (E).

4. (J) *Frivolity* describes a certain playful giddiness that lacks any type of seriousness, and so its opposite would be *seriousness* (J).

5. (C) The opposite of *grandiose*, which describes anything flamboyant or extravagant, would be something plain, ordinary, or *simple* (C).

6. (B) To have an extreme passion or intensity about someone or something is to be *fervent*. Therefore its opposite could best be described as *dispassionate* (B).

7. (D) Things that are basic and necessary are described as *fundamental*. The opposite would be anything that is not necessary or essential, and *extraneous* (D).

8. (I)   *Furtive* describes anything that is done secretively and slyly, the opposite of which is *openly* (I) or candid.

9. (F)   Something that is *futile* is said to be a lost cause, a worthless endeavor that will have no benefits. The opposite would then be something that is worthwhile and *beneficial* (F).

10. (H)   *Haphazard* describes anything that is unplanned, disorganized, and done without preparation. Therefore the opposite would be anything planned, prepared, or *organized* (H).

11. (D)   By definition, a *glutton* is an *overeater* (D).

12. (E)   *Heed* means to take the advice of; take into consideration and *obey* (E).

13. (A)   *Hamper* means to get in the way of or to interfere with deleterious effects. *Hinder* (A) is the best response.

14. (C)   *Hackneyed* describes anything that is commonplace, dull, boring or *trite* (C).

15. (B)   A *hindrance* is anything that gets in the way of something, an *obstacle* (B).

Drill: Group 7

1. (F)   Since *immutable* describes anything that is unchanging or permanent, its opposite would describe anything that is not permanent, or *changeable* (F).

2. (E)   *Impartial* describes anything that is fair, objective, and unbiased. Therefore the opposite would describe anything that is unfair, subjective, and *biased* (E).

3. (A)   Something that occurs by accident is said to be *inadvertent*. The opposite would be something done on purpose, or *intentional* (A).

4. (B)   Since *incoherent* refers to unclear and illogical ramblings, its opposite would refer to logical, clear, and succinct speech. Therefore, *articulate* (B) is the best response.

5. (H)   Anything that is disagreeing or discordant is considered *incompatible*. The opposite would be compatibility, or *harmonious* agreement (H).

6. (I)   *Innate* refers to certain talents or qualities that people are born with. The opposite would refer to talents or qualities that people *learn* (I).

7. (C)   *Incredulous* describes people who are unwilling to believe or are skeptical of certain ideas or facts. The opposite would be someone who willingly believes anything they are told. Therefore, *gullible* (C) is the best response.

8. (G)   Something that is unavoidable, or has a 100% certainty of happening, is considered to be *inevitable*. Therefore the opposite would be something that is not certain to happen or something that is *avoidable* (G).

9. (D)   Something that is *intangible* cannot be touched; does not exist of physical material. The opposite would then be something that can be touched and does exist of physical *material* (D).

10. (J)   *Indolent* describes anyone who is lazy or inactive. Therefore the opposite would be someone who is very active or *energetic* (J).

11. (B)   *Impetuous* describes anything that is rash, and *impulsive* (B).

12. (E) Something that is *incidental* is thought to be an unexpected bonus, is more than required, and therefore, *extraneous* (E).

13. (D) The meaning of *infer* is to form an opinion, or to *conclude* (D) something from the facts presented.

14. (C) *Instigate* means to start something, or *provoke* (C) something to happen.

15. (A) *Indulgent* describes anyone who is patient or *lenient* (A).

Drill: Group 8

1. (D) Since *irrational* means not logical, the opposite must be *logical* (D).

2. (A) *Kindle* means to nurture into a fire, or to ignite, so the opposite would be to put out a fire, or *extinguish* (A).

3. (H) *Meticulous* describes someone who is precise, someone who shows a close attention to detail. Therefore the opposite would be someone who is less exacting, or *sloppy* (H).

4. (G) *Malicious* describes someone or something that is spiteful and vengeful. The opposite would be someone who is forgiving, loving, and *kindly* (G).

5. (B) *Morose* describes someone who is sad, gloomy, depressing, or despondent. The opposite would be someone who is happy, optimistic, and *jovial* (B).

6. (C) Someone who is very forgiving and unselfish about wrongs committed against him is said to be *magnanimous*. The opposite of this is to be unforgiving and *selfish* (C) in search of retribution.

7. (E) *Levity* refers to a lightness of heart, or lack of seriousness about a situation. Therefore the opposite is to be very grave and *serious* about a situation (E).

8. (I) *Minute* describes a very small or tiny amount. The opposite would simply be a very large or *huge* (I) amount.

9. (F) Since *laud* refers to the act of praising or commending someone, the opposite would mean to criticize, condemn, or *ridicule* (F) someone.

10. (J) *Novel* is used to describe something that is new, fresh, and original. Therefore the opposite would be something that is old, trite, and *stale* (J).

11. (C) *Ironic* describes anything that is contradictory, inconsistent, or *sarcastic* (C).

12. (B) *Marred* is used to describe anything that is in any way *damaged* (B).

13. (A) *Mitigate* refers to the action of alleviating, or making a situation better. It *lessens* (A) the seriousness of a thing or act.

14. (E) Far removed from its origin in the contemporary world of gameshows, *jeopardy* simply means *danger* (E).

15. (D) *Negligence* refers to any act of *carelessness* (D).

Drill: Group 9

1. (D) *Objective* is used to describe someone who is open-minded and impartial. Therefore the opposite would be someone who is closed-minded, partial, and *biased* (D).

2. (I) Something is said to be *obsolete* when it is considered out of date or no longer in fashion. The opposite would then be something that is contemporary or *modern* (I).

3. (G) *Placate* refers to the act of bringing peace to, or pacifying someone or something. The opposite would be to incite or bring to *anger* (G).

4. (A) *Profusion* refers to a great amount or overabundance of a particular thing. Therefore the opposite would refer to the lack of or *scantiness* (A) of a thing.

5. (J) *Peripheral* describes something on the outer edges, marginal in the sense of less importance. The opposite would then be of major importance, *central* (J).

6. (E) If something is *plausible*, it means that it could possibly happen. It is feasible. The opposite would be not feasible or *improbable* (E).

7. (B) *Preclude* means to inhibit or make something impossible. Therefore the opposite must mean to make possible; help or *assist* (B).

8. (F) *Prodigious* describes anything that is exceptional in size or amount, tremendous in extent. The opposite would mean anything that is small or *minute* (F) in size or amount.

9. (C) Since *profound* describes something that is deep or knowledgeable, the opposite would be something that means shallow, ignorant, or *superficial* (C).

10. (H) An *optimist* is a person who always hopes for the best and tries to see the good in everything. The opposite would be a person who is overly negative and always without hope. *Pessimism* (H) is the best response.

11. (A) *Nullify* means to cancel out, make *invalid* (A).

12. (D) *Ominous* is used to describe something that is *threatening* (D).

13. (B) A *partisan* is a *follower* (B) or supporter of an idea or ideology.

14. (E) *Pernicious* is used to describe anything that is persistently dangerous or *harmful* (E).

15. (C) *Prodigal* describes someone who is wasteful, especially on *lavish* (C) and unnecessary things.

Drill: Group 10

1. (H) *Provincial* refers to the bucolic, rural areas that are located away from the culturally sophisticated cities. The correct answer, *sophisticated* (H), best reflects the opposite meaning.

2. (I) A person who is silent, reserved, or shy is considered *reticent*. The opposite would be someone who is outspoken, unreserved, or *forward* (I).

3. (E) *Prudent* describes someone who is wise, prepared, and careful. Therefore the opposite would be rash, hasty, and *careless* (E).

4. (A) Since *qualified* means to have experience, the opposite must mean to have no experience, or *inexperience* (A).

5. (J) *Relegate* is to banish, or demote to a lower position than was already obtained. The opposite would then be to *promote* (J) to a higher position.

6. (B) *Remorse* is a show of guilt or sorrow. Therefore the opposite would be a show of happiness or *joy* (B).

7. (F) *Repudiate* means to reject previously held beliefs or ideas. The opposite would be to accept, or *affirm* (F) those beliefs.

8. (C) A person who is red with cheerful enthusiasm or energetic optimism is said to be *sanguine*. Its opposite would be sorrowful resignation or *pessimism* (C).

9. (D) *Relevant* refers to something that is significant to the topic at hand and related to the matter of discussion. Therefore the opposite would be anything insignificant or *unrelated* (D) to a topic or discussion.

10. (G) *Prosaic* describes anything that is common, dull, ordinary, or boring. The opposite must be uncommon, exciting, and *extraordinary* (G).

11. (B) Anything that entices or tempts one to do something he or she would normally not do is considered *provocative* (B).

12. (D) *Rigor* refers to the quality of being strict, inflexible, and of great *severity* (D).

13. (A) *Saturate* means to soak thoroughly, to *drench* (A).

14. (C) *Rescind* refers to the action of taking back what was already said or given; to *retract* (C).

15. (E) *Reprehensible* describes anything that is wicked or *disgraceful* (E).

Drill: Group 11

1. (F) *Scrutinize* means to study something very closely; to examine the tiniest detail. The opposite would be to glance over quickly or *skim* (F).

2. (I) A *skeptic* is a person who is not easily convinced to believe; a doubter. Therefore the opposite would be someone who very readily believes, someone who is a *believer* (I).

3. (A) *Solemnity* refers to anything that is of utmost importance or seriousness. The opposite is anything that is of a silly or inconsequential nature. *Frivolity* is the best response.

4. (H) When something is *static*, it is considered inactive and unchanging. Therefore the opposite would be anything that is *active* (H).

5. (B) *Tedious* describes anything that is burdensome, time-consuming, and uninteresting. Therefore its opposite would be interesting, pleasant, and *enjoyable* (B).

6. (J) *Tentative* is used to describe things that are unconfirmed or not definite. Its opposite is something that is definite, officially scheduled, or *confirmed* (J).

7. (C) A *thrifty* person is someone who is economical and not wasteful; restrains themselves from lavish spending. Therefore the opposite must be someone who is uneconomical and wasteful, or *prodigal* (C).

8. (D) *Tranquility* is a state of peace and harmony, in which everything is in its right place. The opposite is a state of turmoil and *chaos* (D).

9. (E) To *solicit* means to ask or seek someone or something. The opposite is to be presented or *given* something (E).

10. (G) *Stagnant* describes anything that is motionless or not circulating, such as air or water. Therefore its opposite would be something constantly moving or *turbulent* (G).

11. (C) *Symmetry* refers to a correspondence of parts; a harmony that is achieved when things are in *balance* (C).

12. (B) *Superfluous* describes everything that is extra or *unnecessary* (B).

13. (E) A *sycophant* is someone who tries to win favor by flattering, and thus is considered a *flatterer* (E).

14. (A) Something that is *subtle* has the characteristics of not being stated directly, but rather hinted at through the use of tones and gestures. *Subtlety* is the art of *understatement* (A).

15. (D) *Trepidation* refers to the apprehension and uneasiness that is caused due to *fear* (D).

Drill: Group 12

1. (J) Something that is *uniform* is considered unchanging and consistent. The opposite would be something that is constantly changing, or *varied* (J).

2. (A) A *virtuoso* is the highest level of skill an artist can obtain. Therefore the opposite would be the lowest level of skill, or a beginner or *amateur* (A).

3. (B) *Vital* describes anything that is of great importance or necessary for life. The opposite must describe something that is not of importance or necessity; something that is superfluous or *trivial* (B).

4. (I) *Wane* means to grow gradually smaller; to lessen in importance and strength, and decline inevitably to an end. The opposite would be to grow larger, to increase in importance and strength, and to rise up. *Wax* (I) best reflects the opposite meaning.

5. (C) Someone who is *unobtrusive* is inconspicuous and not noticed. Therefore the opposite would be someone who is very noticeable or *visible* (C).

6. (H) *Vigor* refers to a high level of energy or forcefulness. The opposite would refer to a low level of energy or apathy. *Lethargy* (H) best reflects the opposite meaning.

7. (D) Something that is unstable, quickly changing, and easily agitated is considered *volatile*. Therefore the opposite would be anything that is stable, unchanging, and calm. *Placid* (D) best reflects the opposite meaning.

8. (G) *Vacillation* refers to something that is constantly moving back and forth; always fluctuating. The opposite would be something that is unwavering, steady, and *constant*. (G).

9. (F) *Undermine* is the act of weakening or ruining the authority or prestige of a person or thing. The opposite would be the act of bolstering or *supporting* (F).

10. (E) Anything considered legal, acceptable, or appropriate is said to be *valid*. Therefore the opposite would be something inappropriate, illegal, or *unacceptable* (E).

11. (E) *Wither* means to wilt, die, or *shrivel* (E) up.

12. (C) *Whimsical* describes any kind of fanciful or *amusing* (C) idea.

13. (D) *Viable* describes anything that is attainable or *possible* (D).

14. (A) *Vehement* refers to the qualities of displaying intensity, excitability, and *intense* (A) enthusiasm.

15. (B) *Virulent* describes things that are harmful, malicious, and *deadly* (B).

Drill: Prefixes

1. *pro–* in favor of: for
2. *com–* with
3. *epi–* upon; among
4. *ob–* against
5. *ad–* to; toward

6. *efface-* ef– (out, from)
7. *hypothetical-* hypo– (beneath, lower)
8. *permeate-* per– (through)
9. *contrast-* contra– (against)
10. *inevitable-* in– (not)

Drill: Roots

1. *cede* - to go; to yield
2. *fact* - to do; to make
3. *path* - to feel
4. *ject* - to throw
5. *ver* - true

6. *acclaim-* claim (shout)
7. *verbatim-* verb (word)
8. *benefactor-* bene (good) fact (to do; to make)
9. *relegate-* leg (law)
10. *tension-* ten (to hold)

Drill: Suffixes

1. *–ant, –ent* - full of
2. *–tude* - state
3. *–ile* - pertaining to; capable of
4. *–fy* - to make
5. *–ary* - connected with

6. *audacious-* acious (full of)
7. *expedient-* ent (full of)
8. *gullible-* ible (capable of)
9. *grandiose-* ose (full of)
10. *antagonism-* ism (belief, condition)

CHAPTER 4

MASTERING SENTENCE
COMPLETION QUESTIONS

CHAPTER 4

MASTERING SENTENCE COMPLETION QUESTIONS

Regardless of the verbal PSAT section in which one is working, all problem-solving techniques should be divided into two main categories: skills and strategies. This chapter will present skills and strategies that are effective in helping the test-taker successfully answer Sentence Completions. These techniques include the recognition of a context clue, a knowledge of the levels of difficulty in a Sentence Completion section, the application of deductive reasoning, and familiarity with the logical structure of sentence completions. You will encounter 13 Sentence Completion questions on the PSAT/NMSQT.

Success on the verbal PSAT begins with one fundamental insight: the underlying intent is to test your vocabulary. No matter what section you are working in, you will be expected to demonstrate a command of a wide array of vocabulary words drawn from a treasury of Greek and Latin roots and prefixes. Devote as much time as possible to strengthening your vocabulary, especially by studying the prefixes and roots of Greek- and Latin-derived words. The Vocabulary Enhancer section of the Basic Verbal Skills Review should be studied thoroughly.

ABOUT THE DIRECTIONS

The directions for Sentence Completion questions are relatively straightforward.

DIRECTIONS: Each sentence below has one or two blanks, each blank indicating that something has been omitted. Beneath the sentence are five lettered words or sets of words. Choose the word or set of words that BEST fits the meaning of the sentence as a whole.

Although the critics found the book _____, many of the readers found it rather _____.

(A) obnoxious . . . perfect

(B) spectacular . . . interesting

(C) boring . . . intriguing

(D) comical . . . persuasive

(E) popular . . . rare

ABOUT THE QUESTIONS

You will encounter two main types of questions in the Sentence Completion section of the PSAT. In addition, the questions will appear in varying difficulties which we will call Level I (easy), Level II (average), and Level III (difficult). The following explains the structure of the questions.

Question Type 1: One-Word Completions

One-Word Completions will require you to fill in one blank. The one-word completion can appear as a Level I, II, or III question depending on the difficulty of the vocabulary included.

Question Type 2: Two-Word Completions

Two-Word Completions will require you to fill in two blanks. As with the one-word completion, this type may be a Level I, II, or III question. This will depend not only on the difficulty of the vocabulary, but also on the relationship between the words and between the words and the sentence.

The remainder of this review will provide explicit details on what you will encounter when dealing with Sentence Completion questions, in addition to strategies for correctly completing these sentences.

POINTS TO REMEMBER

- Like other verbal sections of the test, Sentence Completions can be divided into three basic levels of difficulty, and, as a general rule, PSAT verbal exercises increase in difficulty as they progress through a section.

- Level I exercises allow you to rely on your instincts and common sense. You should not be obsessed with analysis or second-guessing in Level I problems.

- In Level II questions, the PSAT often presents words that appear easy at first glance but that may have secondary meanings. Be wary of blindly following your gut reactions and common sense.

- All PSAT word problems contain "magnet words," answer choices that look good but are designed to draw the student away from the correct answer. Magnet words can effectively mislead you in Level III questions. Always watch for them. Remember that

Level III questions are intentionally designed to work against your common sense and natural inclinations.

- Deductive reasoning is a tool that will be of constant assistance to you as you work through PSAT word problems. To deduce means to derive a truth (or answer) through a reasoning process.

- Sentence Completion questions are puzzles, and they are put together with a certain amount of predictability. One such predictable characteristic is the structure of a PSAT word exercise. Since there are always five possible answers from which to choose, you must learn to see which answers are easy to eliminate first. Use the process of elimination.

- Most PSAT word problems are designed around a "three-two" structure. This means that there are three easier answers to eliminate before you have to make the final decision between the remaining two.

- Use word roots, prefixes, and suffixes to find the meanings of words you do not know.

ANSWERING SENTENCE COMPLETION QUESTIONS

Follow these steps as you attempt to answer each question.

 Identifying context clues is one of the most successful ways for students to locate correct answers in Sentence Completions. Practicing constantly in this area will help you strengthen one of your main strategies in this type of word problem. The sentence completion below is an example of a Level I question.

Pamela played her championship chess game _____, avoiding all traps and making no mistakes.

(A) hurriedly

(B) flawlessly

(C) prodigally

(D) imaginatively

(E) aggressively

The phrase "avoiding all traps and making no mistakes" is your context clue. Notice that the phrase both follows *and* modifies the word in question. Since you know that Sentence Completions are exercises seeking to test your vocabulary knowledge, attack these problems accordingly. For example, ask yourself what word means "avoiding all traps and making no mistakes." In so doing, you discover the answer flawlessly (B), which means perfectly or without mistakes. If Pamela played hurriedly (A), she might well make mistakes. Difficult words are seldom the answer in easier questions; therefore, prodigally (C) stands out as a suspicious word. This could be a magnet word. However, before you eliminate it, ask yourself whether you know its meaning. If so, does it surpass flawlessly (B) in defining the context clue, "making no mistakes"? It does not. Imaginatively (D) is a tempting answer, since one might associate a perfect game of chess as one played imaginatively; however, there is no connection between the imagination and the absence of mistakes. Aggressively (E) playing a game may, in fact, cause you to make mistakes.

Here is an example of a Level II Sentence Completion. Try to determine the context clue.

Although most people believe the boomerang is the product of a _____ design, that belief is deceptive; in fact, the boomerang is a _____ example of the laws of aerodynamics.

(A) foreign . . . modern   (D) primitive . . . sophisticated

(B) symbolic . . . complex   (E) faulty . . . invalid

(C) practical . . . scientific

The most important context clue in this sentence is the opening word "although," which indicates that some kind of antonym relationship is present in the sentence. It tells us there is a reversal in meaning. Therefore, be on the lookout for words which will form an opposite relationship. The phrase "that belief is deceptive" makes certain the idea that there will be an opposite meaning between the missing words. Primitive . . . sophisticated (D) is the best answer, since the two are exact opposites. "Primitive" means crude and elementary, whereas "sophisticated" means refined and advanced. Foreign . . . modern (A) and symbolic . . . complex (B) have no real opposite relationship. Also, "complex" is a magnet word that sounds right in the context of scientific laws, but "symbolic" is not its counterpart.

Practical . . . scientific (C) and faulty . . . invalid (E) are rejectable because they are generally synonymous pairs of relationships.

The following is an example of a Level III question:

The weekly program on public radio is the most _____ means of educating the public about pollution.

(A) proficient   (D) capable

(B) effusive   (E) competent

(C) effectual

The context clue in this sentence is "means of educating the public about pollution." Effectual (C) is the correct answer. Effectual means having the power to produce the exact effect or result. Proficient (A) is not correct as it implies competency above the average—radio programs are not described in this manner. Effusive (B) does not fit the sense of the sentence. Both capable (D) and competent (E) are incorrect because they refer to people, not things.

 Since the verbal PSAT is fundamentally a vocabulary test, it must resort to principles and techniques necessary for testing your vocabulary. Therefore, certain dynamics like antonyms (word opposites) and synonyms (word similarities) become very useful in setting up a question or word problem. This idea can be taken one step further.

Another type of technique that utilizes the tension of opposites and the concurrence of similarities is *word values*. Word values begin with the recognition that most pivotal words in a PSAT word problem can be assigned a positive or negative value. Marking a "+" or "–" next to choices may help you eliminate inappropriate choices. In turn, you will be able to more quickly identify possible correct answers.

Dealing with Positive Value Words

Positive value words are usually easy to recognize. They usually convey a meaning which can be equated with gain, advantage, liveliness, intelligence, virtue, and positive emotions, conditions, or actions.

The ability to recognize positive and negative word values, however, will not bring you very far if you do not understand how to apply it to your advantage in Sentence Completions. Below you will find examples of how to do this, first with a study of positive value Sentence Completions, then with a study of negative value Sentence Completions. The following is an example of a Level I question.

An expert skateboarder, Tom is truly _____ ; he smoothly blends timing with balance.

(A) coordinated   (D) supportive

(B) erudite   (E) casual

(C) a novice

As you know, the context clue is the clause after the word in question, which acts as a modifier. Naturally, anyone who "smoothly blends" is creating a *positive* situation. Look for the positive answer.

An expert skateboarder, Tom is truly __+__ ; *he smoothly blends timing with balance.*

+(A) coordinated   +(D) supportive

+(B) erudite   –(E) casual

–(C) a novice

Coordinated (A), a positive value word that means ordering two or more things, fits the sentence perfectly. Erudite (B) is positive, but it is too difficult to be a Level I answer. A novice (C) in this context is negative. Supportive (D) and casual (E) don't fulfill the definition of the context clue, and casual is negative, implying a lack of attention. Notice that eliminating negatives *immediately reduces the number of options from which you have to choose.* This raises the odds of selecting the correct answer. (One of the analytic skills you should develop for the PSAT is being able to see the hidden vocabulary question in any exercise.)

A Level II question may appear as follows:

Despite their supposedly primitive lifestyle, Australian aborigines developed the boomerang, a _____ and _____ hunting tool that maximizes gain with minimum effort.

(A) ponderous . . . expensive   (D) sophisticated . . . efficient

(B) clean . . . dynamic   (E) useful . . . attractive

(C) dangerous . . . formidable

In this case, the context clues (in italics) begin and end the sentence.

Despite their supposedly primitive lifestyle, Australian aborigines developed the boomerang, a __+__ and __+__ hunting *tool that maximizes gain with minimum effort.*

–(A) ponderous . . . expensive   +(D) sophisticated . . . efficient

+(B) clean . . . dynamic   +(E) useful . . . attractive

–(C) dangerous . . . formidable

The first context clue (*despite*) helps you determine that this exercise entails an antonym relationship with the word primitive, which means simple or crude. The second context clue offers a definition of the missing words. Since the meaning of primitive in this context is a negative word value, you can be fairly confident that the answer will be a pair of positive word values. Sophisticated . . . efficient (D) is positive *and* it satisfies the definition of the latter context clue. This is the best answer. Ponderous . . . expensive (A) is not correct. Clean . . . dynamic (B) is positive, but does not meet the definition of the latter context clue. Dangerous . . . formidable (C) is negative. Useful . . . attractive (E) is positive, but it does not work with the latter context clue.

Here is a Level III example.

When a physician describes an illness to a colleague, he must speak an _____ language, using professional terms and concepts understood mostly by members of his profession.

(A) extrinsic   (D) esoteric

(B) inordinate   (E) abbreviated

(C) ambulatory

Looking at this question, we can see an important context clue. This appears in italics below.

When a physician describes an illness to a colleague, he must speak an __+__ language, *using professional terms and concepts understood mostly by members of his profession.*

+(A) extrinsic   +(D) esoteric

–(B) inordinate   –(E) abbreviated

+(C) ambulatory

This clue gives us a definition of the missing word. Begin by eliminating the two obvious negatives, inordinate (B) and abbreviated (E). This leaves us with three positives. Since this is a Level III exercise, at first you may be intimidated by the level of vocabulary. In the section on etymology you will be given insights into how to handle difficult word problems. For now, note that esoteric (D) is the best answer, since it is an adjective that means *inside* or *part of a group*. Ambulatory (C) is positive, but it is a trap. It seems like an easy association with the world of medicine. In Level III there are *no* easy word associations. Extrinsic (A) is positive, but it means *outside of*, which would not satisfy the logic of the sentence.

Dealing with Negative-Value Words

Here are examples of how to work with negative-value Sentence Completion problems. The first example is Level I.

Although Steve loves to socialize, his fellow students find him _____ and strive to _____ his company

(A) generous . . . enjoy   (D) sinister . . . delay

(B) boring . . . evade   (E) weak . . . limit

(C) altruistic . . . accept

The context clue (in italics) tells us that a reversal is being set up between what Steve thinks and what his fellow students think.

Although Steve loves to socialize, his fellow students find him __–__ and strive to __–__ his company.

+(A) generous . . . enjoy   –(D) sinister . . . delay

–(B) boring . . . evade   –(E) weak . . . limit

+(C) altruistic . . . accept

Boring . . . evade (B) is the best answer. The words appearing in Level 1 questions are not overly difficult, and they satisfy the logic of the sentence. Generous . . . enjoy (A) is positive. Altruistic . . . accept (C) is not only positive but contains a very difficult word (altruistic), and it would be unlikely that this would be a Level I answer. The same is true of sinister . . . delay (D), even though it is negative. Weak . . . limit (E) does not make sense in the context of the sentence.

This next example is Level II.

Because they reject _____, conscientious objectors are given jobs in community work as a substitute for participation in the armed services.

(A) labor   (D) dictatorships

(B) belligerence (E) poverty

(C) peace

Essentially, this example is a synonym exercise. The description of conscientious objectors (in italics) acts as a strong context clue. Conscientious objectors avoid ("reject") militancy.

Because they reject __–__, conscientious objectors *are given jobs in community work as a substitute for participation in the armed services.*

+(A) labor   –(D) dictatorships

–(B) belligerence   –(E) poverty

+(C) peace

Since we are looking for a negative word value (something to do with militancy), labor (A) is incorrect since it is positive. Belligerence (B) fits perfectly, as this is a negative value word having to do with war. Not only is peace (C) a positive value word, it is hardly something to be rejected by conscientious objectors. Dictatorships (D), although a negative word value, has no logical place in the context of this sentence. The same is true of poverty (E).

Here is a Level III example:

Dictators understand well how to centralize power, and that is why they combine a(n) _____ political process with military _____.

(A) foreign . . . victory   (D) domestic . . . decreases

(B) electoral . . . escalation   (E) totalitarian . . . coercion

(C) agrarian . . . strategies

Totalitarian . . . coercion (E) is the best answer. These are difficult words, and both have to do with techniques useful in the centralizing of power by a dictator. *Totalitarian* means centralized, and *coercion* means force.

Dictators understand well how to *centralize power*, and that is why they combine a(n) __–__ political process with military __–__.

+(A) foreign . . . victory   +(D) domestic . . . decreases

+(B) electoral . . . escalation   –(E) totalitarian . . . coercion

+(C) agrarian . . . strategies

Foreign . . . victory (A) are not only easy words, they do not appear to be strictly negative. Remember that easy word answers should be suspect in Level III. Agrarian . . . strategies (C) is positive. Domestic . . . decreases (D) is a positive combination. Since you are searching for two negatives, this answer is incorrect. There will be more about this in the next section.

Dealing with Mixed-Value Words

In examples with two-word answers so far, you have searched for answers composed with identical word values, such as negative/negative and positive/positive. However, every PSAT Sentence Completion section will have exercises in which two-word answers are found in combinations. Below you will find examples of how to work with these. Here is a Level I example:

Despite a healthy and growing environmental _____ in America, there are many people who prefer to remain _____ .

(A) awareness . . . ignorant   (D) crisis . . . unencumbered

(B) movement . . . enlightened (E) industry . . . satisfied

(C) bankruptcy . . . wealthy

The context clue *despite* sets up the predictable antonym warning. In this case, the sentence seems to call for a positive and then a negative-value word answer.

Chapter 4—Mastering Sentence Completion Questions   **135**

Despite a healthy and growing environmental __+__ in America, there are many people who prefer to remain __–__.

+/–(A)   awareness . . . ignorant

+/+(B)   movement . . . enlightened

–/+(C)   bankruptcy . . . wealthy

–/+(D)   crisis . . . unencumbered

+/+(E)   industry . . . satisfied

Awareness . . . ignorant (A) is the best answer. These are logical antonyms, and they fit the meaning of the sentence. Notice that the order of the missing words is positive, *then* negative. This should help you eliminate (C) and (D) immediately, as they are a reversal of the correct order. Furthermore, industry . . . satisfied (E) and movement . . . enlightened (B) are both identical values, and so are eliminated. Practice these techniques until you confidently can recognize word values *and* the order in which they appear in a sentence.

Here is a Level II example:

Prone to creating characters of _____ quality, novelist Ed Abbey cannot be accused of writing _____ stories.

(A)   measly . . . drab

(B)   romantic . . . imaginative

(C)   mythic . . .mundane

(D)   sinister . . . complete

(E)   two-dimensional . . . flat

The best answer is mythic . . . mundane (C). Measly . . . drab (A) does not make sense when you consider the context clue *cannot*, which suggests the possibility of antonyms. The same is true for sinister . . . complete (D), romantic . . . imaginative (B), and two-dimensional . . . flat (E).

Prone to creating characters of __+__ quality, novelist Ed Abbey *cannot* be accused of writing __–__ stories.

–/–(A)   measly . . . drab

+/+(B)   romantic . . . imaginative

+/–(C)   mythic . . .mundane

–/+(D)   sinister . . . complete

–/–(E)   two-dimensional . . . flat

Notice that the value combinations help you determine where to search for the correct answer.

Here is a Level III example:

Reminding his students that planning ahead would protect them from _____ , Mr. McKenna proved to be a principal who understood the virtues of _____ .

(A)   exigency . . . foresight

(B)   grades . . . examinations

(C)   poverty . . . promotion

(D)   deprivation . . . abstinence

(E)   turbulence . . . amelioration

The best answer is exigency . . . foresight (A). The first context clue tells us that we are looking for a negative value word. The second context clue tells us the missing word is most likely positive. Furthermore, exigency. . . foresight is a well-suited antonym combination. Exigencies are emergencies, and foresight helps to lessen their severity, if not their occurrence.

Reminding his students that planning ahead would *protect them* from __–__ , Mr. McKenna proved to be a principal who understood the *virtues* of __+__ .

–/+(A)   exigency . . . foresight

0/0(B)   grades . . . examinations

–/+(C)   poverty . . . promotion

–/–(D)   deprivation . . . abstinence

–/+(E)   turbulence . . . amelioration

Grades . . . examinations (B) are a trap, since they imply school matters. Furthermore, they are neutrals. There will be more on this below. Poverty . . . promotion (C) is an easy word answer and should be immediately suspect, especially if there are no difficult words in the sentence completion itself. Also, this answer does not satisfy the logic of the sentence. Turbulence . . . amelioration (E) is a negative/positive combination, but it does not make sense in this sentence. Even if you are forced to guess between this answer and exigency . . . foresight (A), you have narrowed the field to two. These are excellent odds for success.

Dealing with Neutral Value Words

There is another category of word values that will help you determine the correct answer in a Sentence Completion problem. These are neutral word values. Neutral words are words that convey neither loss nor gain, advantage nor disadvantage, etc. Consider the example above, once again:

Reminding his students that planning ahead would *protect them* from ___–___ , Mr. McKenna proved to be a principal who understood the *virtues* of ___+___ .

–/+(A)   exigency . . . foresight

0/0(B)   grades . . . examinations

–/+(C)   poverty . . . promotion

–/–(D)   deprivation . . . abstinence

–/+(E)   turbulence . . . amelioration

Notice that grades . . . examinations (B) is rated as neutral. In fact, in this case, both words are considered of neutral value. This is because neither word conveys a usable value. Grades in and of themselves are not valued until a number is assigned. Examinations are not significant until a passing or failing value is implied or applied.

Neutral word values are significant because they are *never* the correct answer. Therefore, when you identify a neutral word or combination of words, you may eliminate that choice from your selection. You may eliminate a double-word answer even if only one of the words is obviously neutral.

Neutral words are rare, and you should be careful to measure their value before you make a choice. Here is another example from an exercise seen previously (Note: The answer choices have been altered.):

Dictators understand well how to *centralize power*, and that is why they combine a(n) ___–___ political process with military ___–___.

0/+(A)   foreign . . . victory

0/+(B)   electoral . . . escalation

0/+(C)   agrarian . . . strategies

0/0(D)   current . . . jobs

–/–(E)   totalitarian . . . coercion

Here, current . . . jobs (D) is an obvious neutral word combination, conveying no positive or negative values. You may eliminate this choice immediately. There is no fixed list of words that may be considered neutral. Rather, you should determine *from the context* of a word problem whether you believe a word or word combination is of a neutral value. This ability will come with practice and a larger vocabulary. As before, the correct answer remains totalitarian . . . coercion (E).

STEP 3 *Another way to determine the correct answer is by using etymology. Etymology is the study of the anatomy of words. The most important components of etymology on the PSAT are prefixes and roots. PSAT vocabulary is derived almost exclusively from the etymology of Greek and Latin word origins, and that is where you should concentrate your study. In this section, you will learn how to apply your knowledge of prefixes and roots to Sentence Completion problems.*

Etymological skills will work well in conjunction with other techniques you have learned, including positive/negative word values. Furthermore, the technique of "scrolling" will help you understand how to expand your knowledge of etymology.

Scrolling is a process whereby you "scroll" through a list of known related words, roots, or prefixes to help you discover the meaning of a word. As an example, consider the common PSAT word *apathy*. The prefix of apathy is *a*. This means *without*. To scroll this prefix, think of any other words that may begin with this prefix, such as *a*moral, *a*typical, *a*symmetrical. In each case, the meaning of the word is preceded by the meaning *without*.

At this point, you know that *apathy* means without something. Now try to scroll the root, *path*, which comes from the Greek word *pathos*. Words like pathetic, sympathy, antipathy, and empathy may come to mind. These words all have to do with feeling or sensing. In fact, that is what *pathos* means: *feeling*. So apathy means *without feeling*.

With this process you can often determine the fundamental meaning of a word or part of a word, and this may give you enough evidence with which to choose a correct answer. Consider the following familiar Level I example:

An expert skateboarder, Tom is truly __+__ ; he smoothly blends timing with balance.

+(A) coordinated   +(D) supportive

+(B) erudite   –(E) casual

–(C) a novice

As you should remember, the correct answer is coordinated (A). The prefix of this word is *co*, meaning together, and the root is *order*. Something that is "ordered together" fits the context clue perfectly. Combining that with the knowledge that you are looking for a positive value word certifies coordinated (A) as the correct answer.

Here is a Level II example:

Because they reject __+__ , conscientious objectors *are given jobs in community work as a substitute for participation in the armed services.*

+(A) labor   –(D) dictatorships

–(B) belligerence   –(E) poverty

+(C) peace

From working with this example previously, you know that the correct answer is belligerence (B). The root of this word is *bellum*, Latin for war. Belligerence is an inclination toward war. Other words that may be scrolled from this are bellicose, belligerent, and antebellum, all of which have to do with war. Study your roots and prefixes well. A casual knowledge is not good enough. Another root, *bellis*, might be confused with *bellum*. *Bellis* means beauty. Is it logical that a conscientious objector would reject beauty? Know when to use which root and prefix. This ability will come with study and practice.

Here is a Level III example:

When a physician describes an illness to a colleague, he must speak an __+__ language, *using professional terms and concepts understood mostly by members of his profession.*

+(A) extrinsic   +(D) esoteric

−(B) inordinate   −(E) abbreviated

+(C) ambulatory

Recalling this example, you will remember that the context clue defines the missing word as one meaning language that involves a special group of people, i.e., "inside information." The correct answer is esoteric (D). *Eso* is a prefix that means *inside*. The prefix of extrinsic (A) is *ex*, which means *out*, the opposite of the meaning you seek. Inordinate (B) means *not ordered*. In this case, the prefix *in* means *not*. This is Level III, so beware of easy assumptions! The root of ambulatory (C) is *ambulare*, which means *to walk*. Abbreviated (E) breaks down to *ab*, meaning *to*; and *brevis*, Latin for brief or short.

In many Level III words you may not be able to scroll or break down a word completely. However, often, as in the example above, a partial knowledge of the etymology may be enough to find the correct answer.

Now, take what you have learned and apply it to the questions appearing in the following drill. If you are unsure of an answer, refer back to the review material for help.

DRILL: SENTENCE COMPLETIONS

DIRECTIONS: Each sentence below has one or two blanks, each blank indicating that something has been omitted. Beneath the sentence are five lettered words or sets of words. Choose the word or set of words that BEST fits the meaning of the sentence as a whole.

EXAMPLE

Although the critics found the book _____, many of the readers found it rather _____.

(A) obnoxious . . . perfect   (D) comical . . . persuasive

(B) spectacular . . . interesting   (E) popular . . . rare

(C) boring . . . intriguing

1. The problems of the homeless were so desperate that he felt a need to help _____ them.

   (A) increase   (D) collaborate
   (B) ameliorate   (E) justify
   (C) authenticate

2. The activities of the business manager were so obviously unethical that the board had no choice but to _____ him.

   (A) censure   (D) censor
   (B) commend   (E) reiterate
   (C) consecrate

3. _____ people often are taken in by _____ salespeople.

   (A) Suave . . . futile   (D) Erratic . . . passive
   (B) Benevolent . . . inept   (E) Pious . . . obstinate
   (C) Gullible . . . larcenous

4. The speaker _____ the work of environmentalists as ineffective.

   (A) dissented   (D) conceded
   (B) savored   (E) tantalized
   (C) disparaged

5. Her exceptionally well-written first novel was happily reviewed by the critics with _____ .

   (A) ennui   (D) acclaim
   (B) pessimism   (E) chagrin
   (C) remorse

6. That commentator never has anything good to say; every remark is _____ .

   (A) inept   (D) bombastic
   (B) frivolous   (E) caustic
   (C) aberrant

Chapter 4—Mastering Sentence Completion Questions **141**

7. The principal's plan to gain students' and parents' cooperation by forming small work groups has worked well; it is both creative and _____ .

(A) sagacious   (D) erroneous
(B) ignoble   (E) conventional
(C) dissonant

8. My boss is so arrogant that we're surprised when he _____ to speak to us in the cafeteria.

(A) forbears   (D) delays
(B) declines   (E) deigns
(C) abhors

9. Scientists and environmentalists are very concerned about the _____ of the ozone layer.

(A) depletion   (D) defamation
(B) dissonance   (E) enhancement
(C) conglomeration

10. Resolving racist attitudes seems to happen most successfully in communities where different ethnic groups _____ around issues of justice.

(A) educe   (D) coalesce
(B) collapse   (E) diverge
(C) dissolve

11. One obstacle to solving the mass transit problem is a _____ of funds to build and repair systems.

(A) euphony   (D) dearth
(B) profusion   (E) vindication
(C) periphery

12. Terrorists, who are usually _____ , seldom can be dealt with _____ .

(A) rabid . . . timorously   (D) blasphemous . . . tersely
(B) unruly . . . fairly   (E) hedonistic . . . honestly
(C) zealots . . . rationally

13. The candidate argued that it was _____ to _____ democracy and yet not vote.

    (A) malicious . . . denounce   (D) inarticulate . . . defend

    (B) lucrative . . . allocate   (E) hypocritical . . . advocate

    (C) commendable . . . delineate

14. Of all the boring speeches I have ever heard, last night's address had to be the most _____ yet!

    (A) arrogant   (D) fervent

    (B) insipid   (E) indolent

    (C) effervescent

15. Malcolm X was a _____ of Martin Luther King, Jr., yet he had a _____ different view of integration.

    (A) disciple . . . reciprocally

    (B) codependent . . . uniquely

    (C) contemporary . . . radically

    (D) fanatic . . . futilely

    (E) biographer . . . unrealistically

16. In order to pass the hearing test, you have to be able to _____ high pitch tones from low pitch tones.

    (A) surmise   (D) document

    (B) define   (E) vindicate

    (C) discriminate

17. The committee _____ carefully before making the final report; nevertheless, a minority report _____ its conclusions.

    (A) deliberated . . . refuted   (D) gloated . . . implemented

    (B) analyzed . . . abased   (E) argued . . . accepted

    (C) discerned . . .emulated

18. In general, _____ behavior will bring rewards.

    (A) languid   (D) disruptive

    (B) rhetorical   (E) exemplary

    (C) questionable

19. Colonial Americans, who had little extra money or leisure time, built simple and _____ homes.

(A) baroque
(B) unpretentious
(C) grandiose
(D) prodigious
(E) disreputable

20. Communist countries today are trying to _____ the ineffective economic policies of the past.

(A) ignore
(B) rectify
(C) reiterate
(D) condone
(E) provoke

21. Albert Einstein is the _____ of a genius.

(A) rebuttal
(B) digression
(C) antithesis
(D) mentor
(E) epitome

22. He was tempted to cheat but did not want to _____ his morals.

(A) obscure
(B) refute
(C) compromise
(D) concede
(E) succumb

23. Religious services have spiritual significance for those who are _____ .

(A) fastidious
(B) pessimistic
(C) pragmatic
(D) pious
(E) phlegmatic

24. Her _____ remarks seemed innocent enough, but in reality they were _____ .

(A) caustic . . . fallacious
(B) acrid . . . insipid
(C) magnanimous . . . affable
(D) innocuous . . . malicious
(E) ebullient . . . frivolous

25. The legend of Beowulf is a famous Norse _____ .

    (A) saga   (D) utopia
    (B) reverie   (E) satire
    (C) soliloquy

26. An effective way to prevent the spread of infectious disease is to _____ the sick person.

    (A) alleviate   (D) salvage
    (B) efface   (E) absolve
    (C) quarantine

27. In international business and politics, English is virtually a _____ language.

    (A) mundane   (D) palpable
    (B) finite   (E) universal
    (C) dead

28. Spring break is a welcome _____ from _____ school work.

    (A) dichotomy . . . garbled   (D) liaison . . . difficult
    (B) quandary . . . lax   (E) zenith . . . phenomenal
    (C) respite . . . arduous

29. If you can't find an original form, just prepare a reasonable _____ .

    (A) paradigm   (D) aberration
    (B) facsimile   (E equivocation
    (C) facade

30. Their generous donation provided the _____ needed to raise the entire goal.

    (A) catalyst   (D) ideology
    (B) alacrity   (E) plethora
    (C) duress

31. The protestors got a better response to their requests when they _____ their anger.

    (A) invoked   (D) tempered
    (B) appeased   (E) censured
    (C) condoned

32. Carelessly dumping chemicals has created many _____ waste sites.

    (A) choleric   (D) toxic
    (B) utopian   (E) vaunted
    (C) torpid

33. The investment counselor had a _____ reputation for purchasing companies and then stripping them of all the assets.

    (A) potent   (D) notorious
    (B) commendable   (E) pervasive
    (C) subtle

34. Staying active is important for people of all ages, so that neither the brain nor the muscles _____ .

    (A) expand   (D) vacillate
    (B) atrophy   (E) condescend
    (C) endure

35. When a student consistently does not turn in homework, the teacher often _____ that the student is _____ .

    (A) implies . . . zealous   (D) assures . . . taciturn
    (B) concludes . . . ambitious (E) infers . . . indolent
    (C) assumes . . . depraved

36. Looking through the photo album brought warm feelings of _____ .

    (A) remorse   (D) ambiguity
    (B) nostalgia   (E) deference
    (C) complacence

37. There is a marked _____ between the salaries of skilled and unskilled workers.

   (A) disparity   (D) calamity

   (B) increase   (E) amorphousness

   (C) cohesion

38. Although the chairperson seemed to be neutral in her support of the plan, they suspected she had _____ motives.

   (A) satirical   (D) guileless

   (B) palpable   (E) ulterior

   (C) occult

39. They were elated to learn that the salary increases were _____ to the beginning of the year.

   (A) reciprocal   (D) germane

   (B) recessive   (E) subsidiary

   (C) retroactive

40. Scientists debate whether it is possible to even _____ exactly how life begins.

   (A) fathom   (D) rebut

   (B) juxtapose   (E) suppress

   (C) gloat

SENTENCE COMPLETIONS

ANSWER KEY

Drill: Sentence Completions

1.	(B)	11.	(D)	21.	(E)	31	(D)
2.	(A)	12.	(C)	22.	(C)	32.	(D)
3.	(C)	13.	(E)	23.	(D)	33.	(D)
4.	(C)	14.	(B)	24.	(D)	34.	(B)
5.	(D)	15.	(C)	25.	(A)	35.	(E)
6.	(E)	16.	(C)	26.	(C)	36.	(B)
7.	(A)	17	(A)	27.	(E)	37.	(A)
8.	(E)	18.	(E)	28.	(C)	38.	(E)
9.	(A)	19.	(B)	29.	(B)	39.	(C)
10.	(D)	20.	(B)	30.	(A)	40.	(A)

DETAILED EXPLANATIONS

SENTENCE COMPLETIONS

1. (B) The blank in this sentence describes the action the individual wanted to take concerning the problems of the homeless. The context clue is the phrase "so desperate," which modifies "the problems of the homeless." The best answer expresses how people would react to a desperate problem or situation. Naturally, people would want to help bring a desperate situation to an end. Ameliorate (B) is the best answer because it means to help in a way that relieves pain and suffering. Answer (A), increase, is counter-intuitive; no one would want to increase a desperate situation to make things worse. Authenticate (C) and justify (E) both insinuate that the person wanted to prove or legitimize the problems of the homeless, which is unrelated to our context clue "desperate." Finally, collaborate (D) suggests that the person wanted the problems of the homeless to work together, which is nonsensical.

2. (A) The blank refers to the action the board is going to take towards the business manager. The context clue is the "unethical activities" of the manager. The correct answer reflects the appropriate action taken towards someone who has acted unethically. Censure (A) is the best answer because it means to scold or condemn the actions of someone. Commend (B) and consecrate (C) both refer to the opposite meaning of censure; someone who has acted unethically does not deserve praise or holiness. If the board chose to censor (D) the manager they would be deleting or hiding his unethical practices instead of condemning them, therefore censor (D) is incorrect. Finally, reiterate (E) means to restate or say again, which makes no sense in the context of the sentence.

3. (C) The context clue for this sentence is "taken in by," which refers to the action of being fooled or scammed. The second blank, therefore, must be a word that describes salespeople in a lying or scamming way. Gullible . . . larcenous (C) is the best answer because it correctly describes the salespeople as scamming and thieving and portrays their customers as readily believing the scam. No other answer choice reflects this opposite relationship between the blanks.

4. (C) The context clue is "ineffective." By calling the work of environmentalists ineffective, the speaker is criticizing and placing little value in their work. The correct answer best reflects this tone. Disparaged (C) is the best answer because it means to belittle or undervalue, thus creating an environment in which to criticize as ineffective. Dissented (A), savored (B), conceded (D), and tantalized (E) are all unrelated to ineffective.

5. **(D)** The context clue is that the novel was "exceptionally well written" and was "happily reviewed," therefore the critics would look on it with something very positive and good. Ennui (A) reflects a boredom with modern things and cannot be considered positive and good. Pessimism (B) means to look on things in a negative light and is therefore the opposite of the correct meaning. Remorse (C) is incorrect because it refers to sadness and grieving. Acclaim (D) is the best response because it means praise and applause, both of which reflect the "exceptionally well written" and "happily reviewed" clues of the sentence. Chagrin (E) refers to shame and distress, which is incorrect.

6. **(E)** The context clue "never has anything good to say" defines what the commentators' remarks are for the blank. Caustic (E), or harshly critical, is the best answer because it most nearly means "never has anything good to say." Inept (A) and aberrant (C) are not usually used to describe remarks or speech. Frivolous (B) refers to a lack of seriousness and bombastic (D) describes anything that is pompous or grandiose.

7. **(A)** The first part of the sentence describes the principal's plan and states that it worked well. The second part describes this plan as "creative" and something else. The most important context clue is the word "both" in the second part of the sentence. The use of "both" signifies that the meaning of the blank is similar to creative, since both words describe the "well worked" plan. Sagacious (A), which means wise or smart, is the only answer choice that reflects the same positive meaning as creative, and is the best answer. Ignoble (B), dissonant (C), and erroneous (D) all have negative meanings and conventional (E) simply means common or everyday, not creative.

8. **(E)** The context clue is "arrogant," but the meaning of the blank is going to be the opposite of this because the workers are "surprised" when the boss "stoops down" and lets go of his arrogance to speak to them. Deigns (E) is the best response because it most nearly reflects this idea of stooping down or stepping to a lower level. Declines (B) and abhors (C) are incorrect because the boss would no longer be letting go of his arrogance and would still not be speaking to them, both of which would not surprise the workers.

9. **(A)** The decrease in size of the ozone layer would be the only thing that both scientists and environmentalists would be concerned about. So far there have been no reports of a contradiction or dissonance (B) in the ozone layer. There have been no reports of a gathering or conglomeration (C), slander or defamation (D), or an artificial improvement or enhancement (E) of the ozone layer either. Therefore the correct the answer means decrease in size. Depletion (A) is the best response.

10. **(D)** The sentence implies that, to resolve racist attitudes, different ethnic groups must do something about issues of justice. Any type of resolution on racist attitudes between different ethnic groups would most likely involve an agreement between them rather than a disagreement, especially when the issue is justice. Therefore the answer is the word that most closely means "agreement." Coalesce (D), which means to form together, is the best response. Diverge (E), which means to separate, would be the opposite of the correct answer.

11. **(D)** The context clue for this sentence is "obstacle," and this prevents the mass transit problem from being solved. The second part of the sentence explains that this problem has to do with funds to build and repair systems. The blank, therefore, will explain the problem with the funds. Euphony (A), periphery (B), and vindication (E) do not sensibly describe a condition of funds or money. Profusion (B) is incorrect because it is difficult to understand how an excess of money can be an obstacle to building and re-

pairing transit systems. Therefore, dearth (D) is the best answer because it adequately describes a lack of funds as an obstacle to solving the mass transit problem.

12. (C) In this two-blank sentence completion, the relationship between the two blanks is the context clue that will lead to the correct answer. The first blank is a word that describes terrorists. The second blank describes the way terrorists are seldom or rarely dealt with. Therefore the relationship between the blanks is opposite. Blasphemous . . . tersely (D) and hedonistic . . . honestly (E) are incorrect because they are not opposite in meaning. Rabid . . . timorously (A) is incorrect because even if a terrorist has a lot of anger, they can still be quiet and reserved. Unruly . . . fairly (B) is incorrect as well, because although a terrorist can be unruly, it does not mean they must be unfair. Zealots . . . rationally (A) is the best answer because it correctly expresses the opposite dynamic of the two blanks. A zealot is someone who is ruled by their passions or emotions, which means they can rarely be rational or devoid of passion or emotions.

13. (E) The first part of the sentence focuses on democracy, a system of government that is maintained through active participation of its citizens through voting. The second half of the sentence provides the context clue "yet not vote." The word "yet" indicates an antonym relationship between "not vote" and the blank before "democracy." Hypocritical . . . advocate (E) is the best answer because it clarifies this antonym relationship. Hypocritical means to say one thing while doing the opposite, therefore it would be hypocritical to advocate, or support, democracy and yet not participate in it. Answer (A), malicious . . . denounce, is incorrect because it would be expected for a person to denounce or speak out against democracy and not vote, not vindictive or malicious. The second word in answer (D), inarticulate . . . defend, makes sense, but it would not be inarticulate, or the inability to speak clearly, to defend democracy and not vote. Lucrative . . . allocate (B) and commendable . . . delineate (C) are incorrect because democracy can be neither allocated nor delineated.

14. (B) The sentence is comparing last night's speech to all the "boring" speeches the speaker had heard before. Therefore "boring" is the context clue and the blank must be a synonym of boring. Insipid (B) is the best answer because it means boring and dull. Effervescent (C) and fervent (D) are the opposites of boring, while indolent (E) expresses more laziness than boringness. Arrogant (A), to be full of pride, has nothing to do with boring.

15. (C) The context clue is the word "yet" which suggests that the first half of the sentence and the second half of the sentence have opposite relationships. The second half of the sentence describes how different Malcolm X's view of integration was compared to that of Dr. King. Therefore the first half of the sentence must describe how Malcolm X and Dr. King were the same. Contemporary . . . radically (C) is the best answer because it sufficiently expresses how Malcolm X and Dr. King were similar and how their views were different. Since they were contemporaries, they existed and worked at the same time, but their views on integration were radically, or extremely, different. Answer (A), disciple . . . reciprocally, suggests that Malcolm X was a follower of Dr. King's. If this were true, Malcolm would not have had a different view of integration at all. The same applies to answer (D), fanatic . . . futilely. A fanatic would have an extreme view of its leader, not a different one. Answers (B), codependent . . . uniquely, and (E), biographer . . . unrealistically, also do not fit the opposite paradigm of the blanks.

16. (C) The first half of the sentence gives the context clue "to pass the hearing test." The second half of the sentence gives the blank that describes the requirement needed "to pass the hearing test." The second half of the sentence also states that the requirement needed to pass involves "high pitch tones" and "low pitch tones." Therefore, in order to pass a hearing test, one most likely will need to distinguish or tell the difference between the two tones. Discriminate (C) is the best answer because it most nearly means distinguish. Define (B) and document (C) would help if it was a written exam about hearing, but the exam is to determine if one can hear. Surmise (A), which means to guess, and vindicate (E), which means to free from blame, make no sense.

17. (A) The context clue is "nevertheless" which indicates that the first and second half of the sentence will show a contrast rather than a similarity. Answers (C), discerned . . . emulated, and (E), argued . . . accepted, insinuate that the minority report agreed with the conclusions of the committee, which is incorrect because we are looking for contrast, or disagreement. Answer (B), analyzed . . . abased, is too extreme because a minority report would never humiliate a committee or report. Answer (A), deliberated . . . refuted, is the best answer because it insinuates that the committee thought long and hard before making its conclusions and that the minority report still disagreed with it. Answer (D), gloated . . . implemented, is wrong because a committee would not gloat, or boast, before making any conclusion or report. Also, implemented makes no sense in the second blank.

18. (E) The context clue is "bring rewards." What kind of behavior will "bring rewards"? Exemplary (E) behavior, or outstanding behavior, will usually bring rewards and is the correct answer. Rhetorical (B) does not make sense as an answer choice. Languid (A), questionable (C), and disruptive (D) describe behavior that is usually scolded or advised against, thus not enticing any types of rewards.

19. (B) The first half of the sentence informs us that early Americans had "little money or leisure time." As a result of this, their homes were usually "simple." The correct answer will be synonymous with the context clue, "simple." Baroque (A), grandiose (C), and prodigious (D) all refer to things that are wealthy, grand, and not simple and therefore are incorrect. Disreputable (E) can describe either a simple or complex home and is not similar or opposite of "simple." Unpretentious (B), which means quaint or plain, is the best answer because it is most similar to "simple."

20. (B) The context clue is in the second half of the sentence, "the ineffective economic policies of the past." Since "ineffective economic policies" are a bad thing that should be avoided, reiterate (C), condone (D), and provoke (E) are incorrect, because not even a communist country would want to reinstate, approve, or bring about ineffective economic policies. Rectify (B) is the best answer because it insinuates that the communist countries are trying to fix or repair the old, ineffective economic systems. Ignore (A) is incorrect because ignoring ineffective economic policies does not correct or solve them.

21. (E) The context clue is "Albert Einstein," a Nobel Prize winner who revolutionized physics in the twentieth century. Because of his genius and intellect, he is a model for other scientists to look up to. Therefore epitome (E), a model or essence of, is the best answer. Rebuttal (A) and antithesis (C) imply that Einstein was not a genius and are incorrect. Digression (B) and mentor (D) imply that Einstein was smart but not a genius, which is false.

22. (C) The first half of the sentence gives the context clue "tempted to cheat." The second half of the sentence begins with "but," which indicates that the second half will contrast with the first half. Therefore, someone who was tempted to cheat, but did not, would still have high, or secure, morals. Compromise (C), the correct answer, best implies this idea, since because the individual did not cheat, his morals were not readjusted or compromised to reflect cheating tendencies. Refute (B), concede (D), and succumb (E) imply that by cheating, all the morality would be lost in the individual, and so these choices are too extreme. Obscure (A) is incorrect because by cheating, an individual does not confuse or blur his morals, but rather compromises them.

23. (D) The entire sentence is the context clue for the meaning of the blank. What answer choice best describes someone who believes "religious services have spiritual significance"? Pious (D) is the correct answer because it describes someone who is devoutly religious, and as such would find spiritual significance in a religious service. Fastidious (A) describes someone who is hard to please. Pessimistic (B) describes someone who is overly negative, religiously or not. Pragmatic (C) describes someone who is concerned with practical things, and thus would not be concerned with spiritual matters. Phlegmatic (E) describes sickly people who could, or could not, find spiritual significance in religion.

24. (D) The first half of the sentence deals with a type of remark that appears "innocent." The second half of the sentence, beginning with the word "but," suggests that the meaning is opposite of "innocent." Innocuous . . . malicious (D) is the best answer because it reflects this contrast of meaning. Innocuous refers to something that is harmless or innocent while malicious describes something that is harmful or dangerous. Not only are caustic . . . fallacious (A), acrid . . . insipid (B), and ebullient . . . frivolous (E) not opposites in meaning, but caustic, acrid, and ebullient do not have the same meaning as innocent. Magnanimous . . . affable (C) have similar meanings and do not reflect the contrast of the sentence.

25. (A) "Beowulf," the context clue of this sentence, is an ancient, epic story. The answer would then be the closest to meaning ancient, epic story. Saga (A) is the best answer because it refers to legends or stories. Reverie (B) has nothing to do with stories or legends. Soliloquy (C) is a talk given to oneself, which is usually associated with stage drama. Utopia (D) and satire (E) deal with other types of writing than legends and epic stories.

26. (C) The blank in this sentence is referring to an action taken towards a sick person in order to, as the context clue states, "prevent the spread of infectious disease." Quarantine (C), the correct answer, means just that; to isolate an individual to prevent the spread of disease. Although it would help a sick person to alleviate (A) their ailments, it would not prevent the spread of disease while they are still infected. Efface (B) is an extreme answer choice because even though wiping out the sick person would prevent the spread of the disease, it would be an ineffective solution, especially if you were the sick person. To salvage (D) the sick person makes no sense. To forgive, or absolve (E), the sick person to prevent the spread of disease would also be ineffective.

27. (E) The first half of the sentence sets up the context clue "international business and politics." The second half of the sentence tries to describe the position of English within that area. Understanding that the United States and Great Britain, both English speaking countries, lead the world in business and politics, the position of English could be considered prevalent, or widespread. Universal (E) is the correct answer because it correctly implies a prevalent or widespread use of English in international business

and politics. Finite (B) and palpable (E) do not describe languages, and mundane (A) and dead (C) both imply an opposite meaning to prevalent or universal.

28. (C) The context clue, "welcome," helps define the first blank as a word with positive or good meaning because something that is welcome is usually looked forward to or sought after. The second blank would then have a negative or bad meaning because of the contrast in the sentence between spring break, which is welcome, and school work, which is usually not. Respite . . . arduous (C) is the correct answer because respite refers to the welcome break from the hard or arduous schoolwork. Dichotomy (A), liaison (D), and zenith (E) have neither positive nor negative meanings and the entire answers can be eliminated. Both words in answer (B) quandary . . . lax have negative meanings.

29. (B) If the "original form" cannot be found, then the only thing to use in its place would be a copy. Facsimile (B) is the correct answer because it most closely means copy. Paradigm (A) refers to a model on which other designs or ideas are based, and does not imply a direct copy, which is needed to replace a missing original. Facade (C) describes a false appearance for the use of fooling or deceiving, not the intent of making a copy of the original form. Aberration (D) and equivocation (E) are unrelated to the topic of the sentence.

30. (A) According to the context of the sentence, a goal was reached, and a generous donation played a role in reaching that goal. The blank describes what role the donation played. Catalyst (A) is the best response because it correctly suggests that the donation provided a starting point upon which the goal was reached. Alacrity (B) would more appropriately describe the efforts of the volunteers in reaching the goal, which is not mentioned here. Duress (C), which means excessive stress, would most likely hinder the attainment of the goal. Ideology (D) is irrelevant concerning the amount of a donation and the attainment of a goal. Plethora (E), or overabundance, is nonsensical.

31. (D) It is always easier and preferable to deal with people who are calm, level-headed and cordial. When the context of this sentence suggests that the protesters did something to their anger in order to get "a better response to their requests," it can be reasoned that they lessened, or got rid of, their anger. Tempered (D) is the best response because it insinuates a reducing or softening of their anger. Invoke (A) means to call upon their anger, which would have the opposite effect of receiving a better response. Appeased (B) implies that the protestors already received their desired response. Condoned (C) and censured (E) are nonsensical, implying that the protestors received better responses when they agreed with or criticized their anger.

32. (D) The blank in this sentence describes what is created when chemicals are carelessly thrown away. Since most chemicals are of an inorganic or synthetic nature, they do not react well with organic or natural environments, and as a result end up poisoning the land and waters. Therefore if they are not properly disposed of, they will create poisonous waste sites. Toxic (D) is the best response because it means poisonous. Choleric (A) incorrectly personifies the waste site as bitter or cranky. Utopian (B) is the opposite response because it refers to an ideal, perfect place, not poisonous and intoxicated. Torpid (C) and vaunted (E) do not appropriately describe any waste site.

33. (D) The blank in this sentence describes the reputation of the investment counselor. The context clue in the second half defines the counselor's reputation as "purchasing companies and then stripping them of all the assets." Therefore we can conclude that the counselor's reputation is not good, and even call it bad and scary. Notorious (D) is the best response because it means popular through bad or evil acts. The counselor was notorious because he was known for buying companies and parting them out to the highest bidder. Commendable (B) is the opposite of this meaning and therefore incorrect. The counselor could have a potent (A) or subtle (C) reputation, but there is not enough information to determine this from the sentence. Pervasive (E), or present everywhere, does not work in describing the counselor's reputation.

34. (B) "Staying active" is the context clue. The use of "neither . . . nor" in the second half defines the meaning of the blank as the opposite of "staying active." By staying active, neither the brain nor the muscles will become "inactive." The answer is a word that means inactive. Atrophy (B) is the best response because it refers to the loss or deterioration of muscle tissue usually associated with inactivity. Expand (A) and endure (C) imply the opposite meaning of weaken and are incorrect. Vacillate (D) and condescend (E) are not used to describe the state of muscle tissue.

35. (E) The first half of the sentence provides the context clue of the student's scholastic habits as "consistently not turning in homework." Therefore, the word for the second blank would appropriately describe a student who does not turn in homework. Answer (E), infers . . . indolent, is the best response because the teacher correctly infers, or draws the conclusion that the student is lazy, based on the context clue of "not turning in homework." None of the other answer choices for the second blank appropriately describe the action of "consistently not turning in homework."

36. (B) The answer refers to remembering the past in a way that brings up warm feelings. Nostalgia (B) is the best response because it specifically refers to fond or warm recollections of the past. Remorse (A) is incorrect because it deals with feeling of guilt or sadness. Complacence (C) and ambiguity (D) have neutral tones and therefore would describe only neutral feelings. Deference (E) does not appropriately describe feelings.

37. (A) The topic of the sentence deals with the salaries of skilled workers and unskilled workers, and the blank represents something that is between them. Disparity (A) is the best answer because it denotes that there is a marked difference between the two salaries. Increase (B) is incorrect because the sentence is conveying a distinction between two things and not the growth between two things. Cohesion (C), calamity (D), and amorphousness (E) are not used to distinguish between two separate things.

38. (E) The most important context clue in this sentence is the first word "although," which indicates that the first half of the sentence will contrast with the second half. In the first half the chairperson appeared to be neutral, so the second half should express that she was not neutral. Ulterior (E) is the best answer because it indicates that the chairperson had hidden, or non-neutral motives. Palpable (B) and guileless (D) express the opposite of the intended meaning, while satirical (A) and occult (C) do not properly describe motives.

39. (C) The blank in this sentence completion explains what the employees were happy to learn about their salary increases. It is very doubtful that the employees would be happy to learn that their salary increases were reciprocal (A), or mutual, to the beginning of the year. It is also doubtful that the salary increases would be either germane (D), or subsidiary (E) to the beginning of the year. It is possible that the salary increases could be recessive (B) to the beginning of the year, but that would not make the employees elated or happy. Retroactive (C) is the best response because it explains that the employees will receive a pay raise for hours already worked, which is the reason for their happiness.

40. (A) The blank represents the point of issue that is up for debate among scientists. Fathom (A) is the best answer because it reasonably defines that the debate is about whether scientists can even comprehend or understand how life begins. Rebut (D) and suppress (E) do not define a sensible debate. It is highly improbable to juxtapose (B), or place side-by-side, how life began or gloat (C), or brag, about how life began.

CHAPTER 5

MASTERING CRITICAL READING QUESTIONS

CHAPTER 5

MASTERING CRITICAL READING QUESTIONS

The Critical Reading sections of the PSAT are indeed critical, for they make up over 50 percent of the entire verbal section content. In all, you will encounter 35 Critical Reading questions. "Why," you must wonder, "would this much importance be attached to reading?" The reason is simple. Your ability to read at a strong pace while grasping a solid understanding of the material is a key factor in your high school performance and your potential college success. But "critical" can be taken in another sense, for the PSAT will ask you to be a reading critic. You'll be required not only to summarize the material but analyze it, make judgments about it, and make educated guesses about what the writer implies and infers. Even your ability to understand vocabulary in context will come under scrutiny. "Can I," you ask yourself, "meet the challenge?" *Yes*, and preparation is the means!

CRITICAL READING PASSAGES AND QUESTIONS

Within the PSAT critical reading section you will be given 5–7 Critical Reading passages, ranging in length from 250–850 words apiece. The shortest passages will be brief paragraphs followed by 3–4 questions. The medium length passages will consist of 2–5 paragraphs followed by 6–10 questions. The longest passage is the dual or double passage followed by 10–13 questions. The double passage will be composed of two separate works which you will be asked to compare or contrast. The reading content of the passages will cover:

- the humanities (philosophy, the fine arts)

- the social sciences (psychology, archaeology, anthropology, economics, political science, sociology, history)

- the natural sciences (biology, geology, astronomy, chemistry, physics)

- narration (fiction, nonfiction)

These Critical Reading questions are of four types:

1.   Synthesis/Analysis

2.   Evaluation

3.   Vocabulary-in-Context

4.   Interpretation

Through this review, you'll learn not only how to identify these types of questions, but how to successfully attack each one. Familiarity with the test format, combined with solid reading strategies, will prove invaluable in answering the questions quickly and accurately.

ABOUT THE DIRECTIONS

Make sure to study and learn the directions to save yourself time during the actual test. You should simply skim them when beginning the section. The directions will read much like the following.

DIRECTIONS: Read each passage and answer the questions that follow. Each question will be based on the information stated or implied in the passage or its introduction.

A variation of these directions will be presented as follows for the double passage.

DIRECTIONS: Read the passages and answer the questions that follow. Each question will be based on the information stated or implied in the selections or their introductions, and may be based on the relationship between the passages.

ABOUT THE PASSAGES

You may encounter any of a number of passage types in the Critical Reading section. These passages may consist of straight text, dialogue and text, or narration. A passage may appear by itself or as part of a pair in a double passage. A brief introduction will be provided for each passage to set the scene for the text being presented.

To familiarize yourself with the types of passages you will encounter, review the examples that follow. The content of the passages will include the humanities, social sciences, natural sciences, and also narrative text.

A **humanities passage** may discuss such topics as philosophy, the fine arts, and language. The following is an example of such a passage. It falls into the 550- to 700-word range.

Throughout his pursuit of knowledge and enlightenment, the philosopher Socrates made many enemies among the Greek citizens. The following passage is an account of the trial resulting from their accusations.

1   The great philosopher Socrates was put on trial in Athens in 400 B.C. on charges of corrupting the youth and of impiety. As recorded in Plato's dialogue *The Apology*, Socrates began his defense by saying he was going to "speak plainly and honestly," unlike the eloquent sophists the Athenian jury was accustomed to hearing. His appeal to
5   unadorned language offended the jurors, who were expecting to be entertained.

Socrates identified the two sets of accusers that he had to face: the past and the present. The former had filled the jurors' heads with lies about him when they were young, and was considered by Socrates to be the most dangerous. The accusers from the past could not be cross-examined, and they had already influenced the jurors when
10 they were both naive and impressionable. This offended the jury because it called into question their ability to be objective and render a fair judgment.

The philosopher addressed the charges himself, and dismissed them as mere covers for the deeper attack on his philosophical activity. That activity, which involved questioning others until they revealed contradictions in their beliefs, had given rise to Socrates' motto,
15 "The unexamined life is not worth living," and the "Socratic Method," which is still employed in many law schools today. This critical questioning of leading Athenians had made Socrates very unpopular with those in power and, he insisted, was what led to his trial. This challenge to the legitimacy of the legal system itself further alienated his judges.

Socrates tried to explain that his philosophical life came about by accident. He had
20 been content to be a humble stone mason until the day a friend informed him that the Oracle of Delphi had said that "Socrates is the wisest man in Greece." Socrates had been so surprised by this statement, and so sure of its inaccuracy, that he set about disproving it by talking to the reputed wise men of Athens and showing how much more knowledge they possessed. Unfortunately, as he told the jury, those citizens reputed to
25 be wise (politicians, businessmen, artists) turned out to be ignorant, either by knowing absolutely nothing, or by having limited knowledge in their fields of expertise and assuming knowledge of everything else. Of these, Socrates had to admit, "I am wiser, because although all of us have little knowledge, I am aware of my ignorance, while they are not." But this practice of revealing prominent citizens' ignorance and arrogance
30 did not earn Socrates their affection, especially when the bright young men of Athens began following him around and delighting in the disgracing of their elders. Hence, in his view, the formal charges of "corrupting the youth" and "impiety" were a pretext to retaliate for the deeper offense of challenging the pretensions of the establishment.

Although Socrates viewed the whole trial as a sham, he cleverly refuted the charges
35 by using the same method of questioning that got him in trouble in the first place. Against the charges of corrupting the youth, Socrates asked his chief accuser, Meletus, if any wanted to arm himself, to which Meletus answered, "no." Then, Socrates asked if one's associates had an effect on one: Good people for good, and evil people for evil, to which Meletus answered, "yes." Next, Socrates asked if corrupting one's companions makes
40 them better or worse, to which Meletus responded, "worse." Finally Socrates set the trap by asking Meletus if Socrates had corrupted the youth intentionally or unintentionally. Meletus, wanting to make the charges as bad as possible, answered, "intentionally." Socrates showed the contradictory nature of the charge, since by intentionally corrupting his companions he made them worse, thereby bringing harm on himself. He also refuted
45 the second charge of impiety in the same manner, by showing that its two components (teaching about strange gods and atheism) were inconsistent.

Although Socrates had logically refuted the charges against him, the Athenian jury found him guilty, and Meletus proposed the death penalty. The defendant Socrates was allowed to propose an alternative penalty and Socrates proposed a state pension, so he
50 could continue his philosophical activity to the benefit of Athens. He stated that this is what he deserved. The Athenian jury, furious over his presumption, voted the death penalty and, thus, one of the great philosophers of the Western heritage was executed.

The **social science passage** may discuss such topics as psychology, archaeology, anthropology, economics, political science, sociology, and history. The following is an example of such a passage. It falls into the 400- to 550-word range.

Not only does music have the ability to entertain and enthrall, but it also has the capacity to heal. The following passage illustrates the recent indoctrination of music therapy.

1   Music's power to affect moods and stir emotions has been well known for as long as music has existed. Stories about the music of ancient Greece tell of the healing powers of Greek music. Leopold Mozart, the father of Wolfgang, wrote that if the Greeks' music could heal the sick, then our music should be able to bring the dead back to life.
5   Unfortunately, today's music cannot do quite that much.

The healing power of music, taken for granted by ancient man and by many primitive societies, is only recently becoming accepted by medical professionals as a new way of healing the emotionally ill.

Using musical activities involving patients, the music therapist seeks to restore
10   mental and physical health. Music therapists usually work with emotionally disturbed patients as part of a team of therapists and doctors. Music therapists work together with physicians, psychiatrists, psychologists, physical therapists, nurses, teachers, recreation leaders, and families of patients.

The rehabilitation that a music therapist gives to patients can be in the form of listen-
15   ing, performing, taking lessons on an instrument, or even composing. A therapist may help a patient regain lost coordination by teaching the patient how to play an instrument. Speech defects can sometimes be helped by singing activities. Some patients need the social awareness of group activities, but others may need individual attention to build self-confidence. The music therapist must learn what kinds of activities are best for each patient.

20   In addition to working with patients, the music therapist has to attend meetings with other therapists and doctors that work with the same patients to discuss progress and plan new activities. Written reports to doctors about patients' responses to treatment are another facet of the music therapist's work.

Hospitals, schools, retirement homes, and community agencies and clinics are
25   some of the sites where music therapists work. Some music therapists work in private studies with patients that are sent to them by medical doctors, psychologists, and psychiatrists. Music therapy can be done in studios, recreation rooms, hospital wards, or classrooms depending on the type of activity and needs of the patients.

Qualified music therapists have followed a four-year course with a major emphasis
30   in music plus courses in biological science, anthropology, sociology, psychology, and music therapy. General studies in English, history, speech, and government complete the requirements for a Bachelor of Music Therapy. After college training, a music therapist must participate in a six-month training internship under the guidance of a registered music therapist.

35   Students who have completed college courses and have demonstrated their ability during the six-month internship can become registered music therapists by applying to the National Association for Music Therapy, Inc. New methods and techniques of music therapy are always being developed, so the trained therapist must continue to study new articles, books, and reports throughout his/her career.

The **natural science passage** may discuss such topics as biology, geology, astronomy, chemistry, and physics. The following is an example of such a passage. It falls into the 550- to 700-word range.

The following article was written by a physical chemist and recounts the conflict between volcanic matter in the atmosphere and airplane windows. It was published in a scientific periodical in 1989.

(Reprinted by permission of American Heritage Magazine, a division of Forbes Inc., © Forbes Inc., 1989.)

1   Several years ago the airlines discovered a new kind of problem—a window problem. The acrylic windows on some of their 747s were getting hazy and dirty-looking. Suspicious travelers thought the airlines might have stopped cleaning them, but the windows were not dirty; they were inexplicably deteriorating within as little as 390
5   hours of flight time, even though they were supposed to last for five to ten years. Boeing looked into it.

     At first the company thought the culprit might be one well known in modern technology, the component supplier who changes materials without telling the customer. Boeing quickly learned this was not the case, so there followed an extensive investiga-
10 tion that eventually brought in the Air Transport Association, geologists, and specialists in upper-atmosphere chemistry, and the explanation turned out to be not nearly so mundane. Indeed, it began to look like a grand reenactment of an ancient Aztec myth: the struggle between the eagle and the serpent, which is depicted on the Mexican flag.

     The serpent in this case is an angry Mexican volcano, El Chichon. Like its reptilian
15 counterpart, it knows how to spit venom at the eyes of its adversary. In March and April of 1982 the volcano, in an unusual eruption pattern, ejected millions of tons of sulfur-rich material directly into the stratosphere. In less than a year, a stratospheric cloud had blanketed the entire Northern Hemisphere. Soon the photochemistry of the upper atmosphere converted much of the sulfur into tiny droplets of concentrated sulfuric acid.

20 The eagle in the story is the 747, poking occasionally into the lower part of the stratosphere in hundreds of passenger flights daily. Its two hundred windows are made from an acrylic polymer, which makes beautifully clear, strong windows but was never intended to withstand attack by strong acids.

     The stratosphere is very different from our familiar troposphere environment.
25 Down here the air is humid, with a lot of vertical convection to carry things up and down; the stratosphere is bone-dry, home to the continent-striding jet stream, with unceasing horizontal winds at an average of 120 miles per hour. A mist of acid droplets accumulated gradually near the lower edge of the stratosphere, settling there at a thickness of about a mile a year, was able to wait for planes to come along.

30 As for sulfuric acid, most people know only the relatively benign liquid in a car battery: 80 percent water and 20 percent acid. The stratosphere dehydrated the sulfuric acid into a persistent, corrosive mist 75 percent pure acid, an extremely aggressive liquid. Every time the 747 poked into the stratosphere—on almost every long flight—acid droplets struck the windows and began to react with their outer surface, causing it to swell. This
35 built up stresses between the softened outer layer and the underlying material. Finally, parallel hairline cracks developed, creating the hazy appearance. The hazing was sped up by the mechanical stresses always present in the windows of a pressurized cabin.

The airlines suffered through more than a year of window replacements before the acid cloud finally dissipated. Ultimately the drops reached the lower edge of the strato-
40 sphere, were carried away into the lower atmosphere, and finally came down in the rain. In the meantime, more resistant window materials and coatings were developed. (As for the man-made sulfur dioxide that causes acid rain, it never gets concentrated enough to attack the window material. El Chichon was unusual in its ejection of sulfur directly into the stratosphere, and the 747 is unusual in its frequent entrance into the
45 stratosphere.)

As for the designers of those windows, it is hard to avoid the conclusion that a perfectly adequate engineering design was defeated by bad luck. After all, this was the only time since the invention of the airplane that there were acid droplets of this concentration in the upper atmosphere. But reliability engineers, an eminently rational breed, are very
50 uncomfortable when asked to talk about luck. In principle it should be possible to anticipate events, and the failure to do so somehow seems like a professional failure. The cosmos of the engineer has no room for poltergeists, demons, or other mystic elements. But might it accommodate the inexorable scenario of an ancient Aztec myth?

A **narrative passage dealing with fictional material** may be in the form of dialogue between characters, or one character speaking to the reader. The following is an example of the latter. It falls into the 700- to 850-word range.

In this passage, the narrator discovers that he has been transported to King Arthur's court in the year A.D. 528

1   The moment I got a chance I slipped aside privately and touched an ancient common-looking man on the shoulder and said, in an insinuating, confidential way—

"Friend, do me a kindness. Do you belong to the asylum, or are you just here on a visit or something like that?"

5   He looked me over stupidly, and said— "Marry, fair sir, me seemeth—"

"That will do," I said; "I reckon you are a patient."

I moved away, cogitating, and at the same time keeping an eye out for any chance passenger in his right mind that might come along and give me some light. I judged I had found one, presently; so I drew him aside and said in his ear—

10   "If I could see the head keeper a minute—only just a minute—"

"Prithee do not let me."

"Let you *what*?"

"*Hinder* me, then, if the word please thee better." Then he went on to say he was an under-cook and could not stop to gossip, though he would like it another time; for
15 it would comfort his very liver to know where I got my clothes. As he started away he pointed and said yonder was one who was idle enough for my purpose, and was seeking me besides, no doubt. This was an airy slim boy in shrimp-colored tights that made him look like a forked carrot; the rest of his gear was blue silk and dainty laces and ruffles; and he had long yellow curls, and wore a plumed pink satin cap tilted compla-
20 cently over his ear. By his look, he was good-natured; by his gait, he was satisfied with himself. He was pretty enough to frame. He arrived, looked me over with a smiling and impudent curiosity; said he had come for me, and informed me that he was a page.

"Go 'long," I said; "you ain't more than a paragraph."

It was pretty severe, but I was nettled. However, it never phazed him; he didn't
25 appear to know he was hurt. He began to talk and laugh, in happy, thoughtless, boy-
ish fashion, as we walked along, and made himself old friends with me at once; asked
me all sorts of questions about myself and about my clothes, but never waited for an
answer—always chattered straight ahead, as if he didn't know he had asked a question
and wasn't expecting any reply, until at last he happened to mention that he was born
30 in the beginning of the year 513.

It made the cold chills creep over me! I stopped, and said, a little faintly:

"Maybe I didn't hear you just right. Say it again—and say it slow. What year was it?"

"513."

"513! You don't look it! Come, my boy, I am a stranger and friendless: be honest
35 and honorable with me. Are you in your right mind?"

He said he was.

"Are these other people in their right minds?"

He said they were.

"And this isn't an asylum? I mean, it isn't a place where they cure crazy people?"

40 He said it wasn't.

"Well, then," I said, "either I am a lunatic, or something just as awful has happened. Now tell me, honest and true, where am I?"

"In King Arthur's Court."

I waited a minute, to let that idea shudder its way home, and then said:

45 "And according to your notions, what year is it now?"

"528—nineteenth of June."

I felt a mournful sinking at the heart, and muttered: "I shall never see my friends
again—never, never again. They will not be born for more than thirteen hundred years
yet."

50 I seemed to believe the boy, I didn't know why. *Something* in me seemed to
believe him—my consciousness, as you may say; but my reason didn't. My reason
straightway began to clamor; that was natural. I didn't know how to go about satisfying it, because I knew that the testimony of men wouldn't serve—my reason would say
they were lunatics, and throw out their evidence. But all of a sudden I stumbled on the
55 very thing, just by luck. I knew that the only total eclipse of the sun in the first half of
the sixth century occurred on the 21st of June, A. D. 528, o. s., and began at 3 minutes
after 12 noon. I also knew that no total eclipse of the sun was due in what to *me* was
the present year—*i.e.*, 1879. So, if I could keep my anxiety and curiosity from eating
the heart out of me for forty-eight hours, I should then find out for certain whether this
60 boy was telling me the truth or not.

A narrative passage dealing with nonfiction material may appear in the form of a speech or any such discourse in which one person speaks to a group of people or to the reader. The following two selections are examples of nonfiction narratives. Together, they are also an example of a double passage, in which the subject matter in the selections can be either compared or contrasted. As you will recall, the two selections will total 700 to 850.

The following passages are excerpts from two different Presidential Inaugural Addresses. Passage 1 comes from President John F. Kennedy's Inaugural Address, given on January 20, 1961. Passage 2 was given by President Franklin D. Roosevelt on March 4, 1933.

Passage 1

1   Let every nation know, whether it wishes us well or ill, that we shall pay any price, bear any burden, meet any hardship, support any friend, oppose any foe to assure the survival and the success of liberty.

This much we pledge—and more. To those old allies whose cultural and spiritual
5   origins we share, we pledge the loyalty of faithful friends. United, there is little we cannot do in a host of cooperative ventures. Divided, there is little we can do, for we dare not meet a powerful challenge at odds and split asunder.

To those new states whom we welcome to the ranks of the free, we pledge our word that one form of colonial control shall not have passed away merely to be re-
10   placed by a far more iron tyranny. We shall not always expect to find them supporting our view. But we shall always hope to find them strongly supporting their own freedom, and to remember that, in the past, those who foolishly sought power by riding the back of the tiger ended up inside.

To those peoples in the huts and villages of half the globe struggling to break the
15   bonds of mass misery, we pledge our best efforts to help them help themselves, for whatever period is required, not because the Communists may be doing it, not because we seek their votes, but because it is right. If a free society cannot help the many who are poor, it cannot save the few who are rich.

Passage 2

20   This is preeminently the time to speak the truth, the whole truth, frankly and boldly. Nor need we shrink from honestly facing conditions in our country today. This great nation will endure as it has endured, will revive, and will prosper.

So first of all let me assert my firm belief that the only thing we have to fear is fear itself—nameless, unreasoning, unjustified terror, which paralyzes needed efforts to
25   convert retreat into advance.

In every dark hour of our national life a leadership of frankness and vigor has met with that understanding and support of the people themselves which is essential to victory. I am convinced that you will again give that support to leadership in these critical days.

In such a spirit on my part and yours we face our common difficulties. They con-
30   cern, thank God, only material things. Values have shrunken to fantastic levels; taxes have risen; our ability to pay has fallen; government of all kinds is faced by serious curtailment of income; the means of exchange are frozen in the currents of trade; the

withered leaves of industrial enterprise lie on every side; farmers find no markets
for their produce; the savings of many years in thousands of families are gone. More
35 important, a host of unemployed citizens face the grim problem of existence, and an
equally great number toil with little return. Only a foolish optimist can deny the dark
realities of the moment.

Yet our distress comes from no failure of substance. We are stricken by no plague of
locusts. Compared with the perils which our forefathers conquered because they believed
40 and were not afraid, we have still much to be thankful for. Nature still offers her bounty,
and human efforts have multiplied it. Plenty is at our doorstep, but a generous use of it lan-
guishes in the very sight of the supply.

Primarily, this is because the rulers of the exchange of mankind's goods have
failed through their own stubbornness and their own incompetence, have admitted their
45 failure and abdicated. Practices of the unscrupulous money changers stand indicted in
the court of public opinion, rejected by the hearts and minds of men.

ABOUT THE QUESTIONS

As previously mentioned, there are four major question types which appear in the Critical
Reading section. The following explains what these questions will cover.

Question Type 1: Synthesis/Analysis

Synthesis/analysis questions deal with the structure of the passage and how one part relates
to another part or to the text as a whole. These questions may ask you to look at passage details
and from them, point out general themes or concepts. They might ask you to trace problems,
causes, effects, and solutions or to understand the points of an argument or persuasive passage.
They might ask you to compare or contrast different aspects of the passage. Synthesis/analysis
questions may also involve inferences, asking you to decide what the details of the passage imply
about the author's general tone or attitude. Key terms in synthesis/analysis questions are example, difference, general, compare, contrast, cause, effect, and result.

Question Type 2: Evaluation

Evaluation questions involve judgments about the worth of the essay as a whole. You may be asked
to consider concepts the author assumes rather than factually proves and to judge whether or not the
author presents a logically consistent case. Does he/she prove the points through generalization, citing
an authority, use of example, implication, personal experience, or factual data? You'll need to be able to
distinguish the supportive bases for the argumentative theme. Almost as a book reviewer, you'll also be
asked to pinpoint the author's writing techniques. What is the style, the tone? Who is the intended audience? How might the author's points relate to information outside the essay, itself? Key terms you'll often see in evaluation questions and answer choices are generalization, implication, and support.

Question Type 3: Vocabulary-in-Context

Vocabulary-in-context questions occur in several formats. You'll be given easy words with challenging choices or the reverse. You'll need to know multiple meanings of words. You'll encounter
difficult words and difficult choices. In some cases, your knowledge of prefixes-roots-suffixes will
gain you clear advantage. In addition, connotations will be the means of deciding, in some cases,
which answer is the best. Of course, how the term works in the textual context is the key to the issue.

Question Type 4: Interpretation

Interpretation questions ask you to decide on a valid explanation or clarification of the author's points. Based on the text, you'll be asked to distinguish probable motivations and effects or actions not stated outright in the essay. Furthermore, you'll need to be familiar with clichés, euphemisms, catch phrases, colloquialisms, metaphors, and similes, and be able to explain them in straightforward language. Interpretation question stems usually have a word or phrase enclosed in quotation marks.

Keep in mind that being able to categorize accurately is not of prime importance. What is important, however, is that you are familiar with all the types of information you will be asked and that you have a set of basic strategies to use when answering questions. The remainder of this review will give you these skills.

POINTS TO REMEMBER

- Do not spend too much time answering any one question.

- Vocabulary plays a large part in successful critical reading. As a long-term approach to improving your ability and therefore your test scores, read as much as you can of any type of material. Your speed, comprehension, and vocabulary will grow.

- Be an engaged reader. Don't let your mind wander. Focus through annotation and key terms.

- Time is an important factor on the PSAT. Therefore, the rate at which you are reading is very important. If you are concerned that you may be reading too slow, try to compete with yourself. For example, if you are reading at 120 words per minute, try to improve your speed to 250 words per minute (without decreasing your understanding). Remember that improving reading speed is not a means in itself. Improved comprehension with fewer regressions must accompany this speed increase. Make sure to read, read, read. The more you read, the more you will sharpen your skills.

ANSWERING CRITICAL READING QUESTIONS

You should follow these steps as you begin each critical reading passage. They will act as a guide when answering the questions.

 Before you address the critical reading, answer all sentence completions within the given section. You can answer more questions per minute in this short section than in the reading, and since all answers are credited equally, you'll get the most for your time here.

Now, find the Critical Reading passage(s). If more than one passage appears, give each a brief overview. Attack the shortest passages first. Critical Reading passages are not automatically presented in the order of least-to-most difficult. The difficulty or ease of a reading selection is an individual matter, determined by the reader's own specific interests and past experience, so what you might consider easy, someone else might consider hard, and *vice-versa*. Again, time is an issue, so you need to begin with something you can quickly understand in order to get to the questions, where the pay-off lies.

STEP 2 *First, read the question stems following the passage, making sure to block out the answer choices with your free hand. (You don't want to be misled by incorrect choices.)*

In question stems, underline key words, phrases, and dates. For example:

1. In line 27, "<u>stand</u>" means:

2. From <u>1776</u> <u>to</u> <u>1812,</u> <u>King</u> <u>George</u> did:

3. <u>Lincoln</u> was <u>similar</u> to <u>Pericles</u> in that:

The act of underlining takes little time and will force you to focus first on the main ideas in the questions, then in the essays.

You will notice that questions often note a line number for reference. Place a small mark by the appropriate lines in the essay itself to remind yourself to read those parts very carefully. You'll still have to refer to these lines upon answering the questions, but you'll be able to find them quickly.

STEP 3 *If the passage is not divided into paragraphs, read the first 10 lines. If the passage is divided into manageable paragraphs, read the first paragraph. Make sure to read at a moderate pace, as fast skimming will not be sufficient for comprehension, while slow, forced reading will take too much time and yield too little understanding of the overall passage.*

In the margin of your test booklet, using two or three words, note the main point of the paragraph/section. Don't labor long over the exact wording. Underline key terms, phrases, or ideas when you notice them. If a sentence is particularly difficult, don't spend too much time trying to figure it out. Bracket it, though, for easy reference in the remote instance that it might serve as the basis for a question.

You should proceed through each paragraph/section in a similar manner. Don't read the whole passage with the intention of going back and filling in the main points. Read carefully and consistently, annotating and underlining to keep your mind on the context.

Upon finishing the entire passage, quickly review your notes in the margin. They should give you main ideas and passage structure (chronological, cause and effect, process, comparison-contrast). Ask yourself what the author's attitude is toward his/her subject. What might you infer from the selection? What might the author say next? Some of these questions may appear, and you'll be immediately prepared to answer.

STEP 4 *Start with the first question and work through to the last question. The order in which the questions are presented follows the order of the passage, so going for the "easy" questions first rather than answering the questions consecutively will cost you valuable time in searching and backtracking.*

Be sure to block the answer choices for each question before you read the question, itself. Again, you don't want to be misled.

If a line number is mentioned, quickly reread that section. In addition, circle your own answer to the question *before* viewing the choices. Then, carefully examine each answer choice, eliminating those which are obviously incorrect. If you find a close match to your own answer, don't assume that it is the best answer, as an even better one may be among the last choices. Remember, in the PSAT, only one answer is correct, and it is the *best* one, not simply one that will work.

Once you've proceeded through all the choices, eliminating incorrect answers as you go, choose from among those remaining. If the choice is not clear, reread the question stem and the referenced passage lines to seek tone or content you might have missed. If the answer now is not readily obvious and you have reduced your choices by eliminating at least one, then simply choose one of the remaining and proceed to the next question. Place a small mark in your test booklet to remind you, should you have time at the end of this test section, to review the question and seek a more accurate answer.

Now, let's go back to our natural sciences passage. Read the passage, and then answer the questions that follow using the skills gained through this review.

The following article was written by a physical chemist and recounts the conflict between volcanic matter in the atmosphere and airplane windows. It was published in a scientific periodical in 1989.

(Reprinted by permission of American Heritage Magazine, a division of Forbes Inc., © Forbes Inc., 1989.)

1   Several years ago the airlines discovered a new kind of problem—a window problem. The acrylic windows on some of their 747s were getting hazy and dirty-looking. Suspicious travelers thought the airlines might have stopped cleaning them, but the windows were not dirty; they were inexplicably deteriorating within as little as 390
5   hours of flight time, even though they were supposed to last for five to ten years. Boeing looked into it.

At first the company thought the culprit might be one well known in modern technology, the component supplier who changes materials without telling the customer. Boeing quickly learned this was not the case, so there followed an extensive investiga-
10 tion that eventually brought in the Air Transport Association, geologists, and specialists in upper-atmosphere chemistry, and the explanation turned out to be not nearly so mundane. Indeed, it began to look like a grand reenactment of an ancient Aztec myth: the struggle between the eagle and the serpent, which is depicted on the Mexican flag.

The serpent in this case is an angry Mexican volcano, El Chichon. Like its reptilian
15 counterpart, it knows how to spit venom at the eyes of its adversary. In March and April of 1982 the volcano, in an unusual eruption pattern, ejected millions of tons of sulfur-rich material directly into the stratosphere. In less than a year, a stratospheric cloud had blanketed the entire Northern Hemisphere. Soon the photochemistry of the upper atmosphere converted much of the sulfur into tiny droplets of concentrated sulfuric acid.

20 The eagle in the story is the 747, poking occasionally into the lower part of the stratosphere in hundreds of passenger flights daily. Its two hundred windows are made from an acrylic polymer, which makes beautifully clear, strong windows but was never intended to withstand attack by strong acids.

The stratosphere is very different from our familiar troposphere environment.
25 Down here the air is humid, with a lot of vertical convection to carry things up and down; the stratosphere is bone-dry, home to the continent-striding jet stream, with unceasing horizontal winds at an average of 120 miles per hour. A mist of acid droplets accumulated gradually near the lower edge of the stratosphere, settling there at a thickness of about a mile a year, was able to wait for planes to come along.

30 As for sulfuric acid, most people know only the relatively benign liquid in a car battery: 80 percent water and 20 percent acid. The stratosphere dehydrated the sulfuric acid into a persistent, corrosive mist 75 percent pure acid, an extremely aggressive liquid.

Every time the 747 poked into the stratosphere—on almost every long flight—acid droplets struck the windows and began to react with their outer surface, causing it to swell.
35 This built up stresses between the softened outer layer and the underlying material. Finally, parallel hairline cracks developed, creating the hazy appearance. The hazing was sped
up by the mechanical stresses always present in the windows of a pressurized cabin.

The airlines suffered through more than a year of window replacements before the
acid cloud finally dissipated. Ultimately the drops reached the lower edge of the strato-
40 sphere, were carried away into the lower atmosphere, and finally came down in the
rain. In the meantime, more resistant window materials and coatings were developed.
(As for the man-made sulfur dioxide that causes acid rain, it never gets concentrated
enough to attack the window material. El Chichon was unusual in its ejection of sulfur
directly into the stratosphere, and the 747 is unusual in its frequent entrance into the
45 stratosphere.)

As for the designers of those windows, it is hard to avoid the conclusion that a
perfectly adequate engineering design was defeated by bad luck. After all, this was
the only time since the invention of the airplane that there were acid droplets of this
concentration in the upper atmosphere. But reliability engineers, an eminently rational
50 breed, are very uncomfortable when asked to talk about luck. In principle it should
be possible to anticipate events, and the failure to do so somehow seems like a professional failure. The cosmos of the engineer has no room for poltergeists, demons, or
other mystic elements. But might it accommodate the inexorable scenario of an ancient
Aztec myth?

1.　Initially the hazy windows were thought by the company to be a result of

(A) small particles of volcanic glass abrading their surfaces.
(B) substandard window material substituted by the parts supplier.
(C) ineffectual cleaning products used by the maintenance crew.
(D) a buildup of the man-made sulfur dioxide that also causes acid rain.
(E) the humidity.

2.　When first seeking a reason for the abraded windows, both the passengers and Boeing management exhibited attitudes of

(A) disbelief.　　　　(D) pacifism.
(B) optimism.　　　　(E) disregard.
(C) cynicism.

3.　In line 12, "mundane" means

(A) simple.　　　　(D) ordinary.
(B) complicated.　　(E) important.
(C) far-reaching.

4. In what ways is El Chichon like the serpent on the Mexican flag, knowing how to "spit venom at the eyes of its adversary" (lines 14–15)?

(A) It seeks to poison its adversary with its bite.

(B) It carefully plans its attack on an awaited intruder.

(C) It ejects tons of destructive sulfuric acid to damage jet windows.

(D) It angrily blankets the Northern Hemisphere with sulfuric acid.

(E) It protects itself with the acid rain it produces.

5. The term "photochemistry" in line 18 refers to a chemical change caused by

(A) the proximity of the sun.

(B) the drop in temperature at stratospheric altitudes.

(C) the jet stream's "unceasing horizontal winds."

(D) the vertical convection of the troposphere.

(E) the amount of sulfur present in the atmosphere.

6. Unlike the troposphere, the stratosphere

(A) is extremely humid as it is home to the jet stream.

(B) contains primarily vertical convections to cause air particles to rise and fall rapidly.

(C) is approximately one mile thick.

(D) contains powerful horizontal winds resulting in an excessively dry atmosphere.

(E) contains very little wind activity.

7. In line 32, "aggressive" means

(A) exasperating.   (D) assertive.

(B) enterprising.   (E) surprising.

(C) prone to attack.

8. As the eagle triumphed over the serpent in the Mexican flag,

(A) El Chichon triumphed over the plane, as the 747s had to change their flight altitudes.

(B) the newly designed window material deflected the damaging acid droplets.

(C) the 747 was able to fly unchallenged by acid droplets a year later as they drifted away to the lower atmosphere.

(D) the reliability engineers are now prepared for any run of "bad luck" which may approach their aircraft.

(E) the component supplier of the windows changed materials without telling the customers.

9.   The reliability engineers are described as people who

   (A)   are uncomfortable considering natural disasters.

   (B)   believe that all events are predictable through scientific methodology.

   (C)   accept luck as an inevitable and unpredictable part of life.

   (D)   easily accept their failure to predict and protect against nature's surprises.

   (E)   are extremely irrational and are comfortable speaking about luck.

   The questions following the passage which you just read are typical of those in the Critical Reading section. After carefully reading the passage, you can begin to answer these questions. Let's look again at the questions.

1.   Initially the hazy windows were thought by the company to be a result of

   (A)   small particles of volcanic glass abrading their surfaces.

   (B)   substandard window material substituted by the parts supplier.

   (C)   ineffectual cleaning products used by the maintenance crew.

   (D)   a buildup of the man-made sulfur dioxide that also causes acid rain.

   (E)   the humidity.

   As you read the question stem, blocking the answer choices, you'll note the key term "result" which should alert you to the question category *synthesis/analysis*. Argument structure is the focus here. Ask yourself what part of the argument is being questioned: cause, problem, result, or solution. Careful reading of the stem and perhaps mental rewording to "_____ caused hazy windows" reveals cause is the issue. Once you're clear on the stem, proceed to the choices.

   The word "initially" clues you in to the fact that the correct answer should be the first cause considered. Answer choice (B) is the correct response, as "substandard window material" was the *company's* first (initial) culprit, as explained in the first sentence of the second paragraph. They had no hint of (A) a volcanic eruption's ability to cause such damage. In addition, they were not concerned, as were the *passengers*, that (C) the windows were not properly cleaned. Answer (D) is not correct since scientists had yet to consider testing the atmosphere. Along the same lines, answer choice (E) is incorrect.

2.   When first seeking a reason for the abraded windows, both the passengers and Boeing management exhibited attitudes of

   (A)   disbelief.   (D)   pacifism.

   (B)   optimism.   (E)   disregard.

   (C)   cynicism.

   As you read the stem before viewing the choices, you'll know you're being asked to judge or *evaluate* the tone of a passage. The tone is not stated outright, so you'll need to rely on your perception as you reread that section, if necessary. Remember, questions follow the order of the passage, so you know to look after the initial company reaction to the windows, but not far after, as many more questions are to follow. Now, formulate your own word for the attitude of the passengers and employees. "Skepticism" or "criticism" work well. If you can't come up with a term, at least note if the tone is negative or positive. In this case, negative is clearly indicated as the passengers are distrustful of the maintenance crew and the company mistrusts the window supplier. Proceed to each choice, seeking the closest match to your term and/or eliminating words with positive connotations.

Choice (C) is correct because "cynicism" best describes the skepticism and distrust with which the passengers view the cleaning company and the parts suppliers. Choice (A) is not correct because both Boeing and the passengers believed the windows were hazy, they just didn't know why. Choice (B) is not correct because people were somewhat agitated that the windows were hazy—certainly not "optimistic." Choice (D), "pacifism," has a rather positive connotation, which the tone of the section does not. Choice (E) is incorrect because the people involved took notice of the situation and did not disregard it. In addition to the ability to discern tone, of course, your vocabulary knowledge is being tested. "Cynicism," should you be unsure of the term, can be viewed in its root, "cynic," which may trigger you to remember that it is negative, and therefore, appropriate in tone.

3. In line 12, "mundane" means

    (A) simple.   (D) ordinary.
    (B) complicated.   (E) important.
    (C) far-reaching.

This question obviously tests vocabulary-in-context. Your strategy here should be quickly to view line 12 to confirm usage, block answer choices while devising your own synonym for "mundane," perhaps "common," and then viewing each choice separately, looking for the closest match. Although you might not be familiar with "mundane," the choices are all relatively simple terms. Look for contextual clues in the passage if you can't define the term outright. While the "component supplies" explanation is "mundane," the Aztec myth is not. Perhaps, you could then look for an opposite of mythical; "real" or "down-to-earth" comes to mind.

Choice (D), "ordinary," fits best as it is clearly the opposite of the extraordinary Aztec myth of the serpent and the eagle, which is not as common as a supplier switching materials. Choice (A), "simple," works contextually, but not as an accurate synonym for the word "mundane"; it does not deal with "mundane's" "down-to-earth" definition. Choice (B), "complicated," is inaccurate because the parts switch is anything but complicated. Choice (C), "far-reaching," is not better as it would apply to the myth rather than the common, everyday action of switching parts. Choice (E), "important," does not work either, because the explanation was an integral part of solving the problem. Had you eliminated (B), (C), and (E) due to contextual inappropriateness, you were left with "ordinary" and "simple." A quick rereading of the section, then, should clarify the better choice. But, if the rereading did not clarify the better choice, your strategy would be to choose one answer, place a small mark in the booklet, and proceed to the next question. If time is left at the end of the test, you can then review your answer choice.

4.   In what ways is El Chichon like the serpent on the Mexican flag, knowing how to "spit venom at the eyes of its adversary" (lines 14–15)?

(A)   It seeks to poison its adversary with its bite.

(B)   It carefully plans its attack on an awaited intruder.

(C)   It ejects tons of destructive sulfuric acid to damage jet windows.

(D)   It angrily blankets the Northern Hemisphere with sulfuric acid.

(E)   It protects itself with the acid rain it produces.

As you view the question, note the word "like" indicates a comparison is being made. The quoted simile forms the comparative basis of the question, and you must *interpret* that phrase with respect to the actual process. You must carefully seek to duplicate the tenor of the terms, coming close to the spitting action in which a harmful substance is expelled in the direction of an object similar to the eyes of an opponent. Look for key words when comparing images. "Spit," "venom," "eyes," and "adversary" are these keys.

In choice (C), the verb that is most similar to the serpent's "spitting" venom is the sulfuric acid "ejected" from the Mexican volcano, El Chichon. Also, the jet windows most closely resemble the "eyes of the adversary" that are struck by El Chichon. Being a volcano, El Chichon is certainly incapable of injecting poison into an adversary, as in choice (A), or planning an attack on an intruder, as in choice (B). In choice (D), although the volcano does indeed "blanket the Northern Hemisphere" with sulfuric acid, this image does not coincide with the "spitting" image of the serpent. Finally, in choice (E), although a volcano can indirectly cause acid rain, it cannot produce acid rain on its own and then spew it out into the atmosphere.

5.   The term "photochemistry" in line 18 refers to a chemical change caused by

(A)   the proximity of the sun.

(B)   the drop in temperature at stratospheric altitudes.

(C)   the jet stream's "unceasing horizontal winds."

(D)   the vertical convection of the troposphere.

(E)   the amount of sulfur present in the atmosphere.

Even if you are unfamiliar with the term "photochemistry," you probably know its root or its prefix. Clearly, this question fits in the *vocabulary-in-context* mode. Your first step may be a quick reference to line 18. If you don't know the term, context may provide you a clue. The conversion of sulfur-rich *upper* atmosphere into droplets may help. If context does not yield information, look at the term "photochemistry," itself. "Photo" has to do with light or sun, as in photosynthesis. Chemistry deals with substance composition and change. Knowing these two parts can take you a long way toward a correct answer.

Answer choice (A) is the correct response, as the light of the sun closely compares with the prefix "photo." Although choice (B), "the drop in temperature," might lead you to associate the droplet formation with condensation, light is not a factor here, nor is it in choice (C), "the jet stream's winds"; choice (D), "the vertical convection"; or choice (E), "the amount of sulfur present."

6. Unlike the troposphere, the stratosphere

    (A)   is extremely humid as it is home to the jet stream.

    (B)   contains primarily vertical convections to cause air particles to rise and fall rapidly.

    (C)   is approximately one mile thick.

    (D)   contains powerful horizontal winds resulting in an excessively dry atmosphere.

    (E)   contains very little wind activity.

"Unlike" should immediately alert you to a *synthesis/analysis* question asking you to contrast specific parts of the text. Your margin notes should take you right to the section contrasting the atmospheres. Quickly scan it before considering the answers. Usually you won't remember this broad type of comparison from your first passage reading. Don't spend much time, though, on the scan before beginning to answer, as time is still a factor.

This question is tricky because all the answer choices contain key elements/ phrases in the passage, but again, a quick, careful scan will yield results. Answer (D) proves best as the "horizontal winds" dry the air of the stratosphere. Choices (A), (B), (C), and (E) are all characteristic of the troposphere, while only the acid droplets accumulate at the rate of one mile per year within the much larger stratosphere. As you answer such questions, remember to eliminate incorrect choices as you go; don't be misled by what seems familiar, yet isn't accurate—read all the answer choices.

7.   In line 32, "aggressive" means

    (A)   exasperating.   (D)   assertive.

    (B)   enterprising.   (E)   surprising.

    (C)   prone to attack.

Another *vocabulary-in-context* surfaces here; yet, this time, the word is probably familiar to you. Again, before forming a synonym, quickly refer to the line number, aware that perhaps a secondary meaning is appropriate as the term already is a familiar one. Upon reading the line, you'll note "persistent" and "corrosive," both strong terms, the latter being quite negative in its destruction. Now, form an appropriate synonym for aggressive, one that has a negative connotation. "Hostile" might come to mind. You are ready at this point to view all choices for a match.

Using your vocabulary knowledge, you can answer this question. "Hostile" most closely resembles choice (C), "prone to attack," and is therefore the correct response. Choice (A), "exasperating," or irritating, is too weak a term, while choice (B), "enterprising," and (D), "assertive," are too positive. Choice (E), "surprising," is not a synonym for "aggressive."

8.   As the eagle triumphed over the serpent in the Mexican flag,

    (A)   El Chichon triumphed over the plane, as the 747s had to change their flight altitudes.

    (B)   the newly designed window material deflected the damaging acid droplets.

    (C)   the 747 was able to fly unchallenged by acid droplets a year later as they drifted away to the lower atmosphere.

    (D)   the reliability engineers are now prepared for any run of "bad luck" which may approach their aircraft.

    (E)   the component supplier of the windows changed materials without telling the customer.

This question asks you to compare the eagle's triumph over the serpent to another part of the text. "As" often signals comparative relationships, so you are forewarned of the *synthesis/analysis* question. You are also dealing again with a simile, so, of course, the question can also be categorized as *interpretation*. The eagle-serpent issue is a major theme in the text. You are being asked, as you will soon discover in the answer choices, what this general theme is. Look at the stem keys: eagle, triumphed, and serpent. Ask yourself to what each corresponds. You'll arrive at the eagle and the 747, some sort of victory, and the volcano or its sulfur. Now that you've formed that corresponding image in your own mind, you're ready to view the choices.

Choice (C) is the correct choice because we know the statement "the 747 was able to fly unchallenged . . . " to be true. Not only do the remaining choices fail to reflect the eagle-triumphs-over-serpent image, but choice (A) is inaccurate because the 747 did not "change its flight altitudes." In choice (B), the windows did not deflect "the damaging acid droplets." Furthermore, in choice (D), "the reliability engineers" cannot be correct because they cannot possibly predict the future, and therefore, cannot anticipate what could go wrong in the future. Finally, we know that in (E) the window materials were never changed.

9.   The reliability engineers are typified as people who

(A)   are uncomfortable considering natural disasters.

(B)   believe that all events are predictable through scientific methodology.

(C)   accept luck as an inevitable and unpredictable part of life.

(D)   easily accept their failure to predict and protect against nature's surprises.

(E)   are extremely irrational and are comfortable speaking about luck.

When the question involves such terms as type, kind, example, or typified, be aware of possible *synthesis/analysis* or *interpretation* issues. Here the question deals with implications: what the author means but doesn't state outright. Types can also lead you to situations which ask you to make an unstated generalization based on specifically stated details. In fact, this question could even be categorized as evaluation because specific detail to generalization is a type of argument/ essay structure. In any case, before viewing the answer choices, ask yourself what general traits the reliability engineers portray. You may need to check back in the text for typical characteristics. You'll find the engineers to be rational unbelievers in luck. These key characteristics will help you to make a step toward a correct answer.

Choice (B) is the correct answer because the passage specifically states that the reliability engineers "are very uncomfortable when asked to talk about luck" and believe "it should be possible to anticipate events" scientifically. The engineers might be uncomfortable, as in choice (A), but this is not a main concern in the passage. Choice (C) is obviously incorrect, because the engineers do not believe in luck at all, and choice (D) is not correct because "professional failure" is certainly unacceptable to these scientists. There is no indication in the passage that (E) the scientists are "irrational and are comfortable speaking about luck."

The following drill should be used to test what you have just learned. Read the passages and answer the questions. If you are unsure of an answer, refer back to the review for help.

DRILL: CRITICAL READING

DIRECTIONS: Read each passage and answer the questions that follow. Each question will be based on the information stated or implied in the passage or its introduction.

The following passage looks at the relationship between two great jazz musicians.

1   Bud Powell and Thelonious Monk have a long history together. It was Thelonious Monk who first realized Bud Powell's great talent and took him under his wing, promoting him when other club owners were dubious. In 1944, Powell played with the Cootie Williams band that made the first recording of "'Round Midnight." Even
5 though Powell was not featured on the track, Williams used the recording as a lure to get Monk to sign over half the royalties on the tune. Monk would later correct this error in judgment. A few years later when Powell began to record on his own, he chose Monk's "Off Minor" as part of his sessions. Monk would later comment that Powell was one of the few musicians that was capable of doing his music justice. The two
10 musicians complimented each other. The combinations of Monk's "weird" harmonic structures and Powell's harmonically advanced melodic lines produced a sound that was easy and swinging. Powell continued to play and record Monk's music until his death. In one of Powell's last recordings, "Portrait of Thelonious," recorded in 1966 or 1967, Powell plays in a more angular manner than he did in the 1940's, adding a new,
15 Monk-like dimension to the songs.

1.   The author would most likely agree with which statement?

   (A) Bud Powell stole his music from Thelonious Monk.
   (B) Bud Powell's career was cut short before he was able to develop his skills.
   (C) Thelonious Monk and Bud Powell spent most of their careers tied up in legal copywrite matters.
   (D) Thelonious Monk and Bud Powell influenced each other's musical style.
   (E) Thelonious Monk's "weird" harmonic structures were incompatible with Bud Powell's melodic lines.

2.   In line 3, *dubious* most nearly means

   (A) ignorant.
   (B) supportive.
   (C) doubtful.
   (D) conceited.
   (E) destitute.

3. The purpose of the passage is to

    (A) give the history and development of jazz from 1940's to the 1960's.

    (B) give a brief account of the relationship between Thelonious Monk and Bud Powell.

    (C) detail the economics of jazz musicians incomes.

    (D) prove that jazz music is not original.

    (E) show how Thelonious Monk helped develop Bud Powell's career.

4. The result of the combination of Thelonious Monk's "weird" harmonic structure and Bud Powell's harmonically advanced melodic lines was

    (A) unusual and not very popular.

    (B) a cacophony of discordant sounds.

    (C) appreciated only by the trained ear.

    (D) received with reserved skepticism.

    (E) a tune that was natural and melodic.

In this excerpt from Dickens's Oliver Twist, we read the early account of Oliver's birth and the beginning of his impoverished life.

1   Although I am not disposed to maintain that the being born in a workhouse, is in itself the most fortunate and enviable circumstance that can possibly befall a human being, I do mean to say that in this particular instance, it was the best thing for Oliver Twist that could by possibility have occurred. The fact is, that there was considerable difficulty in
5 inducing Oliver to take upon himself the office of respiration,—a troublesome practice, but one which custom has rendered necessary to our easy existence; and for some time he lay gasping on a little flock mattress, rather unequally poised between this world and the next: the balance being decidedly in favour of the latter. Now, if, during this brief period, Oliver had been surrounded by careful grandmothers, anxious aunts, experienced nurses,
10 and doctors of profound wisdom, he would most inevitably and indubitably have been killed in no time. There being nobody by, however, but a pauper old woman, who was rendered rather misty by an unwonted allowance of beer; and a parish surgeon who did such matters by contract; Oliver and Nature fought out the point between them. The result was, that, after a few struggles, Oliver breathed, sneezed, and proceeded to advertise
15 to the inmates of the workhouse the fact of a new burden having been imposed upon the parish, by setting up as loud a cry as could reasonably have been expected from a male infant who had not been possessed of that very useful appendage, a voice, for a much longer space of time than three minutes and a quarter. . . .

    For the next eight or ten months, Oliver was the victim of a systematic course of
20 treachery and deception. He was brought up by hand. The hungry and destitute situation of the infant orphan was duly reported by the workhouse authorities to the parish authorities. The parish authorities inquired with dignity of the workhouse authorities, whether there was no female then domiciled in 'the house' who was in a situation to impart to Oliver Twist, the consolation and nourishment of which he stood in need.
25 The workhouse authorities replied with humility, that there was not. Upon this, the par-

ish authorities magnanimously and humanely resolved, that Oliver should be 'farmed,' or, in other words, that he should be despatched to a branchworkhouse some three miles off, where twenty or thirty other juvenile offenders against the poor-laws, rolled about the floor all day, without the inconvenience of too much food or too much cloth-
30 ing, under the parental superintendence of an elderly female, who received the culprits at and for the consideration of sevenpence-halfpenny per small head per week. Seven-pence-halfpenny's worth per week is a good round diet for a child; a great deal may be got for sevenpence-halfpenny: quite enough to overload its stomach, and make it uncomfortable. The elderly female was a woman of wisdom and experience; she knew
35 what was good for children; and she had a very accurate perception of what was good for herself. So, she appropriated the greater part of the weekly stipend to her own use, and consigned the rising parochial generation to even a shorter allowance than was originally provided for them. Thereby finding in the lowest depth a deeper still; and proving herself a very great experimental philosopher.

40   Everybody knows the story of another experimental philosopher, who had a great theory about a horse being able to live without eating, and who demonstrated it so well, that he got his own horse down to a straw a day, and would most unquestionably have rendered him a very spirited and rampacious animal on nothing at all, if he had not died, just four-and-twenty hours before he was to have had his first comfortable bait of air. Unfortunately
45 for the experimental philosophy of the female to whose protecting care Oliver Twist was delivered over, a similar result usually attended the operation of *her* system . . .

   It cannot be expected that this system of farming would produce any very extraor-dinary or luxuriant crop. Oliver Twist's ninth birth-day found him a pale thin child, somewhat diminutive in stature, and decidedly small in circumference. But nature or
50 inheritance had implanted a good sturdy spirit in Oliver's breast. It had had plenty of room to expand, thanks to the spare diet of the establishment; and perhaps to this cir-cumstance may be attributed his having any ninth birth-day at all.

5.   After Oliver was born, he had an immediate problem with his

   (A) heart rate.   (D) hearing.
   (B) breathing.   (E) memory.
   (C) vision.

6.   What are the two worlds that Oliver stands "unequally poised between" in lines 7–8?

   (A) Poverty and riches
   (B) Infancy and childhood
   (C) Childhood and adolescence
   (D) Love and hatred
   (E) Life and death

7.   What does the author imply about "careful grandmothers, anxious aunts, experienced nurses, and doctors of profound wisdom" in lines 9–13?

    (A)   They can help nurse sick children back to health.

    (B)   They are necessary for every being's survival.

    (C)   They are the pride of the human race.

    (D)   They tend to adversely affect the early years of children.

    (E)   Their involvement in Oliver's birth would have had no outcome on his survival.

8.   What is the outcome of Oliver's bout with Nature?

    (A)   He is unable to overcome Nature's fierceness.

    (B)   He loses, but gains some dignity from his will to fight.

    (C)   It initially appears that Oliver has won, but moments later he cries out in crushing defeat.

    (D)   Oliver cries out with the breath of life in his lungs.

    (E)   There is no way of knowing who won the struggle.

9.   What is the "systematic course of treachery and deception" that Oliver falls victim to in the early months of his life?

    (A)   He is thrown out into the streets.

    (B)   His inheritance is stolen by caretakers of the workhouse.

    (C)   He is relocated by the uncaring authorities of the workhouse and the parish.

    (D)   The records of his birth are either lost or destroyed.

    (E)   He is publicly humiliated by the parish authorities.

10.   What is meant when the residents of the branch-workhouse are referred to by the phrase "juvenile offenders against the poor-laws" (line 28)?

    (A)   They are children who have learned to steal early in life.

    (B)   They are adolescents who work on probation.

    (C)   They are infants who have no money to support them.

    (D)   They are infants whose parents were law offenders.

    (E)   They are adults who have continuously broken the law.

11. What is the author's tone when he writes that the elderly caretaker "knew what was good for children" (lines 34–35)?

   (A) Sarcastic   (D) Astonished

   (B) Complimentary   (E) Outraged

   (C) Impressed

12. What does the author imply when he further writes that the elderly caretaker "had a very accurate perception of what was good for herself" (lines 35–36)?

   (A) She knew how to keep herself groomed and clean.

   (B) She knew how to revenge herself on her enemies.

   (C) She had a sense of confidence that inspired others.

   (D) She really had no idea how to take care of herself.

   (E) She knew how to selfishly benefit herself despite the cost to others.

13. Why is the elderly caretaker considered "a very great experimental philosopher" (lines 38–39)?

   (A) She was scientifically weaning the children off of food trying to create stronger humans.

   (B) She experimented with the survival of the children in her care.

   (C) She thought children were the key to a meaningful life.

   (D) She made sure that the children received adequate training in philosophy.

   (E) She often engaged in parochial and philosophical discussions.

14. In line 44, "bait" most nearly means

   (A) worms.   (D) trap.

   (B) a hook.   (E) meal.

   (C) a breeze.

15. To what does the author attribute Oliver's survival to his ninth year?

   (A) A strong, healthy diet

   (B) Money from an anonymous donor

   (C) Sheer luck

   (D) His diminutive stature

   (E) His sturdy spirit

16. Based upon the passage, what is the author's overall attitude concerning the city where Oliver lives?

   (A) It is the best of all possible worlds.

   (B) It should be the prototype for future cities.

   (C) It is a dark place filled with greedy, selfish people.

   (D) Although impoverished, most of its citizens are kind.

   (E) It is a flawed place, but many good things often happen there.

The following passage is adapted from the author's introduction to "The Scarlet Letter" by Nathaniel Hawthorne.

1   The life of the Custom House lies like a dream behind me. The old Inspector,—who, I regret to say, was overthrown and killed by a horse, some time ago; else he would certainly have lived forever,—he, and all those other venerable personages who sat with him at the receipt of custom, are but shadows in my view. They are whiteheaded and wrinkled
5 images, which my fancy used to sport with, and has now flung aside forever. The merchants—Pingree, Phillips, Shepard, Upton, Kimball, Bertram, Hunt,—these, and many other names, which had such a classic familiarity for my ear six months ago—how little time has it required to disconnect me from them all, not merely in act, but recollection! It is with an effort that I recall the figures and appellations of these few.

10   Soon, likewise, my old native town will loom upon me through the haze of memory, a mist brooding over and around it. It will appear as if it were no portion of the real earth, but an overgrown village in cloud-land, with only imaginary inhabitants to people its wooden houses and walk its homely lanes. Henceforth it ceases to be a reality of my life. I am a citizen of somewhere else. My good townspeople will not much re-
15 gret me; for there has never been, for me, the genial atmosphere, which a literary man requires, in order to ripen the best harvest of his mind. I shall do better amongst other faces; and these familiar ones, it need hardly be said, will do just as well without me.

17. The author remembers the old Inspector with

   (A) disdainful reproach.

   (B) fearful agony.

   (C) reverential fondness.

   (D) loving kindness.

   (E) respectful disassociation.

18. The author leaves his town and job because

   (A) he was deported for not being a citizen.

   (B) he wants to write.

   (C) he was mistreated by his coworkers.

   (D) all his friends and family have left.

   (E) the townspeople kicked him out.

19. The phrase "to ripen the best harvest of his mind," (line 19) means

   (A) the knowledge required to pick the best fruits.

   (B) the ability to read about nature to produce better crops.

   (C) to obtain the best results from one's intellectual and creative endeavors.

   (D) the ability to write successfully about crop rotation.

   (E) to understand and get along with one's fellow townspeople.

20. From the information in the passage, it is most likely that the author

   (A) is homesick and will return to his hometown soon.

   (B) hopes the merchants are doing well without him.

   (C) wishes that Main Street had not changed.

   (D) will never return to live or work in his hometown again.

   (E) was a pallbearer at the Inspector's funeral.

The following passage analyzes the legal and political philosophy of John Marshall, a chief justice of the Supreme Court in the nineteenth century.

1   As chief justice of the Supreme Court from 1801 until his death in 1835, John Marshall was a staunch nationalist and upholder of property rights. He was not, however, as the folklore of American politics would have it, the lonely and embattled Federalist defending these values against the hostile forces of Jeffersonian democracy. On the
5   contrary, Marshall's opinions dealing with federalism, property rights, and national economic development were consistent with the policies of the Republican Party in its mercantilist phase from 1815 to 1828. Never an extreme Federalist, Marshall opposed his party's reactionary wing in the crisis of 1798-1800. Like almost all Americans of his day, Marshall was a Lockean republican who valued property not as an economic
10 end in itself, but rather as the foundation of civil liberty and a free society. Property was the source both of individual happiness and social stability and progress.

    Marshall evinced strong centralizing tendencies in his theory of federalism and completely rejected the compact theory of the Union expressed in the Virginia and Kentucky Resolutions. Yet his outlook was compatible with the Unionism that formed
15 the basis of the post-1815 American System of the Republican Party. Not that Marshall shared the democratic sensibilities of the Republicans; like his fellow Federalists, he tended to distrust the common people and saw in legislative majoritarianism a force that was potentially hostile to constitutionalism and the rule of law. But aversion to democracy was not the hallmark of Marshall's constitutional jurisprudence. Its central
20 features rather were a commitment to federal authority versus states' rights and a socially productive and economically dynamic conception of property rights. Marshall's support of these principles placed him near the mainstream of American politics in the years between the War of 1812 and the conquest of Jacksonian Democracy.

    In the long run, the most important decisions of the Marshall Court were those up-
25 holding the authority of the federal government against the states. *Marbury v. Madison* provided a jurisprudential basis for this undertaking, but the practical significance of

judicial review in the Marshall era concerned the state legislatures rather than Congress. The most serious challenge to national authority resulted from state attempts to administer their judicial systems independent of the Supreme Court's appellate super-
30 visions as directed by the Judiciary Act of 1789. In successfully resisting this challenge, the Marshall Court not only averted a practical disruption of the federal system, but it also evolved doctrines of national supremacy which helped preserve the Union during the Civil War.

21. The primary purpose of this passage is to

 (A) describe Marshall's political jurisprudence.
 (B) discuss the importance of centralization to the preservation of the Union.
 (C) criticize Marshall for being disloyal to his party.
 (D) examine the role of the Supreme Court in national politics.
 (E) chronicle Marshall's tenure on the Supreme Court.

22. According to the author, Marshall viewed property as

 (A) an investment.
 (B) irrelevant to constitutional liberties.
 (C) the basis of a stable society.
 (D) inherent to the upper class.
 (E) an important centralizing incentive.

23. In line 13, the "compact theory" was most likely a theory

 (A) supporting states' rights.
 (B) of the extreme Federalists.
 (C) of the Marshall Court's approach to the Civil War.
 (D) supporting centralization.
 (E) advocating jurisprudential activism.

24. According to the author, Marshall's attitude toward mass democratic politics can best be described as

 (A) hostile.   (D) nurturing.
 (B) supportive.   (E) distrustful.
 (C) indifferent.

25. In line 18, the word "aversion" means

   (A) loathing.   (D) forbidding.

   (B) acceptance.   (E) misdirection.

   (C) fondness.

26. The author argues the Marshall Court

   (A) failed to achieve its centralizing policies.

   (B) failed to achieve its decentralizing policies.

   (C) helped to bring on the Civil War.

   (D) supported federalism via judicial review.

   (E) had its greatest impact on Congress.

27. According to the author, Marshall's politics were

   (A) extremist.   (D) moderate.

   (B) right-wing.   (E) majoritarian.

   (C) democratic.

1   By the beginning of the nineteenth century, Britain had complete control over the
island of Ireland. English Protestants owned all the land. Irish Catholics were not
allowed to own land or vote. The language of government, business, and trade was officially English, and the dissolution of the Irish Parliament in 1800 granted complete
5 political control of the island to the British crown. The indigenous Catholics who spoke
Gaelic, a Celtic language that dates back to antiquity, were allowed to "rent" land from
the Protestant landlords if they gave over 90% of their harvests in payment of the
"rent." They were allowed to keep what was left over for their own sustenance. Since
this was hardly enough food to survive on, the Irish needed to find another source of
10 food that could be grown off the landlords' land.

     This is how the potato became a vital food crop to the natives. Because of the potato's
versatility it was able to be harvested from the rocky hills and mountainsides and would
keep all winter long. For millions of Irish, the potato was the sole staple of their daily diet.

     The Irish reliance on the potato had drastic repercussions when the Great Potato
15 Blight of 1846 occurred. Popularly known today as the potato famine, the blight was
immediately responsible for death, disease, and mass emigration from the homeland.
Other, far-reaching repercussions were the loss of the Irish native language (Gaelic),
and a bitter animosity, still present today, between the Irish and British cultures. For,
although the British were not directly responsible for the Blight, their colonial structure
20 over the island made many of the symptoms worse. For example, the British imported
corn to sell to the native population without understanding that there was no currency
with which to buy it. The British then funded construction projects, later called "Famine Roads," intended as a way for the natives to "earn" currency to pay for the imported food. These difficult projects often killed more Irish than the famine alone.

28. The overall purpose of the passage is to

   (A) explain the ramifications of the Irish potato famine.

   (B) discuss the economic system of Ireland in the mid-nineteenth century.

   (C) explain the causes of the potato famine.

   (D) present an overview of the potato famine.

   (E) describe the relief efforts of the British to the Irish famine.

29. How did the potato become a vital food source to the Irish?

   (A) It was able to grow on land that was not part of the landlords' "rent" collection, and would keep for a long time before it spoiled.

   (B) It was given to them by the Protestant landlords.

   (C) It had been a part of the island since antiquity.

   (D) The Protestant landlords did not desire it as a part of the rent agreement.

   (E) The Protestant landlords had set up a lucrative potato export business that was often pilfered by the Irish farmers.

30. In line 12, the word "versatility" most nearly means

   (A) tractable.

   (B) adaptable.

   (C) delectable.

   (D) curable.

   (E) potable.

31. According to the second paragraph, all of the following are results of the potato blight EXCEPT:

   (A) mass emigration from the Irish homeland.

   (B) the loss of the Gaelic language.

   (C) construction projects such as building roads and canals.

   (D) an increase in the sale of wholegrain corn.

   (E) starvation and disease.

In this passage, the author discusses the properties and uses of selenium cells, which convert sunlight to energy, creating solar power.

1   The physical phenomenon responsible for converting light to electricity—the photovoltaic effect—was first observed in 1839 by the renowned French physicist, Antoine-César Becquerel. Becquerel noted that a voltage appeared when one of two identical electrodes in a weak conducting solution was illuminated. The PV effect was
5   first studied in solids, such as selenium, in the 1870s. In the 1880s, selenium photovoltaic cells were built that exhibited 1%-2% efficiency in converting light to electricity. Selenium converts light in the visible part of the sun's spectrum; for this reason, it was quickly adopted by the then merging field of photography for photometric (light-measuring) devices. Even today, the light-sensitive cells on cameras used for adjusting
10   shutter speed to match illumination are made of selenium.

     Selenium cells have never become practical as energy converters because their cost is too high relative to the tiny amount of power they produce (at 1% efficiency). Meanwhile, work on the physics of PV phenomena has expanded. In the 1920s and 1930s, quantum mechanics laid the theoretical foundation for our present understanding of
15   PV. A major step forward in solar-cell technology came in the 1940s and early 1950s when a new method (called the Czochralski method) was developed for producing highly pure crystalline silicon. In 1954, work at Bell Telephone Laboratories resulted in a silicon photovoltaic cell with a 4% efficiency. Bell Labs soon bettered this to a 6% and then 11% efficiency, heralding an entirely new era of power-producing cells. A
20   few schemes were tried in the 1950s to use silicon PV cells commercially. Most were for cells in regions geographically isolated from electric utility lines. But an unexpected boom in PV technology came from a different quarter. In 1958, the U.S. Vanguard space satellite used a small (less than one-watt) array of cells to power its radio. The cells worked so well that space scientists soon realized the PV could be an effective
25   power source for many space missions. Technology development of the solar cell has been a part of the space program ever since.

     Today, photovoltaic systems are capable of transforming one kilowatt of solar energy falling on one square meter into about a hundred watts of electricity. One hundred watts can power most household appliances: a television, a stereo, an electric type-
30   writer, or a lamp. In fact, standard solar cells covering the sun-facing roof space of a typical home can provide about 8,500-kilowatt-hours of electricity annually, which is about the average household's yearly electric consumption. By comparison, a modern, 200-ton electric-arc steel furnace, demanding 50,000 kilowatts of electricity, would require about a square kilometer of land for a PV power supply.

35   Certain factors make capturing solar energy difficult. Besides the sun's low illuminating power per square meter, sunlight is intermittent, affected by time of day, climate, pollution, and season. Power sources based on photovoltaics require either back-up from other sources or storage for times when the sun is obscured.

     In addition, the cost of a photovoltaic system is far from negligible (electricity
40   from PV systems in 1980 cost about 20 times more than that from conventional fossil-fuel-powered systems).

     Thus, solar energy for photovoltaic conversion into electricity is abundant, inexhaustible, and clean; yet, it also requires special techniques to gather enough of it effectively.

32. To the author, Antoine-César Becquerel's research was

    (A) unimportant.
    (B) of some significance.
    (C) not recognized in its time.
    (D) weak.
    (E) an important breakthrough.

33. In the first paragraph, it can be concluded that the photovoltaic effect is the result of

    (A) two identical negative electrodes.
    (B) one weak solution and two negative electrodes.
    (C) two positive electrodes of different qualities.
    (D) positive electrodes interacting in a weak environment.
    (E) one negative electrode and one weak solution.

34. The author establishes that selenium was used for photometric devices because

    (A) selenium was the first solid to be observed to have the PV effect.
    (B) selenium is inexpensive.
    (C) selenium converts the visible part of the sun's spectrum.
    (D) selenium can adjust shutter speeds on cameras.
    (E) selenium is abundant.

35. Which of the following can be concluded from the passage?

    (A) Solar energy is still limited by problems of technological efficiency.
    (B) Solar energy is the most efficient source of heat for most families.
    (C) Solar energy represents the PV effect in its most complicated form.
    (D) Solar energy is 20 percent cheaper than fossil-fuel-powered systems.
    (E) Solar energy is 40 percent more expensive than fossil-fuel-powered systems.

36. In line 19, the word "heralding" most nearly means

    (A) celebrating.   (D) anticipating.
    (B) observing.   (E) introducing.
    (C) commemorating.

37. According to the passage, commercially used PV cells have powered

    (A) car radios.   (D) electric utility lines.

    (B) space satellite radios.   (E) space stations.

    (C) telephones.

38. Through the information in lines 27–28, it can be inferred that two kilowatts of solar energy transformed by a PV system equal

    (A) 200 watts of electricity.

    (B) 100 watts of electricity.

    (C) no electricity.

    (D) two square meters.

    (E) 2,000 watts of electricity.

39. Sunlight is difficult to procure for transformation into solar energy. Which of the following statements most accurately supports this belief derived from the passage?

    (A) Sunlight is erratic and subject to variables.

    (B) Sunlight is steady but never available.

    (C) Sunlight is not visible because of pollution.

    (D) Sunlight would have to be artificially produced.

    (E) Sunlight is never erratic.

40. The author's concluding paragraph would be best supported with additional information regarding

    (A) specific benefits of solar energy for photovoltaic conversion into electricity.

    (B) the negative effects of solar energy for photovoltaic conversion into electricity.

    (C) the negative effects of photovoltaic conversion.

    (D) why solar energy is clean.

    (E) why solar energy is abundant.

The following passage is on the Phoenicians, a sea-faring civilization that existed over 2,500 years ago.

1   Although Phoenicians are mentioned frequently in ancient texts as traders and sailors, we know little about these puzzling people. They were known as Canaanites before 1200 B.C., and the name Phoenicians was derived from the Greek word *phoinikes*, meaning "red people," based on the prized reddish purple cloth the Phoeni-
5 cians exported. They never referred to themselves as Phoenicians, or considered themselves a united people. Instead, they considered themselves citizens of the ports from which they set sail, cities such as Byblos, Sidon, and Tyre. The culture later referred to as Phoenician was established as early as the third millennium B.C. in the Levant, a coastal region located in between Israel, Lebanon, and Syria. Around 1100 B.C.,
10 after a period of general disorder throughout the region, they emerged as a significant cultural and political force. For 300 years, the ninth to sixth centuries B.C., the Phoenicians dominated the Mediterranean Sea. They established colonies from Cyprus in the east, to the Aegean Sea, Italy, North Africa and Spain in the west. They grew rich trading precious metals from abroad and products such as wine, olive oil, and, most
15 notably, timber from the famous cedar trees of Lebanon. The armies and empires that eventually conquered the Phoenicians either destroyed or built over their cities. Nothing remains of their writings, so the written history of Phoenicia is recorded only in the biased reports of their enemies. It is ironic that the rich literature of Phoenicia has also been totally lost in antiquity since they developed the modern alphabet and spread it to
20 the world through their ports of call.

41.   According to the passage, Phoenicians thought of themselves as

    (A)   the most powerful empire on the Mediterranean.

    (B)   Canaanites, the rightful heirs to the Levant.

    (C)   citizens of their native port town.

    (D)   a united Phoenician empire.

    (E)   inventors of the modern alphabet.

42.   What reasons are given in the passage for the little knowledge we have of Phoenician civilization?

    (A)   The destruction of their cities by invading armies and the disintegration of their written texts.

    (B)   Their lack of appearances in ancient texts and their illiteracy.

    (C)   Their illiteracy and lack of political and cultural strength.

    (D)   Their disunity and lack of a common language.

    (E)   The usurpation of their alphabet by invading armies has blurred the distinction between Phoenician writing and their enemies'.

43. The main purpose of the passage is to

    (A) give the origins of the name Phoenician.

    (B) detail the expansion of the Phoenician empire.

    (C) discuss the causes of the decline of the Phoenician empire.

    (D) outline the history of the Phoenicians.

    (E) discuss the contributions Phoenicians made to the modern world.

44. The author would consider which of the following to be a great legacy of the Phoenician civilization?

    (A) The timber from the cedar trees.

    (B) Their prized reddish purple cloth.

    (C) The development of the Levant.

    (D) The development of the alphabet.

    (E) Their literature.

DIRECTIONS: Read the passages and answer the questions that follow. Each question will be based on the information stated or implied in the selections or their introductions, and may be based on the relationship between the passages.

In Passage 1, the author writes a general summary about the nature of comedy. In Passage 2, the author sums up the essentials of tragedy.

Passage 1

1   The primary aim of comedy is to amuse us with a happy ending, although comedies can vary according to the attitudes they project, which can be broadly identified as either high or low, terms having nothing to do with an evaluation of the play's merit. Generally, the amusement found in comedy comes from an eventual victory
5 over threats or ill fortune. Much of the dialogue and plot development might be laughable, yet a play need not be funny to be comic. In fact, some critics in the Renaissance era thought that the highest form of comedy should elicit no laughter at all from its audience. A comedy that forced its audience into laughter failed in the highest comic endeavor, whose purpose was to amuse as subtly as possible. Note that Shakespeare's
10 comedies themselves were often under attack for their appeal to laughter.

    Farce is low comedy intended to make us laugh by means of a series of exaggerated, unlikely situations that depend less on plot and character than on gross absurdities, sight gags, and coarse dialogue. The "higher" a comedy goes, the more natural the characters seem and the less boisterous their behavior. The plots become more
15 sustained, and the dialogue shows more weighty thought. As with all dramas, comedies are about things that go wrong. Accordingly, comedies create deviations from accepted normalcy, presenting problems which we might or might not see as harmless. If these problems make us judgmental about the involved characters and events, the play takes

on the features of satire, a rather high comic form implying that humanity and human
20 institutions are in need of reform. If the action triggers our sympathy for the characters,
we feel even less protected from the incongruities as the play tilts more in the direction
of tragicomedy. In other words, the action determines a figurative distance between the
audience and the play. Such factors as characters' personalities and the plot's predictability influence this distance. The farther away we sit, the more protected we feel and
25 usually the funnier the play becomes. Closer proximity to believability in the script
draws us nearer to the conflict, making us feel more involved in the action and less safe
in its presence.

Passage 2

The term "tragedy" when used to define a play has historically meant something
very precise, not simply a drama which ends with unfortunate consequences. This defi-
30 nition originated with Aristotle, who insisted that the play be an imitation of complex
actions which should arouse an emotional response combining fear and pity. Aristotle believed that only a certain kind of plot could generate such a powerful reaction.
Comedy shows us a progression from adversity to prosperity. Tragedy must show the
reverse; moreover, this progression must be experienced by a certain kind of character,
35 says Aristotle, someone whom we can designate as the tragic hero. This central figure
must be basically good and noble: "good" because we will not be aroused to fear and
pity over the misfortunes of a villain, and "noble" both by social position and moral
stature because the fall to misfortune would not otherwise be great enough for tragic
impact. These virtues do not make the tragic hero perfect, however, for he must also
40 possess hamartia—a tragic flaw—the weakness which leads him to make an error in
judgment which initiates the reversal in his fortunes, causing his death or the death of
others or both. These dire consequences become the hero's catastrophe. The most common tragic flaw is hubris; an excessive pride that adversely influences the protagonist's
judgment.

45   Often the catastrophic consequences involve an entire nation because the tragic
hero's social rank carries great responsibilities. Witnessing these events produces the
emotional reaction Aristotle believed the audience should experience, the catharsis.
Although tragedy must arouse our pity for the tragic hero as he endures his catastrophe and must frighten us as we witness the consequences of a flawed behavior which
50 anyone could exhibit, there must also be a purgation, "a cleansing," of these emotions
which should leave the audience feeling not depressed but relieved and almost elated.
The assumption is that while the tragic hero endures a crushing reversal, somehow he
is not thoroughly defeated as he gains new stature through suffering and the knowledge
that comes with suffering. Classical tragedy insists that the universe is ordered. If truth
55 or universal law is ignored, the results are devastating, causing the audience to react
emotionally; simultaneously, the tragic results prove the existence of truth, thereby re-
assuring our faith that existence is sensible.

45. In Passage 1, the term "laughable" (lines 5–6) suggests that on occasion comic dialogue and plot development can be

   (A) senselessly ridiculous.
   (B) foolishly stupid.
   (C) amusingly droll.
   (D) theoretically depressing.
   (E) critically unsavory.

46. The author of Passage 1 makes an example of Shakespeare (lines 9–10) in order to

   (A) make the playwright look much poorer in our eyes.
   (B) emphasize that he wrote the highest form of comedy.
   (C) degrade higher forms of comedy.
   (D) suggest the foolishness of Renaissance critics.
   (E) show that even great authors do not always use high comedy.

47. The protagonist in a play discovers he has won the lottery, only to misplace the winning ticket. According to the author's definition, this situation would be an example of which type of comedy?

   (A) Satire   (D) Sarcasm
   (B) Farce   (E) Slapstick
   (C) Tragicomedy

48. In line 22, the phrase "figurative distance" suggests

   (A) the distance between the seats in the theater and the stage.
   (B) the lengths the comedy will go to elicit laughter.
   (C) the years separating the composition of the play and the time of its performance.
   (D) the degree to which an audience relates to the play's action.
   (E) that the play's subject matter is too high for the audience to grasp.

49. What is the author trying to espouse in lines 24–27?

   (A) He warns us not to get too involved with the action of the drama.
   (B) He wants the audience to immerse itself in the world of the drama.
   (C) He wants us to feel safe in the presence of the drama.
   (D) He wants us to be critical of the drama's integrity.
   (E) He feels that we should not enjoy the drama overly much.

50. In Passage 2, the author introduces Aristotle as a leading source for the definition of tragedy. He does this

   (A) to emphasize how outdated the tragedy is for the modern audience.

   (B) because Greek philosophy is the only way to truly understand the world of the theater.

   (C) because Aristotle was one of Greece's greatest actors.

   (D) because Aristotle instituted the definition of tragedy still used widely today.

   (E) in order to prove that Aristotle's sense of tragedy was based on false conclusions.

51. In line 37, "noble" most nearly means

   (A) of high degree and superior virtue.

   (B) of great wealth and self-esteem.

   (C) of quick wit and high intelligence.

   (D) of manly courage and great strength.

   (E) of handsome features and social charm.

52. Which of the following is an example of *harmatia* (line 40)?

   (A) Courtesy to the lower class

   (B) The ability to communicate freely with others

   (C) A refusal to acknowledge the power of the gods

   (D) A weak, miserly peasant

   (E) A desire to do penance for one's crimes

53. Which of the following best summarizes the idea of catharsis explained in lines 45–47?

   (A) All of the tragic consequences are reversed at the last moment; the hero is rescued from certain doom and is allowed to live happily for the rest of his life.

   (B) The audience gains a perverse pleasure from watching another's suffering.

   (C) The play's action ends immediately, unresolved, and the audience is left in a state of blissful confusion.

   (D) When the play ends, the audience is happy to escape the drudgery of the tragedy's depressing conclusion.

   (E) The audience lifts itself from a state of fear and pity for the tragic hero to a sense of renewal and absolution for the hero's endurance of great suffering.

54. The authors of both passages make an attempt to

   (A) ridicule their subject matter.
   (B) outline the general terms and guidelines of a particular aspect of drama.
   (C) thrill their readers with sensational information.
   (D) draw upon Shakespeare as an authority to back up their work.
   (E) persuade their readers to study only one or the other type of drama (i.e., comedy or tragedy).

55. Which of the following best describes the differences between the structure of both passages?

   (A) Passage 1 is concerned primarily with the Renaissance era. Passage 2 is concerned primarily with Classical Greece.
   (B) Passage 1 is concerned with dividing its subject into subcategories. Passage 2 is concerned with extracting its subject's individual elements.
   (C) Passage 1 makes fun of its subject matter. Passage 2 treats its subject matter very solemnly.
   (D) Passage 1 draws upon a series of plays that serve as examples. Passage 2 draws upon no outside sources.
   (E) Passage 1 introduces special vocabulary to illuminate the subject matter; Passage 2 fails to do this.

56. What assumption do both passages seem to draw upon?

   (A) Tragedy is a higher form of drama than comedy.
   (B) Tragedy is on the decline in modern society; comedy, however, is on the rise.
   (C) *Catharsis* is an integral part of both comedy and tragedy.
   (D) An audience's role in the performance of either comedy or tragedy is a vital one.
   (E) The tragicomedy is a form that is considered greater than drama that is merely comic or tragic.

The following passage discusses the new discoveries that scientists are making about our star, the sun.

1   By galactic standards the sun, our star, is quite undistinguished. Even though it is so big that a million Earths would fit comfortably inside, it falls into the general stellar category of yellow runts called type G, a species so monotonously common that there are billions of them in the Milky Way. But nothing else in the universe is more imme-
5 diately important to us. Besides being the origin of virtually all the energy that sustains life, the sun is also the source of our weather and climate, and our closest connection to the power of the cosmos. Four centuries after Galileo and others stunned the world by revealing that spots moved across the solar surface, many of the most profound aspects of our local star remain shadowed in mystery. Thanks to advances in computer

10 modeling and new, high-tech instruments, scientists are now on the cusp of finding
answers to the nature of solar behavior. However, much finer telescopic resolution is
still needed to discern fundamental solar structure, which is believed to be only a few
miles wide. The best resolution to date is only 50 miles. Another advance in the study
of solar behavior is the new initiative to understand and forecast space weather, the
15 effects created by the billions of tons of plasma that can erupt from the sun and cause
magneto-electrical squalls throughout the solar system.

57. According to the passage, compared to other stars, the Earth's star is

(A) rare in size and color.

(B) common in size and number.

(C) one of the few rare giants capable of supporting life.

(D) distinguished by its size and number.

(E) referred to as type G because it is "golden" in color.

58. The overall tone of the passage could best be described as

(A) impassioned objectivity.

(B) impassioned subjectivity.

(C) detached objectivity.

(D) nostalgic subjectivity.

(E) reasoned objectivity.

59. It can be inferred from the passage that

(A) the sun affects the oceanic tides.

(B) type G stars are so common that they do not need to be studied.

(C) fundamental solar structure is less than 50 miles wide.

(D) the sun has little effect on our weather and climate.

(E) the sun has only been studied for 400 years.

60. In line 10, the phrase "on the cusp" most nearly means

(A) at the beginning.

(B) at the end.

(C) at the top.

(D) on the edge.

(E) in the middle.

DETAILED EXPLANATIONS

CRITICAL READING

Drill: Critical Reading

1. (D) This *evaluation* question is asking you to find the one answer choice that the author would agree with. Since the answer is based solely on what is presented in the passage, you are looking for the one answer choice that is entirely supported by the information in the passage. Nowhere in the passage does the author talk about Bud Powell stealing his music from Thelonious Monk, so answer (A) is incorrect. The passage does give the relative dates of Bud Powell's career, 1940's–1960's, but does not insinuate or suggest that his career ended before it should have, so answer (B) is incorrect. The passage does mention royalties and the borrowing of music between the two musicians, but nothing was mentioned about copyright issues, so answer (C) is incorrect. In line 8, the author does mention that Powell used Monk's "Off Minor" as part of his recording sessions, and in lines 10–12, the author mentions how "easy and swinging" the combination of the two musicians music was, thus insinuating that each built on the other's contribution to jazz. Answer (D) is best. Lines 11–12 states that the combination of the two styles produced an "easy and swinging" sound, or a very compatible sound, making answer (E) is incorrect.

2. (C) This is a *vocab-in-context* question. Reread the sentence in line 3 to have an understanding of the context in which the word *dubious* is being used. According to the sentence, Thelonious Monk realized Bud Powell's great talent and decided to promote him in clubs when other club owners were *dubious*, or not so certain of his talent. The one answer choice that most nearly means "not so certain of his talent" is (C), doubtful. The club owners were uncertain or doubtful whether Bud's talent would bring a profit to their club.

3. (B) The question is asking you to *evaluate* the entire passage and determine what its purpose is. One paragraph, or 15 lines, is way too short to give the history and development of jazz for two decades, so answer (A) is incorrect. Answer (B) is correct because the passage briefly discussed the relationship between Thelonious Monk and Bud Powell and nothing else. Economics were not discussed, so answer (C) is incorrect. The passage did not debunk the originality of jazz, nor could this be done in 15 lines, meaning answer (D) is wrong. Although the second sentence mentions how Thelonious Monk helped start Bud Powell's career, it was not the purpose of the entire passage and therefore answer (E) is incorrect.

4. **(E)** The question is asking you to *analyze* certain pieces of information in the passage. Specifically, what was the result of the combination of the two styles of music? Starting on line 10, the passage discusses the combination of Monk's weird harmonic structures and Powell's harmonically advanced melodic lines. On line 12, the passage states that the combination produced a sound that was "easy and swinging." Answer (E), a tune that was natural and melodic, is the closest in meaning to "easy and swinging" and is correct. All other answer choices are unrelated to the said result.

5. **(B)** The question type is *synthesis/analysis* because the question requires you to identify or analyze the immediate problem Oliver had at birth. Remember that the questions are arranged in chronological order in accordance with the passage, so the answer to the first question should be at the beginning of the passage. The second sentence of the passage explains that there was "considerable difficulty in inducing Oliver to take upon himself the office of respiration" (lines 4 and 5). The phrase "considerable difficulty in inducing Oliver to take upon himself the office of respiration" is a long and convoluted way of saying Oliver had trouble breathing. Answer choice (B) is the correct response. The rest of the paragraph elaborates upon the breathing trouble Oliver had at birth and nothing is mentioned of his (A) heart rate, (C) vision, (D) hearing, or (E) memory.

6. **(E)** The question is asking for an *interpretation* of a quotation in the passage. The line reference mentioned in the question gives you a good idea as to where to find the answer in the passage. The first paragraph talks about the trouble Oliver had breathing after he was born, and line 7 refers to him "gasping" for breath on a mattress. What two worlds would a newborn child be poised between if he were laying on a mattress gasping for breath? Most likely between life and death, answer choice (E). Since we know Oliver is only a newborn child in this paragraph, we know he could not be poised between (B) infancy and childhood or (C) childhood and adolescence. Also, his breathing problems would not adequately explain being poised between (A) poverty and riches or (D) love and hatred.

7. **(D)** The key term "imply" indicates that the question category is *synthesis/analysis* and that the answer requires you to discern how the author feels about the "careful grandmothers, anxious aunts, experienced nurses, and doctors of profound wisdom." The line reference (9–10) mentioned in the question informs you where in the passage to find the answer. The paragraph still talks about Oliver's breathing problem after he was born, and the author writes that during this difficulty, if he was surrounded by grandmothers, aunts, nurses, and doctors he would have been "inevitably and indubitably . . . killed in no time." The author feels they have a bad or negative effect. Answer choice (D), they tend to adversely affect the early years of children, is the best response because it reflects the negative feeling the author has towards them. Answers (A) and (B) state the opposite feeling of the author, while answer (E) refers to a neutral effect, which the author disagrees with. Answer (C) was not mentioned or referred to and is therefore wrong.

8. **(D)** The key term "outcome" indicates that the question category is *synthesis/analysis* and the answer requires you to determine the result of Oliver's struggle with nature. There is no line reference directly stated, but based on the chronology of the questions the answer should be found somewhere shortly after line 13, referenced from question 7. Skimming the passage, line 13 informs us of the fight between Oliver and Nature, and the next sentence describes the result. "The result was, that...Oliver breathed, sneezed . . . setting up as loud a cry . . ." (lines 13–18). In other words, the result of Oliver's

fight with nature was that he lived. Answer (D), "Oliver cries out with the breath of life in his lungs" is the best response because it most closely reflects the idea that he lived. Answers (A), (B), and (C) insinuate that Nature won the battle, in which case Oliver would be dead, and are incorrect. Answer (E) indicates the outcome of the struggle is uncertain, which is incorrect because once Oliver breathed it was known he would live and thus he won the struggle.

9. (C) The question type is *synthesis/analysis* because it requires you to identify or analyze the "treachery and deception" that Oliver fell victim to in the early months of his life. The chronology of the questions indicates that the answer will be found somewhere after line 16, referenced from question 8. In the beginning of the second paragraph, line 19, is the quoted line from the question, "systematic course of treachery and deception," and indicates that the answer to the question will be found in the same paragraph. Lines 20–31 give the description that Oliver was passed on from one authority to another and was finally placed in a branch-workhouse. Answer (C) is the best response because it most closely relates that Oliver was unwanted and passed along from one authority to another. Nothing in the paragraph mentions his inheritance (B), birth records (D), and humiliation (E). The fact that he ended up in a workhouse proves that he was not "thrown out into the streets" (A).

10. (C) The question type is *interpretation*, since it is asking for the meaning of the phrase "juvenile offenders against the poor-laws" (line 28) in reference to the residents of the branch-workhouse. From the entire sentence, starting on line 25, we know that Oliver is being sent to this branch-workhouse, where he will be placed with "other" juvenile offenders. The word "other" indicates that Oliver is part of the same category as the offenders; they are all offenders against the poor laws. We know that Oliver has not stolen anything, so answer (A) is incorrect. Answer (B) is incorrect because none of the other residents are working, lines 28–29 says they "rolled about the floor all day." Nothing in the passage talks about Oliver's parents or the other residents' parents, so answer (D) is incorrect. Answer (E) is incorrect because from the quotation we know everyone is a "juvenile offender," therefore no adults are present. We know from the passage that Oliver is only a few months old and that he is an orphan with no money or relatives, so answer (C) is the best response.

11. (A) The key term "tone" indicates that the question type is *evaluation* and your response is based not only on what the author states directly, but also what is implied through the structure and tone. According to the reference in the question, the author talks about the caretaker around lines 34–35. The quote in the question, "knew what was good for children," is in reference to the topic of how much money was given to the children to pay for the costs of feeding and clothing them. The author states that the amount, sevenpence-halfpenny, was quite enough to feed the children properly but that the elderly woman, in knowing "what was good for children," thought the amount was too much and gave herself the greater part of the money. The author's tone would be sarcastic, answer (A), because he does not really believe she "knew what was good for children," but rather she did not know or care and was selfish. Complimentary (B) and impressed (C) are incorrect because they imply the old caretaker was right in taking money from the orphans. Astonished (D) and outraged (E) would naturally be reactions to learning of the caretaker's selfish disregard for the orphans, but do not properly describe the author's tone in saying she "knew what was good for children."

12. (E) The term "imply" indicates that the question type is *synthesis/analysis* and the answer requires you to discern what the author means by the phrase "(the caretaker) had a very accurate perception of what was good for herself." The line reference directs us to the same place in the passage as the last question, and therefore it deals with the same subject matter; the caretaker taking the majority of the money that was to be used for the benefit of the orphans. The fact that the caretaker "appropriated the greater part of the weekly stipend to her own use" (line 36) shows that she had selfish motives and a disregard for the wellbeing of the children she was taking care of. Answer (E) best reflects the author's intended meaning of the phrase. Answers (A), (B), and (C) are not mentioned anywhere in the passage and are therefore incorrect. Answer (D) is wrong because the author was implying that the caretaker did know how to take care of herself.

13. (B) This is an *interpretation* question since you are asked to clarify, or give a reason, for why the caretaker is considered "a very great experimental philosopher." The line reference (line 39) is located at the end of the second paragraph, but the explanation is given in the third paragraph, where the author gives an example of what an experimental philosopher does. The example of the horse indicates that an experimental philosopher is someone who tests a theory on living creatures and will only admit failure upon the death of the creature. Therefore the author considered the caretaker an experimental philosopher because she experimented with the survival of the children in her care, answer (B). The last sentence of the third paragraph reinforces this view by suggesting that the caretaker followed the same philosophy as the horse owner – that creatures can live without eating. Answers (C), (D), and (E) are unrelated to the topic of the paragraphs and are incorrect. Answer (A) is incorrect because we know she was unconcerned with the wellbeing of the children and had only selfish motives; there was nothing scientific about it.

14. (E) This is a *vocab-in-context* question since it is clearly asking for the meaning of the word "bait" in line 44. The best strategy is to locate the sentence by the line reference and read enough around the sentence to understand the context of the topic at hand. Once you have done this, reread the sentence and substitute your own word in place of the word "bait." Compare the word you came up with to those in the answer choices and choose the one that is closest in meaning. The sentence in which the word is located is discussing the horse owner who was weaning his horse off of food. He had gotten the horse down to a straw a day, but the horse died 24 hours before it had its first "meal" of air. Answer (E) is the best response.

15. (E) The question is asking to identify a cause for Oliver surviving to his ninth year and is therefore a *synthesis/analysis* question. There is no line reference, but based on the chronology of the questions, the answer can be found in the fourth paragraph were the passage talks about Oliver's ninth year. Line 50 mentions the "good sturdy spirit" implanted in Oliver's breast. The last sentence of the passage states that "it" (the sturdy spirit) "may be attributed (to) his having any ninth birthday at all." Answer (E) is the best response. Answer (A) is incorrect because he had a very weak and unhealthy diet due to the caretaker's selfishness. His diminutive stature (D) would have been a detriment to his survival. Sheer luck (C), is a tempting answer but incorrect because the author did not attribute it to his survival. Anonymous money from a donor, answer (B) is not mentioned in the passage.

16. (C) The term "overall attitude" indicates that the question type is *evaluation* and deals with the entire passage. The actual city where the passage takes place is not mentioned, but

you can still determine the author's attitude by examining the whole passage and evaluating the individual events that make up the passage. Oliver is born in a workhouse where he struggles for life. He is then handed over to different authorities because no one wants to care for him, and then ends up in a branch-workhouse. The caretaker of the workhouse malnourished the orphans for her own profit, and Oliver survives to his ninth birthday solely because of his strong, sturdy spirit. There was nothing good in the entire passage about the environment or city that Oliver grew up in. Answer (C) is the best response because all other answers reflect some good or positive aspect about the city.

17. (E) The question is asking for you to *evaluate*, or identify, the tone of the author as he remembers the old Inspector. The author recalls the old Inspector at the beginning of the passage, so you will want to reread and note the style and words used in the author's reflection. The author uses words like "venerable" and refers to the inspector and other coworkers as "shadows in my view," and "images...now flung aside forever." This description implies the idea that the inspector is part of the past that the author cannot go back to. Respectful disassociation, answer (E), is the best answer because it combines the author's feelings of "venerable" with his view of "images...now flung aside forever." Answer (A), disdainful reproach, and answer (B), fearful agony, do not reflect the "venerable" feelings of the author. Reverential fondness, answer (C), and loving kindness, answer (D), reflect a closer friendship than someone who has "flung aside (their images) forever," and are incorrect.

18. (B) The question is asking you to *analyze*, or find the reason stated in the passage for the author leaving his hometown. In lines 15–16 he states his town lacks the "atmosphere which a literary man requires," and because of this no one will "regret" his leaving. Therefore the author then is leaving for a literary endeavor. Answer (B) he wants to write, is the best response. There was no question of his citizenship in the passage, therefore answer (A) is incorrect. He remembers his coworkers and townspeople with indifference, not the attitude of someone who had been mistreated, answer (C), or kicked out, answer (E), by them. Although the author does refer to the town as the town of his forefathers, there was no reference to the absence of his friends and family as the reason for his leaving, so answer (D) is wrong.

19. (C) The question is asking you to best *interpret* the phrase "to ripen the best harvest of his mind" (line 16). From the previous question, you know the sentence that contains the phrase is also the one that gave the author's reason for leaving the town, to pursue literary endeavors. Therefore "ripen the best harvest of his mind" is a metaphor comparing the mind to a crop, and his leaving the town will produce the best fruits of his mind. Answer (C) obtain the best results from ones intellectual and creative endeavors, is the best response. Answers (A), (B) and (D) treat the metaphor literally, and are therefore irrelevant to the meaning of the passage. Answer (E) is also incorrect because the author is not trying to improve his relationship with his townspeople.

20. (D) This question is asking you to *evaluate* the passage as a whole and determine which answer choice most closely supports the author's feelings or opinions. We know the author is not homesick because in lines 13 and 14 he writes that the town "ceases to be a reality of my life" and "I am a citizen of somewhere else," therefore answer (A) is incorrect. The author mentions the merchants only in reference to how he has disconnected himself from them (lines 4–9), so answer (B) is incorrect. Since there was no mention in the passage of the town physically changing, answer (C) is incorrect. The author does mention his old job as a

"dream behind me," and says the town "will loom upon me in the haze of memory." Combine these quotes with his statement "I am a citizen of somewhere else," and you could conclude that the author will never return to live or work in his hometown again, making answer (D) correct. Although the Inspector is dead (lines 1–3), there was no mention of a funeral in the passage, and therefore answer (E) is incorrect.

21. (A) The term "purpose of this passage" indicates that the question type is *evaluation* and deals with the entire passage. From the *introduction*—the few lines at the beginning of the passage that tell you what the passage is about and are written in italics—you know that the passage is going to "analyze the legal and political philosophy of John Marshall." The next three paragraphs describe Marshall's personal political beliefs and what effect they had on his job as Supreme Court judge. Answer (A), "describe Marshall's political jurisprudence," is the best answer because "political jurisprudence" means how politics effects the interpretation of the law, which is what the three paragraphs in the passage describe. Answer (B) is incorrect because although the Union was mentioned, it was not the primary focus of the passage. Answer (C) is wrong because there was no criticizing of Marshall in the passage and (D) and (E) are wrong because the passage did not chronicle any years of the Supreme Court.

22. (C) The question is asking for the view that Marshall had on property. Based on the chronology of the questions, you know that the answer must be somewhere in the beginning of the passage. Read through the first paragraph, keeping an eye out for where it talks about what Marshall thought about property. Starting on line 9 the passage states, "Marshall was a Lockean republican who valued property . . . as the foundation of civil liberty and a free society." Answer (C), "the basis of a free society," best reflects the meaning of the quoted passage.

23. (A) The question is asking for the meaning of "compact theory" based on the information in the passage, therefore it is an *interpretation* question. From the question you know that "compact theory" is found in line 13 and therefore an example or interpretation of its meaning will be found in the same vicinity. The first sentence in the paragraph states that Marshall had strong centralizing tendencies in his idea of federalism, and because of this, he rejected, or disagreed with the "compact theory." Therefore you can interpret the "compact theory" as having weak centralizing tendencies, or not supporting a strong central government. The "compact theory" would be one that "supports states' rights," answer (A). Since federalists supported the idea of a strong, centralized government, answers (B) and (D) are incorrect. Answers (C) and (E) are not mentioned in the passage and are therefore incorrect.

24. (E) The question wants you to determine what Marshall's attitude was toward mass democratic politics, so you will need to analyze the passage where it talks about mass democratic politics in relation to Marshall. According to the chronology of the questions and the lines referenced in Questions 23 (line 13) and 25 (line 18), you know the answer will be somewhere in the middle of the second paragraph. Starting on line 16 it states "he (Marshall) tended to distrust the common people and saw in legislative majoritarianism a (hostile force that threatened the rule of law.)" In other words, he did not trust democracy in the hands of the masses. Answer (E), distrustful, is the best answer because line 17 states Marshall "distrusts the common people." Answer (A) is incorrect because hostile is too extreme, and the passage does not imply that Marshall was at war with the masses. Answers (A), (B), and (C) imply the opposite of Marshall's attitude.

25. (A) This is a *vocab-in-context* question. Read enough of the second paragraph to get an understanding of the main idea and to understand the context in which line 18 is written. The sentence before line 18 discusses Marshall's distrust of the common people to govern themselves in a democratic society, which insinuates a dislike of democratic principles. Line 18 changes the tone by talking about the positive aspects of the Marshall court, and begins by stating that Marshall's *aversion*, or dislike, of democracy was not what he was remembered for. Answer (A), loathing, is the best answer because it most closely means dislike. Answers (B) and (C) imply the opposite meaning, while (D) and (E) are nonsensical.

26. (D) The question wants to know what point the author made about the Marshall Court. Following the chronology of the questions, you know the answer will be somewhere near the end of the passage, and it is in the last paragraph where the Marshall Court is discussed. The first sentence of the last paragraph states that the most important decisions of the Marshall Court were those "upholding the authority of the federal government." The rest of the paragraph then discusses the significance of judicial review in the Marshall Court concerning decisions made by separate state legislatures. In other words, the Supreme Court had the ultimate say in determining the constitutionality of state laws, not the state legislatures. Therefore the author agues that the Marshall Court supported federalism via judicial review, answer (D). The paragraph does not mention any failures of the Court, therefore answer (A) and (B) are incorrect. It was stated at the end of the passage that the court's decisions helped preserve the Union during the Civil War, not, as answer (C) states, bring about the Civil War. Finally, the paragraph suggests that the Court had its greatest impact on state legislators, not, as answer (E) states, Congress.

27. (D) Since Marshall's politics were discussed throughout the entire passage, the question requires you to *evaluate* the passage to determine what answer choice best describes his politics. Looking back over the passage, note key terms such as "consistent with the policies of the Republican Party" (line 6), "Never an extreme Federalist" (line 7) and "Marshall's support of these principles placed him near the mainstream of American politics" (line 22). Marshall's politics were near the middle of the road, or mainstream. Answer (D), moderate, is the best choice. Both (A) and (B) denote an extreme bias or leaning and are incorrect. Answer (C), democratic, describes a political system, not someone's personal politics. Answer (E) is incorrect because the second paragraph states that Marshall distrusted majoritarianism.

28. (D) The question wants you to *evaluate* the purpose of the two short paragraphs. Answer (D), present an overview of the potato famine, is the best response because it adequately incorporates both paragraphs in the summary. Answers (B) and (C) were not mentioned in the passage and answers (A) and (E) are mentioned in the second paragraph, but are not referred to in enough detail to be considered the purpose of the whole passage.

29. (A) The question is asking you to evaluate the reasons behind the emergence of the potato as a vital food source for the Irish. The end of the second paragraph discusses how the native farmers had to pay over 90% of their crop to the landlords for rent, and that they had to look to other sources for food that was not controlled by the landlord. The second-to-last sentence in the paragraph explains that the potato became a vital food source because it was able to grow on the hillsides (land not controlled by the landlords), and it was able to be stored for a long time before spoiling, thus it could feed

the farmers year round. Answer (A) is the best response. The remaining answer choices were not mentioned in the passage.

30. **(B)** This is a *vocab-in-context question.* "Versatility" is being used in line 12 to describe the potato that grows on rocky hills and mountainsides and could be kept for very long periods before spoiling. The best answer is (B) because adaptable is the best choice to describe the enduring or versatile qualities of the potato. Answer (A), tractable, refers to the quality of bending, or easily shaped, which does not apply to the potato. Answer (C), delectable, may be used to describe a potato, but it does not fit the context of the sentence. Answer (D), curable, is not a quality of the potato. Answer (E), potable, refers to drinking, which also does not fit in with the qualities of a potato.

31. **(D)** All the answer choices mentioned were results of the blight EXCEPT answer (D). The second paragraph does mention the importation of corn by the British to relieve the famine; however, the lack of currency in Ireland prevented anyone from buying it. Therefore, if no one could pay for the corn, there could not be an increase in the sale of it.

32. **(E)** The question is asking you to *evaluate* how the author feels about Edmund Becquerel's research. Since this is the first question, you know it relates to the beginning of the passage. In the first paragraph it is noted that Edmund Becquerel was the first to observe the photovoltaic effect and began the research in the field of solar power. Since the passage is concerned with the development of solar power from its beginnings to the present day, the author would most likely feel that Becquerel's research was answer (E), an important breakthrough. Without Becquerel's research, there would be no solar power to write about. Answers (A), (B), and (D) downplay Becquerel's contributions which the author would not agree with. Answer (C) is wrong because the photovoltaic effect has been studied since its discovery, and therefore was recognized in its time.

33. **(D)** This question is asking you to *analyze* the cause of the photovoltaic effect as it was observed in the first paragraph. According to Becquerel's research, the photovoltaic effect was first observed when "one of two identical electrodes in a weak conducting solution was illuminated." (lines 3–4) Therefore the cause of the photovoltaic effect requires positive electrodes interacting in a weak environment, answer (D). Answers (A) and (C) mention the required electrodes, but leave out the environment in which those electrodes need to interact. Answers (B) and (E) mention "one weak solution" which is incorrect because the electrodes are interacting in a weak environment which could be made up of any number of weak solutions.

34. **(C)** This question wants to know why selenium was used for cameras (photometric devices), and requires you to *analyze,* or identify the reason. Starting on line 6, the passage states that selenium "converts light in the visible part of the spectrum; for this reason, it was adopted by . . . field of photography for photometric devices." Therefore, the reason cameras used selenium was because it converts the visible part of the sun's spectrum into electricity, answer (C). Answers (A), (B), and (C) are not directly stated in paragraph and are clearly not given as the reason selenium is used in cameras. They are incorrect. Answer (D) is tricky because selenium is used in the cells that adjust shutter speeds, but it does not adjust the shutter speeds on it own. (D) is therefore incorrect.

35. **(A)** The term "concluded" indicates the question is *evaluation,* and requires you to choose the one answer that is best supported by the information in the passage. Answer (A), solar energy is still limited by problems of technological efficiency, is the best conclu-

sion because the fourth paragraph talks about the capabilities of solar energy systems and the last three paragraph state the limitations of the same systems. Therefore a strong conclusion would be that solar energy is still limited by certain problems. Answers (B) and (C) are not stated in the passage and therefore there is no support for these conclusions in the passage. Answers (D) and (E) misstate information that was given in the passage and cannot be proper conclusions.

36. (E) This is a *vocab-in-context* question. Be sure to read enough of the passage around line 18 to understand the context of the sentence. The last lines in the second paragraph talk about the new increases in efficiency in the silicon photovoltaic cells, "heralding," or beginning an entirely new era of power producing cells. Answer (E), introducing, most nearly means beginning and is the correct answer. No other answer choice conveys the idea that a new era has started in developing photovoltaic cells.

37. (B) For this question you are looking for an example of what a PV cell has powered. Keep in mind the chronology of the questions and the answer should be somewhere after line 19 in Question 36. Line 23 talks about a space satellite that used an array of cells to power its radio. Therefore a space satellite radio, answer (B), is an example of what a PV cell has powered. Answers (A) and (C) were not mentioned in the passage, and therefore can not be used as examples of what a PV cell has powered. Electric utility lines, answer (D), carry power and would not need to be powered by PV cells. PV cells would probably power space stations, answer (E), but it is not an example stated in the passage and therefore incorrect.

38. (A) This is a math question in disguise. Lines 26–27 state that 1 kilowatt of solar energy will yield 100 watts of electricity through the photovoltaic effect. The question wants to know how much electricity 2 kilowatts of solar energy will yield. Since the solar energy has been doubled, the electricity should also be doubled to yield 200 watts of electricity, answer (A).

39. (A) The question gives you a statement and asks you for the one answer choice, derived from the passage, that most supports it. The statement claims that sunlight is difficult to procure, or collect for use in solar energy. The paragraph starting on line 34 talks about the difficulties in capturing, or collecting solar energy. Some of the reasons are that the sun has low illuminating power, sunlight is intermittent and effected by the time of day, climate, pollution, and season. Therefore sunlight is difficult to procure because it is erratic and subject to variables, answers (A). All the remaining answer choices are not stated or derived from the passage.

40. (A) In this *evaluation* question, you are asked to supply the concluding paragraph with additional information that best supports its main idea. The concluding paragraph states the benefits of solar energy by claiming it is abundant, inexhaustible, and clean, but yet does not give any specific examples of its benefits. Therefore the best additional information to support the paragraph would deal with the specific benefits of solar energy, answer (A). Answers (D) and (E) are too specific, whereas all the benefits need to be elaborated on. Answers (B) and (C) run contrary to the main idea of the concluding paragraph, which is to endorse solar energy.

41. (C) The question is asking you to *analyze* the information in the passage to determine which answer choice best reflects how the Phoenicians regarded themselves. The passage states that the Phoenicians emerged around 1100 B.C. as a powerful political

force (line 11), but this does not insinuate that they thought of themselves as an all-powerful empire, therefore answer (A) is incorrect. Line 2 states that they were known as Canaanites, not that they referred to themselves as Canaanites, so answer (B) is incorrect. Line 5 states that they never thought of themselves as Phoenicians, and therefore they could not consider themselves a united Phoenician empire, making answer (D) wrong. Lines 19–20 mention that the Phoenicians developed the modern alphabet, but this does not imply that they thought of themselves as inventors of the alphabet, so answer (E) is incorrect. Lines 6–7 state that, instead of thinking of themselves as Phoenicians, they "considered themselves citizens of the ports from which they set sail," so they thought of themselves as citizens of their hometowns, answer (C), and not as citizens of a nation.

42. (A) This question is asking you to *analyze* the passage to find the reasons for the lack of knowledge on Phoenician civilization. The first sentence of the passage informs you that little is known about these "puzzling people" and then recounts what little information there is. Towards the end of the passage (line 15) the author details the end of the Phoenician civilization by stating that armies and empires destroyed or built over their cities and that their writings had disintegrated. This information suggests that not much was left behind to help scholars and archeologists learn about the Phoenician civilization. Therefore, answer (A) is correct. The first sentence of the passage states that the Phoenicians appear frequently in ancient texts, therefore answer (B) is incorrect. Answer (C) is incorrect on both accounts; the Phoenicians had writings and literature and therefore were not illiterate, and they also "emerged as a cultural and political force," proving they did not lack strength. The fact that the Phoenicians developed an alphabet and had literature suggests that there was a common language between the Phoenician people, so answer (D) is incorrect. Answer (E) is not only contrary to the facts presented in the passage, but also not a valid reason the question is looking for.

43. (D) The question is asking you to *evaluate* the passage as a whole to determine its purpose. Answers (A), (B), and (C) are mentioned in the passage, but they are referred to as parts of the passage, not the purpose of the whole passage. Answer (D), outline the history of the Phoenicians, is the best response because the passage does briefly give an account of the Phoenician civilization. Answer (E) is mentioned at the end of the passage, but it is not the topic of the entire passage, and therefore incorrect.

44. (D) The question is asking you to *analyze* the passage to determine what the author would consider to be the greatest contribution or legacy of the Phoenician civilization. You can eliminate answer (E) because their literature was lost, and therefore cannot be remembered or traced to the Phoenicians. The passage states that the Phoenicians inhabited the region known as the Levant, not that they developed it in such a way that it was their legacy to future generations, eliminating answer (C). Answer (A), cedar timber, and answer (B), reddish purple cloth, were items that the Phoenicians traded, not a legacy or contribution that future generations would remember them for. Answer (D), the development of the alphabet, is the best answer because in the last sentence the author states that the Phoenicians developed the modern alphabet, something that future generations would remember them for.

45. (C) This is a *vocab-in-context* question. The passage begins by stating that the purpose of a comedy is to "amuse" the audience. The sentence in line 6 states that the dialogue and plot development may be "laughable," but a play does not need to be "funny" to be

comic. Therefore the term "laughable" most closely relates to the meanings of "amuse" and "funny." Answer (C), amusingly droll, is the best response because it most closely relates to the meaning of "amuse" and "funny." Answers (A) and (B) are too extreme and suggest a lack of seriousness that the author believes comedies must have. Answers (D) and (E) are too serious and reflect no amusement whatsoever.

46. **(E)** This question is asking you to *analyze* the Shakespeare example the author uses. In the first paragraph, the author differentiates between the two types of comedy, low and high. He states that high comedy should "elicit no laughter at all from its audience," and its purpose was to "amuse as subtly as possible." These types of comedies could be thought of as highbrow, or highly sophisticated. The author then suggests that comedies that did elicit outright laughter from its audience were considered a low comedy. These could be thought of as lowbrow or unsophisticated. He then ends the paragraph by stating that highbrow Renaissance critics criticized Shakespeare for some of his plays appealing to laughter. The author uses this example to show that even the even Shakespeare, a great writer, was capable of writing low quality comedies. Answer (E) best reflects this idea. Answer (B) reflects the opposite meaning and is incorrect. Since the author is trying to define the comedy genre, he has no need to make Shakespeare look like a poor writer, answer (A), or criticize the Renaissance critics, answer (D). Also, the author is not judging either high or low comedy types, answer (C).

47. **(C)** The question is asking you to identify which type of comedy, discussed in passage 1, best reflects the situation in the question. If a friend or relative told you of the loss of a winning lottery ticket it would not elicit from you a sense of laughter, but rather sympathy, or a sharing of remorse with the individual. Lines 23–26 state that if the action "triggers our sympathy for the characters...the play tilts more in the direction of tragicomedy." Therefore answer (C), tragicomedy, is the correct response. Sarcasm (D) and slapstick (E) were not types of comedy mentioned in the passage. Nothing about losing a lottery ticket suggest judgement or reform, which are the requirements of satire, answer (A), and there is nothing overly exaggerated about the loss of a winning lottery ticket, so farce (B) is incorrect.

48. **(D)** The question is asking for the meaning of the phrase "figurative distance" and is thus an *interpretation* question. The line reference tells you where in the passage you will need to look to find the meaning of the phrase. From lines 26–32 the author discusses how the involvement of the audience determines the type of comedy. If the audience feels removed from the characters the comedy tends to be funnier than if the audience feels a close connection to the characters. Therefore the "figurative distance" refers to answer (D), the degree to which an audience relates to the play's action. Answer (A) reflects the "literal" distance, and answers (B), (C), and (E) are not mentioned in the passage and therefore do not relate to the "figurative distance" at all.

49. **(B)** This question is dealing with *evaluation* because you are to determine what the author would espouse, or support, according to the lines referenced. At the end of the first passage, the author is discussing the involvement of the audience in any given comedy. He states that the level of connectedness between the audience and the characters or actions of the play determines how the audience will view the play. Answer (A) is incorrect because the author would want us to get involved with the action—that is the purpose of a comedy. Answer (B) would be the best response, because the author would support the audience getting immersed in the world of drama. That is what he

talks about in the last five lines. Feeling safe, answer (C), is one of many feelings that an audience is likely to have, therefore the answer is incomplete. Answers (D) and (E) are not mentioned in the last lines of the passage and there is no evidence that the author would or would not support these contentions.

50. (D) The question switches over to the second passage and wants to know why the author uses Aristotle as a leading source for the definition of tragedy. The author begins by explaining that the term "tragedy" has a very precise meaning and then defines the term as it "originated with Aristotle." (line 35) Answer (D) is the best response because it explains that the author introduces Aristotle as the source of the definition because Aristotle created the definition. All other answer choices are not stated or suggested in the passage.

51. (A) This is a *vocab-in-context* question. Familiarize yourself with the content around line 42 to understand the context of the sentence. The sentence in line 42 describes the qualities of the central character in a tragedy as good and noble. The sentence continues to define what is meant by "good," and in line 44 the author defines what is meant by "noble." "Noble" involves both "social stature" and "moral stature." Answer (A), high degree and superior virtue, is the best response because it most closely reflects the meaning of high social stature and high moral stature. Answer (B) is incorrect because "moral stature" does not have any relation to self-esteem. Answers (C), (D), and (E) are incorrect because neither of their meanings reflect "social stature" or "moral stature."

52. (C) In line 47, *harmatia* is defined as "a tragic flaw." It is a weakness that leads the hero to "make an error in judgement that initiates the reversal in his fortunes." In line 50, the author gives an example of the most common flaw, hubris, or excessive pride. Answer (C), a refusal to acknowledge the power of the gods, is the best response because it most closely reflects the error of the hero's judgement due to his pride. By not acknowledging the power of the gods, the hero would believe he is more powerful than they are, and would be guilty of hubris. Answers (A), (B), and (E) do not reflect an error in judgement that will eventually lead to a reversal of fortunes, since they are beneficial qualities to have. Answer (D) describes a person not a quality of a person.

53. (E) In lines 52–55, the author defines *catharsis* as the emotional reaction the audience should experience in witnessing the events of a tragedy. The remainder of the paragraph explains exactly what that emotional reaction should be. Starting with line 55 the tragedy is said to arouse feelings of pity and fear for the tragic hero as the audience witnesses the consequences of his flawed behavior. There also must be "a cleansing" of these emotions which will leave the audience feeling "not depressed but relieved and almost elated." This is the emotional reaction, or catharsis, that the audience should experience when watching a tragedy. Answer (E) best summarizes this idea. Answer (A) does not define the actions of a tragedy, while answers (B), (C), and (D) are reactions that are not referred to in the passage.

54. (B) The question is asking for you to *compare* the two passages and identify what both authors have in common in writing the passages. You will need to go through each answer choice and determine if it is reflected in both passages. Neither author ridiculed their subject matter, so answer (A) is incorrect. The author of the first passage did outline the terms and guidelines of the comedy and the author of the second passage also outlined the terms and guidelines of the tragedy; therefore answer (B) is correct. No one is ever thrilled to read Critical Reading passages, so answer (C) is incorrect. The

author of the second passage did not mention Shakespeare, so answer (D) is incorrect. Both passages were informative, not persuasive, which means answer (E) is incorrect.

55. (B) This question is asking you to determine the main difference in how the passages were put together, or structured. Passage 1 is a general summary about the nature of comedy, while passage 2 sums up the essentials of tragedy. There is no specific time period given for either passage. Although temporal references were given in each passage, the discussions in each passage were not limited to those particular time frames, so answer (A) is incorrect. Passage 1 does divide its subject into subcategories, such as farce, satire, and tragicomedy. Passage 2 does extract its subject's individual elements, such as harmatia and catharsis, so answer (B) is correct. Passage 1 does not make fun of its subject matter, therefore answer (C) is incorrect. Passage 1 does not draw on a series of plays as examples, meaning answer (D) is incorrect. Passage 1 may introduce special vocabulary, but passage 2 definitely does (harmatia and catharsis). Answer (E) is incorrect because it states that passage 2 fails to introduce special vocabulary.

56. (D) This question is asking for the assumption, or the one thing that both passages will agree on. Nothing in passage 1 indicates that it would agree with answer (A). Nothing in passage 2 suggests that tragedy is on the decline, so answer (B) is incorrect. Catharsis was not mentioned in passage 1 and therefore cannot be an integral part of comedy, answer (C) is incorrect. Both passages do mention the importance of the audience's role in both comedy and tragedy, so answer (D) is correct. The tragicomedy was not mentioned or referred to in passage 2, therefore answer (E) is incorrect.

57. (B) The question is asking you to *analyze* the passage to determine how the Earth's star compares with other stars in the galaxy. In lines 2–4, the passage states that our star "falls into a category of yellow runts . . . a species so monotonously common that there are billions of them." Answer (B), common in size and number, best reflects our sun when compared with other stars. Answers (A) and (C) use the adjective "rare," which is not true since there are billions of them. Answer (D) is also incorrect because the first sentence states that our star is "quite undistinguished." Answer (E) is not mentioned in the passage at all.

58. (E) The question is asking you to *evaluate* the tone the author uses throughout the entire passage. Since this is a science passage, you should be wary of answers that are "impassioned," therefore you can eliminate answers (A) and (B). Answer (C), detached objectivity, may be incorrect because if an author were detached from the issue, he would not care enough to even write about it. It might be the right answer, but only if another choice is not better. Answer (D), nostalgic subjectivity, is incorrect because the passage does not insinuate that the study of the sun should go back to the way it was done in the past. Answer (E), reasoned objectivity, is the best response because the passage was detailed with facts, i.e. reasoned, and scientifically unemotional, i.e. objective.

59. (C) The question is asking you to *analyze* the passage to determine the one answer choice that can be proven from the information in the passage. Nothing in the passage connects the sun with ocean tides, so answer (A) is incorrect. The entire passage is about the study of our sun, a type G star, so answer (B) is wrong. If finer resolution is needed to study fundamental solar structure (line 11) and the best resolution to date is 50 miles wide (line 13), it can be concluded that fundamental solar structure is less than 50 miles wide, otherwise finer resolution would not be needed to study the solar structure. Answer (C) is the best response. Line 6 states the opposite of answer (D), and therefore

it cannot be inferred. The passage states that it has only been 400 years since the discovery of sun spots, not the total time the sun has been studied, answer (E) is incorrect.

60. (D) This is a *vocab-in-context* question. You are looking for the one answer choice that best reflects the meaning of "on the cusp" as found in line 10. The sentence is explaining that now, thanks to computers and high-tech instruments, scientists are "on the cusp" of finding answers, or on the verge of finding answers to questions they have been studying for over 400 years. Answers (B), (C), and (E) do not reflect the intended meaning of "on the verge" and are incorrect. Answer (A) is incorrect because it suggests that scientists have just begun to study and find answers, when in fact they have been studying the sun for over 400 years. Answer (D), on the edge, is the best response because it suggests that the scientists are about to reach a breakthrough that will reveal a number of answers that were before hidden from them.

CHAPTER 6

BASIC MATH SKILLS REVIEW

CHAPTER 6

BASIC MATH SKILLS REVIEW

I. ARITHMETIC

II. ALGEBRA

III. GEOMETRY

IV. WORD PROBLEMS

Are you ready to tackle the math sections of the PSAT? Well, the chances are that you will be, but only after some reviewing of basic concepts in arithmetic, algebra, and geometry. The more familiar you are with these fundamental principles, the better you will do on the math sections of the PSAT. Our math review represents the various mathematical topics that will appear on the PSAT. You will not find any calculus, trigonometry, or even imaginary numbers in our math review. Why? Because these concepts are not tested on the math sections of the PSAT. The mathematical concepts presented on the PSAT are ones with which you are already familiar and simply need to review in order to score well.

Along with a knowledge of these topics, how quickly and accurately you can answer the math questions will have an effect upon your success. Therefore, memorize the directions in order to save time and decrease your chances of making careless mistakes. Then, complete the practice drills that are provided for you in our review. Even if you are sure you know your fundamental math concepts, the drills will help to warm you up so that you can go into the math sections of the PSAT with quick, sharp math skills.

REFERENCE TABLE

SYMBOLS AND THEIR MEANINGS

$=$	is equal to	$\leq$	is less than or equal to
$\neq$	is unequal to	$\geq$	is greater than or equal to
$<$	is less than	$\parallel$	is parallel to
$>$	is greater than	$\perp$	is perpendicular to

FORMULAS

DESCRIPTION	FORMULA
Area (A) of a:	
square	$A = s^2$; where $s =$ side
rectangle	$A = lw$; where $l =$ length, $w =$ width
parallelogram	$A = bh$; where $b =$ base, $h =$ height
triangle	$A = \frac{1}{2}bh$; where $b =$ base, $h =$ height
circle	$A = \pi r^2$; where $\pi = 3.14$, $r =$ radius
Perimeter (P) of a:	
square	$P = 4s$; where $s =$ side
rectangle	$P = 2l + 2w$; where $l =$ length, $w =$ width
triangle	$P = a + b + c$; where a, b, and c are the sides
circumference (C) of a circle	$C = \pi d$; where $\pi = 3.14$, $d =$ diameter $= 2r$
Volume (V) of a:	
cube	$V = s^3$; where $s =$ side
rectangular container	$V = lwh$; where $l =$ length, $w =$ width, $h =$ height
Pythagorean Theorem	$c^2 = a^2 + b^2$; where $c =$ hypotenuse, a and b are legs of a right triangle
Distance (d):	
between two points in a plane	$d = \sqrt{(x_2 - x_1)^2 + (y_2 - y_1)^2}$ where (x_1, y_1) and (x_2, y_2) are two points in a plane
as a function of rate and time	$d = rt$; where $r =$ rate, $t =$ time
Mean	$\text{mean} = \dfrac{x_1 + x_2 + ... + x_n}{n}$ where the x's are the values for which a mean is desired, and $n =$ number of values in the series
Median	median $=$ the point in an ordered set of numbers at which half of the numbers are above and half of the numbers are below this value
Simple Interest (i)	$i = prt$; where $p =$ principal, $r =$ rate, $t =$ time
Total Cost (c)	$c = nr$; where $n =$ number of units, $r =$ cost per unit

I. ARITHMETIC

INTEGERS AND REAL NUMBERS

Most of the numbers used in algebra belong to a set called the **real numbers** or **reals**. This set can be represented graphically by the real number line.

Given the number line below, we arbitrarily fix a point and label it with the number 0. In a similar manner, we can label any point on the line with one of the real numbers, depending on its position relative to 0. Numbers to the right of 0 are positive, while those to the left are negative. Value increases from left to right, so that if *a* is to the right of *b*, it is said to be greater than *b*.

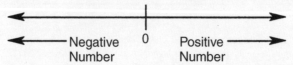

If we now divide the number line into equal segments, we can label the points on this line with real numbers. For example, the point 2 lengths to the left of 0 is –2, while the point 3 lengths to the right of 0 is + 3 (the + sign is usually assumed, so + 3 is written simply as 3). The number line now looks like this:

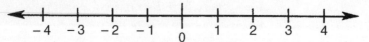

These boundary points represent the subset of the reals known as the **integers**. The set of integers is made up of both the positive and negative whole numbers:

$$\{\dots, -4, -3, -2, -1, 0, 1, 2, 3, 4, \dots\}.$$

Some subsets of integers are:

Natural Numbers or Positive Numbers—the set of integers starting with 1 and increasing:

$$N = \{1, 2, 3, 4, \dots\}.$$

Whole Numbers—the set of integers starting with 0 and increasing:

$$W = \{0, 1, 2, 3, \dots\}.$$

Negative Numbers—the set of integers starting with – 1 and decreasing:

$$Z = \{-1, -2, -3, \dots\}.$$

Prime Numbers—the set of positive integers greater than 1 that are divisible only by 1 and themselves:

$$\{2, 3, 5, 7, 11, \dots\}.$$

Even Integers—the set of integers divisible by 2:

$$\{\dots, -4, -2, 0, 2, 4, 6, \dots\}.$$

Odd Integers—the sct of integers not divisible by 2:

$$\{\dots, -3, -1, 1, 3, 5, 7, \dots\}.$$

Consecutive Integers—the set of integers that differ by 1:

$$\{n, n + 1, n + 2, \dots\} \ (n = \text{an integer}).$$

Classify each of the following numbers into as many different sets as possible. Example: real, integer …

(1) 0   (3) $\sqrt{6}$ (5) $\dfrac{2}{3}$

(2) 9   (4) $\dfrac{1}{2}$ (6) 1.5

SOLUTION

(1) 0 is a real number, an integer, and a whole number.

(2) 9 is a real number, an odd number, and a natural number.

(3) $\sqrt{6}$ is a real number.

(4) $\frac{1}{2}$ is a real number.

(5) $\frac{2}{3}$ is a real number.

(6) 1.5 is a real number and a decimal.

ABSOLUTE VALUE

The **absolute value** of a number is represented by two vertical lines around the number, and is equal to the given number, regardless of sign.

The absolute value of a real number A is defined as follows:

$$|A| = \begin{cases} A \text{ if } A \geq 0 \\ -A \text{ if } A < 0 \end{cases}$$

EXAMPLES

$$|5| = 5, |-8| = -(-8) = 8$$

Absolute values follow the given rules:

(A) $|-A| = |A|$

(B) $|A| \geq 0$, equality holding only if A = 0

(C) $\left|\dfrac{A}{B}\right| = \dfrac{|A|}{|B|}$, $B \neq 0$

(D) $|AB| = |A| \times |B|$

(E) $|A|^2 = A^2$

Absolute value can also be expressed on the real number line as the distance of the point represented by the real number from the point labeled 0.

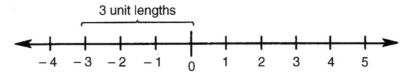

3 unit lengths

So $|-3| = 3$ because -3 is 3 units to the left of 0.

PROBLEM

Classify each of the following statements as true or false. If it is false, explain why.

(1) $\left|-120\right| > 1$ (4) $\left|12-3\right| = 12-3$

(2) $\left|4-12\right| = \left|4\right| - \left|12\right|$ (5) $\left|-12a\right| = 12\left|a\right|$

(3) $\left|4-9\right| = 9-4$

SOLUTION

(1) True

(2) False, $\left|4-12\right| = \left|4\right| - \left|12\right|$

$\qquad\qquad \left|-8\right| = 4-12$

$\qquad\qquad\quad 8 \neq -8$

In general, $\left|a+b\right| \neq \left|a\right| + \left|b\right|$

(3) True

(4) True

(5) True

PROBLEM

Find the absolute value for each of the following:

(1) 0   (3) $-\pi$

(2) 4   (4) a, where a is a real number

SOLUTION

(1) $\left|0\right| = 0$

(2) $\left|4\right| = 4$

(3) $\left|-\pi\right| = \pi$

(4) for $a > 0$, $\left|a\right| = a$

      for $a = 0$, $\left|a\right| = 0$

      for $a < 0$, $\left|a\right| = a$

$$\text{i.e., } \left|a\right| = \begin{cases} a & \text{if } a > 0 \\ 0 & \text{if } a = 0 \\ -a & \text{if } a < 0 \end{cases}$$

POSITIVE AND NEGATIVE NUMBERS

A) **To add two numbers with like signs,** add their absolute values and write the sum with the common sign. So, $6 + 2 = 8$, $(-6) + (-2) = -8$

B) **To add two numbers with unlike signs,** find the difference between their absolute values, and write the result with the sign of the number with the greater absolute value. So,

$$(-4) + 6 = 2, \quad 15 + (-19) = -4$$

C) **To subtract a number b from another number a,** change the sign of b and add to a. Examples:

$$10 - (3) = 10 + (-3) = 7 \tag{1}$$
$$2 - (-6) = 2 + 6 = 8 \tag{2}$$
$$(-5) - (-2) = -5 + 2 = -3 \tag{3}$$

D) **To multiply (or divide) two numbers having like signs,** multiply (or divide) their absolute values and write the result with a positive sign. Examples:

$$(5)(3) = 15 \tag{1}$$
$$(-6) \div (-3) = 2 \tag{2}$$

E) **To multiply (or divide) two numbers having unlike signs,** multiply (or divide) their absolute values and write the result with a negative sign. Examples:

$$(-2)(8) = -16 \tag{1}$$
$$9 \div (-3) = -3 \tag{2}$$

According to the law of signs for real numbers, the square of a positive or negative number is always positive. This means that it is impossible to take the square root of a negative number in the real number system.

PROBLEM

Calculate the value of each of the following expressions:

(1) $\left| |2-5| + 6 - 14 \right|$ (2) $|-5| \times 4 + \dfrac{|-12|}{4}$

SOLUTION

Before solving this problem, one must use the rules for the **order of operations**. Always work within the parentheses or with absolute values first while keeping in mind that multiplication and division are carried out before addition and subtraction.

(1) $\left| |-3| + 6 - 14 \right| = |3 + 6 - 14|$

$$= |9 - 14|$$
$$= |-5|$$
$$= 5$$

$$(2) \quad (5 \times 4) + \frac{12}{4} = 20 + 3$$
$$= 23$$

ODD AND EVEN NUMBERS

When dealing with odd and even numbers keep in mind the following:

Adding:

$$even + even = even$$

$$odd + odd = even$$

$$even + odd = odd$$

Multiplying:

$$even \times even = even$$

$$even \times odd = even$$

$$odd \times odd = odd$$

DRILL: INTEGERS AND REAL NUMBERS

Addition

1.   Simplify $4 + (-7) + 2 + (-5)$.

   (A) -6 (B) -4
   (C) 0 (D) 6
   (E) 18

2.   Simplify $144 + (-317) + 213$.

   (A) -357 (B) -40
   (C) 40 (D) 357
   (E) 674

3.   Simplify $|4 + (-3)| + |-2|$.

   (A) -2 (B) -1
   (C) 1 (D) 3
   (E) 9

4.   What integer makes the equation $-13 + 12 + 7 + ? = 10$ a true statement?

(A)   −22   (B)   −10
(C)   4   (D)   6
(E)   10

5.   Simplify $4 + 17 + (-29) + 13 + (-22) + (-3)$.

(A)   − 44   (B)   − 20
(C)   23   (D)   34
(E)   78

Subtraction

6.   Simplify $319 - 428$.

(A)   − 111   (B)   − 109
(C)   − 99   (D)   109
(E)   747

7.   Simplify $91,203 - 37,904 + 1,073$.

(A)   54,372   (B)   64,701
(C)   128,034   (D)   129,107
(E)   130,180

8.   Simplify $|43 - 62| - |-17 - 3|$.

(A)   − 39   (B)   − 19
(C)   − 1   (D)   1
(E)   39

9.   Simplify $-(-4 - 7) + (-2)$.

(A)   − 22   (B)   − 13
(C)   − 9   (D)   7
(E)   9

10. In the St. Elias Mountains, Mt. Logan rises from 1,292 meters above sea level to 7,243 meters above sea level. How tall is Mt. Logan?

(A) 4,009 m
(B) 5,951 m
(C) 5,699 m
(D) 6,464 m
(E) 7,885 m

Multiplication

11. Simplify $(-3) \times (-18) \times (-1)$.

(A) -108
(B) -54
(C) -48
(D) 48
(E) 54

12. Simplify $|-42| \times |7|$.

(A) -294
(B) -49
(C) -35
(D) 284
(E) 294

13. Simplify $(-6) \times 5 \times (-10) \times (-4) \times 0 \times 2$.

(A) $-2,400$
(B) -240
(C) 0
(D) 280
(E) 2,700

14. Simplify $-|-6 \times 8|$.

(A) -48
(B) -42
(C) 2
(D) 42
(E) 48

15. A city in Georgia had a record low temperature of $-3°F$ one winter. During the same year, a city in Michigan experienced a record low that was nine times the record low set in Georgia. What was the record low in Michigan that year?

(A) $-31°F$
(B) $-27°F$
(C) $-21°F$
(D) $-12°F$
(E) $-6°F$

Division

16. Simplify $(-24) \div 8$.

    (A) -4 (B) -3
    (C) -2 (D) 3
    (E) 4

17. Simplify $(-180) \div (-12)$.

    (A) -30 (B) -15
    (C) 1.5   (D) 15
    (E) 216

18. Simplify $|-76| \div |-4|$.

    (A) -21 (B) -19
    (C) 13   (D) 19
    (E) 21.5

19. Simplify $|216 \div (-6)|$.

    (A) -36 (B) -12
    (C) 36   (D) 38
    (E) 43

20. At the end of the year, a small firm has \$2,996 in its account for bonuses. If the entire amount is equally divided among the 14 employees, how much does each one receive?

    (A) \$107   (B) \$114
    (C) \$170   (D) \$210
    (E) \$214

Order of Operations

21. Simplify $\dfrac{4 + 8 \times 2}{5 - 1}$

    (A) 4   (B) 5
    (C) 6   (D) 8
    (E) 12

22. $96 \div 3 \div 4 \div 2 =$

    (A) 65   (B) 64

    (C) 16   (D) 8

    (E) 4

23. $3 + 4 \times 2 - 6 \div 3 =$

    (A) −1   (B) $\dfrac{5}{3}$

    (C) $\dfrac{8}{3}$ (D) 9

    (E) 12

24. $[(4 + 8) \times 3] \div 9 =$

    (A) 4   (B) 8

    (C) 12   (D) 24

    (E) 36

25. $18 + 3 \times 4 \div 3 =$

    (A) 3   (B) 5

    (C) 10   (D) 22

    (E) 28

26. $(29 - 17 + 4) \div 4 + |-2| =$

    (A) $2\dfrac{2}{3}$ (B) 4

    (C) $4\dfrac{2}{3}$ (D) 6

    (E) 15

27. $(-3) \times 5 - 20 \div 4 =$

    (A) −75   (B) −20

    (C) −10   (D) $-8\dfrac{3}{4}$

    (E) 20

28. $\dfrac{11\times 2+2}{16-2\times 2}$

   (A) $\dfrac{11}{16}$ (B) 1

   (C) 2   (D) $3\dfrac{2}{3}$

   (E) 4

29. $|-8-4|\div 3\times 6+(-4)=$

   (A) 20   (B) 26
   (C) 32   (D) 62
   (E) 212

30. $32\div 2+4-15\div 3=$

   (A) 0   (B) 7
   (C) 15   (D) 23
   (E) 63

FRACTIONS

The fraction, a/b, where the numerator is a and the denominator is b, implies that a is being divided by b. The denominator of a fraction can never be zero since a number divided by zero is not defined. If the numerator is greater than the denominator, the fraction is called an **improper fraction**. A **mixed number** is the sum of a whole number and a fraction, i.e.,

$$4\dfrac{3}{8}=4+\dfrac{3}{8}$$

OPERATIONS WITH FRACTIONS

A) **To change a mixed number to an improper fraction**, simply multiply the whole number by the denominator of the fraction and add the numerator. This product becomes the numerator of the result and the denominator remains the same, e.g.,

$$5\dfrac{2}{3}=\dfrac{(5\times 3)+2}{3}=\dfrac{15+2}{3}=\dfrac{17}{3}$$

To change an improper fraction to a mixed number, simply divide the numerator by the denominator. The remainder becomes the numerator of the fractional part of the mixed number, and the denominator remains the same, e.g.,

$$\dfrac{35}{4}=35\div 4=8\dfrac{3}{4}$$

To check your work, change your result back to an improper fraction to see if it matches the original fraction.

B) To find the sum of fractions having a common denominator, simply add together the numerators of the given fractions and put this sum over the common denominator.

$$\frac{11}{3} + \frac{5}{3} = \frac{11+5}{3} = \frac{16}{3}$$

Similarly for subtraction,

$$\frac{11}{3} - \frac{5}{3} = \frac{11-5}{3} = \frac{6}{3} = 2$$

C) **To find the sum of two fractions having different denominators**, it is necessary to find the **lowest common denominator (LCD)** of the different denominators using a process called **factoring**.

To **factor** a number means to find two numbers that when multiplied together have a product equal to the original number. These two numbers are then said to be **factors** of the original number; e.g., the factors of 6 are

(1)   1 and 6 since $1 \times 6 = 6$.

(2)   2 and 3 since $2 \times 3 = 6$.

Every number is the product of itself and 1. A **prime factor** is a number that does not have any factors besides itself and 1. This is important when finding the LCD of two fractions having different denominators.

To find the LCD of $\frac{11}{6}$ and $\frac{5}{16}$, we must first find the prime factors of each of the two denominators.

$$6 = 2 \times 3$$
$$16 = 2 \times 2 \times 2 \times 2$$
$$LCD = 2 \times 2 \times 2 \times 2 \times 3 = 48$$

Note that we do not need to repeat the 2 that appears in both the factors of 6 and 16.

Once we have determined the LCD of the denominators, each of the fractions must be converted into equivalent fractions having the LCD as a denominator.

Rewrite $\frac{11}{6}$ and $\frac{5}{16}$ to have 48 as their denominators.

$$6 \times ? = 48 \qquad\qquad 16 \times ? = 48$$
$$6 \times 8 = 48 \qquad\qquad 16 \times 3 = 48$$

If the numerator and denominator of each fraction is multiplied (or divided) by the same number, the value of the fraction will not change. This is because a fraction $\frac{b}{b}$, b being any number, is equal to the multiplicative identity, 1.

Therefore,

$$\frac{11}{6} \times \frac{8}{8} = \frac{88}{48} \qquad\qquad \frac{5}{16} \times \frac{3}{3} = \frac{15}{48}$$

We may now find

$$\frac{11}{6} + \frac{5}{16} = \frac{88}{48} + \frac{15}{48} = \frac{103}{48}$$

Similarly for subtraction,

$$\frac{11}{6} - \frac{5}{16} = \frac{88}{48} - \frac{15}{48} = \frac{73}{48}$$

D) **To find the product of two or more fractions**, simply multiply the numerators of the given fractions to find the numerator of the product and multiply the denominators of the given fractions to find the denominator of the product, e.g.,

$$\frac{2}{3} \times \frac{1}{5} \times \frac{4}{7} = \frac{2 \times 1 \times 4}{3 \times 5 \times 7} = \frac{8}{105}$$

E) **To find the quotient of two fractions**, simply invert (or flip-over) the divisor and multiply; e.g.,

$$\frac{8}{9} \div \frac{1}{3} = \frac{8}{9} \times \frac{3}{1} = \frac{24}{9} = \frac{8}{3}$$

F) **To simplify a fraction** is to convert it into a form in which the numerator and denominator have no common factor other than 1; e.g.,

$$\frac{12}{18} = \frac{12 \div 6}{18 \div 6} = \frac{2}{3}$$

G) A **complex fraction** is a fraction whose numerator and/or denominator is made up of fractions. To simplify the fraction, find the LCD of all the fractions. Multiply both the numerator and denominator by this number and simplify.

PROBLEM

If $a = 4$ and $b = 7$, find the value of $\dfrac{a + \frac{a}{b}}{a - \frac{a}{b}}$.

SOLUTION

By substitution,

$$\frac{a + \frac{a}{b}}{a - \frac{a}{b}} = \frac{4 + \frac{4}{7}}{4 - \frac{4}{7}}$$

In order to combine the terms, we must find the LCD of 1 and 7. Since both are prime factors, the LCD $= 1 \times 7 = 7$.

Multiplying both the numerator and denominator by 7, we get

$$\frac{7\left(4 + \frac{4}{7}\right)}{7\left(4 - \frac{4}{7}\right)} = \frac{28 + 4}{28 - 4} = \frac{32}{24}$$

By dividing both the numerator and denominator by 8, $\frac{32}{24}$ can be reduced to $\frac{4}{3}$.

DRILL: FRACTIONS

Changing an Improper Fraction to a Mixed Number

<u>DIRECTIONS</u>: Write each improper fraction as a mixed number in simplest form.

1. $\dfrac{50}{4}$

   (A) $10\dfrac{1}{4}$ (B) $11\dfrac{1}{2}$ (C) $12\dfrac{1}{4}$ (D) $12\dfrac{1}{2}$ (E) 25

2. $\dfrac{17}{5}$

   (A) $3\dfrac{2}{5}$ (B) $3\dfrac{3}{5}$ (C) $3\dfrac{4}{5}$ (D) $4\dfrac{1}{5}$ (E) $4\dfrac{2}{5}$

3. $\dfrac{42}{3}$

   (A) $10\dfrac{2}{3}$ (B) 12 (C) $13\dfrac{1}{3}$ (D) 14 (E) $21\dfrac{1}{3}$

4. $\dfrac{85}{6}$

   (A) $9\dfrac{1}{6}$ (B) $10\dfrac{5}{6}$ (C) $11\dfrac{1}{2}$ (D) 12 (E) $14\dfrac{1}{6}$

5. $\dfrac{151}{7}$

   (A) $19\dfrac{6}{7}$ (B) $20\dfrac{1}{7}$ (C) $21\dfrac{4}{7}$ (D) $31\dfrac{2}{7}$ (E) $31\dfrac{4}{7}$

Changing a Mixed Number to an Improper Fraction

<u>DIRECTIONS</u>: Change each mixed number to an improper fraction in simplest form.

6. $2\dfrac{3}{5}$

   (A) $\dfrac{4}{5}$ (B) $\dfrac{6}{5}$ (C) $\dfrac{11}{5}$ (D) $\dfrac{13}{5}$ (E) $\dfrac{17}{5}$

7. $4\dfrac{3}{4}$

   (A) $\dfrac{7}{4}$ (B) $\dfrac{13}{4}$ (C) $\dfrac{16}{3}$ (D) $\dfrac{19}{4}$ (E) $\dfrac{21}{4}$

8. $6\dfrac{7}{6}$

   (A) $\dfrac{13}{6}$ (B) $\dfrac{43}{6}$ (C) $\dfrac{19}{36}$ (D) $\dfrac{42}{36}$ (E) $\dfrac{48}{6}$

9. $12\dfrac{3}{7}$

   (A) $\dfrac{87}{7}$ (B) $\dfrac{164}{14}$ (C) $\dfrac{34}{3}$ (D) $\dfrac{187}{21}$ (E) $\dfrac{252}{7}$

10. $21\dfrac{1}{2}$

    (A) $\dfrac{11}{2}$ (B) $\dfrac{22}{2}$ (C) $\dfrac{24}{2}$ (D) $\dfrac{42}{2}$ (E) $\dfrac{43}{2}$

Adding Fractions with the Same Denominator

DIRECTIONS: Add and write the answer in its simplest form.

11. $\dfrac{5}{12}+\dfrac{3}{12}=$

    (A) $\dfrac{5}{24}$ (B) $\dfrac{1}{3}$ (C) $\dfrac{8}{12}$ (D) $\dfrac{2}{3}$ (E) $1\dfrac{1}{3}$

12. $\dfrac{5}{8}+\dfrac{7}{8}+\dfrac{3}{8}=$

    (A) $\dfrac{15}{24}$ (B) $\dfrac{3}{4}$ (C) $\dfrac{5}{6}$ (D) $\dfrac{7}{8}$ (E) $1\dfrac{7}{8}$

13. $131\dfrac{2}{15}+28\dfrac{3}{15}=$

    (A) $159\dfrac{1}{6}$ (B) $159\dfrac{1}{5}$ (C) $159\dfrac{1}{3}$ (D) $159\dfrac{1}{2}$ (E) $159\dfrac{3}{5}$

14. $3\dfrac{5}{18} + 2\dfrac{1}{18} + 8\dfrac{7}{18} =$

   (A) $13\dfrac{13}{18}$ (B) $13\dfrac{3}{4}$ (C) $13\dfrac{7}{9}$ (D) $14\dfrac{1}{6}$ (E) $14\dfrac{2}{9}$

15. $17\dfrac{9}{20} + 4\dfrac{3}{20} + 8\dfrac{11}{20} =$

   (A) $29\dfrac{23}{60}$ (B) $29\dfrac{23}{20}$ (C) $30\dfrac{3}{20}$ (D) $30\dfrac{1}{5}$ (E) $30\dfrac{3}{5}$

Subtracting Fractions with the Same Denominator

DIRECTIONS: Subtract and write the answer in simplest form.

16. $4\dfrac{7}{8} - 3\dfrac{1}{8} =$

   (A) $1\dfrac{1}{4}$ (B) $1\dfrac{3}{4}$ (C) $1\dfrac{12}{16}$ (D) $1\dfrac{7}{8}$ (E) 2

17. $132\dfrac{5}{12} - 37\dfrac{3}{12} =$

   (A) $94\dfrac{1}{6}$ (B) $95\dfrac{1}{12}$ (C) $95\dfrac{1}{6}$ (D) $105\dfrac{1}{6}$ (E) $169\dfrac{2}{3}$

18. $19\dfrac{1}{3} - 2\dfrac{2}{3} =$

   (A) $16\dfrac{2}{3}$ (B) $16\dfrac{5}{6}$ (C) $17\dfrac{1}{3}$ (D) $17\dfrac{2}{3}$ (E) $17\dfrac{5}{6}$

19. $\dfrac{8}{21} - \dfrac{5}{21} =$

   (A) $\dfrac{1}{21}$ (B) $\dfrac{1}{7}$ (C) $\dfrac{3}{21}$ (D) $\dfrac{2}{7}$ (E) $\dfrac{3}{7}$

20. $82\dfrac{7}{10} - 38\dfrac{9}{10} =$

   (A) $43\dfrac{4}{5}$ (B) $44\dfrac{1}{5}$ (C) $44\dfrac{2}{5}$ (D) $45\dfrac{1}{5}$ (E) $45\dfrac{2}{10}$

Finding the LCD

DIRECTIONS: Find the lowest common denominator of each group of fractions.

21. $\frac{2}{3}$, $\frac{5}{9}$, and $\frac{1}{6}$

    (A) 9   (B) 18   (C) 27   (D) 54   (E) 162

22. $\frac{1}{2}$, $\frac{5}{6}$, and $\frac{3}{4}$

    (A) 2   (B) 4   (C) 6   (D) 12   (E) 48

23. $\frac{7}{16}$, $\frac{5}{6}$, and $\frac{2}{3}$

    (A) 3   (B) 6   (C) 12   (D) 24   (E) 48

24. $\frac{8}{15}$, $\frac{2}{5}$, and $\frac{12}{25}$

    (A) 5   (B) 15   (C) 25   (D) 75   (E) 375

25. $\frac{2}{3}$, $\frac{1}{5}$, and $\frac{5}{6}$

    (A) 15   (B) 30   (C) 48   (D) 90   (E) 120

26. $\frac{1}{3}$, $\frac{9}{42}$, and $\frac{4}{21}$

    (A) 21   (B) 42   (C) 126   (D) 378   (E) 4,000

27. $\frac{4}{9}$, $\frac{2}{5}$, and $\frac{1}{3}$

    (A) 15   (B) 17   (C) 27   (D) 45   (E) 135

28. $\frac{7}{12}$, $\frac{11}{36}$, and $\frac{1}{9}$

    (A) 12   (B) 36   (C) 108   (D) 324   (E) 432

29. $\frac{3}{7}$, $\frac{5}{21}$, and $\frac{2}{3}$

    (A) 21   (B) 42   (C) 31   (D) 63   (E) 441

30. $\dfrac{13}{16}, \dfrac{5}{8},$ and $\dfrac{1}{4}$

    (A) 4   (B) 8   (C) 16   (D) 32   (E) 64

Adding Fractions with Different Denominators

DIRECTIONS: Add and write the answer in simplest form.

31. $\dfrac{1}{3} + \dfrac{5}{12} =$

    (A) $\dfrac{2}{5}$ (B) $\dfrac{1}{2}$ (C) $\dfrac{9}{12}$ (D) $\dfrac{3}{4}$ (E) $1\dfrac{1}{3}$

32. $3\dfrac{5}{9} + 2\dfrac{1}{3} =$

    (A) $5\dfrac{1}{2}$ (B) $5\dfrac{2}{3}$ (C) $5\dfrac{8}{9}$ (D) $6\dfrac{1}{9}$ (E) $6\dfrac{2}{3}$

33. $12\dfrac{9}{16} + 17\dfrac{3}{4} + 8\dfrac{1}{8} =$

    (A) $37\dfrac{7}{16}$ (B) $38\dfrac{7}{16}$ (C) $38\dfrac{1}{2}$ (D) $38\dfrac{2}{3}$ (E) $39\dfrac{3}{16}$

34. $28\dfrac{4}{5} + 11\dfrac{16}{25} =$

    (A) $39\dfrac{2}{3}$ (B) $39\dfrac{4}{5}$ (C) $40\dfrac{9}{25}$ (D) $40\dfrac{2}{5}$ (E) $40\dfrac{11}{25}$

35. $2\dfrac{1}{8} + 1\dfrac{3}{16} + \dfrac{5}{12} =$

    (A) $3\dfrac{35}{48}$ (B) $3\dfrac{3}{4}$ (C) $3\dfrac{19}{24}$ (D) $3\dfrac{13}{16}$ (E) $4\dfrac{1}{12}$

Subtracting Fractions with Different Denominators

DIRECTIONS: Subtract and write the answer in simplest form.

36. $8\dfrac{9}{12} - 2\dfrac{2}{3} =$

    (A) $6\dfrac{1}{12}$ (B) $6\dfrac{1}{6}$ (C) $6\dfrac{1}{3}$ (D) $6\dfrac{7}{12}$ (E) $6\dfrac{2}{3}$

37. $185\dfrac{11}{15} - 107\dfrac{2}{5} =$

    (A) $77\dfrac{2}{15}$ (B) $78\dfrac{1}{5}$ (C) $78\dfrac{3}{10}$ (D) $78\dfrac{1}{3}$ (E) $78\dfrac{9}{15}$

38. $34\dfrac{2}{6} - 16\dfrac{5}{6} =$

    (A) 16 (B) $16\dfrac{1}{3}$ (C) $17\dfrac{1}{2}$ (D) 17 (E) $17\dfrac{5}{6}$

39. $3\dfrac{11}{48} - 2\dfrac{3}{16} =$

    (A) $\dfrac{47}{48}$ (B) $1\dfrac{1}{48}$ (C) $1\dfrac{1}{24}$ (D) $1\dfrac{8}{48}$ (E) $1\dfrac{7}{24}$

40. $81\dfrac{4}{21} - 31\dfrac{1}{3} =$

    (A) $47\dfrac{3}{7}$ (B) $49\dfrac{6}{7}$ (C) $49\dfrac{1}{6}$ (D) $49\dfrac{5}{7}$ (E) $49\dfrac{13}{21}$

Multiplying Fractions

DIRECTIONS: Multiply and reduce the answer.

41. $\dfrac{2}{3} \times \dfrac{4}{5} =$

    (A) $\dfrac{6}{8}$ (B) $\dfrac{3}{4}$ (C) $\dfrac{8}{15}$ (D) $\dfrac{10}{12}$ (E) $\dfrac{6}{5}$

42. $\frac{7}{10} \times \frac{4}{21} =$

(A) $\frac{2}{15}$ (B) $\frac{11}{31}$ (C) $\frac{28}{210}$ (D) $\frac{1}{6}$ (E) $\frac{4}{15}$

43. $5\frac{1}{3} \times \frac{3}{8} =$

(A) $\frac{4}{11}$ (B) 2 (C) $\frac{8}{5}$ (D) $5\frac{1}{8}$ (E) $5\frac{17}{24}$

44. $6\frac{1}{2} \times 3 =$

(A) $9\frac{1}{2}$ (B) $\frac{1}{6}$ (C) $19\frac{1}{2}$ (D) 20 (E) $12\frac{1}{2}$

45. $3\frac{1}{4} \times 2\frac{1}{3} =$

(A) $5\frac{7}{12}$ (B) $6\frac{2}{7}$ (C) $6\frac{5}{7}$ (D) $7\frac{7}{12}$ (E) $7\frac{11}{12}$

Dividing Fractions

DIRECTIONS: Divide and reduce the answer.

46. $\frac{3}{16} \div \frac{3}{4} =$

(A) $\frac{9}{64}$ (B) $\frac{1}{4}$ (C) $\frac{6}{16}$ (D) $\frac{9}{16}$ (E) $\frac{3}{4}$

47. $\frac{4}{9} \div \frac{2}{3} =$

(A) $\frac{1}{3}$ (B) $\frac{1}{2}$ (C) $\frac{2}{3}$ (D) $\frac{7}{11}$ (E) $\frac{8}{9}$

48. $5\frac{1}{4} \div \frac{7}{10} =$

(A) $2\frac{4}{7}$ (B) $3\frac{27}{40}$ (C) $5\frac{19}{20}$ (D) $7\frac{1}{2}$ (E) $8\frac{1}{4}$

49. $4\dfrac{2}{3} \div \dfrac{7}{9} =$

   (A) $2\dfrac{24}{27}$ (B) $3\dfrac{2}{9}$ (C) $4\dfrac{14}{27}$ (D) $5\dfrac{12}{27}$ (E) 6

50. $3\dfrac{2}{5} \div 1\dfrac{7}{10} =$

   (A) 2 (B) $3\dfrac{4}{7}$ (C) $4\dfrac{7}{25}$ (D) $5\dfrac{1}{10}$ (E) $5\dfrac{2}{7}$

DECIMALS

When we divide the denominator of a fraction into its numerator, the result is a **decimal**. The decimal is based upon a fraction with a denominator of 10, 100, 1,000, … and is written with a **decimal point**. Whole numbers are placed to the left of the decimal point where the first place to the left is the units place; the second to the left is the tens; the third to the left is the hundreds, etc. The fractions are placed on the right where the first place to the right is the tenths; the second to the right is the hundredths, etc.

EXAMPLES

$$12\dfrac{3}{10} = 12.3 \qquad 4\dfrac{17}{100} = 4.17 \qquad \dfrac{3}{100} = .03$$

Since a **rational number** is of the form $\dfrac{a}{b}$, $b \neq 0$, then all rational numbers can be expressed as decimals by dividing b into a. The result is either a **terminating decimal**, meaning that b divides a with a remainder of 0 after a certain point; or a **repeating decimal**, meaning that b continues to divide a so that the decimal has a repeating pattern of integers.

EXAMPLES

   (A) $\dfrac{1}{2} = .5$

   (B) $\dfrac{1}{3} = .333…$

   (C) $\dfrac{11}{16} = .6875$

   (D) $\dfrac{2}{7} = .285714285714…$

(A) and (C) are terminating decimals; (B) and (D) are repeating decimals. This explanation allows us to define **irrational numbers** as numbers whose decimal form is non-terminating and non-repeating, e.g.,

$$\sqrt{2} = 1.414...$$
$$\sqrt{3} = 1.732...$$

PROBLEM

Express $-\frac{10}{20}$ as a decimal.

SOLUTION

$$-\frac{10}{20} = -\frac{50}{100} = -.5$$

PROBLEM

Write $\frac{2}{7}$ as a repeating decimal.

SOLUTION

To write a fraction as a repeating decimal divide the numerator by the denominator until a pattern of repeated digits appears.

$$2 \div 7 = .285714285714...$$

Identify the entire portion of the decimal which is repeated. The repeating decimal can then be written in the shortened form:

$$\frac{2}{7} = .\overline{285714}$$

OPERATIONS WITH DECIMALS

A) **To add numbers containing decimals**, write the numbers in a column making sure the decimal points are lined up, one beneath the other. Add the numbers as usual, placing the decimal point in the sum so that it is still in line with the others. It is important not to mix the digits in the tenths place with the digits in the hundredths place, and so on.

EXAMPLES

$$2.558 + 6.391 \qquad\qquad 57.51 + 6.2$$

$$
\begin{array}{r}
2.558 \\
+\ 6.391 \\
\hline
8.949
\end{array}
\qquad\qquad
\begin{array}{r}
57.51 \\
+\ 6.20 \\
\hline
63.71
\end{array}
$$

Similarly with subtraction,

$$78.54 - 21.33 \qquad\qquad 7.11 - 4.2$$

$$\begin{array}{r} 78.54 \\ -\,21.33 \\ \hline 57.21 \end{array} \qquad\qquad \begin{array}{r} 7.11 \\ -\,4.20 \\ \hline 2.91 \end{array}$$

Note that if two numbers differ according to the number of digits to the right of the decimal point, zeros must be added.

$$.63 - .214 \qquad\qquad 15.224 - 3.6891$$

$$\begin{array}{r} .630 \\ -\,.214 \\ \hline .416 \end{array} \qquad\qquad \begin{array}{r} 15.2240 \\ -\,3.6891 \\ \hline 11.5349 \end{array}$$

B) **To multiply numbers with decimals**, simply multiply as usual. Then, to figure out the number of decimal places that belong in the product, find the total number of decimal places in the numbers being multiplied.

EXAMPLES

6.555	(3 decimal places)	5.32	(2 decimal places)
× 4.5	(1 decimal place)	× .04	(2 decimal places)

$$\begin{array}{r} 6.555 \\ \times\; 4.5 \\ \hline 32775 \\ 26220 \\ \hline 294975 \end{array} \qquad\qquad \begin{array}{r} 5.32 \\ \times\; .04 \\ \hline 2128 \\ 000 \\ \hline 2128 \end{array}$$

29.4975 (4 decimal places)   .2128 (4 decimal places)

C) **To divide numbers with decimals**, you must first make the divisor a whole number by moving the decimal point the appropriate number of places to the right. The decimal point of the dividend should also be moved the same number of places. Place a decimal point in the quotient, directly in line with the decimal point in the dividend.

EXAMPLES

$$12.92 \div 3.4 \qquad\qquad 40.376 \div 7.21$$

$$\begin{array}{r} 3.8 \\ 3.4.\overline{)\,12.9.2} \\ -102 \\ \hline 272 \\ -272 \\ \hline 0 \end{array} \qquad\qquad \begin{array}{r} 5.6 \\ 7.21.\overline{)\,40.37.6} \\ -3605 \\ \hline 4326 \\ -4326 \\ \hline 0 \end{array}$$

If the question asks you to find the correct answer to two decimal places, simply divide until you have three decimal places and then round off. If the third decimal place is a 5 or larger, the number in the second decimal place is increased by 1. If the third decimal place is less than 5, that number is simply dropped.

Find the answer to the following to two decimal places:

(1) $44.3 \div 3$ (2) $56.99 \div 6$

SOLUTION

(1)
```
        14.766
    3) 44.300
       -3
       ___
       14
      -12
      ___
       23
      -21
      ___
       20
      -18
      ___
       20
      -18
      ___
        2
```

(2)
```
        9.498
    6) 56.990
      -54
      ___
       29
      -24
      ___
       59
      -54
      ___
       50
      -48
      ___
        2
```

14.766 can be rounded off to 14.77

9.498 can be rounded off to 9.50

D) When comparing two numbers with decimals to see which is the larger, first look at the tenths place. The larger digit in this place represents the larger number. If the two digits are the same, however, take a look at the digits in the hundredths place, and so on.

EXAMPLES

.518 and .216

.723 and .726

5 is larger than 2, therefore .518 is larger than .216

6 is larger than 3, therefore .726 is larger than .723

DRILL: DECIMALS

Addition

DIRECTIONS: Solve the following equations.

1. $1.032 + 0.987 + 3.07 =$

(A) 4.089   (B) 5.089   (C) 5.189   (D) 6.189   (E) 13.972

2. $132.03 + 97.1483 =$

   (A)   98.4686   (B)   110.3513
   (C)   209.1783   (D)   229.1486
   (E)   229.1783

3. $7.1 + 0.62 + 4.03827 + 5.183 =$

   (A)   0.2315127   (B)   16.45433
   (C)   16.94127   (D)   18.561
   (E)   40.4543

4. $8 + 17.43 + 9.2 =$

   (A)   34.63   (B)   34.86   (C)   35.63   (D)   176.63   (E)   189.43

5. $1,036.173 + 289.04 =$

   (A)   382.6573   (B)   392.6573
   (C)   1,065.077   (D)   1,325.213
   (E)   3,926.573

Subtraction

DIRECTIONS: Solve the following equations.

6. $3.972 - 2.04 =$

   (A)   1.932   (B)   1.942   (C)   1.976   (D)   2.013   (E)   2.113

7. $16.047 - 13.06 =$

   (A)   2.887   (B)   2.987   (C)   3.041   (D)   3.141   (E)   4.741

8. $87.4 - 56.27 =$

   (A)   30.27   (B)   30.67   (C)   31.1   (D)   31.13   (E)   31.27

9. $1{,}046.8 - 639.14 =$

    (A) 303.84   (B) 313.74   (C) 407.66   (D) 489.74   (E) 535.54

10. $10{,}000 - 842.91 =$

    (A) 157.09   (B) 942.91   (C) 5,236.09 (D) 9,057.91 (E) 9,157.09

Multiplication

DIRECTIONS: Solve the following equations.

11. $1.03 \times 2.6 =$

    (A) 2.18   (B) 2.678   (C) 2.78   (D) 3.38   (E) 3.63

12. $93 \times 4.2 =$

    (A) 39.06   (B) 97.2   (C) 223.2   (D) 390.6   (E) 3,906

13. $0.04 \times 0.23 =$

    (A) 0.0092   (B) 0.092   (C) 0.27   (D) 0.87   (E) 0.920

14. $0.0186 \times 0.03 =$

    (A) 0.000348   (B) 0.000558
    (C) 0.0548   (D) 0.0848
    (E) 0.558

15. $51.2 \times 0.17 =$

    (A) 5.29   (B) 8.534   (C) 8.704   (D) 36.352   (E) 36.991

Division

DIRECTIONS: Solve the following equations.

16. $123.39 \div 3 =$

    (A) 31.12   (B) 41.13   (C) 401.13   (D) 411.3   (E) 4,113

17. $1{,}428.6 \div 6 =$

   (A) 0.2381   (B) 2.381   (C) 23.81   (D) 238.1   (E) 2,381

18. $25.2 \div 0.3 =$

   (A) 0.84   (B) 8.04   (C) 8.4   (D) 84   (E) 840

19. $14.95 \div 6.5 =$

   (A) 2.3   (B) 20.3   (C) 23   (D) 230   (E) 2,300

20. $46.33 \div 1.13 =$

   (A) 0.41   (B) 4.1   (C) 41   (D) 410   (E) 4,100

Comparing

DIRECTIONS: Solve the following equations.

21. Which is the **largest** number in this set—{0.8, 0.823, 0.089, 0.807, 0.852}?

   (A) 0.8   (B) 0.823   (C) 0.089   (D) 0.807   (E) 0.852

22. Which is the **smallest** number in this set—{32.98, 32.099, 32.047, 32.5, 32.304}?

   (A) 32.98   (B) 32.099   (C) 32.047   (D) 32.5   (E) 32.304

23. In which set below are the numbers arranged correctly from smallest to largest?

   (A)   {0.98, 0.9, 0.993}   (B)   {0.113, 0.3, 0.31}
   (C)   {7.04, 7.26, 7.2}   (D)   {0.006, 0.061, 0.06}
   (E)   {12.84, 12.801, 12.6}

24. In which set below are the numbers arranged correctly from largest to smallest?

   (A)   {1.018, 1.63, 1.368}   (B)   {4.219, 4.29, 4.9}
   (C)   {0.62, 0.6043, 0.643}   (D)   {16.34, 16.304, 16.3}
   (E)   {12.98, 12.601, 12.86}

25. Which is the **largest** number in this set—{0.87, 0.89, 0.889, 0.8, 0.987}?

    (A) 0.87   (B) 0.89   (C) 0.889   (D) 0.8   (E) 0.987

Changing a Fraction to a Decimal

DIRECTIONS: Solve the following equations.

26. What is $\frac{1}{4}$ written as a decimal?

    (A) 1.4   (B) 0.14   (C) 0.2   (D) 0.25   (E) 0.3

27. What is $\frac{3}{5}$ written as a decimal?

    (A) 0.3   (B) 0.35   (C) 0.6   (D) 0.65   (E) 0.8

28. What is $\frac{7}{20}$ written as a decimal?

    (A) 0.35   (B) 0.4   (C) 0.72   (D) 0.75   (E) 0.9

29. What is $\frac{2}{3}$ written as a decimal?

    (A) 0.23   (B) 0.33   (C) 0.5   (D) 0.6   (E) $0.6\overline{6}$

30. What is $\frac{11}{25}$ written as a decimal?

    (A) 0.1125   (B) 0.25   (C) 0.4   (D) 0.44   (E) 0.5

PERCENTAGES

A **percent** is a way of expressing the relationship between part and whole, where whole is defined as 100%. A percent can be defined by a fraction with a denominator of 100. Decimals can also represent a percent. For instance,

$$56\% = 0.56 = \frac{56}{100}$$

PROBLEM

Compute the value of

(1) 90% of 400   (3) 50% of 500

(2) 180% of 400   (4) 200% of 4

SOLUTION

The symbol % means per hundred, therefore $5\% = \frac{5}{100}$

(1) 90% of 400 = 90 ÷ 100 × 400 = 90 × 4 = 360

(2) 180% of 400 = 180 ÷ 100 × 400 = 180 × 4 = 720

(3) 50% of 500 = 50 ÷ 100 × 500 = 50 × 5 = 250

(4) 200% of 4 = 200 ÷ 100 × 4 = 2 × 4 = 8

PROBLEM

What percent of

(1) 100 is 99.5   (2) 200 is 4

SOLUTION

(1) $99.5 = x \times 100$

$99.5 = 100x$

$.995 = x$; but this is the value of x per hundred. Therefore, $99.5\% = x$

(2) $4 = x \times 200$

$4 = 200x$

$.02 = x$. Again this must be changed to percent, so $2\% = x$

EQUIVALENT FORMS OF A NUMBER

Some problems may call for converting numbers into an equivalent or simplified form in order to make the solution more convenient.

A) **Converting a fraction to a decimal:**

$\frac{1}{2} = 0.50$

Divide the numerator by the denominator:

```
      .50
  2)1.00
     -10
      00
```

B) **Converting a number to a percent:**

$0.50 = 50\%$

Multiply by 100:

$0.50 = (0.50 \times 100)\% = 50\%$

C) **Converting a percent to a decimal:**

$30\% = 0.30$

Divide by 100:

$$30\% = 30 \div 100 = 0.30$$

D) **Converting a decimal to a fraction:**

$$0.500 = \frac{1}{2}$$

Convert .500 to $\frac{500}{1000}$ and then simplify the fraction by dividing the numerator and denominator by common factors:

$$\frac{\cancel{2} \times \cancel{2} \times \cancel{5} \times \cancel{5} \times \cancel{5}}{\cancel{2} \times \cancel{2} \times 2 \times \cancel{5} \times \cancel{5} \times \cancel{5}}$$

and then cancel out the common numbers to get $\frac{1}{2}$.

PROBLEM

Express

(1)   1.65 as a percent

(2)   0.7 as a fraction

(3) $-\frac{10}{20}$ as a decimal

(4) $\frac{4}{2}$ as an integer

SOLUTION

(1) $1.65 \times 100 = 165\%$

(2) $0.7 = \frac{7}{10}$

(3) $-\frac{10}{20} = -0.5$

(4) $\frac{4}{2} = 2$

DRILL: PERCENTAGES

Finding Percents

DIRECTIONS: **Solve to find the correct percentages.**

1.   Find 3% of 80.

(A) 0.24   (B) 2.4   (C) 24   (D) 240   (E) 2,400

2.   Find 50% of 182.

(A) 9   (B) 90   (C) 91   (D) 910   (E) 9,100

3. Find 83% of 166.

    (A) 0.137   (B) 1.377   (C) 13.778   (D) 137   (E) 137.78

4. Find 125% of 400.

    (A) 425   (B) 500   (C) 525   (D) 600   (E) 825

5. Find 300% of 4.

    (A) 12   (B) 120   (C) 1,200   (D) 12,000   (E) 120,000

6. Forty-eight percent of the 1,200 students at Central High are males. How many male students are there at Central High?

    (A) 57   (B) 576   (C) 580   (D) 600   (E) 648

7. For 35% of the last 40 days, there has been measurable rainfall. How many days out of the last 40 days have had measurable rainfall?

    (A) 14   (B) 20   (C) 25   (D) 35   (E) 40

8. Of every 1,000 people who take a certain medicine, 0.2% develop severe side effects. How many people out of every 1,000 who take the medicine develop the side effects?

    (A) 0.2   (B) 2   (C) 20   (D) 22   (E) 200

9. Of 220 applicants for a job, 75% were offered an initial interview. How many people were offered an initial interview?

    (A) 75   (B) 110   (C) 120   (D) 155   (E) 165

10. Find 0.05% of 4,000.

    (A) 0.05   (B) 0.5   (C) 2   (D) 20   (E) 400

Changing Percents to Fractions

DIRECTIONS: Solve to find the correct fractions.

11. What is 25% written as a fraction?

    (A) $\frac{1}{25}$ (B) $\frac{1}{5}$ (C) $\frac{1}{4}$ (D) $\frac{1}{3}$ (E) $\frac{1}{2}$

12. What is $33\frac{1}{3}$% written as a fraction?

    (A) $\frac{1}{4}$ (B) $\frac{1}{3}$ (C) $\frac{1}{2}$ (D) $\frac{2}{3}$ (E) $\frac{5}{9}$

13. What is 200% written as a fraction?

    (A) $\frac{1}{2}$ (B) $\frac{2}{1}$ (C) $\frac{20}{1}$ (D) $\frac{200}{1}$ (E) $\frac{2,000}{1}$

14. What is 84% written as a fraction?

    (A) $\frac{1}{84}$ (B) $\frac{4}{8}$ (C) $\frac{17}{25}$ (D) $\frac{21}{25}$ (E) $\frac{44}{50}$

15. What is 2% written as a fraction?

    (A) $\frac{1}{50}$ (B) $\frac{1}{25}$ (C) $\frac{1}{10}$ (D) $\frac{1}{4}$ (E) $\frac{1}{2}$

Changing Fractions to Percents

DIRECTIONS: Solve to find the following percentages.

16. What is $\frac{2}{3}$ written as a percent?

    (A) 23%   (B) 32%   (C) $33\frac{1}{3}$%   (D) $57\frac{1}{3}$%   (E) $66\frac{2}{3}$%

17. What is $\frac{3}{5}$ written as a percent?

    (A) 30%   (B) 35%   (C) 53%   (D) 60%   (E) 65%

18. What is $\frac{17}{20}$ written as a percent?

    (A) 17%   (B) 70%   (C) 75%   (D) 80%   (E) 85%

19. What is $\frac{45}{50}$ written as a percent?

    (A) 45%   (B) 50%   (C) 90%   (D) 95%   (E) 97%

20. What is $1\frac{1}{4}$ written as a percent?

    (A) 114%   (B) 120%   (C) 125%   (D) 127%   (E) 133%

Changing Percents to Decimals

DIRECTIONS: Convert the percentages to decimals.

21. What is 42% written as a decimal?

    (A) 0.42   (B) 4.2   (C) 42   (D) 420   (E) 422

22. What is 0.3% written as a decimal?

    (A) 0.0003   (B) 0.003   (C) 0.03   (D) 0.3   (E) 3

23. What is 8% written as a decimal?

    (A) 0.0008   (B) 0.008   (C) 0.08   (D) 0.80   (E) 8

24. What is 175% written as a decimal?

    (A) 0.175   (B) 1.75   (C) 17.5   (D) 175   (E) 17,500

25. What is 34% written as a decimal?

    (A) 0.00034   (B) 0.0034   (C) 0.034   (D) 0.34   (E) 3.4

Changing Decimals to Percents

DIRECTIONS: Convert the following decimals to percents.

26. What is 0.43 written as a percent?

    (A) 0.0043% (B) 0.043% (C) 4.3% (D) 43% (E) 430%

27. What is 1 written as a percent?

    (A) 1% (B) 10% (C) 100% (D) 111% (E) 150%

28. What is 0.08 written as a percent?

    (A) 0.08% (B) 8% (C) 8.8% (D) 80% (E) 800%

29. What is 3.4 written as a percent?

    (A) 0.0034% (B) 3.4% (C) 34% (D) 304% (E) 340%

30. What is 0.645 written as a percent?

    (A) 64.5% (B) 65% (C) 69% (D) 70% (E) 645%

RADICALS

The **square root** of a number is a number that when multiplied by itself results in the original number. Thus, the square root of 81 is 9 since $9 \times 9 = 81$. However, -9 is also a root of 81 since $(-9)(-9) = 81$. Every positive number will have two roots. The principal root is the positive one. Zero has only one square root, while negative numbers do not have real numbers as their roots.

A **radical sign** indicates that the root of a number or expression will be taken. The **radicand** is the number of which the root will be taken. The **index** tells how many times the root needs to be multiplied by itself to equal the radicand, e.g.,

index↘
radical sign → $\sqrt{}$ radicand

(1) $\sqrt[3]{64}$

   3 is the index and 64 is the radicand. Since $4 \times 4 \times 4 = 64$, then $\sqrt[3]{64} = 4$.

(2) $\sqrt[5]{32}$;

     5 is the index and 32 is the radicand. Since $2 \times 2 \times 2 \times 2 \times 2 = 32$, then $\sqrt[5]{32} = 2$.

OPERATIONS WITH RADICALS

A) **To multiply two or more radicals**, we utilize the law that states,

$$\sqrt{a} \times \sqrt{b} = \sqrt{ab}.$$

Simply multiply the whole numbers as usual. Then, multiply the radicands and put the product under the radical sign and simplify, e.g.,

(1) $\sqrt{12} \times \sqrt{5} = \sqrt{60} = 2\sqrt{15}$

(2) $3\sqrt{2} \times 4\sqrt{8} = 12\sqrt{16} = 48$

(3) $2\sqrt{10} \times 6\sqrt{5} = 12\sqrt{50} = 60\sqrt{2}$

B) **To divide radicals**, simplify both the numerator and the denominator. By multiplying the radical in the denominator by itself, you can make the denominator a rational number. The numerator, however, must also be multiplied by this radical so that the value of the expression does not change. You must choose as many factors as necessary to rationalize the denominator, e.g.,

(1) $\dfrac{\sqrt{128}}{\sqrt{2}} = \dfrac{\sqrt{64} \times \sqrt{2}}{\sqrt{2}} = \dfrac{8\sqrt{2}}{\sqrt{2}} = 8$

(2) $\dfrac{\sqrt{10}}{\sqrt{3}} = \dfrac{\sqrt{10} \times \sqrt{3}}{\sqrt{3} \times \sqrt{3}} = \dfrac{\sqrt{30}}{3}$

(3) $\dfrac{\sqrt{8}}{2\sqrt{3}} = \dfrac{\sqrt{8} \times \sqrt{3}}{2\sqrt{3} \times \sqrt{3}} = \dfrac{\sqrt{24}}{2 \times 3} = \dfrac{2\sqrt{6}}{6} = \dfrac{\sqrt{6}}{3}$

C) **To add two or more radicals**, the radicals must have the same index and the same radicand. Only where the radicals are simplified can these similarities be determined.

EXAMPLES

(1) $6\sqrt{2} + 2\sqrt{2} = (6 + 2)\sqrt{2} = 8\sqrt{2}$

(2) $\sqrt{27} + 5\sqrt{3} = \sqrt{9}\sqrt{3} + 5\sqrt{3} = 3\sqrt{3} + 5\sqrt{3} = 8\sqrt{3}$

(3) $7\sqrt{3} + 8\sqrt{2} + 5\sqrt{3} = 12\sqrt{3} + 8\sqrt{2}$

Similarly, to subtract,

(1) $12\sqrt{3} - 7\sqrt{3} = (12 - 7)\sqrt{3} = 5\sqrt{3}$

(2) $\sqrt{80} - \sqrt{20} = \sqrt{16}\sqrt{5} - \sqrt{4}\sqrt{5} = 4\sqrt{5} - 2\sqrt{5} = 2\sqrt{5}$

(3) $\sqrt{50} - \sqrt{3} = 5\sqrt{2} - \sqrt{3}$

DRILL: RADICALS

Multiplication

DIRECTIONS: Multiply and simplify each answer.

1. $\sqrt{6} \times \sqrt{5} =$

   (A) $\sqrt{11}$ (B) $\sqrt{30}$ (C) $2\sqrt{5}$ (D) $3\sqrt{10}$ (E) $2\sqrt{3}$

2. $\sqrt{3} \times \sqrt{12} =$

   (A) 3   (B) $\sqrt{15}$ (C) $\sqrt{36}$ (D) 6   (E) 8

3. $\sqrt{7} \times \sqrt{7} =$

   (A) 7   (B) 49   (C) $\sqrt{14}$ (D) $2\sqrt{7}$ (E) $2\sqrt{14}$

4. $3\sqrt{5} \times 2\sqrt{5} =$

   (A) $5\sqrt{5}$ (B) 25   (C) 30   (D) $5\sqrt{25}$ (E) $6\sqrt{5}$

5. $4\sqrt{6} \times \sqrt{2} =$

   (A) $4\sqrt{8}$ (B) $8\sqrt{2}$ (C) $5\sqrt{8}$ (D) $4\sqrt{12}$ (E) $8\sqrt{3}$

Division

DIRECTIONS: Divide and simplify the answer.

6. $\sqrt{10} \div \sqrt{2} =$

   (A) $\sqrt{8}$ (B) $2\sqrt{2}$ (C) $\sqrt{5}$ (D) $2\sqrt{5}$ (E) $2\sqrt{3}$

7. $\sqrt{30} \div \sqrt{15} =$

   (A) $\sqrt{2}$ (B) $\sqrt{45}$ (C) $3\sqrt{5}$ (D) $\sqrt{15}$ (E) $5\sqrt{3}$

8. $\sqrt{100} \div \sqrt{25}$

    (A) $\sqrt{4}$ (B) $5\sqrt{5}$ (C) $5\sqrt{3}$ (D) 2   (E) 4

9. $\sqrt{48} \div \sqrt{8} =$

    (A) $4\sqrt{3}$ (B) $3\sqrt{2}$ (C) $\sqrt{6}$ (D) 6   (E) 12

10. $3\sqrt{12} \div \sqrt{3} =$

    (A) $3\sqrt{15}$ (B) 6   (C) 9   (D) 12   (E) $3\sqrt{36}$

ADDITION

DIRECTIONS: Simplify each radical and add.

11. $\sqrt{7} + 3\sqrt{7} =$

    (A) $3\sqrt{7}$ (B) $4\sqrt{7}$ (C) $3\sqrt{14}$ (D) $4\sqrt{14}$ (E) $3\sqrt{21}$

12. $\sqrt{5} + 6\sqrt{5} + 3\sqrt{5} =$

    (A) $9\sqrt{5}$ (B) $9\sqrt{15}$ (C) $5\sqrt{10}$ (D) $10\sqrt{5}$ (E) $18\sqrt{15}$

13. $3\sqrt{32} + 2\sqrt{2} =$

    (A) $5\sqrt{2}$ (B) $\sqrt{34}$ (C) $14\sqrt{2}$ (D) $5\sqrt{34}$ (E) $6\sqrt{64}$

14. $6\sqrt{15} + 8\sqrt{15} + 16\sqrt{15} =$

    (A) $15\sqrt{30}$ (B) $30\sqrt{45}$ (C) $30\sqrt{30}$ (D) $15\sqrt{45}$ (E) $30\sqrt{15}$

15. $6\sqrt{5} + 2\sqrt{45} =$

    (A) $12\sqrt{5}$ (B) $8\sqrt{50}$ (C) $40\sqrt{2}$ (D) $12\sqrt{50}$ (E) $8\sqrt{5}$

Subtraction

DIRECTIONS: Simplify each radical and subtract.

16. $8\sqrt{5} - 6\sqrt{5} =$

(A) $2\sqrt{5}$ (B) $3\sqrt{5}$ (C) $4\sqrt{5}$ (D) $14\sqrt{5}$ (E) $48\sqrt{5}$

17. $16\sqrt{33} - 5\sqrt{33} =$

(A) $3\sqrt{33}$ (B) $33\sqrt{11}$ (C) $11\sqrt{33}$ (D) $11\sqrt{0}$ (E) $\sqrt{33}$

18. $14\sqrt{2} - 19\sqrt{2} =$

(A) $5\sqrt{2}$ (B) $-5\sqrt{2}$ (C) $-33\sqrt{2}$ (D) $33\sqrt{2}$ (E) $-4\sqrt{2}$

19. $10\sqrt{2} - 3\sqrt{8} =$

(A) $6\sqrt{6}$ (B) $-2\sqrt{2}$ (C) $7\sqrt{6}$ (D) $4\sqrt{2}$ (E) $-6\sqrt{6}$

20. $4\sqrt{3} - 2\sqrt{12} =$

(A) $-2\sqrt{9}$ (B) $-6\sqrt{15}$ (C) 0 (D) $6\sqrt{15}$ (E) $2\sqrt{12}$

EXPONENTS

When a number is multiplied by itself a specific number of times, it is said to be **raised to a power**. The way this is written is $a^n = b$ where a is the number or **base**, n is the **exponent** or **power** that indicates the number of times the base is to be multiplied by itself, and b is the product of this multiplication.

In the expression 3^2, 3 is the base and 2 is the exponent. This means that 3 is multiplied by itself 2 times and the product is 9.

An exponent can be either positive or negative. A negative exponent implies a fraction such that if n is a negative integer

$$a^{-n} = \frac{1}{a^n}, \ a \neq 0. \ \text{So}, \ 2^{-4} - \frac{1}{2^4} = \frac{1}{16}.$$

An exponent that is 0 gives a result of 1, assuming that the base is not equal to 0.

$$a^0 = 1, \ a \neq 0.$$

An exponent can also be a fraction. If m and n are positive integers,

$$a^{\frac{m}{n}} = \sqrt[n]{a^m}$$

The numerator remains the exponent of a, but the denominator tells what root to take. For example,

(1) $4^{\frac{3}{2}} = \sqrt[2]{4^3} = \sqrt{64} = 8$ (2) $3^{\frac{4}{2}} = \sqrt[2]{3^4} = \sqrt{81} = 9$

If a fractional exponent were negative, the same operation would take place, but the result would be a fraction. For example,

(1) $27^{-\frac{2}{3}} = \dfrac{1}{27^{\frac{2}{3}}} = \dfrac{1}{\sqrt[3]{27^2}} = \dfrac{1}{\sqrt[3]{729}} = \dfrac{1}{9}$

PROBLEM

Simplify the following expressions:

(1) -3^{-2} (3) $\dfrac{-3}{4^{-1}}$

(2) $(-3)^{-2}$

SOLUTION

(1)   Here the exponent applies only to 3. Since
$$x^{-y} = \frac{1}{x^y}, -3^{-2} = -(3)^{-2} = -\left(\frac{1}{3^2}\right) = -\frac{1}{9}$$

(2)   In this case the exponent applies to the negative base. Thus,
$$(-3)^{-2} = \frac{1}{(-3)^2} = \frac{1}{(-3)(-3)} = \frac{1}{9}$$

(3) $\dfrac{-3}{4^{-1}} = \dfrac{-3}{\left(\dfrac{1}{4}\right)^1} = \dfrac{-3}{\dfrac{1^1}{4^1}} = \dfrac{-3}{\dfrac{1}{4}}$

Division by a fraction is equivalent to multiplication by that fraction's reciprocal, thus
$$\frac{-3}{\frac{1}{4}} = -3 \times \frac{4}{1} = -12 \text{ and } \frac{-3}{4^{-1}} = -12$$

General Laws of Exponents

A) $a^p a^q = a^{p+q}$

  $4^2 4^3 = 4^{2+3} = 1{,}024$

B) $(a^p)^q = a^{pq}$

  $(2^3)^2 = 2^6 = 64$

C) $\dfrac{a^p}{a^q} = a^{p-q}$

  $\dfrac{3^6}{3^2} = 3^4 = 81$

D) $(ab)^p = a^p b^p$

$(3 \times 2)^2 = 3^2 \times 2^2 = (9)(4) = 36$

E) $\left(\dfrac{a}{b}\right)^p = \dfrac{a^p}{b^p}, b \neq 0$

$\left(\dfrac{4}{5}\right)^2 = \dfrac{4^2}{5^2} = \dfrac{16}{25}$

DRILL: EXPONENTS

Multiplication

DIRECTIONS: Simplify.

1. $4^6 \times 4^2 =$

   (A) 4^4 (B) 4^8 (C) 4^{12} (D) 16^8 (E) 16^{12}

2. $2^2 \times 2^5 \times 2^3 =$

   (A) 2^{10} (B) 4^{10} (C) 8^{10} (D) 2^{30} (E) 8^{30}

3. $6^6 \times 6^2 \times 6^4 =$

   (A) 18^8 (B) 18^{12} (C) 6^{12} (D) 6^{48} (E) 18^{48}

4. $a^4 b^2 \times a^3 b =$

   (A) ab (B) $2a^7 b^2$ (C) $2a^{12}b$ (D) $a^7 b^3$ (E) $a^7 b^2$

5. $m^8 n^3 \times m^2 n \times m^4 n^2 =$

   (A) $3m^{16}n^6$ (B) $m^{14}n^6$ (C) $3m^{17}n^5$ (D) $3m^{14}n^5$ (E) m^2

Division

DIRECTIONS: Simplify.

6. $6^5 \div 6^3 =$

    (A) 0   (B) 1   (C) 6   (D) 12   (E) 36

7. $11^8 \div 11^5 =$

    (A) 1^3 (B) 11^3 (C) 11^{13} (D) 11^{40} (E) 88^5

8. $x^{10}y^8 \div x^7 y^3 =$

    (A) $x^2 y^5$ (B) $x^3 y^4$ (C) $x^3 y^5$ (D) $x^2 y^4$ (E) $x^5 y^3$

9. $a^{14} \div a^9 =$

    (A) 1^5 (B) a^5 (C) $2a^5$ (D) a^{23} (E) $2a^{23}$

10. $c^{17}d^{12}e^4 \div c^{12}d^8 e =$

    (A) $c^4 d^5 e^3$ (B) $c^4 d^4 e^3$ (C) $c^5 d^8 e^4$ (D) $c^5 d^4 e^3$ (E) $c^5 d^4 e^4$

Power to a Power

DIRECTIONS: Simplify.

11. $(3^6)^2 =$

    (A) 3^4 (B) 3^8 (C) 3^{12} (D) 9^6 (E) 9^8

12. $(4^3)^5 =$

    (A) 4^2 (B) 2^{15} (C) 4^8 (D) 20^3 (E) 4^{15}

13. $(a^4 b^3)^2 =$

    (A) $(ab)^9$ (B) $a^8 b^6$ (C) $(ab)^{24}$ (D) $a^6 b^5$ (E) $2a^4 b^3$

14. $(r^3p^6)^3 =$

(A) r^9p^{18} (B) $(rp)^{12}$ (C) r^6p^9 (D) $3r^3p^6$ (E) $3r^9p^{18}$

15. $(m^6n^5q^3)^2 =$

(A) $2m^6n^5q^3$ (B) m^4n^3q (C) $m^8n^7q^5$ (D) $m^{12}n^{10}q^6$ (E) $2m^{12}n^{10}q^6$

MEAN, MEDIAN, MODE

MEAN

The mean is the arithmetic average. It is the sum of the variables divided by the total number of variables. For example, the mean of 4, 3, and 8 is

$$\frac{4+3+8}{3} = \frac{15}{3} = 5$$

PROBLEM

Find the mean salary for four company employees who make $5/hr., $8/hr., $12/hr., and $15/hr.

SOLUTION

The mean salary is the average.

$$\frac{\$5 + \$8 + \$12 + \$15}{4} = \frac{\$40}{4} = \$10/hr$$

PROBLEM

Find the mean length of five fish with lengths of 7.5 in., 7.75 in., 8.5 in., 8.5 in., 8.25 in.

SOLUTION

The mean length is the average length.

$$\frac{7.5 + 7.75 + 8.5 + 8.5 + 8.25}{5} = \frac{40.5}{5} = 8.1 \text{ in}$$

MEDIAN

The median is the middle value in a set when there is an odd number of values. There is an equal number of values larger and smaller than the median. When the set is an even number of values, the average of the two middle values is the median. For example:

The median of (2, 3, 5, 8, 9) is 5.

The median of (2, 3, 5, 9, 10, 11) is $\dfrac{5+9}{2} = 7$.

MODE

The mode is the most frequently occurring value in the set of values. For example, the mode of 4, 5, 8, 3, 8, 2 would be 8, since it occurs twice while the other values occur only once.

PROBLEM

For this series of observations find the mean, median, and mode.

500, 600, 800, 800, 900, 900, 900, 900, 900, 1,000, 1,100

SOLUTION

The mean is the value obtained by adding all the measurements and dividing by the number of measurements.

$$\frac{500 + 600 + 800 + 800 + 900 + 900 + 900 + 900 + 900 + 1,000 + 1,100}{11}$$

$$= \frac{9,300}{11} = 845.45.$$

The median is the value appearing in the middle. We have 11 values, so here the sixth, 900, is the median.

The mode is the value that appears most frequently. That is also 900, which has five appearances.

All three of these numbers are measures of central tendency. They describe the "middle" or "center" of the data.

PROBLEM

Nine rats run through a maze. The time each rat took to traverse the maze is recorded and these times (in minutes) are listed below.

1 min, 2.5 min, 3 min, 1.5 min, 2 min, 1.25 min, 1 min, .9 min, 30 min

Which of the three measures of central tendency would be the most appropriate in this case?

SOLUTION

We will calculate the three measures of central tendency and then compare them to determine which would be the most appropriate in describing these data.

The mean is the sum of the values listed divided by the number of values. In this case

$$\frac{1 + 2.5 + 3 + 1.5 + 2 + 1.25 + 1 + .9 + 30}{9} = \frac{43.15}{9} = 4.79.$$

The median is the "middle number" in an array of the values from the lowest to the highest.

$$0.9, 1.0, 1.0, 1.25, 1.5, 2.0, 2.5, 3.0, 30.0$$

The median is the fifth value in this ordered array or 1.5. There are four values larger than 1.5 and four values smaller than 1.5.

The mode is the most frequently occurring value in the sample. In this data set the mode is 1.0.

$$\text{mean} = 4.79$$

$$\text{median} = 1.5$$

$$\text{mode} = 1.0$$

The mean is not appropriate here. Only one rat took more than 4.79 minutes to run the maze and this rat took 30 minutes. We see that the mean has been distorted by this one large value.

The median or mode seems to describe this data set better and would be more appropriate to use.

DRILL: AVERAGES

Mean

DIRECTIONS: Find the mean of each set of numbers.

1. 18, 25, and 32

    (A) 3   (B) 25   (C) 50   (D) 75   (E) 150

2. $\frac{4}{9}, \frac{2}{3},$ and $\frac{5}{6}$

    (A) $\frac{11}{18}$ (B) $\frac{35}{54}$ (C) $\frac{41}{54}$ (D) $\frac{35}{18}$ (E) $\frac{54}{18}$

3. 97, 102, 116, and 137

    (A) 40   (B) 102   (C) 109   (D) 113   (E) 116

4. 12, 15, 18, 24, and 31

    (A) 18   (B) 19.3   (C) 20   (D) 25   (E) 100

5. 7, 4, 6, 3, 11, and 14

    (A) 5   (B) 6.5   (C) 7   (D) 7.5   (E) 8

Median

DIRECTIONS: Find the median value of each set of numbers.

6. 3, 8, and 6

   (A) 3   (B) 6   (C) 8   (D) 17   (E) 20

7. 19, 15, 21, 27, and 12

   (A) 19   (B) 15   (C) 21   (D) 27   (E) 94

8. $1\frac{2}{3}$, $1\frac{7}{8}$, $1\frac{3}{4}$, and $1\frac{5}{6}$

   (A) $1\frac{30}{48}$ (B) $1\frac{2}{3}$ (C) $1\frac{3}{4}$ (D) $1\frac{19}{24}$ (E) $1\frac{21}{24}$

9. 29, 18, 21, and 35

   (A) 29   (B) 18   (C) 21   (D) 35   (E) 25

10. 8, 15, 7, 12, 31, 3, and 28

   (A) 7   (B) 11.6   (C) 12   (D) 14.9   (E) 104

Mode

DIRECTIONS: Find the mode(s) of each set of numbers.

11. 1, 3, 7, 4, 3, and 8

   (A) 1   (B) 3   (C) 7   (D) 4   (E) None

12. 12, 19, 25, and 42

   (A) 12   (B) 19   (C) 25   (D) 42   (E) None

13. 16, 14, 12, 16, 30, and 28

   (A) 6   (B) 14   (C) 16   (D) $19.\overline{3}$ (E) None

14. 4, 3, 9, 2, 4, 5, and 2

    (A) 3 and 9 (B) 5 and 9 (C) 4 and 5 (D) 2 and 4 (E) None

15. 87, 42, 111, 116, 39, 111, 140, 116, 97, and 111

    (A) 111   (B) 116   (C) 39   (D) 140   (E) None

ARITHMETIC DRILLS

ANSWER KEY

Drill: Integers and Real Numbers

1.	(A)	9.	(E)	17.	(D)	25.	(D)
2.	(C)	10.	(B)	18.	(D)	26.	(D)
3.	(D)	11.	(B)	19.	(C)	27.	(B)
4.	(C)	12.	(E)	20.	(E)	28.	(C)
5.	(B)	13.	(C)	21.	(B)	29.	(A)
6.	(B)	14.	(A)	22.	(E)	30.	(C)
7.	(A)	15.	(B)	23.	(D)		
8.	(C)	16.	(B)	24.	(A)		

Drill: Fractions

1.	(D)	14.	(A)	27.	(D)	40.	(B)
2.	(A)	15.	(C)	28.	(B)	41.	(C)
3.	(D)	16.	(B)	29.	(A)	42.	(A)
4.	(E)	17.	(C)	30.	(C)	43.	(B)
5.	(C)	18.	(A)	31.	(D)	44.	(C)
6.	(D)	19.	(B)	32.	(C)	45.	(D)
7.	(D)	20.	(A)	33.	(B)	46.	(B)
8.	(B)	21.	(B)	34.	(E)	47.	(C)
9.	(A)	22.	(D)	35.	(A)	48.	(D)
10.	(E)	23.	(E)	36.	(A)	49.	(E)
11.	(D)	24.	(D)	37.	(D)	50.	(A)
12.	(E)	25.	(B)	38.	(E)		
13.	(C)	26.	(B)	39.	(C)		

Drill: Decimals

1.	(B)	9.	(C)	17.	(D)	25.	(E)
2.	(E)	10.	(E)	18.	(D)	26.	(D)
3.	(C)	11.	(B)	19.	(A)	27.	(C)
4.	(A)	12.	(D)	20.	(C)	28.	(A)
5.	(D)	13.	(A)	21.	(E)	29.	(E)
6.	(A)	14.	(B)	22.	(C)	30.	(D)
7.	(B)	15.	(C)	23.	(B)		
8.	(D)	16.	(B)	24.	(D)		

Drill: Percentages

1.	(B)	9.	(E)	17.	(D)	25.	(D)
2.	(C)	10.	(C)	18.	(E)	26.	(D)
3.	(E)	11.	(C)	19.	(C)	27.	(C)
4.	(B)	12.	(B)	20.	(C)	28.	(B)
5.	(A)	13.	(B)	21.	(A)	29.	(E)
6.	(B)	14.	(D)	22.	(B)	30.	(A)
7.	(A)	15.	(A)	23.	(C)		
8.	(B)	16.	(E)	24.	(B)		

Drill: Radicals

1.	(B)	6.	(C)	11.	(B)	16.	(A)
2.	(D)	7.	(A)	12.	(D)	17.	(C)
3.	(A)	8.	(D)	13.	(C)	18.	(B)
4.	(C)	9.	(C)	14.	(E)	19.	(D)
5.	(E)	10.	(B)	15.	(A)	20.	(C)

Drill: Exponents

1.	(B)	9.	(B)
2.	(A)	10.	(D)
3.	(C)	11.	(C)
4.	(D)	12.	(E)
5.	(B)	13.	(B)
6.	(E)	14.	(A)
7.	(B)	15.	(D)
8.	(C)		

Drill: Averages

1.	(B)	9.	(E)
2.	(B)	10.	(C)
3.	(D)	11.	(B)
4.	(C)	12.	(E)
5.	(D)	13.	(C)
6.	(B)	14.	(D)
7.	(A)	15.	(A)
8.	(D)		

II. ALGEBRA

In algebra, letters or variables are used to represent numbers. A **variable** is defined as a placeholder, which can take on any of several values at a given time. A **constant**, on the other hand, is a symbol which takes on only one value at a given time. A **term** is a constant, a variable, or a combination of constants and variables. For example: 7.76, $3x$, xyz, $\frac{5z}{x}$, $(0.99)x^2$ are terms. If a term is a combination of constants and variables, the constant part of the term is referred to as the **coefficient** of the variable. If a variable is written without a coefficient, the coefficient is assumed to be 1.

EXAMPLES

$3x^2$ y^3

coefficient: 3   coefficient: 1

variable: x variable: y

An **expression** is a collection of one or more terms. If the number of terms is greater than 1, the expression is said to be the sum of the terms.

EXAMPLES

$9, 9xy, 6x + \dfrac{x}{3}, 8yz - 2x$

An algebraic expression consisting of only one term is called a **monomial**; of two terms is called a **binomial**; of three terms is called a **trinomial**. In general, an algebraic expression consisting of two or more terms is called a **polynomial**.

OPERATIONS WITH POLYNOMIALS

A) **Addition of polynomials** is achieved by combining like terms, terms which differ only in their numerical coefficients, e.g.,

$$P(x) = (x^2 - 3x + 5) + (4x^2 + 6x - 3)$$

Note that the parentheses are used to distinguish the polynomials.

By using the commutative and associative laws, we can rewrite $P(x)$ as:

$$P(x) = (x^2 + 4x^2) + (6x - 3x) + (5 - 3)$$

Using the distributive law, $ab + ac = a(b + c)$, yields:

$$(1 + 4)x^2 + (6 - 3)x + (5 - 3)$$
$$= 5x^2 + 3x + 2$$

B) **Subtraction of two polynomials** is achieved by first changing the sign of all terms in the expression which are being subtracted and then adding this result to the other expression, e.g.,

$$(5x^2 + 4y^2 + 3z^2) - (4xy + 7y^2 - 3z^2 + 1)$$
$$= 5x^2 + 4y^2 + 3z^2 - 4xy - 7y^2 + 3z^2 - 1$$
$$= 5x^2 + (4y^2 - 7y^2) + (3z^2 + 3z^2) - 4xy - 1$$
$$= 5x^2 + (-3y^2) + 6z^2 - 4xy - 1$$

C) **Multiplication of two or more polynomials** is achieved by using the laws of exponents, the rules of signs, and the communicative and associative laws of multiplication. Begin by multiplying the coefficients and then multiply the variables according to the laws of exponents, e.g.,

$$(y^2)\,(5)\,(6y^2)\,(yz)\,(2z^2)$$
$$= (1)\,(5)\,(6)\,(1)\,(2)\,(y^2)\,(y^2)\,(yz)\,(z^2)$$
$$= 60[(y^2)\,(y^2)\,(y)]\,[(z)\,(z^2)]$$
$$= 60\,(y^5)\,(z^3)$$
$$= 60y5z^3$$

D) **Multiplication of a polynomial by a mononomial** is achieved by multiplying each term of the polynomial by the mononomial and combining the results, e.g.,

$$(4x^2 + 3y)\,(6xz^2)$$
$$= (4x^2)\,(6xz^2) + (3y)\,(6xz^2)$$
$$= 24x^3z^2 + 18xyz^2$$

E) **Multiplication of a polynomial by a polynomial** is achieved by multiplying each of the terms of one polynomial by each of the terms of the other polynomial and combining the results, e.g.,

$$(5y + z + 1)\,(y^2 + 2y)$$
$$= [(5y)\,(y^2) + (5y)\,(2y)] + [(z)\,(y^2) + (z)\,(2y)] + [(1)\,(y^2) + (1)\,(2y)]$$
$$= (5y^3 + 10y^2) + (y^2z + 2yz) + (y^2 + 2y)$$
$$= (5y^3) + (10y^2 + y^2) + (y^2z) + (2yz) + (2y)$$
$$= 5y^3 + 11y^2 + y^2z + 2yz + 2y$$

F) **Division of a monomial by a monomial** is achieved by first dividing the constant coefficients and the variable factors separately, and then multiplying these quotients, e.g.,

$$6xyz^2 \div 2y^2z$$
$$= \left(\frac{6}{2}\right)\left(\frac{x}{1}\right)\left(\frac{y}{y^2}\right)\left(\frac{z^2}{z}\right)$$
$$= 3xy^{-1}z$$
$$= \frac{3xz}{y}$$

G) **Division of a polynomial by a polynomial** is achieved by following the given procedure, called long division.

Step 1: The terms of both the polynomials are arranged in order of ascending or descending powers of one variable.

Step 2: The first term of the dividend is divided by the first term of the divisor which gives the first term of the quotient.

Step 3: This first term of the quotient is multiplied by the entire divisor and the result is subtracted from the dividend.

Step 4: Using the remainder obtained from Step 3 as the new dividend, Steps 2 and 3 are repeated until the remainder is zero or the degree of the remainder is less than the degree of the divisor.

Step 5: The result is written as follows:

$$\frac{\text{dividend}}{\text{divisor}} = \text{quotient} + \frac{\text{remainder}}{\text{divisor}}$$

$\text{divisor} \neq 0$

e.g., $(2x^2 + x + 6) \div (x + 1)$

$$\begin{array}{r} 2x - 1 \\ (x+1)\overline{\smash{\big)}\,2x^2 + x + 6} \\ \underline{-(2x^2 + 2x)} \\ -x + 6 \\ \underline{-(-x - 1)} \\ 7 \end{array}$$

The result is $(2x^2 + x + 6) \div (x + 1) = 2x - 1 + \dfrac{7}{x+1}$

DRILL: OPERATIONS WITH POLYNOMIALS

Addition

<u>DIRECTIONS</u>: Add the following polynomials.

1. $9a^2b + 3c + 2a^2b + 5c =$

   (A) $19a^2bc$
   (B) $11a^2b + 8c$
   (C) $11a^4b^2 + 8c^2$
   (D) $19a^4b^2c^2$
   (E) $12a^2b + 8c^2$

2. $14m^2n^3 + 6m^2n^3 + 3m^2n^3 =$

   (A) $20m^2n^3$
   (B) $23m^6n^9$
   (C) $23m^2n^3$
   (D) $32m^6n^9$
   (E) $23m^8n^{27}$

3. $3x + 2y + 16x + 3z + 6y =$

   (A) $19x + 8y$
   (B) $19x + 11yz$
   (C) $19x + 8y + 3z$
   (D) $11xy + 19xz$
   (E) $30xyz$

4. $(4d^2 + 7e^3 + 12f) + (3d^2 + 6e^3 + 2f) =$

    (A) $23d^2e^3f$ (B) $33d^2e^2f$ (C) $33d^4e^6f^2$

    (D) $7d^2 + 13e^3 + 14f$ (E) $23d^2 + 11e^3f$

5. $3ac^2 + 2b^2c + 7ac^2 + 2ac^2 + b^2c =$

    (A) $12ac^2 + 3b^2c$ (B) $14ab^2c^2$ (C) $11ac^2 + 4ab^2c$

    (D) $15ab^2c^2$ (E) $15a^2b^4c^4$

Subtraction

DIRECTIONS: Subtract the following polynomials.

6. $14m^2n - 6m^2n =$

    (A) $20m^2n$ (B) $8m^2n$ (C) $8m$ (D) 8 (E) $8m^4n^2$

7. $3x^3y^2 - 4xz - 6x^3y^2 =$

    (A) $-7x^2y2z$ (B) $3x^3y^2 - 10x^4y^2z$ (C) $-3x^3y^2 - 4xz$

    (D) $-x^2y^2z - 6x^3y^2$ (E) $-7xyz$

8. $9g^2 + 6h - 2g^2 - 5h =$

    (A) $15g^2h - 7g^2h$ (B) $7g^4h^2$ (C) $11g^2 + 7h$

    (D) $11g^2 - 7h^2$ (E) $7g^2 + h$

9. $7b^3 - 4c^2 - 6b^3 + 3c^2 =$

    (A) $b^3 - c^2$ (B) $-11b^2 - 3c^2$ (C) $13b^3 - c$

    (D) $7b - c$ (E) 0

10. $11q^2r - 4q^2r - 8q^2r =$

    (A) $22q^2r$ (B) q^2r (C) $-2q^2r$

    (D) $-q^2r$ (E) $2q^2r$

Multiplication

DIRECTIONS: Multiply the following polynomials.

11. $5p^2t \times 3p^2t =$

(A) $15p^2t$ (B) $15p^4t$ (C) $15p^4t^2$

(D) $8p^2t$ (E) $8p^4t^2$

12. $(2r + s)\,14r =$

(A) $28rs$ (B) $28r^2 + 14sr$ (C) $16r^2 + 14rs$

(D) $28r + 14sr$ (E) $17r^2s$

13. $(4m + p)\,(3m - 2p) =$

(A) $12m^2 + 5mp + 2p^2$ (B) $12m^2 - 2mp + 2p^2$ (C) $7m - p$

(D) $12m - 2p$ (E) $12m^2 - 5mp - 2p^2$

14. $(2a + b)\,(3a^2 + ab + b^2) =$

(A) $6a^3 + 5a^2b + 3ab^2 + b^3$ (B) $5a^3 + 3ab + b^3$ (C) $6a^3 + 2a^2b + 2ab^2$

(D) $3a^2 + 2a + ab + b + b^2$ (E) $6a^3 + 3a^2b + 5ab^2 + b^3$

15. $(6t^2 + 2t + 1)\,3t =$

(A) $9t^2 + 5t + 3$ (B) $18t^2 + 6t + 3$ (C) $9t^3 + 6t^2 + 3t$

(D) $18t^3 + 6t^2 + 3t$ (E) $12t^3 + 6t^2 + 3t$

Division

DIRECTIONS: Divide the following polynomials.

16. $(x^2 + x - 6) \div (x - 2) =$

(A) $x - 3$ (B) $x + 2$ (C) $x + 3$ (D) $x - 2$ (E) $2x + 2$

17. $24b^4c^3 \div 6b^2c =$

    (A) $3b^2c^2$ (B) $4b^4c^3$ (C) $4b^3c^2$ (D) $4b^2c^2$ (E) $3b^4c^3$

18. $(3p^2 + pq - 2q^2) \div (p + q) =$

    (A) $3p + 2q$ (B) $2q - 3p$ (C) $3p - q$ (D) $2q + 3p$ (E) $3p - 2q$

19. $(y^3 - 2y^2 - y + 2) \div (y - 2) =$

    (A) $(y - 1)^2$ (B) $y^2 - 1$ (C) $(y + 2)(y - 1)$
    (D) $(y + 1)^2$ (E) $(y + 1)(y - 2)$

20. $(m^2 + m - 14) \div (m + 4) =$

    (A) $m - 2$ (B) $m - 3 + \dfrac{-2}{m + 4}$ (C) $m - 3 + \dfrac{4}{m + 4}$

    (D) $m - 3$ (E) $m - 2 + \dfrac{-3}{m + 4}$

FACTORING ALGEBRAIC EXPRESSIONS

To factor a polynomial completely is to find the prime factors of the polynomial with respect to a specified set of numbers.

The following concepts are important while factoring or simplifying expressions.

A) The factors of an algebraic expression consist of two or more algebraic expressions which, when multiplied together, produce the given algebraic expression.

B) A **prime factor** is a polynomial with no factors other than itself and 1. The **least common multiple (LCM)** for a set of numbers is the smallest quantity divisible by every number of the set. For algebraic expressions the least common numerical coefficients for each of the given expressions will be a factor.

C) The **greatest common factor (GCF)** for a set of numbers is the largest factor that is common to all members of the set.

D) For algebraic expressions, the greatest common factor is the polynomial of highest degree and the largest numerical coefficient which is a factor of all the given expressions.

Some important formulas, useful for the factoring of polynomials, are listed below.

$$a(c + d) = ac + ad$$

$$(a + b)(a - b) = a^2 - b^2$$

$$(a + b)(a + b) = (a + b)^2 = a^2 + 2ab + b^2$$

$$(a - b)(a - b) = (a - b)^2 = a^2 - 2ab + b^2$$

$$(x + a)(x + b) = x^2 + (a + b)x + ab$$

$$(ax + b)(cx + d) = acx^2 + (ad + bc)x + bd$$

$$(a + b)(c + d) = ac + bc + ad + bd$$

$$(a + b)(a + b)(a + b) = (a + b)^3 = a^3 + 3a^2b + 3ab^2 + b^3$$

$$(a - b)(a - b)(a - b) = (a - b)^3 = a^3 - 3a^2b + 3ab^2 - b^3$$

$$(a - b)(a^2 + ab + b^2) = a^3 - b^3$$

$$(a + b)(a^2 - ab + b^2) = a^3 + b^3$$

$$(a + b + c)^2 = a^2 + b^2 + c^2 + 2ab + 2ac + 2bc$$

$$(a - b)(a^3 + a^2b + ab^2 + b^3) = a^4 - b^4$$

$$(a - b)(a^4 + a^3b + a^2b^2 + ab^3 + b^4) = a^5 - b^5$$

$$(a - b)(a^5 + a^4b + a^3b^2 + a^2b^3 + ab^4 + b^5) = a^6 - b^6$$

$$(a - b)(a^{n-1} + a^{n-2}b + a^{n-3}b^2 + \ldots + ab^{n-2} + b^{n-1}) = a^n - b^n$$

where n is any positive integer $(1, 2, 3, 4, \ldots)$.

$$(a + b)(a^{n-1} - a^{n-2}b + a^{n-3}b^2 - \ldots - ab^{n-2} + b^{n-1}) = a^n + b^n$$

where n is any positive odd integer $(1, 3, 5, 7, \ldots)$.

The procedure for factoring an algebraic expression completely is as follows:

Step 1: First find the greatest common factor if there is any. Then examine each factor remaining for greatest common factors.

Step 2: Continue factoring the factors obtained in Step 1 until all factors other than monomial factors are prime.

EXAMPLE

Factoring $4 - 16x^2$,

$$4 - 16x^2 = 4(1 - 4x^2) = 4(1 + 2x)(1 - 2x)$$

PROBLEM

Express each of the following as a single term.

(1) $3x^2 + 2x^2 - 4x^2$ (2) $5axy^2 - 7axy^2 - 3xy^2$

SOLUTION

(1)   Factor x^2 in the expression.

$$3x^2 + 2x^2 - 4x^2 = (3 + 2 - 4)x^2 = 1x^2 = x^2$$

(2)   Factor xy^2 in the expression and then factor a.

$$5axy^2 - 7axy^2 - 3xy^2 = (5a - 7a - 3)xy^2$$
$$= [(5 - 7)a - 3]xy^2$$
$$= (-2a - 3)xy^2$$

PROBLEM

Simplify $\dfrac{\frac{1}{x-1} - \frac{1}{x-2}}{\frac{1}{x-2} - \frac{1}{x-3}}$.

SOLUTION

Simplify the expression in the numerator by using the addition rule:

$$\frac{a}{b} + \frac{c}{d} = \frac{ad + bc}{bd}$$

Notice bd is the Least Common Denominator, LCD. We obtain

$$\frac{x - 2 + (x - 1)}{(x - 1)(x - 2)} = \frac{-1}{(x - 1)(x - 2)}$$

in the numerator.

Repeat this procedure for the expression in the denominator:

$$\frac{x - 3 - (x - 2)}{(x - 2)(x - 3)} = \frac{-1}{(x - 2)(x - 3)}$$

We now have

$$\frac{\frac{-1}{(x-1)(x-2)}}{\frac{-1}{(x-2)(x-3)}}$$

which is simplified by inverting the fraction in the denominator and multiplying it by the numerator and cancelling like terms

$$\frac{-1}{(x - 1)(x - 2)} \times \frac{(x - 2)(x - 3)}{-1} = \frac{x - 3}{x - 1}.$$

DRILL: SIMPLIFYING ALGEBRAIC EXPRESSIONS

DIRECTIONS: Simplify the following expressions.

1. $16b^2 - 25z^2 =$

(A) $(4b - 5z)^2$ (B) $(4b + 5z)^2$ (C) $(4b - 5z)(4b + 5z)$

(D) $(16b - 25z)^2$ (E) $(5z - 4b)(5z + 4b)$

2. $x^2 - 2x - 8 =$

   (A) $(x-4)^2$ (B) $(x-6)(x-2)$ (C) $(x+4)(x-2)$
   (D) $(x-4)(x+2)$ (E) $(x-4)(x-2)$

3. $2c^2 + 5cd - 3d^2 =$

   (A) $(c-3d)(c+2d)$ (B) $(2c-d)(c+3d)$ (C) $(c-d)(2c+3d)$
   (D) $(2c+d)(c+3d)$ (E) Not possible.

4. $4t^3 - 20t =$

   (A) $4t(t^2-5)$ (B) $4t^2(t-20)$ (C) $4t(t+4)(t-5)$
   (D) $2t(2t^2-10)$ (E) Not possible.

5. $x^2 + xy - 2y^2 =$

   (A) $(x-2y)(x+y)$ (B) $(x-2y)(x-y)$ (C) $(x+2y)(x+y)$
   (D) $(x+2y)(x-y)$ (E) Not possible.

6. $5b^2 + 17bd + 6d^2 =$

   (A) $(5b+d)(b+6d)$ (B) $(5b+2d)(b+3d)$ (C) $(5b-2d)(b-3d)$
   (D) $(5b-2d)(b+3d)$ (E) Not possible.

7. $x^2 + x + 1 =$

   (A) $(x+1)^2$ (B) $(x+2)(x-1)$ (C) $(x-2)(x+1)$
   (D) $(x+1)(x-1)$ (E) Not possible.

8. $3z^3 + 6z^2 =$

   (A) $3(z^3+2z^2)$ (B) $3z^2(z+2)$ (C) $3z(z^2+2z)$
   (D) $z^2(3z+6)$ (E) $3z^2(1+2z)$

9. $m^2p^2 + mpq - 6q^2 =$

   (A) $(mp-2q)(mp+3q)$ (B) $mp(mp-2q)(mp+3q)$
   (C) $mpq(1-6q)$ (D) $(mp+2q)(mp+3q)$
   (E) Not possible.

10. $2h^3 + 2h^2t - 4ht^2 =$

   (A) $2(h^3 - t)(h + t)$ (B) $2h(h - 2t)^2$ (C) $4h(ht - t^2)$

   (D) $2h(h + t) - 4ht^2$ (E) $2h(h + 2t)(h - t)$

EQUATIONS

An **equation** is defined as a statement that two separate expressions are equal.

A **solution** to an equation containing a single variable is a number that makes the equation true when it is substituted for the variable. For example, in the equation $3x = 18$, 6 is the solution since $3(6) = 18$. Depending on the equation, there can be more than one solution. Equations with the same solutions are said to be **equivalent equations**. An equation without a solution is said to have a solution set that is the **empty** or **null** set and is represented by ϕ.

Replacing an expression within an equation by an equivalent expression will result in a new equation with solutions equivalent to the original equation. Suppose we are given the equation

$$3x + y + x + 2y = 15.$$

By combining like terms we get

$$3x + y + x + 2y = 4x + 3y.$$

Since these two expressions are equivalent, we can substitute the simpler form into the equation to get

$$4x + 3y = 15$$

Performing the same operation to both sides of an equation by the same expression will result in a new equation that is equivalent to the original equation.

A)   **Addition or subtraction**

   $$y + 6 = 10$$

   We can add (-6) to both sides

   $$y + 6 + (-6) = 10 + (-6)$$
   $$\text{to get } y + 0 = 10 - 6 \rightarrow y = 4$$

B)   **Multiplication or division**

   $$3x = 6$$
   $$\frac{3z}{3} = \frac{6}{3}$$
   $$x = 2$$
   $$3x = 6 \text{ is equivalent to } x = 2.$$

C)   **Raising to a power**

   $$a = x^2y$$
   $$a^2 = (x^2y)^2$$

$$a^2 = x^4y^2$$

This can be applied to negative and fractional powers as well, e.g.,

$$x^2 = 3y^4$$

If we raise both sides to the –2 power, we get

$$(x^2)^{-2} = (3y^4)^{-2}$$

$$\frac{1}{(x^2)^2} = \frac{1}{(3y^4)^2}$$

$$\frac{1}{x^4} = \frac{1}{9y^8}$$

If we raise both sides to the $\frac{1}{2}$ power, which is the same as taking the square root, we get

$$(x^2)^{\frac{1}{2}} = (3y^4)^{\frac{1}{2}}$$

$$x = \pm\sqrt{3}y^2$$

D) The **reciprocal** of both sides of an equation are equivalent to the original equation. Note: The reciprocal of zero is undefined.

$$\frac{2x+y}{z} = \frac{5}{2} \qquad\qquad \frac{z}{2x+y} = \frac{2}{5}$$

PROBLEM

Solve for x, justifying each step.

$$3x - 8 = 7x + 8$$

SOLUTION

$$3x - 8 = 7x + 8$$

Add 8 to both sides:	$3x - 8 + 8 = 7x + 8 + 8$
Additive inverse property:	$3x + 0 = 7x + 16$
Additive identity property:	$3x = 7x + 16$
Add ($-7x$) to both sides:	$3x - 7x = 7x + 16 - 7x$
Commute:	$-4x = 7x - 7x + 16$
Additive inverse property:	$-4x = 0 + 16$
Additive identity property:	$-4x = 16$
Divide both sides by -4:	$x = \dfrac{16}{-4}$

Check: Replacing x with -4 in the original equation:

$$3x - 8 = 7x + 8$$

$$3(-4) - 8 = 7(-4) + 8$$
$$-12 - 8 = -28 + 8$$
$$-20 = -20$$

LINEAR EQUATIONS

A linear equation with one unknown is one that can be put into the form $ax + b = 0$, where a and b are constants, $a \neq 0$.

To solve a linear equation means to transform it in the form $x = -\frac{b}{a}$.

A) If the equation has unknowns on both sides of the equality, it is convenient to put similar terms on the same sides. Refer to the following example.

$$4x + 3 = 2x + 9$$
$$4x + 3 - 2x = 2x + 9 - 2x$$
$$(4x - 2x) + 3 = (2x - 2x) + 9$$
$$2x + 3 = 0 + 9$$
$$2x + 3 - 3 = 0 + 9 - 3$$
$$2x = 6$$
$$\frac{2x}{2} = \frac{6}{2}$$
$$x = 3$$

B) If the equation appears in fractional form, it is necessary to transform it, using cross-multiplication, and then repeating the same procedure as in A), we obtain:

$$\frac{3x + 4}{3} \qquad \frac{7x + 2}{5}$$

By using cross-multiplication we would obtain:

$$3(7x + 2) = 5(3x + 4).$$

This is equivalent to:

$$21x + 6 = 15x + 20,$$

which can be solved as in A).

$$21x + 6 = 15x + 20$$
$$21x - 15x + 6 = 15x - 15x + 20$$
$$6x + 6 - 6 = 20 - 6$$
$$6x = 14$$
$$x = \frac{14}{6}$$
$$x = \frac{7}{3}$$

C) If there are radicals in the equation, it is necessary to square both sides and then apply A).

$$\sqrt{3x+1} = 5$$
$$\left(\sqrt{3x+1}\right)^2 = 5^2$$
$$3x+1 = 25$$
$$3x+1-1 = 25-1$$
$$3x = 24$$
$$x = \frac{24}{3}$$
$$x = 8$$

PROBLEM

Solve the equation $2(x + 3) = (3x + 5) - (x - 5)$.

SOLUTION

We transform the given equation to an equivalent equation in which we can easily recognize the solution set.

$$2(x + 3) = 3x + 5 - (x - 5)$$

Distribute: $\qquad\qquad 2x + 6 = 3x + 5 - x + 5$

Combine terms: $\qquad\quad 2x + 6 = 2x + 10$

Subtract $2x$ from both sides: $\qquad 6 = 10$

Since $6 = 10$ is not a true statement, there is no real number x which will make the original equation true. The equation is inconsistent and the solution set is ϕ, the empty set.

PROBLEM

Solve the equation $2(\frac{2}{3}y + 5) + 2(y + 5) = 130$.

SOLUTION

The procedure for solving this equation is as follows:

Distribute: $\qquad\qquad\qquad\qquad\qquad\qquad \frac{4}{3}y + 10 + 2y + 10 = 130$

Combine like terms: $\qquad\qquad\qquad\qquad\quad \frac{4}{3}y + 2y + 20 = 130$

Subtract 20 from both sides: $\qquad\qquad\qquad \frac{4}{3}y + 2y = 110$

Convert 2y into a fraction with denominator 3:

$$\frac{4}{3}y + \frac{6}{3}y = 110$$

Combine like terms:

$$\frac{10}{3}y = 110$$

Divide by $\frac{10}{3}$:

$$y = 110 \times \frac{3}{10} = 33$$

Check: Replace y with 33 in the original equation.

$$2(\frac{2}{3}(33) + 5) + 2(33 + 5) = 130$$
$$2(22 + 5) + 2(38) = 130$$
$$2(27) + 76 = 130$$
$$54 + 76 = 130$$
$$130 = 130$$

Therefore, the solution to the given equation is $y = 33$.

DRILL: LINEAR EQUATIONS

<u>DIRECTIONS</u>: Solve for x.

1. $4x - 2 = 10$

    (A) -1 (B) 2   (C) 3   (D) 4   (E) 6

2. $7z + 1 - z = 2z - 7$

    (A) -2 (B) 0   (C) 1   (D) 2   (E) 3

3. $\frac{1}{3}b + 3 = \frac{1}{2}b$

    (A) $\frac{1}{2}$ (B) 2   (C) $3\frac{3}{5}$ (D) 6   (E) 18

4. $0.4p + 1 = 0.7p - 2$

    (A) 0.1   (B) 2   (C) 5   (D) 10   (E) 12

5. $4(3x + 2) - 11 = 3(3x - 2)$

    (A) -3 (B) -1 (C) 2   (D) 3   (E) 7

TWO LINEAR EQUATIONS

Equations of the form $ax + by = c$, where a, b, c are constants and a, $b \neq 0$ are called **linear equations** with two unknown variables.

There are several ways to solve systems of linear equations with two variables.

Method 1: **Addition or subtraction**—if necessary, multiply the equations by numbers that will make the coefficients of one unknown in the resulting equations numerically equal. If the signs of equal coefficients are the same, subtract the equation, otherwise add.

The result is one equation with one unknown; we solve it and substitute the value into the other equations to find the unknown that we first eliminated.

Method 2: **Substitution**—find the value of one unknown in terms of the other. Substitute this value in the other equation and solve.

Method 3: **Graph**—graph both equations. The point of intersection of the drawn lines is a simultaneous solution for the equations and its coordinates correspond to the answer that would be found analytically.

If the lines are parallel they have no simultaneous solution.

Dependent equations are equations that represent the same line; therefore, every point on the line of a dependent equation represents a solution. Since there is an infinite number of points on a line there is an infinite number of simultaneous solutions, for example,

$$2x + y = 8$$
$$4x + 2y = 16$$

The equations on the previous page are dependent. Since they represent the same line, all points that satisfy either of the equations are solutions of the system.

A system of linear equations is consistent if there is only one solution for the system.

A system of linear equations is inconsistent if it does not have any solutions.

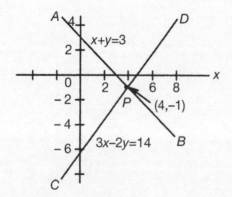

EXAMPLE

Find the point of intersection of the graphs of the equations as shown in the previous figure.

$$x + y = 3$$

$$3x - 2y = 14$$

To solve these linear equations, solve for y in terms of x. The equations will be in the form $y = mx + b$, where m is the slope and b is the intercept on the y-axis.

$$x + y = 3$$

Subtract x from both sides: $\qquad y = 3 - x$

Subtract $3x$ from both sides: $\qquad 3x - 2y = 14$

Divide by –2: $\qquad -2y = 14 - 3x$

$$y = -7 + \frac{3}{2}x$$

The graphs of the linear functions, $y = 3 - x$ and $y = 7 + \frac{3}{2}x$ can be determined by plotting only two points. For example, for $y = 3 - x$, let $x = 0$, then $y = 3$. Let $x = 1$, then $y = 2$. The two points on this first line are $(0, 3)$ and $(1, 2)$. For $y = -7 + \frac{3}{2}x$, let $x = 0$, then $y = -7$. Let $x = 1$, then $y = -5\frac{1}{2}$. The two points on this second line are $(0, -7)$ and $(1, -5\frac{1}{2})$.

To find the point of intersection P of

$$x + y = 3 \text{ and } 3x - 2y = 14,$$

solve them algebraically. Multiply the first equation by 2. Add these two equations to eliminate the variable y.

$$2x + 2y = 6$$
$$\underline{3x - 2y = 14}$$
$$5x \qquad = 20$$

Solve for x to obtain $x = 4$. Substitute this into $y = 3 - x$ to get $y = 3 - 4 = -1$. P is $(4, -1)$. AB is the graph of the first equation, and CD is the graph of the second equation. The point of intersection P of the two graphs is the only point on both lines. The coordinates of P satisfy both equations and represent the desired solution of the problem. From the graph, P seems to be the point $(4, -1)$. These coordinates satisfy both equations, and hence are the exact coordinates of the point of intersection of the two lines.

To show that $(4, -1)$ satisfies both equations, substitute this point into both equations.

$$x + y = 3 \qquad\qquad 3x - 2y = 14$$
$$4 + (-1) = 3 \qquad\qquad 3(4) - 2(-1) = 14$$
$$4 - 1 = 3 \qquad\qquad 12 + 2 = 14$$
$$3 = 3 \qquad\qquad 14 = 14$$

EXAMPLE

Solve the equations $2x + 3y = 6$ and $4x + 6y = 7$ simultaneously.

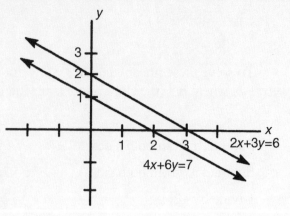

We have 2 equations and 2 unknowns,

$$2x + 3y = 6 \quad (1)$$

and

$$4x + 6y = 7 \quad (2)$$

There are several methods to solve this problem. We have chosen to multiply each equation by a different number so that when the two equations are added, one of the variables drops out. Thus,

Multiply equation (1) by 2: $4x + 6y = 12$ (3)

Multiply equation (2) by –1: $\underline{-4x - 6y = -7}$ (4)

Add equations (3) and (4): $0 = 5$

We obtain a peculiar result!

Actually, what we have shown in this case is that if there were a simultaneous solution to the given equations, then 0 would equal 5. But the conclusion is impossible; therefore there can be no simultaneous solution to these two equations, hence no point satisfying both.

The straight lines which are the graphs of these equations must be parallel if they never intersect, but not identical, which can be seen from the graph of these equations (see the accompanying diagram).

EXAMPLE

Solve the equations $2x + 3y = 6$ and $y = -\frac{2x}{3} + 2$ simultaneously.

We have 2 equations and 2 unknowns.

$$2x + 3y = 6 \qquad (1)$$

and

$$y = -\left(\frac{2x}{3}\right) + 2 \qquad (2)$$

There are several methods of solution for this problem. Since equation (2) already gives us an expression for y, we use the method of substitution. Substitute: $-\frac{2x}{3} + 2$ for y in the first equation:

$$2x + 3\left(-\frac{2x}{3} + 2\right) = 6$$

Distribute: $2x - 2x + 6 = 6$

$$6 = 6$$

Apparently we have gotten nowhere! The result $6 = 6$ is true, but indicates no solution. Actually, our work shows that no matter what real number x is, if y is determined by the second equation, then the first equation will always be satisfied.

The reason for this peculiarity may be seen if we take a closer look at the equation $y = -\frac{2x}{3} + 2$. It is equivalent to $3y = -2x + 6$, or $2x + 3y = 6$.

In other words, the two equations are equivalent. Any pair of values for x and y which satisfies one satisfies the other.

It is hardly necessary to verify that in this case the graphs of the given equations are identical lines, and that there are an infinite number of simultaneous solutions of these equations.

A system of three linear equations in three unknowns is solved by eliminating one unknown from any two of the three equations and solving them. After finding two unknowns substitute them in any of the equations to find the third unknown.

PROBLEM

Solve the system

$$2x + 3y - 4z = -8 \qquad (1)$$
$$x + y - 2z = -5 \qquad (2)$$
$$7x - 2y + 5z = 4 \qquad (3)$$

SOLUTION

We cannot eliminate any variable from two pairs of equations by a single multiplication. However, both x and z may be eliminated from equations (1) and (2) by multiplying equation (2) by -2. Then

$$2x + 3y - 4z = -8 \qquad (1)$$
$$-2x - 2y + 4z = 10 \qquad (4)$$

By addition, we have $y = 2$. Although we may now eliminate either x or z from another pair of equations, we can more conveniently substitute $y = 2$ in equations (2) and (3) to get two equations in two variables. Thus, making the substitution $y = 2$ in equations (2) and (3), we have

$$x - 2z = -7 \qquad (5)$$
$$7x + 5z = 8 \qquad (6)$$

Multiply equation (5) by 5 and multiply (6) by 2. Then add the two new equations. Then $x = -1$. Substitute x in either equation (5) or (6) to find z.

The solution of the system is $x = -1$, $y = 2$, and $z = 3$. Check by substitution.

A system of equations, as shown below, that has all constant terms b_1, b_2, ..., b_n equal to zero is said to be a homogeneous system.

$$\begin{cases} a_{11}x_1 + a_{12}x_2 + \ldots + a_{1n}x_m = b_1 \\ a_{21}x_1 + a_{22}x_2 + \ldots + a_{2n}x_m = b_2 \\ \quad \vdots \qquad \quad \vdots \qquad \qquad \vdots \quad \vdots \\ a_{n1}x_1 + a_{n2}x_2 + \ldots + a_{nn}x_m = b_n \end{cases}$$

A homogeneous system (one in which each variable can be replaced by a constant and the constant can be factored out) always has at least one solution which is called the trivial solution that is $x_1 = 0$, $x_2 = 0$, ..., $x_m = 0$.

For any given homogeneous system of equations, in which the number of variables is greater than or equal to the number of equations, there are nontrivial solutions.

Two systems of linear equations are said to be equivalent if and only if they have the same solution set.

PROBLEM

Solve for x and y.

$$x + 2y = 8 \tag{1}$$

$$3x + 4y = 20 \tag{2}$$

SOLUTION

Solve equation (1) for x in terms of y: $\qquad x = 8 - 2y \tag{3}$

Substitute $(8 - 2y)$ for x in (2): $\quad 3(8 - 2y) + 4y = 20 \tag{4}$

Solve (4) for y as follows:

Distribute: $\quad 24 - 6y + 4y = 20$

Combine like terms and then subtract 24 from both sides:

$$24 - 2y = 20$$

$$24 - 24 - 2y = 20 - 24$$

$$-2y = -4$$

Divide both sides by –2: $\qquad\qquad\qquad\qquad y = 2$

Substitute 2 for y in equation (1): $\qquad x + 2(2) = 8$

$$x = 4$$

Thus, our solution is $x = 4$, $y = 2$

Check: Substitute $x = 4$, $y = 2$ in equations (1) and (2):

$$4 + 2(2) = 8$$

$$8 = 8$$

$$3(4) + 4(2) = 20$$

$$20 = 20$$

Solve algebraically.

$$4x + 2y = -1 \tag{1}$$

$$5x - 3y = 7 \tag{2}$$

SOLUTION

We arbitrarily choose to eliminate x first.

Multiply (1) by 5:	$20x + 10y = -5$	(3)
Multiply (2) by 4:	$20x - 12y = 28$	(4)
Subtract (3) from (4):	$22y = -33$	(5)
Divide (5) by 22:	$y = \dfrac{33}{22} = -\dfrac{3}{2},$	

To find x, substitute $y = -\frac{3}{2}$ in either of the original equations. If we use equation (1), we obtain $4x + 2(-\frac{3}{2}) = -1$, $4x - 3 = -1$, $4x = 2$, $x = \frac{1}{2}$.

The solution $(\frac{1}{2}, -\frac{3}{2})$ should be checked in both equations of the given system.

Replacing $(\frac{1}{2}, -\frac{3}{2})$ in equation (1):

$$4x + 2y = -1$$

$$4\left(\frac{1}{2}\right) + 2\left(-\frac{3}{2}\right) = -1$$

$$\frac{4}{2} - 3 = -1$$

$$2 - 3 = -1$$

$$-1 = -1$$

Replacing $(\frac{1}{2}, -\frac{3}{2})$ in equation (2):

$$5x - 3y = 7$$

$$5\left(\frac{1}{2}\right) - 3\left(-\frac{3}{2}\right) = 7$$

$$\frac{5}{2} + \frac{9}{2} = 7$$

$$\frac{14}{2} = 7$$

$$7 = 7$$

(Instead of eliminating x from the two given equations, we could have eliminated y by multiplying equation (1) by 3, multiplying equation (2) by 2, and then adding the two derived equations.)

DRILL: TWO LINEAR EQUATIONS

DIRECTIONS: Find the solution set for each pair of equations.

1. $3x + 4y = -2$
    $x - 6y = -8$

    (A) $(2, -1)$ (B) $(1, -2)$ (C) $(-2, -1)$

    (D) $(1, 2)$ (E) $(-2, 1)$

2. $2x + y = -10$
    $-2x - 4y = 4$

    (A) $(6, -2)$ (B) $(-6, 2)$ (C) $(-2, 6)$

    (D) $(2, 6)$ (E) $(-6, -2)$

3. $6x + 5y = -4$
    $3x - 3y = 9$

    (A) $(1, -2)$ (B) $(1, 2)$ (C) $(2, -1)$

    (D) $(-2, 1)$ (E) $(-1, 2)$

4. $4x + 3y = 9$
    $2x - 2y = 8$

    (A) $(-3, 1)$ (B) $(1, -3)$ (C) $(3, 1)$

    (D) $(3, -1)$ (E) $(-1, 3)$

5. $x + y = 7$
    $x = y - 3$

    (A) $(5, 2)$ (B) $(-5, 2)$ (C) $(2, 5)$

    (D) $(-2, 5)$ (E) $(2, -5)$

6. $5x + 6y = 4$
    $3x - 2y = 1$

    (A) $(3, 6)$ (B) $\left(\dfrac{1}{2}, \dfrac{1}{4}\right)$ (C) $(-3, 6)$

    (D) $(2, 4)$ (E) $\left(\dfrac{1}{3}, \dfrac{3}{2}\right)$

7. $x - 2y = 7$
    $x + y = -2$

    (A) (−2, 7)   (B) (3, −1)   (C) (−7, 2)

    (D) (1, −3)   (E) (1, −2)

8. $4x + 3y = 3$
    $-2x + 6y = 3$

    (A) $\left(\dfrac{1}{2}, \dfrac{2}{3}\right)$ (B) (−0.3, 0.6)   (C) $\left(\dfrac{2}{3}, -1\right)$

    (D) (−0.2, 0.5)   (E) (0.3, 0.6)

9. $4x - 2y = -14$
    $8x + y = 7$

    (A) (0, 7)   (B) (2, −7)   (C) (7, 0)

    (D) (−7, 2)   (E) (0, 2)

10. $6x - 3y = 1$
     $-9x + 5y = -1$

    (A) (1, −1)   (B) $\left(\dfrac{2}{4}, 1\right)$ (C) $\left(1, \dfrac{2}{3}\right)$

    (D) (−1, 1)   (E) $\left(\dfrac{2}{3}, -1\right)$

QUADRATIC EQUATIONS

A second degree equation in x of the type $ax^2 + bx + c = 0$, $a \neq 0$, a, b and c are real numbers, is called a **quadratic equation**.

To solve a quadratic equation is to find values of x which satisfy $ax^2 + bx + c = 0$. These values of x are called **solutions**, or **roots**, of the equation.

A quadratic equation has a maximum of two roots. Methods of solving quadratic equations:

A) **Direct solution**: Given $x^2 - 9 = 0$.

    We can solve directly by isolating the variable x.

        $x^2 = 9$

        $x = \pm 3$

B) **Factoring**: Given a quadratic equation $ax^2 + bx + c = 0$, a, b, $c \neq 0$, to factor means to express it as the product $a(x - r_1)(x - r_2) = 0$, where r_1 and r_2 are the two roots.

Some helpful hints to remember are

a) $r_1 + r_2 = -\dfrac{b}{a}$.

b) $r_1 r_2 = \dfrac{c}{a}$.

Given $x^2 - 5x + 4 = 0$.

Since

$$r_1 + r_2 = -\frac{b}{a} = -\frac{(-5)}{1} = 5,$$

the possible solutions are $(3, 2)$, $(4, 1)$, and $(5, 0)$. Also

$$r_1 r_2 = \frac{c}{a} = \frac{4}{1} = 4;$$

this equation is satisfied only by the second pair, so $r_1 = 4$, $r_2 = 1$, and the factored form is $(x - 4)(x - 1) = 0$.

If the coefficient of x^2 is not 1, it is necessary to divide the equation by this coefficient and then factor.

Given $2x^2 - 12x + 16 = 0$.

Dividing by 2, we obtain

$$x^2 - 6x + 8 = 0.$$

Since

$$r_1 + r_2 = -\frac{b}{a} = 6,$$

the possible solutions are $(6, 0)$, $(5, 1)$, $(4, 2)$, and $(3, 3)$. Also $r_1 r_2 = 8$, so the only possible answer is $(4, 2)$ and the expression $x^2 - 6x + 8 = 0$ can be factored as $(x - 4)(x - 2)$.

C) **Completing the Squares**: If it is difficult to factor the quadratic equation using the previous method, we can complete the squares.

Given $x^2 - 12x + 8 = 0$.

We know that the two roots added up should be 12 because

$$r_1 + r_2 = -\frac{b}{a} = \frac{-(-12)}{1} = 12.$$

The possible roots are $(12, 0)$, $(11, 1)$, $(10, 2)$, $(9, 3)$, $(8, 4)$, $(7, 5)$, and $(6, 6)$.

But none of these satisfy $r_1 r_2 = 8$, so we cannot use (B).

To complete the square, it is necessary to isolate the constant term,

$$x^2 - 12x = -8.$$

Then take $\frac{1}{2}$ coefficient of x, square it and add to both sides.

$$x^2 - 12x + \left(\frac{-12}{2}\right)^2 = -8 + \left(\frac{-12}{2}\right)^2$$

$$x^2 - 12x + 36 = -8 + 36 = 28$$

Now we can use the previous method to factor the left side.

$$r_1 + r_2 = 12, r_1r_2 = 36$$

is satisfied by the pair (6, 6), so we have

$$(x - 6)2 = 28.$$

Now extract the root of both sides and solve for x.

$$(x - 6) = \pm\sqrt{28} = \pm2\sqrt{7}$$
$$x = \pm2\sqrt{7} + 6$$

So the roots are

$$x = 2\sqrt{7} + 6, \, x = -2\sqrt{7} + 6.$$

PROBLEM

Solve the equation $x^2 + 8x + 15 = 0$.

SOLUTION

Since

$$(x + a)(x + b) = x^2 + bx + ax + ab$$
$$= x^2 + (a + b)x + ab,$$

we may factor the given equation,

$$0 = x^2 + 8x + 15,$$

replacing $a + b$ by 8 and ab by 15. Thus,

$$a + b = 8, \text{ and } ab = 15.$$

We want the two numbers a and b whose sum is 8 and whose product is 15. We check all pairs of numbers whose product is 15.

(a) $1 \times 15 = 15$; thus, $a = 1$, $b = 15$, and $ab = 15$.

$1 + 15 = 16$; therefore, we reject these values because $a + b \neq 8$.

(b) $3 \times 5 = 15$; thus, $a = 3$, $b = 5$, and $ab = 15$.

$3 + 5 = 8$; therefore, $a + b = 8$, and we accept these values.

Hence, $x^2 + 8x + 15 = 0$ is equivalent to

$$0 = x^2 + (3 + 5)x + 3 \times 5 = (x + 3)(x + 5)$$

Hence, $x + 5 = 0$ or $x + 3 = 0$

since the product of these two numbers is zero, one of the numbers must be zero. Hence, $x = -5$, or $x = -3$, and the solution set is $x = \{-5, -3\}$.

The student should note that $x = -5$ or $x = -3$. We are certainly not making the statement that $x = -5$ and $x = -3$. Also, the student should check that both these numbers do actually satisfy the given equations and hence are solutions.

Check: Replacing x by (-5) in the original equation:

$$x^2 + 8x + 15 = 0$$

$$(-5)^2 + 8(-5) + 15 = 0$$

$$25 - 40 + 15 = 0$$

$$15 + 15 = 0$$

$$0 = 0$$

Replacing x by (-3) in the original equation:

$$x^2 + 8x + 15 = 0$$

$$(-3)^2 + 8(-3) + 15 = 0$$

$$9 - 24 + 15 = 0$$

$$15 + 15 = 0$$

$$0 = 0$$

PROBLEM

Solve the following equations by factoring.

(1) $2x^2 + 3x = 0$ (2) $y^2 - 2y - 3 = y - 3$

(3) $z^2 - 2z - 3 = 0$ (4) $2m^2 - 11m - 6 = 0$

SOLUTION

(1) $2x^2 + 3x = 0$. Factor out the common factor of x from the left side of the given equation.

$$x(2x + 3) = 0$$

Whenever a product $ab = 0$, where a and b are any two numbers, either $a = 0$ or $b = 0$. Then, either

$$x = 0 \quad \text{or} \quad 2x + 3 = 0$$

$$2x = -3$$

$$x = -\frac{3}{2}$$

Hence, the solution set to the original equation $2x^2 + 3x = 0$ is: $\{-\frac{3}{2}, 0\}$.

(2) $y^2 - 2y - 3 = y - 3$. Subtract $(y - 3)$ from both sides of the given equation:

$$y^2 - 2y - 3 - (y - 3) = y - 3 - (y - 3)$$

$$y^2 - 2y - 3 - y + 3 = y - 3 - y + 3$$

$$y^2 - 2y - \cancel{3} - y + \cancel{3} = \cancel{y} - \cancel{3} - \cancel{y} + \cancel{3}$$

$$y^2 - 3y = 0$$

Factor out a common factor of y from the left side of this equation:

$$y(y-3) = 0$$

Thus, $y = 0$ or $y - 3 = 0$, $y = 3$.

Therefore, the solution set to the original equation $y^2 - 2y - 3 = y - 3$ is $\{0, 3\}$.

(3) $z^2 - 2z - 3 = 0$. Factor the original equation into a product of two polynomials.

$$z^2 - 2z - 3 = (z - 3)(z + 1) = 0$$

Hence,

$$(z - 3)(z + 1) = 0; \text{ and } \quad z - 3 = 0 \text{ or } z + 1 = 0$$

$$z = 3 \qquad\qquad\qquad z = -1$$

Therefore, the solution set to the original equation $z^2 - 2z - 3 = 0$ is $\{-1, 3\}$.

(4) $2m^2 - 11m - 6 = 0$. Factor the original equation into a product of two polynomials.

$$2m^2 - 11m - 6 = (2m + 1)(m - 6) = 0$$

Thus,

$$2m + 1 = 0 \quad \text{ or } \quad m - 6 = 0$$

$$2m = -1 \qquad\qquad m = 6$$

$$m = -\frac{1}{2}$$

Therefore, the solution set to the original equation $2m^2 - 11m - 6 = 0$ is $\{-\frac{1}{2}, 6\}$.

DRILL: QUADRATIC EQUATIONS

__DIRECTIONS__: Solve for all values of *x*.

1. $x^2 - 2x - 8 = 0$

   (A)   4 and –2   (B)   4 and 8   (C)   4
   (D)   –2 and 8   (E)   –2

2. $x^2 + 2x - 3 = 0$

   (A)   –3 and 2   (B)   2 and 1   (C)   3 and 1
   (D)   –3 and 1   (E)   –3

3. $x^2 - 7x = -10$

   (A)   –3 and 5   (B)   2 and 5   (C)   2
   (D)   –2 and –5   (E)   5

4. $x^2 - 8x + 16 = 0$

(A) 8 and 2 (B) 1 and 16 (C) 4
(D) −2 and 4 (E) 4 and −4

5. $3x^2 + 3x = 6$

(A) 3 and −6 (B) 2 and 3 (C) −3 and 2
(D) 1 and −3 (E) 1 and −2

6. $x^2 + 7x = 0$

(A) 7 (B) 0 and −7 (C) −7
(D) 0 and 7 (E) 0

7. $x^2 - 25 = 0$

(A) 5 (B) 5 and −5 (C) 15 and 10
(D) −5 and 10 (E) −5

8. $2x^2 + 4x = 16$

(A) 2 and −2 (B) 8 and −2 (C) 4 and 8
(D) 2 and −4 (E) 2 and 4

9. $6x^2 - x - 2 = 0$

(A) 2 and 3 (B) $\dfrac{1}{2}$ and $\dfrac{1}{3}$ (C) $-\dfrac{1}{2}$ and $\dfrac{2}{3}$
(D) $\dfrac{2}{3}$ and 3 (E) 2 and $-\dfrac{1}{3}$

10. $12x^2 + 5x = 3$

(A) $\dfrac{1}{3}$ and $\dfrac{1}{4}$ (B) 4 and −3 (C) 4 and $\dfrac{1}{6}$
(D) $\dfrac{1}{3}$ and −4 (E) $-\dfrac{3}{4}$ and $\dfrac{1}{3}$

ABSOLUTE VALUE EQUATIONS

The absolute value of a, $|a|$, is defined as

$$|a| = a \text{ when } a > 0,$$

$$|a| = -a \text{ when } a < 0,$$

$$|a| = 0 \text{ when } a = 0.$$

When the definition of absolute value is applied to an equation, the quantity within the absolute value symbol is considered to have two values. This value can be either positive or negative before the absolute value is taken. As a result, each absolute value equation actually contains two separate equations.

When evaluating equations containing absolute values, proceed as follows:

EXAMPLE

$|5 - 3x| = 7$ is valid if either

$$5 - 3x = 7 \qquad \text{or} \qquad 5 - 3x = -7$$
$$-3x = 2 \qquad\qquad\qquad -3x = -12$$
$$x = -\frac{2}{3} \qquad\qquad\qquad x = 4$$

The solution set is therefore $x = (-\frac{2}{3}y, 4)$.

Remember, the absolute value of a number cannot be negative. So, for the equation $|5x + 4| = -3$, there would be no solution.

EXAMPLE

Solve for x in $|2x - 6| = |4 - 5x|$.

There are four possibilities here. $2x - 6$ and $4 - 5x$ can be either positive or negative. Therefore,

$$2x - 6 = 4 - 5x \qquad\qquad\qquad (1)$$

$$-(2x - 6) = 4 - 5x \qquad\qquad\qquad (2)$$

$$2x - 6 = -(4 - 5x) \qquad\qquad\qquad (3)$$

$$-(2x - 6) = -(4 - 5x) \qquad\qquad\qquad (4)$$

Equations (2) and (3) result in the same solution, as do equations (1) and (4). Therefore, it is necessary to solve only for equations (1) and (2). This gives

$$2x - 6 = 4 - 5x \quad \text{or} \quad -(2x - 6) = 4 - 5x$$
$$7x = 10 \qquad\qquad -2x + 6 = 4 - 5x$$
$$x = \frac{10}{7} \qquad\qquad\qquad x = -\frac{2}{3}$$

The solution set is $(\frac{10}{7}, -\frac{2}{3})$.

DRILL: ABSOLUTE VALUE EQUATIONS

DIRECTIONS: Find the appropriate solutions.

1. $|4x - 2| = 6$

   (A) -2 and -1 (B) -1 and 2   (C) 2

   (D) $\dfrac{1}{2}$ and -2 (E) No solution

2. $\left|3 - \dfrac{1}{2}y\right| = -7$

   (A) -8 and 20   (B) 8 and -20 (C) 2 and -5
   (D) 4 and -2 (E) No solution

3. $2|x + 7| = 12$

   (A) -13 and -1 (B) -6 and 6   (C) -1 and 13
   (D) 6 and -13 (E) No solution

4. $|5x| - 7 = 3$

   (A) 2 and 4   (B) $\dfrac{4}{5}$ and 3   (C) -2 and 2

   (D) 2   (E) No solution

5. $\left|\dfrac{3}{4}m\right| = 9$

   (A) 24 and -16 (B) $\dfrac{4}{27}$ and $-\dfrac{4}{3}$ (C) $\dfrac{4}{3}$ and 12

   (D) -12 and 12   (E) No solution

INEQUALITIES

An inequality is a statement where the value of one quantity or expression is greater than (>), less than (<), greater than or equal to (≥), less than or equal to (≤), or not equal to (≠) that of another.

EXAMPLE

   $5 > 4$

The expression above means that the value of 5 is greater than the value of 4.

A **conditional inequality** is an inequality whose validity depends on the values of the variables in the sentence. That is, certain values of the variables will make the sentence true, and others will make it false.

$$3 - y > 3 + y$$

is a conditional inequality for the set of real numbers, since it is true for any replacement less than zero and false for all others.

$$x + 5 > x + 2$$

is an **absolute inequality** for the set of real numbers, meaning that for any real value x, the expression on the left is greater than the expression on the right.

$$5y < 2y + y$$

is inconsistent for the set of non-negative real numbers. For any y greater than 0 the sentence is always false. A sentence is inconsistent if it is always false when its variables assume allowable values.

The solution of a given inequality in one variable x consists of all values of x for which the inequality is true.

The graph of an inequality in one variable is represented by either a ray or a line segment on the real number line.

The endpoint is not a solution if the variable is strictly less than or greater than a particular value.

EXAMPLE

$x > 2$

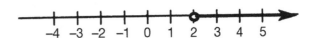

2 is not a solution and should be represented as shown.

The endpoint is a solution if the variable is either (1) less than or equal to or (2) greater than or equal to, a particular value.

EXAMPLE

$5 > x \geq 2$

In this case 2 is the solution and should be represented as shown.

PROPERTIES OF INEQUALITIES

If x and y are real numbers, then one and only one of the following statements is true.

$x > y$, $x = y$, or $x < y$.

This is the order property of real numbers.

If a, b, and c are real numbers, the following are true:

A) If $a < b$ and $b < c$ then $a < c$.

B) If $a > b$ and $b > c$ then $a > c$.

This is the transitive property of inequalities.

If a, b, and c are real numbers and $a > b$, then $a + c > b + c$ and $a - c > b - c$. This is the **addition property of inequality**.

Two inequalities are said to have the same **sense** if their signs of inequality point in the same direction.

The sense of an inequality remains the same if both sides are multiplied or divided by the same positive real number.

EXAMPLE

$$4 > 3$$

If we multiply both sides by 5, we will obtain

$$4 \times 5 > 3 \times 5$$

$$20 > 15$$

The sense of the inequality does not change.

The sense of an inequality becomes opposite if each side is multiplied or divided by the same negative real number.

EXAMPLE

$$4 > 3$$

If we multiply both sides by -5, we would obtain

$$4 \times -5 < 3 \times -5$$

$$-20 < -15$$

The sense of the inequality becomes opposite.

If $a > b$ and a, b, and n are positive real numbers, then

$$a^n > b^n \text{ and } a^{-n} < b^{-n}$$

If $x > y$ and $q > p$, then $x + q > y + p$.

If $x > y > 0$ and $q > p > 0$, then $xq > yp$.

Inequalities that have the same solution set are called **equivalent inequalities**.

PROBLEM

Solve the inequality $2x + 5 > 9$.

SOLUTION

Add -5 to both sides:	$2x + 5 + (-5) > 9 + (-5)$
Additive inverse property:	$2x + 0 > 9 + (-5)$
Additive identity property:	$2x > 9 + (-5)$

Combine terms: $2x > 4$

Multiply both sides by $\dfrac{1}{2}$: $\dfrac{1}{2}(2x) > \dfrac{1}{2} \times 4$

$x > 2$

The solution set is

$$X = \{x \mid 2x + 5 > 9\}$$
$$= \{x \mid x > 2\}$$

(that is all x, such that x is greater than 2).

PROBLEM

Solve the inequality $4x + 3 < 6x + 8$.

SOLUTION

In order to solve the inequality $4x + 3 < 6x + 8$, we must find all values of x which make it true. Thus, we wish to obtain x alone on one side of the inequality.

Add -3 to both sides:

$$4x + 3 < 6x + 8$$
$$\underline{ - 3 \phantom{<6x+}- 3}$$
$$4x < 6x + 5$$

Add $-6x$ to both sides:

$$4x < 6x + 8$$
$$\underline{ - 6x \phantom{<6x+}- 6x}$$
$$-2x < 5$$

In order to obtain x alone we must divide both sides by (-2). Recall that dividing an inequality by a negative number reverses the inequality sign, hence

$$\frac{-2x}{-2} > \frac{5}{-2}$$

Cancelling $\frac{-2}{-2}$ we obtain, $x > -\frac{5}{2}$.

Thus, our solution is $\{x : x > -\frac{5}{2}\}$ (the set of all x such that x is greater than $-\frac{5}{2}$).

DRILL: INEQUALITIES

DIRECTIONS: Find the solution set for each inequality.

1. $3m + 2 < 7$

   (A) $m \geq \dfrac{5}{3}$ (B) $m \leq 2$ (C) $m < 2$

   (D) $m > 2$ (E) $m < \dfrac{5}{3}$

2. $\dfrac{1}{2}x - 3 \leq 1$

   (A) $-4 \leq x \leq 8$ (B) $x \geq -8$ (C) $x \leq 8$

   (D) $2 \leq x \leq 8$ (E) $x \geq 8$

3. $-3p + 1 \geq 16$

   (A) $p \geq -5$ (B) $p \geq \dfrac{-17}{3}$ (C) $p \leq \dfrac{-17}{3}$

   (D) $p \leq -5$ (E) $p \geq 5$

4. $-6 < \dfrac{2}{3}r + 6 \leq 2$

   (A) $-6 < r \leq -3$ (B) $-18 < r \leq -6$ (C) $r \geq -6$

   (D) $-2 < r \leq -\dfrac{4}{3}$ (E) $r \leq -6$

5. $0 < 2 - y < 6$

   (A) $-4 < y < 2$ (B) $-4 < y < 0$ (C) $-4 < y < -2$

   (D) $-2 < y < 4$ (E) $0 < y < 4$

RATIOS AND PROPORTIONS

The ratio of two numbers x and y written $x : y$ is the fraction $\frac{x}{y}$ where $y \neq 0$. A ratio compares x to y by dividing one by the other. Therefore, in order to compare ratios, simply compare the fractions.

A proportion is an equality of two ratios. The laws of proportion are listed below.

If $\dfrac{a}{b} = \dfrac{c}{d}$, then

   (A) $ad = bc$

   (B) $\dfrac{b}{a} = \dfrac{d}{c}$

(C) $\dfrac{a}{c} = \dfrac{b}{d}$

(D) $\dfrac{a+b}{b} = \dfrac{c+d}{d}$

(E) $\dfrac{a-b}{b} = \dfrac{c-d}{d}$

Given a proportion $a : b = c : d$, then a and d are called extremes, b and c are called the means, and d is called the fourth proportion to a, b, and c.

PROBLEM

Solve the proportion $\dfrac{x+1}{4} = \dfrac{15}{12}$.

SOLUTION

Cross-multiply to determine x; that is, multiply the numerator of the first fraction by the denominator of the second, and equate this to the product of the numerator of the second and the denominator of the first.

$$(x + 1)\,12 = 4 \times 15$$
$$12x + 12 = 60$$
$$x = 4$$

PROBLEM

Find the ratios of $x : y : z$ from the equations

$$7x = 4y + 8z, \quad 3z = 12x + 11y.$$

SOLUTION

By transposition we have

$$7x - 4y - 8z = 0$$
$$12x + 11y - 3z = 0$$

To obtain the ratio of $x : y$, we convert the given system into an equation in terms of just x and y. We may eliminate z as follows: Multiply each term of the first equation by 3 and each term of the second equation by 8 (because they are both z variables which we wish to eliminate), and then subtract the second equation from the first. We thus obtain

$$21x - 12y - 24z = 0$$
$$\underline{-(96x + 88y - 24z = 0)}$$
$$-75x - 100y = 0$$

Dividing each term of the last equation by 25, we obtain

$$-3x - 4y = 0$$

or, $\quad -3x = 4y$

Dividing both sides of this equation by 4 and by –3, we have the proportion

$$\frac{x}{4} = \frac{y}{-3}$$

We are now interested in obtaining the ratio of $y : z$. To do this we convert the given system of equations into an equation in terms of just y and z, by eliminating x as follows: Multiply each term of the first equation by 12, and each term of the second equation by 7, and then subtract the second equation from the first. We thus obtain

$$84x - 48y - 96z = 0$$
$$\underline{-(84x + 77y - 21z = 0)}$$
$$-125y - 75z = 0$$

Dividing each term of the last equation by 25, we obtain

$$-5y - 3z = 0$$

or, $\quad -3z = 5y$

Dividing both sides of this equation by 5 and by – 3, we have the proportion

$$\frac{z}{5} = \frac{y}{-3}.$$

From this result and our previous result we obtain

$$\frac{x}{4} = \frac{y}{-3} = \frac{z}{5}$$

as the desired ratios.

DRILL: RATIOS AND PROPORTIONS

<u>DIRECTIONS</u>: **Find the appropriate solutions.**

1.   Solve for n: $= \dfrac{4}{n} = \dfrac{8}{5}$.

    (A) 10   (B) 8   (C) 6   (D) 2.5   (E) 2

2.   Solve for n: $= \dfrac{2}{3} = \dfrac{n}{72}$.

    (A) 12   (B) 48   (C) 64   (D) 56   (E) 24

3. Solve for n: $n : 12 = 3 : 4$.

   (A) 8   (B) 1   (C) 9   (D) 4   (E) 10

4. Four out of every five students at West High take a mathematics course. If the enrollment at West is 785, how many students take mathematics?

   (A) 628   (B) 157   (C) 705   (D) 655   (E) 247

5. At a factory, three out of every 1,000 parts produced are defective. In a day, the factory can produce 25,000 parts. How many of these parts would be defective?

   (A) 7   (B) 75   (C) 750   (D) 7,500   (E) 75,000

6. A summer league softball team won 28 out of the 32 games they played. What is the ratio of games won to games played?

   (A) 4 : 5   (B) 3 : 4   (C) 7 : 8   (D) 2 : 3   (E) 1 : 8

7. A class of 24 students contains 16 males. What is the ratio of females to males?

   (A) 1 : 2   (B) 2 : 1   (C) 2 : 3   (D) 3 : 1   (E) 3 : 2

8. A family has a monthly income of $1,250, but they spend $450 a month on rent. What is the ratio of the amount of income to the amount paid for rent?

   (A) 16 : 25 (B) 25 : 9   (C) 25 : 16 (D) 9 : 25   (E) 36 : 100

9. A student attends classes 7.5 hours a day and works a part-time job for 3.5 hours a day. She knows she must get 7 hours of sleep a night. Write the ratio of the number of free hours in this student's day to the total number of hours in a day.

   (A) 1 : 3   (B) 4 : 3   (C) 8 : 24   (D) 1 : 4   (E) 5 : 12

10. In a survey by mail, 30 out of 750 questionnaires were returned. Write the ratio of question-naires returned to questionnaires mailed (write in simplest form).

    (A) 30 : 750 (B) 24 : 25   (C) 3 : 75   (D) 1 : 4   (E) 1 : 25

ALGEBRA DRILLS

ANSWER KEY

Drill: Operations with Polynomials

1.	(B)	6.	(B)	11.	(C)	16.	(C)
2.	(C)	7.	(C)	12.	(B)	17.	(D)
3.	(C)	8.	(E)	13.	(E)	18.	(E)
4.	(D)	9.	(A)	14.	(A)	19.	(B)
5.	(A)	10.	(D)	15.	(D)	20.	(B)

Drill: Simplifying Algebraic Expressions

1.	(C)	6.	(B)
2.	(D)	7.	(E)
3.	(B)	8.	(B)
4.	(A)	9.	(A)
5.	(D)	10.	(E)

Drill: Linear Equations

1.	(C)
2.	(A)
3.	(E)
4.	(D)
5.	(B)

Drill: Two Linear Equations

1.	(E)	6.	(B)
2.	(B)	7.	(D)
3.	(A)	8.	(E)
4.	(D)	9.	(A)
5.	(C)	10.	(B)

Drill: Quadratic Equations

1.	(A)	6.	(B)
2.	(D)	7.	(B)
3.	(B)	8.	(D)
4.	(C)	9.	(C)
5.	(E)	10.	(E)

Drill: Absolute Value Equations

1. (B)   4. (C)
2. (E)   5. (D)
3. (A)

Drill: Inequalities

1. (E)   4. (B)
2. (C)   5. (A)
3. (D)

Drill: Ratios and Proportions

1. (D)   4. (A)   7. (A)   10. (E)
2. (B)   5. (B)   8. (B)
3. (C)   6. (C)   9. (D)

III. GEOMETRY

POINTS, LINES, AND ANGLES

Geometry is built upon a series of undefined terms. These terms are those which we accept as known in order to define other undefined terms.

A) **Point**: Although we represent points on paper with small dots, a point has no size, thickness, or width.

B) **Line**: A line is a series of adjacent points which extends indefinitely. A line can be either curved or straight; however, unless otherwise stated, the term "line" refers to a straight line.

C) **Plane**: A plane is a collection of points lying on a flat surface, which extends indefinitely in all directions.

If A and B are two points on a line, then the **line segment** $\overline{AB}$ is the set of points on that line between A and B and including A and B, which are endpoints. The line segment is referred to as $\overline{AB}$.

A **ray** is a series of points that lie to one side of a single endpoint.

PROBLEM

How many lines can be found that contain (a) one given point (b) two given points (c) three given points?

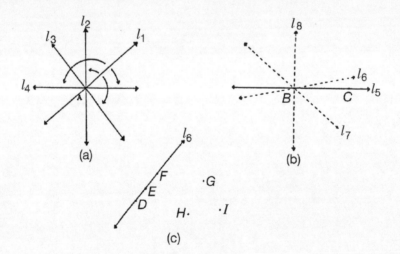

(a)
(b)
(c)

SOLUTION

(a) *Given one point A*, there are an infinite number of distinct lines that contain the given point. To see this, consider line l_1 passing through point A. By rotating l_1 around A like the hands of a clock, we obtain different lines l_2, l_3, etc. Since we can rotate l_1 in infinitely many ways, there are infinitely many lines containing A.

(b) *Given two distinct points B and C*, there is one and only one straight line passing through both. To see this, consider all the lines containing point B: l_5, l_6, l_7, and l_8. Only

l_5 contains both points B and C. Thus, there is only one line containing both points B and C. Since there is always at least one line containing two distinct points and never more than one, the line passing through the two points is said to be determined by the two points.

(c)   Given three distinct points, there may be one line or none. If a line exists that contains the three points, such as D, E, and F, then the points are said to be **colinear**. If no such line exists (as in the case of points G, H, and I) then the points are said to be **noncolinear**.

INTERSECTION LINES AND ANGLES

An **angle** is a collection of points which is the union of two rays having the same endpoint. An angle such as the one illustrated below can be referred to in any of the following ways:

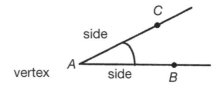

A)   by a capital letter which names its vertex, i.e., $\angle A$;

B)   by a lowercase letter or number placed inside the angle, i.e., $\angle x$;

C)   by three capital letters, where the middle letter is the vertex and the other two letters are not on the same ray, i.e., $\angle CAB$ or $\angle BAC$, both of which represent the angle illustrated in the figure.

TYPES OF ANGLES

A)   **Vertical angles** are formed when two lines intersect. These angles are equal.

B)   **Adjacent angles** are two angles with a common vertex and a common side, but no common interior points. In the following figure, $\angle DAC$ and $\angle BAC$ are adjacent angles. $\angle DAB$ and $\angle BAC$ are not.

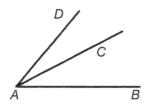

C)   A **right angle** is an angle whose measure is 90°.

D)   An **acute angle** is an angle whose measure is larger than 0°, but less than 90°.

E)   An **obtuse angle** is an angle whose measure is larger than 90° but less than 180°.

F)   A **straight angle** is an angle whose measure is 180°. Such an angle is, in fact, a straight line.

G)   A **reflex angle** is an angle whose measure is greater than 180° but less than 360°.

H) **Complementary angles** are two angles whose measures total 90°.

I) **Supplementary angles** are two angles whose measures total 180°.

J) **Congruent angles** are angles of equal measure.

PROBLEM

In the figure, we are given $\overline{AB}$ and triangle ABC. We are told that the measure of $\angle 1$ is five times the measure of $\angle 2$. Determine the measures of $\angle 1$ and $\angle 2$.

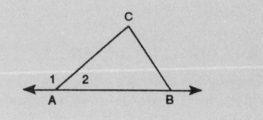

SOLUTION

Since $\angle 1$ and $\angle 2$ are adjacent angles whose non-common sides lie on a straight line, they are, by definition, supplementary. As supplements, their measures must total 180°.

If we let x = the measure of $\angle 2$, then $5x$ = the measure of $\angle 1$.

To determine the respective angle measures, set $x + 5x = 180$ and solve for x. $6x = 180$. Therefore, $x = 30$ and $5x = 150$.

Therefore, the measure of $\angle 1 = 150$ and the measure of $\angle 2 = 30$.

PERPENDICULAR LINES

Two lines are said to be **perpendicular** if they intersect and form right angles. The symbol for perpendicular (or, is therefore perpendicular to) is $\perp$; $\overline{AB}$ is perpendicular to $\overline{CD}$ is written $AB \perp CD$.

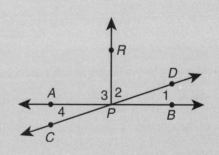

PROBLEM

We are given straight lines $\overline{AB}$ and $\overline{CD}$ intersecting at point P. $\overline{PR} \perp \overline{AB}$ and the measure of $\angle APD$ is 170°. Find the measures of $\angle 1$, $\angle 2$, $\angle 3$, and $\angle 4$.

SOLUTION

This problem will involve making use of several of the properties of supplementary and vertical angles, as well as perpendicular lines.

$\angle APD$ and $\angle 1$ are adjacent angles whose non-common sides lie on a straight line, $\overline{AB}$. Therefore, they are supplements and their measures total 180°.

$$m \angle APD + m \angle 1 = 180°.$$

We know $m \angle APD = 170°$. Therefore, by substitution, $170° + m \angle 1 = 180°$. This implies $m \angle 1 = 10°$.

$\angle 1$ and $\angle 4$ are vertical angles because they are formed by the intersection of two straight lines, $\overline{CD}$ and $\overline{AB}$, and their sides form two pairs of opposite rays. As vertical angles, they are, by theorem, of equal measure. Since $m \angle 1 = 10°$, then $m \angle 4 = 10°$.

Since $\overline{PR} \perp \overline{AB}$, at their intersection the angles formed must be right angles. Therefore, $\angle 3$ is a right angle and its measure is 90°. $m \angle 3 = 90°$.

The figure shows us that $\angle APD$ is composed of $\angle 3$ and $\angle 2$. Since the measure of the whole must be equal to the sum of the measures of its parts, $m \angle APD = m \angle 3 + m \angle 2$. We know the $m \angle APD = 170°$ and $m \angle 3 = 90°$, therefore, by substitution, we can solve for $m \angle 2$, our last unknown.

$$170° = 90° + m \angle 2$$

$$80° = m \angle 2$$

Therefore, $m \angle 1 = 10°$, $m \angle 2 = 80°$,

$m \angle 3 = 90°$, $m \angle 4 = 10°$.

PROBLEM

In the accompanying figure $\overline{SM}$ is the perpendicular bisector of $\overline{QR}$, and $\overline{SN}$ is the perpendicular bisector of $\overline{QP}$. Prove that $SR = SP$.

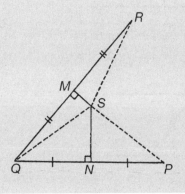

SOLUTION

Every point on the perpendicular bisector of a segment is equidistant from the endpoints of the segment.

Since point S is on the perpendicular bisector of $\overline{QR}$,

$$SR = SQ. \qquad\qquad (1)$$

Also, since point S is on the perpendicular bisector of $\overline{QP}$,

$$SQ = SP. \tag{2}$$

By the transitive property (quantities equal to the same quantity are equal), we have

$$SR = SP. \tag{3}$$

PARALLEL LINES

Two lines are called **parallel lines** if, and only if, they are in the same plane (coplanar) and do not intersect. The symbol for parallel, or is parallel to, is $\|$; $\overleftrightarrow{AB}$ is parallel to $\overleftrightarrow{CD}$ is written $\overleftrightarrow{AB} \parallel \overleftrightarrow{CD}$.

The distance between two parallel lines is the length of the perpendicular segment from any point on one line to the other line.

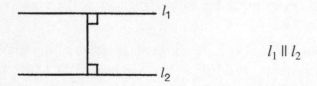

$$l_1 \parallel l_2$$

Given a line l and a point P not on line l, there is one and only one line through point P that is parallel to line l.

Two coplanar lines are either intersecting lines or parallel lines.

If two (or more) lines are perpendicular to the same line, then they are parallel to each other.

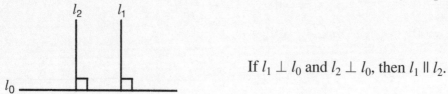

If $l_1 \perp l_0$ and $l_2 \perp l_0$, then $l_1 \parallel l_2$.

If two lines are cut by a transversal (a line intersecting two or more other lines) so that alternate interior angles are equal, the lines are parallel.

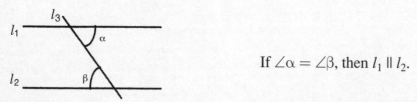

If $\angle\alpha = \angle\beta$, then $l_1 \parallel l_2$.

If two lines are parallel to the same line, then they are parallel to each other.

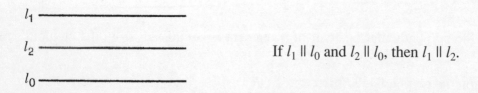

If $l_1 \parallel l_0$ and $l_2 \parallel l_0$, then $l_1 \parallel l_2$.

If a line is perpendicular to one of two parallel lines, then it is perpendicular to the other line, too.

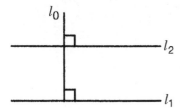

If $l_1 \parallel l_2$ and $l_1 \perp l_0$, then $l_0 \perp l_2$

If two lines being cut by a transversal form congruent corresponding angles, then the two lines are parallel.

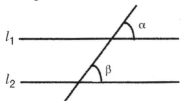

If $\angle\alpha = \angle\beta$, then $l_1 \parallel l_2$.

If two lines being cut by a transversal form interior angles on the same side of the transversal that are supplementary, then the two lines are parallel.

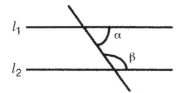

If $m\angle\alpha + m\angle\beta = 180°$, then $l_1 \parallel l_2$.

If a line is parallel to one of two parallel lines, it is also parallel to the other line.

$$l_0$$

$$l_1$$

If $l_1 \parallel l_2$ and $l_0 \parallel l_1$, then $l_0 \parallel l_2$.

$$l_2$$

If two parallel lines are cut by a transversal, then:

A)   The alternate interior angles are congruent.

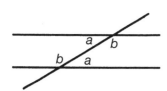

B)   The corresponding angles are congruent.

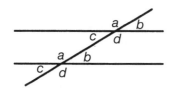

C) The consecutive interior angles are supplementary.

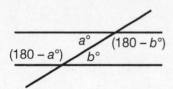

D) The alternate exterior angles are congruent.

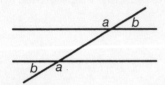

PROBLEM

Given: ∠2 is supplementary to ∠3.
Prove: $l_1 \parallel l_2$.

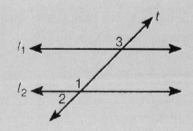

SOLUTION

Given two lines intercepted by a transversal, if a pair of corresponding angles are congruent, then the two lines are parallel. In this problem, we will show that since ∠1 and ∠2 are supplementary and ∠2 and ∠3 are supplementary, ∠1 and ∠3 are congruent. Since corresponding angles ∠1 and ∠3 are congruent, it follows $l_1 \parallel l_2$.

Statement	Reason
1. ∠2 is supplementary to ∠3.	1. Given.
2. ∠1 is supplementary to ∠2.	2. Two angles that form a linear pair are supplementary.
3. ∠1 ≅ ∠3.	3. Angles supplementary to the same angle are congruent.
4. $l_1 \parallel l_2$.	4. Given two lines intercepted by a transversal, if a pair of corresponding angles are congruent, then the two lines are parallel.

PROBLEM

If line $\overline{AB}$ is parallel to line $\overline{CD}$ and line $\overline{EF}$ is parallel to line $\overline{GH}$, prove that $m\angle 1 = m\angle 2$.

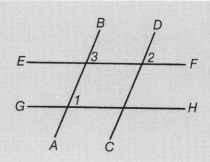

SOLUTION

To show $\angle 1 \cong \angle 2$, we relate both to $\angle 3$. Because $\overline{EF} \parallel \overline{GH}$, corresponding angles 1 and 3 are congruent. Since $\overline{AB} \parallel \overline{CD}$, corresponding angles 3 and 2 are congruent. Because both $\angle 1$ and $\angle 2$ are congruent to the same angle, it follows that $\angle 1 \cong \angle 2$.

	Statement		**Reason**
1.	$\overline{EF} \parallel \overline{GH}$	1.	Given.
2.	$m\angle 1 = m\angle 3$	2.	If two parallel lines are cut by a transversal, corresponding angles are of equal measure.
3.	$\overline{AB} \parallel \overline{CD}$	3.	Given
4.	$m\angle 2 = m\angle 3$	4.	If two parallel lines are cut by a transversal, corresponding angles are of equal measure.
5.	$m\angle 1 = m\angle 2$	5.	If two quantities are equal to the same quantity, they are equal to each other.

DRILL: LINES AND ANGLES

Intersecting Lines

<u>DIRECTIONS</u>: Refer to the diagram and find the appropriate solution.

1. Find a.

   (A) 38°   (B) 68°   (C) 78°

   (D) 90°   (E) 112°

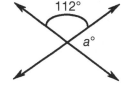

2. Find *c*.

    (A) 32° (B) 48° (C) 58°

    (D) 82° (E) 148°

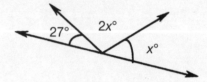

3. Determine *x*.

    (A) 21° (B) 23° (C) 51°

    (D) 102° (E) 153°

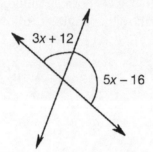

4. Find *x*.

    (A) 8 (B) 11.75 (C) 21

    (D) 23 (E) 32

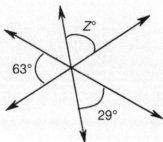

5. Find *z*.

    (A) 29° (B) 54° (C) 61°

    (D) 88° (E) 92°

Perpendicular Lines

DIRECTIONS: Refer to the diagram and find the appropriate solution.

6. $\overrightarrow{BA} \perp \overrightarrow{BC}$ and $m \angle DBC = 53°$. Find $m \angle ABD$.

    (A) 27° (B) 33° (C) 37°

    (D) 53° (E) 90°

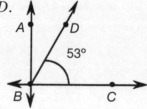

7. $m \angle 1 = 90°$. Find $m \angle 2$.

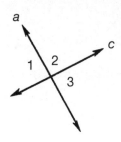

   (A) 80°   (B) 90°   (C) 100°

   (D) 135°   (E) 180°

8. If $n \perp p$, which of the following statements is true?

   (A) $\angle 1 \cong \angle 2$

   (B) $\angle 4 \cong \angle 5$

   (C) $m \angle 4 + m \angle 5 > m \angle 1 + m \angle 2$

   (D) $m \angle 3 > m \angle 2$

   (E) $m \angle 4 = 90°$

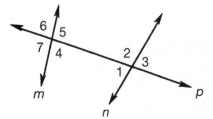

9. $\overline{CD} \perp \overline{EF}$. If $m \angle 1 = 2x$, $m \angle 2 = 30°$, and $m \angle 3 = x$, find x.

   (A) 5°

   (B) 10°

   (C) 12°

   (D) 20°

   (E) 25°

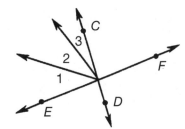

10. In the figure, $p \perp t$ and $q \perp t$, which of the following statements is false?

   (A) $\angle 1 \cong \angle 4$

   (B) $\angle 2 \cong \angle 3$

   (C) $m \angle 2 + m \angle 3 = m \angle 4 + m \angle 6$

   (D) $m \angle 5 + m \angle 6 = 180°$

   (E) $m \angle 2 > m \angle 5$

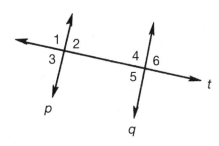

Parallel Lines

DIRECTIONS: Refer to the diagram and find the appropriate solution.

11. If $a \parallel b$, find z.

    (A) 26°   (B) 32°   (C) 64°
    (D) 86°   (E) 116°

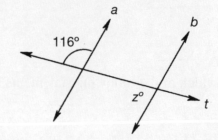

12. In the figure, $p \parallel q \parallel r$. Find $m \angle 7$.

    (A) 27°   (B) 33°   (C) 47°
    (D) 57°   (E) 64°

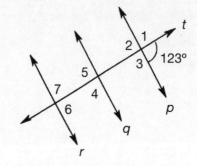

13. If $m \parallel n$, which of the following statements is not necessarily true?

    (A) $\angle 2 \cong \angle 5$
    (B) $\angle 3 \cong \angle 6$
    (C) $m \angle 4 + m \angle 5 = 180°$
    (D) $\angle 1 \cong \angle 6$
    (E) $m \angle 7 + m \angle 3 = 180°$

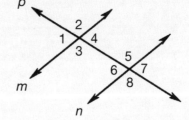

14. If $r \parallel s$, find $m \angle 2$.

    (A) 17°   (B) 27°   (C) 43°
    (D) 67°   (E) 73°

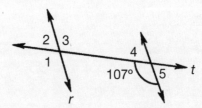

15. If $a \parallel b$ and $c \parallel d$, find $m \angle 5$.

    (A) 55°   (B) 65°   (C) 75°
    (D) 95°   (E) 125°

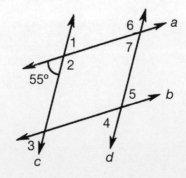

POLYGONS (CONVEX)

A **polygon** is a figure with the same number of sides as angles.

An **equilateral polygon** is a polygon all of whose sides are of equal measure.

An **equiangular polygon** is a polygon all of whose angles are of equal measure.

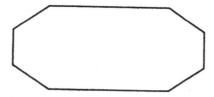

A **regular polygon** is a polygon that is both equilateral and equiangular.

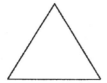

PROBLEM

Each interior angle of a regular polygon contains 120°. How many sides does the polygon have?

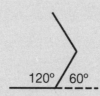

SOLUTION

At each vertex of a polygon, the exterior angle is supplementary to the interior angle, as shown in the diagram.

Since we are told that the interior angles measure 120°, we can deduce that the exterior angle measures 60°.

Each exterior angle of a regular polygon of n sides measure $\frac{360°}{n}$ degrees. We know that each exterior angle measures 60°, and, therefore, by setting $\frac{360°}{n}$ equal to 60°, we can determine the number of sides in the polygon. The calculation is as follows:

$$\frac{360°}{n} = 60°$$
$$60°n = 360°$$
$$n = 6$$

Therefore, the regular polygon, with interior angles of 120°, has six sides and is called a hexagon.

The area of a regular polygon can be determined by using the **apothem** and **radius** of the polygon. The apothem (a) of a regular polygon is the segment from the center of the polygon perpendicular to a side of the polygon. The radius (r) of a regular polygon is the segment joining any vertex of a regular polygon with the center of that polygon.

(1) All radii of a regular polygon are congruent.

(2) The radius of a regular polygon is congruent to a side.

(3) All apothems of a regular polygon are congruent.

The **area** of a regular polygon equals one-half the product of the length of the apothem and the perimeter.

$$\text{Area} = \frac{1}{2}a \times p$$

PROBLEM

Find the area of the regular pentagon whose radius is 8 and whose apothem is 6.

SOLUTION

If the radius is 8, the length of a side is also 8. Therefore, the perimeter of the polygon is 40.

$$A = \frac{1}{2}a \times p$$

$$A = \frac{1}{2}(6)(40)$$

$$A = 120$$

PROBLEM

Find the area of a regular hexagon if one side has length 6.

SOLUTION

Since the length of a side equals 6, the radius also equals 6 and the perimeter equals 36. The base of the right triangle, formed by the radius and apothem, is half the length of a side, or 3. You can find the length of the apothem by using what is known as the Pythagorean Theorem (discussed further in the next section).

$$a^2 + b^2 = c^2$$

$$a^2 + (3)^2 = (6)^2$$

$$a^2 = 36 - 9$$

$$a^2 = 27$$

$$a = 3\sqrt{3}$$

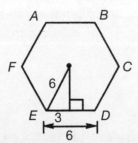

The apothem equals $3\sqrt{3}$. Therefore, the area of the hexagon

$$= \frac{1}{2}a \times p$$

$$= \frac{1}{2}\left(3\sqrt{3}\right)(36)$$

$$= 54\sqrt{3}$$

DRILL: REGULAR POLYGONS

Angle Measures

DIRECTIONS: Find the appropriate solution.

1. Find the measure of an interior angle of a regular pentagon.

    (A) 55°   (B) 72°   (C) 90°   (D) 108°   (E) 540°

2. Find the measure of an exterior angle of a regular octagon.

    (A) 40°   (B) 45°   (C) 135°   (D) 540°   (E) 1,080°

3. Find the sum of the measures of the exterior angles of a regular triangle.

    (A) 90°   (B) 115°   (C) 180°   (D) 250°   (E) 360°

Area(s) and Perimeter(s)

DIRECTIONS: Find the appropriate solution.

4. Find the area of a square with a perimeter of 12 cm.

    (A) 9 cm²   (B) 12 cm²   (C) 48 cm²   (D) 96 cm²   (E) 144 cm²

5. A regular triangle has sides of 24 mm. If the apothem is $4\sqrt{3}$ mm, find the area of the tri-angle.

    (A) 72 mm²   (B) $96\sqrt{3}$ mm²   (C) 144 mm²

    (D) $144\sqrt{3}$ mm²   (E) 576 mm²

6. Find the area of a regular hexagon with sides of 4 cm.

(A) $12\sqrt{3}$ cm^2 (B) 24 cm^2 (C) $24\sqrt{3}$ cm^2

(D) 48 cm^2 (E) $48\sqrt{3}$ cm^2

7. Find the area of a regular decagon with sides of length 6 cm and an apothem of length 9.2 cm.

(A) 55.2 cm^2 (B) 60 cm^2 (C) 138 cm^2

(D) 138.3 cm^2 (E) 276 cm^2

8. The perimeter of a regular heptagon (7-gon) is 36.4 cm. Find the length of each side.

(A) 4.8 cm   (B) 5.2 cm   (C) 6.7 cm   (D) 7 cm   (E) 10.4 cm

9. The apothem of a regular quadrilateral is 4 in. Find the perimeter.

(A) 12 in.   (B) 16 in.   (C) 24 in.   (D) 32 in.   (E) 64 in.

10. A regular triangle has a perimeter of 18 cm; a regular pentagon has a perimeter of 30 cm; a regular hexagon has a perimeter of 33 cm. Which figure (or figures) have sides with the longest measure?

(A) Regular triangle

(B) Regular triangle and regular pentagon

(C) Regular pentagon

(D) Regular pentagon and regular hexagon

(E) Regular hexagon

TRIANGLES

A closed three-sided geometric figure is called a **triangle**. The points of the intersection of the sides of a triangle are called the **vertices** of the triangle.

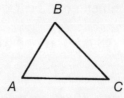

The **perimeter** of a triangle is the sum of the measures of the sides of the triangle.

A triangle with no equal sides is called a **scalene** triangle.

A triangle having at least two equal sides is called an **isosceles** triangle. The third side is called the **base** of the triangle.

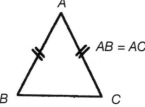

A side of a triangle is a line segment whose endpoints are the vertices of two angles of the triangle.

An **interior angle** of a triangle is an angle formed by two sides and includes the third side within its collection of points.

An **equilateral triangle** is a triangle having three equal sides. $\overline{AB} = \overline{AC} = \overline{BC}$.

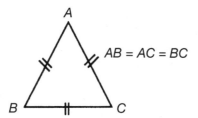

The sum of the measures of the interior angles of a triangle is 180°.

A triangle with one obtuse angle greater than 90° is called an **obtuse triangle**.

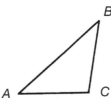

An **acute triangle** is a triangle with three acute angles (less than 90°).

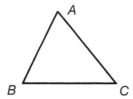

A triangle with a right angle is called a **right triangle**. The side opposite the right angle in a right triangle is called the hypotenuse of the right triangle. The other two sides are called arms or legs of the right triangle.

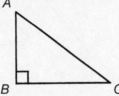

An **altitude** of a triangle is a line segment from a vertex of the triangle perpendicular to the opposite side.

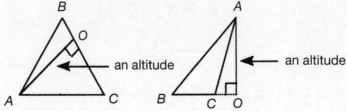

A line segment connecting a vertex of a triangle and the midpoint of the opposite side is called a **median** of the triangle.

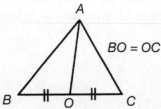

A line that bisects and is perpendicular to a side of a triangle is called a **perpendicular bisector** of that side.

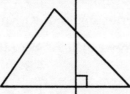

An **angle bisector** of a triangle is a line that bisects an angle and extends to the opposite side of the triangle.

The line segment that joins the midpoints of two sides of a triangle is called a **midline** of the triangle.

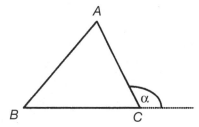

$AD = DC$
$BE = EC$

midline: DE

An **exterior angle** of a triangle is an angle formed outside a triangle by one side of the triangle and the extension of an adjacent side.

A triangle whose three interior angles have equal measure (60° each) is said to be **equiangular**.

Two triangles are **similar** if their corresponding sides are proportional.

Three or more lines (or rays or segments) are concurrent if there exists one point common to all of them, that is, if they all intersect at the same point.

RIGHT TRIANGLES

A right triangle is any triangle with a 90° angle. The PSAT loves to test you on right triangles because it gives them a chance to use the *Pythagorean theorem*. This theorem states that in any right triangle the lengths of any two sides can be used to solve for the third. It is expressed as

$$a^2 + b^2 = c^2$$

where a and b are the perpendicular sides and c is the hypotenuse—the side opposite the 90° angle.

There are four types of right triangles that occur on the test more often than others. If you take the time to familiarize yourself with them now, you will be able to determine the length of the missing side without using the Pythagorean theorem, saving both time and the possibility of careless errors.

3:4:5 Right Triangle This ratio expresses the relationship of the three sides to each other, where 3 and 4 are the perpendicular sides and 5 is the hypotenuse. The test refers to this type of triangle because when these numbers are used in the Pythagorean theorem the solution will always be a whole number. So when you recognize this type of triangle, you won't actually have to use the theorem to solve. Any multiple of this ratio is also acceptable, such as 6:8:10, 9:12:15, 30:40:50, and so on.

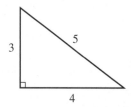

5:12:13 Right Triangle Similar to the 3:4:5 triangle, this ratio expresses the relationship of the three sides to each other, where 5 and 12 are the perpendicular sides and 13 is the hypotenuse. The test will use this type of triangle because when these numbers are used in the Pythagorean theorem the solution will always be a whole number. Familiarize yourself with this ratio so when it comes up on the test you won't have to waste time solving the theorem. Multiples of this ratio are also acceptable, such as 10:24:26, 50:120:130, and so forth.

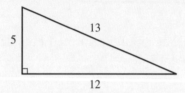

30° 60° 90° Right Triangle Whenever the three angles of a right triangle measure 30°, 60°, and 90°, the lengths of the sides correspond as follows: the side opposite of the 30° angle is said to be x, the side opposite the 60° angle is $x\sqrt{3}$, and the side opposite the 90° angle, the hypotenuse, is twice the smaller side, or $2x$. Note: an equilateral triangle split in two creates two 30° 60° 90° triangles, where the side opposite the 60° angle becomes the height of the entire triangle.

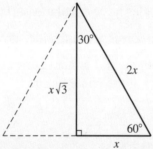

45° 45° 90° Right Triangle Often referred to as an isosceles right triangle, when the angles of a right triangle measure 45°, 45°, and 90° the lengths of the sides correspond as follows: the two perpendicular and equal sides are said to be of length x, and the hypotenuse is $x\sqrt{2}$. Note: the diagonal of a square is also the hypotenuse of an isosceles right triangle.

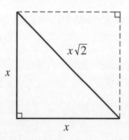

PROBLEM

The measure of the vertex angle of an isosceles triangle exceeds the measurement of each base angle by 30°. Find the value of each angle of the triangle.

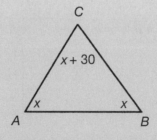

SOLUTION

We know that the sum of the values of the angles of a triangle is 180°. In an isosceles triangle, the angles opposite the congruent sides (the base angles) are, themselves, congruent and of equal value.

Therefore,

(1) Let x = the measure of each base angle.

(2) Then $x + 30$ = the measure of the vertex angle.

We can solve for x algebraically by keeping in mind the sum of all the measures will be 180°.

$$x + x + (x + 30) = 180$$
$$3x + 30 = 180$$
$$3x = 150$$
$$x = 50$$

Therefore, the base angles each measure 50°, and the vertex angle measures 80°.

PROBLEM

Prove that the base angles of an isosceles right triangle measure 45° each.

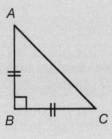

SOLUTION

As drawn in the figure, $\triangle ABC$ is an isosceles right triangle with base angles BAC and BCA. The sum of the measures of the angles of any triangle is 180°. For $\triangle ABC$, this means

$$m \angle BAC + m \angle BCA + m \angle ABC = 180° \qquad (1)$$

But $m \angle ABC = 90°$ because ABC is a right triangle. Furthermore, $m \angle BCA = m \angle BAC$, since the base angles of an isosceles triangle are congruent. Using these facts in equation (1)

$$m \angle BAC + m \angle BCA + 90° = 180°$$

or $\qquad 2m \angle BAC = 2m \angle BCA = 90°$

or $\qquad m \angle BAC = m \angle BCA = 45°.$

Therefore, the base angles of an isosceles right triangle measure 45° each.

The area of a triangle is given by the formula $A = \frac{1}{2}bh$, where b is the length of a base, which can be any side of the triangle, and h is the corresponding height of the triangle, which is the perpendicular line segment that is drawn from the vertex opposite the base to the base itself.

$$A = \frac{1}{2}bh$$

$$A = \frac{1}{2}(10)(3)$$

$$A = 15$$

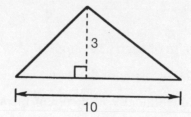

The area of a right triangle is found by taking $\frac{1}{2}$ the product of the lengths of its two arms.

$$A = \frac{1}{2}(5)(12)$$

$$A = 30$$

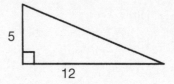

DRILL: TRIANGLES

Angle Measures

<u>DIRECTIONS</u>: Refer to the diagram and find the appropriate solution.

1. In $\triangle PQR$, $\angle Q$ is a right angle. Find $m \angle R$.

    (A) 27°   (B) 33°   (C) 54°

    (D) 67°   (E) 157°

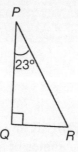

2. $\triangle MNO$ is isosceles. If the vertex angle, $\angle N$, has a measure of 96°, find the measure of $\angle M$.

    (A) 21°   (B) 42°   (C) 64°

    (D) 84°   (E) 96°

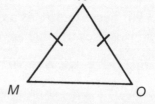

3. Find x.

    (A) 15°   (B) 25°   (C) 30°

    (D) 45°   (E) 90°

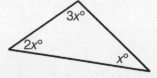

4. Find $m \angle 1$.

    (A) 40°   (B) 66°   (C) 74°

    (D) 114°   (E) 140°

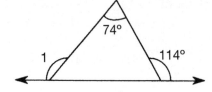

5. $\triangle ABC$ is a right triangle with a right angle at B. $\triangle BDC$ is a right triangle with right angle $\angle BDC$. If $m \angle C = 36°$, find $m \angle A$.

    (A) 18°   (B) 36°   (C) 54°

    (D) 72°   (E) 180°

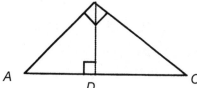

Similar Triangles

DIRECTIONS: Refer to the diagram and find the appropriate solution.

6. The two triangles shown are similar. Find b.

    (A) $2\frac{2}{3}$ (B) 3   (C) 4

    (D) 16   (E) 24

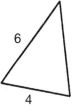

7. The two triangles shown are similar. Find $m \angle 1$.

    (A) 48°   (B) 53°   (C) 74°

    (D) 127°   (E) 180°

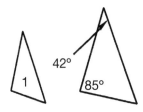

8. The two triangles shown are similar. Find a and b.

    (A) 5 and 10   (B) 4 and 8   (C) $4\frac{2}{3}$ and $7\frac{1}{3}$

    (D) 5 and 8   (E) $5\frac{1}{3}$ and 8

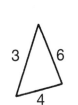 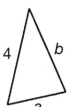

9. The perimeter of $\triangle LXR$ is 45 and the perimeter of $\triangle ABC$ is 27. If $LX = 15$, find the length of AB.

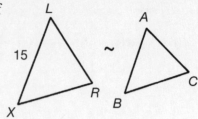

(A) 9   (B) 15   (C) 27

(D) 45   (E) 72

10. Find b.

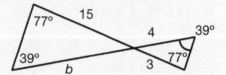

(A) 9   (B) 15   (C) 20

(D) 45   (E) 60

Area

DIRECTIONS: Refer to the diagram and find the appropriate solution.

11. Find the area of $\triangle MNO$.

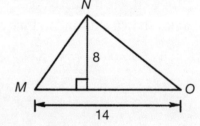

(A) 22   (B) 49   (C) 56

(D) 84   (E) 112

12. Find the area of $\triangle PQR$.

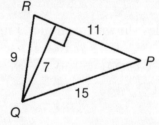

(A) 31.5   (B) 38.5   (C) 53

(D) 77   (E) 82.5

13. Find the area of $\triangle STU$.

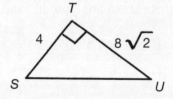

(A) $4\sqrt{2}$ (B) $8\sqrt{2}$ (C) $12\sqrt{2}$

(D) $16\sqrt{2}$ (E) $32\sqrt{2}$

14. Find the area of $\triangle ABC$.

    (A) 54 cm²   (B) 81 cm²   (C) 108 cm²

    (D) 135 cm²   (E) 180 cm²

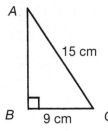

15. Find the area of $\triangle XYZ$.

    (A) 20 cm²   (B) 50 cm²   (C) $50\sqrt{2}$ cm²

    (D) 100 cm²   (E) 200 cm²

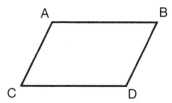

QUADRILATERALS

A **quadrilateral** is a polygon with four sides.

PARALLELOGRAMS

A **parallelogram** is a quadrilateral whose opposite sides are parallel.

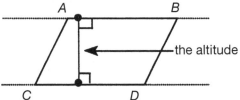

Two angles that have their vertices at the endpoints of the same side of a parallelogram are called **consecutive angles**.

The perpendicular segment connecting any point of a line containing one side of the parallelogram to the line containing the opposite side of the parallelogram is called the **altitude** of the parallelogram.

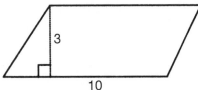

A diagonal of a polygon is a line segment joining any two nonconsecutive vertices.

The area of a parallelogram is given by the formula $A = bh$, where b is the base and h is the height drawn perpendicular to that base. Note that the height equals the altitude of the parallelogram.

$A = bh$

$A = (10)(3)$

$A = 30$

RECTANGLES

A rectangle is a parallelogram with right angles.

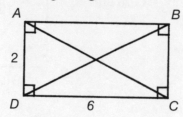

The diagonals of a rectangle are equal.

If the diagonals of a parallelogram are equal, the parallelogram is a rectangle.

If a quadrilateral has four right angles, then it is a rectangle.

The area of a rectangle is given by the formula $A = lw$, where l is the length and w is the width.

$A = lw$

$A = (3)(10)$

$A = 30$

RHOMBI

A rhombus is a parallelogram which has two adjacent sides that are equal.

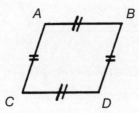

All sides of a rhombus are equal.

The diagonals of a rhombus are perpendicular to each other.

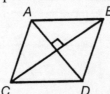

The diagonals of a rhombus bisect the angles of the rhombus.

If the diagonals of a parallelogram are perpendicular, the parallelogram is a rhombus.

If a quadrilateral has four equal sides, then it is a rhombus.

A parallelogram is a rhombus if either diagonal of the parallelogram bisects the angles of the vertices it joins.

SQUARES

A square is a rhombus with a right angle.

A square is an equilateral quadrilateral.

A square has all the properties of parallelograms and rectangles.

A rhombus is a square if one of its interior angles is a right angle.

In a square, the measure of either diagonal can be calculated by multiplying the length of any side by the square root of 2.

The area of a square is given by the formula $A = s^2$, where s is the side of the square. Since all sides of a square are equal, it does not matter which side is used.

$A = s^2$

$A = 6^2$

$A = 36$

The area of a square can also be found by taking $\frac{1}{2}$ the product of the length of the diagonal squared.

$A = \frac{1}{2}d^2$

$A = \frac{1}{2}(8)^2$

$A = 32$

TRAPEZOIDS

A **trapezoid** is a quadrilateral with two and only two sides parallel. The parallel sides of a trapezoid are called **bases**.

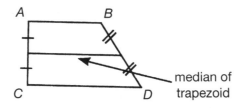

The **median** of a trapezoid is the line joining the midpoints of the non-parallel sides.

The perpendicular segment connecting any point in the line containing one base of the trapezoid to the line containing the other base is the **altitude** of the trapezoid.

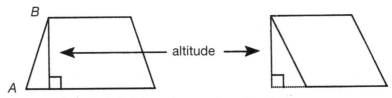

An **isosceles trapezoid** is a trapezoid whose non-parallel sides are equal. A pair of angles including only one of the parallel sides is called **a pair of base angles**.

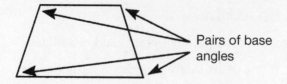

Pairs of base angles

The median of a trapezoid is parallel to the bases and equal to one-half their sum.

The base angles of an isosceles trapezoid are equal.

The diagonals of an isosceles trapezoid are equal.

The opposite angles of an isosceles trapezoid are supplementary.

The area of a trapezoid is equal to one-half the product of the length of its altitude and the sum of its bases.

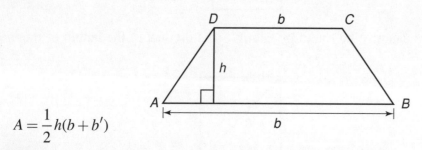

$$A = \frac{1}{2}h(b + b')$$

PROBLEM

Prove that all pairs of consecutive angles of a parallelogram are supplementary.

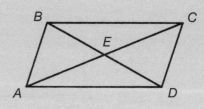

SOLUTION

We must prove that the pairs of angles $\angle BAD$ and $\angle ADC$, $\angle ADC$ and $\angle DCB$, $\angle DCB$ and $\angle CBA$, and $\angle CBA$ and $\angle BAD$ are supplementary. (This means that the sum of their measures is 180°.)

Because $ABCD$ is a parallelogram, $\overline{AB} \parallel \overline{CD}$. Angles BAD and ADC are consecutive interior angles, as are $\angle CBA$ and $\angle DCB$. Since the consecutive interior angles formed by two parallel lines and a transversal are supplementary, $\angle BAD$ and $\angle ADC$ are supplementary, as are $\angle CBA$ and $\angle DCB$.

Similarly, $\overline{AD} \parallel \overline{BC}$. Angles ADC and DCB are consecutive interior angles, as are $\angle CBA$ and $\angle BAD$. Since the consecutive interior angles formed by two parallel lines and a transversal are supplementary, $\angle CBA$ and $\angle BAD$ are supplementary, as are $\angle ADC$ and $\angle DCB$.

In the accompanying figure, $\triangle ABC$ is given to be an isosceles right triangle with $\angle ABC$ a right angle and $\overline{AB} \cong \overline{BC}$. Line segment $\overline{BD}$ which bisects $\overline{CA}$, is extended to E so that $\overline{BD} \cong \overline{DE}$. Prove $BAEC$ is a square.

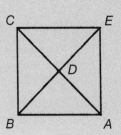

SOLUTION

A square is a rectangle in which two consecutive sides are congruent. This definition will provide the framework for the proof in this problem. We will prove that $BAEC$ is a parallelogram that is specifically a rectangle with consecutive sides congruent, namely a square.

Statement	Reason
1. $\overline{BD} \cong \overline{DE}$ and $\overline{AD} \cong \overline{DC}$	1. Given ($\overline{BD}$ bisects $\overline{CA}$).
2. $BAEC$ is a parallelogram.	2. If diagonals of a quadrilateral bisect each other, then the quadrilateral is a parallelogram.
3. $\angle ABC$ is a right angle.	3. Given
4. $BAEC$ is a rectangle.	4. A parallelogram, one of whose angles is a right angle, is a rectangle.
5. $\overline{AB} \cong \overline{BC}$.	5. Given
6. $BAEC$ is a square.	6. If a rectangle has two congruent consecutive sides, then the rectangle is a square.

DRILL: QUADRILATERALS

Parallelograms, Rectangles, Rhombi, Squares, Trapezoids

DIRECTIONS: Refer to the diagram and find the appropriate solution.

1. In parallelogram $WXYZ$, $\overline{WX} = 14$, $\overline{WZ} = 6$, $\overline{ZY} = 3x + 5$, and $\overline{XY} = 2y - 4$. Find x and y.

    (A) 3 and 5   (B)   4 and 5   (C)   4 and 6

    (D)   6 and 10   (E)   6 and 14

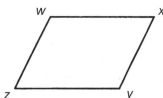

2. Quadrilateral *ABCD* is a parallelogram.
   If $m \angle B = 6x + 2$ and $m \angle D = 98$, find x.

   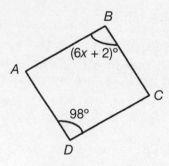

   (A) 12 (B) 16 (C) $16\frac{2}{3}$

   (D) 18 (E) 20

3. Find the area of parallelogram *STUV*.

   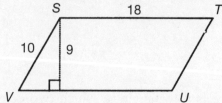

   (A) 56 (B) 90 (C) 108

   (D) 162 (E) 180

4. Find the area of parallelogram *MNOP*.

   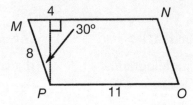

   (A) 19 (B) 32 (C) $32\sqrt{3}$

   (D) 44 (E) $44\sqrt{3}$

5. If the perimeter of rectangle *PQRS* is 40, find x.

   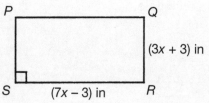

   (A) 31 (B) 38 (C) 2

   (D) 44 (E) 121

6. In rectangle *ABCD*, $\overline{AD} = 6$ cm and $\overline{DC} = 8$ cm.
   Find the length of the diagonal $\overline{AC}$.

   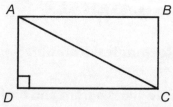

   (A) 10 cm (B) 12 cm (C) 20 cm

   (D) 28 cm (E) 48 cm

7. Find the area of rectangle *UVXY*.

   (A) 17 cm² (B) 34 cm² (C) 35 cm²

   (D) 70 cm² (E) 140 cm²

8. Find the length of $\overline{BO}$ in rectangle $BCDE$ if the diagonal $\overline{EC}$ is 17 mm.

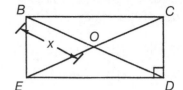

(A) 6.55 mm (B) 8 mm   (C) 8.5 mm

(D) 17 mm   (E) 34 mm

9. In rhombus $DEFG$, $\overline{DE} = 7$ cm. Find the perimeter of the rhombus.

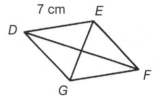

(A) 14 cm   (B) 28 cm   (C) 42 cm

(D) 49 cm   (E) 56 cm

10. In rhombus $RHOM$, the diagonal $\overline{RO}$ is 8 cm and the diagonal $\overline{HM}$ is 12 cm. Find the area of the rhombus.

(A) 20 cm² (B) 40 cm² (C) 48 cm²

(D) 68 cm² (E) 96 cm²

11. In rhombus $GHIJ$, $\overline{GI} = 6$ cm and $\overline{HJ} = 8$ cm. Find the length of $\overline{GH}$.

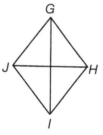

(A) 3 cm   (B) 4 cm   (C) 5 cm

(D) $4\sqrt{3}$ cm (E) 14 cm

12. In rhombus $CDEF$, $\overline{CD}$ is 13 mm and $\overline{DX}$ is 5 mm. Find the area of the rhombus.

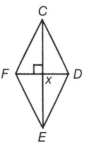

(A) 31 mm² (B) 60 mm² (C) 78 mm²

(D) 120 mm² (E) 260 mm²

13. Quadrilateral $ATUV$ is a square. If the perimeter of the square is 44 cm, find the length of $\overline{AT}$.

(A) 4 cm   (B) 11 cm   (C) 22 cm   (D) 30 cm   (E) 40 cm

14. The area of square *XYZW* is 196 cm². Find the perimeter of the square.

    (A)   28 cm   (B)   42 cm   (C)   56 cm
    (D)   98 cm   (E)   196 cm

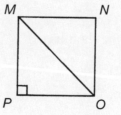

15. In square *MNOP*, $\overline{MN}$ is 6 cm. Find the length of diagonal $\overline{MO}$.

    (A)   6 cm   (B) $6\sqrt{2}$ cm (C) $6\sqrt{3}$ cm
    (D) $6\sqrt{6}$ cm (E)   12 cm

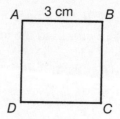

16. In square *ABCD*, $\overline{AB} = 3$ cm. Find the area of the square.

    (A)   9 cm²   (B)   12 cm²   (C)   15 cm²
    (D)   18 cm²   (E)   21 cm²

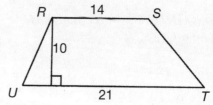

17. Find the area of trapezoid *RSTU*.

    (A)   80 cm²   (B)   87.5 cm² (C)   140 cm²
    (D)   147 cm² (E)   175 cm²

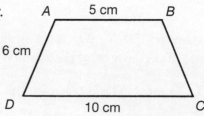

18. *ABCD* is an isosceles trapezoid. Find the perimeter.

    (A)   21 cm   (B)   27 cm   (C)   30 cm
    (D)   50 cm   (E)   54 cm

19. Find the area of trapezoid *MNOP*.

(A) $(17 + 3\sqrt{3})$ mm²

(B) $\dfrac{33}{2}$ mm²

(C) $\dfrac{33\sqrt{3}}{2}$ mm²

(D) 33 mm²

(E) $33\sqrt{3}$ mm²

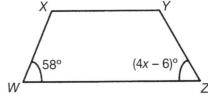

20. Trapezoid *XYZW* is isosceles. If $m \angle W = 58°$ and $m \angle Z = (4x - 6)$, find $x°$.

(A) 8°   (B) 12°   (C) 13°

(D) 16°   (E) 58°

CIRCLES

A **circle** is a set of points in the same plane equidistant from a fixed point, called its center.

A **radius** of a circle is a line segment drawn from the center of the circle to any point on the circle.

A portion of a circle is called an **arc** of the circle.

A line that intersects a circle in two points is called a **secant**.

A line segment joining two points on a circle is called a **chord** of the circle.

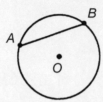

A chord that passes through the center of the circle is called a **diameter** of the circle.

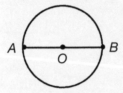

The line passing through the centers of two (or more) circles is called the **line of centers**.

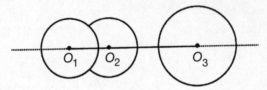

An angle whose vertex is on the circle and whose sides are chords of the circle is called an **inscribed angle**.

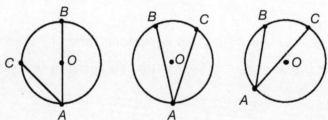

An angle whose vertex is at the center of a circle and whose sides are radii is called a **central angle**.

The measure of a minor arc is the measure of the central angle that intercepts that arc.

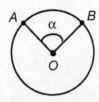

$$m\widehat{AB} = \alpha = m\angle AOB$$

The distance from a point P to a given circle is the distance from that point to the point where the circle intersects with a line segment with endpoints at the center of the circle and point P.

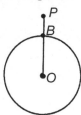

The distance of point P to the diagrammed circle with center O is the line segment $\overline{PB}$ of line segment $\overline{PO}$.

A line that has one and only one point of intersection with a circle is called a tangent to that circle, while their common point is called a **point of tangency**.

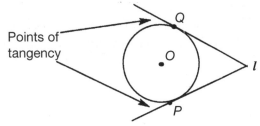

Congruent circles are circles whose radii are congruent.

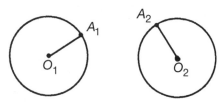

If $O_1A_1 > O_2A_2$, then $O_1 > O_2$.

The measure of a semicircle is 180°.

A **circumscribed circle** is a circle passing through all the vertices of a polygon.

Circles that have the same center and unequal radii are called **concentric circles**.

A and B are points on circle Q such that $\triangle AQB$ is equilateral. If the length of side $\overline{AB} = 12$, find the length of arc AB.

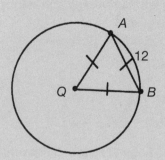

SOLUTION

To find the arc length of arc AB, we must find the measure of the central angle $\angle AQB$ and the measure of the radius $\overline{QA}$. $\angle AQB$ is an interior angle of the equilateral triangle $\triangle AQB$. Therefore,

$$m \angle AQB = 60°.$$

Similarly, in the equilateral $\triangle AQB$,

$$\overline{AQ} = \overline{AB} = \overline{QB} = 12.$$

Given the radius, r, and the central angle, n, the arc length is given by

$$\frac{n}{360} \times 2\pi r$$

Therefore, by substitution,

$$\angle AQB = \frac{60}{360} \times 2\pi \times 12 = \frac{1}{6} \times 2\pi \times 12 = 4\pi.$$

Therefore, the length of arc $AB = 4\pi$.

PROBLEM

In circle O, the measure of arc AB is 80°. Find the measure of $\angle A$.

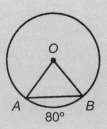

SOLUTION

The accompanying figure shows that arc AB is intercepted by central angle AOB. By definition, we know that the measure of the central angle is the measure of its intercepted arc. In this case, arc $mAB = m\angle AOB = 80°$.

Radius $\overline{OA}$ and radius $\overline{OB}$ are congruent and form two sides of $\triangle OAB$. By a theorem, the angles opposite these two congruent sides must, themselves, be congruent. Therefore, $m\angle A = m\angle B$.

The sum of the measures of the angles of a triangle is 180°. Therefore,

$$m\angle A + m\angle B + \angle AOB = 180°.$$

Since $m\angle A = m\angle B$, we can write

$$m\angle A + m\angle A + 80° = 180°$$

or $$2m\angle A = 100°$$

or $$m\angle A = 50°.$$

Therefore, the measure of $\angle A$ is 50°.

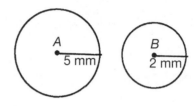

DRILL: CIRCLES

Circumference, Area, Concentric Circles

DIRECTIONS: Determine the accurate measure.

1. Find the circumference of circle A if its radius is 3 mm.

   (A) 3π mm   (B) 6π mm   (C) 9π mm   (D) 12π mm   (E) 15π mm

2. The circumference of circle H is 20π cm. Find the length of the radius.

   (A) 10 cm   (B) 20 cm   (C) 10π cm   (D) 15π cm   (E) 20π cm

3. The circumference of circle A is how many millimeters larger than the circumference of circle B?

   (A) 3 mm   (B) 6 mm   (C) 3π mm   (D) 6π mm   (E) 7π mm

4. If the diameter of circle X is 9 cm and if $\pi = 3.14$, find the circumference of the circle to the nearest tenth.

   (A) 9 cm   (B) 14.1 cm   (C) 21.1 cm   (D) 24.6 cm   (E) 28.3 cm

5.   Find the area of circle *I*.

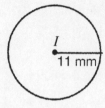

(A)   22 mm²

(D)   132 mm²

(B)   121 mm²

(E)   132π mm²

(C)   121π mm²

6.   The diameter of circle *Z* is 27 mm. Find the area of the circle.

(A)   91.125 mm²

(B)   182.25 mm²

(C)   191.5π mm²

(D)   182.25π mm²

(E)   729 mm²

7.   The area of circle *B* is 225π cm². Find the length of the diameter of the circle.

(A)   15 cm   (B)   20 cm   (C)   30 cm   (D)   20π cm   (E)   25 π cm

8.   The area of circle *X* is 144π mm² while the area of circle *Y* is 81π mm². Write the ratio of the radius of circle *X* to that of circle *Y*.

(A)   3 : 4   (B)   4 : 3   (C)   9 : 12   (D)   27 : 12   (E)   18 : 24

9.   The circumference of circle *M* is 18π cm. Find the area of the circle.

(A)   18π cm²   (B)   81cm²   (C)   36cm²   (D)   36π cm²   (E)   81π cm²

10.   In two concentric circles, the smaller circle has a radius of 3 mm while the larger circle has a radius of 5 mm. Find the area of the shaded region.

(A)   2π mm²

(D)   16π mm²

(B)   8π mm²

(E)   26π mm²

(C)   13π mm²

11.   The radius of the smaller of two concentric circles is 5 cm while the radius of the larger circle is 7 cm. Determine the area of the shaded region.

(A)   7π cm²

(D)   36π cm²

(B)   24π cm²

(E)   49π cm²

(C)   25π cm²

12. Find the measure of arc *MN* if *m* ∠*MON* = 62°.

    (A) 16°   (B) 32°   (C) 59°
    (D) 62°   (E) 124°

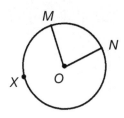

13. Find the measure of arc *AXC*.

    (A) 150°   (B) 160°   (C) 180°
    (D) 270°   (E) 360°

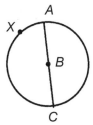

14. If arc *MXP* = 236°, find the measure of arc *MP*.

    (A) 62°   (B) 124°   (C) 236°
    (D) 270°   (E) 360°

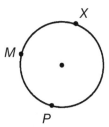

15. In circle *S*, major arc *PQR* has a measure of 298°.
    Find the measure of the central angle ∠*PSR*.

    (A) 62°   (B) 124°   (C) 149°
    (D) 298°   (E) 360°

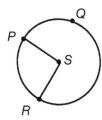

16. Find the measure of arc *XY* in circle *W*.

    (A) 40°   (B) 120°   (C) 140°
    (D) 180°   (E) 220°

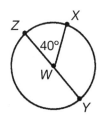

17. Find the area of the sector shown.

    (A) 4 cm²   (B) 2π cm² (C) 16 cm²
    (D) 8π cm²   (E) 16π cm²

18. Find the area of the shaded region.

    (A) 10   (B) 5π (C) 25

    (D) 20π (E) 25π

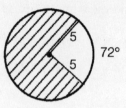

19. Find the area of the shaded sector shown.

    (A) $\dfrac{9\pi\,\text{mm}^2}{4}$ (B) $\dfrac{9\pi\,\text{mm}^2}{2}$

    (C) 18 mm^2 (D) 6π mm^2

    (E) 9π mm^2

20. If the area of the square is 100 cm^2, find the area of the shaded sector.

    (A) 10π cm^2 (B) 25 cm^2

    (C) 25π cm^2 (D) 100 cm^2

    (E) 100π cm^2

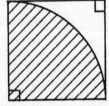

SOLIDS

Solid geometry is the study of figures which consist of points not all in the same plane.

RECTANGULAR SOLIDS

A solid with lateral faces and bases that are rectangles is called a **rectangular solid**.

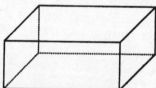

The surface area of a rectangular solid is the sum of the areas of all the faces.

The volume of a rectangular solid is equal to the product of its length, width, and height.

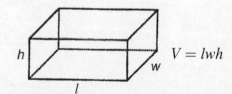

$V = lwh$

What are the dimensions of a solid cube whose surface area is numerically equal to its volume?

SOLUTION

The surface area of a cube of edge length a is equal to the sum of the areas of its six faces. Since a cube is a regular polygon, all six faces are congruent. Each face of a cube is a square of edge length a. Hence, the surface area of a cube of edge length a is

$S = 6a^2$.

The volume of a cube of edge length a is

$V = a^3$.

We require that $A = V$, or that

$6a^2 = a^3$ or $a = 6$.

Hence, if a cube has edge length 6, its surface area will be numerically equal to its volume.

DRILL: SOLIDS

Area and Volume

DIRECTIONS: Refer to the diagram and find the appropriate solution.

1. Find the surface area of the rectangular prism shown.

    (A)   138 cm² (B)   336 cm² (C)   381 cm²

    (D)   426 cm² (E)   540 cm²

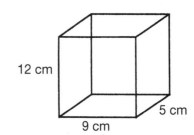

12 cm

9 cm

5 cm

2. Find the volume of the rectangular storage tank shown.

    (A)   24 m³   (B)   36 m³   (C)   38 m³

    (D)   42 m³   (E)   45 m³

    1.5 m

    4 m

    6 m

3. The area of a side of a cube is 100 cm². Find the length of an edge of the cube.

    (A)   4 cm   (B)   5 cm   (C)   10 cm   (D)   12 cm   (E)   15 cm

COORDINATE GEOMETRY

Coordinate geometry refers to the study of geometric figures using algebraic principles.

The graph shown is called the Cartesian coordinate plane. The graph consists of a pair of perpendicular lines called coordinate axes. The **vertical axis** is the *y*-axis and the **horizontal axis** is the *x*-axis. The point of intersection of these two axes is called the **origin**; it is the zero point of both axes. Furthermore, points to the right of the origin on the *x*-axis and above the origin on the *y*-axis represent positive real numbers. Points to the left of the origin on the *x*-axis or below the origin on the *y*-axis represent negative real numbers.

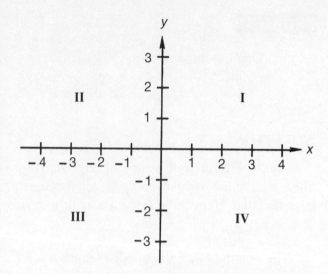

The four regions cut off by the coordinate axes are, in counterclockwise direction from the top right, called the first, second, third, and fourth quadrant, respectively. The first quadrant contains all points with two positive coordinates.

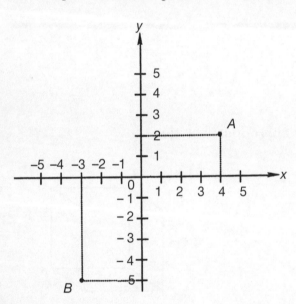

In the graph shown, two points are identified by the ordered pair, (*x*, *y*), of numbers. The *x*-coordinate is the first number and the *y*-coordinate is the second number.

To plot a point on the graph when given the coordinates, draw perpendicular lines from the number-line coordinates to the point where the two lines intersect.

To find the coordinates of a given point on the graph, draw perpendicular lines from the point to the coordinates on the number line. The *x*-coordinate is written before the *y*-coordinate and a comma is used to separate the two.

In this case, point *A* has the coordinates (4, 2) and the coordinates of point *B* are (−3, −5).

For any two points *A* and *B* with coordinates (X_A, Y_A) and (X_B, Y_B), respectively, the distance between *A* and *B* is represented by:

$$AB = \sqrt{(X_A - X_B)^2 + (Y_A - Y_B)^2}$$

This is commonly known as the distance formula.

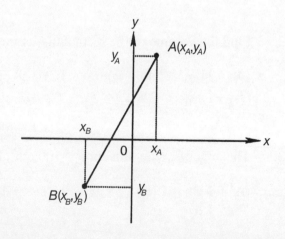

Find the distance between the point $A(1, 3)$ and $B(5, 3)$.

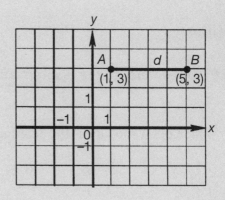

SOLUTION

In this case, where the ordinate of both points is the same, the distance between the two points is given by the absolute value of the difference between the two abscissas. In fact, this case reduces to merely counting boxes as the figure shows.

Let, $x_1 = $ abscissa of A $\qquad$ $y_1 = $ ordinate of A

$\qquad$ $x_2 = $ abscissa of B $\qquad$ $y_2 = $ ordinate of B

$\qquad$ $d = $ the distance

Therefore, $d = |x_1 - x_2|$. By substitution, $d = |1 - 5| = |-4| = 4$. This answer can also be obtained by applying the general formula for distance between any two points.

$$d = \sqrt{(x_1 - x_2)^2 + (y_1 - y_2)^2}$$

By substitution,

$$d = \sqrt{(1-5)^2 + (3-3)^2}$$
$$= \sqrt{(-4)^2 + (0)^2}$$
$$= \sqrt{16}$$
$$= 4$$

The distance is 4.

To find the midpoint of a segment between the two given endpoints, use the formula

$$MP = \left(\frac{x_1 + x_2}{2}, \frac{y_1 + y_2}{2}\right)$$

where x_1 and y_1 are the coordinates of one point; x_2 and y_2 are the coordinates of the other point.

DRILL: COORDINATE GEOMETRY

Coordinates

DIRECTIONS: Refer to the diagram and find the appropriate solution.

1. Which point shown has the coordinates (– 3, 2)?

   (A) A   (B) B   (C) C

   (D) D   (E) E

2. Name the coordinates of point A.

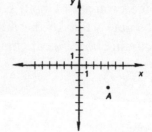

   (A) (4, 3)   (B) (3, – 4)   (C) (3, 4)

   (D) (– 4, 3)   (E) (4, – 3)

3. Which point shown has the coordinates (2.5, – 1)?

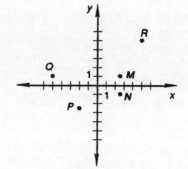

   (A) M   (B) N   (C) P

   (D) Q   (E) R

4. The correct *x*-coordinate for point *H* is what number?

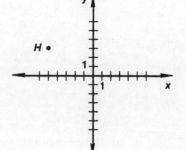

   (A) 3   (B) 4   (C) – 3

   (D) – 4   (E) – 5

5. The correct y-coordinate for point R is what number?

    (A) –7   (B) 2   (C) – 2
    (D) 7   (E) 8

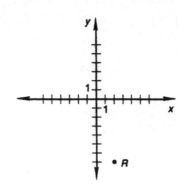

Distance

DIRECTIONS: Determine the distance or value as appropriate.

6. Find the distance between $(4, -7)$ and $(-2, -7)$.

    (A) 4   (B) 6   (C) 7   (D) 14   (E) 15

7. Find the distance between $(3, 8)$ and $(5, 11)$.

    (A) 2   (B) 3   (C) $\sqrt{13}$ (D) $\sqrt{13}$ (E) $3\sqrt{3}$

8. How far from the origin is the point $(3, 4)$?

    (A) 3   (B) 4   (C) 5   (D) $5\sqrt{3}$ (E) $4\sqrt{5}$

9. Find the distance between the point $(-4, 2)$ and $(3, -5)$.

    (A) 3   (B) $3\sqrt{3}$ (C) 7   (D) $7\sqrt{2}$ (E) $7\sqrt{3}$

10. The distance between points A and B is 10 units. If A has coordinates $(4, -6)$ and B has co-ordinates $(-2, y)$, determine the value of y.

    (A) – 6   (B) – 2   (C) 0   (D) 1   (E) 2

Midpoints and Endpoints

DIRECTIONS: Determine the coordinates or value as appropriate.

11. Find the midpoint between the points $(-2, 6)$ and $(4, 8)$.

    (A) $(3, 7)$ (B) $(1, 7)$ (C) $(3, 1)$ (D) $(1, 1)$ (E) $(-3, 7)$

12. Find the coordinates of the midpoint between the points $(-5, 7)$ and $(3, -1)$.

(A) $(-4, 4)$ (B) $(3, -1)$ (C) $(1, -3)$ (D) $(-1, 3)$ (E) $(4, -4)$

13. The y-coordinate of the midpoint of segment $\overline{AB}$ if A has coordinates $(-3, 7)$ and B has coordinates $(-3, -2)$ is what value?

(A) $\dfrac{5}{2}$ (B) 3 (C) $\dfrac{7}{2}$ (D) 5 (E) $\dfrac{15}{2}$

14. One endpoint of a line segment is $(5, -3)$. The midpoint is $(-1, 6)$. What is the other endpoint?

(A) $(7, 3)$ (D) $(-2, 1.5)$
(B) $(2, 1.5)$ (E) $(-7, 12)$
(C) $(-7, 15)$

15. The point $(-2, 6)$ is the midpoint for which of the following pair of points?

(A) $(1, 4)$ and $(-3, 8)$ (D) $(-1, 4)$ and $(3, -8)$
(B) $(-1, -3)$ and $(5, 9)$ (E) $(1, 3)$ and $(-5, 9)$
(C) $(1, 4)$ and $(5, 9)$

GEOMETRY DRILLS

ANSWER KEY

Drill: Lines and Angles

1.	(B)	5.	(D)	9.	(D)	13.	(B)
2.	(A)	6.	(C)	10.	(E)	14.	(E)
3.	(C)	7.	(B)	11.	(C)	15.	(A)
4.	(D)	8.	(A)	12.	(D)		

Drill: Regular Polygons

1.	(D)	4.	(A)	7.	(E)	10.	(B)
2.	(B)	5.	(D)	8.	(B)		
3.	(E)	6.	(C)	9.	(D)		

Drill: Triangles

1.	(D)	5.	(C)	9.	(A)	13.	(D)
2.	(B)	6.	(A)	10.	(C)	14.	(A)
3.	(C)	7.	(B)	11.	(C)	15.	(B)
4.	(E)	8.	(E)	12.	(B)		

Drill: Quadrilaterals

1.	(A)	6.	(A)	11.	(C)	16.	(A)
2.	(B)	7.	(D)	12.	(D)	17.	(E)
3.	(D)	8.	(C)	13.	(B)	18.	(B)
4.	(E)	9.	(B)	14.	(C)	19.	(C)
5.	(C)	10.	(C)	15.	(B)	20.	(D)

Drill: Circles

1.	(B)	6.	(D)	11.	(B)	16.	(C)
2.	(A)	7.	(C)	12.	(D)	17.	(B)
3.	(D)	8.	(B)	13.	(C)	18.	(D)
4.	(E)	9.	(E)	14.	(B)	19.	(A)
5.	(C)	10.	(D)	15.	(A)	20.	(C)

Drill: Solids

1.	(D)	2.	(B)	3.	(C)

Drill: Coordinate Geometry

1.	(C)	5.	(A)	9.	(D)	13.	(A)
2.	(E)	6.	(B)	10.	(E)	14.	(C)
3.	(B)	7.	(C)	11.	(B)	15.	(E)
4.	(E)	8.	(C)	12.	(D)		

IV. WORD PROBLEMS

One of the main problems students have in mathematics involves solving word problems. The secret to solving these problems is being able to convert words into numbers and variables in the form of an algebraic equation.

The easiest way to approach a word problem is to read the question and ask yourself what you are trying to find. This unknown quantity can be represented by a variable.

Next, determine how the variable relates to the other quantities in the problem. More than likely, these quantities can be explained in terms of the original variable. If not, a separate variable may have to be used to represent a quantity.

Using these variables and the relationships determined among them, an equation can be written. Solve for a particular variable and then plug this number in for each relationship that involves this variable in order to find any unknown quantities.

Lastly, re-read the problem to be sure that you have answered the questions correctly and fully.

ALGEBRAIC

The following illustrates how to formulate an equation and solve the problem.

EXAMPLE

Find two consecutive odd integers whose sum is 36.

Let $x =$ the first odd integer

Let $x + 2 =$ the second odd integer

The sum of the two numbers is 36. Therefore,

$$x + (x + 2) = 36$$

Simplifying,

$$2x + 2 = 36$$
$$2x + 2 + (-2) = 36 + (-2)$$
$$2x = 34$$
$$x = 17$$

Plugging 17 in for x, we find the second odd integer $= (x + 2) = (17 + 2) = 19$. Therefore, we find that the two consecutive odd integers whose sum is 36 are 17 and 19, respectively.

DRILL: ALGEBRAIC

Algebraic Word Problems

<u>DIRECTIONS</u>: Solve the following word problems algebraically.

1. The sum of two numbers is 41. One number is one less than twice the other. Find the larger of the two numbers.

   (A) 13   (B) 14   (C) 21   (D) 27   (E) 41

2. The sum of two consecutive integers is 111. Three times the larger integer less two times the smaller integer is 58. Find the value of the smaller integer.

   (A) 55   (B) 56   (C) 58   (D) 111   (E) 112

3. The difference between two integers is 12. The sum of the two integers is 2. Find both integers.

   (A) 7 and 5   (B) 7 and – 5   (C) – 7 and 5
   (D) 2 and 12   (E) – 2 and 12

RATE

One of the formulas you will use for rate problems will be

Rate × Time = Distance

PROBLEM

If a plane travels five hours from New York to California at a speed of 600 miles per hour, how many miles does the plane travel?

SOLUTION

Using the formula rate × time = distance, multiply 600 mph × 5 hours = 3,000 miles.

The average rate at which an object travels can be solved by dividing the total distance traveled by the total amount of time.

PROBLEM

On a 40-mile bicycle trip, Cathy rode half the distance at 20 mph and the other half at 10 mph. What was Cathy's average speed on the bike trip?

SOLUTION

First you need to break down the problem. On half of the trip, which would be 20 miles, Cathy rode 20 mph. Using the rate formula,

$$\frac{\text{distance}}{\text{rate}} = \text{time},$$

you would compute,

$$\frac{20 \text{ miles}}{20 \text{ miles per hour}} = 1 \text{ hour}$$

to travel the first 20 miles. During the second 20 miles, Cathy traveled at 10 miles per hour, which would be

$$\frac{20 \text{ miles}}{10 \text{ miles per hour}} = 2 \text{ hour}$$

Thus, the average speed Cathy traveled would be $\frac{40}{3} = 13.3$ miles per hour.

In solving for some rate problems you can use cross multiplication involving ratios to solve for x.

PROBLEM

If 2 pairs of shoes cost $52, then what is the cost of 10 pairs of shoes at this rate?

SOLUTION

$$\frac{2}{52} = \frac{10}{x}, \; 2x = 52 \times 10, \; x = \frac{520}{2}, \; x = \$260$$

DRILL: RATE

Rate Word Problems

<u>**DIRECTIONS**</u>: **Solve to find the rate.**

1. Two towns are 420 miles apart. A car leaves the first town traveling toward the second town at 55 mph. At the same time, a second car leaves the other town and heads toward the first town at 65 mph. How long will it take for the two cars to meet?

    (A) 2 hr   (B) 3 hr   (C) 3.5 hr   (D) 4 hr   (E) 4.25 hr

2. A camper leaves the campsite walking due east at a rate of 3.5 mph. Another camper leaves the campsite at the same time but travels due west. In two hours the two campers will be 15 miles apart. What is the walking rate of the second camper?

    (A) 2.5 mph   (B) 3 mph   (C) 3.25 mph

    (D) 3.5 mph   (E) 4 mph

3. A bicycle racer covers a 75 mile training route to prepare for an upcoming race. If the racer could increase his speed by 5 mph, he could complete the same course in 3/4 of the time. Find his average rate of speed.

    (A) 15 mph   (B) 15.5 mph   (C) 16 mph

    (D) 18 mph   (E) 20 mph

WORK

In work problems, one of the basic formulas is

$$\frac{1}{x} + \frac{1}{y} = \frac{1}{z}$$

where x and y represent the number of hours it takes two objects or people to complete the work and z is the total number of hours when both are working together.

PROBLEM

Otis can seal and stamp 400 envelopes in 2 hours while Elizabeth seals and stamps 400 envelopes in 1 hour. In how many hours can Otis and Elizabeth, working together, complete a 400-piece mailing at these rates?

SOLUTION

$$\frac{1}{2} + \frac{1}{1} = \frac{1}{z}$$

$$\frac{1}{2} + \frac{2}{2} = \frac{3}{2}$$

$$\frac{3}{2} = \frac{1}{z}$$

$$3z = 2$$

$z = \frac{2}{3}$ of an hour or 40 minutes. Working together, Otis and Elizabeth can seal and stamp 400 envelopes in 40 minutes.

DRILL: WORK

Work Word Problems

__DIRECTIONS__: Solve to find amount of work.

1. It takes Marty 3 hours to type the address labels for his club's newsletter. It only takes Pat $2\frac{1}{4}$ hours to type the same amount of labels. How long would it take them working together to complete the address labels?

    (A) $\frac{7}{9}$ hr (B) $1\frac{2}{7}$ hr (C) $1\frac{4}{5}$ hr (D) $2\frac{5}{8}$ hr (E) $5\frac{1}{4}$ hr

2. It takes Troy 3 hours to mow his family's large lawn. With his little brother's help, he can finish the job in only 2 hours. How long would it take the little brother to mow the entire lawn alone?

    (A) 4 hr   (B) 5 hr   (C) 5.5 hr   (D) 6 hr   (E) 6.75 hr

3. A tank can be filled by one inlet pipe in 15 minutes. It takes an outlet pipe 75 minutes to drain the tank. If the outlet pipe is left open by accident, how long would it take to fill the tank?

    (A) 15.1 min   (B) 15.9 min   (C) 16.8 min
    (D) 18.75 min   (E) 19.3 min

MIXTURE

Mixture problems present the combination of different products and ask you to solve for different parts of the mixture.

__PROBLEM__

A chemist has an 18% solution and a 45% solution of a disinfectant. How many ounces of each should be used to make 12 ounces of a 36% solution?

SOLUTION

Let x = Number of ounces from the 18% solution, and

             y = Number of ounces from the 45% solution.

$x + y = 12$ (1)

$.18x + .45y = .36(12)$ (2)

Note that .18 of the first solution is pure disinfectant and that .45 of the second solution is pure disinfectant. When the proper quantities are drawn from each mixture the result is 12 ounces of mixture which is .36 pure disinfectant.

The second equation cannot be solved with two unknowns. Therefore, write one variable in terms of the other and plug it into the second equation.

$$x = 12 - y \tag{1}$$

$$.18(12 - y) + .45y = .36(12) \tag{2}$$

Simplifying,

$$2.16 - .18y + .45y = 4.32$$

$$.27y = 4.32 - 2.16$$

$$27y = 2.16$$

$$y = 8$$

Plugging in for y in the first equation,

$$x + 8 = 12$$

$$x = 4$$

Therefore, 4 ounces of the first and 8 ounces of the second solution should be used.

PROBLEM

> Clark pays $2.00 per pound for 3 pounds of peanut butter chocolates and then decides to buy 2 pounds of chocolate covered raisins at $2.50 per pound. If Clark mixes both together, what is the cost per pound of the mixture?

SOLUTION

The total mixture is 5 pounds and the total value of the chocolates is

$$3(\$2.00) + 2(\$2.50) = \$11.00$$

The price per pound of the chocolates is

$$\frac{\$11.00}{5 \text{ pounds}} = \$2.20.$$

DRILL: MIXTURE

Mixture Word Problems

<u>DIRECTIONS</u>: Find the appropriate solution.

1. How many liters of a 20% alcohol solution must be added to 80 liters of a 50% alcohol solution to form a 45% solution?

    (A) 4   (B) 8   (C) 16   (D) 20   (E) 32

2. How many kilograms of water must be evaporated from 50 kg of a 10% salt solution to obtain a 15% salt solution?

    (A) 15   (B) 15.75   (C) 16   (D) $16.\overline{66}$ (E) 16.75

3. How many pounds of coffee A at $3.00 a pound should be mixed with 2.5 pounds of coffee B at $4.20 a pound to form a mixture selling for $3.75 a pound?

    (A) 1   (B) 1.5   (C) 1.75   (D) 2   (E) 2.25

INTEREST

If the problem calls for computing simple interest, the interest is computed on the principal alone. If the problem involves compounded interest, then the interest on the principal is taken into account in addition to the interest earned before.

PROBLEM

How much interest will Jerry pay on his loan of $400 for 60 days at 6% per year?

SOLUTION

Use the formula:

Interest $=$ Principal $\times$ Rate $\times$ Time $(I = P \times R \times T)$.

$400 \times 6\%/\text{year} \times 60 \text{ days} = \$400 \times .06 \times \dfrac{60}{365}$

$= \$400 \times 0.00986 = \$3.94$

Jerry will pay $4.00.

Mr. Smith wishes to find out how much interest he will receive on $300 if the rate is 3% compounded annually for three years.

SOLUTION

Compound interest is interest computed on both the principal and the interest it has previously earned. The interest is added to the principal at the end of every year. The interest on the first year is found by multiplying the rate by the principal. Hence, the interest for the first year is

$$3\% \times \$300 = .03 \times \$300 = \$9.00.$$

The principal for the second year is now $309, the old principal ($300) plus the interest ($9). The interest for the second year is found by multiplying the rate by the new principal. Hence, the interest for the second year is

$$3\% \times \$309 = .03 \times \$309 = \$9.27.$$

The principal now becomes $309 + $9.27 = $318.27.

The interest for the third year is found using this new principal. It is

$$3\% \times \$318.27 = .03 \times \$318.27 = \$9.55.$$

At the end of the third year his principal is $318.27 + $9.55 = $327.82. To find how much interest was earned, we subtract his starting principal ($300) from his ending principal ($327.82), to obtain

$$\$327.82 - \$300.00 = \$27.82.$$

DRILL: INTEREST

Interest Word Problems

DIRECTIONS: Determine the amount of money invested or possible amount earned as appropriate.

1. A man invests $3,000, part in a 12-month certificate of deposit paying 8% and the rest in municipal bonds that pay 7% a year. If the yearly return from both investments is $220, how much was invested in bonds?

    (A) $80   (B) $140   (C) $220   (D) $1,000   (E) $2,000

2. A sum of money was invested at 11% a year. Four times that amount was invested at 7.5%. How much was invested at 11% if the total annual return was $1,025?

    (A) $112.75   (B) $1,025   (C) $2,500
    (D) $3,400   (E) $10,000

3. One bank pays 6.5% a year simple interest on a savings account while a credit union pays 7.2% a year. If you had $1,500 to invest for three years, how much more would you earn by putting the money in the credit union?

   (A) $10.50   (B) $31.50   (C) $97.50   (D) $108   (E) $1,500

DISCOUNT

If the discount problem asks to find the final price after the discount, first multiply the original price by the percent of discount. Then subtract this result from the original price.

If the problem asks to find the original price when only the percent of discount and the discounted price are given, simply subtract the percent of discount from 100% and divide this percent into the sale price. This will give you the original price.

PROBLEM

> A popular bookstore gives a 10% discount to students. What does a student actually pay for a book costing $24.00?

SOLUTION

10% of $24 is $2.40 and hence the student pays

$24 – $2.40 = $21.60.

PROBLEM

> Eugene paid $100 for a business suit. The suit's price included a 25% discount. What was the original price of the suit?

SOLUTION

Let x represent the original price of the suit and take the complement of .25 (discount price) which is .75.

$.75x = 100 or $x = 133.34$.

So, the original price of the suit is $133.34.

DRILL: DISCOUNT

Discount Word Problems

<u>DIRECTIONS</u>: **Find cost, price, or discount as appropriate.**

1. A man bought a coat marked 20% off for $156. How much had the coat cost originally?

    (A) $136   (B) $156   (C) $175   (D) $195   (E) $205

2. A woman saved $225 on the new sofa which was on sale for 30% off. What was the original price of the sofa?

    (A) $25   (B) $200   (C) $225   (D) $525   (E) $750

3. At an office supply store, customers are given a discount if they pay in cash. If a customer is given a discount of $9.66 on a total order of $276, what is the percent of discount?

    (A) 2%   (B) 3.5%   (C) 4.5%   (D) 9.66%   (E) 276%

PROFIT

The formula used for the profit problems is

    Profit = Revenue – Cost

or   Profit = Selling Price – Expenses.

PROBLEM

Four high school and college friends started a business of remodeling and selling old automobiles during the summer. For this purpose they paid $600 to rent an empty barn for the summer. They obtained the cars from a dealer for $250 each, and it takes an average of $410 in materials to remodel each car. How many automobiles must the students sell at $1,440 each to obtain a gross profit of $7,000?

SOLUTION

    Total Revenues – Total Cost = Gross Profit

    Revenue – [Variable Cost + Fixed Cost] = Gross Profit

    Let a = number of cars

        Revenue = $1,440a$

     Variable Cost = ($250 + 410)a$

      Fixed Cost = $600

The desired gross profit is $7,000.

Using the equation for the gross profit,

$$1,440a - [660a + 600] = 7,000$$

$$1,440a - 660a - 600 = 7,000$$

$$780a = 7,000 + 600$$

$$780a = 7,600$$

$$a = 9.74$$

or to the nearest car, $a = 10$.

PROBLEM

A glass vase sells for $25.00. The net profit is 7%, and the operating expenses are 39%. Find the gross profit on the vase.

SOLUTION

The gross profit is equal to the net profit plus the operating expenses. The net profit is 7% of the selling cost; thus, it is equal to

$$7\% \times \$25.00 = .07 \times \$25 = \$1.75.$$

The operating expenses are 39% of the selling price, thus equal to

$$39\% \times \$25 = .39 \times \$25 = \$9.75.$$

$1.75	net profit
+ $9.75	operating expenses
$11.50	gross profit

DRILL: PROFIT

Profit Word Problems

DIRECTIONS: Determine profit or stock value as appropriate.

1. An item cost a store owner $50. She marked it up 40% and advertised it at that price. How much profit did she make if she later sold it at 15% off the advertised price?

    (A) $7.50   (B) $9.50   (C) $10.50   (D) $39.50   (E) $50

2. An antique dealer makes a profit of 115% on the sale of an oak desk. If the desk cost her $200, how much profit did she make on the sale?

    (A) $230   (B) $315   (C) $430   (D) $445   (E) $475

3. As a graduation gift, a young man was given 100 shares of stock worth $27.50 apiece. Within a year the price of the stock had risen by 8%. How much more were the stocks worth at the end of the first year than when they were given to the young man?

(A) $110   (B) $220   (C) $1,220   (D) $2,750   (E) $2,970

SETS

A **set** is any collection of well defined objects called elements.

A set which contains only a finite number of elements is called a **finite set**; a set which contains an infinite number of elements is called an **infinite set**. Often the sets are designated by listing their elements. For example:

{a, b, c, d} is the set which contains elements a, b, c, and d.

The set of positive integers is {1, 2, 3, 4, ...}.

Venn diagrams can represent sets. These diagrams are circles which help to visualize the relationship between members or objects of a set.

PROBLEM

In a certain Broadway show audition, it was asked of 30 performers if they knew how to either sing or dance, or both. If 20 auditioners said they could dance and 14 said they could sing, how many could sing and dance?

SOLUTION

Divide the 30 people into 3 sets: those who dance, those who sing, and those who dance and sing. S is the number of people who both sing and dance. So $20 - S$ represents the number of people who dance and $14 - S$ represents the number of people who sing.

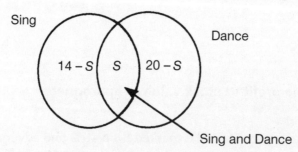

The equation for this problem is as follows:

$$(20 - S) + S + (14 - S) = 30$$
$$20 + 14 - 30 = S$$
$$34 - 30 = S$$
$$4 = S$$

So, 4 people in the audition both sing and dance.

DRILL: SETS

Set Word Problems

DIRECTIONS: Determine the appropriate set.

1. In a small school there are 147 sophomores. Of this number, 96 take both Biology and Technology I. Eighty-three take both Chemistry and Technology I. How many students are taking Technology I?

   (A) 32   (B) 51   (C) 64   (D) 83   (E) 96

2. In a survey of 100 people, 73 owned only stocks. Six of the people invested in both stocks and bonds. How many people owned bonds only?

   (A) 6   (B) 21   (C) 73   (D) 94   (E) 100

3. On a field trip, the teachers counted the orders for a snack and sent the information in with a few people. The orders were for 77 colas only and 39 fries only. If there were 133 orders, how many were for colas and fries?

   (A) 17   (B) 56   (C) 77   (D) 95   (E) 150

GEOMETRY

PROBLEM

A boy knows that his height is 6 ft. and his shadow is 4 ft. long. At the same time of day, a tree's shadow is 24 ft. long. How high is the tree? (See the figure.)

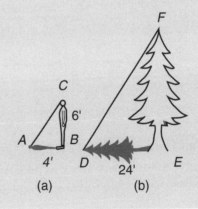

(a)   (b)

SOLUTION

Show that $\triangle ABC \approx \triangle DEF$, and then set up a proportion between the known sides $\overline{AB}$ and $\overline{DE}$, and the sides $\overline{BC}$ and $\overline{EF}$.

First, assume that both the boy and the tree are $\perp$ to the earth. Then, $\overline{BC} \perp \overline{BA}$ and $\overline{EF} \perp \overline{ED}$. Hence,

$$\angle ABC \cong \angle DEF.$$

Since it is the same time of day, the rays of light from the sun are incident on both the tree and the boy at the same angle, relative to the earth's surface. Therefore,

$$\angle BAC \cong \angle EDF.$$

We have shown, so far, that two pairs of corresponding angles are congruent. Since the sum of the angles of any triangle is 180°, the third pair of corresponding angles is congruent (i.e., $\angle ACB > \angle DFE$). By the Angle-Angle-Angle Theorem

$$\angle ABC \approx \angle DEF.$$

By definition of similarity,

$$\frac{\overline{FE}}{\overline{CB}} = \frac{\overline{ED}}{\overline{BA}}$$

$\overline{CB} = 6'$, $\overline{ED} = 24'$, and $\overline{BA} = 4'$. Therefore,

$$FE = (6')\left(\frac{24'}{4'}\right) = 36'.$$

DRILL: GEOMETRY

Geometry Word Problems

<u>DIRECTIONS</u>: **Find the appropriate measurements.**

1. $\triangle PQR$ is a scalene triangle. The measure of $\angle P$ is 8 more than twice the measure of $\angle R$. The measure of $\angle Q$ is two less than three times the measure of $\angle R$. Determine the measure of $\angle Q$.

    (A) 29°   (B) 53°   (C) 60°

    (D) 85°   (E) 174°

2. Angle A and angle B are supplementary. The measure of angle B is 5 more than four times the measure of angle A. Find the measure of angle B.

    (A) 35°   (B) 125°   (C) 140°   (D) 145°   (E) 155°

3. Triangle RUS is isosceles with base $\overline{SU}$. Each leg is 3 less than 5 times the length of the base. If the perimeter of the triangle is 60 cm, find the length of a leg.

    (A) 6 cm   (B) 12 cm   (C) 27 cm   (D) 30 cm   (E) 33 cm

MEASUREMENT

When measurement problems are presented in either metric or English units which involve conversion of units, the appropriate data will be given in the problem.

PROBLEM

The Eiffel Tower is 984 feet high. Express this height in meters, in kilometers, in centimeters, and in millimeters.

SOLUTION

A meter is equivalent to 39.370 inches. In this problem, the height of the tower in feet must be converted to inches and then the inches can be converted to meters. There are 12 inches in 1 foot. Therefore, feet can be converted to inches by using the factor $\frac{12\ inches}{1\ foot}$.

$$984 \text{ feet} \times \frac{12 \text{ in}}{1 \text{ ft}} = 118 \times 10^2 \text{ inches.}$$

Once the height is found in inches, this can be converted to meters by the factor $\frac{1\ meter}{39.370\ inches}$.

$$11,808 \text{ in} \times \frac{1 \text{ m}}{39.370 \text{ inches}} = 300 \text{ m.}$$

Therefore, the height in meters is 300 m.

There are 1,000 meters in one kilometer. Meters can be converted to kilometers by using the factor $\frac{1\ meter}{39.370\ inches}$.

$$300 \text{ m} \times \frac{1 \text{ km}}{1,000 \text{ m}} = .300 \text{ km}$$

As such, there are .300 kilometers in 300 m.

There are 100 centimeters in 1 meter, thus meters can be converted to centimeters by multiplying by the factor $\frac{100\ cm}{1\ m}$.

$$300 \text{ m} \times \frac{100 \text{ cm}}{1 \text{ m}} = 300 \times 10^2 \text{ cm.}$$

There are 30,000 centimeters in 300 m.

There are 1,000 millimeters in 1 meter; therefore, meters can be converted to millimeters by the factor $\frac{1,000\ mm}{1\ m}$.

$$300 \text{ m} \times \frac{1,000 \text{ mm}}{1 \text{ m}} = 300 \times 10^3 \text{ mm.}$$

There are 300,000 millimeters in 300 meters.

PROBLEM

The unaided eye can perceive objects which have a diameter of 0.1 mm. What is the diameter in inches?

SOLUTION

From a standard table of conversion factors, one can find that 1 inch = 2.54 cm. Thus, cm can be converted to inches by multiplying by $\frac{1 \text{ inch}}{2.54 \text{ cm}}$. Here, one is given the diameter in mm, which is .1 cm. Millimeters are converted to cm by multiplying the number of mm by $\frac{.1 \text{ cm}}{1 \text{ mm}}$. Solving for cm, you obtain

$$0.1 \text{ mm} \times \frac{.1 \text{ cm}}{1 \text{ mm}} = .01 \text{ cm}.$$

Solving for inches:

$$0.01 \text{ cm} \times \frac{1 \text{ inch}}{2.54 \text{ cm}} = 3.94 = 10^{-3} \text{ inches}.$$

DRILL: MEASUREMENT

Measurement Word Problems

<u>DIRECTIONS</u>: Determine the appropriate solution from the information provided.

1. A brick walkway measuring 3 feet by 11 feet is to be built. The bricks measure 4 inches by 6 inches. How many bricks will it take to complete the walkway?

   (A) 132   (B) 198   (C) 330   (D) 1,927   (E) 4,752

2. A wall to be papered is three times as long as it is wide. The total area to be covered is 192 ft^2. Wallpaper comes in rolls that are 2 feet wide by 8 feet long. How many rolls will it take to cover the wall?

   (A) 8   (B) 12   (C) 16   (D) 24   (E) 32

3. A bottle of medicine containing 2 kg is to be poured into smaller containers that hold 8 grams each. How many of these smaller containers can be filled from the 2 kg bottle?

   (A) 0.5   (B) 1   (C) 5   (D) 50   (E) 250

DATA INTERPRETATION

Some of the problems test ability to apply information given in graphs and tables.

PROBLEM

In which year was the least number of bushels of wheat produced? (See figure below)

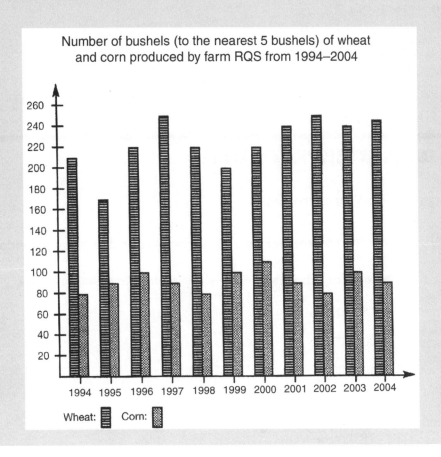

Number of bushels (to the nearest 5 bushels) of wheat and corn produced by farm RQS from 1994–2004

SOLUTION

By inspection of the graph, we find that the shortest bar representing wheat production is the one representing the wheat production for 1995. Thus, the least number of bushels of wheat was produced in 1995.

PROBLEM

What was the ratio of wheat production in 2004 to that of 1994?

SOLUTION

From the graph representing wheat production, the number of bushels of wheat produced in 1994 is equal to 210 bushels. This number can be found by locating the bar on the graph representing wheat production in 1994 and then drawing a horizontal line from the top of that bar to the vertical axis. The point where this horizontal line meets the vertical axis represents the number of bushels of wheat produced in 1994. This number on the vertical axis is 210. Similarly, the graph indicates that the number of bushels of wheat produced in 2004 is equal to 245 bushels.

Thus, the ratio of wheat production in 2004 to that of 1994 is 245 to 210, which can be written as $\frac{245}{210}$. Simplifying this ratio to its simplest form yields

$$\frac{245}{210} = \frac{5 \times 7 \times 7}{2 \times 3 \times 5 \times 7}$$
$$= \frac{7}{2 \times 3}$$
$$= \frac{7}{6} \text{ or } 7{:}6$$

DRILL: DATA INTERPRETATION

Data Interpretation Word Problems

<u>DIRECTIONS</u>: Determine the correct response from the information provided.

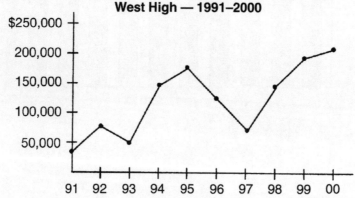

Amount of Scholarship Money Awarded to Graduating Senior
West High — 1991–2000

1. What was the approximate amount of scholarship money awarded in 1995?

(A) $150,000   (B) $155,000   (C) $165,000
(D) $175,000   (E) $190,000

2. By how much did the scholarship money increase between 1997 and 1998?

(A) $25,000   (B) $30,000   (C) $50,000
(D) $55,000   (E) $75,000

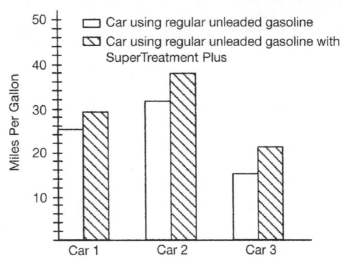

Changes in Average Mileage

Miles Per Gallon

☐ Car using regular unleaded gasoline

▨ Car using regular unleaded gasoline with SuperTreatment Plus

Car 1   Car 2   Car 3

3. By how much did the mileage increase for Car 2 when the new product was used?

   (A) 5 mpg   (B) 6 mpg   (C) 7 mpg   (D) 10 mpg   (E)   12 mpg

4. Which car's mileage increased the most in this test?

   (A) Car 1   (B) Car 2   (C) Car 3
   (D) Cars 1 and 2   (E) Cars 2 and 3

5. According to the bar graph, if your car averages 25 mpg, what mileage might you expect with the new product?

   (A) 21 mpg   (B) 30 mpg   (C) 31 mpg   (D) 35 mpg   (E)   37 mpg

Sample Family Budget

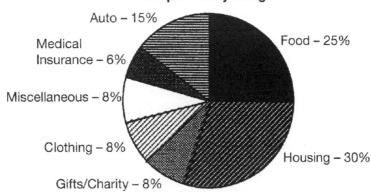

Auto – 15%

Medical
Insurance – 6%

Miscellaneous – 8%

Clothing – 8%

Gifts/Charity – 8%

Food – 25%

Housing – 30%

6. Using the budget shown, a family with an income of $1,500 a month would plan to spend what amount on housing?

   (A) $300   (B) $375   (C) $450   (D) $490   (E) $520

7. In this sample family budget, how does the amount spent on an automobile compare to the amount spent on housing?

(A) $\dfrac{1}{3}$ (B) $\dfrac{1}{2}$ (C) $\dfrac{2}{3}$ (D) $1\dfrac{1}{2}$ (E) 2

8. A family with a monthly income of $1,240 spends $125 a month on clothing. By what amount do they exceed the sample budget?

(A) $1.00   (B) $5.20   (C) $10.00   (D) $25.80   (E) $31.75

CALORIE CHART — BREADS

Bread	Amount	Calories
French Bread	2 oz	140
Bran Bread	1 oz	95
Whole Wheat Bread	1 oz	115
Oatmeal Bread	0.5 oz	55
Raisin Bread	1 oz	125

9. One dieter eats two ounces of French bread. A second dieter eats two ounces of bran bread. The second dieter has consumed how many more calories than the first dieter?

(A) 40   (B) 45   (C) 50   (D) 55   (E) 65

10. One ounce of whole wheat bread has how many more calories than an ounce of oatmeal bread?

(A) 5   (B) 15   (C) 60   (D) 75   (E) 125

WORD PROBLEM DRILLS

ANSWER KEY

Drill: Algebraic

1. (D)   2. (A)   3. (B)

Drill: Rate

1. (C)   2. (E)   3. (A)

Drill: Work

1. (B)   2. (D)   3. (D)

Drill: Mixture

1. (C)   2. (D)   3. (B)

Drill: Interest

1. (E)   2. (C)   3. (B)

Drill: Discount

1. (D)   2. (E)   3. (B)

Drill: Profit

1. (B)   2. (A)   3. (B)

Drill: Sets

1. (A)   2. (B)   3. (A)

Drill: Geometry

1. (D)   2. (D)   3. (C)

Drill: Measurement

1. (B)   2. (B)   3. (E)

Drill: Data Interpretation

1. (D)   4. (E)   7. (B)   10. (A)
2. (E)   5. (B)   8. (D)
3. (B)   6. (C)   9. (C)

CHAPTER 7

MASTERING REGULAR
MATH QUESTIONS

CHAPTER 7

MASTERING REGULAR MATH QUESTIONS

The Regular Math questions of the PSAT are designed to test your ability to solve problems involving arithmetic, algebra, and geometry. A few of the problems may be similar to those found in a math textbook and will require nothing more than the use of basic rules and formulas. Most of the problems, however, will require more than that. Regular Math questions will ask you to think creatively and apply basic skills to solve problems.

All Regular Math questions are in a multiple-choice format with five possible responses. There are a number of advantages and disadvantages associated with multiple-choice math tests. Learning what some of these advantages and disadvantages are can help you improve your test performance.

The greatest disadvantage of a multiple-choice math test is that every question presents you with four wrong answers. These wrong answers are not randomly chosen numbers—they are the answers that students are most likely to get if they make certain mistakes. They also tend to be answers that "look right" to someone who does not know how to solve the problem. Thus, on a particular problem, you may be relieved to find "your" answer among the answer choices, only to discover later that you fell into a common error trap. Wrong answer choices can also distract or confuse you when you are attempting to solve a problem correctly, causing you to question your answer even though it is right.

The greatest *advantage* of a multiple-choice math test is that the *right* answer is also presented to you. This means that you may be able to spot the right answer even if you do not understand a problem completely or do not have time to finish it. It means that you may be able to pick the right answer by guessing intelligently. It also means that you may be saved from getting a problem wrong when the answer you obtain is not among the answer choices—and you have to go back and work the problem again.

Keep in mind, also, that the use of a calculator is permitted during the test. Do not be tempted, however, to use this as a crutch. Some problems can actually be solved more quickly without a calculator, and you still have to work through the problem to know what numbers to punch. No calculator in the world can solve a problem for you.

ABOUT THE DIRECTIONS

The directions found at the beginning of each Regular Math section are simple—solve each problem, then mark the best of five answer choices on your answer sheet. Following these instructions, however, is important information that you should understand thoroughly before you attempt to take a test. This information includes definitions of standard symbols and formulas that you may need in order to solve Regular Math problems. The formulas are given so that you don't have to memorize them—however, in order to benefit from this information, you need to know what is and what is not included. Otherwise, you may waste time looking for a formula that is not listed, or you may fail to look for a formula that is listed. The formulas given to you at the beginning of a Regular Math section include:

- The number of degrees in a straight line

- Area and circumference of a circle; number of degrees in a circle

- Area of a triangle; Pythagorean Theorem for a right triangle; sum of angle measures of a triangle

Following the formulas and definitions of symbols is a very important statement about the diagrams, or figures, that may accompany Regular Math questions. This statement tells you that, unless stated otherwise in a specific question, figures are drawn to scale.

ABOUT THE QUESTIONS

Most Regular Math questions on the PSAT fall into one of three categories: arithmetic, algebra, and geometry. In the following three sections, we will review the kinds of questions you will encounter on the actual test.

ARITHMETIC QUESTIONS

Most arithmetic questions on the PSAT fall into one of the following four question types. For each question type, an example and solution will be given, highlighting strategies and techniques for completing the problems as quickly as possible.

Question Type 1: Evaluating Expressions

Arithmetic questions on the PSAT often ask you to find the value of an arithmetic expression or to find the value of a missing term in an expression. The temptation when you see one of these expressions is to calculate its value—a process that is time-consuming and can easily lead to an error. A better way to approach an arithmetic expression is to use your knowledge of properties of numbers to spot shortcuts.

PROBLEM

$7(8 + 4) - (3 \times 12) =$

(A) 24

(B) 48

(C) 110

(D) 144

(E) 3,024

SOLUTION

Before you jump into multiplication, look at the numbers inside the first parentheses. This is the sum $(8 + 4) = 12$, which makes the entire expression equal to $7(12) - (3 \times 12)$. The distributive property tells you that $a(b + c) = ab + ac$ and $a(b - c) = ab - ac$. The expression $7(12) - (3 \times 12)$ can be made to fit the second formula, with a equal to 12 and 7 and 3 equal to b and c, respectively. Thus, $7(12) - (3 \times 12)$ becomes $12(7 - 3)$, and the answer is simply 12×4, or 48.

Question Type 2: Undefined Symbols

Most PSAT math sections include problems that involve undefined symbols. In some problems, these symbols define a value by asking you to perform several arithmetic operations. For example, the symbol $\boxed{x}$ may tell you to square some number x then subtract 3: $\boxed{x} = x^2 - 3$. In other problems, a symbol may represent a missing numeral, such as $10 - \Delta = 7$. By looking at the arithmetic, you can see that Δ must equal 3.

PROBLEM

Let $[n] = n^2 + 1$ for all numbers n. Which of the following is equal to the product of [2] and [3]?

(A) [A]   (D) [9]

(B) [7]   (E) [11]

(C) [8]

SOLUTION

The newly defined symbol is [ ]. To find the values for [2] and [3], plug them into the formula $[n] = n^2 + 1$:

$$[2] = 2^2 + 1 = 4 + 1 = 5$$

$$[3] = 3^2 + 1 = 9 + 1 = 10$$

Since, [2] = 5, and [3] = 10, we can compute the product: $5 \times 10 = 50$.

Now look at the answers. You will see that the answers are given in terms of [ ]. Once again, you must plug them into the formula $[n] = n^2 + 1$. If we plug each answer choice into the equation, we get:

$$[6] = 6^2 + 1 = 36 + 1 = 37$$

$$[7] = 7^2 + 1 = 49 + 1 = 50$$

$$[8] = 8^2 + 1 = 64 + 1 = 65$$

$$[9] = 9^2 + 1 = 81 + 1 = 82$$

$$[11] = 11^2 + 1 = 121 + 1 = 122$$

Question Type 3: Averages

Some PSAT math problems ask you to simply compute the average of a given set of values. More challenging problems ask you to apply the definition of *average*. You will recall that the average of a given set of values is equal to the sum of the values divided by the number of values in the set.

PROBLEM

The average of 10 numbers is 53. What is the sum of the numbers?

(A)   106   (D)   530

(B)   350   (E)   615

(C)   363

SOLUTION

You can solve this problem using the formula:

$$\text{Average} = \frac{\text{sum of values}}{\text{number of values}}$$

In this question,

$$53 = \frac{\text{sum of values}}{10}$$

Therefore, the sum of the numbers is 530:

$$10 \times 53 = \text{sum of values}$$

$$530 = \text{sum of values}$$

PROBLEM

The average of three numbers is 16. If one of the numbers is 5, what is the sum of the other two?

(A)   11   (D)   38

(B)   24   (E)   43

(C)   27

SOLUTION

In this problem, if we plug in the numbers we know we get

$$16 = \frac{a+b+c}{3}$$

This can be converted to

$$3 \times 16 = a + b + c,$$

which means that

$$48 = a + b + c.$$

If $a = 5$, we can solve:

$$48 = 5 + b + c, \text{ or } 48 - 5 = b + c,$$

and finally $43 = b + c$. Therefore, the sum of the other two numbers is 43 which is choice (E). Notice that choice (A) is waiting for the person who fails to work the formula and simply subtracts 5 from 16.

Question Type 4: Data Interpretation

Data interpretation problems usually require two basic steps. First, you have to read a chart or graph in order to obtain certain information. Then you have to apply or manipulate the information in order to obtain an answer.

PROBLEM

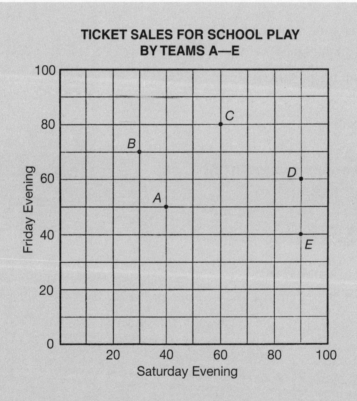

Which team sold the greatest number of tickets for Friday evening and Saturday evening combined?

(A) Team A   (D) Team D

(B) Team B   (E) Team E

(C) Team C

SOLUTION

Glancing over the data, you see that the number of tickets sold for Friday evening is represented vertically, while the number of tickets sold for Saturday evening is represented horizontally. Points placed on the grid represent each team's ticket sales for the two evenings.

Read the graph to determine the number of tickets sold by each team for Friday evening and Saturday evening.

Add each pair of numbers to find the total number of tickets sold by each team for both evenings.

Compare the totals to see which team sold the most tickets.

The answer is (D), since team D sold 60 tickets for Friday evening and 90 tickets for Saturday evening for a highest total of 150.

ALGEBRA QUESTIONS

Algebra problems use letters or variables to represent numbers. In these types of problems, you will be required to solve existing algebraic expressions or translate word problems into algebraic expressions.

Question Type 1: Algebraic Expressions

Problems involving algebraic expressions often contain hidden shortcuts. You can find these shortcuts by asking yourself, "How can this expression be rearranged?" Often rearrangement will cause an answer to appear almost magically.

There are three basic ways in which you can rearrange an algebraic expression. You can

1. combine like terms

2. factor the expression

3. multiply out the expression

PROBLEM

If $x = \frac{1}{2}$, which of the following equals $x^2 - x + \frac{1}{4}$?

(A) $-\dfrac{1}{2}$ (D) $\dfrac{1}{2}$

(B) 0   (E) 1

(C) $\dfrac{1}{4}$

SOLUTION

You can find the answer by substituting $x = \frac{1}{2}$ into the given expression, but there is an easier way. Look at $x^2 - x + \frac{1}{4}$. Remembering the strategy tip, this expression is equal to the trinomial square $(x - \frac{1}{2})^2$. Now you can see at a glance that since you are told that

$$x = \tfrac{1}{2}, \left(x - \tfrac{1}{2}\right)^2$$

must equal 0. Thus, the answer is (B).

Question Type 2: Word Problems

Among the most common types of word problems found on the PSAT are age problems, mixture problems, distance problems, and percent problems. You can find detailed explanations of these and other problem types in the Basic Math Skills Review. There is a strategy, however, that can help you to solve all types of word problems—learning to recognize "keywords."

Keywords are words or phrases that can be translated directly into a mathematical symbol, expression, or operation. As you know, you usually cannot solve a word problem without writing some kind of equation. Learning to spot keywords will enable you to write the equations you need more easily.

Listed below are some of the most common keywords. As you practice solving word problems, you will probably find others.

Keyword	Mathematical Equivalent
is	equals
sum	add
plus	add
more than, older than	add
difference	subtract
less than, younger than	subtract
twice, double	multipy by 2
half as many	divided by 2
increase by 3	add 3
decrease by 3	subtract 3

PROBLEM

Adam has 50 more than twice the number of "frequent flier" miles that Erica has. If Adam has 200 frequent flier miles, how many does Erica have?

(A) 25   (D) 100

(B) 60   (E) 250

(C) 75

SOLUTION

The keywords in this problem are "more" and "twice." If you let a = the number of frequent flier miles that Adam has and e = the number of frequent flier miles that Erica has, you can write: $a = 50 + 2e$. Since $a = 200$, the solution becomes: $200 = 50 + 2e$. Therefore, $200 - 50 = 2e$, or $150 = 2e$, and $\frac{150}{2} = e$ or $75 = e$, which is choice (C).

GEOMETRY QUESTIONS

PSAT geometry questions require you to find the area or missing sides of figures given certain information. These problems require you to use "if . . . then" reasoning or to draw figures based on given information.

Question Type 1: "If . . . Then" Reasoning

You will not have to work with geometric proofs on the PSAT, but the logic used in proofs can help you enormously when it comes to solving PSAT geometry problems. This type of logic is often referred to as "If . . . then" reasoning. In "if . . . then" reasoning, you say to yourself, "If A is true, then B must be true." By using "if . . . then" reasoning, you can draw conclusions based on the rules and definitions that you know. For example, you might say, "If ABC is a triangle, then the sum of its angles must equal 180."

PROBLEM

If triangle QRS is an equilateral triangle, what is the value of $a + b$?

(A) 60°

(B) 80°

(C) 85°

(D) 100°

(E) 120°

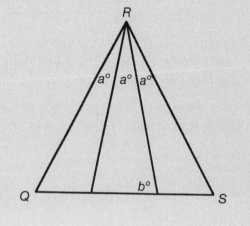

SOLUTION

You can obtain the information that you need to solve this problem by using a series of "if . . . then" statements: "If QRS is an equilateral triangle, then each angle must equal 60°." "If angle $R = 60°$, then a must equal 20°." "If $a = 20°$, then b must equal half of $(180° - 20°)$ or 80°." "If $a = 20°$ and $b = 80°$, then $a + b - 100°$." Therefore, answer (D) is correct.

Question Type 2: Drawing Diagrams

Among the most difficult geometry problems on the PSAT are those that describe a geometric situation without providing a diagram. For these problems, you must learn to draw your own diagram based on the information that is given. The best way to do this is step-by-step, using each piece of information that the problem provides. As you draw, you should always remember to:

1. label all points, angles, and line segments according to the information provided.

2. indicate parallel or perpendicular lines.

3. write in any measures that you are given.

If vertical line segment $\overline{AB}$ is perpendicular to line segment $\overline{CD}$ at point O and if ray OE bisects angle BOD, what is the value of angle AOE?

(A) 45°   (D) 135°

(B) 90°   (E) 180°

(C) 120°

SOLUTION

Draw as follows:

Draw and label vertical line segment $\overline{AB}$.

Draw and label line segment $\overline{CD}$ perpendicular to $\overline{AB}$. Label the right angle that is formed. Label point O.

Locate angle BOD. Draw and label ray OE so that it bisects, or cuts into two equal parts, angle BOD. Use equal marks to show that the two parts of the angle are equal. Since you are bisecting a right angle, you can write in the measure 45°.

Your diagram should resemble that shown below. Now you can evaluate your drawing to answer the question. Angle AOE is equal to 90° + 45°, or 135°. The answer is (D).

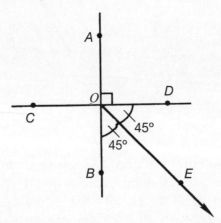

POINTS TO REMEMBER

- Certain patterns of factoring appear so often on the PSAT that you should learn to spot them in every possible form. These include: difference of squares, where $x^2 - y^2 = (x + y)(x - y)$; and trinomial squares, where $(x + y)^2 = x^2 + 2xy + y^2$ or $(x - y)^2 = x^2 - 2xy + y^2$.

- When solving data interpretation problems, you should take a moment to look at the graph or chart in order to see how it is set up and what types of information are displayed. You should not, however, waste time reading or analyzing the data until you read the question(s) and find out what is being asked.

- If you are dealing with a geometry question that refers to a figure and the question does not provide the figure, draw the figure. This will help you visualize the problem. In addition, if a figure is provided, note whether or not it is drawn to size.

- Do not use your calculator for simple mathematic calculations. Using your calculator for such purposes may waste more time than it saves.

- Be sure to review the reference information. It provides some common formulas that may prove valuable when you are answering the questions.

ANSWERING REGULAR MATH QUESTIONS

The following steps should be used to help guide you through answering Regular Math questions. Combined with the review material which you have just studied, these steps will provide you with the tools necessary to correctly answer the questions you will encounter.

STEP 1   *Try to determine the type of question with which you are dealing. This will help you focus in on how to attack the question.*

STEP 2   *Carefully read all of the information presented. Make sure you are answering the question, and not incorrectly reading the question. Look for key words that can help you determine what the question is asking.*

STEP 3   *Perform the operations indicated, but be sure you are taking the easiest approach. Simplify all expressions and equations before performing your calculations. Draw your own figures if a question refers to them, but does not provide them.*

STEP 4   *Try to work backwards from the answer choices if you are having difficulty determining an answer.*

STEP 5   *If you are still having difficulty determining an answer, use the process of elimination. If you can eliminate at least two choices, you will greatly increase your chances of correctly answering the question. Eliminating three choices means that you have a fifty-fifty chance of correctly answering the question if you guess.*

STEP 6   *Once you have chosen an answer, fill in the oval which corresponds to the question and answer which you have chosen. Beware of stray lines on your answer sheet, as they may cause your answers to be scored incorrectly.*

Now, use the information you have just learned to answer the following drill questions. Doing so will help reinforce the material learned, and will better prepare you for the actual test.

DRILL: REGULAR MATH

<u>DIRECTIONS</u>: Choose the best answer choice and fill in the corresponding oval on the answer sheet.

1. If $8 - (7 - 6 - 5) = 8 - 7 - (x - 5)$, what is the value of x?

    (A) -6 (B) -16 (C) -18 (D) 4   (E) 6

2. The average (arithmetic mean) volume of 4 containers is 40 liters. If 3 of these containers each has a volume of 35 liters, what is the volume in liters of the fourth container?

    (A) 40   (B) 50   (C) 55   (D) 105   (E) 160

3.
$$
\begin{array}{r}
2 \blacklozenge 5 \\
\times \quad 7 \\
\hline
1{,}8 \oplus 5
\end{array}
$$

    In the correctly computed multiplication problem above, if $\blacklozenge$ and $\oplus$ are different digits, then $\blacklozenge =$

    (A) 2.   (B) 6   (C) 5   (D) 4.   (E) 7.

4. If for any number n, $[n]$ is defined as the least whole number that is greater than or equal to n, then $[-3.7] + 14 =$

    (A) 10.3   (B) 17.7   (C) 18   (D) 10   (E) 11

5. How many tenths of a kilometer will a cyclist travel in 1 minute if she cycles at a rate of 30 km/hour?

    (A) 0.5   (B) 1   (C) 2   (D) 5   (E) $\dfrac{1}{30}$

6. If $\overline{DE}$ is parallel to $\overline{ST}$ and triangle RST is an isoceles triangle, then $\angle E$ is

    (A) 50°.
    (B) 40°.
    (C) 70°.
    (D) 90°.
    (E) 75°.

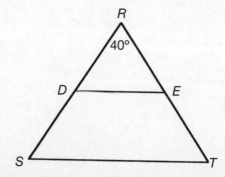

7. If 20 students share the cost equally of a gift for Coach Brown, what percent of the total cost do 5 of the students share?

   (A) 5%   (B) 10%   (C) 25%   (D) 40%   (E) 50%

8. If $n \div 5 = 150 \div 25$, then $n =$

   (A) 5.   (B) 6.   (C) 25.   (D) 30.   (E) 125.

9. If the average (arithmetic mean) of -9 and s is -9, then $s =$

   (A) -9 (B) 0   (C) 9   (D) -18 (E) -4.5

10. If $x \blacklozenge y = (x - 3)y$, then $8 \blacklozenge 3 + 5 \blacklozenge 2 =$

    (A) 34.   (B) 50.   (C) 0.   (D) -5.   (E) 19.

11. If $22 \times 3 \times R = 6$, then $R =$

    (A) $\dfrac{1}{9}$.   (B) $\dfrac{1}{11}$.   (C) $\dfrac{1}{8}$.   (D) 11.   (E) 9.

12. What is the total area, in square meters, of two adjacent square garden plots with sides 4 meters and 1 meter, respectively?

    (A) 1   (B) 4   (C) 16   (D) 17   (E) 20

13. If line m is parallel to line n as shown, then $\angle b =$

    (A) 30°.
    (B) 45°.
    (C) 55°.
    (D) 60°.
    (E) 120°.

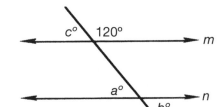

14. If $\frac{6m}{9} = 4$, then $18m =$

    (A) 6.   (B) 24.   (C) 36.   (D) 72.   (E) 108.

15. During a local high school track meet, all three contestants earn points. Olivia earns 12 times more points than Barbara, and Diane earns 8 times more points than Barbara. What is the ratio of Diane's points to Olivia's points?

(A) 96 : 1   (B) 8 : 1   (C) 3 : 2   (D) 2 : 3   (E) 1 : 8

16. If $x^2 - z^2 = 130$, and $x - z = 10$, then $x + z =$

(A) 10.   (B) 13.   (C) 36.   (D) 30.   (E) 120.

17. In the figure shown here, what does x equal?

(A) 80
(B) 90
(C) 100
(D) 110
(E) 120

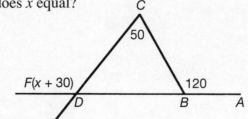

18. In triangle ABC, $\angle ABC$ is 53° and $\angle BCA$ is 37°, $\overline{BC} = 5$ inches and $\overline{AC} = 4$ inches, what is the length of the shortest side?

(A) 2 inches   (D) 5 inches
(B) 3 inches   (E) 6 inches
(C) 4 inches

19. If 22 is the average of $n, n, n, 15,$ and 35, then $n =$

(A) 16.   (B) 18.   (C) 20.   (D) 50.   (E) 110.

20. If $7x + 18 = 16x$, then $x =$

(A) -2.   (B) $\dfrac{18}{23}$.   (C) $\dfrac{23}{18}$.   (D) 2.   (E) 36.

21. A circular piece of turquoise with radius 5 inches is inscribed in a square piece of tile, where the piece of turquoise touches each side of the square only once. What is the area in square inches of the tile?

(A) 25   (B) 78.5   (C) 50   (D) 10   (E) 100

22. If the area of the shaded region is 24π, then the radius of circle O is

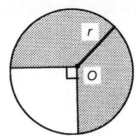

(A) 4.

(B) 16.

(C) $2\sqrt{6}$.

(D) $4\sqrt{2}$.

(E) $2\sqrt{2}$.

23. If, in the triangle shown here, $\overline{AS} < \overline{ST}$ which of the following <u>cannot</u> be the value of t?

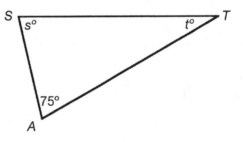

(A) 20   (E) 80

(B) 36   (D) 71

(C) 65

24. If $R \# S = \dfrac{R+2}{S}$, then $(4 \# 3) \# k =$

(A) $\dfrac{5}{4}$.   (B) 2.   (C) $\dfrac{2}{k}$.   (D) $\dfrac{4}{k}$.   (E) $4k$.

25. If $48x - 6y = 1$, then $16x - 2y =$

(A) -3.   (B) 0.   (C) $\dfrac{1}{3}$.   (D) $\dfrac{1}{2}$.   (E) 1.

26. Sam is 5 years older than Marcia, and Marcia is 6 years older than Jack. How many years older than Jack is Sam?

(A) 11   (B) 9   (C) 7   (D) 6   (E) 2

27. A cat ate $\frac{1}{2}$ of the food in its dish in the morning, and 2 ounces of food in the afternoon. The cat's owner came home to find $\frac{2}{5}$ of the original amount of food in the dish. How many ounces of food were in the dish at the start of the day?

(A)   4 ounces   (D)   16 ounces

(B)   5 ounces   (E)   20 ounces

(C)   8 ounces

28. The average value of A, B, and C is 8, and $2(A + C) = 24$. What is the value of B?

(A) 0   (B) 3   (C) -16 (D) 32   (E) 12

29. If S is the sum of the positive integers from 1 to n, inclusive, then the average (arithmetic mean), k, of these integers can be represented by the formula

(A) $S \times n$.   (B) $\dfrac{S}{n}$.   (C) $\dfrac{k}{n}$.   (D) $S + n$.   (E) $n + 1$.

30. If $3a + 4a = 14$, and $b + 6b = 20$, then $7(a + b) =$

(A) 21.   (B) 28.   (C) 34.   (D) 40.   (E) 42.

31. The perimeter of an equilateral triangle is 18. What is the altitude of the triangle?

(A) 3   (B) 6   (C) 9   (D) $\sqrt{3}$ (E) $3\sqrt{3}$

32. A truck driver covered 450 miles during a 9-hour period, stopped for one hour, then drove 90 miles in 2 hours. What was the driver's average rate, in miles per hour, for the total distance traveled?

(A) 45   (B) 49   (C) 50   (D) 54   (E) 60

33. If $x + y = 7$ and $x - y = 3$, then $x^2 - y^2 =$

(A) 4.   (B) 10.   (C) 16.   (D) 21.   (E) 40.

34. If $a \times b = 6a \,\square\, 5b$, then $(5 \,\square\, 5) \times (3 \,\square\, 2) =$

(A) 4.   (C) 180.   (C) 66.   (D) 7.   (E) 9.

35. If $m < n < 0$, which expression must be < 0?

(A) The product of m and n
(B) The square of the product of m and n
(C) The sum of m and n
(D) The result of subtracting m from n
(E) The quotient of dividing n by m

36. In the figure shown, if $\overline{BD}$ is the bisector of angle *ABC*, and angle *ABD* is one-fourth the size of angle *XYZ*, what is the size of angle *ABC*?

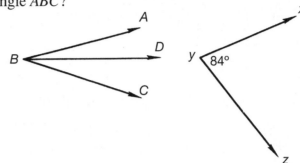

(A) 21°

(B) 28°

(C) 42°

(D) 63°

(E) 168°

37. A cube of volume 8 cubic centimeters is placed directly next to a cube of volume 125 cubic centimeters. What is the perpendicular distance in centimeters from the top of the larger cube to the top of the smaller cube?

(A) 7   (B) 5   (C) 3   (D) 2   (E) 0

38. If Company A's November income is $1 million less than the average income of July and September, what will the November income be?

Income for Company A
July–October 2005
(in millions of dollars)

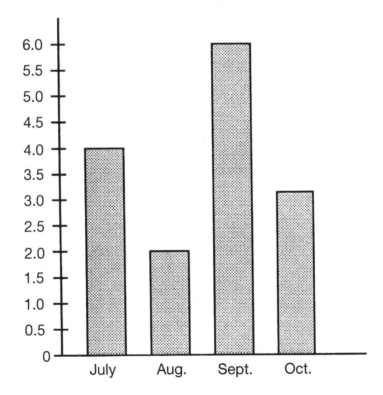

(A) $2 million   (D) $5 million

(B) $3 million   (E) $10 million

(C) $4 million

39. If $21 - (a - b) = 2(b + 9)$, and $a = 8$, what is the value of b?

(A) 31   (B) 13   (C) 4   (D) $-\dfrac{5}{3}$ (E) -5

40.

Employees in Division R of Corporation S

Year	1999	2000	2001	2002	2003
Number of Employees	1,900	2,200	2,500	2,800	3,100

Based on the increase in employees over the past 5 years, how many employees can Division R expect to have by 2005?

(A) 3,100   (B) 3,400   (C) 3,550   (D) 3,700   (E) 4,000

REGULAR MATH

ANSWER KEY

Drill: Regular Math

1.	(A)	11.	(B)	21.	(E)	31.	(E)
2.	(C)	12.	(D)	22.	(D)	32.	(A)
3.	(B)	13.	(D)	23.	(E)	33.	(D)
4.	(E)	14.	(E)	24.	(D)	34.	(A)
5.	(A)	15.	(D)	25.	(C)	35.	(C)
6.	(C)	16.	(B)	26.	(A)	36.	(C)
7.	(C)	17.	(A)	27.	(E)	37.	(C)
8.	(D)	18.	(B)	28.	(E)	38.	(C)
9.	(A)	19.	(C)	29.	(B)	39	(E)
10.	(E)	20.	(D)	30.	(C)	40.	(D)

DETAILED EXPLANATIONS

REGULAR MATH

1. **(A)** The question involves both algebra and arithmetic concepts. Remember the Order of Operations (PEMDAS) for the left side of the equation and reduce the expression in the parenthesis $(7 - 6 - 5)$ to -4. You are left with $8 - (-4)$, which is the same as $8 + 4$, or 12. On the right side of the equation, multiply the expression in parenthesis by the negative next to it to get $-x + 5$, then add up all the integers to reduce the expression to $6 - x$. The reduced equation is now $12 = 6 - x$. Subtracting 6 from both sides gives us $6 = -x$. Since the question is asking for the value of positive x, multiply the entire equation by -1 to get $x = -6$, answer (A).

2. **(C)** If the average volume of 4 containers is 40 liters, then you know that the total sum of all 4 containers must be 160 liters—the product of the number of containers (4) and the average (40). If three containers each have an individual volume of 35 liters, then their sum will be $35 + 35 + 35$, or 105. The question is asking for the volume of the fourth container, which, when added to the volumes of the other 3 must equal 160. The equation is $105 + x = 160$. Subtract 105 from both sides of the equation and the volume of the fourth container (x) is 55, answer (C).

3. **(B)** This arithmetic question is testing your ability to multiply without a calculator and your understanding of number placement. The symbols ◆ and ⊕ stand for different single digits—which could be anything from 0 to 9—but the question is asking for the specific value of ◆ which is represented in the five different answer choices. Start by substituting answer (A), 2, for ◆ and multiply out. $225 \times 7 = 1{,}575$. Since the thousands digit (1), hundreds digit (8), and units digit (5) cannot change, answer (A), which has a hundreds digit of (5), is incorrect. Substitute answer (B), 6, for ◆ and multiply out. $265 \times 7 = 1855$. All the permanent digits match up, and the digits used in place of ◆ and ⊕ are different, therefore answer (B) is correct.

4. **(E)** The definition of $[n]$ as the least whole number that is greater than or equal to n means that the number inside the brackets [ ] will be rounded **up** to the nearest whole number, unless n is equal to a whole number. If $n = 4.2$, then $[4.2]$ would be rounded up to 5. The question gives you $[-3.7]$. Since this is a negative number, the greatest whole number would be -3, NOT -4. The arithmetic equation will then look like $-3 + 14$, which equals 11, answer (E).

5. **(A)** A cyclist traveling at a rate of $\frac{30 \text{ km}}{1 \text{ hr}}$ is the same as traveling at a rate of $\frac{30 \text{ km}}{60 \text{ min}}$. Since the question is asking for the distance traveled in 1 minute, you can set up a simple proportion that looks like this: $\frac{30 \text{ km}}{60 \text{ min}} = \frac{x \text{ km}}{1 \text{ min}}$. Cross multiply and you come up with $60x = 30$. Divide both sides by 60 and you get 0.5 km as the distance traveled, answer (A).

6. (C)   Since triangle *RST* is isosceles, and *DE* is parallel to *ST*, then triangle *RDE* is also isosceles. Remember that an isosceles triangle has two equal sides and corresponding equal angles, and all the angles in a triangle must add up to 180°. Since $\angle R$ equals 40°, $\angle D$ and $\angle E$ must add up to 140°. The two angles are equal, so divide 140° by 2 and then both $\angle D$ and $\angle E$ equal 70°, answer (C).

7. (C)   If all the students share equally in the cost of the gift, then each student pays $\frac{1}{20}$ of the cost individually. Five students would then pay $\frac{5}{20}$ of the cost, or, reduced, $\frac{1}{4}$. To get the percent, divide 1 by 4 and multiply by 100, which would be .25 × 100, or 25%, answer (C). Another way to approach this problem would be to recognize that the total cost of the gift is spread equally among 20 people and the question wants to know what percent of the 20 people is 5 people. Since percent means to divide by 100, the equation would look like this: $\frac{x}{100} \times 20$. Isolate the variable by multiplying both sides by 100 and then dividing both sides by 20. You then get $x = \frac{500}{20}$, or 25%, answer (C).

8. (D)   Simplify the right side of the equation (150 ÷ 25) to 6. Rewrite the remainder of the equation as follows: $\frac{x}{5} = 6$. Multiply both sides by 5 to isolate the variable, and the result is $x = 30$, answer (D).

9. (A)   If the average of two numbers is –9, then the sum of the two numbers must be the average multiplied by the number of things being averaged, –9 × 2, or –18. From this we can determine the value of *s* by the equation –9 + *s* = –18. Add 9 to both sides and *s* = –9, answer (A).

10. (E)   The function $x \blacklozenge y$ is defined by the equation $(x - 3)y$. This means that in any given function, the number to the left of $\blacklozenge$ will be used in the place of variable *x* and the number to the right of $\blacklozenge$ will be used in the place of variable *y*. Therefore the first function of $8 \blacklozenge 3$ simply means $(8 - 3)3 = (5)3$, or 15. The second function of $5 \blacklozenge 2$ simply means $(5 - 3)2 = (2)2$, or 4. The answer to the equation is 15 + 4 = 19, answer (E).

11. (B)   In this simple algebra expression, you are looking to isolate variable *R*. Simplify the left side of the equation to $66 \times R$. Divide both sides of the equation by 66 to get: $R = \frac{6}{66}$, or $\frac{1}{11}$, answer (B).

12. (D)   Since the garden plots are square, all the sides must be equal. The area of one garden plot is 4 × 4, or 16, and the area of the second plot is 1 × 1, or 1. The total area of the two garden plots would be 16 + 1, or 17, answer (D). The fact that the two plots are adjacent is superfluous and unnecessary to answer the question.

13. (D)   When a line intersects two parallel lines, two types of angles are created; big angles (greater than 90°) and small angles (less than 90°). All big angles are of equal measure and all small angles are of equal measure. From the information in the diagram, $\angle c = 60°$ because a straight line must have 180°. All other small angles in the diagram will also equal 60° because the lines are parallel. $\angle a$ and $\angle b$ are both small angles and will both equal 60°, answer (D).

14. (E)   There are two parts to this equation, first you need to solve for *m* and then multiply that value by 18. In the first part, multiply both sides of the equation by 9. This gives you $6m = 36$. Divide both sides by 6 and you get $m = 6$. Careful, 6 is not the answer you are looking for, but it is an answer choice (A) that is there to trick you. Remember the question is asking for the value of 18*n*, so multiply the value of *m*, 6, by 18 and you come up with 108, answer (E).

15. **(D)**   The word problem is asking for the ratio of Diane's points to Olivia's points. The tricky part is that there is no way of determining what the actual number of points are, since both contestants points are based on Barbara's points, which are not stated. But for ratio problems you don't need to know the actual numbers, just the relationship between the numbers. Diane's points are 8 times more than Barbara's, therefore write out Diane's points as $8B$. Olivia's points are 12 times more than Barbara's, therefore write out Olivia's points as $12B$. Remember that a ratio can be expressed as a fraction and the ratio of Diane's points to Olivia's can be expressed as:

$$\frac{8B}{12B} = \frac{8}{12} = \frac{2}{3}$$

Since Barbara's points are the same for the numerator and the denominator, they can be cancelled out and the remaining fraction reduced, leaving 2 : 3, answer (D).

16. **(B)**   In this question you are given two equations and asked to solve for a third. One of the equations involves exponents, which should tip you off that you are dealing with quadratic equations. If you expand the first equation into the quadratic form you get $x^2 - y^2 = (x - y)(x + y)$. Now we can rewrite the first equation as $(x - y)(x + y) = 130$. The second equation tells us that $x - z = 10$, so if you substitute this value into the first parenthesis you get $(10)(x + y) = 130$. Divide both sides by 10 and you come up with the answer, $x + y = 13$ (B).

17. **(A)**   Remember that all the angles in a triangle must add up to $180°$ and a straight line also consists of $180°$. $\angle B$ must equal $60°$ so that the line has $180°$, and so $\angle D$ can be solved with the following equation: $50° + 60° + \angle D = 180°$. If $\angle D = 70°$, then adjacent $\angle F$ must equal $110°$ so the line has $180°$. Now we can solve for x with the equation $\angle F = (x + 30) = 110°$. Subtract 30 from both sides of the equation and $x = 80$, answer (A).

18. **(B)**   In this question the triangle is not provided for you, but rather described, therefore you will need to draw a sketch of it yourself for a visual aid. Two angles are given to you, so you will need to find the third. Since all angles in a triangle add up to $180°$, $\angle BAC = 180° - 53° + 37° = 90°$. Now you know you are dealing with a right triangle where the hypotenuse has a length of 5, the base has a length of 4, and you need to solve for the third side. Remember the Pythagorean theorem, $a^2 + b^2 = c^2$, where c is the hypotenuse. The equation for the third side is now $4^2 + b^2 = 5^2$, or $16 + b^2 = 25$. Subtract 16 from both sides of the equation and you get $b^2 = 9$. Take the square root from both sides of the equation and up with the third side (b) = 3, answer (B). This is one of the 3:4:5 special case right triangles that appear quite often on the PSAT.

19. **(C)**   Five numbers average out to 22, therefore the sum of the five numbers must equal 22 × 5, or 110. You can now write an algebraic expression to solve for n: $35 + 15 + n + n + n = 110$, or $50 + 3n = 110$. Subtract 50 from both sides of the equation to get $3n = 60$. Divide both sides of the equation by 3 and you get $n = 20$, answer (C).

20. **(D)**   In this algebraic expression you need to have all the variables on one side of the equation and the integers on the other. Subtract $7x$ from both sides of the equation and you end up with $18 = 9x$. Divide both sides by 9 and you end up with $x = 2$, answer (D).

21. (E) Since the circle is inscribed inside the tile in such a way that the circumference touches each side of the square exactly once, the diameter of the circle must equal the length of one side of the square. The diameter is twice the radius, which is equal to 5. Therefore the diameter and the length of one side of the square is 10. The question is asking for the area of the square, which is length × width, or side^2. $10 \times 10 = 100$, answer (E).

22. (D) In order to find the radius, you will need to find the area of the entire circle. Remember that there are 360° in a circle. The unshaded portion of the circle takes up 90°, or $\frac{1}{4}$ of the area of the circle, therefore the shaded region of the circle accounts for $\frac{3}{4}$ of the area, which is equal to 24π. The area of the entire circle, (A), can now be solved for with the following equation: $\frac{3}{4}A = 24\pi$. Multiply both sides of the equation by $\frac{4}{3}$ and the area of the entire circle is $A = 32\pi$. Use the formula for finding the area of a circle (Area = πr^2) to find the radius of circle O. $\pi32 = \pi r^2$. Divide both sides by π and you get $32 = r^2$, and then when you extract the square from both sides you should come up with $r = \sqrt{32} = \sqrt{16 \times 2} = 4\sqrt{2}$, answer (D).

23. (E) In triangles the longest side is always opposite the longest angle and the shortest side is always opposite the shortest angle. Since $\overline{AS} < \overline{ST}$, the angle opposite of $\overline{AS}$, t, will also have to be less than the angle opposite of $\overline{ST}$, 75°. Therefore t cannot be greater than 75° and the answer is 80 (E).

24. (D) This function means that whenever you see two numbers on either side of the # symbol, add 2 to the number on the left and divide this new number by the number on the right side of the symbol. Start with the numbers in parenthesis first (remember the order of operations?). Since 4 is on the left of the # symbol, it can be substituted for R and since 3 is to the right of the # symbol, it can substituted for S. Now you can solve the equation (4 # 3) = $\frac{4+2}{3}$ = 2. Substituting 2 for the value in the parenthesis, your new equation is now 2 # k. Go back and place these new values into the function and you come up with $\frac{2+2}{k}$, or $\frac{4}{k}$, answer (D).

25. (C) Since you don't know the exact values of x and y, you are going to need to factor both equations to see what they have in common. If you factor out the 6 in the first equation you come up with $6(8x - y) = 1$. Factor out the 2 in the second equation and you get $2(8x - y)$. Now you can see that both equations have $(8x - y)$ in common. Divide both sides of the first equation by 6 and you get $(8x - y) = \frac{1}{6}$. Substitute $\frac{1}{6}$ in for the value of $(8x - y)$ in the second equation and you get $2(\frac{1}{6}) = \frac{2}{6}$, or $\frac{1}{3}$, answer (C).

26. (A) The ages of Sam, Marcia, and Jack are not given, so go ahead and make them up yourself following the requirements of the problem. Say Sam is 18 years old, which is 5 years older than Marcia. This means that Marcia would have to be 13. If Marcia is 13, which is 6 years older than Jack, then Jack must be 7. The question is asking for the difference between Sam and Jack's age, which is 11, answer (A).

27. (E)   Since you are dealing with fractions and the question wants to know whole amount of food in the cat dish, go ahead and use 1 to represent the whole amount. The cat ate $\frac{1}{2}$ the food, plus 2 ounces and there was $\frac{2}{5}$ remaining. Therefore you can set up the equation $\frac{1}{2} + \frac{2}{5} + 2$ ounces = whole amount (1). Add the fractions and you get $\frac{1}{2} + \frac{2}{5} = \frac{5}{10} + \frac{4}{10} = \frac{9}{10}$. Now the equation is $\frac{9}{10} + 2$ ounces = whole amount (1). Subtract $\frac{9}{10}$ from both sides of the equation and you get: 2 ounces = whole amount (1) $- \frac{9}{10}$, or 2 ounces = $\frac{1}{10}$. Now that you know the fractional portion of the 2 ounces, you can use the equation $\frac{1}{10}x = 2$, where x is the total amount of food in ounces. Multiply both sides by 10 and you come up with $x = 20$, answer (E).

28. (E)   The average of 3 numbers—A, B, and C—is 8, therefore the sum of these numbers is 8×3, or 24. If $2(A + C) = 24$, then divide both sides by 2 and you get $A + C = 12$. Since the question is asking for the value of B, use the expression $A + C + B = 24$. Substitute the value of 12 for $(A + C)$ and you get $12 + B = 24$. Subtract 12 from both sides and you get $B = 12$, answer (E).

29. (B)   The average, or arithmetic mean, is defined as the sum of the things being averaged divided by the number of things being averaged. The question already informs you that S represents the sum. The number of things being averaged would be represented by n, since it defines the range of the numbers being added together. So the average would be represented by the formula $\frac{S}{n}$, answer (B).

30. (C)   Simplify the first two equations by adding together like variables and you get $7a = 14$ and $7b = 20$. Before you solve for the solution of both variables, look at what the question is asking for, the answer to $7(a + b)$. If you expand out the equation you can rewrite it to look like $7a + 7b$. Now you can substitute in 14 for the amount of $7a$ and 20 for the amount of $7b$ from the previous equations and you get $14 + 20 = 34$, answer (C). If you try to solve for the individual variables you would fall for the test writer's trick. Since b would equal a number with a very long and convoluted decimal you would not only waste valuable time, but also eventually get frustrated and choose the wrong answer. Always keep in mind what the question is asking for.

31. (E)   Since a figure is not provided for you, it would be best to draw one out in the space provided next to the question. Since all sides are equal in an equilateral triangle, the length of one side would be $18 \div 3$, or 6. The question is asking for the height of the triangle, which is defined as the perpendicular distance from the base to the highest point. In an equilateral triangle, this distance splits the triangle right down the middle, creating two separate 30°, 60°, 90° triangles. You need to be familiar with the relationship between the lengths of the sides on a 30°, 60°, 90° triangle. The smallest side, opposite the smallest angle, 30°, can be represented as x; the longest side or the hypotenuse, opposite the 90° angle, can be represented as $2x$; and last side, opposite the 60° angle, can be represented as $x\sqrt{3}$. Looking at half of the equilateral triangle, the base has been split in half as well which gives a distance of 3, opposite the 30°. The hypotenuse was not changed and remains 6, twice the value of the new base. The height is the side opposite the 60° angle and is the smallest side (x) times $\sqrt{3}$, or $3\sqrt{3}$, answer (E).

32. (A)   Remember the formula for rate, $rate = \frac{distance}{time}$. The sum of the two separate distances give you the total distance traveled. $450 + 90 = 540$. Including the one hour of rest taken in the middle, it took the driver a total of 12 hours $(9 + 1 + 2)$ to complete the total distance of 540 miles. Therefore the driver's average rate for the entire distance traveled is $r = \frac{540 \text{ miles}}{12 \text{ hours}}$, or 45 miles/hour, answer (A).

33. (D)   You are given three separate equations and one of them involves exponents, therefore you are dealing with quadratic equations. Look at the third equation, $x^2 - y^2$. First you want to expand it out into two separate expressions to factor out the exponents, giving you $(x + y)(x - y)$. The first two equations already give you the values of $(x + y)$ and $(x - y)$ as 7 and 3 respectively. Substitute these values into the equation and you get $(7)(3) = 21$, answer (D).

34. (A)   This function equation requires you to multiply the number to the left of the box by 6 and divide by the number to the right of the box. Solve the functions in parenthesis first. The first function should give you $(\frac{6 \cdot 5}{5}) = 6$. The second function gives you $(\frac{6 \cdot 3}{2}) = 9$. Now you end up with $6 \ \square \ 9$, which gives you $(\frac{6 \cdot 6}{9}) = 4$. Answer (A) is correct.

35. (C)   If $m < n < 0$, then both m and n must be negative numbers. When any two negative numbers are added together, the result will ALWAYS be negative, so answer (C) is correct. Two negative numbers multiplied together will yield a positive result; therefore both (A) and (B) are incorrect. When you divide a negative number by another negative number, the result must be a positive number; answer (E) is incorrect. By subtracting m from n, m becomes a positive number that is greater than n, and thus the result will be positive, eliminating answer (D).

36. (C)   Angle ABD is $\frac{1}{4}$ the size of $\angle XYZ$, which is 84°. Therefore $\angle ABD = \frac{84}{4} = 21°$. The bisector is the line that cuts the angle in half, so $\angle ABD$ is half of $\angle ABC$, so you double 21° to get 42°, answer (C).

37. (C)   A figure is not provided in the question, so you will need to draw one out in the space next to the question. A cube is a three dimensional object in which the length, width, and height are all of equal measure. The volume of a cube is length × width × height, or length of side cubed (s^3). To find the length of one side of the cubes, you will need to take the cube root of the volumes. The larger cube would be $\sqrt[3]{125} = 5$, and the smaller cube is $\sqrt[3]{8} = 2$. When the two cubes are placed next to each other, one with a height of 5 and the other with a height of 2, the difference between the two tops would be $5 - 2$, or 3, answer (C).

38. (C)   According to the chart, July's income was 4 million dollars and September's income was 6 million. The average would be the sum of the two months divided by the number of months being averaged, 2. $\frac{6 + 4}{2} = 5$. The question is asking for the value of November's income, if that income is 1 million less than the average. So the average for the two months is 5 million, and November's income is 1 million less, or 4 million, answer (C).

39. (E)   This algebraic expression is asking for the value of b, so you will want to manipulate the equation to isolate b on one side and the rest on the opposite side. Start by substituting 8 for the value of a, $21 - (8 - b) = 2(b + 9)$, and expand out the two expressions in parentheses, $32 - 8 + b = 2b + 18$. Simplify the integers on the left side of the equation and subtract b from both sides and you get $13 = b + 18$. Subtract 18 from both sides and you get $b = -5$, answer (E).

40. (D)   This question is asking you to identify a pattern in the given chart of data. Every year Division R grew by 300 employees. If this pattern was to continue, in 2004 Division R could expect to have 3,400 employees, and in 2005 they could expect to have 300 more, or 3,700, answer (D).

CHAPTER 8

MASTERING STUDENT-PRODUCED RESPONSE QUESTIONS

CHAPTER 8

MASTERING STUDENT-PRODUCED RESPONSE QUESTIONS

The Student-Produced Response format of the PSAT is designed to give the student a certain amount of flexibility in answering questions. In this section the student must calculate the answer to a given question and then enter the solution into a grid. The grid is constructed so that a solution can be given in either decimal or fraction form. Either form is acceptable unless otherwise stated.

The problems in the Student-Produced Response section try to reflect situations arising in the real world. Here calculations will involve objects occurring in everyday life. There is also an emphasis on problems involving data interpretation. In keeping with this emphasis, students will be allowed the use of a calculator during the exam.

Through this review, you will learn how to successfully attack Student-Produced Response questions. Familiarity with the test format combined with solid math strategies will prove invaluable in answering the questions quickly and accurately.

ABOUT THE DIRECTIONS

Each Student-Produced Response question will require you to solve the problem and enter your answer in a grid. There are specific rules you will need to know for entering your solution. If you enter your answer in an incorrect form, you will not receive credit, even if you originally solved the problem correctly. Therefore, you should carefully study the following rules now, so you don't have to waste valuable time during the actual test:

DIRECTIONS: Each of the following questions requires you to solve the problem and enter your answer in the ovals in the special grid:

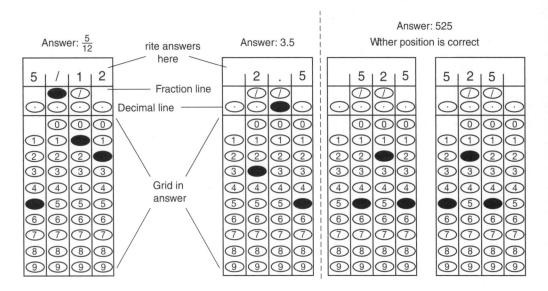

- You may begin filling in your answer in any column, space permitting. Columns not needed should be left blank.

- Answers may be entered in either decimal or fraction form. For example, ³⁄₁₂ or .25 are equally acceptable.

- A mixed number, such as 4 ½ , must be entered either as 4.5 or ⁹⁄₂ . If you entered 41/2, the machine would interpret your answer as ⁴¹⁄₂ , not 4 ½ .

- There may be some instances where there is more than one correct answer to a problem. Should this be the case, grid only one answer.

- Be very careful when filling in ovals. Do not fill in more than one oval in any column, and make sure to completely darken the ovals.

- It is suggested that you fill in your answer in the boxes above each column. Although you will not be graded incorrectly if you do not write in your answer, it will help you fill in the corresponding ovals.

- If your answer is a decimal, grid the most accurate value possible. For example, if you need to grid a repeating decimal such as 0.6666̄ , enter the answer as .666 or .667. A less accurate value, such as .66 or .67, is not acceptable.

- A negative answer cannot appear for any question.

How many pounds of apples can be bought with $5.00 if apples cost $.40 a pound?

SOLUTION

Converting dollars to cents we obtain the equation

$x = 500 \div 40$

$x = 12.5$

The solution to this problem would be gridded as

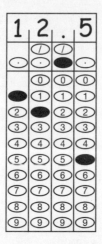

ABOUT THE QUESTIONS

Within the PSAT Student-Produced Response section you will be given 10 grid-in questions and 8 multiple-choice questions. You will have 25 minutes to complete this section. Therefore, you should work quickly.

The Student-Produced Response questions will come from the areas of arithmetic, algebra, and geometry. There is an emphasis on word problems and on data interpretation, which usually involves reading tables to answer questions. Many of the geometry questions will refer to diagrams or will ask you to create a figure from information given in the question.

The following will detail the different types of questions you should expect to encounter on the Student-Produced Response section.

ARITHMETIC QUESTIONS

These arithmetic questions test your ability to perform standard manipulations and simplifications of arithmetic expressions. For some questions, there is more than one approach. There are six kinds of arithmetic questions you may encounter in the Student-Produced Response section. For each type of question, we will show how to solve the problem and grid your answer.

Question Type 1: Properties of a Whole Number N

This problem tests your ability to find a whole number with a given set of properties. You will be given a list of properties of a whole number and asked to find that number.

PROBLEM

The properties of a whole number N are

(A) N is a perfect square.

(B) N is divisible by 2.

(C) N is divisible by 3.

Grid in the second smallest whole number with the above properties.

SOLUTION

Try to first obtain the smallest number with the above properties. The smallest number with properties (B) and (C) is 6. Since property (A) says the number must be a perfect square, the smallest number with properties (A), (B), and (C) is 36.

$6^2 = 36$ is the smallest whole number with the above properties. The second smallest whole number (the solution) is

$$2^2 6^2 = 144.$$

The correct answer entered into the grid is

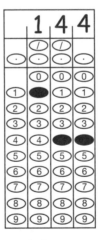

Question Type 2: Simplifying Fractions

This type of question requires you to simplify fractional expressions and grid the answer in the format specified. By canceling out terms common to both the numerator and denominator, we can simplify complex fractional expressions.

Change $\frac{1}{2} \times \frac{3}{7} \times \frac{2}{8} \times \frac{14}{10} \times \frac{1}{3}$ to decimal form.

SOLUTION

The point here is to cancel out terms common to both the numerator and denominator. Once the fraction is brought down to lowest terms, the result is entered into the grid as a decimal.

After cancellation we are left with the fraction $\frac{1}{40}$. Equivalently,

$$\frac{1}{40} = \frac{1}{10} \times \frac{1}{4} = \frac{1}{10}(.25) = .025$$

Hence, in our grid we enter

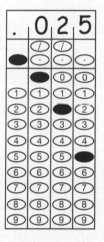

Note: If "decimal" was not specified, any correct version of the answer could be entered into the grid.

Question Type 3: Prime Numbers of a Particular Form

Here, you will be asked to find a prime number with certain characteristics. Remember—a prime number is a number that can only be divided by itself and 1.

Find a prime number of the form $7k + 1 < 50$.

SOLUTION

This is simply a counting problem. The key is to list all the numbers of the form $7k + 1$ starting with $k = 0$. The first one that is prime is the solution to the problem.

The whole numbers of the form $7k + 1$ which are less than 50 are 1, 8, 15, 22, 29, 36, and 43. Of these, 29 and 43 are prime numbers. The possible solutions are 29 and 43.

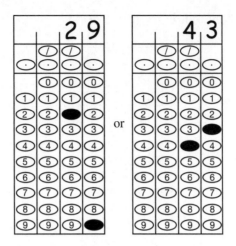

Question Type 4 : Order of Operations

The following question type tests your knowledge of the arithmetic order of operations. Always work within the parentheses or with absolute values first, while keeping in mind that multiplication and division are carried out before addition and subtraction.

PROBLEM

Find a solution to the equation $x \div 3 \times 4 \div 2 = 6$.

SOLUTION

The key here is to recall the order of precedence for arithmetic operations. After simplifying the expression one can solve for x.

Since multiplication and division have the same level of precedence, we simplify the equation from left to right to obtain

$$\frac{x}{3} \times 4 \div 2 = 6$$

$$\frac{4x}{3} \div 2 = 6$$

$$\frac{2x}{3} = 6$$

$$x = 9$$

As 9 solves the above problem, our entry in the grid is

Question Type 5: Solving for Ratios

This type of question tests your ability to manipulate ratios given a set of constraints.

PROBLEM

Let A, B, C, and D be positive integers. Assume that the ratio of A to B is equal to the ratio of C to D. Find a possible value for A if the product of $BC = 24$ and D is odd.

SOLUTION

The quickest way to find a solution is to list the possible factorizations of 24:

1×24

2×12

3×8

4×6

Since $AD = BC = 24$ and D is odd, the only possible solution is $A = 8$ (corresponding to $D = 3$). In the following grid we enter

Question Type 6: Simplifying Arithmetic Expressions

Here you will be given an arithmetic problem that is easier to solve if you transform it into a basic algebra problem. This strategy saves valuable time by cutting down on the number and complexity of computations involved.

PROBLEM

Simplify $1 - \left(\dfrac{1}{2} + \dfrac{1}{4} + \dfrac{1}{8} + \dfrac{1}{16} + \dfrac{1}{32} + \dfrac{1}{64} \right)$.

SOLUTION

This problem can be done one of two ways. The "brute force" approach would be to get a common denominator and simplify. An approach involving less computation is given below.

Set $S = 1 - \left(\dfrac{1}{2} + \dfrac{1}{4} + \dfrac{1}{8} + \dfrac{1}{16} + \dfrac{1}{32} + \dfrac{1}{64} \right)$

Multiplying this equation by 2 we obtain

$$2S = 2 - \left(1 + \dfrac{1}{2} + \dfrac{1}{4} + \dfrac{1}{8} + \dfrac{1}{16} + \dfrac{1}{32} \right)$$

$$2S = 1 - \left(\dfrac{1}{2} + \dfrac{1}{4} + \dfrac{1}{8} + \dfrac{1}{16} + \dfrac{1}{32} \right)$$

$$2S = 1 - \left(\dfrac{1}{2} + \dfrac{1}{4} + \dfrac{1}{8} + \dfrac{1}{16} + \dfrac{1}{32} + \dfrac{1}{64} \right) + \dfrac{1}{64}$$

$$2S = S + \dfrac{1}{64}$$

$$S = \dfrac{1}{64}$$

We enter into the grid

ALGEBRA QUESTIONS

Within the Student-Produced Response section, you will also encounter algebra questions which will test your ability to solve algebraic expressions in the setting of word problems. You may encounter the following six types of algebra questions during the PSAT. As in the previous section, we provide methods for approaching each type of problem.

Question Type 1: Solving a System of Linear Equations

This is a standard question which will ask you to find the solution to a system of two linear equations with two unknowns.

PROBLEM

Consider the system of simultaneous equations given by

$$y - 2 = x - 4$$
$$y + 3 = 6 - x$$

Solve for the quantity $6y + 3$.

SOLUTION

This problem can be solved by taking the first equation given and solving for x. This would yield

$$x = y + 2.$$

Next, we plug this value for x into the second equation, giving us

$$y + 3 = 6 - (y + 2).$$

Solve this equation for y and we get

$$y = \frac{1}{2}.$$

We are asked to solve for $6y + 3$, so we can plug our value for y in and get

$$6(\frac{1}{2}) + 3 = 6.$$

Our answer is 6 and gridded correctly it is

Question Type 2: Word Problems Involving Age

When dealing with this type of question, you will be asked to solve for the age of a particular person. The question may require you to determine how much older one person is, how much younger one person is, or the specific age of the person.

PROBLEM

Tim is 2 years older than Jane and Joe is 4 years younger than Jane. If the sum of the ages of Jane, Joe, and Tim is 28, how old is Joe?

SOLUTION

Define Jane's age to be the variable x and work from there.

Let

Jane's age $= x$

Tim's age $= x + 2$

Joe's age $= x - 4$

Summing up the ages we get

$$x + x + 2 + x - 4 = 28$$
$$3x - 2 = 28$$
$$3x = 30$$
$$x = 10$$

Joe's age $= 10 - 4 = 6$.

Hence, we enter into the grid

Question Type 3: Word Problems Involving Money

Word problems involving money will test your ability to translate the information given into an algebraic statement. You will also be required to solve your algebraic statement.

PROBLEM

After receiving his weekly paycheck on Friday, a man buys a television for $100, a suit for $200, and a radio for $50. If the total money he spent amounts to 40% of his paycheck, what is his weekly salary?

SOLUTION

Simply set up an equation involving the man's expenditures and the percentage of his paycheck that he used to buy them.

Let the amount of the man's paycheck equal x. We then have the equation

$$40\%x = 100 + 200 + 50$$
$$0.4x = 350$$
$$x = \$875$$

In the grid we enter

Question Type 4: Systems of Non-Linear Equations

This type of question will test your ability to perform the correct algebraic operations for a given set of equations in order to find the desired quantity.

PROBLEM

Consider the system of equations

$x^2 + y^2 = 8$

$xy = 4$

Solve for the quantity $3x + 3y$.

SOLUTION

Solve for the quantity $x + y$ and not for x or y individually.

First, multiply the equation $xy = 4$ by 2 to get $2xy = 8$. Adding this to $x^2 + y^2 = 8$ we obtain

$$x^2 + 2xy + y^2 = 16$$

$$(x + y)^2 = 16$$

$$x + y = 4$$

or $\quad x + y = -4$

Hence, $3x + 3y = 12$ or $3x + 3y = -12$. We enter 12 for a solution since -12 cannot be entered into the grid.

Question Type 5: Word Problems Involving Hourly Wage

When dealing with this type of question, you will be required to form an algebraic expression from the information based on a person's wages. You will then solve the expression to determine the person's wages (i.e., hourly, daily, annually, etc.).

Jim works 25 hours a week earning $10 an hour. Sally works 50 hours a week earning y dollars an hour. If their combined income every two weeks is $2,000, find the amount of money Sally makes an hour.

SOLUTION

Be careful. The combined income is given over a two-week period. Simply set up an equation involving income. We obtain

$$2[(25)\,(10) + (50)\,(y)] = 2,000$$

$$[(25)\,(10) + (50)\,(y)] = 1,000$$

$$250 + 50y = 1,000$$

$$50y = 750$$

$$y = \$15 \text{ an hour}$$

We enter in the grid

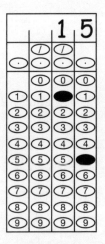

Question Type 6: Word Problems Involving Consecutive Integers

In this type of question, you will need to set up an equation involving consecutive integers based on the product of the integers, which is given.

PROBLEM

Consider two positive consecutive odd integers such that their product is 143. Find their sum.

SOLUTION

Be careful. Notice x and y are consecutive odd integers.

Let

1st odd integer $= x$

2nd odd integer $= x + 2$.

We get

$$x(x + 2) = 143$$

$$x^2 + 2x - 143 = 0$$

$$(x - 11)(x + 13) = 0$$

Hence $\qquad x = 11$

and $\qquad x = -13$.

From the above we obtain the solution sets $\{11, 13\}$ and $\{-13, -11\}$ whose sums are 24 and –24, respectively. Since the problem specifies that the integers are positive, we enter 24.

GEOMETRY QUESTIONS

In this section, we will explain how to solve questions which test your ability to find the area of various geometric figures. There are six types of questions you may encounter.

Question Type 1: Area of an Inscribed Triangle

This question asks you to find the area of a triangle which is inscribed in a square. By knowing certain properties of both triangles and squares, we can deduce the necessary information.

Consider the triangle inscribed in the square.

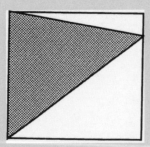

If the area of the square is 36, find the area of the triangle.

SOLUTION

Find the height of the triangle.

Let x be the length of the square. Since the four sides of a square are equal, and the area of a square is the length of a side squared, $x^2 = 36$. Therefore, $x = 6$.

The area of a triangle is given by

$\frac{1}{2}$ (base)(height).

Here x is both the base and height of the triangle. The area of the triangle is

$\frac{1}{2}$ (6)(6) = 18.

This is how the answer would be gridded.

```
        1 8
     / / /
   . . . .
    0 0 0 0
  1 1 ● 1
  2 2 2 2
  3 3 3 3
  4 4 4 4
  5 5 5 5
  6 6 6 6
  7 7 7 7
  8 8 8 ●
  9 9 9 9
```

Question Type 2: Length of the Side of a Triangle

For this type of question, one must find the length of a right triangle given information about the other sides. The key here is to apply the Pythagorean Theorem, which states that the square of the hypotenuse of a right triangle is equal to the sum of the squares of the other two sides.

Consider the line given below

A   B   C   D

where $\overline{AD} = 30$ and $\overline{AB} = 5$. What length is $\overline{BC}$ if the sides $\overline{AB}$, $\overline{BC}$, and $\overline{CD}$ form the sides of a right triangle?

SOLUTION

Draw a diagram and fill in the known information.

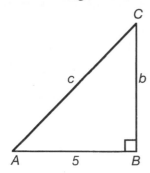

Next, apply the Pythagorean Theorem ($a^2 + b^2 = c^2$), filling in the known variables. Here, we are solving for BC (b in our equation). We know that $a = 5$, and since $AD = 30$ and $AB = 5$, $BD = 25$. Filling in these values, we obtain this equation:

$$5^2 + x^2 = (25 - x)^2$$
$$25 + x^2 = 625 - 50x + x^2$$
$$50x = 600$$
$$x = 12$$

This is one possible solution. If we had chosen $x = CD$ and $25 - x = BC$, one obtains $BC = 13$, which is another possible solution. The possible grid entries are shown here.

or

Question Type 3: Solving for the Degree of an Angle

Here you will be given a figure with certain information provided. You will need to deduce the measure of an angle based both on this information, as well as other geometric principles. The easiest way to do this is by setting up an algebraic expression.

PROBLEM

Find the angle y in the diagram below.

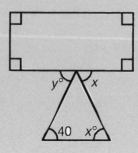

SOLUTION

Use the fact that the sum of the angles on the bottom side of the box is 180°.

Let z be the angle at the top of the triangle. Since we know the sum of the angles of a triangle is 180°,

$$z = 180 - (x + 40).$$

Summing all the angles at the bottom of the square, we get

$$y + [180 - (x + 40)] + x = 180$$

$$y + 140 - x + x = 180$$

$$y + 140 = 180$$

$$y = 40$$

In the grid we enter

Question Type 4: Solving for the Length of a Side

For this type of question, you will be given a figure with certain measures of sides filled in. You will need to apply geometric principles to find the missing side.

PROBLEM

Consider the figure below.

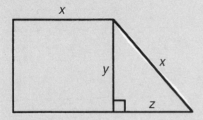

In the figure let x and y be whole numbers where $xy = 65$. Also assume the area of the whole figure is 95 square inches. Find z.

SOLUTION

The key point here is that x and y are whole numbers. Using the figure we only have a finite number of possibilities for z.

The equation for the area of the above figure is

$$xy + yz = 95.$$

Substituting $xy = 65$ into the above equation we get

$$yz = 30.$$

Using the fact that $xy = 65$ we know y can be either 1, 5, or 13. As $y = 13$ does not yield a factorization for $yz = 30$, y is either 1 or 5. If $y = 1$ this implies $x = 65$ and $z = 60$ which contradicts the Pythagorean Theorem (i.e., $1^2 + 60^2 = 13^2$). If $y = 5$ this implies $x = 13$ and $z = 12$ which satisfies $y^2 + z^2 = x^2$; hence, the solution is $y = 5$.

In our grid we enter

$$5$$

Question Type 5: Solving for the Area of a Region

Here, you will be given a figure with a shaded region. Given certain information, you will need to solve for the area of that region.

PROBLEM

Consider the concentric squares drawn below.

Assume that the side of the larger square is length 1. Also assume that the smaller square's perimeter is equal to the diameter of the larger square. Find the area of the shaded region.

SOLUTION

The key here is to find the length of the side for the smaller square. By the Pythagorean Theorem the diameter of the square is

$$d^2 = 1^2 + 1^2$$

which yields $d = \sqrt{2}$. Similarly, the smaller square's perimeter is $\sqrt{2}$; hence, the smaller square's side

$$= \frac{\sqrt{2}}{4}.$$

Calculating the area for the shaded region we get

$$A = A_{\text{large}} - A_{\text{small}}$$

$$A = 1 - \left(\frac{\sqrt{2}}{4}\right)^2$$

$$A = 1 - \frac{2}{16}$$

$$A = \frac{7}{8}$$

In the grid we enter

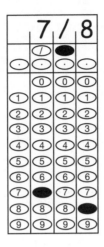

Question Type 6: Solve for a Sum of Lengths

The question here involves solving for a sum of lengths in the figure given knowledge pertaining to its area.

PROBLEM

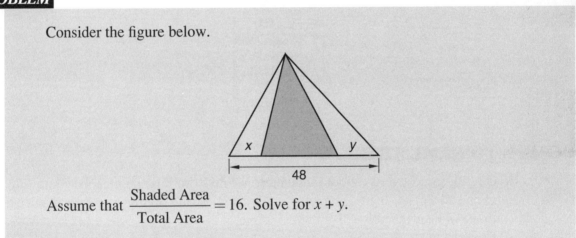

Consider the figure below.

Assume that $\dfrac{\text{Shaded Area}}{\text{Total Area}} = 16$. Solve for $x + y$.

SOLUTION

Solve for $x + y$ and not for x or y individually. Denote by b the base of the smaller triangle. Then

$$48 - b = x + y.$$

From the information given

$$\frac{\frac{1}{2}48h}{\frac{1}{2}bh} = 16$$

$$\frac{1}{2}48h = 16\left(\frac{1}{2}bh\right)$$

$$24 = 8b$$

$$3 = b$$

This yields

$$x + y = 48 - 3 = 45.$$

We enter in the grid

POINTS TO REMEMBER

- Be careful not to overuse your calculator. While it may be helpful in computing large sums and decimals, many problems, such as those involving common denominators, would be more efficiently solved without one.

- Immediately plug the values of all specific information into your equation.

- To visualize exactly what the question is asking and what information you need to find, draw a sketch of the problem.

- Even though you may think you have the equation worked out, make sure your result is actually answering the question. For example, although you may solve an equation for a specific variable, this may not be the final answer. You may have to use this answer to find another quantity.

- Make sure to work in only one unit, and convert if more than one is presented in the problem. For example, if a problem gives numbers in decimals and fractions, convert one in terms of the other and then work out the problem.

- Eliminate all dollar and percent signs when gridding your answers.

ANSWERING STUDENT-PRODUCED RESPONSE QUESTIONS

When answering Student-Produced Response questions, you should follow these steps.

STEP 1   *Identify the type of question with which you are presented (i.e., arithmetic, algebra, or geometry).*

STEP 2   *Once you have determined if the question deals with arithmetic, algebra, or geometry, further classify the question. Then, try to determine what type of arithmetic (or algebra or geometry) question is being presented.*

STEP 3   *Solve the question using the techniques explained in this review. Make sure your answer can be gridded.*

STEP 4   *Grid your answer in the question's corresponding answer grid. Make sure you are filling in the correct grid. Keep in mind that it is not mandatory to begin gridding your answer on any particular side of the grid. Fill in the ovals as completely as possible, and beware of stray lines—stray lines may cause your answer to be marked incorrect.*

The drill questions which follow should be completed to help reinforce the material which you have just studied. Be sure to refer back to the review if you need help answering the questions.

DRILL: STUDENT-PRODUCED RESPONSE QUESTIONS

(An answer key appears at the end of this chapter.)

DIRECTIONS: Each of the following questions requires you to solve the problem and enter your answer in the ovals in the special grid:

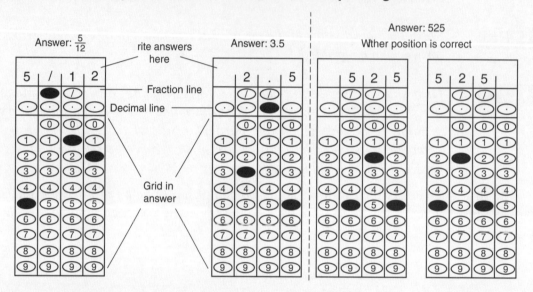

- You may begin filling in your answer in any column, space permitting. Columns not needed should be left blank.

- Answers may be entered in either decimal or fraction form. For example, $\frac{3}{12}$ or .25 are equally acceptable.

- A mixed number, such as $4\frac{1}{2}$, must be entered either as 4.5 or $\frac{9}{2}$. If you entered 41/2, the machine would interpret your answer as $\frac{41}{2}$, not $4\frac{1}{2}$.

- There may be some instances where there is more than one correct answer to a problem. Should this be the case, grid only one answer.

- Be very careful when filling in ovals. Do not fill in more than one oval in any column, and make sure to completely darken the ovals.

- It is suggested that you fill in your answer in the boxes above each column. Although you will not be graded incorrectly if you do not write in your answer, it will help you fill in the corresponding ovals.

- If your answer is a decimal, grid the most accurate value possible. For example, if you need to grid a repeating decimal such as $0.666\overline{6}$, enter the answer as .666 or .667. A less accurate value, such as .66 or .67, is not acceptable.

1.   At the end of the month, a woman pays $714 in rent. If the rent constitutes 21% of her monthly income, what is her hourly wage given the fact that she works 34 hours per week?

2.   Find the largest integer which is less than 100 and divisible by 3 and 7.

3.   The radius of the smaller of two concentric circles is 5 cm while the radius of the larger circle is 7 cm. Determine the area of the shaded region.

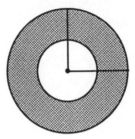

4. $\dfrac{1}{6}+\dfrac{2}{3}+\dfrac{1}{6}-\dfrac{1}{3}+1-\dfrac{3}{4}-\dfrac{1}{4}=$

5.   The sum of the squares of two consecutive integers is 41. What is the sum of their cubes?

6.   Find x.

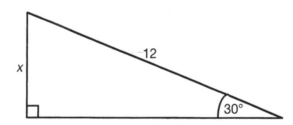

7. $|-8-4|\div 3 \times 6 + (-4) =$

8.   A class of 24 students contains 16 males. What is the ratio of females to males?

9.   At an office supply store, customers are given a discount if they pay in cash. If a customer is given a discount of $9.66 on a total order of $276, what is the percent of discount?

10. Let $\overline{RO} = 16$, $\overline{HM} = 30$. Find the perimeter of rhombus $HOMR$.

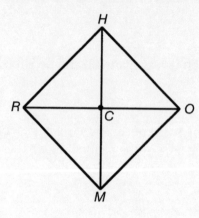

11. Solve for x.

$$x + 2y = 8$$
$$3x + 4y = 20$$

12. Six years ago, Henry's mother was nine times as old as Henry. Now she is only three times as old as Henry. How old is Henry now?

13. Find a prime number less than 40 which is of the form $5k + 1$.

14. If the radius of the circle is 6, find the area of the shaded triangles.

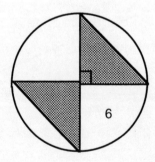

15. $\dfrac{7}{10} \times \dfrac{4}{21} \times \dfrac{25}{36} =$

16. Find the solution for x in the pair of equations.

$$x + y = 7$$
$$x = y - 3$$

17. Given the square $RHOM$, find the length of the diagonal $\overline{RO}$.

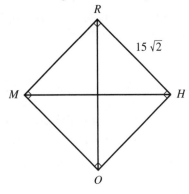

18. $\triangle MNO$ is isosceles. If the vertex angle, $\angle N$, has a measure of 96°, find the measure of $\angle M$.

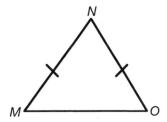

19. Simplify $\dfrac{\dfrac{1}{2} + \dfrac{1}{3}}{\dfrac{1}{6}}$.

20. In the diagram shown, ABC is an isosceles triangle. Sides $\overline{AC}$ and $\overline{BC}$ are extended through C to E and D to form triangle CDE. What is the sum of the measures of angles D and E?

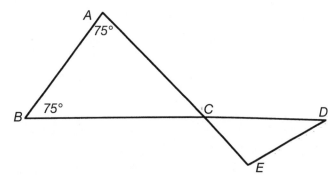

21.

Number of Muffins	Total Price
1	$0.55
Box of 4	$2.10
Box of 8	$4.00

According to the information in the table above, what would be the *least* amount of money needed to purchase exactly 19 muffins? (Disregard the dollar sign when gridding your answer.)

22. Several people rented a van for $30, sharing the cost equally. If there had been one more person in the group, it would have cost each $1 less. How many people were there in the group originally?

23. For the triangle pictured below, the degree measures of the three angles are x, $3x$, and $3x + 5$. Find x.

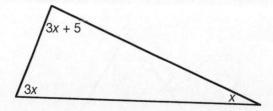

24. $\triangle PQR$ is a scalene triangle. The measure of $\angle P$ is 8 more than twice the measure of $\angle R$. The measure of $\angle Q$ is two less than three times the measure of $\angle R$. Determine the measure of $\angle Q$.

25. A mother is now 24 years older than her daughter. In 4 years, the mother will be 3 times as old as the daughter. What is the present age of the daughter?

26. John is 4 times as old as Harry. In six years John will be twice as old as Harry. What is Harry's age now?

27. What is the area of the shaded region?

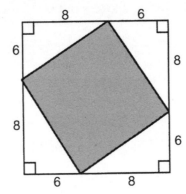

28. In an apartment building there are 9 apartments having terraces for every 16 apartments. If the apartment building has a total of 144 apartments, how many apartments have terraces?

29. If arc *AB* is a perfect semicircle, what is the area of the figure below?

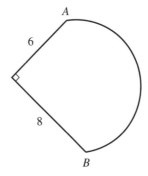

30. Find the length of a side of an equilateral triangle whose area is $4\sqrt{3}$.

31. Solve $\dfrac{3}{x-1} + \dfrac{1}{x-2} = \dfrac{5}{(x-1)(x-2)}$.

32. Solve the proportion $\dfrac{x+1}{4} = \dfrac{15}{12}$.

33. In an isosceles triangle, the length of each of the congruent sides is 10 and the length of the base is 12. Find the length of the altitude drawn to the base.

34. The following are three students' scores on Mr. Page's Music Fundamentals midterm. The given score is the number of correct answers out of 55 total questions.

Liz   48
Jay   45
Carl   25

What is the *average* percentage of questions correct for the three students?

35. Reserved seat tickets to a football game are $6 more than general admission tickets. Mr. Jones finds that he can buy general admission tickets for his whole family of five for only $3 more than the cost of reserved seat tickets for himself and Mrs. Jones. How much do the general admission tickets cost?

36. The sum of three numbers is 96. The ratio of the first to the second is 1 : 2, and the ratio of the second to the third is 2 : 3. What is the third number?

37. What is the smallest even integer n for which $(.5)^n$ is less than .01?

38. The mean (average) of the numbers 50, 60, 65, 75, x, and y is 65. What is the mean of x and y?

39. The ages of the students enrolled at XYZ University are given in the following table:

Age	Number of students
18	750
19	1,600
20	1,200
21	450

What percent of students are 19 and 20 years old?

40. Find the larger side of a rectangle whose area is 24 and whose perimeter is 22.

STUDENT-PRODUCED RESPONSE

ANSWER KEY

1. **2 5**

2. **8 4**

3. **7 5 . 4**

4. **2 / 3**

5. **1 8 9**

6. **6**

7. **2 0**

8. **1 / 2**

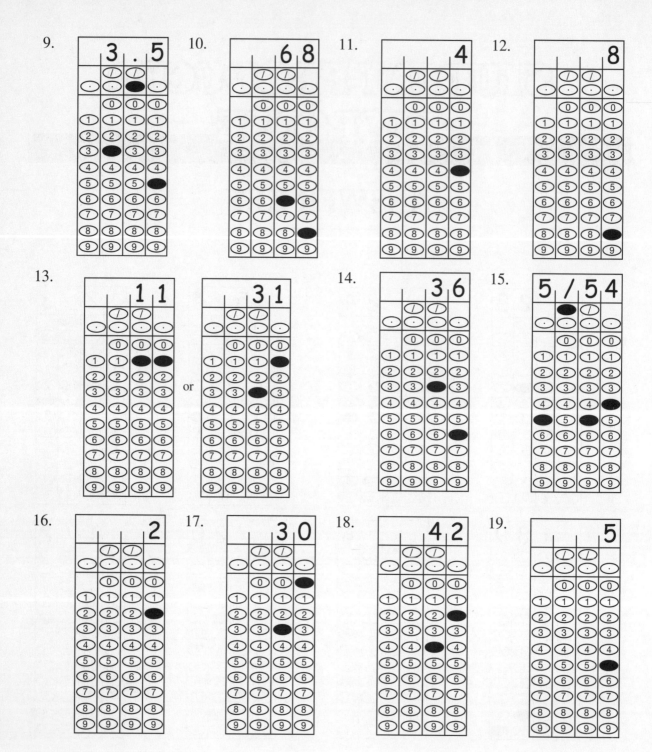

20. 150

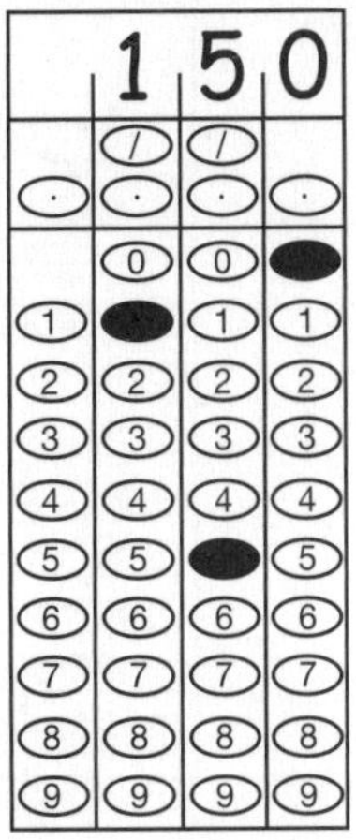

21. 9.65

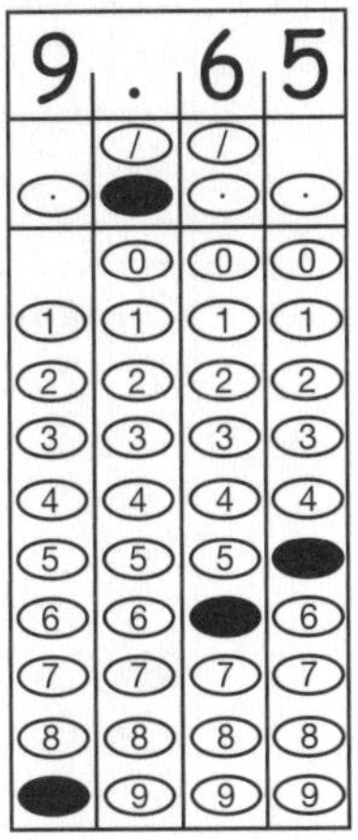

22. 5

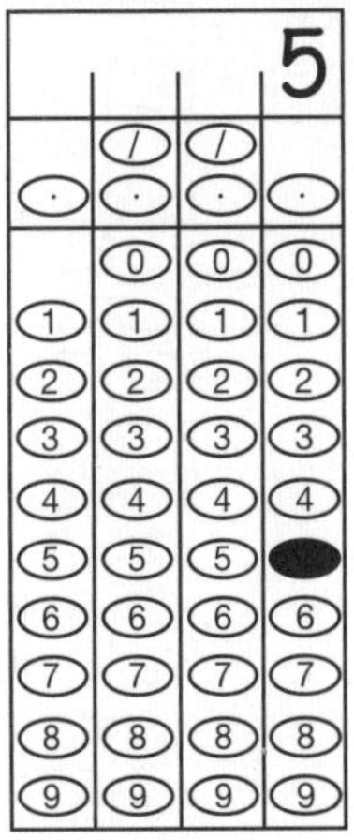

23. 25

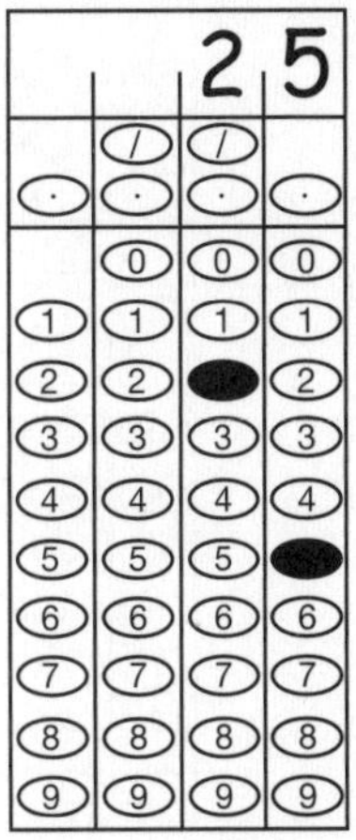

24. 85

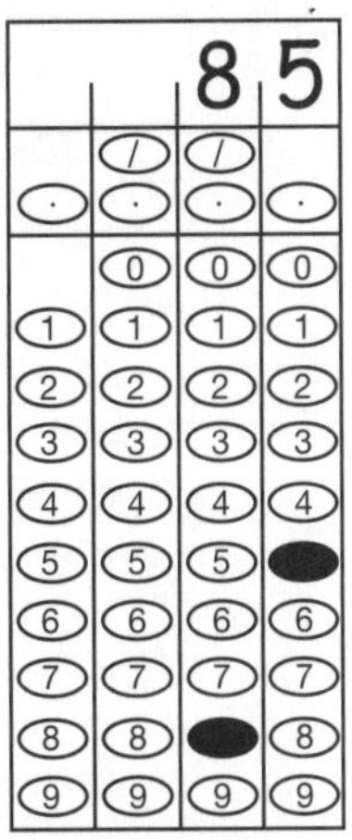

25. 8

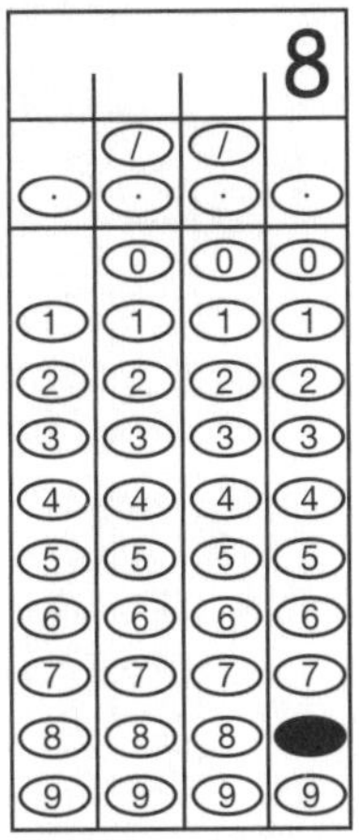

26. 3

27. 100

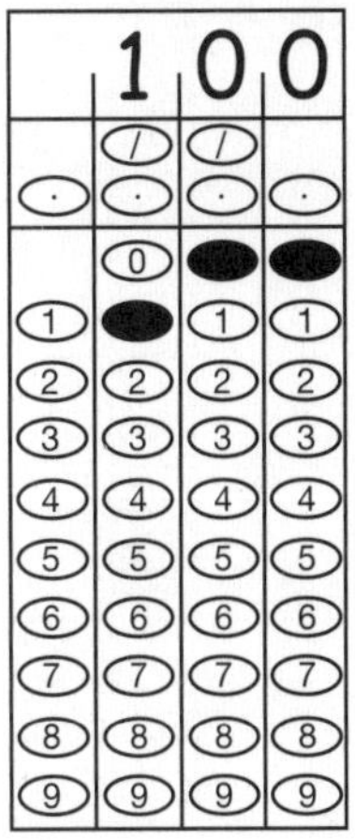

28. 81

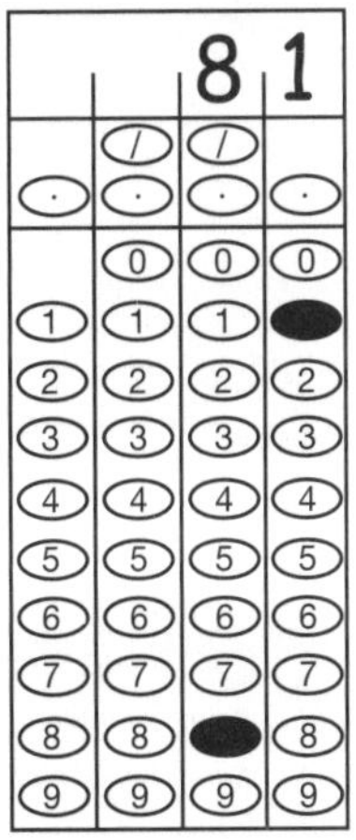

29. 63.2

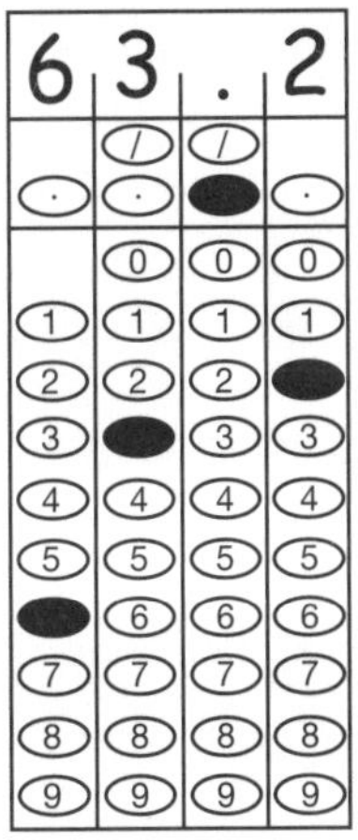

30. 4

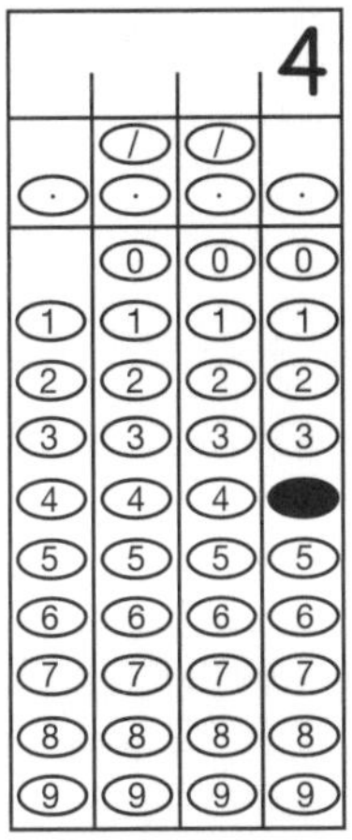

31. 3

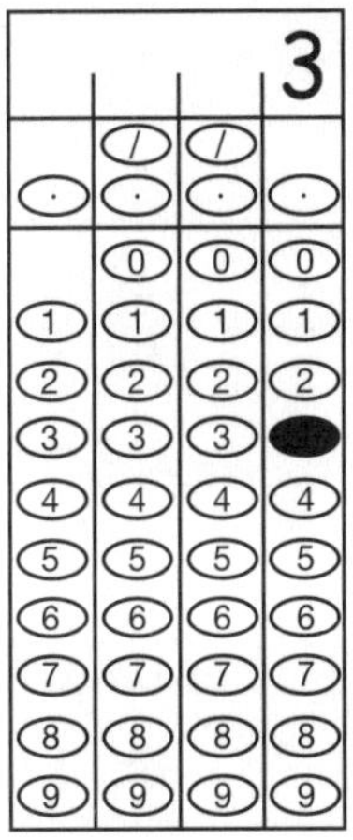

32. **4**

33. **8**

34. **71.5**

35. **5**

36. **48**

37. **8**

38. **70**

39. **70**

40. **8**

DETAILED EXPLANATIONS

STUDENT-PRODUCED RESPONSE

1. (25) If the rent makes up 21% of the woman's monthly income, you can solve for her total monthly income with the following equation: $\frac{21}{100}$ × monthly income = \$714. Multiply both sides of the equation by $\frac{100}{21}$ and you get the monthly income to equal $\frac{71400}{21}$, or \$3,400. Working 34 hours a week for four weeks (one month) comes out to 34 × 4, or 136 hours a month. The woman's hourly wage is determined by dividing her monthly income, \$3,400, by the number of hours she worked in a month, 136. $\frac{\$3,400}{136} = \$25$.

2. (84) A number that is divisible by both 3 and 7 means that the number must be a multiple of 3 × 7, or 21. The largest multiple of 21 that is less than 100 is 84.

3. (75.4) To find the area of the shaded region, you will first need to find the area of the entire region. The area of a circle is always equal to πr^2, so the area of the entire circle must be $\pi 7^2$, or 49π. By subtracting the area of the unshaded region you will be left with the area of the shaded region. The area of the unshaded region is $\pi 5^2$, or 25π. The larger area minus the unshaded area is $49\pi - 25\pi = 24\pi$. Since you are unable to grid in variables, including π, you will need to substitute an estimated value for $\pi(3.14)$ to complete your answer: 24 × 3.14 = 75.36. There are only four available columns for your answer choice, so round your response to 75.4.

4. ($\frac{2}{3}$) By adding together the fractions that have common denominators, you can reduce the expression to $\frac{2}{6} + \frac{1}{3} + 1 - \frac{4}{4}$. $\frac{2}{6}$ will reduce to $\frac{1}{3}$, and $\frac{4}{4}$ will reduce to 1, which simplifies the expression to $\frac{1}{3} + \frac{1}{3} + 1 - 1 = \frac{2}{3}$.

5. (189) Since $7^2 = 49$, and the sum of the squares of the two consecutive numbers is 41, the two numbers must be somewhere in the range of 1-6. The two consecutive integers end up being 4 and 5, since 16 + 25 = 41. The answer is looking for the value of $4^3 + 5^3$, or 64 + 125 = 189.

6. (6) If two angles of a triangle are 90° and 30°, the third angle must be 180° − (90° + 30°) = 60°. In any 30°, 60°, 90° triangle, the length of the sides have the set ratio of $x : 2x : x\sqrt{3}$, where x is the side opposite of the 30° angle, $2x$ is opposite of the 90° angle, and $x\sqrt{3}$ is opposite of the 60° angle. The opposite of the 90° angle is 12, therefore $2x = 12$, or $x = 6$. Since the question is asking for the side opposite of the 30° angle, or x, the answer remains unchanged, $x = 6$.

7. (20) For this question you need to remember the order of operations. Parentheses or brackets are solved first, so $|-8-4|=|-12|$, and the absolute value is simply the positive value of the number within the brackets, so the equation now looks like this: $12 \div 3 \times 6 - 4$. Next, solve out all the multiplication and division parts of the equation, $12 \div 3 = 4$, and $4 \times 6 = 24$. Now the equation has been reduced to $24 - 4 = 20$.

8. $(\frac{1}{2})$ If a class has 24 students and 16 are males, then the remaining 8 must be females. Ratios are expressed as fractions, so the ratio of females to males is $\frac{F}{M}=\frac{8}{16}=\frac{1}{2}$.

9. (3.5) The question wants to know what percent of $276 is $9.66. Since percent means to divide by 100, the algebraic expression would look like this: $\frac{x}{100} \times 276 = 9.66$. Multiply both sides of the equation by 100 and you get $x \times 276 = 966$. Divide both sides by 276 and you get $x = \frac{966}{276} = 3.5$.

10. (68) Lines $\overline{RO}$ and $\overline{HM}$ divide rhombus $HOMR$ into four equal triangles, each with a base of 8 and a height of 15. The perimeter of the rhombus is the sum of the four individual hypotenuses. Therefore you will need to use the Pythagorean theorem, $a^2 + b^2 = c^2$, to determine the length of the hypotenuse, or one side of the rhombus. Remember side c represents the hypotenuse, so the equation should look like this: $8^2 + 15^2 = c^2$. Once you square and add the two sides you get: $289 = c^2$. Once you take the square root of both sides you get $c = 17$. Since the two sides of all four triangles are 8 and 15, the hypotenuse will be 17 for each triangle, and the sides of the rhombus will also equal 17. Therefore the perimeter would be $17 + 17 + 17 + 17 = 4(17) = 68$.

11. (4) Multiply the first equation by 2 to get $2x + 4y = 16$. Now you can subtract the second equation from the first to eliminate the y term. It will look like this:

$$
\begin{array}{r}
2x + 4y = 16 \\
-\ 3x - 4y = -20 \\
\hline
-x + 0 = -4
\end{array}
$$

Multiply both sides by -1 and you get $x = 4$.

12. (8) In this algebra problem, you will need to create two separate equations and solve for one of their variables. Start with their current ages: Henry's mother is three times as old as Henry. This can be expressed as $M = 3H$. The second piece of information states that six years ago, Henry's mother was nine times as old as Henry. This can be expressed as the mother's age minus six equals nine times Henry's age minus six, or $M - 6 = 9(H - 6)$. Multiply out the second part of the equation to get $M - 6 = 9H - 54$. Add 6 to both sides and you get $M = 9H - 48$. Now that you have two different equations for the mother's age you can set the equations to be equal to one another, $3H = 9H - 48$. Subtract $9H$ from both sides of the equation and you come up with $-6H = -48$. Divide by -6 and you get $H = 8$.

13. (11, 31) This is simply a counting problem. The term "of the form" means the number you come up with when you substitute a value for x. For example, if $x = 1$, then the "of the form" number would be $5(1) + 1$, or 6. Since 6 is not a prime number, it is not the answer you are looking for. If $x = 2$, then the "of the form" number would be $5(2) + 1$, or 11. 11 is prime and less than 40, therefore it is a correct answer choice. If $x = 6$, then the "of the form" number would be 31, also prime and less than 40 and also a correct answer choice. For all other values of x, no other "of the form" numbers would be prime and less than 40.

14. (36) Since the base and height intersect at 90° angles and the two perpendicular sides originate at the center of the circle, the length of the sides of the triangles must equal the radius. If the radius is 6 the area of each triangle must be $\frac{6 \times 6}{2} = 18$. There are two triangles, so the area of both would be $18 \times 2 = 36$.

15. $(\frac{5}{54})$ The best way to approach this multiplication problem is to reduce as much as you can before you multiply. $\frac{7}{10} \times \frac{4}{21} \times \frac{25}{36} = \frac{7 \times 4 \times 25}{10 \times 21 \times 36}$. Remember that when you multiply fractions, you are able to reduce anything in the numerator with anything in the denominator, therefore 7 and 21 will reduce to 1 and 3, 25 and 10 will reduce to 5 and 2, and 4 and 36 will reduce to 2 and 18, so that the expression now looks like $\frac{1 \times 2 \times 5}{3 \times 2 \times 18}$. The two 2's will cancel each other out and you are left with $\frac{1 \times 5}{3 \times 18} = \frac{5}{54}$.

16. (2) In the equation $x = y - 3$, subtract y from both sides and you get $x - y = -3$. Stack the two equations on top of each other and add:

$$\begin{array}{r} x + y = 7 \\ + x - y = -3 \\ \hline 2x + 0 = 4 \end{array}$$

Divide both sides by 2 and you get $x = 2$.

17. (30) Quadrilateral *ROHM* is a square, which makes all sides equal $15\sqrt{2}$. Line segment $\overline{RO}$ is the diagonal that splits the square into two equal isosceles right triangles. Therefore, $\overline{RO}$ is the hypotenuse of the isosceles right triangle and is equal to the length of the perpendicular side ($15\sqrt{2}$) times $\sqrt{2}$, or $15\sqrt{2} \times \sqrt{2} = 30$.

18. (42) An isosceles triangle is a triangle in which two sides are equal, and the angles opposite the equal sides are also equal. From the diagram, $\overline{MN}$ and $\overline{NO}$ are equal, therefore $\angle M$ and $\angle O$ are also equal. If $\angle N = 96°$, then $\angle M + \angle O = 180° - 96° = 84°$. Since $\angle M$ and $\angle O$ are of equal measure and the sum of the two angles is 84°, the measure of each angle would be $\frac{84°}{2} = 42°$.

19. (5) Remember that you must have common denominators when you add fractions. Start with the numerator first, $\frac{1}{2} = \frac{3}{6}$, and $\frac{1}{3} = \frac{2}{6}$, so $\frac{3}{6} + \frac{2}{6} = \frac{5}{6}$. Now the equation is

$$\frac{\frac{5}{6}}{\frac{1}{6}}.$$

When you divide by a fraction, such as $\frac{1}{6}$, remember that you are actually multiplying by its reciprocal, so that $\frac{5}{6} \div \frac{1}{6} = \frac{5}{6} \times \frac{6}{1} = 5$.

20. (150) If $\angle A$ and $\angle B$ are each 75°, then $\angle C = 180° - (75° + 75°) = 30°$. Whenever any two lines intersect, the opposite or reciprocal angles are always going to be equal, so that $\angle C$ in the smaller triangle must also equal 30°. Therefore the sum of $\angle D$ and $\angle E = 180° - 30° = 150°$.

21. (9.65) The key term to this question is "exactly 19 muffins," which means you CANNOT add up the cost of two boxes of 8 and one box of 4. Instead you need to add up the cost of two boxes of 8, for 16 donuts, and add to it the cost of 3 individual donuts. So you get $4.00 + $4.00 + $0.55 + $0.55 + $0.55 = $9.65.

22. (5) To find the original number of people in the group, you will need to create two different equations with variable n for the number of people and variable c for the cost of each person. If n people share equally in the cost of renting a \$30 van, then the cost per person could be expressed as $\frac{30}{n} = c$. If one more person had been in the group, the cost per person would have been \$1 less; therefore you can use the expression $\frac{30}{n+1} = c - 1$. Since you are looking to solve for the original number of people, n, you can substitute $\frac{30}{n}$ for c in the second equation to come up with $\frac{30}{n+1} = \frac{30}{n} - 1$. Change -1 to $-\frac{n}{n}$ to create a common denominator that gives you $\frac{30}{n} - \frac{n}{n}$, or $\frac{30-n}{n}$. Now the entire equation looks like $\frac{30}{n+1} = \frac{30-n}{n}$. To eliminate the denominator n, multiply both sides by n and to get $\frac{30n}{n+1} = 30 - n$. Now multiply both sides by $n + 1$ to eliminate the denominator on the left side, and you get $30n = (30 - n)(n + 1)$. Expanding out the right side of the equation through the use of FOIL, you come up with $30n = 30n + 30 - n^2 - n$. Subtract $30n$ from both sides of the equation and multiply by -1 to get $n^2 + n - 30 = 0$. Solve for roots by contracting the equation to $(n - 5)(n + 6) = 0$, and the two values of n are 5 and -6. Since you are unable to grid in negative numbers, the answer is 5.

23. (25) All three angles of a triangle must add up to $180°$. Therefore to find the value of x, you can write out the equation $x + 3x + 3x + 5 = 180$. Add together all values of x to come up with $7x + 5 = 180$. Subtract both sides by 5 and divide by 7 to get $x = \frac{175}{7}$, or $x = 25$.

24. (85) There are three angles in $\triangle PQR$, and the sum of all three must equal $180°$, or $\angle P + \angle Q + \angle R = 180°$. If $\angle P = 2R + 8$ and $\angle Q = 3R - 2$, then the value of $\angle R$ can be determined by the equation $2R + 8 + 3R - 2 + R = 180$. Add together like terms to get $6R = 174$, divide by 6 and $\angle R = 29$. Remember that the question is asking for the value of $\angle Q$, so substitute the value of $\angle R$ into the equation for $\angle Q$ and you come up with $\angle Q = 3(29) - 2$, or $\angle Q = 85$.

25. (8) To find the present age of the daughter, you will need to create two separate equations using m for the mother's age and d for the daughter's age. The first equation states that the mother is 24 years older than the daughter, or $m = d + 24$. The second equation deals with both of their ages 4 years from now, so you will need to add 4 to both variables to get $m + 4 = 3(d + 4)$. Since you are solving for the daughter's age, go ahead and substitute $d + 24$ for m in the second equation to get $d + 24 + 4 = 3(d + 4)$. Add like terms and multiply out the right side to come up with $28 + d = 3d + 12$. Subtract 12 from both sides and subtract d from both sides and you get $16 = 2d$. Divide by 2 and $d = 8$, the current age of the daughter.

26. (3) To find the age of Harry, you will need to create two separate equations using j for John's age and h for Harry's age. The first part of the problem tells you that John is 4 times as old as Harry, or $j = 4h$. The second piece of the problem deals with their ages 6 years from now, so you will need to add 6 to both variables to get $j + 6 = 2(h + 6)$. Since the question is asking for Harry's age, you can substitute $4h$ for j in the second equation to get $4h + 6 = 2(h + 6)$. Multiply out the right side to get $4h + 6 = 2h + 12$. Subtract 6 from both sides and subtract $2h$ from both sides and you come up with $2h = 6$. Divide both sides by 2 and $h = 3$, the current age of Harry.

27. (100) The lengths of the sides of the shaded region are equal to the hypotenuse of the corner right triangles. Therefore you can use the Pythagorean theorem, $a^2 + b^2 = c^2$, to determine the length of the side of the shaded region. $8^2 + 6^2 = c^2$ is equal to $64 + 36 = c^2$, or $100 = c^2$. Take the square root of both sides and you come up with $10 = c$. Since the smaller triangles are right triangles, the sum of the two remaining angles, $\angle$small and $\angle$big, must be 90° as well, since all the angles must add up to 180°. A straight line also has 180°, so the angle of the shaded region would be $\angle$small + $\angle$big + $\angle$shaded region = 180°, or 90° + $\angle$shaded region = 180°, or $\angle$shaded region = 90°. If all the sides of the shaded region are equal to 10, and the angles are 90°, then the area of the shaded region will be $l \times w$, or $10 \times 10 = 100$.

28. (81) This question is asking about proportions. If 9 out of 16 apartments have terraces, you can express the ratio as the fraction $\frac{9}{16}$. The question wants to know how many apartments have terraces if there are a total of 144 apartments. To set up the proportion, keep the total number of apartments in the denominator and the apartments with terraces in the numerator, and you get $\frac{9}{16} = \frac{x}{144}$. Cross multiply and you get $16x = 9 \times 144$. Divide both sides by 16 and you will get the number of apartments that have terraces, $x = \frac{9 \times 144}{16} = 9 \times 9 = 81$.

29. (63.2 or 63.3) The figure is an odd, unfamiliar shape. You need to break it up into smaller, more familiar shapes. If you draw a line opposite the 90° angle, you will create a right triangle and a half circle. To find the area of the triangle, simply multiply the base and height together and divide by 2, $\frac{6 \times 8}{2} = 24$. To find the area of the half circle, you must first determine the length of the diameter, which is the same line as the hypotenuse of the triangle. Remember the right triangles that you should be familiar with? The two perpendicular sides are 6 and 8, therefore the hypotenuse must be 10 since it is a multiple of the 3:4:5 right triangle. If you did not remember this, using the Pythagorean theorem ($a^2 + b^2 = c^2$) would also give you 10 for the hypotenuse/diameter. The radius of a circle with a diameter of 10 is 5, so the area would be 25π. Since you are solving for half the area, divide by 2, which gives you 12.5π, or $12.5 \times 3.14 = 39.23$. Add together the two separate areas to find the area of the whole region, $39.23 + 24 = 63.2$.

30. (4) The formula for the area of a triangle is $\frac{1}{2}b \times h$. If you substitute the area into the formula, you get $4\sqrt{3} = \frac{1}{2}b \times h$, which tells you that $b \times h = 8\sqrt{3}$. Remember, if you split an equilateral triangle in half, from top to bottom, you form two 30°, 60°, and 90° triangles. The length of the sides are all proportional to the angle they are opposite of, so the side opposite of the 30° angle is said to be x, and the side opposite the 60° angle is said to be $x\sqrt{3}$, and the side opposite of the 90° angle is said to be $2x$, which happens to be the length of the side of the equilateral triangle. Since all sides of an equilateral triangle are equal, the base of the triangle must also be $2x$ and the height is the value opposite the 60° angle, or $x\sqrt{3}$, so you can substitute these values into the $b \times h$ equation above and get $2x \times x\sqrt{3} = 8\sqrt{3}$. Divide both sides by $\sqrt{3}$ and then divide both sides again by 2 and you get $x \times x = 4$, or $x^2 = 4$. Now that you have $x = 2$, remember that the question is asking for the length of a side, which was already determined to be $2x$, or 4.

31. (3) Before you add any fractions together, you must first have a common denominator. The common denominator for the left side of the equation would simply be the two denominators multiplied together, or $(x-1)(x-2)$. This means that the fraction $\frac{3}{(x-1)}$ must be multiplied by $\frac{(x-2)}{(x-2)}$ and $\frac{1}{(x-2)}$ must be multiplied by $\frac{(x-1)}{(x-1)}$. After this is done, you get the equation $\frac{3x-6}{(x-1)(x-2)} + \frac{x-1}{(x-1)(x-2)} = \frac{5}{(x-1)(x-2)}$. Since the denominators remain constant when you add or subtract fractions, you can solve for x by simply using the values in the numerators. This gives you $3x - 6 + x - 1 = 5$. Adding like terms gives you $4x - 7 = 5$, adding 7 to both sides gives you $4x = 12$, and dividing by 4 gives you $x = 3$.

32. (4) To solve for the missing value in a proportion you need to cross-multiply the fractions. This gives you $12(x + 1) = 4(15)$, or $12x + 12 = 60$. Subtract 12 from both sides of the equation to get $12x = 48$. Divide both sides by 12 and you get $x = 4$.

33. (8) The altitude, drawn perpendicularly from the apex of the triangle to the base, will split the isosceles triangle in half, creating two right triangles with a hypotenuse of 10 and a base 6. Remember that the third side of any right triangle can be solved by using the Pythagorean theorem, $a^2 + b^2 = c^2$, where c is always the hypotenuse. To find the height of a triangle with a base of 6 and a hypotenuse of 10, the equation will look like this: $6^2 + b^2 = 10^2$, or $36 + b^2 = 100$. Subtract 36 from both sides to get $b^2 = 64$. Take the square root of both sides and you get the height, b, to equal 8.

34. (71.5) "Percentage of questions correct" means to divide the total number of correct questions by the total number of questions given. Start by adding together the total number of correct questions, $48 + 45 + 25 = 118$. Divide this number by the total number of questions, or $55 \times 3 = 165$, and multiply by 100 to get the percent. $\frac{118}{165} \times 100 = 71.51$, which can be rounded to the nearest tenth in order to fit into the grid, 71.5.

35. (5) For this question you will need to create two algebraic equations for the constant variables g, for general admission, and r, for reserved seating. The first piece of information tells you that reserved seats are \$6 more than general admission, which translates into $r = g + 6$. The second part of the question tells you that the cost of five general admission tickets is 3 more than the cost of two reserved seat tickets. This can be expressed as $5g = 2r + 3$. Since the question is asking for the cost of the general admission tickets, substitute $g + 6$ for r in the second equation to get $5g = 2(g + 6) + 3$. Multiply the right side to get $5g = 2g + 12 + 3$. Subtract $2g$ from both sides and you get $3g = 15$. Divide both sides by 3 to get the price of one general admission ticket, $g = 5$.

36. (48) Ratios express the relationship of a part to other parts. Since the ratio for the second number remains 2 for both ratios, you can combine the two separate ratios so that it reads $1 : 2 : 3$. The key to solving ratio problems is to determine what the constant multiplier is for the entire ratio. If you add up the different ratios, you get a total of $1 + 2 + 3 = 6$. You know the sum of the three numbers is 96 and the sum of the ratios is 6, so now divide 96 by 6 and you get: $96 \div 6 = 16$. The number 16 is referred to as the constant multiplier because any part of the ratio multiplied by it will give you the actual, or real value of the number. Since the third number is represented by the ratio 3, multiply it by 16 to find out its real value, $3 \times 16 = 48$.

37. (8) The easiest way to visualize this problem would be to convert the decimal values into fraction values. The question wants to know what smallest even integer n will let $(\frac{1}{2})^n < \frac{1}{100}$? If $n = 2$, you get $\frac{1}{4}$, which is not less than $\frac{1}{100}$. If $n = 6$, you get $\frac{1}{64}$, which is also not less than $\frac{1}{100}$. If $r = 8$, you get $\frac{1}{256}$, which is less than $\frac{1}{100}$.

38. (70) The formula for averages is ($\frac{sum}{\# \, of \, things}$ = average), so if the average of 6 numbers is 65, their sum must be 65×6, or 390. Four of the numbers add up to 250, therefore the sum of the remaining two numbers must be $390 - 250 = 140$. Since the sum of x and y is 140, their average would be $\frac{140}{2} = 70$.

39. (70) To find the percent, you simply divide the part by the whole and multiply by 100. There are 2,800 students who are 19 and 20 years old, and the total number of students is 4,000. Therefore the percent of 19 and 20 year olds would be $\frac{2,800}{4,000} \times 100 = .7 \times 100 = 70$.

40. (8) The opposite sides of a rectangle are always equal. The formula for the area is $A = l \times w$, and the formula for perimeter is $P = 2l + 2w$. From the information in the question, you know that $l \times w = 24$ and $2l + 2w = 22$, which can be reduced to $l + w = 11$. The values for the length and width must satisfy each equation. Starting with the first equation, list all the possible factors of 24 that l and w could equal. You should get (1, 24), (2, 12), (3, 8), and (4, 6). Now substitute these numbers into the second equation and the one that satisfies the perimeter equation is (3, 8), which are the lengths and widths of the rectangle. Since the question is asking for the distance of the longer side, the only answer choice is 8.

CHAPTER 9

MASTERING WRITING
SKILLS QUESTIONS

MASTERING WRITING SKILLS QUESTIONS

There is one 30 minute, 39 question Writing Skills section on the PSAT, consisting of three types of questions: Identifying Sentence Errors (14), Improving Sentences (20), and Improving Paragraphs (5). All question types test your knowledge of word use, syntax, meaning, and grammar.

Since all question types test your knowledge on the conventions of standard written English, you can prepare for the entire section by following a few study suggestions.

1. Read material that reflects proper grammar usage. Suitable material may be found in good magazines (news magazines, *National Geographic*, science journals) and nonfiction books. Editorials from outstanding national newspapers (*New York Times, Washington Post, Boston Globe, Miami Herald*) are an excellent source of standard written English. Finally, ask your English or Grammar teacher to recommend a list of writers and essays that are commonly used in high school and college writing courses. Literature (the works of fiction that are studied in the universities and colleges and in the majority of high schools) is also an acceptable grammar guide. **It is important to note that not all published material uses correct grammar. The majority of action/adventure, mystery, and romance novels that are on the bestsellers lists do not reflect the standards of written English, and should not be referred to as a guide to the Writing Skills section on the PSAT.**

2. Review the basic rules of grammar. The chapter in this book titled "English Language Skills Review" is a great place to start. Be careful to not just read through the rules and move on to the next section. Unlike the math and verbal sections on the PSAT, the rules of grammar that are tested in the Writing Skills section are necessary not just for the test, but for your entire academic career. Study and learn them now so they will not come back to haunt you later on. Flash cards would be a terrific way to organize and memorize all the different rules. Another way to memorize the rules is to start consciously using them in your own writing. Whether you are writing for school, for fun,

or to a friend, you should try to implement the conventions of standard written English. Not only will it help your PSAT score, but it will also greatly increase your communication skills in every other aspect of your life!

Let's take a closer look at each question type and the strategies you will want to employ to answer them.

IDENTIFYING SENTENCE ERRORS

As stated earlier, there will be 14 Identifying Sentence Error questions in the Writing Skills section. Since the instructions will always be the same, familiarize yourself with them now so you don't waste valuable test time reading them on the day of the exam.

<u>**DIRECTIONS**</u>: **Each of the following sentences may contain an error in diction, usage, idiom, or grammar. Some of the sentences are correct. Some sentences contain one error. No sentence contains more than one error.**

If there is an error, it will appear in one of the underlined portions labeled A, B, C, or D. If there is no error, choose the portion labeled E. If there is an error, select the letter of the portion that must be changed in order to correct the sentence.

EXAMPLE

He drove <u>slowly</u> and <u>cautiously</u> in order to <u>hopefully</u> avoid having an <u>accident</u>. <u>No error</u>.
      A   B   C   D   E

Take a look at the example in the directions. The question presents a sentence with four different words underlined. Under each underlined portion of the sentence are the letters A, B, C, or D (E is always under the end of the sentence that states No error) and these letters correspond to the letters on your answer sheet. Your job is to bubble in the letter that is underneath the underlined portion of the sentence that is grammatically incorrect, or E if the whole sentence is grammatically sound.

Take a look at the following steps and strategies that will help you answer these question types and the example that follows:

1. Read the entire sentence carefully. Try to understand the context or idea that the sentence is trying to express. A good place to start is to identify the subject and the verb, since these are the two building blocks of all sentences. Once you have done that, you can begin to understand how the different parts of the sentence should relate to each other.

2. Concentrate on the underlined portions of the sentence to see if they are being used correctly. *If* there is anything wrong with the sentence, it must be one of the underlined portions.

3. Use the non-underlined portion of the sentence to guide you. The non-underlined portion of the sentence *must* be grammatically correct, so use it as a guide to determine if the underlined portions are grammatically accurate or not.

4. Remember that there can be at most one error per sentence. To save time and prevent careless mistakes, if there is one answer choice that you are certain is ungrammatical, choose it and move on to the next question. Don't waste time by studying the other underlined portions of the sentence when you are pretty certain that you have already found the answer—this usually leaves students second guessing themselves and choosing the wrong answer. There is only one possible error per sentence, so if you recognize it on the first read through don't bother with the other answer choices.

5. Finally, don't be afraid to choose answer E. Most students will only choose answer E after brooding over the sentence for minutes, wasting valuable time. Statistically speaking, E is correct 20% of the time, so if you don't see any grammatical errors, go ahead and choose E with confidence. It is not a trick answer choice.

Work through this example using the strategies outlined above:

Contrary to the city council reports, the city's landfills will be completely full by 2021,
       A   B   C
leaving no space available for the cities' trash. No error.
       D   E

The sentence is trying to convey the idea that the space in the city's landfills will be filled by a certain date, and that the city council does not agree with this information. Does anything jump out at you or sound conspicuous about the grammatical make up of the sentence? If not, move on to the next step.

Look closely at the underlined parts of the sentence and try to determine how they relate to the whole sentence. The first part, "Contrary to the city council reports," has no subject and therefore must modify or describe the first noun that appears in the sentence. In this case it would be "the city's landfills." The structure of the sentence implies that the city's landfills are contrary to the city council report, which is nonsensical. How can a landfill not agree with a report? The intended meaning is rather that the space available in the landfills is contrary, or in disagreement with, the city council reports. Therefore, answer A is correct, because it does not properly modify, as it should, the city's landfills.

Work the following drill using the techniques that were just discussed. Answers and explanations can be found at the end of this chapter. Note what grammar rules you need help on and work on them in the "English Language Skills Review" chapter.

DRILL: IDENTIFYING SENTENCE ERRORS

1. Some people fail to realize that a twice-yearly dental cleaning and exam are a relatively
     A   B   C
painless way to avoid more serious complications later. No error.
                           D   E

2. On vacation, Sue <u>plans</u> on <u>eating</u>, sleeping, <u>exercise</u>, and forgetting about <u>work</u>. <u>No error</u>.
                      A   B   C   D   E

3. <u>Considered a dolt as child</u>, <u>Claudius;</u> became emperor of <u>the entire</u> Roman Empire
            A   B   C
    <u>at the age of 51</u>. <u>No error</u>.
            D   E

4. <u>The cost of 8 – track tapes</u>, though not manufactured for years due to <u>poor</u> sales and sound
                A   B
    quality, <u>are</u> gradually <u>increasing</u> due to their new status as antiques. <u>No error</u>.
              C   D   E

5. The term Orwellian <u>refers to</u> the <u>dystopian</u> events that <u>take place</u> in <u>George Orwell's</u> timeless
                          A   B   C   D
    classic *1984*. <u>No error</u>.
                        E

6. <u>Although</u> James Madison debated his point <u>goodly</u>, his resolution <u>still failed</u> to pass <u>in</u> the
          A   B   C   D
    House of Representatives. <u>No error</u>.
                                  E

7. <u>Not knowing</u> where to buy a car, <u>Jane</u> contacted five different auto dealerships before <u>she</u>
          A   B   C
    found the closest one to <u>him</u>. <u>No error</u>.
                                D   E

8. The new school policy requiring everyone to wear name tags had three distinct <u>results;</u>
                                                                                      A
    <u>an increase</u> in friendliness among the students, <u>an increase</u> in respect towards the faculty,
          B   C
    and <u>a decrease</u> in name calling. <u>No error</u>.
            D   E

9. The name-calling and finger pointing had gotten <u>so bad</u> that Carol, <u>a naturally shy person</u>,

                                                        A   B

   stood up <u>to ask</u> the candidates to address the issues and <u>not each other</u>. <u>No error</u>.

               C   D   E

10. Everyone <u>involved</u> in the election campaigns for more than three months <u>are</u> going <u>to receive</u>

                   A   B   C

    a compensation check for <u>their</u> time. <u>No error</u>.

                                    D   E

11. Steve and Dan <u>had been</u> good friends <u>for over 10 years</u>, so it was surprising when <u>he</u> was

                               A   B   C

    not invited <u>to the wedding</u>. <u>No error</u>.

                           D   E

12. <u>Found only in</u> the Caspian Sea, <u>sturgeon</u> are sought after <u>worldwide</u> for their eggs, a gourmet

             A   B   C

    delicacy <u>selling for</u> well over $100 a pound. <u>No error</u>.

                     D   E

13. The more Tim practices <u>his</u> free throws, <u>the more</u> chance <u>his</u> team has <u>to win</u> the championship.

                                     A   B   C   D

    <u>No error</u>.

     E

14. The debate <u>about</u> whether or not <u>to install</u> a crosswalk signal <u>across from</u> city hall was cancelled;

                       A   B   C

    everyone agreed that <u>it</u> should be installed. <u>No error</u>.

                            D   E

15. Mercury travels around the sun <u>faster</u> than the Earth, but <u>it</u> rotates <u>much slowly</u> than the

                                      A   B   C

    Earth; <u>one</u> day on Mercury lasts 176 Earth days. <u>No error</u>.

                 D   E

IMPROVING SENTENCES

As mentioned earlier, there will be 20 Improving Sentence questions in the Writing Skills section. Go ahead and familiarize yourself with the instructions so you don't waste valuable test time reading them on the day of the exam. On the exam, the instructions look like this:

DIRECTIONS: **In each of the following sentences, some portion of the sentence is underlined. Under each sentence are five choices. The first choice has the same wording as the original. The other four choices are reworded. Sometimes the first choice containing the original wording is the best; sometimes one of the other choices is the best. Choose the letter of the best choice. Your choice should produce a sentence which is not ambiguous or awkward and which is correct, clear, and precise.**

This is a test of correct and effective English expression. Keep in mind the standards of English usage, punctuation, grammar, word choice, and construction.

EXAMPLE

When you listen to opera, <u>a person may not appreciate it</u>.

(A) a person may not appreciate it.

(B) it may not be appreciated by a person.

(C) which may not be appreciated by one.

(D) you may not appreciate it.

(E) appreciating it may be a problem for you.

These directions never change. In the following sentences some part of the sentence, or the entire sentence, is underlined. The answer choices are different revisions of the underlined portion of the sentence. You are to choose the best answer choice or revision for the underlined portion of the sentence. Your answer should be based on the rules of standard written English and should deviate as little as possible from the intended meaning of the original sentence. The best answer choice is neither awkward nor ambiguous, but clear and concise in meaning and grammatically sound. Answer choice (A) is always the exact same as the original underlined portion of the sentence. Choose (A) if there is nothing wrong with the original sentence.

Take a look at the following steps and strategies that will help you answer these questions types:

1. Read the entire sentence carefully. Try to understand the context or idea that the sentence is trying to express. A good place to start is to identify the subject and the verb, since these are the two building blocks of all sentences. Once you have done that, you can begin to understand how the different parts of the sentence should relate to each other.

2. Evaluate the underlined portion of the sentence for errors and possible corrections before you look at your answer choices. This will make reading through your answer choices easier and efficacious, since you can eliminate any answer choice that does not reflect your correction. Remember that any non-underlined portion of the sentence can be considered grammatically correct, so use it to determine the proper usage of the underlined portion.

3. If you can't identify any errors on your own, read the answer choices carefully. Look for differences among the answer choices to determine which grammar rule is being tested. Once you eliminate one answer choice due to an infraction of a certain grammar rule, eliminate all other answer choices that repeat the same infraction.

Read the following sentence carefully:

<u>Intelligence is determined contrary to public opinion not by</u> the size of the brain but by the number and complexity of dendrites in the brain.

(A) Intelligence is determined contrary to public opinion not by

(B) Intelligence is contrary to public opinion and determined not by

(C) Contrary to public opinion, intelligence is determined not by

(D) Not by popular opinion is intelligence determined but by

(E) Contrary to public opinion, intelligence determines not by

The underlined portion of the sentence is awkward and a bit unclear, therefore go ahead and eliminate answer (A), which is always an exact restatement of the original sentence. If you do not notice the particular grammar rule being tested, go ahead and review your remaining answer choices. Answer (B) changes the meaning of the original sentence by suggesting that intelligence disagrees or is contrary to public opinion, when it is how intelligence is determined that is contrary. Answer (E) is awkward and clouds the meaning of the sentence. Answer (D) is also incorrect because it is unclear what actually determines intelligence. Answer (C) is the best response because it effectively expresses what determines intelligence and relates how that is contrary to public opinion.

Remember, if you cannot find an error in the sentence, look over the answer choices and compare what is changed to the original sentence. If the original sentence seems best, choose answer (A), the restatement of the original sentence.

Work the following drill using the techniques that were just discussed. Answers and explanations can be found at the end of this chapter. Note what grammar rules you need help on and work on them in the "English Language Skills Review" chapter.

DRILL: IMPROVING SENTENCES

1. According to the school health instructor, <u>the eating of highly nutritional foods</u> helps improve your athletics.

(A) the eating of highly nutritional foods

(B) highly nutritional foods, eaten,

(C) if you eat nutritional foods it

(D) eating highly nutritional foods

(E) foods of highly nutritional value that will be consumed by you

2. <u>Great Britain's withdrawal from the province of Hong Kong, an occasion for joy and sorrow, in 1997.</u>

   (A) Great Britain's withdrawal from the province of Hong Kong, an occasion for joy and sorrow, in 1997.

   (B) 1997, an occasion for joy and sorrow, Great Britain withdrew from Hong Kong.

   (C) Great Britain's withdrawal from the province of Hong Kong in 1997 was an occasion for joy and sorrow.

   (D) Withdrawing from the province of Hong Kong, an occasion of joy and sorrow in 1997, was Great Britain.

   (E) Although it was an occasion for joy and sorrow, Great Britain withdrew in 1997 from Hong Kong.

3. Used now more for flavoring, <u>the long cold winters of the northern climates required salt for preserving meats.</u>

   (A) the long cold winters of the northern climates required salt for preserving meats.

   (B) salt was a necessary staple for preserving meats in the long cold winters of the northern climates.

   (C) preserved meats required salt to make it through the long cold winters of the northern climates.

   (D) the northern climates utilized salt as a preservative for meats during the long cold winters.

   (E) salts preserved meats in the northern climates' long cold winters.

4. After a long and exciting trip, everyone in the camp counselor groups <u>were happy to be going home.</u>

   (A) were happy to be going home.

   (B) were happy going home.

   (C) was going to be happy home.

   (D) were going to be happy home.

   (E) was happy to be going home.

5. Remembering that he had Katie's eyeglasses, <u>Jonathan quickly ran to the end of the terminal</u> to give them to her before she left.

   (A) Jonathan quickly ran to the end of the terminal

   (B) Jonathan ran fast to the terminal

   (C) running to the end of the terminal Jonathan wanted

   (D) Jonathan was the fastest runner in the terminal

   (E) to the end of the terminal Jonathan quickly ran

6. Jorge was so nervous before the recital that his stomach <u>was twisting and turning, such as</u> a washing machine full of dirty towels.

   (A) was twisting and turning, such as

   (B) twisting and turning, was

   (C) was twisting and turning, like

   (D) was twisting and turning, in the manner of

   (E) twisted and turned, such as

7. Often romanticized as a tale of courage and sacrifice against fatal odds, <u>the charge of the Light Brigade was, in reality, neither courageous or sacrificial</u>; the Light Brigade sustained less than a 5% casualty rate, a light skirmish by modern warfare standards.

   (A) the charge of the Light Brigade was, in reality, neither courageous or sacrificial

   (B) but in reality it was not courageous nor sacrificial

   (C) the charge of the Light Brigade, neither courageous nor sacrificial

   (D) the Light Brigade, courageous and sacrificial in reality, did not charge

   (E) the charge of the Light Brigade was, in reality, neither courageous nor sacrificial

8. Although never a great military power, the Phoenicians were the first great merchant naval power; <u>their ships traded goods all over the Mediterranean World over 2,500 years before the British Empire.</u>

   (A) their ships traded goods all over the Mediterranean World over 2,500 years before the British Empire.

   (B) their ships were trading goods all over the Mediterranean World over 2,500 years before the British Empire.

   (C) trading goods over 2,500 years before the British Empire all over the Mediterranean World.

   (D) 2,500 years before the British Empire was trading goods all the Mediterranean World.

   (E) their ships having traded goods all over the Mediterranean World over 2,500 years before the British Empire.

9. The moon Europa's icy shell both protects <u>the warm salty ocean below the icy shell from</u> <u>the deadening vacuum of space and allowing sunlight entering in</u>, two necessary components for life.

    (A) the warm salty ocean below the icy shell from the deadening vacuum of space and allowing sunlight entering in

    (B) salty warm oceans below the icy shell from dead vacuums in space and allows sunlight entering in

    (C) the warm salty ocean below from the vacuum of space and sunlight entering in

    (D) the warm salty ocean below from the vacuum of space and allows sunlight in

    (E) salty warm oceans below icy shells and allow space for sunlight to enter upon

10. It was a foolish decision for King George to allow the English colonies to be taxed so severely; <u>he neither diminished</u> the colonial dislike for the crown nor allowed greater colonial representation in Parliament.

    (A) he neither diminished

    (B) he had either diminished

    (C) it neither diminished

    (D) it diminishing neither

    (E) it had diminished

11. When you buy a new car, it immediately <u>loses over 35% of its value due to depreciation</u> <u>when you drive it</u> off the lot.

    (A) loses over 35% of its value due to depreciation when you drive it

    (B) loses over 35% of its value to depreciation when you drive it

    (C) loses over 35% of its valued price due to depreciation when you drive it

    (D) depreciates by 35% when you drive it

    (E) depreciates by losing over 35% of its value when you drive it

12. According to the new by-laws in the railway charter, <u>vendors are now prohibited to selling</u> their products in the passenger cars.

    (A) vendors are now prohibited to selling

    (B) vendors are now prohibited from selling

    (C) vendors are prohibiting the sale of

    (D) the selling is now prohibited from

    (E) prohibition now affects vendors from selling

13. Unlike the Mars day, the Mars year is twice as long as the Earth's.

(A) Unlike the Mars day, the Mars year is twice as long as the Earth's.

(B) Not like a Mars day, the year is twice as long as the Earth year.

(C) The Mars year is twice as long as the Earth, which is different from the Mars day.

(D) Unlike the Mars day, which is almost the same length as the Earth day, the Mars year is twice as long as the Earth year.

(E) Twice as long as the Earth, the Mars year is different than the Mars day.

14. Although many consider Shakespeare to be the greatest English writer in history, evidence has surfaced that questions the authenticity of his works.

(A) Although many consider Shakespeare to be the greatest English writer in history

(B) Considered by many to be the greatest English writer in history, Shakespeare,

(C) Once Shakespeare was considered the greatest English writer in history, but

(D) Shakespeare was once considered to be the greatest English writer in history, until

(E) Although many consider Shakespeare the greatest English writer in history,

15. The Supreme Court of the United States is independent from partisan politics and laws and relies solely on the Constitution to render its judgments.

(A) independent from partisan politics and laws and relies solely on

(B) independent of partisan politics and laws and interprets

(C) independent of partisan politics and partisan laws and relies on

(D) independent from partisan political laws and interprets

(E) independent to partisan politics and laws and relies solely on

16. The British colonial system exploited the natural resources and the labor of the indigenous people of the British colonies, and it was only when this system became unprofitable that serious reforms began to take shape.

(A) the British

(B) its

(C) their

(D) its own

(E) their own

17. Johannes Kepler's discovery of the elliptical orbits of the planets in the 16th century <u>centers around the then recently new Galilean</u> view of the solar system; that all planets revolve around the sun.

   (A) centers around the then recently new Galilean
   (B) centers on the recently new Galilean
   (C) centers on the then recently new Galilean
   (D) is set around the then Galilean
   (E) is set on the then recently new Galilean

18. Although President Wilson conceived of the League of Nations, the predecessor to the modern United Nations, <u>he was never able to convince his country to join it.</u>

   (A) he was never able to convince his country to join it.
   (B) he never convinced the country to join it.
   (C) his country ended up never joining it.
   (D) he was never able to convince anyone to join it.
   (E) he was never able to convince his own country to join the League of Nations.

19. Joan of Arc is considered the savior of France; she turned the tide of war in France's favor by recapturing the city of Orleans and <u>convincing Charles VII to claim his throne.</u>

   (A) convincing Charles VII to claim his throne.
   (B) by convincing Charles VII to claim his throne.
   (C) convinced Charles VII into claiming his throne.
   (D) convincing Charles VII into claiming his throne.
   (E) convinced Charles VII to claim his throne.

20. Last year, property values in the city rose <u>so fast than what they did</u> in the suburbs.

   (A) so fast than what they did
   (B) almost as fast as those
   (C) so fast as
   (D) faster than what they did
   (E) so faster that they did not

IMPROVING PARAGRAPHS

As stated earlier, there will be 5 Improving Paragraph questions in the Writing Skills section. Since the instructions will always be the same, familiarize yourself with them now so you don't waste valuable test time reading them on the day of the exam.

DIRECTIONS: The following passages are considered early draft efforts of a student. Some sentences need to be rewritten to make the ideas clearer and more precise.

Read each passage carefully and answer the questions that follow. Some of the questions are about particular sentences or parts of sentences and ask you to make decisions about sentence structure, diction, and usage. Some of the questions refer to the entire essay or parts of the essay and ask you to make decisions about organization, development, appropriateness of language, audience, and logic. Choose the answer that most effectively makes the intended meaning clear and follows the requirements of standard written English. After you have chosen your answer, fill in the corresponding oval on your answer sheet.

EXAMPLE

(1) On the one hand, I think television <u>is bad, But it also</u> does some good things for all of us. (2) For instance, my little sister thought she wanted to be a policeman until she saw police shows on television.

Which of the following is the best revision of the underlined portion of sentence 1 below?

On the one hand, I thing television <u>is bad, But it also</u> does some good things for all of us.

(A) is bad; But it also

(B) is bad. but is also

(C) is bad, and it also

(D) is bad, but it also

(E) is bad because it also

Basically, Improving Paragraphs is the same as Improving Sentences except that you will need to understand and correct the structure and meaning of an essay as well as the grammar of the individual sentences. The questions will ask you to do one of a few things:

Correct the grammar of a sentence (exactly like Improving Sentences)

Add a sentence to the paragraph to strengthen the meaning or logic of the essay

Evaluate the paragraph as a whole and render a verdict on its construction.

For any Improving Paragraph questions, follow these steps and strategies:

1. Skim the paragraph. Don't bother to read it in detail. It is supposed to be a first draft riddled with grammatical and stylistic errors. There is no reason for you to identify everything that is wrong with the paragraph when you first read it because you will not be asked about everything. Remember that there are only five questions to this section, so concentrate on the questions rather than the entire essay.

2. Identify the question type. Make sure you read the question carefully and understand what it is asking for. If it is asking about grammar or sentence construction, remember your grammar rules. If it is asking you to add a sentence, understand the context of the passage where the sentence is to be placed so you will understand what purpose the sentence you are to choose from serves. If it asks you to evaluate the paragraph or passage as a whole, go back to make sure you understand the main topic and how the passage was constructed around that topic.

3. Read through ALL the answer choices. Since the questions are usually asking for the answer that will most improve the sentence or paragraph, more than one answer choice might work, so check them all to decide which is best.

Let's go ahead and take a look at an example with some sample questions:

The following essay was written by a student in response to an essay question about how his/her use of language differs from proper English when speaking with a friend.

(1) The language I would use in talking to a friend would certainly differ from standard English. (2) In talking with a friend I would be prone to phrases drawn from popular culture that we are both aware of. (3) I would know that by employing certain phrases that my friends and I were members of a peer group, and thus friends.

(4) In talking with friends I would be more prone to use certain words and phrases, such as "hey," "like," and "you know," in ways that are both unconventional and grammatically incorrect. (5) This informal use of language implies the casualness and familiarity that I feel when among my friends.

(6) I would pepper my vocabulary with words that have set meaning on their own, such as "like." (7) "Like" functions as an intensifier; "He was, like, so dumb," would imply that the person of whom I was speaking was quite stupid. (8) My friends would easily understand what I was saying.

1. Which of the following revisions most clearly states the meaning of sentence 3?

   (A) As it is now.
   (B) I would know, by employing certain phrases, that my friends and I shared similar interests.
   (C) My friends and I would be peers by employing certain phrases that show we are friends.
   (D) I would know that my friends and I had things in common by our similar uses of language.
   (E) I would know, that by employing certain phrases and words, that my friends and I shared common interests and were, because of this knowledge, peers.

   This question is asking you if it is necessary to revise sentence 3, and if so, which revision would be most appropriate to clarify the meaning. Since this is exactly like the improving sentence question, choose (A) if there is no need for revision. However, if you go back and reread sentence 3, you will notice that it is repetitive and employs circular reasoning, therefore you can eliminate (A). Look through the remaining answer choices and eliminate the obviously incorrect ones. Answer (D) changes the meaning of the idea implied in sentence 3—the use of phrases helps the author express himself to his peers, not identify their common interests. Answer (E) is verbose and a repetitive run-on sentence. Now compare the two remaining choices, (B) and (C), and look for the one that is most clear, concise, and conveys the intended meaning. Answer (B) best expresses the idea that the author and his/her friends use certain phrases that help express their shared interests to one another.

2.   Which sentence would best follow sentence 8?

   (A)   And that is all that matters.

   (B)   Furthermore, my friends and I would employ many more non-standard usages.

   (C)   The language I would use in talking to a friend would certainly be different than standard English.

   (D)   My friends and I have our own way of speaking.

   (E)   My use of language among friends would be casual, informal and idiosyncratic, reflecting these same qualities in our relationship.

Since the question is asking you to add a sentence, the first thing you need to do is locate where the sentence is going to be added. The last sentence in the passage is sentence 8, therefore you are adding the concluding sentence to the passage. Concluding sentences need to organize and summarize the main idea of the essay. Answers (A) and (B) end the essay abruptly and do not summarize the main ideas. Answer (C) restates the opening sentence, which is a good introduction, but NOT conclusion. Answer (D) restates one main point, but fails to give a sense of finality, or summary. Answer (E) would be the best response because it properly organizes the main points in a summary fashion.

3.   How could the author make paragraph 1 stronger?

   (A)   By using concrete examples, as in the second and third paragraph.

   (B)   By combining sentences (2) and (3).

   (C)   By focusing on the meaning of standard English.

   (D)   By switching the order of paragraph 1 and paragraph 2.

   (E)   By clearly stating a thesis in the paragraph.

The question is asking you to evaluate the first paragraph to determine what could make it stronger. Since your own ideas will probably not correspond to the one correct answer choice, it will be necessary for you to read through all the answer choices and choose the one that will strengthen the paragraph. Answer (A) makes sense, since the opening paragraph does lack concrete examples that were employed in the second and third paragraphs. Answer (B) would create an unnecessarily long and confusing sentence, and would not help strengthen the paragraph. Answer (C) does not relate to the main idea, and would not strengthen the paragraph. Answer (D) would harm the essay, since the opening paragraph states the main idea of the essay. Answer (E) is unnecessary because the thesis or main idea has already been clearly stated in the first paragraph. Answer (A) would be best.

Work the following drill using the techniques that were just discussed. Answers and explanations can be found at the end of this chapter. Note what grammar rules you need help on and work on them in the "English Language Skills Review" chapter.

DRILL: IMPROVING PARAGRAPHS

(1) Computers have shaped our society for over 50 years. (2) Everything from elevators to space travel has been made possible through research in computer technology and perhaps their most humane advantages have been in medical science and research. (3) Diseases that once wiped out entire populations have been rendered extinct thanks to computers.

(4) But computers are not as perfect as society believes. (5) How many disasters and deaths have been caused by computer malfunction?

1.   What would be the best way to improve the second paragraph?

   (A)   Combine sentences (4) and (5) with the conjunction "and."
   (B)   Delete the second paragraph because it disproves the thesis proposed in the first paragraph.
   (C)   Add examples that illustrate the effects of computer malfunctions.
   (D)   Explain how computer malfunctions are always the fault of human operators.
   (E)   Combine sentences (4) and (5) with a comma ",".

2.   Which of the following would be the best improvement to the underlined portion of sentence (2) below?

   Everything from elevators to space travel has been made possible through research in computer technology and perhaps their most humane advantages have been in medical science and research.

   (A)   technology. Perhaps their most humane advantages have been
   (B)   technology, perhaps its most humane advantages has been
   (C)   technology, perhaps their most humane advantages have been
   (D)   technology. But perhaps their most humane advantages has been
   (E)   technology, but perhaps its most humane advantages have been

3.   Which sentence would best follow sentence (3)?

   (A)   They have truly saved humanity from extinction.
   (B)   Hospital survival rates have more than doubled thanks to the advancements in surgery and recovery that computers helped develop.
   (C)   If only there was a way to make computer viruses extinct.
   (D)   Computers have made mistakes in the past.
   (E)   Now computers are on the verge of curing all known diseases, saving humanity from certain extinction.

(1) Freedom of expression is protected by the first amendment of the United States Constitution. (2) The new school policy of mandatory uniforms for its students violates the first amendment of the United States Constitution. (3) Rather than create a more equal learning environment where students are judged on their personalities and intellect instead of their appearance, it will create an expressionless and dull atmosphere where students feel more like prisoners than students. (4) Uniforms are a very bad idea.

4. Which of the following would be the best revision of the underlined portion of sentence (3) below?

    Rather than create a more equal learning environment were students are judged on their personalities and intellect instead of their appearance, it will create an expressionless and dull atmosphere were students feel more like prisoners than students.

    (A) As it is now.
    (B) intellect, it will have created an
    (C) intellect instead of their appearance. It will create an
    (D) intellect instead of their appearance, but it will create an
    (E) intellect instead of their appearance. It creates an

5. Which of the following would best replace sentence (4) as the concluding sentence?

    (A) For these reasons uniforms are a very bad idea.
    (B) Students should not be made to feel like prisoners in school.
    (C) Uniforms are the first step to a tyrannical and despotic society.
    (D) Since uniforms violate our first amendment rights and create an unimaginative and boring learning environment, they should not be imposed on the students.
    (E) The first amendment is the most sacred of all the amendments and therefore should protect the students from mandatory uniforms.

DETAILED EXPLANATIONS

WRITING SKILLS

Drill: Identifying Sentence Errors

1. (C) This sentence is testing you on verb tense and agreement. The "twice-yearly dental cleaning and exam" refers to a single visit that occurs twice a year. The article "a" helps denotes that it is singular. Therefore the verb should be singular, or "is."

2. (C) Sue plans on doing four different actions while on vacation. The proper way to express this is for all the actions to have the same verb form. This is referred to stylistically as parallel construction. Therefore Sue must plan on eating, sleeping, "exercising," and forgetting. Since the two verbs "sleeping" and "eating" were not underlined, you know that the other verbs must copy their form and structure.

3. (B) Who was considered a dolt as a child? Claudius was. Therefore the opening descriptive phrase properly modifies Claudius. However the semicolon is improperly used after the noun Claudius. There is no need for any punctuation that separates the subject from the body of the sentence unless subordinate clauses are involved. There are none in this sentence.

4. (C) Be aware of long prepositional phrases that separate the subject from the verb. They are usually there to confuse the subject/verb agreement. Are 8 – track tapes gradually increasing? No, "the cost" is gradually increasing. Therefore the proper verb should be "is."

5. (E) This sentence is grammatically sound. The verb "refers to" properly agrees with the subject "the term," "dystopian" properly modifies the noun "events," nothing is wrong with "take place," and "George Orwell's" is in the proper possessive case to refer to his book, "1984."

6. (B) Remember that adjectives describe nouns and adverbs describe everything else, including other adverbs. "Goodly" is not a proper word. The sentence tries to modify the action of how Madison debated his point, and should use the proper adverb "well." "Good" is an adjective.

7. (D) Pronouns must clearly and unambiguously refer back to their antecedents (the word the pronoun is taking the place of.) "She" clearly refers to Jane, who was contacting all the auto dealerships, but who does "him" refer to? There is no proper antecedent for "him" and is therefore incorrect usage.

8. (A) Whenever there is a list in a sentence, everything in the list should be of the same form and tense, referred to as parallel construction. "an increase," "an increase," and "a decrease" are all nouns in the same form, therefore they are grammatically correct. However, a list is always introduced into a sentence by a colon, not a semicolon. Look in the "English Language Review Skills" chapter for the proper use of colon and semicolon.

9. (E) This sentence is grammatically sound. "So bad" correctly describes how bad the finger pointing and name-calling got, while "a naturally shy person" properly modifies Carol. "To ask" is in the proper infinitive form following "stood up" and "not each other" correctly completes the idea of who the candidates were not to talk to.

10. (B) The subject "everyone" is singular, referring to individual people, therefore the verb should also be singular. "Are" should be changed to "is." Remember to be aware of the prepositional phrase separating the subject from the verb, it is usually used as a distractor to blur the agreement between the subject and verb.

11. (C) Pronouns need to clearly and unambiguously refer to their antecedent. The subjects are Steve and Dan and it is unclear to which one answer (C), "he," refers. Therefore (C) is the best response.

12. (E) This sentence is grammatically sound. The descriptive clause at the beginning of the sentence clearly modifies the noun "sturgeon." "Worldwide" correctly modifies the verb *sought after* and "selling for" is correctly used in the dependent clause describing the sturgeon eggs.

13. (B) The correct idiomatic expression describing the relationship between Tim's practicing and his teams chances of winning is "the more (Tim practices) the better (chance his team has to win)." So answer (B) is correct because "the more" is unidiomatic.

14. (A) Idiomatically speaking, people debate "over" an issue, not "about" an issue. Therefore answer (A) is correct since it should be "over." Everything else is grammatically sound.

15. (C) Since one day on Mercury lasts 176 Earth days, Mercury must rotate "much more slowly" than the Earth. Answer (C) is correct because it misuses the adverb to describe Mercury's rotation.

Drill: Improving Sentences

1. (D) Stylistically, the term "the eating" is an unnecessary use of the gerund, especially when the intended meaning is the action or verb form of eating. Answer (A) is incorrect. Answer (B) is awkward and (E) uses the passive voice unnecessarily. Between answers (C) and (D), answer (D) is more clear, concise and direct, and is the best choice.

2. (C) The subject "Great Britain's withdrawal" never completes an action or thought and therefore the sentence is a fragment. Answer (A) is incorrect. In order for a sentence not to be a fragment it must have both a subject, consisting of a noun, and a predicate, consisting of a verb. Answer (B) incorrectly implies that the year 1997 was an occasion for joy and sorrow. Answer (D) is in the passive voice and answer (E) improperly uses the subordinating clause "although" which suggests a contradiction between the two parts of the sentence. Answer (C), the best response, properly and effectively implies the intended meaning that Great Britain's withdrawal was an occasion for joy and sorrow.

3. (B) The sentence starts out with a descriptive phrase with no object, so the first noun after the phrase must be the object of the modifier. Clearly the long cold winters are not used more for flavoring, therefore there is a misplaced modifier and answer (A) is incorrect. From the context, salt should be the object of the modifying phrase, therefore salt should be the first noun after the phrase. This eliminates answers (C) and (D). Answer (B) is the best response because it most effectively explains the origins of salt in relation to the modifying phrase. Answer (E) improperly attributes human qualities to the salt and the northern climate.

4. (E) The answer choices are split between was and were, so you will need to identify the subject in order to determine the proper tense of the verb. The subject is everyone, which is singular, therefore the verb must also be singular. You can eliminate (A), (B), and (D). Answer (E) best expresses the mood of the counselors as they were going home.

5. (A) Answer (A) is the best choice because it expresses the intended meaning that Jonathan, upon remembering he had the glasses, quickly ran to give them to Katie. Jonathan is the correct object of the introductory modifying phrase and *quickly* is the proper modifier to describe how he ran. Answers (B) and (D) change the meaning of the sentence, and answers (C) and (E) are not the proper objects of the introductory modifying phrase.

6. (C) The purpose of the underlined portion of the sentence is to describe the condition of Jorge's stomach and then compare it to a washing machine. Idiomatically speaking, the phrase "such as" is used only when listing examples, where the word "like" is used to establish a metaphor. The description of the washing machine is used metaphorically as a way to understand how Jorge's stomach felt. Therefore answer (A) is incorrect, as well as answers (B), (D), and (E). Only answer (C) correctly uses the idiomatic phrase "like" to express the comparison.

7. (E) The underlined portion of the sentence expresses an opposition to the opening descriptive phrase. However, it is grammatically incorrect because it uses the unidiomatic phrase "neither...or." The correct idiomatic phrase to negate two separate instances is "neither...nor." Answers (A) and (B) are incorrect. Answer (D) changes the original meaning of the sentence. Answer (C) creates a sentence fragment because it lacks a predicate verb. Answer (E) is the best response because it properly negates the two adjectives and relates "the charge" to the opening descriptive phrase.

8. (A) The underlined portion of the sentence needs to be an independent clause since it follows a semicolon and it should unambiguously relate to the first half of the sentence. Answer (A) is the best response because the underlined portion clearly refers back to the Phoenicians and elaborates on their merchant naval power. Answers (B) and (E) use the improper verb tense since the trading took place and ended in the past. Answer (C) lacks punctuation and creates an awkward and confusing sentence. Answer (D) is a subordinate clause and cannot stand alone.

9. (D) Whenever there is a list of verbs, they should be in the same form and tense. The second part of the sentence explains the two independent functions of the ice shell, it "protects the oceans" and "allows sunlight in." Therefore, answers (A), (C), and (E) do not show parallel verb form. Answer (B) alters the meaning of the sentence by suggesting that there is more than one vacuum in space and by the redundant use of "entering in." Answer (D) is the best response because it has parallel verb form and clearly expresses the two distinct functions of the ice shell.

10. (C) The idiomatic phrase "neither...nor" is correct, so you can eliminate answers (B), (D), and (E). Now you need to determine what or who neither diminished dislike nor allowed representation. Since the king allowed the tax, it can be interpreted that the tax was supposed to have the predicted effects, and it was foolish for the king to think so. Answer (C) is the best response because "it" clearly refers to the tax.

11. (D) The definition of depreciate is to lose value. Therefore the underlined portion of the sentence is redundant because to lose over 35% of its value means to depreciate in value, it does not need to be stated twice. Answer (D) is the only answer choice that corrects the redundancy and expresses the idea of the sentence both succinctly and clearly.

12. (B) The correct preposition to use with "prohibit" is "from." Answers (A) and (C) use the idiom incorrectly. Answer (D) is nonsensical and answer (E) changes the meaning of the sentence. Answer (B) is the best response because it most clearly relates the message that vendors are prohibited from selling things in the passenger cars.

13. (D) Whenever a comparison is made in a sentence, there can be no doubt as to what is being compared and the two or more things must be comparable (apples compared to apples and oranges compared to oranges). Is the Mars year twice as long as the Earth's year or day? How is the Mars day different than the Mars year? Only answer (D) states the comparison clearly and correctly. Answers (C) and (E) incorrectly compare the Mars year to the actual size of the Earth. Answers (A) and (B) have unmodified years and days, thus confusing what is being compared.

14. (E) A common mistake with the use of the word "consider" is that it is followed by "to be." However, the correct use of "consider" is that it stands alone. No special prepositions or verb forms are required when it is used, so you can eliminate answers (A), (B), and (D) since they all use "to be." Answer (E) best conforms to the original meaning that at the present time, many people consider Shakespeare the greatest English writer. Answer (C) places Shakespeare's greatness in the past tense, which deviates from the intended meaning.

15. (A) This sentence is grammatically sound as it is. The correct idiomatic expression is to be independent "from" someone or something. Therefore you can eliminate answers (B), (C), and (E). Answer (D) changes the intended meaning, suggesting that the court is only independent from "political laws" and that it does not "rely" on the constitution to render its judgments. Answer (A) is the best response.

16. (B) The sentence is redundant. Since it is the British colonial system, it is understood that the colonies being exploited are British. Answer (B) is the best response because it uses the appropriate pronoun to refer the antecedent "British." Answer (C) and (E) are incorrect because the pronoun "their" refers to people, and countries are referred to as things. Answer (D) is redundant since the possessive form of "its" already implies ownership.

17. (C) Idiomatically, when you are referring to the focus of a plan or idea, the word centers is always followed by the preposition "on." As Kepler's discovery "centered on" the Galilean view of the solar system, you can eliminate answers (A), (D), and (E). Answer (B) changes the meaning to imply that the Galilean view is new in terms of present time, not, as the sentence suggests, that the view was new in conjunction with the 16th century when Kepler made his discovery. Answer (C) is the best response.

18. (A) This sentence is grammatically sound. Answer (B) is incorrect because it is unclear what country "the country" refers to. Answer (C) is awkward and distorts the meaning of the context. Answer (D) refers to individuals joining the League of Nations, when it was meant for countries to join. Answer (E) needlessly restates League of Nations when the pronoun "it" works just fine.

19. (E) Joan of Arc did two distinct things to be considered the savior of France; she turned the tide of war and "convinced" Charles VII to be king. In order to maintain parallel construction, the correct response must have "convinced." Eliminate answers (A), (B), and (D). Answer (C) is incorrect because "convinced . . . into" is unidiomatic and awkward. Answer (E) is the best response; it is parallel, succinct, and clear.

20. (B) The sentence is comparing the property values, so it is appropriate to use "those" to refer to the property values in the comparison. Answer (B) is the best response because it clearly compares the rate of increase in the property values in the city to "those" in the suburbs. Answers (A), (C), and (E) are nonsensical and answer (D) incorrectly insinuates that the property values in the city were rising in the suburbs.

Drill: Improving Paragraphs

1. (C) Since there are numerous ways to improve the given paragraph, your own ideas probably will not correspond with the one correct answer choice. You will need to go through all five answer choices to determine which one would best improve the paragraph. Answer (A) creates a run-on sentence that obfuscates the meaning of the paragraph. Answer (B) changes the entire meaning of the essay and no longer presents a balanced view of computers. Answer (C) is the best choice because it adds more depth and conviction to its main idea of the paragraph. Answer (D) also changes the meaning of the essay by suggesting that computers are infallible. Answer (E) creates a run-on sentence.

2. (E) This question wants you to revise sentence (2). The entire sentence consists of two independent clauses connected by the conjunctive "and." Looking at the answer choices you will notice that the differences are how the two clauses should be separated, and what verb and pronoun form to use. Start with the pronoun since it must clearly and unambiguously refer to its antecedent. The antecedent is computer technology, which is singular. Therefore you can eliminate answers (A), (C), and (D). The subject of the verb form in question is "the advantages" which is plural, so the verb must also be plural; therefore you can eliminate answer (B). Answer (E) has the proper pronoun, verb form, and correctly coordinates the two independent clauses.

3. (B) Sentence (3) ends by talking about the health benefits of computer technology, therefore it would be logical to end the paragraph with another example of how computers directly save lives. Answer (B) is the only answer choice that does this effectively and with relevance.

4. (A) Answer (B) is incorrect because it leaves out pertinent information and uses an incorrect verb form. By creating two sentences, the first half of the sentence becomes a sentence fragment and is ungrammatical, thus answers (C) and (E) are incorrect. Answer (D) disrupts the style of the sentence by adding the conjunction "but," which does not coordinate with the "rather" at the beginning of the sentence. Answer (A) is best, since the sentence is grammatical and clear the way it is written.

5. **(D)** Concluding sentences need to summarize and organize the main idea of an essay. Two points were made in the paragraph, that uniforms are unconstitutional and they fail to produce their intended results. Answers (B), (C), and (E) mention one, but not both main points. Answer (A) simply restates the original sentence. Answer (D) is best because it summarizes the two main points the paragraph made and organizes what the points prove—that uniforms should not be mandatory.

CHAPTER 10

ENGLISH LANGUAGE
SKILLS REVIEW

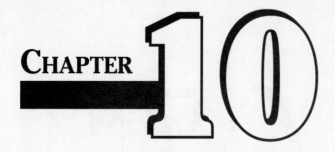

CHAPTER 10

ENGLISH LANGUAGE SKILLS REVIEW

The requirements for informal spoken English are much more relaxed than the rigid rules for "standard written English." While slang, colloquialisms, and other informal expressions are acceptable and sometimes very appropriate in casual speech, they are inappropriate in academic and business writing. More often than not, writers, especially student writers, do not make a distinction between the two: they use the same words, grammar, and sentence structure from their everyday speech in their college papers, albeit unsuccessfully.

The PSAT Writing Skills section does not require you to know grammatical terms such as *gerund, subject complement,* or *dependent clause*, although general familiarity with such terms may be helpful to you in determining whether a sentence or part of a sentence is correct or incorrect. You should watch for errors in grammar, punctuation, sentence structure, and word choice. Remember: this is a test of written language skills; therefore, your responses should be based on what you know to be correct for written work, not what you know to be appropriate for a casual conversation. For instance, in informal speech, you might say "Who are you going to choose?" But in formal academic writing, you would write "Whom are you going to choose?" Your choices, then, should be dictated by requirements for *written*, not *conversational* English.

WORD CHOICE SKILLS

Connotative and Denotative Meanings

The denotative meaning of a word is its *literal* dictionary definition: what the word denotes or "means." The connotative meaning of a word is what the word connotes or "suggests"; it is a meaning apart from what the word literally means. A writer should choose a word based on the tone and context of the sentence; this ensures that a word bears the appropriate connotation while still conveying some exactness in denotation. For example, a gift might be described as "cheap," but the directness of this word has a negative connotation—something cheap is something of little or no value. The word "inexpensive" has a more positive connotation, though "cheap" is a synonym for "inexpensive." Questions of this type require you to make a decision regarding the appropriateness of words and phrases for the context of a sentence.

Wordiness and Conciseness

Effective writing is concise. Wordiness, on the other hand, decreases the clarity of expression by cluttering sentences with unnecessary words.

Wordiness questions test your ability to detect redundancies (unnecessary repetitions), circumlocution (failure to get to the point), and padding with loose synonyms. Wordiness questions require you to choose sentences that use as few words as possible to convey a message clearly, economically, and effectively.

Notice the difference in impact between the first and second sentences in the following pairs:

INCORRECT: The medical exam that he gave me was entirely complete.

    CORRECT: The medical exam he gave me was complete.

INCORRECT: Larry asked his friend John, who was a good, old friend, if he would join him and go along with him to see the foreign film made in Japan.

    CORRECT: Larry asked his good, old friend John if he would join him in seeing the Japanese film.

INCORRECT: I was absolutely, totally happy with the present that my parents gave to me at 7 a.m. on the morning of my birthday.

    CORRECT: I was happy with the present my parents gave me on the morning of my birthday.

DRILL: WORD CHOICE SKILLS

DIRECTIONS: Choose the correct option.

1.   His <u>principal</u> reasons for resigning were his <u>principles</u> of right and wrong.

    (A) principal . . . principals   (C) principle . . . principles

    (B) principle . . . principals   (D) No change is necessary.

2.   The book tells about Alzheimer's disease—how it <u>affects</u> the patient and what <u>effect</u> it has on the patient's family.

    (A) effects . . . affect   (C) effects . . . effects

    (B) affects . . . affect   (D) No change is necessary.

3.   The <u>amount</u> of homeless children we can help depends on the <u>number</u> of available shelters.

    (A)   number . . . number   (C)   number . . . amount

    (B)   amount . . . amount   (D)   No change is necessary.

4.   All students are <u>suppose to</u> pass the test before <u>achieving</u> upper-division status.

    (A)   suppose to . . . acheiving

    (B)   suppose to. . . being achieved

    (C)   supposed to . . . achieving

    (D)   No change is necessary.

5.   The reason he <u>succeeded</u> is <u>because</u> he worked hard.

    (A)   succeeded . . . that   (C)   succede . . . because of

    (B)   seceded . . . that   (D)   No change is necessary.

DIRECTIONS: **Select the sentence that clearly and effectively states the idea and has no structural errors.**

6.   (A)   South of Richmond, the two roads converge together to form a single highway.

    (B)   South of Richmond, the two roads converge together to form an interstate highway.

    (C)   South of Richmond, the two roads converge to form an interstate highway.

    (D)   South of Richmond, the two roads converge to form a single interstate highway.

7.   (A)   The student depended on his parents for financial support.

    (B)   The student lacked the ways and means to pay for his room and board, so he depended on his parents for this kind of money and support.

    (C)   The student lacked the ways and means or the wherewithal to support himself, so his parents provided him with the financial support he needed.

    (D)   The student lacked the means to pay for his room and board, so he depended on his parents for financial support.

8. (A) Vincent van Gogh and Paul Gauguin were close personal friends and companions who enjoyed each other's company and frequently worked together on their artwork.

    (B) Vincent van Gogh and Paul Gauguin were friends who frequently painted together.

    (C) Vincent van Gogh was a close personal friend of Paul Gauguin's, and the two of them often worked together on their artwork because they enjoyed each other's company.

    (D) Vincent van Gogh, a close personal friend of Paul Gauguin's, often worked with him on their artwork.

9. (A) A college education often involves putting away childish thoughts, which are characteristic of youngsters, and concentrating on the future, which lies ahead.

    (B) A college education involves putting away childish thoughts, which are characteristic of youngsters, and concentrating on the future.

    (C) A college education involves putting away childish thoughts and concentrating on the future.

    (D) A college education involves putting away childish thoughts and concentrating on the future which lies ahead.

10. (A) I had the occasion to visit an Oriental pagoda while I was a tourist on vacation and visiting in Kyoto, Japan.

    (B) I visited a Japanese pagoda in Kyoto.

    (C) I had occasion to visit a pagoda when I was vacationing in Kyoto, Japan.

    (D) On my vacation, I visited a Japanese pagoda in Kyoto.

SENTENCE STRUCTURE SKILLS

Parallelism

Parallel structure is used to express matching ideas. It refers to the grammatical balance of a series of any of the following:

Phrases:

> The squirrel ran *along the fence*, *up the tree*, and *into his burrow* with a mouthful of acorns.

Adjectives:

> The job market is flooded with *very talented*, *highly motivated*, and *well-educated* young people.

Nouns:

> You will need a *notebook*, *pencil*, and *dictionary* for the test.

Clauses:

> The children were told to decide which toy they would keep and which toy they would give away.

Verbs:

> The farmer *plowed*, *planted*, and *harvested* his corn in record time.

Verbals:

> *Reading*, *writing*, and *calculating* are fundamental skills that all of us should possess.

Correlative conjunctions:

> *Either* you will do your homework *or* you will fail.

Repetition of structural signals:

> (such as articles, auxiliary verbs, prepositions, and conjunctions)

> INCORRECT: I have quit my job, enrolled in school, and am looking for a reliable babysitter.

> CORRECT: I have quit my job, have enrolled in school, and am looking for a reliable babysitter.

Note: Repetition of prepositions is considered formal and is not necessary.

> You can travel *by car*, *by plane*, or *by train*; it's all up to you.

OR

> You can travel *by car*, *plane*, or *train*; it's all up to you.

When a sentence contains items in a series, check for both punctuation and sentence balance. When you check for punctuation, make sure the commas are used correctly. When you check for parallelism, make sure that the conjunctions connect similar grammatical constructions, such as all adjectives or all clauses.

Misplaced and Dangling Modifiers

A misplaced modifier is one that is in the wrong place in the sentence. Misplaced modifiers come in all forms—words, phrases, and clauses. Sentences containing misplaced modifiers are often very comical: *Mom made me eat the spinach instead of my brother.* Misplaced modifiers, like the one in this sentence, are usually too far away from the word or words they modify. This sentence should read: *Mom made me, instead of my brother, eat the spinach.*

Modifiers like *only*, *nearly*, and *almost* should be placed next to the word they modify and not in front of some other word, especially a verb, that they are not intended to modify.

A modifier is misplaced if it appears to modify the wrong part of the sentence or if we cannot be certain what part of the sentence the writer intended it to modify. To correct a misplaced modifier, move the modifier next to the word it describes.

INCORRECT: He served hamburgers to the guests on paper plates.

CORRECT: He served hamburgers on paper plates to the guests.

Split infinitives also result in misplaced modifiers. Infinitives consist of the marker *to* plus the plain form of the verb. The two parts of the infinitive make up a grammatical unit that should not be split. Splitting an infinitive is placing an adverb between the *to* and the verb.

INCORRECT: The weather service expects temperatures to not rise.

CORRECT: The weather service expects temperatures not to rise.

Sometimes a split infinitive may be natural and preferable, though it may still bother some readers.

EXAMPLE: Several U.S. industries expect *to* more than *triple* their use of robots within the next decade.

A squinting modifier is one that may refer to either a preceding or a following word, leaving the reader uncertain about what it is intended to modify. Correct a squinting modifier by moving it next to the word it is intended to modify.

INCORRECT: Snipers who often fired on the soldiers escaped capture.

CORRECT: Snipers who fired on the soldiers often escaped capture.

OR   Snipers who fired on the soldiers escaped capture often.

A dangling modifier is a modifier or verb in search of a subject: the modifying phrase (usually an *-ing* word group, an *-ed* or *-en* word group, or a *to + a verb* word group—participle phrase or infinitive phrase respectively) either appears to modify the wrong word or has nothing to modify. It is literally dangling at the beginning or the end of a sentence. The sentences often look and sound correct: *To be a student government officer, your grades must be above average.* (However, the verbal modifier has nothing to describe. Who is *to be a student government officer*? Your grades?) Questions of this type require you to determine whether a modifier has a headword or whether it is dangling at the beginning or the end of the sentence.

To correct a dangling modifier, reword the sentence by either: 1) changing the modifying phrase to a clause with a subject, or 2) changing the subject of the sentence to the word that should be modified. The following are examples of a dangling gerund, a dangling infinitive, and a dangling participle:

INCORRECT: Shortly after leaving home, the accident occurred.

Who is <u>leaving home</u>, the accident?

CORRECT: Shortly after we left home, the accident occurred.

INCORRECT: To get up on time, a great effort was needed.

<u>To get up</u> needs a subject.

CORRECT: To get up on time, I made a great effort.

Fragments

A fragment is an incomplete construction which may or may not have a subject and a verb. Specifically, a fragment is a group of words pretending to be a sentence. Not all fragments appear as separate sentences, however. Often, fragments are separated by semicolons.

INCORRECT: Traffic was stalled for ten miles on the freeway. Because repairs were being made on potholes.

CORRECT: Traffic was stalled for ten miles on the freeway because repairs were being made on potholes.

INCORRECT: It was a funny story; one that I had never heard before.

CORRECT: It was a funny story, one that I had never heard before.

Run-on/Fused Sentences

A run-on/fused sentence is not necessarily a long sentence or a sentence that the reader considers too long; in fact, a run-on may be two short sentences: *Dry ice does not melt it evaporates.* A run-on results when the writer fuses or runs together two separate sentences without any correct mark of punctuation separating them.

INCORRECT: Knowing how to use a dictionary is no problem each dictionary has a section in the front of the book telling how to use it.

CORRECT: Knowing how to use a dictionary is no problem. Each dictionary has a section in the front of the book telling how to use it.

Even if one or both of the fused sentences contains internal punctuation, the sentence is still a run-on.

INCORRECT: Bob bought dress shoes, a suit, and a nice shirt he needed them for his sister's wedding.

CORRECT: Bob bought dress shoes, a suit, and a nice shirt. He needed them for his sister's wedding.

Comma Splices

A comma splice is the unjustifiable use of only a comma to combine what really is two separate sentences.

INCORRECT: One common error in writing is incorrect spelling, the other is the occasional use of faulty diction.

CORRECT: One common error in writing is incorrect spelling; the other is the occasional use of faulty diction.

Both run-on sentences and comma splices may be corrected in one of the following ways:

RUN-ON: Neal won the award he had the highest score.

COMMA SPLICE: Neal won the award, he had the highest score.

Separate the sentences with a period:

Neal won the award. He had the highest score.

Separate the sentences with a comma and a coordinating conjunction (*and, but, or, nor, for, yet, so*):

Neal won the award, for he had the highest score.

Separate the sentences with a semicolon:

Neal won the award; he had the highest score.

Separate the sentences with a subordinating conjunction such as *although, because, since, if*:

Neal won the award because he had the highest score.

Subordination, Coordination, and Predication

Suppose, for the sake of clarity, you wanted to combine the information in these two sentences to create one statement:

I studied a foreign language. I found English quite easy.

How you decide to combine this information should be determined by the relationship you'd like to show between the two facts. *I studied a foreign language, and I found English quite easy* seems rather illogical. The **coordination** of the two ideas (connecting them with the coordinating conjunction *and*) is ineffective. Using **subordination** instead (connecting the sentences with a subordinating conjunction) clearly shows the degree of relative importance between the expressed ideas:

After I studied a foreign language, I found English quite easy.

When using a conjunction, be sure that the sentence parts you are joining are in agreement.

INCORRECT: She loved him dearly but not his dog.

CORRECT: She loved him dearly but she did not love his dog.

A common mistake that is made is to forget that each member of the pair must be followed by the same kind of construction.

INCORRECT: They complimented them both for their bravery and they thanked them for their kindness.

CORRECT: They both complimented them for their bravery and thanked them for their kindness.

While refers to time and should not be used as a substitute for *although, and,* or *but*.

INCORRECT: While I'm usually interested in Fellini movies, I'd rather not go tonight.

CORRECT: Although I'm usually interested in Fellini movies, I'd rather not go tonight.

Where refers to time and should not be used as a substitute for *that*.

INCORRECT: We read in the paper where they are making great strides in DNA research.

CORRECT: We read in the paper that they are making great strides in DNA research.

After words like reason and explanation, use *that*, not *because*.

INCORRECT: His explanation for his tardiness was because his alarm did not go off.

CORRECT: His explanation for his tardiness was that his alarm did not go off.

DRILL: SENTENCE STRUCTURE SKILLS

DIRECTIONS: Choose the sentence that expresses the thought most clearly and that has no error in structure.

1. (A)   Many gases are invisible, odorless, and they have no taste.

   (B)   Many gases are invisible, odorless, and have no taste.

   (C)   Many gases are invisible, odorless, and tasteless.

2. (A)   Everyone agreed that she had neither the voice or the skill to be a speaker.

   (B)   Everyone agreed that she had neither the voice nor the skill to be a speaker.

   (C)   Everyone agreed that she had either the voice nor the skill to be a speaker.

3. (A)   The mayor will be remembered because he kept his campaign promises and because of his refusal to accept political favors.

   (B)   The mayor will be remembered because he kept his campaign promises and because he refused to accept political favors.

   (C)   The mayor will be remembered because of his refusal to accept political favors and he kept his campaign promises.

4. (A)   While taking a shower, the doorbell rang.

   (B)   While I was taking a shower, the doorbell rang.

   (C)   While taking a shower, someone rang the doorbell.

5. (A)   He swung the bat, while the runner stole second base.

   (B)   The runner stole second base while he swung the bat.

   (C)   While he was swinging the bat, the runner stole second base.

DIRECTIONS: Choose the correct option.

6. Nothing grows as well in Mississippi as <u>cotton. Cotton</u> being the state's principal crop.

    (A) cotton, cotton   (C) cotton cotton

    (B) cotton; cotton   (D) No change is necessary.

7. It was a heartwrenching <u>movie; one</u> that I had never seen before.

    (A) movie and   (C) movie. One

    (B) movie, one   (D) No change is necessary.

8. Traffic was stalled for three miles on the <u>bridge. Because</u> repairs were being made.

    (A) bridge because   (C) bridge, because

    (B) bridge; because   (D) No change is necessary.

9. The ability to write complete sentences comes with <u>practice writing</u> run-on sentences seems to occur naturally.

    (A) practice, writing   (C) practice and

    (B) practice. Writing   (D) No change is necessary.

10. Even though she had taken French classes, she could not understand native French <u>speakers they</u> all spoke too fast.

    (A) speakers, they   (C) speaking

    (B) speakers. They   (D) No change is necessary.

VERBS

Verb Forms

This section covers the principal parts of some irregular verbs including troublesome verbs like *lie* and *lay*. The use of regular verbs like *look* and *receive* poses no real problem to most writers since the past and past participle forms end in -*ed*; it is the irregular forms which pose the most serious problems—for example, *seen*, *written*, and *begun*.

Verb Tenses

Tense sequence indicates a logical time sequence.

Use present tense

in statements of universal truth:

> I learned that the sun *is* ninety-million miles from the earth.

in statements about the contents of literature and other published works:

> In this book, Sandy *becomes* a nun and *writes* a book on psychology.

Use past tense

in statements concerning writing or publication of a book:

> He *wrote* his first book in 1949, and it *was published* in 1952.

Use present perfect tense

for an action that began in the past but continues into the future:

> I *have lived* here all my life.

Use past perfect tense

for an earlier action that is mentioned in a later action:

> Cindy ate the apple that she *had picked*.

(First she picked it, then she ate it.)

Use future perfect tense

for an action that will have been completed at a specific future time:

> By May, I shall have graduated.

Use a present participle

for action that occurs at the same time as the verb:

> *Speeding* down the interstate, I saw a cop's flashing lights.

Use a perfect participle

for action that occurred before the main verb:

> *Having read* the directions, I started the test.

Use the subjunctive mood

to express a wish or state a condition contrary to fact:

> *If it were not raining*, we could have a picnic.

in *that* clauses after verbs like *request*, *recommend*, *suggest*, *ask*, *require*, and *insist*; and after such expressions as *it is important* and *it is necessary*:

> It is necessary that all papers *be* submitted on time.

Subject-Verb Agreement

Agreement is the grammatical correspondence between the subject and the verb of a sentence: *I do, we do, they do, he, she, it does.*

Every English verb has five forms, two of which are the bare form (plural) and the *-s* form (singular). Simply put, singular verb forms end in *-s*; plural forms do not.

Study these rules governing subject-verb agreement:

A verb must agree with its subject, not with any additive phrase in the sentence such as a prepositional or verbal phrase. Ignore such phrases.

> Your *copy* of the rules *is* on the desk.

> Ms. Craig's *record* of community service and outstanding teaching *qualifies* her for promotion.

In an inverted sentence beginning with a prepositional phrase, the verb still agrees with its subject.

> At the end of the summer *come* the best *sales*.

> Under the house *are* some old Mason *jars*.

Prepositional phrases beginning with compound prepositions such as *along with, together with, in addition to,* and *as well as* should be ignored, for they do not affect subject-verb agreement.

> *Gladys Knight*, as well as the Pips, *is* riding the midnight train to Georgia.

A verb must agree with its subject, not its subject complement.

> *Taxes are* a problem.

> A *problem is* taxes.

> His main *source* of pleasure *is* food and sleep.

> *Food and sleep are* his main source of pleasure.

When a sentence begins with an expletive such as *there, here*, or *it*, the verb agrees with the subject, not the expletive.

> Surely, there *are* several *alumni* who would be interested in forming a group.

> There *are* 50 *students* in my English class.

> There *is* a horrifying *study* on child abuse in *Psychology Today*.

Indefinite pronouns such as *each, either, one, everyone, everybody,* and *everything* are singular.

> *Somebody* in Detroit *loves* me.

> *Does either*[one] of you have a pencil?

> *Neither* of my brothers *has* a car.

Indefinite pronouns such as *several, few, both,* and *many* are plural.

> *Both* of my sorority sisters *have* decided to live off campus.

> *Few seek* the enlightenment of transcendental meditation.

Indefinite pronouns such as *all, some, most,* and *none* may be singular or plural depending on their referents.

> *Some* of the food *is* cold.

> *Some* of the vegetables *are* cold.

> I can think of some retorts, but *none seem* appropriate.

> *None* of the children *is* as sweet as Sally.

Fractions such as *one-half* and *one-third* may be singular or plural depending on the referent.

> *Half* of the mail *has* been delivered.

> *Half* of the letters *have* been read.

Subjects joined by *and* take a plural verb unless the subjects are considered one item or unit.

> *Jim* and *Tammy were* televangelists.

> *Simon and Garfunkel is* my favorite group.

In cases when the subjects are joined by *or, nor, either . . . or,* or *neither . . . nor,* the verb must agree with the subject closer to it.

> Either the teacher or the *students are* responsible.

> Neither the students nor the *teacher is* responsible.

Relative pronouns, such as *who, which,* or *that,* which refer to plural antecedents require plural verbs. However, when the relative pronoun refers to a singular subject, the pronoun takes a singular verb.

> She is one of the girls *who play basketball* on Friday nights.

> She is the only basketball player *who has* a broken leg.

Subjects preceded by *every, each,* and *many a* are singular.

> *Every* man, woman, and child *was* given a life preserver.

> *Each* undergraduate *is* required to pass a proficiency exam.

> *Many a* tear *has* to fall before one matures.

A collective noun, such as *audience, faculty, jury,* etc., requires a singular verb when the group is regarded as a whole, and a plural verb when the members of the group are regarded as individuals.

> The *jury has* made its decision.

> The *faculty are* preparing their grade rosters.

Subjects preceded by *the number of* or *the percentage of* are singular, while subjects preceded by *a number of* or *a percentage of* are plural.

> *The number of* vacationers in Florida *increases* every year.

> *A number of* vacationers *are* young couples.

Titles of books, companies, name brands, and groups are singular or plural depending on their meaning.

> *Great Expectations is* my favorite novel.

> The *Rolling Stones are* performing in the Super Dome.

Certain nouns of Latin and Greek origin have unusual singular and plural forms.

Singular	Plural
criterion	criteria
alumnus	alumni
datum	data
medium	media

> The *data are* available for inspection.

> The only *criterion* for membership *is* a high GPA.

Some nouns such as *deer*, *shrimp*, and *sheep* have the same spellings for both their singular and plural forms. In these cases, the meaning of the sentence will determine whether they are singular or plural.

> *Deer are* beautiful animals.

> The spotted *deer is* licking the sugar cube.

Some nouns like *scissors*, *jeans*, and *wages* have plural forms but no singular counterparts. These nouns almost always take plural verbs.

> The *scissors are* on the table.

> My new *jeans fit* me like a glove.

Words used as examples, not as grammatical parts of the sentence, require singular verbs.

> *Can't is* the contraction for "cannot."

> *Cats is* the plural form of "cat."

Mathematical expressions of subtraction and division require singular verbs, while expressions of addition and multiplication take either singular or plural verbs.

> Ten *divided* by two *equals* five.

> Five *times* two *equals* ten.

OR   Five times two *equal* ten.

Nouns expressing time, distance, weight, and measurement are singular when they refer to a unit and plural when they refer to separate items.

> *Fifty yards is* a short distance.

> *Ten years have* passed since I finished college.

Expressions of quantity are usually plural.

> *Nine out of ten* dentists *recommend* that their patients floss.

Some nouns ending in *-ics*, such as *economics* and *ethics*, take singular verbs when they refer to principles or a field of study; however, when they refer to individual practices, they usually take plural verbs.

> *Ethics is* being taught in the spring.

> His unusual business *ethics are* what got him into trouble.

Some nouns like *measles*, *news*, and *calculus* appear to be plural but are actually singular in number. These nouns require singular verbs.

> *Measles is* a very contagious disease.

> *Calculus requires* great skill in algebra.

A verbal noun (infinitive or gerund) serving as a subject is treated as singular, even if the object of the verbal phrase is plural.

> *Hiding* your mistakes does *not* make them go away.

> *To run* five miles *is* my goal.

A noun phrase or clause acting as the subject of a sentence requires a singular verb.

> What I need is to be loved.

> Whether there is any connection between them is unknown.

Clauses beginning with *what* may be singular or plural depending on the meaning, that is, whether *what* means "the thing" or "the things."

> What I want for Christmas is a new motorcycle.

> What matters are Clinton's ideas.

A plural subject followed by a singular appositive requires a plural verb; similarly, a singular subject followed by a plural appositive requires a singular verb.

> When the girls throw a party, *they* each bring a *gift*.

> The *board*, all ten members, *is* meeting today.

DRILL: VERBS

DIRECTIONS: Choose the correct option.

1. If you <u>had been concerned</u> about Marilyn, you <u>would have went</u> to greater lengths to ensure her safety.

    (A) had been concern . . . would have gone
    (B) was concerned . . . would have gone
    (C) had been concerned . . . would have gone
    (D) No change is necessary.

2. Susan <u>laid</u> in bed too long and missed her class.

    (A) lays   (C) lied
    (B) lay   (D) No change is necessary.

3. The Great Wall of China <u>is</u> fifteen hundred miles long; it <u>was built</u> in the third century B.C.

    (A) was . . . was built   (C) has been . . . was built
    (B) is . . . is built   (D) No change is necessary.

4. Joe stated that the class <u>began</u> at 10:30 a.m.

    (A) begins   (C) was beginning
    (B) had begun   (D) No change is necessary.

5. The ceiling of the Sistine Chapel <u>was</u> painted by Michelangelo; it <u>depicted</u> scenes from the Creation in the Old Testament.

    (A) was . . . depicts   (C) has been . . . depicting
    (B) is . . . depicts   (D) No change is necessary.

6. After Christmas <u>comes</u> the best sales.

    (A) has come   (C) is coming
    (B) come   (D) No change is necessary.

7. The bakery's specialty <u>are</u> wedding cakes.

   (A) is   (C) be
   (B) were   (D) No change is necessary.

8. Every man, woman, and child <u>were given</u> a life preserver.

   (A) have been given   (C) was given
   (B) had gave   (D) No change is necessary.

9. Hiding your mistakes <u>don't</u> make them go away.

   (A) doesn't   (C) have not
   (B) do not   (D) No change is necessary.

10. The Board of Regents <u>has recommended</u> a tuition increase.

   (A) have recommended   (C) had recommended
   (B) has recommend   (D) No change is necessary.

PRONOUNS

Pronoun Case

Pronoun case questions test your knowledge of the use of nominative

Nominative Case	Objective Case
I	me
he	him
she	her
we	us
they	them
who	whom

This review section answers the most frequently asked grammar questions: when to use *I* and when to use *me*; when to use *who* and when to use *whom*. Some writers avoid *whom* altogether, and instead of distinguishing between *I* and *me*, many writers incorrectly use *myself*.

Use the nominative case (subject pronouns)

for the subject of a sentence:

> *We* students studied until early morning for the final.

> Alan and *I* "burned the midnight oil," too.

for pronouns in apposition to the subject:

> Only two students, Alex and *I*, were asked to report on the meeting.

for the predicate nominative/subject complement:

> The actors nominated for the award were *she* and *I*.

for the subject of an elliptical clause:

> Molly is more experienced than *he*.

for the subject of a subordinate clause:

> Robert is the driver *who* reported the accident.

for the complement of an infinitive with no expressed subject:

> I would not want to be *he*.

Use the objective case (object pronouns)

for the direct object of a sentence:

> Mary invited *us* to her party.

for the object of a preposition:

> The books that were torn belonged to *her*.

> Just between you and *me*, I'm bored.

for the indirect object of a sentence:

> Walter gave a birthday gift to *her*.

for the appositive of a direct object:

> The committee elected two delegates, Barbara and *me*.

for the object of an infinitive:

> The young boy wanted to help *us* paint the fence.

for the object of a gerund:

> Enlisting *him* was surprisingly easy.

for the object of a past participle:

> Having called the other students and *us*, the secretary went home for the day.

for a pronoun that precedes an infinitive (the subject of an infinitive):

> The supervisor told *him* to work late.

for the complement of an infinitive with an expressed subject:

The fans thought the best player to be *him*.

for the object of an elliptical clause:

Bill tackled Joe harder than *me*.

for the object of a verb in apposition:

Charles invited two extra people, Carmen and *me*, to the party.

When a conjunction connects two pronouns or a pronoun and a noun, remove the "and" and the other pronoun or noun to determine what the correct pronoun form should be:

Mom gave ~~Tom and~~ myself a piece of cake.

Mom gave ~~Tom and~~ I a piece of cake

Mom gave ~~Tom and~~ me a piece of cake.

Removal of these words reveals what the correct pronoun should be:

Mom gave *me* a piece of cake.

The only pronouns that are acceptable after *between* and other prepositions are: *me, her, him, them,* and *whom*. When deciding between *who* and *whom*, try substituting *he* for *who* and *him* for *whom*; then follow these easy transformation steps:

1. Isolate the *who* clause or the *whom* clause:

    whom we can trust

2. Invert the word order, if necessary. Place the words in the clause in the natural order of an English sentence, subject followed by the verb:

    we can trust whom

3. Read the final form with the *he* or *him* inserted:

    We can trust ~~whom~~ him.

When a pronoun follows a comparative conjunction like *than* or *as*, complete the elliptical construction to help you determine which pronoun is correct.

EXAMPLE: She has more credit hours than me [do].

She has more credit hours than I [do].

Pronoun-Antecedent Agreement

These kinds of questions test your knowledge of using an appropriate pronoun to agree with its antecedent in number (singular or plural form) and gender (masculine, feminine, or neuter). An antecedent is a noun or pronoun to which another noun or pronoun refers.

Here are the two basic rules for pronoun reference-antecedent agreement:

1. Every pronoun must have a conspicuous antecedent.

2. Every pronoun must agree with its antecedent in number, gender, and person.

When an antecedent is one of dual gender like *student, singer, artist, person, citizen*, etc., use *his* or *her*. Some careful writers change the antecedent to a plural noun to avoid using the sexist, singular masculine pronoun his:

INCORRECT: Everyone hopes that he will win the lottery.

CORRECT: Most people hope that they will win the lottery.

Ordinarily, the relative pronoun *who* is used to refer to people, *which* to refer to things and places, *where* to refer to places, and *that* to refer to places or things. The distinction between *that* and *which* is a grammatical distinction (see the section on Word Choice Skills).

Many writers prefer to use *that* to refer to collective nouns.

EXAMPLE: A family *that* traces its lineage is usually proud of its roots.

Many writers, especially students, are not sure when to use the reflexive case pronoun and when to use the possessive case pronoun. The rules governing the usage of the reflexive case and the possessive case are quite simple.

Use the possessive case

before a noun in a sentence:

Our friend moved during the semester break.

My dog has fleas, but *her* dog doesn't.

before a gerund in a sentence:

Her running helps to relieve stress.

His driving terrified her.

as a noun in a sentence:

Mine was the last test graded that day.

to indicate possession:

Karen never allows anyone else to drive *her* car.

Brad thought the book was *his,* but it was someone else's.

Use the reflexive case

as a direct object to rename the subject:

I kicked *myself.*

as an indirect object to rename the subject:

Henry bought *himself* a tie.

as an object of a prepositional phrase:

Tom and Lillie baked the pie for *themselves.*

as a predicate pronoun:

She hasn't been *herself* lately.

Do not use the reflexive in place of the nominative pronoun:

INCORRECT: Both Randy and *myself* plan to go.

CORRECT: Both Randy and *I* plan to go.

INCORRECT: *Yourself* will take on the challenges of college.

CORRECT: *You* will take on the challenges of college.

INCORRECT: Either James or *yourself* will paint the mural.

CORRECT: Either James or *you* will paint the mural.

Watch out for careless use of the pronoun form:

INCORRECT: George *hisself* told me it was true.

CORRECT: George *himself* told me it was true.

INCORRECT: They washed the car *theirselves*.

CORRECT: They washed the car *themselves*.

Notice that reflexive pronouns are not set off by commas:

INCORRECT: Mary, *herself*, gave him the diploma.

CORRECT: Mary *herself* gave him the diploma.

INCORRECT: I will do it, *myself*.

CORRECT: I will do it *myself*.

Pronoun Reference

Pronoun reference questions require you to determine whether the antecedent is conspicuously written in the sentence or whether it is remote, implied, ambiguous, or vague, none of which results in clear writing. Make sure that every italicized pronoun has a conspicuous antecedent and that one pronoun substitutes only for another noun or pronoun, not for an idea or a sentence.

Pronoun reference problems occur

when a pronoun refers to either of two antecedents:

INCORRECT: Joanna told Jen that *she* was happy with her weight.

CORRECT: Joanna told Jen, "I'm happy with my weight."

when a pronoun refers to a remote antecedent:

INCORRECT: A strange car followed us closely, and *he* kept blinking his lights at us.

CORRECT: A strange car followed us closely, and its driver kept blinking his lights at us.

when *this*, *that*, and *which* refer to the general idea of the preceding clause or sentence rather than the preceding word:

INCORRECT: The students could not understand the pronoun reference handout, which annoyed them very much.

CORRECT: The students could not understand the pronoun reference handout, a fact which annoyed them very much.

OR   The students were annoyed because they could not understand the pronoun reference handout.

when a pronoun refers to an unexpressed but implied noun:

INCORRECT: My husband wants me to knit a blanket, but I'm not interested in it.

CORRECT: My husband wants me to knit a blanket, but I'm not interested in knitting.

when *it* is used as something other than an expletive to postpone a subject:

INCORRECT: It says in today's paper that the newest shipment of cars from Detroit, Michigan, seems to include outright imitations of European models.

CORRECT: Today's paper says that the newest shipment of cars from Detroit, Michigan, seems to include outright imitations of European models.

INCORRECT: The football game was canceled because it was bad weather.

CORRECT: The football game was canceled because the weather was bad.

when *they* or *it* is used to refer to something or someone indefinitely, and there is no definite antecedent:

INCORRECT: At the job placement office, they told me to stop wearing ripped jeans to my interviews.

CORRECT: At the job placement office, I was told to stop wearing ripped jeans to my interviews.

when the pronoun does not agree with its antecedent in number, gender, or person:

INCORRECT: Any graduate student, if they are interested, may attend the lecture.

CORRECT: Any graduate student, if he or she is interested, may attend the lecture.

OR   All graduate students, if they are interested, may attend the lecture.

INCORRECT: Many Americans are concerned that the overuse of slang and colloquialisms is corrupting the language.

CORRECT: Many Americans are concerned that the overuse of slang and colloquialisms is corrupting their language.

INCORRECT:	The Board of Regents will not make a decision about tuition increase until their March meeting.
CORRECT:	The Board of Regents will not make a decision about tuition increase until its March meeting.

when a noun or pronoun has no expressed antecedent:

INCORRECT:	In the President's address to the union, he promised no more taxes.
CORRECT:	In his address to the union, the President promised no more taxes.

DRILL: PRONOUNS

DIRECTIONS: Choose the correct option.

1. My friend and <u>myself</u> bought tickets for *Cats*.

    (A) I   (C) us

    (B) me   (D) No change is necessary.

2. Alcohol and tobacco are harmful to <u>whomever</u> consumes them.

    (A) whom   (C) whoever

    (B) who   (D) No change is necessary.

3. Everyone is wondering <u>whom</u> her successor will be.

    (A) who   (C) who'll

    (B) whose   (D) No change is necessary.

4. Rosa Lee's parents discovered that it was <u>her who</u> wrecked the family car.

    (A) she who   (C) her whom

    (B) she whom   (D) No change is necessary.

5. A student <u>who</u> wishes to protest <u>his or her</u> grades must file a formal grievance in the Dean's office.

    (A) that . . . their   (C) whom . . . their

    (B) which . . . his   (D) No change is necessary.

6. One of the best things about working for this company is that <u>they</u> pay big bonuses.

   (A) it pays
   (B) they always pay
   (C) they paid
   (D) No change is necessary.

7. Every car owner should be sure that <u>their</u> automobile insurance is adequate.

   (A) your
   (B) his or her
   (C) its
   (D) No change is necessary.

8. My mother wants me to become a teacher, but I'm not interested in <u>it</u>.

   (A) this
   (B) teaching
   (C) that
   (D) No change is necessary.

9. Since I had not paid my electric bill, <u>they</u> sent me a delinquent notice.

   (A) the power company
   (B) he
   (C) it
   (D) No change is necessary.

10. Margaret seldom wrote to her sister when <u>she</u> was away at college.

    (A) who
    (B) her
    (C) her sister
    (D) No change is necessary.

ADJECTIVES AND ADVERBS

Correct Usage

Adjectives are words that modify nouns or pronouns by defining, describing, limiting, or qualifying those nouns or pronouns.

Adverbs are words that modify verbs, adjectives, or other adverbs and that express such ideas as time, place, manner, cause, and degree. Use adjectives as subject complements with linking verbs; use adverbs with action verbs.

EXAMPLE:	The old man's speech was *eloquent*	ADJECTIVE
	Mr. Brown speaks *eloquently*.	ADVERB
	Please be *careful*.	ADJECTIVE
	Please drive *carefully*	ADVERB

Good or well

Good is an adjective; its use as an adverb is colloquial and nonstandard.

INCORRECT: He plays *good.*

   CORRECT: He looks *good* to be an octogenarian.

                      The quiche tastes very *good.*

Well may be either an adverb or an adjective. As an adjective, *well* means "in good health."

   CORRECT: He plays *well.*   ADVERB

                      My mother is not *well.*   ADJECTIVE

Bad or badly

Bad is an adjective used after sense verbs such as *look, smell, taste, feel,* or *sound,* or after linking verbs (*is, am, are, was, were*).

INCORRECT: I feel *badly* about the delay.

   CORRECT: I feel *bad* about the delay.

Badly is an adverb used after all other verbs.

INCORRECT: It doesn't hurt very *bad.*

   CORRECT: It doesn't hurt very *badly.*

Real or really

Real is an adjective; its use as an adverb is colloquial and nonstandard. It means "genuine."

INCORRECT: He writes real *well.*

   CORRECT: This is *real* leather.

Really is an adverb meaning "very."

INCORRECT: This is *really* diamond.

   CORRECT: Have a *really* nice day.

   EXAMPLE: This is *real* amethyst.   ADJECTIVE

                      This is *really* difficult.   ADVERB

                      This is a *real* crisis.   ADJECTIVE

                      This is *really* important.   ADVERB

Sort of and kind of

Sort of and *kind of* are often misused in written English by writers who actually mean *rather* or *somewhat.*

INCORRECT: Jan was *kind of* saddened by the results of the test.

   CORRECT: Jan was *somewhat* saddened by the results of the test.

Faulty Comparisons

Sentences containing a faulty comparison often sound correct because their problem is not one of grammar but of logic. Read these sentences closely to make sure that like things are being compared, that the comparisons are complete, and that the comparisons are logical.

When comparing two persons or things, use the comparative, not the superlative form, of an adjective or an adverb. Use the superlative form for comparison of more than two persons or things. Use *any*, *other*, or *else* when comparing one thing or person with a group of which it/he or she is a part.

Most one- and two-syllable words form their comparative and superlative degrees with -*er* and -*est* suffixes. Adjectives and adverbs of more than two syllables form their comparative and superlative degrees with the addition of *more* and *most*.

Positive	Comparative	Superlative
good	better	best
old	older	oldest
friendly	friendlier	friendliest
lonely	lonelier	loneliest
talented	more talented	most talented
beautiful	more beautiful	most beautiful

A double comparison occurs when the degree of the modifier is changed incorrectly by adding both -*er* and *more* or -*est* and *most* to the adjective or adverb.

INCORRECT: He is the *most nicest* brother.

CORRECT: He is the *nicest* brother.

INCORRECT: She is the *more meaner* of the sisters.

CORRECT: She is the *meaner* sister.

Illogical comparisons occur when there is an implied comparison between two things that are not actually being compared or that cannot be logically compared.

INCORRECT: The interest at a loan company is higher *than* a bank.

CORRECT: The interest at a loan company is higher *than* that *at* a bank.

OR The interest at a loan company is higher *than at* a bank.

Ambiguous comparisons occur when elliptical words (those omitted) create for the reader more than one interpretation of the sentence.

INCORRECT: I like Mary better than you. (than you *what*?)

CORRECT: I like Mary better than I like you.

OR I like Mary better than you do.

Incomplete comparisons occur when the basis of the comparison (the two categories being compared) is not explicitly stated.

INCORRECT: Skywriting is *more* spectacular.

CORRECT: Skywriting is *more* spectacular *than* billboard advertising.

Do not omit the words *other*, *any*, or *else* when comparing one thing or person with a group of which it/he or she is a part.

INCORRECT: Joan writes better *than any* student in her class.

CORRECT: Joan writes better *than any other* student in her class.

Do not omit the second *as* of *as . . .as* when making a point of equal or superior comparison.

INCORRECT: The University of West Florida is *as large* or larger than the University of North Florida.

CORRECT: The University of West Florida is *as large as* or larger than the University of Northern Florida.

Do not omit the first category of the comparison, even if the two categories are the same.

INCORRECT: This is one of the best, if not the best, college in the country.

CORRECT: This is one of the best colleges in the country, if not the best.

The problem with the incorrect sentence is that *one of the best* requires the plural word *colleges*, not *college*.

DRILL: ADJECTIVES AND ADVERBS

DIRECTIONS: Choose the correct option.

1. Although the band performed <u>badly</u>, I feel <u>real bad</u> about missing the concert.

    (A) badly . . . real badly   (C) badly . . .very bad

    (B) bad . . . badly   (D) No change is necessary.

2. These reports are <u>relative simple</u> to prepare.

    (A) relatively simple   (C) relatively simply

    (B) relative simply   (D) No change is necessary.

3. He did <u>very well</u> on the test although his writing skills are not <u>good</u>.

    (A) real well . . . good   (C) good . . . great

    (B) very good . . . good   (D) No change is necessary.

4. Shake the medicine bottle <u>good</u> before you open it.

    (A) very good   (C) well

    (B) real good   (D) No change is necessary.

5. Though she speaks <u>fluently</u>, she writes <u>poorly</u> because she doesn't observe <u>closely</u> or think <u>clear</u>.

    (A) fluently, poorly, closely, clearly

    (B) fluent, poor, close, clear

    (C) fluently, poor, closely, clear

    (D) No change is necessary.

<u>DIRECTIONS</u>: Select the sentence that clearly and effectively states the idea and has no structural errors.

6.   (A) Los Angeles is larger than any city in California.

    (B) Los Angeles is larger than all the cities in California.

    (C) Los Angeles is larger than any other city in California.

7.   (A) Art history is as interesting as, if not more interesting than, music appreciation.

    (B) Art history is as interesting, if not more interesting than, music appreciation.

    (C) Art history is as interesting as, if not more interesting, music appreciation.

8.   (A) The baseball team here is as good as any other university.

    (B) The baseball team here is as good as all the other universities.

    (C) The baseball team here is as good as any other university's.

9.   (A) I like him better than you.

    (B) I like him better than I like you.

    (C) I like him better.

10. (A) You are the most stingiest person I know.

    (B) You are the most stingier person I know.

    (C) You are the stingiest person I know.

PUNCTUATION

Commas

Commas should be placed according to standard rules of punctuation for purpose, clarity, and effect. The proper use of commas is explained in the following rules and examples:

In a series:

When more than one adjective describes a noun, use a comma to separate and emphasize each adjective. The comma takes the place of the word *and* in the series.

> the long, dark passageway
>
> another confusing, sleepless night
>
> an elaborate, complex, brilliant plan
>
> the old, grey, crumpled hat

Some adjective-noun combinations are thought of as one word. In these cases, the adjective in front of the adjective-noun combination needs no comma. If you inserted *and* between the adjective-noun combination, it would not make sense.

> a stately oak tree
>
> an exceptional wine glass
>
> my worst report card
>
> a china dinner plate

The comma is also used to separate words, phrases, and whole ideas (clauses); it still takes the place of *and* when used this way.

> an apple, a pear, a fig, and a banana
>
> a handsome man, an elegant suit, and many admirers
>
> She lowered the shade, closed the curtain, turned off the light, and went to bed.

The only question that exists about the use of commas in a series is whether or not one should be used before the final item. It is standard usage to do so, although many newspapers and magazines have stopped using the final comma. Occasionally, the omission of the comma can be confusing.

> INCORRECT: He got on his horse, tracked a rabbit and a deer and rode on to Canton.
>
> We planned the trip with Mary and Harold, Susan, Dick and Joan, Gregory and Jean and Charles.

With a long introductory phrase:

Usually if a phrase of more than five or six words or a dependent clause precedes the subject at the beginning of a sentence, a comma is used to set it off.

> After last night's fiasco at the disco, she couldn't bear the thought of
>
> looking at him again.

Whenever I try to talk about politics, my husband leaves the room.

Provided you have said nothing, they will never guess who you are.

It is not necessary to use a comma with a short sentence.

In January she will go to Switzerland.

After I rest I'll feel better.

During the day no one is home.

If an introductory phrase includes a verb form that is being used as another part of speech (a *verbal*), it must be followed by a comma.

INCORRECT: When eating Mary never looked up from her plate.

CORRECT: When eating, Mary never looked up from her plate.

INCORRECT: Because of her desire to follow her faith in James wavered.

CORRECT: Because of her desire to follow, her faith in James wavered.

INCORRECT: Having decided to leave Mary James wrote her a letter.

CORRECT: Having decided to leave Mary, James wrote her a letter.

To separate sentences with two main ideas:

To understand this use of the comma, you need to be able to recognize compound sentences. When a sentence contains more than two subjects and verbs (clauses), and the two clauses are joined by a conjunction (*and, but, or, nor, for, yet*), use a comma before the conjunction to show that another clause is coming.

I thought I knew the poem by heart, but he showed me three lines I had forgotten.

Are we really interested in helping the children, or are we more concerned with protecting our good names?

He is supposed to leave tomorrow, but he is not ready to go.

Jim knows you are disappointed, and he has known it for a long time.

If the two parts of the sentence are short and closely related, it is not necessary to use a comma.

He threw the ball and the dog ran after it.

Jane played the piano and Michael danced.

Be careful not to confuse a sentence that has a compound verb and a single subject with a compound sentence. If the subject is the same for both verbs, there is no need for a comma.

INCORRECT: Charles sent some flowers, and wrote a long letter explaining why he had not been able to attend.

CORRECT: Charles sent some flowers and wrote a long letter explaining why he had not been able to attend.

INCORRECT: Last Thursday we went to the concert with Julia, and afterwards dined at an old Italian restaurant.

CORRECT: Last Thursday we went to the concert with Julia and afterwards dined at an old Italian restaurant.

INCORRECT: For the third time, the teacher explained that the literacy level for high school students was much lower than it had been in previous years, and, this time, wrote the statistics on the board for everyone to see.

CORRECT: For the third time, the teacher explained that the literacy level for high school students was much lower than it had been in previous years and this time wrote the statistics on the board for everyone to see.

In general, words and phrases that stop the flow of the sentence or are unnecessary for the main idea are set off by commas.

Abbreviations after names:

Did you invite John Paul, Jr., and his sister?

Martha Harris, Ph.D., will be the speaker tonight.

Interjections (an exclamation without added grammatical connection):

Oh, I'm so glad to see you.

I tried so hard, alas, to do it.

Hey, let me out of here.

Direct address:

Roy, won't you open the door for the dog?

I can't understand, Mother, what you are trying to say.

May I ask, Mr. President, why you called us together?

Hey, lady, watch out for that car!

Tag questions:

I'm really hungry, aren't you?

Jerry looks like his father, doesn't he?

Geographical names and addresses:

The concert will be held in Chicago, Illinois, on August 12.

The letter was addressed to Ms. Marion Heartwell, 1881 Pine Lane, Palo Alto, California 95824.

(Note: No comma is needed before the zip code, because it is already clearly set off from the state name.)

Transitional words and phrases:

On the other hand, I hope he gets better.

In addition, the phone rang constantly this afternoon.

I'm, nevertheless, going to the beach on Sunday.

You'll find, therefore, that no one is more loyal than I am.

Parenthetical words and phrases:

You will become, I believe, a great stateswoman.

We know, of course, that this is the only thing to do.

In fact, I planted corn last summer.

The Mannes affair was, to put it mildly, a surprise.

Unusual word order:

The dress, new and crisp, hung in the closet.

Intently, she stared out the window.

With nonrestrictive elements:

Parts of a sentence that modify other parts are sometimes essential to the meaning of the sentence and sometimes not. When a modifying word or group of words is not vital to the meaning of the sentence, it is set off by commas. Since it does not restrict the meaning of the words it modifies, it is called "nonrestrictive." Modifiers that are essential to the meaning of the sentence are called "restrictive" and are not set off by commas.

| ESSENTIAL: | The woman *who wrote* the story is my sister. |
| NONESSENTIAL: | My sister, *the woman who wrote* the story, has always loved to write. |

| ESSENTIAL: | John Milton's famous poem *Paradise Lost* tells a remarkable story. |
| NONESSENTIAL: | Dante's greatest work, *The Divine Comedy*, marked the beginning of the Renaissance. |

| ESSENTIAL: | The cup *that is on the piano* is the one I want. |
| NONESSENTIAL: | The cup, *which my brother gave me last year*, is on the piano. |

| ESSENTIAL: | The people *who arrived late* were not seated. |
| NONESSENTIAL: | George, *who arrived late*, was not seated. |

To set off direct quotations:

Most direct quotes or quoted materials are set off from the rest of the sentence by commas.

"Please read your part more loudly," the director insisted.

"I won't know what to do," said Michael, "if you leave me."

The teacher said sternly, "I will not dismiss this class until I have silence."

Who was it who said "Do not ask for whom the bell tolls; it tolls for thee"?

Note: Commas always go inside the closing quotation mark, even if the comma is not part of the material being quoted.

Be careful not to set off indirect quotes or quotes that are used as subjects or complements.

"To be or not to be" is the famous beginning of a soliloquy in Shakespeare's *Hamlet*. (subject)

She said she would never come back. (indirect quote)

Back then my favorite poem was "Evangeline." (complement)

To set off contrasting elements:

Her intelligence, not her beauty, got her the job.

Your plan will take you a little further from, rather than closer to, your destination.

It was a reasonable, though not appealing, idea.

He wanted glory, but found happiness instead.

In dates:

Both forms of the date are acceptable.

She will arrive on April 6, 1998.

He left on 5 December 2000.

In January 1997, he handed in his resignation.

On October 22, 1992, Frank and Julie were married.

Usually, when a subordinate clause is at the end of a sentence, no comma is necessary preceding the clause. However, when a subordinate clause introduces a sentence, a comma should be used after the clause. Some common subordinating conjunctions are:

after	so that
although	though
as	till
as if	unless
because	until
before	when
even though	whenever

if	while
inasmuch as	since

Semicolons

Questions testing semicolon usage require you to be able to distinguish between the semicolon and the comma, and the semicolon and the colon. This review section covers the basic uses of the semicolon: to separate independent clauses not joined by a coordinating conjunction, to separate independent clauses separated by a conjunctive adverb, and to separate items in a series with internal commas. It is important to be consistent; if you use a semicolon between *any* of the items in the series, you must use semicolons to separate *all* of the items in the series.

Usually, a comma follows the conjunctive adverb. Note also that a period can be used to separate two sentences joined by a conjunctive adverb. Some common conjunctive adverbs are:

accordingly	nevertheless
besides	next
consequently	nonetheless
finally	now
furthermore	on the other hand
however	otherwise
indeed	perhaps
in fact	still
moreover	therefore

Then is also used as a conjunctive adverb, but it is not usually followed by a comma.

Use the semicolon

to separate independent clauses which are not joined by a coordinating conjunction:

I understand how to use commas; the semicolon I have not yet mastered.

to separate two independent clauses connected by a conjunctive adverb:

He took great care with his work; *therefore*, he was very successful.

to combine two independent clauses connected by a coordinating conjunction if either or both of the clauses contain other internal punctuation:

Success in college, some maintain, requires intelligence, industry, and perseverance; *but* others, fewer in number, assert that only personality is important.

to separate items in a series when each item has internal punctuation:

I bought an old, dilapidated chair; an antique table which was in beautiful condition; and a new, ugly, blue and white rug.

Call our customer service line for assistance: Arizona, 1-800-555-6020; New Mexico, 1-800-555-5050; California, 1-800-555-3140; or Nevada, 1-800-555-3214.

Do not use the semicolon

to separate a dependent and an independent clause:

INCORRECT: You should not make such statements; even though they are correct.

CORRECT: You should not make such statements even though they are correct.

to separate an appositive phrase or clause from a sentence:

INCORRECT: Her immediate aim in life is centered around two things; becoming an engineer and learning to fly an airplane.

CORRECT: Her immediate aim in life is centered around two things: becoming an engineer and learning to fly an airplane.

to precede an explanation or summary of the first clause:

Note: Although the sentence below is punctuated correctly, the use of the semicolon provides a miscue, suggesting that the second clause is merely an extension, not an explanation, of the first clause. The colon provides a better clue.

WEAK: The first week of camping was wonderful; we lived in cabins instead of tents.

BETTER: The first week of camping was wonderful: we lived in cabins instead of tents.

to substitute for a comma:

INCORRECT: My roommate also likes sports; particularly football, basketball, and baseball.

CORRECT: My roommate also likes sports, particularly football, basketball, and baseball.

to set off other types of phrases or clauses from a sentence:

INCORRECT: Being of a cynical mind; I should ask for a recount of the ballots.

CORRECT: Being of a cynical mind, I should ask for a recount of the ballots.

_____

INCORRECT: The next meeting of the club has been postponed two weeks; inasmuch as both the president and vice-president are out of town.

CORRECT: The next meeting of the club has been postponed two weeks, inasmuch as both the president and vice-president are out of town.

Note: The semicolon is not a terminal mark of punctuation; therefore, it should not be followed by a capital letter unless the first word in the second clause ordinarily requires capitalization.

Colons

While it is true that a colon is used to precede a list, one must also make sure that a complete sentence precedes the colon. The colon signals the reader that a list, explanation, or restatement of the preceding will follow. It is like an arrow, indicating that something is to follow. The difference between the colon and the semicolon and between the colon and the period is that the colon is an introductory mark, not a terminal mark. Look at the following examples:

The Constitution provides for a separation of powers among the three branches of government.

government.	The period signals a new sentence.
government;	The semicolon signals an interrelated sentence.
government,	The comma signals a coordinating conjunction followed by another independent clause.
government:	The colon signals a list.

The Constitution provides for a separation of powers among the three branches of *government*: executive, legislative, and judicial.

Ensuring that a complete sentence precedes a colon means following these rules:

Use the colon to introduce a list (one item may constitute a list):

> I hate this one course: English.

> Three plays by William Shakespeare will be presented in repertory this summer at the University of Michigan: *Hamlet, Macbeth,* and *Othello*.

To introduce a list preceded by *as follows* or *the following*:

> The reasons he cited for his success are as follows: integrity, honesty, industry, and a pleasant disposition.

To separate two independent clauses, when the second clause is a restatement or explanation of the first:

> All of my high school teachers said one thing in particular: college is going to be difficult.

To introduce a word or word group which is a restatement, explanation, or summary of the first sentence:

> She asks for two things: a pen and a sheet of paper.

To introduce a formal appositive:

> I am positive there is one appeal which you can't overlook: money.

To separate the introductory words from a quotation which follows, if the quotation is formal, long, or paragraphed separately:

> The actor then stated: "I would rather be able to adequately play the part of Hamlet than to perform a miraculous operation, deliver a great lecture, or build a magnificent skyscraper."

The colon should only be used after statements that are grammatically complete.

Do *not* use a colon after a verb:

INCORRECT: My favorite holidays are: Christmas, New Year's, and Halloween.

CORRECT: My favorite holidays are Christmas, New Year's, and Halloween.

Do *not* use a colon after a preposition:

INCORRECT: I enjoy different ethnic foods such as: Greek, Chinese, and Italian.

CORRECT: I enjoy different ethnic foods such as Greek, Chinese, and Italian.

Do *not* use a colon interchangeably with the dash:

INCORRECT: Mathematics, German, English: These gave me the greatest difficulty of all my studies.

CORRECT: Mathematics, German, English—these gave me the greatest difficulty of all my studies.

Information preceding the colon should be a complete sentence regardless of the explanatory information following the clause.

Do *not* use the colon before the words *for example*, *namely*, *that is*, or *for instance* even though these words may be introducing a list.

INCORRECT: We agreed to it: namely, to give him a surprise party.

CORRECT: There are a number of well-known American women writers: for example, Nikki Giovanni, Phillis Wheatley, Emily Dickinson, and Maya Angelou.

Colon usage questions test your knowledge of the colon preceding a list, restatement, or explanation. These questions also require you to be able to distinguish between the colon and the period, the colon and the comma, and the colon and the semicolon.

Apostrophes

Apostrophe questions require you to know when an apostrophe has been used appropriately to make a noun possessive, not plural. Remember the following rules when considering how to show possession.

Add *'s* to singular nouns and indefinite pronouns:

> Tiffany's flowers
>
> a dog's bark
>
> everybody's computer
>
> at the owner's expense
>
> today's paper

Add *'s* to singular nouns ending in s, unless this distorts the pronunciation:

> Delores's paper
>
> the boss's pen
>
> Dr. Yots' class
>
> for righteousness' sake
>
> Dr. Evans's office OR Dr. Evans' office

Add *an apostrophe* to plural nouns ending in *s* or *es*:

> two cents' worth

ladies' night

thirteen years' experience

two weeks' pay

Add *'s* to plural nouns not ending in *s*:

men's room

children's toys

Add *'s* to the last word in compound words or groups:

brother-in-law's car

someone else's paper

Add *'s* to the last name when indicating joint ownership:

Joe and Edna's home

Julie and Kathy's party

women and children's clinic

Add *'s* to both names if you intend to show ownership by each person:

Joe's and Edna's trucks

Julie's and Kathy's pies

Ted's and Jane's marriage vows

Possessive pronouns change their forms *without* the addition of an apostrophe:

her, his, hers

your, yours

their, theirs

it, its

Use the possessive form of a noun preceding a gerund:

His driving annoys me.

My bowling a strike irritated him.

Do you mind our stopping by?

We appreciate your coming.

Unless confusion will result, add *s* alone to form the plural of single or multiple letters or numerals used as words:

TVs

IRAs

the three Rs

the 1800s

POWs

But:

> SOS's

Use *'s* when forming the plural of abbreviations with periods:

> R.N.'s

Quotation Marks and Italics

These kinds of questions test your knowledge of the proper use of quotation marks with other marks of punctuation, with titles, and with dialogue. These kinds of questions also test your knowledge of the correct use of italics and underlining with titles and words used as sample words (for example, *the word is is a common verb*).

The most common use of double quotation marks (") is to set off quoted words, phrases, and sentences.

> "If everybody minded their own business," said the Duchess in a hoarse growl, "the world would go round a great deal faster than it does."
>
> "Then you would say what you mean," the March Hare went on.
>
> "I do," Alice hastily replied: "at least—at least I mean what I say— that's the same thing, you know."
>
> —from Lewis Carroll's *Alice in Wonderland*

Single quotation marks are used to set off quoted material within a quote.

> "Shall I bring 'Rime of the Ancient Mariner' along with us?" she asked her brother.
>
> Mrs. Green said, "The doctor told me, 'Go immediately to bed when you get home!'"
>
> "If she said that to me," Katherine insisted, "I would tell her, 'I never intend to speak to you again! Goodbye, Susan!'"

When writing dialogue, begin a new paragraph each time the speaker changes.

> "Do you know what time it is?" asked Jane.
>
> "Can't you see I'm busy?" snapped Mary.
>
> "It's easy to see that you're in a bad mood today!" replied Jane.

Use quotation marks to enclose words used as words (sometimes italics are used for this purpose).

> "Judgment" has always been a difficult word for me to spell.
>
> Do you know what "abstruse" means?
>
> "Horse and buggy" and "bread and butter" can be used either as adjectives or as nouns.

If slang is used within more formal writing, the slang words or phrases should be set off with quotation marks.

> Harrison's decision to leave the conference and to "stick his neck out" by flying to Jamaica was applauded by the rest of the conference attendees.

When words are meant to have an unusual or specific significance to the reader—for instance, irony or humor—they are sometimes placed in quotation marks.

> For years, women were not allowed to buy real estate in order to "protect" them from unscrupulous dealers.

> The "conversation" resulted in one black eye and a broken nose.

To set off titles of TV shows, poems, stories, and book chapters, use quotation marks. (Book, motion picture, newspaper, and magazine titles are underlined when handwritten and italicized when printed.)

> The article "Moving South in the Southern Rain," by Jergen Smith in the *Southern News*, attracted the attention of our editor.

> The assignment is "Childhood Development," Chapter 18 of *Human Behavior*.

> My favorite essay by Montaigne is "On Silence."

> "Happy Days" led the TV ratings for years, didn't it?

> You will find Keats' "Ode on a Grecian Urn" in Chapter 3, "The Romantic Era," in Lastly's *Selections from Great English Poets*.

Errors to avoid:

321

Be sure to remember that quotation marks always come in pairs. Do not make the mistake of using only one set.

INCORRECT:	"You'll never convince me to move to the city, said Thurman. I consider it an insane asylum."
CORRECT:	"You'll never convince me to move to the city," said Thurman. "I consider it an insane asylum."

INCORRECT:	"Idleness and pride tax with a heavier hand than kings and parliaments," Benjamin Franklin is supposed to have said. If we can get rid of the former, we may easily bear the latter."
CORRECT:	"Idleness and pride tax with a heavier hand than kings and parliaments," Benjamin Franklin is supposed to have said. "If we can get rid of the former, we may easily bear the latter."

When a quote consists of several sentences, do not put the quotation marks at the beginning and end of each sentence; put them at the beginning and end of the entire quotation.

INCORRECT:	"It was during his student days in Bonn that Beethoven fastened upon Schiller's poem." "The heady sense of liberation in the verses must have appealed to him." "They appealed to every German." —John Burke
CORRECT:	"It was during his student days in Bonn that Beethoven fastened upon Schiller's poem. The heady sense of liberation in the verses must have appealed to him. They appealed to every German." —John Burke

Instead of setting off a long quote with quotation marks, if it is longer than five or six lines you may want to indent and single space it. If you do indent, do not use quotation marks.

> In his *First Inaugural Address*, Abraham Lincoln appeals to the strife-torn American people:

> > We are not enemies, but friends. We must not be enemies. Though passion may have strained, it must not break, our bonds of affection. The mystic chords of memory, stretching from every battlefield and patriot grave to every living heart and hearthstone all over this broad land, will yet swell the chorus of the Union when again touched, as surely they will be, by the better angels of our nature.

Be careful not to use quotation marks with indirect quotations.

INCORRECT: Mary wondered "if she would get over it."

CORRECT: Mary wondered if she would get over it.

———————

INCORRECT: The nurse asked "how long it had been since we had visited the doctor's office."

CORRECT: The nurse asked how long it had been since we had visited the doctor's office.

When you quote several paragraphs, it is not sufficient to place quotation marks at the beginning and end of the entire quote. Place quotation marks at the *beginning of each paragraph*, but only at the *end of the last paragraph*. Here is an abbreviated quotation for an example:

> "Here begins an odyssey through the world of classical mythology, starting with the creation of the world . . .

> "It is true that themes similar to the classical may be found in any corpus of mythology . . . Even technology is not immune to the influence of Greece and Rome . . .

> "We need hardly mention the extent to which painters and sculptors . . . have used and adapted classical mythology to illustrate the past, to reveal the human body, to express romantic or antiromantic ideals, or to symbolize any particular point of view."

Remember that commas and periods are *always* placed inside the quotation marks even if they are not actually part of the quote.

INCORRECT: "Life always gets colder near the summit", Nietzsche is purported to have said, "—the cold increases, responsibility grows".

CORRECT: "Life always gets colder near the summit," Nietzsche is purported to have said, "—the cold increases, responsibility grows."

———————

INCORRECT: "Get down here right away", John cried. "You'll miss the sunset if you don't."

CORRECT: "Get down here right away," John cried. "You'll miss the sunset if you don't."

———————

INCORRECT:	"If my dog could talk", Mary mused, "I'll bet he would say, 'Take me for a walk right this minute'".
CORRECT:	"If my dog could talk," Mary mused, "I'll bet he would say, 'Take me for a walk right this minute'."

Other marks of punctuation, such as question marks, exclamation points, colons, and semi-colons, go inside the quotation marks if they are part of the quoted material. If they are not part of the quotation, however, they go outside the quotation marks. Be careful to distinguish between the guidelines for the comma and period, which always go inside the quotation marks, and those for other marks of punctuation.

INCORRECT:	"I'll always love you"! he exclaimed happily.
CORRECT:	"I'll always love you!" he exclaimed happily.

INCORRECT:	Did you hear her say, "He'll be there early?"
CORRECT:	Did you hear her say, "He'll be there early"?

INCORRECT:	She called down the stairs, "When are you going"?
CORRECT:	She called down the stairs, "When are you going?"

INCORRECT:	"Let me out"! he cried. "Don't you have any pity"?
CORRECT:	"Let me out!" he cried. "Don't you have any pity?"

Remember to use only one mark of punctuation at the end of a sentence ending with a quotation mark.

INCORRECT:	She thought out loud, "Will I ever finish this paper in time for that class?".
CORRECT:	She thought out loud, "Will I ever finish this paper in time for that class?"

INCORRECT:	"Not the same thing a bit!", said the Hatter. "Why, you might just as well say that 'I see what I eat' is the same thing as 'I eat what I see'!".
CORRECT:	"Not the same thing a bit!" said the Hatter. "Why, you might just as well say that 'I see what I eat' is the same thing as 'I eat what I see'!"

DRILL: PUNCTUATION

<u>DIRECTIONS</u>: **Choose the correct option.**

1. Indianola, <u>Mississippi, where B.B. King and my father grew up,</u> has a population of less than 50,000 people.

    (A) Mississippi where, B.B. King and my father grew up,

    (B) Mississippi where B.B. King and my father grew up,

    (C) Mississippi; where B.B. King and my father grew up,

    (D) No change is necessary.

2. John Steinbeck's best known novel *The Grapes of Wrath* is the story of the <u>Joads and Oklahoma family</u> who were driven from their dustbowl farm and forced to become migrant workers in California.

    (A) Joads, an Oklahoma family

    (B) Joads, an Oklahoma family,

    (C) Joads; an Oklahoma family

    (D) No change is necessary.

3. All students who are interested in student teaching next <u>semester, must submit an application to the Teacher Education Office.</u>

    (A) semester must submit an application to the Teacher Education Office.

    (B) semester, must submit an application, to the Teacher Education Office.

    (C) semester: must submit an application to the Teacher Education Office.

    (D) No change is necessary.

4. Whenever you travel by <u>car, or plane, you</u> must wear a seatbelt.

    (A) car or plane you   (C) car or plane, you

    (B) car, or plane you   (D) No change is necessary.

5. Wearing a seatbelt is not just a good <u>idea, it's</u> the law.

    (A) idea; it's   (C) idea. It's

    (B) idea it's   (D) No change is necessary.

6. Senators and representatives can be reelected <u>indefinitely; a</u> president can only serve two terms.

    (A) indefinitely but a   (C) indefinitely a
    (B) indefinitely, a   (D) No change is necessary.

7. Students must pay a penalty for overdue library <u>books, however,</u> there is a grace period.

    (A) books; however, there   (C) books: however, there
    (B) books however, there   (D) No change is necessary.

8. Among the states that seceded from the Union to join the Confederacy in 1860-1861 <u>were:</u> Mississippi, Florida, and Alabama.

    (A) were   (C) were.
    (B) were;   (D) No change is necessary.

9. The art exhibit displayed works by many famous <u>artists such as:</u> Dali, Picasso, and Michelangelo.

    (A) artists such as;   (C) artists. Such as
    (B) artists such as   (D) No change is necessary.

10. The National Shakespeare Company will perform <u>the following plays:</u> *Othello*, *Macbeth*, *Hamlet*, and *As You Like It*.

    (A) the following plays,   (C) the following plays
    (B) the following plays;   (D) No change is necessary.

ENGLISH LANGUAGE SKILLS

ANSWER KEY

Drill: Word Choice Skills

1.	(D)	4.	(C)	7.	(A)	10.	(B)
2.	(D)	5.	(A)	8.	(B)		
3.	(A)	6.	(C)	9.	(C)		

Drill: Sentence Structure Skills

1.	(C)	4.	(B)	7.	(B)	10.	(B)
2.	(B)	5.	(A)	8.	(A)		
3.	(B)	6.	(A)	9.	(B)		

Drill: Verbs

1.	(C)	4.	(A)	7.	(A)	10.	(D)
2.	(D)	5.	(A)	8.	(C)		
3.	(D)	6.	(B)	9.	(A)		

Drill: Pronouns

1.	(A)	4.	(A)	7.	(B)	10.	(C)
2.	(C)	5.	(D)	8.	(B)		
3.	(A)	6.	(A)	9.	(A)		

Drill: Adjectives and Adverbs

1.	(C)	4.	(C)	7.	(A)	10.	(C)
2.	(A)	5.	(A)	8.	(C)		
3.	(D)	6.	(C)	9.	(B)		

Drill: Punctuation

1.	(D)	4.	(C)	7.	(A)	10.	(D)
2.	(A)	5.	(A)	8.	(A)		
3.	(A)	6.	(D)	9.	(B)		

DETAILED EXPLANATIONS OF ANSWERS

Drill: Word Choice Skills

1. (D) Choice (D) is correct. No change is necessary. *Principal* as a noun means "head of a school." *Principle* is a noun meaning "axiom" or "rule of conduct."

2. (D) Choice (D) is correct. No change is necessary. *Affect* is a verb meaning "to influence" or "to change." *Effect* as a noun meaning "result."

3. (A) Choice (A) is correct. Use *amount* with noncountable, mass nouns (*amount* of food, help, money); use *number* with countable, plural nouns (*number* of children, classes, bills).

4. (C) Choice (C) is correct. *Supposed to* and *used to* should be spelled with a final *d*. *Achieving* follows the standard spelling rule—*i* before *e*.

5. (A) Choice (A) is correct. Use *that*, not *because*, to introduce clauses after the word *reason*. Choice (A) is also the only choice that contains the correct spelling of "succeeded."

6. (C) Choice (C) is correct. *Converge together* is redundant, and *single* is not needed to convey the meaning of a *highway*.

7. (A) Choice (A) is correct. It is economical and concise. The other choices contain unnecessary repetition.

8. (B) Choice (B) is correct. Choices (A) and (C) pad the sentences with loose synonyms that are redundant. Choice (D), although a short sentence, does not convey the meaning as clearly as choice (B).

9. (C) Choice (C) is correct. The other choices all contain unnecessary repetition.

10. (B) Choice (B) is correct. Choices (A) and (C) contain circumlocution; they fail to get to the point. Choice (D) does not express the meaning of the sentence as concisely as choice (B).

Drill: Sentence Structure Skills

1. (C) Choice (C) is correct. Each response contains items in a series. In choices (A) and (B), the word group after the conjunction is not an adjective like the first words in the series. Choice (C) contains three adjectives.

2. (B) Choice (B) is correct. Choices (A), (C), and (D) combine conjunctions incorrectly.

3. (B) Choice (B) is correct. Choices (A) and (C) appear to be parallel because the conjunction *and* connects two word groups that both begin with *because*, but the structure on both sides of the conjunction are very different. *Because he kept his campaign promises* is a clause; *because of his refusal to accept political favors* is a prepositional phrase. Choice (B) connects two dependent clauses.

4. (B) Choice (B) is correct. Choices (A) and (C) contain the elliptical clause *While . . . taking a shower*. It appears that the missing subject in the elliptical clause is the same as that in the independent clause—the *doorbell* in choice (A) and *someone* in choice (C), neither of which is a logical subject for the verbal *taking a shower*. Choice (B) removes the elliptical clause and provides the logical subject.

5. (A) Choice (A) is correct. Who swung the bat? Choices (B) and (C) both imply that it is the runner who swung the bat. Only choice (A) makes it clear that as *he* swung the bat, someone else (the *runner*) stole second base.

6. (A) Choice (A) is correct. The punctuation in the original sentence and in choice (B) creates a fragment. *Cotton being the state's principal crop* is not an independent thought because it lacks a complete verb—*being* is not a complete verb.

7. (B) Choice (B) is correct. The punctuation in the original sentence and in choice (A) creates a fragment. Both the semicolon and the period should be used to separate two independent clauses. The word group *one that I have never seen before* does not express a complete thought and therefore is not an independent clause.

8. (A) Choice (A) is correct. The dependent clause *because repairs were being made* in choices (B) and (C) is punctuated as if it were a sentence. The result is a fragment.

9. (B) Choice (B) is correct. Choices (A) and (C) do not separate the complete thoughts in the independent clauses with the correct punctuation.

10. (B) Choice (B) is correct. Choices (A) and (C) do not separate the independent clauses with the correct punctuation.

Drill: Verbs

1. (C) Choice (C) is correct. The past participle form of each verb is required because of the auxiliaries (helping verbs) *had been* (concerned) and *would have* (gone).

2. (D) Choice (D) is correct. The forms of the irregular verb meaning *to rest* are *lie* (rest), *lies* (rests), *lay* (rested), and *has lain* (has rested). The forms of the verb meaning *to put* are *lay* (put), *lays* (puts), *laying* (putting), *laid* (put), and *have laid* (have put).

3. (D) Choice (D) is correct. The present tense is used for universal truths and the past tense is used for historical truths.

4. (A) Choice (A) is correct. The present tense is used for customary happenings. Choice (B), *had begun*, is not a standard verb form. Choice (C), *was beginning*, indicates that 10:30 a.m. is not the regular class time.

5. (A) Choice (A) is correct. The past tense is used for historical statements, and the present tense is used for statements about works of art.

6. (B) Choice (B) is correct. The subject of the sentence is the plural noun *sales*, not the singular noun *Christmas*, which is the object of the prepositional phrase.

7. (A) Choice (A) is correct. The subject *specialty* is singular.

8. (C) Choice (C) is correct. Subjects preceded by *every* are considered singular and therefore require a singular verb form.

9. (A) Choice (A) is correct. The subject of the sentence is the gerund *hiding*, not the object of the gerund phrase *mistakes*. *Hiding* is singular; therefore, the singular verb form *does* should be used.

10. (D) Choice (D) is correct. Though the form of the subject *Board of Regents* is plural, it is singular in meaning.

Drill: Pronouns

1. (A) Choice (A) is correct. Do not use the reflexive pronoun *myself* as a substitute for I.

2. (C) Choice (C) is correct. In the clause *whoever consumes them*, *whoever* is the subject. *Whomever* is the objective case pronoun and should be used only as the object of a sentence, never as the subject.

3. (A) Choice (A) is correct. Use the nominative case pronoun *who* as the subject complement after the verb *is*.

4. (A) Choice (A) is correct. In this sentence use the nominative case/subject pronouns *she who* as the subject complement after the *be* verb *was*.

5. (D) Choice (D) is correct. *Student* is an indefinite, genderless noun that requires a singular personal pronoun. While *his* is a singular personal pronoun, a genderless noun includes both the masculine and feminine forms and requires *his or her* as the singular personal pronoun.

6. (A) Choice (A) is correct. The antecedent *company* is singular, requiring the singular pronoun *it*, not the plural *they*.

7. (B) Choice (B) is correct. Choice (A) contains a person shift: *Your* is a second person pronoun, and *his* and *her* are third person pronouns. The original sentence uses the third person plural pronoun *their* to refer to the singular antecedent *every car owner*. Choice (B) correctly provides the masculine and feminine forms *his or her* required by the indefinite, genderless *every car owner*.

8. (B) Choice (B) is correct. The implied antecedent is *teaching*. Choices (A) and (C) each contain a pronoun with no antecedent. Neither *it* nor *this* are suitable substitutions for *teacher*.

9. (A) Choice (A) is correct. The pronoun *they* in the original sentence has no conspicuous antecedent. Since the doer of the action is obviously unknown (and therefore genderless), choice (B), *he*, is not the correct choice.

10. (C) Choice (C) is correct. The original sentence is ambiguous: the pronoun *she* has two possible antecedents; we don't know whether it is Margaret or her sister who is away at college.

Drill: Adjectives and Adverbs

1. **(C)** Choice (C) is correct. *Bad* is an adjective; *badly* is an adverb. *Real* is an adjective meaning *genuine* (*a real problem, real leather*). To qualify an adverb of degree to express how bad, how excited, how boring, etc., choose *very*.

2. **(A)** Choice (A) is correct. Use an adverb as a qualifier for an adjective. *How simple? Relatively simple.*

3. **(D)** Choice (D) is correct. *Good* is an adjective; *well* is both an adjective and an adverb. As an adjective, *well* refers to health; it means "not ill."

4. **(C)** Choice (C) is correct. All the other choices use *good* incorrectly as an adverb. *Shake* is an action verb that requires an adverb, not an adjective.

5. **(A)** Choice (A) is correct. The action verbs *speaks*, *writes*, *observe*, and *think* each require adverbs as modifiers.

6. **(C)** Choice (C) is correct. The comparisons in choices (A) and (B) are illogical: these sentences suggest that Los Angeles is not in California because it *is larger than any city in California*.

7. **(A)** Choice (A) is correct. Do not omit the second *as* of the correlative pair *as . . . as* when making a point of equal or superior comparison, as in choice (B). Choice (C) omits *than* from "if not more interesting [than]".

8. **(C)** Choice (C) is correct. Choice (A) illogically compares *baseball team* to a *university*, and choice (B) illogically compares *baseball team* to *all the other universities*. Choice (C) logically compares the baseball team here to the one at any other university, as implied by the possessive ending on university—*university's*.

9. **(B)** Choice (B) is correct. Choices (A) and (C) are ambiguous; because these sentences are too elliptical, the reader does not know where to place the missing information.

10. **(C)** Choice (C) is correct. Choice (A) is redundant; there is no need to use *most* with *stingiest*. Choice (B) incorrectly combines the comparative word *more* with the superlative form *stingiest*.

Drill: Punctuation

1. **(D)** Choice (D) is correct. Nonrestrictive clauses, like other nonrestrictive elements, should be set off from the rest of the sentence with commas.

2. **(A)** Choice (A) is correct. Use a comma to separate a nonrestrictive appositive from the word it modifies. "An Oklahoma family" is a nonrestrictive appositive.

3. **(A)** Choice (A) is correct. Do not use unnecessary commas to separate a subject and verb from their complement. Both choices (B) and (C) use superfluous punctuation.

4. **(C)** Choice (C) is correct. Do not separate two items in a compound with commas. The original sentence incorrectly separates "car or plane." Choice (A) omits the comma after the introductory clause.

5. (A) Choice (A) is correct. Use a semicolon to separate two independent clauses/sentences that are not joined by a coordinating conjunction, especially when the ideas in the sentences are interrelated.

6. (D) Choice (D) is correct. Use a semicolon to separate two sentences not joined by a coordinating conjunction.

7. (A) Choice (A) is correct. Use a semicolon to separate two sentences joined by a conjunctive adverb.

8. (A) Choice (A) is correct. Do not use a colon after a verb or a preposition. Remember that a complete sentence must precede a colon.

9. (B) Choice (B) is correct. Do not use a colon after a preposition, and do not use a colon to separate a preposition from its objects.

10. (D) Choice (D) is correct. Use a colon preceding a list that is introduced by words such as *the following* and *as follows*.

PSAT

PRACTICE TEST

SECTION 1

TIME: 25 Minutes
      24 Questions

For each question in this section, select the best answer from among the given choices and fill in the corresponding oval on the answer sheet.

DIRECTIONS: Each sentence below has one or two blanks, each blank indicating that something has been omitted. Beneath the sentence are five lettered words or sets of words. Choose the word or set of words that BEST fits the meaning of the sentence as a whole.

EXAMPLE

Although the critics found the book _____, many of the readers found it rather _____.

(A) obnoxious . . . perfect
(B) spectacular . . . interesting
(C) boring . . . intriguing
(D) comical . . . persuasive
(E) popular . . . rare

Ⓐ Ⓑ ● Ⓓ Ⓔ

1. Frustrated by many _____, the scientist reluctantly _____ his experiment.

   (A) complications . . . terminated
   (B) dangers . . . extended
   (C) successes . . . finished
   (D) situations . . . submitted
   (E) liabilities . . . studied

2. During the Middle Ages, the majority of the population were _____ since working the land was an _____ occupation.

   (A) nobles . . . enjoyable
   (B) serfs . . . endless
   (C) monks . . . everlasting
   (D) merchants . . . impersonal
   (E) knights . . . inconsequential

3. The speaker's monotonous delivery made his hour-long speech seem _____ and the audience became _____ waiting for the end.

   (A) exciting . . . interested
   (B) interminable . . . impatient
   (C) unbelievable . . . skeptical
   (D) long . . . doubtful
   (E) uninteresting . . . grumpy

4. Even though his published verses were _____, the poet received great acclaim for his work.

   (A) grand   (D) inane
   (B) impressive   (E) unlikely
   (C) musical

5. Because the actor's temperament was so _____, directors often rejected him for parts since no one could be sure how he would behave.

   (A) confident   (D) overpowering
   (B) mercurial   (E) inhibited
   (C) pessimistic

6. Finishing a marathon can be a _____ task when leg cramps _____ the runner.

   (A) Herculean . . . debilitate
   (B) hard . . . impel
   (C) frustrating . . . spur
   (D) invigorating. . . slow
   (E) thrilling . . . sedate

7. Scientists warn us that unless we _____ the poisons in the air, global warming could occur as the sun's rays _____ the atmosphere.

   (A) collect . . . destroy
   (B) combine . . . weaken
   (C) restrict . . . expedite
   (D) aggravate . . . permeate
   (E) curtail . . . penetrate

DIRECTIONS: Read each passage and answer the questions that follow. Each question will be based on the information stated or implied in the passage or its introduction.

Questions 8–12 are based on the following passage.

The following passage discusses the exclusion of Catholics from the Eighteenth Century Irish Parliament.

1   The condition of the Irish Parliament all through the eighteenth century is truly pitiable. Its existence as a legislative body is a huge sham, a ghastly simulacrum. The Parliament
5 was one of the most eccentrically composed, most circumscribed, most corrupt legislative assemblies that the ingenuity of man has ever devised. To begin with: no Catholic could sit in Parliament; no Catholic could even record
10 his vote for a Protestant member. The Catholics were as absolutely unrepresented as if they did not exist; and yet they made up the vast majority of the population which the Irish Parliament tried to govern or misgovern, and
15 by an amazing fiction was supposed to represent. "The borough system," says Mr. Lecky, "which had been chiefly the work of the Stuarts—no less than 40 boroughs have been created by James I alone—had been developed
20 to such an extent that out of the 300 members who composed the Parliament"—Mr. Lecky is, of course, speaking of the Lower House— "216 were returned for boroughs or manors. Of these borough members 200 were elected
25 by 100 individuals, and nearly 50 by 10. According to a secret report drawn up by the Irish Government for Pitt in 1784, Lord Shannon at that time returned no less than 16 members, the Ponsonby family 14, Lord Hillsborough
30 nine, and the Duke of Leinster seven."

That borough system was the successful means of corrupting both Houses. James I had been earnestly remonstrated with for calling 40 boroughs into existence at one blow, and
35 we have it on authority of Hely Hutchinson that the king replied: "I have made 40 boroughs, suppose I had made 400—the more the merrier." A pleasant statesmanlike, truly Stuart way of looking at all things, which was
40 destined to prove fatal to the Stuarts and to nobler hearts and heads than theirs. Borough-owners who returned supple lieges to the Irish Parliament generally found their reward in a peerage. Thus, with a simplicity of corruption,
45 the two Houses were undermined at once, for it is said that some half a hundred peers nominated no less than 123 members of the Lower House.

The Irish Parliament was like one of those buried cities dear to Irish legend which lie be-
50 neath the waters of some legend-haunted lake. The dark waters of corruption covered it; there came a moment when those waters fell away and revealed an ancient institution, defaced, indeed, but still honourable and imposing;
55 then the engulfing waves closed over it again, and it vanished—but not forever.

8.   The author describes the Irish Parliament all through the 1700s as being

   (A)   different from that of the eighteenth century.

   (B)   contrived for the benefit of the Catholic clergy.

   (C)   corrupt in the Upper House only; the Lower House was circumspect.

   (D)   a model of decency.

   (E)   corrupt in many respects.

9. The main idea of the passage is to

    (A) point out a truly distinct and admirable system of government.

    (B) point out the sincerity and honesty of those who brought about the system.

    (C) stress again the model Irish Parliament, which many countries could use as a successful system of government.

    (D) bring to the surface the forgotten system with its many attributes.

    (E) raise the sham of the Irish Parliament from the dark waters of the past.

10. The writer attributes corruption in the Parliament to

    (A) the Catholic religion.

    (B) Mr. Lecky.

    (C) the legend-haunted lake.

    (D) a two-house system.

    (E) the borough system.

11. The word "simulacrum" in line 4 can be best defined as

    (A) symmetry, or one side like that of the other.

    (B) a ghost or haunting.

    (C) a type of government of the 1700s.

    (D) a pretense.

    (E) a legislature or law-making body.

12. To give credence to his writings, the author

    (A) calls on the statements of Hely Hutchinson.

    (B) calls on subliminal persuasion.

    (C) gives all facts and figures; no opinions are given at all.

    (D) neglects to consult the voting records.

    (E) ignores the complicated method of corrupting both Houses.

Questions 13–16 are based on the following passage.

The following passage describes architecture in the American Colonies at the beginning of the eighteenth century.

Almost coincidental with the opening of the eighteenth century, Renaissance architecture finally reached the American Colonies. This "severely formal" adaptation of the classic Roman orders and design, born in Italy in the Fifteenth century, first appeared in England around 1570 and reached its mature phase there 50 years later. The time lag of 130 years before it spread to the Colonies is a measure of the economic and social gap between the mother country and her offspring.

Colonial Renaissance architecture, influenced directly by that of the late Stuart period in England, became known as the Georgian after the advent of the Hanoverian dynasty. Its general features included a balanced design; the use of classic orders to embellish doorways and entrance facades; predominantly brick construction, laid in Flemish bond (although the wood-building tradition was so strong in New England that many of the finer Georgian mansions there were clapboarded); low-pitched roofs, frequently hipped; sheathed and highly finished interiors; and such treatment of the entrance hall as to make it a room of major importance. After midcentury the Late Georgian style evolved, with such features as the projecting

central pavilion, giant pilasters at the corners, small entrance portico, larger windowpanes,
30 roofs pitched progressively lower, balustraded roof decks, and dado interior decoration with wallpaper above paneling.

Although adapted from English antecedents, "Georgian architecture in America was
35 singularly free from either the practice or the doctrine of exact imitation." Professional and amateur American architects, and the humbler carpenter-builders who augmented the work of the few architects, all felt free to disregard
40 their handbooks on occasion, "in accordance with necessity, invention, or taste."

In Charleston, South Carolina, the typical eighteenth-century dwelling was Georgian, but with a certain southern flavor. A disastrous
45 fire in 1740 caused the assembly to specify nonflammable future construction. Charleston became a city of brick houses, faced with tinted stucco and covered with red tile roofs, unlike any other colonial metropolis. Many were
50 "double houses" of typical Georgian design; others were of that peculiarly Charleston type called the "single house," standing "with its shoulder to the street," only one room in width and having a long piazza on one side.

13. Factors influencing the time lag in the adoption of Renaissance architecture by the American Colonies

    (A) were primarily political, since Britain rigidly controlled Colonial tastes.

    (B) were neutralized in the case of Charleston, South Carolina, which immediately imported British architecture.

    (C) were both geographical and economic.

    (D) derived from resistance to the Stuart reign in England.

    (E) derived from a series of calamities, like the 1740 fire.

14. One of the singular qualities in the American architects is

    (A) their total fidelity to an already-established style.

    (B) their innovation of the Late Georgian style.

    (C) their complete devotion to the so-called "log cabin" format.

    (D) their commitment to brick as a building material.

    (E) their relative freedom in style from European rules.

15. The appearance of "clapboard" (line 22) in Georgian mansions is due to

    (A) the dearth of lasting building materials in New England.

    (B) the New England predilection for working in wood.

    (C) the respect in New England for English antecedents.

    (D) the need for nonflammable materials.

    (E) the influence of Flemish models.

16. According to the article, Charleston represents

    (A) a Georgian style of architecture unaffected by regional considerations.

    (B) the typical Colonial metropolis of brick and stucco.

    (C) a unique architectural city, blending the South with Georgian ideals.

    (D) a city totally obliged to the single house concept.

    (E) a city totally obliged to the double house concept.

Questions 17–24 are based on the following passage.

The following passage discusses the fertilization of flowers by the class of insects known as Lepidoptera, which includes butterflies and moths.

1   If the chief divisions of insects are to be arranged in the order of their importance as fertilizers of our native flowers, the first place must decidedly be given to bees—while the
5 Lepidoptera take only the second or third place, before or after the flies. But if, as here, we base our arrangement on the degrees of adaptation to flowers, they undoubtedly take the first place, as the only order which throughout,
10 and not only in certain of its families, is fitted for obtaining honey.

In the perfect state, butterflies, so far as they take food at all, which is not the case in all species, restrict themselves almost en-
15 tirely to honey; and since they take no further thought for their young than to lay their eggs sufficiently concealed upon the food-plant, their mouth-parts have been quite free to adapt themselves to the easy winning of honey from
20 the most various flowers. This adaptation is attained by an astonishing development of the maxillary laminae, with suppression of the greater part of the rest of the mouth-organs. The upper lip and mandibles are aborted. The
25 laminae of the maxillae are transformed into two immensely long, hollow, rounded filaments, provided with semicircular grooves on their inner surfaces, and so forming a tube when placed in close apposition; in the state of
30 rest this tube is spirally coiled, and concealed between the labial palps. The maxillary palps, which are not visible in my figure, and also the labium, are usually more or less abortive. The whole mechanism of the mouth, so complex
35 and many-jointed in bees, is thus here reduced to a long, thin, suctorial tube formed of two apposed grooves and capable of being rolled up into small space, and of a protective covering for this tube. With this simple mechanism,
40 Lepidoptera are able to probe the most various flowers, whether flat or long and tubular, and to secure their honey. Peculiar stiff, sharp-pointed appendages at the ends of the laminae enable them also to tear open delicate succu-
45 lent tissues, and make use of the sap in flowers which secrete no free honey. In a former work I have sought to establish the pedigree of Lepidoptera, which has been foreshadowed by entomologists since last century: the subject has
50 been much more thoroughly discussed by my friend Dr. A. Speyer, by Mr. R. MacLachlan, and by my brother Fritz Müller. Apart from tiny midges and from those insects, especially beetles and bees, which occasionally or habitu-
55 ally take up their quarters for the night in flowers, Lepidoptera seem to be the only insects which do not confine their visits to flowers to the daylight: a large number of their species have acquired the habit of seeking their honey
60 in the dusk of summer nights and evenings, free from the competition of other insects. But in our climate, summer evenings on which twilight-loving and nocturnal Lepidoptera fly abundantly are not very numerous. Though the
65 swift and violent movements of these species may be due to the shortness of the period suitable for their flight, or to the pursuit of bats, this peculiarity is of very great importance to the plants they visit; for the more flowers
70 will be visited in a given time, the less time that is spent on each, and the shorter the time that is spent in the flight from one to another. This explains how many flowers have adapted themselves specially to nocturnal insects, both
75 by their light colours, visible in the dusk, and by their time of opening, of secreting honey, or of emitting their odour.

17. The author believes that the order of insects as fertilizers of native flowers in order of their importance is

    (A) flies, butterflies, bees.
    (B) butterflies, Lepidoptera, flies.
    (C) bees, butterflies, Lepidoptera.
    (D) Lepidoptera, then flies or bees.
    (E) bees, Lepidoptera, flies.

18. The only order(s) which is fitted for taking honey from flowers in all its family is the

    (A) bee.
    (B) bee and Lepidoptera.
    (C) Lepidoptera, butterflies, and bees.
    (D) flies, bees, Lepidoptera, and butterflies.
    (E) Lepidoptera.

19. The mouth of the butterfly can be best described as

    (A) simple.
    (B) a long, thin tube which extends in a stiff manner.
    (C) a long, thin tube which can be rolled up into a small space.
    (D) a long, thin tube which can be rolled up into a small space and an upper lip and mandibles which are short.
    (E) a pointed "stinger" for sucking up the pollen.

20. The Lepidoptera, at the time of this writing, had been studied by

    (A) Müller only, up to the time of this writing.
    (B) Müller and his brother.
    (C) the two Müllers, Speyer, and MacLachlan.
    (D) too many scientists to list.
    (E) no one since its work is inconsequential.

21. The main purpose of this passage is to

    (A) emphasize the importance of the mouth parts of the bee.
    (B) show the importance of the bee in fertilization of native flowers.
    (C) show that the butterfly is number one in fertilization of native flowers.
    (D) show the importance and development of the Lepidoptera.
    (E) show that the Lepidoptera seem to be the only insects which do not confine their visits to flowers to the daylight.

22. The writer speculates that there are few nocturnal Lepidoptera in our climate because of

    (A) the pursuit of collectors during nocturnal hours.
    (B) the shortness of the period suitable for their flight.
    (C) the swift movements of the Lepidoptera.
    (D) the violent movements of the Lepidoptera.
    (E) the lack of nocturnal flowers in our climate.

23. Nocturnal flowers to be visited by the Lepidoptera usually

    (A) are dark-colored.

    (B) are without odor.

    (C) open early in the day.

    (D) secrete their nectar early in the day.

    (E) are light-colored.

24. In line 33, "abortive" most nearly means

    (A) shortened.

    (B) imperfect.

    (C) mangled.

    (D) incompletely formed.

    (E) obsolete.

SECTION 2

TIME: 25 Minutes
20 Questions

<u>**DIRECTIONS**</u>**: Solve each problem, using any available space on the page for scratch work. Then decide which answer choice is the best and fill in the corresponding oval on the answer sheet.**

NOTES

(1) The use of a calculator is permitted. All numbers used are real numbers.

(2) Figures that accompany problems in this test are intended to provide information useful in solving the problems. They are drawn as accurately as possible EXCEPT when it is stated in a specific problem that the figure is not drawn to scale. All figures lie in a plane unless otherwise indicated.

REFERENCE INFORMATION

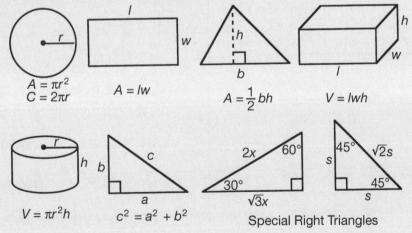

$A = \pi r^2$
$C = 2\pi r$

$A = lw$

$A = \frac{1}{2}bh$

$V = lwh$

$V = \pi r^2 h$

$c^2 = a^2 + b^2$

Special Right Triangles

The number of degrees of arc in a circle is 360.
The measure in degrees of a straight angle is 180.
The sum of the measures in degrees of the angles of a triangle is 180.

1. There were 70 students in a high school graduating class. Of the 70, 40 were members of the French club. Of the 40 members of the French club, $\frac{2}{5}$ were females. Of the remaining students who were not in the French club, $\frac{1}{3}$ were males. How many students in the graduating class were females?

   (A) 16   (D) 28
   (B) 20   (E) 36
   (C) 24

2. One-third of what number is the same as 40 percent of 75?

   (A) 10   (D) 90
   (B) 30   (E) 100
   (C) 60

3. In the figure shown, $ABCD$ is a square and $DEFC$ is a rectangle. What is the area of $DEFC$?

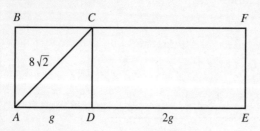

   (A) 32   (D) 72
   (B) 48   (E) 128
   (C) 64

4. If the product of y, $y + 3$, and $y + 5$ is negative and y is an integer, then what is the greatest possible value of y?

   (A) 2   (D) −1
   (B) 1   (E) −2
   (C) 0

5. Five different positive integers have an average (arithmetic mean) of 8. What is the largest that any of the integers could be?

   (A) 20   (D) 35
   (B) 25   (E) 40
   (C) 30

6. A triangle with angles of 45, 45, and 90 degrees has an area of 64. What is the perimeter of the triangle?

   (A) $8 + 8\sqrt{2}$ (D) $16 + 16\sqrt{2}$
   (B) $8 + 16\sqrt{2}$ (E) $24\sqrt{2}$
   (C) $16 + 8\sqrt{2}$

7. If
   $$\frac{m}{g} = \frac{1}{y} \text{ and } \frac{m}{d} = \frac{1}{(y+1)}$$
   which of the following correctly expresses the relationship between g and d?

   (A) $g = d - 1$ (D) $g = d + m$
   (B) $g = \frac{d}{m}$ (E) $g = d - m$
   (C) $g = d + 1$

8. In the figure shown, a and b each represent a side of a square. If

$$o^2 - m^2 = n^2, \quad \frac{ab}{4} = 225$$

and the square and the triangle have equal areas, what does mn equal?

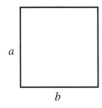 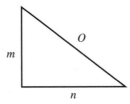

(A) 1,800   (D) 750

(B) 1,000   (E) 500

(C) 900

9. $c = -6$ is *not* a solution for which of the following?

(A) $\frac{1}{2}c + \frac{1}{3}c = -5$

(B) $c^2 + 5c - 6 = 0$

(C) $c^2 - 36 = 0$

(D) $c^2 + 6c = 0$

(E) $c^2 + 36 = 0$

10. From looking at the legend on her map, Cindy notices that one centimeter on the map represents 1,000 kilometers. If her destination is 4.8 centimeters away on the map, how many kilometers must she drive before she arrives at her destination?

(A) 4,000.8   (D) 4,800.0

(B) 4,008.0   (E) 4,800.8

(C) 4,080.0

11. If angle $ABE = 30°$, and angle $ABD = 80°$, what does angle DBC + angle $BCD = ?$

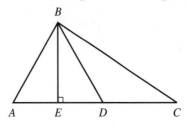

Note: Figure not drawn to scale.

(A) 40°   (D) 75°

(B) 50°   (E) 90°

(C) 60°

12. $\frac{2}{6} \times \frac{3}{9} \times \frac{4}{12} \times \frac{5}{15} \times \frac{6}{18} =$

(A) $\frac{1}{3}$ (D) $\frac{1}{81}$

(B) $\frac{1}{9}$ (E) $\frac{1}{243}$

(C) $\frac{1}{27}$

13. A recipe requires 2 cups of cashews, 6 cups of whole wheat flour, and $\frac{1}{4}$ of a cup of sunflower seeds. The ratio of cashews to whole wheat flour to sunflower seeds could be accurately expressed as which of the following?

(A) 2:6:4   (D) 8:24:1

(B) 2:6:1   (E) 12:24:1

(C) 8:6:4

14. John walks at a pace of 90 feet per minute while Debbie walks at a rate of 65 feet per minute. In a two-hour period, how many more feet will John walk than Debbie?

(A) 1,500   (D) 9,000

(B) 3,000   (E) 15,000

(C) 6,000

15. If $25a^4 - 36b^{18} = 72$, then $4(5a^2 - 6b^9)$ $(5a^2 + 6b^9) =$

(A) 288.   (D) 36.
(B) 126.   (E) 9.
(C) 72.

16. If angles $A + B + C + D = 500°$, what do angles $G + H + I = ?$

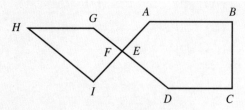

(A) 270°   (D) 400°
(B) 320°   (E) 540°
(C) 360°

17. Change $4\frac{5}{6}$ to an improper fraction.

(A) $\frac{5}{24}$ (D) $\frac{30}{4}$

(B) $\frac{9}{6}$ (E) $\frac{120}{6}$

(C) $\frac{29}{6}$

18. If one side of a right triangle is m, the second is $m - n$, and the longest is $m + n$, what would be the value of n, expressed in terms of m?

(A) $2m$ (D) $\frac{m}{3}$

(B) m (E) $\frac{m}{4}$

(C) $\frac{m}{2}$

19. If $AD \parallel CB$, $AD = CB$, $GM = \frac{3}{4}AD$, and $MY = \frac{4}{5}CE$, what is the ratio of the area of GMY to the area of $ABCD$?

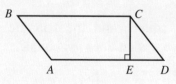

(A) 7:8
(B) 5:8
(C) 1:2
(D) 3:5
(E) 3:10

20. After working for g hours, Mary had earned $75. On the same day, Rosina worked m hours and earned $225. If they receive the same amount of money per hour of work and $g + m = 16$, how many hours did Mary work?

(A) 3   (D) 6
(B) 4   (E) 7
(C) 5

SECTION 3

TIME:	25 Minutes
	24 Questions

For each question in this section, select the best answer from among the given choices and fill in the corresponding oval on the answer sheet.

DIRECTIONS: Each sentence below has one or two blanks, each blank indicating that something has been omitted. Beneath the sentence are five lettered words or sets of words. Choose the word or set of words that BEST fits the meaning of the sentence as a whole.

EXAMPLE

Although the critics found the book _____, many of the readers found it rather _____.

(A) obnoxious . . . perfect

(B) spectacular . . . interesting

(C) boring . . . intriguing

(D) comical . . . persuasive

(E) popular . . . rare

Ⓐ Ⓑ ● Ⓓ Ⓔ

1. People who live in cities in high-rise buildings view country houses with cupolas and white picket fences as _____ and a throwback to another era.

    (A) aloof   (D) ornate
    (B) capricious   (E) quaint
    (C) redundant

2. They hated each other's friends. They liked different books and movies. She preferred outdoor sports; he enjoyed cooking and reading. They got a divorce because they were _____.

    (A) dispassionate (D) meticulous
    (B) incompatible (E) nostalgic
    (C) arbitrary

3. After many years of art school, Marcia could _____ an authentic painting from its copy.

    (A) discern   (D) emulate
    (B) condone   (E) rationalize
    (C) laud

4. The hot summer sun and high humidity left the residents of the town feeling _____ and _____.

    (A) unruly . . . urbane
    (B) pallid . . . vulnerable
    (C) torpid . . . lethargic
    (D) immune . . . articulate
    (E) depleted . . . contrite

5. Not wanting to miss the deadline for submission of his manuscript, the author hurried to _____ the conclusion of his last chapter.

    (A) expand   (D) endorse
    (B) execute   (E) extol
    (C) exhaust

6. Some environmental groups are so _____ in their beliefs that they will face overwhelming forces to protect the environment.

    (A) adamant   (D) fallacious
    (B) deliberate (E) pragmatic
    (C) didactic

DIRECTIONS: Read the passage and answer the questions that follow. Each question will be based on the information stated or implied in the passage or its introduction.

Questions 7–10 are based on the following passage.

The following passage is excerpted from a book of the travels of Theodore F. Wolfe.

From the wilderness to the ocean the course of the lordly Hudson is replete with the enchantments of poetry, romance, and tradition. From the time of Juet's quaint narrative of its first exploration the river has been the scene of events which have been recounted in every form of literature, while its legendary associations and its beauties of flood and shore have inspired many noble works of art. For the literary wayfarer the majestic stream has the added charm of intimate connection with the lives of gifted writers who have found homes as well as themes upon its banks, and have embalmed in their books its scenery and tradi-

tions. Irving gave to it the devotion of a life-
time and, although the tales of Cooper invest
its upper course with the glamour of romance,
yet it is chiefly to the facile pen of Irving that
the Hudson owes its opulence of poetical and
20 sentimental associations; everywhere along
the lower and middle reaches of the river—the
portions traversed in this ramble—we may
find the impress of his genius and love.

Opposite to the city of Irving's birth lies
25 Hoboken, the sometime home of Bryant and
Sands, which gave title to Fay's once popular
romance, and a little way beyond is the spot,
sung by the muse of Sands where, at the foot
of the ledge by the riverside, the great writer
30 of "The Federalist" fell by the hand of Burr.
Above this place tower the cliffs of the Wee-
hawken . . .

From the Manhattan shore at the foot of
Eighty-third Street rises a rocky knoll where
35 Poe often sat and looked upon the river's moving tides while he meditated his compositions;
possibly "The Raven" was pondered here,
since there is some reason to believe it was
written while the poet boarded with the Bren-
40 nans in this neighborhood . . . Poe was once a
cadet in the military school on the rock-bound
promontory of West Point in the heart of the
Highlands, and upon the opposite margin of
the grand river-pass lies historic Constitution
45 Island, long the home of the sisters Warner.
The picturesque island is largely composed
of steep and rude masses of rock, partially
clothed by native trees, and it is now connected with the eastern shore by reedy marshlands.

50 In Irving's early manhood Lindenwald
was the country-seat of Judge Van Ness—the
author of "Aristides"—to whose ancestors
Knickerbocker avers we are indebted for the
invention of buckwheat cakes. The judge, who
55 had been Burr's second in the fateful duel with
Hamilton, was an attached friend of Irving,
and when he suffered the sorrow of his life
in the death of his fair fiancé, Matilda Hoff-
man, he was invited to retire for a time to this

spot, and during the months of his sojourn he 60
sought forgetfulness of his grief in absorbing
literary occupation. Here he revised and complete the peerless "History of New York,"—in
which he mentions his host's family—working
upon it for some hours of each day in the same 65
chamber where Van Buren afterward died.

7. In line 14 the word "embalmed" means

(A) decayed.

(B) exaggerated, as in death.

(C) written about in a boring, deadly
manner.

(D) perfumed, made fragrant, omitted
the faults of.

(E) preserved.

8. The writer's main objective in the writing of the passage is to

(A) present a geographical description
to the reader.

(B) present both a geographical and a
literary description of the area to
the reader.

(C) present both a geographical description and a historical description.

(D) present a fictional narrative to the
reader.

(E) inform the reader of outstanding
literary contributions.

9. The writer would attest that

(A) the gift for writing comes from within.

(B) one can use an element of control to block out external elements and to be able to develop ideas for writing.

(C) Cooper was more influenced by the environment than other writers were influenced.

(D) Irving was more influenced by the environment than other writers were influenced.

(E) such a lovely site on the Hudson could not be the site of crime and violence.

10. The passage describes Constitution Island as

(A) far from the river's moving tides.

(B) beauties of flood and shore.

(C) in the heart of the Highlands.

(D) composed of rude masses of rock.

(E) opulent in poetical and sentimental associations.

Questions 11–15 are based on the following passage.

The following passage is excerpted from a book of literary criticism analyzing the works of George Eliot and others from 1789-1877.

1   [This] personal accent in the writing of George Eliot does not interfere with their dramatic truthfulness; it adds to the power with which they grasp the heart and conscience of
5 the reader. We cannot say with confidence of any of her creations that it is a projection of herself; the lines of their movement are not deflected by hidden powers of attraction or repulsion peculiar to the mind of the author;

most noteworthy is her impartiality towards 10 the several creatures of her imagination; she condemns but does not hate; she is cold or indifferent to none; each lives his own life, good or bad; but the author is present in the midst of them, indicating, interpreting; and we dis- 15 cern in the moral laws, the operation of which presides over the action of each story, those abstractions from the common fund of truth which the author has found most needful to her own deepest life. We feel in reading these 20 works that we are in the presence of a soul, and a soul which has had a history.

At the same time the novels of George Eliot are not didactic treatises. They are primarily works of art and George Eliot herself is artist as 25 much as she is teacher. Many good things in particular passages of her writings are detachable; admirable sayings can be cleared from their surroundings, and presented by themselves, knocked out clean as we knock out fossils from a piece of 30 limestone. But if we separate the moral soul of any complete work of hers from its artistic medium, if we murder to dissect, we lose far more than we gain. When a work of art can be understood only by enjoying it, the art is of a high kind. 35

11. The primary focus of the passage is on the

(A) impressive number of portraitures of men and women created by that great writer George Eliot.

(B) lack of importance of the primary self of Eliot.

(C) evident bias of Eliot toward each of her characters which is "needful to her own deepest life."

(D) writings of George Eliot which are considered by the writer to be inferior since they can be understood only by enjoying them and enjoyment is inferior to cognition.

(E) projection of Eliot which appears in her creations.

12. The author describes George Eliot's writings primarily as

   (A) painful personal recollections.
   (B) compositions which must be kept intact at all cost.
   (C) didactic treatises.
   (D) a revelation of the historical person of George Eliot.
   (E) works of art with a moral soul.

13. In context, the reference to Eliot's works as being "not didactic treatises" (line 24) suggests that they are

   (A) moralistic compositions.
   (B) instructive writing.
   (C) dramatic revelations.
   (D) social criticisms.
   (E) pleasurable readings.

14. The passage indicates that the reader's correct response to Eliot's writing should be to

   (A) analyze it completely.
   (B) enjoy the writings given us by the artist and detach from them what we can.
   (C) search for the glimpses of George Eliot's real self which are hidden there.
   (D) dissect the works until we reach "the moral soul" which we should separate and savor.
   (E) search for Eliot's feelings toward each character which is evident upon careful scrutiny.

15. Eliot's characters can best be described as

   (A) projections of Eliot herself.
   (B) impartial presentations.
   (C) living their own lives without any presence of the author.
   (D) didactic.
   (E) incomplete portraitures.

DIRECTIONS: Read the passages and answer the questions that follow. Each question will be based on the information stated or implied in the selection or its introduction, and may be based on the relationship between the passages.

Questions 16–24 are based on the following passages.

The following passages, written at the turn of the century, present two views toward education. Passage 1 was written by Andrew Carnegie; Passage 2 was written by Alfred Fouillee.

Passage 1

We occasionally find traces even at this day of the old prejudice which existed against educating the masses of the people. I do not wonder that this should exist when I reflect upon what has hitherto passed for education. 5 Men have wasted their precious years trying to extract education from an ignorant past whose chief province is to teach us, not what to adopt, but what to avoid. Men have sent their sons to colleges to waste their energies upon 10 obtaining a knowledge of such languages as Greek and Latin, which are of no more practical use to them than Choctaw. I have known few college graduates that knew Shakespeare or Milton. They might be able to tell you all 15 about Ulysses or Agamemnon or Hector, but what are these compared to the characters that we find in our own classics? One service

Robert Lowell has done, for which he should
20 be thanked—he has boldly said that in Shakespeare alone we have a greater treasure than
in all the classics of ancient time. They have
been crammed with the details of petty and
insignificant skirmishes between savages, and
25 taught to exalt a band of ruffians into heroes;
and we have called them "educated." They
have been "educated" as if they were destined
for life upon some other planet than this. They
have in no sense received instruction. On the
30 contrary, what they have obtained has served
to imbue them with false ideas and to give
them a distaste for practical life. I do not wonder that a prejudice has arisen and still exists
against such education. In my own experience
35 I can say that I have known few young men intended for business who were not injured by a
collegiate education. Had they gone into active
work during the years spent at college they
would have been better educated men in every
40 true sense of that term. The fire and energy
have been stamped out of them, and how to so
manage as to live a life of idleness and not a
life of usefulness has become the chief question with them. But a new idea of education is
45 now upon us. We have begun to realize that a
knowledge of chemistry, for instance, is worth
a knowledge of all the dead languages that
ever were spoken upon the earth; a knowledge
of mechanics more useful than all the classical
50 learning that can be crammed into young men
at college.

Passage 2

Is ignorance of Latin and the substitution
of German and English exercises a sufficient
guarantee of preparation for commerce, of the
55 acquisition of the genius of commerce and
agriculture? "Oh! but we shall include bookkeeping in the program." What! is the unity of
secondary instruction to be sacrificed to bookkeeping? Is your so-called general culture
60 to be subordinated to the requirements of an
office or of a bank? If you are in such a hurry
to teach your children book-keeping—which

can be learned in a few weeks—let them have
special lessons in keeping accounts or let them
have a complementary course at the lyceeum. 65
Let us look a little closer at the program at our
present special instruction, which has a better
claim than "modern humanities" as a preparation for industrial, commercial, and agricultural life, and let us see in what it prepares for it. 70
Classical instruction contains all that is comprised in special instruction….As for the programs of French instruction put forward, there
is nearly as great a medley of the different
subjects as in the present classical programs. 85
With the exception of a few differences in detail in the proportion of the different sciences,
the science subjects appear in the same order
as in the classical course. The only essential difference is the substitution of a second 90
modern language for Latin. So we are saved
by adding Goethe's "Faust" to Shakespeare's
"Hamlet," instead of the "Aeneid"! And for
this magnificent result secondary education is
to be turned upside down, classical training 95
to be disorganized, and to be asphyxiated by
a rarefication of its environment. Instead of
all learning Latin and one modern language
chosen by themselves, our children will learn
a fundamental modern language and a com- 100
plementary modern language. What essential
diversity of aptitudes will be thus satisfied [by
the new program]? What minds are unsuited
to Latin and English and suited to German
and English? I repeat that the whole system 105
of modern humanities is a mass of contradictions—it is a general, special, a disinterested
utilitarian system of instruction.

16. The main idea of Passage 1 is

    (A) to promote a classical education.

    (B) to promote the prejudice against educating the masses.

    (C) to renounce a study of mythology.

    (D) to suggest active work for young men, not a collegiate education.

    (E) to espouse the values of liberal arts.

17. The author of Passage 1 describes the college graduates of today as

    (A) having received valuable instruction.

    (B) having been bettered by collegiate life.

    (C) educated for life in our world.

    (D) ignorant of Shakespeare.

    (E) filled with fire and energy.

18. The main purpose of Passage 2 is to

    (A) renounce the modern humanities.

    (B) present the modern humanities as important general culture.

    (C) ridicule the traditional courses of study.

    (D) advocate the so-called "special education."

    (E) recommend the total reorganization of secondary education.

19. When the writer of Passage 2 states that "we are saved by adding Goethe's 'Faust' to Shakespeare's 'Hamlet,' instead of the 'Aeneid' " (lines 91–93), he is

    (A) using alliteration.

    (B) using a simile.

    (C) employing a tongue-in-cheek attitude.

    (D) using a stylistic device called denotation.

    (E) using an understatement.

20. The best meaning of being "asphyxiated by a rarefication of its environment" (lines 96–97) is

    (A) killed by purification.

    (B) destroying learning through vocational education.

    (C) a reference to Greek mythology where the cure killed.

    (D) being smothered by important concepts.

    (E) being choked with the amount of material to be learned.

21. The main point made by the writer of Passage 2 about "practical" courses like bookkeeping is

(A) subordinate general culture to bookkeeping, a useful course of study.

(B) that they should be provided by the schools and not at special lessons.

(C) they are within the scope of the public schools and not the responsibility of the lyceeum.

(D) that they can be taught at special classes; they are not to be a part of the school curriculum.

(E) that they should be substituted for "dead" courses like Latin.

22. The writer of Passage 1, when questioned about classical education,

(A) would criticize those who say negative things about classical education.

(B) would show the recent research to back up his beliefs.

(C) would point out its inadequacies.

(D) would point out the quality of the structure which has survived for a long period of time.

(E) would show the humility of those who would dispense with the classics.

23. The writer's question as to which minds are insulted by Latin and English

(A) brings out the mistakes made in the past.

(B) indicates why the secondary education program had to be changed.

(C) shows what should be as opposed to what is.

(D) highlights the distinction between the ideal and what was.

(E) criticizes those who seek to change the curriculum.

24. The writer of Passage 2 would agree that modern humanities

(A) should not be employed by secondary education.

(B) includes important classical components, like Latin.

(C) prepares students for industrial, commercial, and agricultural life.

(D) has a superior science component which is evident when compared with the classical course of study.

(E) invokes past errors in order to advocate present improvements.

SECTION 4

TIME: 25 Minutes
18 Questions

<u>DIRECTIONS</u>: **Solve each problem, using any available space on the page for scratch work. Then decide which answer choice is the best and fill in the corresponding oval on the answer sheet.**

NOTES

(1) The use of a calculator is permitted. All numbers used are real numbers.

(2) Figures that accompany problems in this test are intended to provide information useful in solving the problems. They are drawn as accurately as possible EXCEPT when it is stated in a specific problem that the figure is not drawn to scale. All figures lie in a plane unless otherwise indicated.

REFERENCE INFORMATION

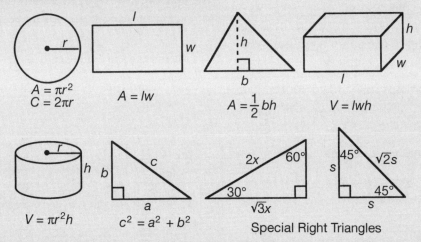

$A = \pi r^2$
$C = 2\pi r$

$A = lw$

$A = \frac{1}{2}bh$

$V = lwh$

$V = \pi r^2 h$

$c^2 = a^2 + b^2$

Special Right Triangles

The number of degrees of arc in a circle is 360.
The measure in degrees of a straight angle is 180.
The sum of the measures in degrees of the angles of a triangle is 180.

DIRECTIONS FOR STUDENT-PRODUCED RESPONSE QUESTIONS

For each of the questions below (1–10), solve the problem and indicate your answer by marking the ovals in the special grid, as shown in the examples below.

Answer: $\frac{9}{5}$ **or 9/5 or 1.8**

Either position is correct.

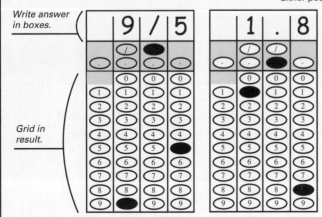

Write answer in boxes.

Grid in result.

— *Fraction line*
— *Decimal point*

NOTE: You may start your anwers in any column, space permitting. Columns not needed should be left blank.

- Mark no more than one oval in any column.

- Because the answer sheet will be machine scored, you will receive credit only if the ovals are filled in correctly.

- Although not required, it is suggested that you write your answer in the boxes at the top of the columns to help you fill in the ovals accurately.

- Some problems may have more than one correct answer. In such cases, grid only one answer.

- No question has a negative answer.

- Mixed numbers such as $3\frac{1}{2}$ must be gridded as 3.5 or 7/2.

  (If [3 1 / 2] is gridded, it will be interpreted as $\frac{31}{2}$, not $3\frac{1}{2}$.)

- **Decimal Accuracy:** If you obtain a decimal answer, enter the most accurate value the grid will accommodate. For example, if you obtain an answer such as 0.6666 …, you should record the result as .666 or .667. Less accurate values such as .66 or .67 are not acceptable.

Acceptable ways to grid $\frac{2}{3}$ = .6666…

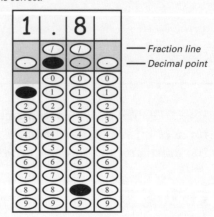

1. If $4^{n+4} = 64$, what is the value of 5^n?

2. Three numbers x, y, and z form a "triple" if $x + y + z = 1$. If A, B, and C form a triple where a) $C = 1$ and b) $3A + 2B + 2C = 5$, find $2A + B$.

3. Find a prime number less than 40 which is of the form $3K + 1$ and $5K + 2$, where $0 \le k < 13$.

4. Consider the figure given below.

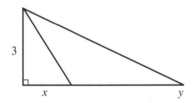

   If the area of the shaded region is 15 square feet and the area of the whole figure is 27 square feet, find y.

5. The product of two consecutive even integers is 1,224. If both numbers are positive, find the smaller number.

6. Find the number(s) that satisfy x in the following:

   (A) $50 < x < 60$

   (B) The prime factorization of x involves primes less than 10.

7. Let x, y, and z be positive integers which satisfy the following conditions:

   a) $x < 10$
   b) $6y < 3x$
   c) $z < y$
   d) $z > 1$

   Find a possible value for z which satisfies these conditions.

8. Consider the system of linear equations given below.

   $3x - y = 2$
   $4x + y = 5$

   Find y.

9. Let $xyz = 24$ where x, y, and z are positive integers greater than or equal to 2. If x is a perfect square find a possible value for z.

10. Consider the triangle inset in the square below.

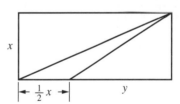

   If $x = 2^3$ ft, find the area of the triangle.

11. The average (arithmetic mean) of nine consecutive integers is 16. What is the average of the four smallest of the integers?

   (A) 9   (D) 12.75
   (B) 10.25   (E) 13.5
   (C) 11

12. A high school biology class had 60 students in it. All the students took a test that was graded from 0 to 100. Precisely 40 students received grades equal to or greater than 75. What is the lowest possible class average for the test?

(A) 60
(B) 50
(C) 40
(D) 30
(E) 20

13. A major league baseball team is considering tearing down the present stadium and building a new stadium. In a survey of 10,000 people, 700 of them said they would support the idea of a new stadium and the rest would not. What percentage of the group surveyed does not support the idea of a new stadium?

(A) 7%
(B) 9.3%
(C) 65%
(D) 70%
(E) 93%

14. A square has a side length of $\frac{3}{4}$. Find the difference between the perimeter and the area ignoring the dimensions associated with the numbers.

(A) $3\frac{9}{16}$
(B) $3\frac{3}{4}$
(C) 3
(D) 2
(E) $2\frac{7}{16}$

15. If two positive integers are in the ratio of 5 : 3 and their difference is 12, find the larger number.

(A) 24
(B) 28
(C) 30
(D) 32
(E) 36

16. If $\frac{m}{9}$ is between 3 and 4, then a possible value of m is which of the following?

(A) 11
(B) 15
(C) 20
(D) 24
(E) 28

17. Which has the largest value?

(A) $\sqrt{\frac{5}{8}}$
(B) $\sqrt{\frac{7}{10}}$
(C) $\sqrt{\frac{6}{13}}$
(D) $\sqrt{\frac{4}{9}}$
(E) $\frac{1}{2}$

18. If $2F = 3G$ and $5G = 7H$, find the ratio of $F : H$.

(A) 21 : 10
(B) 2 : 7
(C) 7 : 2
(D) 3 : 7
(E) 7 : 3

**TIME: 30 Minutes
39 Questions**

<u>DIRECTIONS</u>: Each of the following sentences may contain an error in diction, usage, idiom, or grammar. Some sentences are correct. Some sentences contain one error. No sentence contains more than one error.

If there is an error, it will appear in one of the underlined portions labeled A, B, C, or D. If there is no error, choose the portion labeled E. If there is an error, select the letter of the portion that must be changed in order to correct the sentence.

EXAMPLE

He drove <u>slowly</u> and <u>cautiously</u> in order to <u>hopefully</u> avoid having an <u>accident</u>.
        A   B   C   D

<u>No error.</u>
  E   Ⓐ Ⓑ ● Ⓓ Ⓔ

1. In 1877 Chief Joseph of the Nez Perces,

   together with 250 warriors and 500
          A
   women and children, were praised by
                          B
   newspaper reporters for bravery during
                           C
   the 115-day fight for freedom. No error.
                       D   E

2. The ideals upon which American society
                  A
   is based are primarily those of Europe
   B   C
   and not ones derived from the native Indian
                D
   culture. No error.
            E

3. An astute and powerful woman, Frances
   A
   Nadel was a beauty contest winner before
         B
   she became president of the company
       C
   upon the death of her husband. No error.
   D   E

4. Representative Wilson pointed out, how-
                         A
   ever, that the legislature had not finalized
                              B
   the state budget and salary increases

   had depended on decisions to be made in
   C   D
   a special session. No error.
                      E

5. Now the city librarian, doing more than
            A
   checking out books, must help to plan pup-
                                 B
   pet shows and movies for children, garage

   sales for used books, and arranging for guest
            C   D
   lecturers and exhibits for adults. No error.
                                     E

6. In order to completely understand the
            A
   psychological effects of the Bubonic
                 B
   plague, one must realize that one-fourth
           C
   to one-third of the population in an

   affected area died. No error.
   D   E

7. Rural roads, known in the United States
                A
   as farm to market roads, have always

   been a vital link in the economy of
                 B
   more advanced nations because trans-
   C
   portation of goods to markets is essential.
                                 D
   No error.
   E

8. Many a graduate wishes to return to
      A   B
    college and abide in the protected envi-
                  C
    ronment of a university, particularly if

    someone else pays the bills. No error.
      D   E

9. Confronted with a choice of either
      A
    cleaning up his room or cleaning out the
      B   C
    garage, the teenager became very aggravated
                                    D
    with his parents. No error.
                      E

10. My brother and I dressed as quickly as we
                    A   B
    could, but we missed the school bus, which
                                          C
    made us late for class today. No error.
      D   E

11. Among the activities offered at the local
      A   B
    high school through the community edu-
                  C
    cation program are singing in the couples'
                      D
    chorus, ballroom dancing, and Chinese

    cooking. No error.
             E

12. If you are disappointed by an inexpensive
                A   B
    bicycle, then an option you might consider

    is to work this summer and save your mon-
                                C
    ey for a more expensive model. No error.
             D   E

13. Also being presented to the city council

    this morning is the mayor's city budget for
                A
    next year and plans to renovate the existing
                        B   C
    music theater, so the session will focus on
                                     D
    financial matters. No error.
                       E

14. Even a movement so delicate as a
                      A
    fly's walking triggers the Venus fly-
      B
    trap to grow extra cells on the outside
         C
    of its hinge, immediately closing the
       D
    petals of the trap. No error.
                        E

DIRECTIONS: In each of the following sentences, some portion of the sentence is underlined. Under each sentence are five choices. The first choice has the same wording as the original. The other four choices are reworded. Sometimes the first choice containing the original wording is the best; sometimes one of the other choices is the best. Choose the letter of the best choice. Your choice should produce a sentence which is not ambiguous or awkward and which is correct, clear, and precise.

This is a test of correct and effective English expression. Keep in mind the standards of English usage, punctuation, grammar, word choice, and construction.

EXAMPLE

When you listen to opera, <u>a person may not appreciate it</u>.

(A) a person may not appreciate it.

(B) it may not be appreciated by a person.

(C) which may not be appreciated by one.

(D) you may not appreciate it.

(E) appreciating it may be a problem for you.

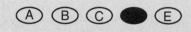

15. <u>Being that you bring home more money than I do</u>, it is only fitting you should pay proportionately more rent.

(A) Being that you bring home more money than I do

(B) Bringing home the more money of the two of us

(C) When more money is made by you than by me

(D) Because you bring home more money than I do

(E) If your bringing home more money than me

16. So tenacious is their grip on life, that sponge cells will regroup and form a new sponge even <u>when they are squeezed</u> through silk.

(A) when they are squeezed

(B) since they have been

(C) as they will be

(D) after they have been

(E) because they should be

17. <u>Seeing as how the plane is late</u>, wouldn't you prefer to wait for a while on the observation deck?

    (A)   Seeing as how the plane is late

    (B)   When the plane comes in

    (C)   Since the plane is late

    (D)   Being as the plane is late

    (E)   While the plane is landing

18. Only with careful environmental planning can we protect the <u>world we live in</u>.

    (A)   world we live in

    (B)   world in which we live in

    (C)   living in this world

    (D)   world's living

    (E)   world in which we live

19. In the last three years we have added more varieties of vegetables to our garden <u>than those you suggested in the beginning</u>.

    (A)   than those you suggested in the beginning

    (B)   than the ones we began with

    (C)   beginning with your suggestion

    (D)   than what you suggested to us

    (E)   which you suggested in the beginning

20. As you know, I am not easily fooled by flattery, and while <u>nice words please you</u>, they don't get the job done.

    (A)   nice words please you

    (B)   nice words are pleasing

    (C)   nice words please a person

    (D)   flattering words please people

    (E)   flattering words are pleasing to some

21. Some pieces of the puzzle, in spite of Jane's search, <u>are still missing and probably will never be found</u>.

    (A)   are still missing and probably will never be found

    (B)   is missing still but never found probably

    (C)   probably will be missing and never found

    (D)   are still probably missing and to never be found

    (E)   probably are missing and will not be found

22. Women live longer and have fewer illnesses than men, <u>which proves that women are the strongest sex.</u>

    (A)   which proves that women are the strongest sex.

    (B)   which proves that women are the stronger sex.

    (C)   facts which prove that women are the stronger sex.

    (D)   proving that women are the strongest sex.

    (E)   a proof that women are the stronger sex.

23. Eighteenth century architecture, with its columns and balanced lines, <u>was characteristic of those of previous times in Greece and Rome</u>.

    (A) was characteristic of those of previous times in Greece and Rome

    (B) is similar to characteristics of Greece and Rome

    (C) is similar to Greek and Roman building styles

    (D) is characteristic with earlier Greek and Roman architecture

    (E) was similar to architecture of Greece and Rome

24. Plato, one of the famous Greek philosophers, won many wrestling prizes when he was a young man, thus <u>exemplifying the Greek ideal of balance between the necessity for physical activity and using one's mind</u>.

    (A) exemplifying the Greek ideal of balance between the necessity for physical activity and using one's mind

    (B) serving as an example of the Greek ideal of balance between physical and mental activities

    (C) an example of balancing Greek mental and athletic games

    (D) this as an example of the Greek's balance between mental physical pursuits

    (E) shown to be exemplifying the balancing of two aspects of Greek life, the physical and the mental

25. Allied control of the Philippine Islands during World War II proved to be <u>another obstacle as the Japanese scattered resistance</u> until the end of the war.

    (A) another obstacle as the Japanese scattered resistance

    (B) difficult because of the Japanese giving resistance

    (C) continuing scattered Japanese resistance as obstacles

    (D) as another scattered obstacle due to Japanese resistance

    (E) difficult because the Japanese gave scattered resistance

26. Flooding abated and the river waters receded as the <u>rainfall finally let up</u>.

    (A) rainfall finally let up

    (B) rain having let up

    (C) letting up of the rainfall

    (D) rainfall, when it finally let up

    (E) raining finally letting up

27. Unless China slows its population growth to zero, that country <u>would still have</u> a problem feeding its people.

    (A) would still have

    (B) will have still had

    (C) might have had still

    (D) will still have

    (E) would have still

28. In *The Music Man* Robert Preston portrays a fast-talking salesman who comes to a small town in Iowa <u>inadvertently falling in love with</u> the librarian.

(A) inadvertently falling in love with

(B) and inadvertently falls in love with

(C) afterwards he inadvertently falls in love with

(D) after falling inadvertently in love with

(E) when he inadvertently falls in love with

29. Two-thirds of American 17-year-olds do not know that the Civil War <u>takes place</u> between 1850 and 1900.

(A) takes place

(B) took place

(C) had taken place

(D) have taken place

(E) is taking place

30. Both professional and amateur ornithologists, <u>people that study birds,</u> recognize the Latin or scientific names of bird species.

(A) people that study birds

(B) people which study birds

(C) the study of birds

(D) people who study birds

(E) in which people study birds

31. Many of the oil-producing states spent their huge surplus tax revenues during the oil boom of the 1970s and early 1980s <u>in spite of the fact that</u> oil production from new wells began to flood the world market as early as 1985.

(A) in spite of the fact that

(B) even in view of the fact that

(C) however clearly it was known that

(D) even though

(E) when it was clear that

32. The president of the community college reported <u>as to the expectability of the tuition increase as well as the actual amount</u>.

(A) as to the expectability of the tuition increase as well as the actual amount

(B) that the tuition will likely increase by a specific amount

(C) as to the expectability that tuition will increase by a specific amount

(D) about the expected tuition increase of five percent.

(E) regarding the expectation of a tuition increase expected to be five percent

33. Although Carmen developed an interest in classical music, <u>she did not read notes and had never played an instrument</u>.

(A) she did not read notes and had never played an instrument

(B) she does not read notes and has never played an instrument

(C) it is without being able to read notes or having played an instrument

(D) she did not read notes nor had she ever played them

(E) it is without reading notes nor having played an instrument

34. Political candidates must campaign on issues and ideas that strike a chord within their constituency but <u>with their goal to sway</u> undecided voters to support their candidacy.

(A) with their goal to sway

(B) need also to sway

(C) aiming at the same time to sway

(D) also trying to sway

(E) its goal should also be in swaying

<u>DIRECTIONS</u>: **The following passages are considered early draft efforts of a student. Some sentences need to be rewritten to make the ideas clearer and more precise.**

Read each passage carefully and answer the questions that follow. Some of the questions are about particular sentences or parts of sentences and ask you to make decisions about sentence structure, diction, and usage. Some of the questions refer to the entire essay or parts of the essay and ask you to make decisions about organization, development, appropriateness of language, audience, and logic. Choose the answer that most effectively makes the intended meaning clear and follows the requirements of standard written English. After you have chosen your answer, fill in the corresponding oval on your answer sheet.

EXAMPLE

(1) On the one hand, I think television is bad, But it also does some good things for all of us. (2) For instance, my little sister thought she wanted to be a policemen until she saw police shows on television.

Which of the following is the best revision of the underlined portion of sentence 1 below?

On the one hand, I think television <u>is bad, But it also</u> does some good things for all of us.

(A) is bad; But it also

(B) is bad. but is also

(C) is bad, and it also

(D) is bad, but it also

(E) is bad because it also

Questions 35–39 are based on the following passage.

(1) In 1840 Dickens came up with the idea of using a raven as a character in his new novel, *Barnaby Rudge*. (2) Soon, the word got out among his friends and neighbors that the famous author was interested in ravens and wanted to know more about them. (3) When someone gave a raven as a pet, he was delighted. (4) The raven was named Grip by Dickens' children and became a successful member of the family. (5) Grip began to get his way around the household, and if he wanted something, he took it, and Grip would bite the children's ankles when he felt displeased. (6) The raven in *Barnaby Rudge* is depicted as a trickster who slept "on horseback" in the stable and "has been known, by the mere superiority of his genius, to walk off unmolested with the dog's dinner." (7) So we get an idea of what life with Grip was like. (8) Poe, however, was dissatisfied. (9) This was a comical presentation of the raven. (10) Poe felt that the large black bird should have a more prophetic use. (10) So, about a year after *Barnaby Rudge* was published, Poe began work on his poem, "The Raven." (11) Any schoolchild can quote the famous line, "Quoth the Raven, 'Nevermore,'" but almost no one knows about Grip. (12) What happened to Grip? (13) Well, when he died, the Dickens family had become so attached to him that they had him stuffed and displayed him in the parlor.

35. Which of the following is the best revision of the underlined portion of sentence 3 below?

When <u>someone gave a raven as a pet, he was delighted</u>.

(A) giving someone a raven as a pet, he was delighted.

(B) someone gave Dickens a raven for a pet, the author was delighted.

(C) someone delightedly gave a raven for a pet to Dickens.

(D) someone gave Dickens a raven as a pet, the result was that the author was delighted with the gift.

(E) receiving a raven as a pet, Dickens was delighted.

36. Which of the following is the best revision of the underlined portion of sentence 5 below?

Grip began to get his way around the household, and <u>if he wanted something, he took it, and Grip would bite the children's ankles when he felt displeased</u>.

(A) if he wanted something, he took it; if he felt displeased, he bit the children's ankles.

(B) if wanting something, he would take, and if unhappy, he would bite.

(C) when he wanted something, he would take it; being displeased, he would bite the children's ankles.

(D) when taking something that he wanted, he would bite the children's ankles.

(E) if displeased and if wanting something, Grip would bite the children's ankles and he would take it.

37. In the context of the sentences preceding and following sentence 7, which of the following is the best revision of sentence 7?

(A) So, you can get an idea of what life with Grip was like.

(B) Therefore, the challenges of living with Grip must have been numerous and varied.

(C) So, an idea of the life with Grip can be gotten.

(D) So, life with Grip must have been entertaining.

(E) These are some examples I have given of what life with Grip was like.

38. Which of the following is the best way to combine sentences 8, 9, and 10?

(A) Having dissatisfaction with the comical presentation of the big black bird, Poe felt it should be more prophetic.

(B) As a result of dissatisfaction, Poe felt the big black bird should be presented more prophetically than comically.

(C) However, Poe felt the comical presentation was not as good as the prophetic one.

(D) Poe, however, dissatisfied with the comical presentation of the big black bird, felt a more prophetic use would be better.

(E) Poe, however, was dissatisfied with this comical presentation and felt that the large black bird should have a more prophetic use.

39. In relation to the passage as a whole, which of the following best describes the writer's intention in the first paragraph?

(A) To provide background information

(B) To provide a concrete example of a humorous episode

(C) To arouse sympathy in the reader

(D) To evaluate the effectiveness of the treatment of the subject

(E) To contrast with treatment of the subject in the second paragraph

Begin with number 1 for each section. If a section has fewer questions than answer spaces, leave the extra answer spaces blank. Be sure to erase any errors or stray marks completely.

SECTION 1

1 (A)(B)(C)(D)(E)	11 (A)(B)(C)(D)(E)	21 (A)(B)(C)(D)(E)	31 (A)(B)(C)(D)(E)
2 (A)(B)(C)(D)(E)	12 (A)(B)(C)(D)(E)	22 (A)(B)(C)(D)(E)	32 (A)(B)(C)(D)(E)
3 (A)(B)(C)(D)(E)	13 (A)(B)(C)(D)(E)	23 (A)(B)(C)(D)(E)	33 (A)(B)(C)(D)(E)
4 (A)(B)(C)(D)(E)	14 (A)(B)(C)(D)(E)	24 (A)(B)(C)(D)(E)	34 (A)(B)(C)(D)(E)
5 (A)(B)(C)(D)(E)	15 (A)(B)(C)(D)(E)	25 (A)(B)(C)(D)(E)	35 (A)(B)(C)(D)(E)
6 (A)(B)(C)(D)(E)	16 (A)(B)(C)(D)(E)	26 (A)(B)(C)(D)(E)	36 (A)(B)(C)(D)(E)
7 (A)(B)(C)(D)(E)	17 (A)(B)(C)(D)(E)	27 (A)(B)(C)(D)(E)	37 (A)(B)(C)(D)(E)
8 (A)(B)(C)(D)(E)	18 (A)(B)(C)(D)(E)	28 (A)(B)(C)(D)(E)	38 (A)(B)(C)(D)(E)
9 (A)(B)(C)(D)(E)	19 (A)(B)(C)(D)(E)	29 (A)(B)(C)(D)(E)	39 (A)(B)(C)(D)(E)
10 (A)(B)(C)(D)(E)	20 (A)(B)(C)(D)(E)	30 (A)(B)(C)(D)(E)	40 (A)(B)(C)(D)(E)

SECTION 2

1 (A)(B)(C)(D)(E)	11 (A)(B)(C)(D)(E)	21 (A)(B)(C)(D)(E)	31 (A)(B)(C)(D)(E)
2 (A)(B)(C)(D)(E)	12 (A)(B)(C)(D)(E)	22 (A)(B)(C)(D)(E)	32 (A)(B)(C)(D)(E)
3 (A)(B)(C)(D)(E)	13 (A)(B)(C)(D)(E)	23 (A)(B)(C)(D)(E)	33 (A)(B)(C)(D)(E)
4 (A)(B)(C)(D)(E)	14 (A)(B)(C)(D)(E)	24 (A)(B)(C)(D)(E)	34 (A)(B)(C)(D)(E)
5 (A)(B)(C)(D)(E)	15 (A)(B)(C)(D)(E)	25 (A)(B)(C)(D)(E)	35 (A)(B)(C)(D)(E)
6 (A)(B)(C)(D)(E)	16 (A)(B)(C)(D)(E)	26 (A)(B)(C)(D)(E)	36 (A)(B)(C)(D)(E)
7 (A)(B)(C)(D)(E)	17 (A)(B)(C)(D)(E)	27 (A)(B)(C)(D)(E)	37 (A)(B)(C)(D)(E)
8 (A)(B)(C)(D)(E)	18 (A)(B)(C)(D)(E)	28 (A)(B)(C)(D)(E)	38 (A)(B)(C)(D)(E)
9 (A)(B)(C)(D)(E)	19 (A)(B)(C)(D)(E)	29 (A)(B)(C)(D)(E)	39 (A)(B)(C)(D)(E)
10 (A)(B)(C)(D)(E)	20 (A)(B)(C)(D)(E)	30 (A)(B)(C)(D)(E)	40 (A)(B)(C)(D)(E)

SECTION 3

1 (A)(B)(C)(D)(E)	11 (A)(B)(C)(D)(E)	21 (A)(B)(C)(D)(E)	31 (A)(B)(C)(D)(E)
2 (A)(B)(C)(D)(E)	12 (A)(B)(C)(D)(E)	22 (A)(B)(C)(D)(E)	32 (A)(B)(C)(D)(E)
3 (A)(B)(C)(D)(E)	13 (A)(B)(C)(D)(E)	23 (A)(B)(C)(D)(E)	33 (A)(B)(C)(D)(E)
4 (A)(B)(C)(D)(E)	14 (A)(B)(C)(D)(E)	24 (A)(B)(C)(D)(E)	34 (A)(B)(C)(D)(E)
5 (A)(B)(C)(D)(E)	15 (A)(B)(C)(D)(E)	25 (A)(B)(C)(D)(E)	35 (A)(B)(C)(D)(E)
6 (A)(B)(C)(D)(E)	16 (A)(B)(C)(D)(E)	26 (A)(B)(C)(D)(E)	36 (A)(B)(C)(D)(E)
7 (A)(B)(C)(D)(E)	17 (A)(B)(C)(D)(E)	27 (A)(B)(C)(D)(E)	37 (A)(B)(C)(D)(E)
8 (A)(B)(C)(D)(E)	18 (A)(B)(C)(D)(E)	28 (A)(B)(C)(D)(E)	38 (A)(B)(C)(D)(E)
9 (A)(B)(C)(D)(E)	19 (A)(B)(C)(D)(E)	29 (A)(B)(C)(D)(E)	39 (A)(B)(C)(D)(E)
10 (A)(B)(C)(D)(E)	20 (A)(B)(C)(D)(E)	30 (A)(B)(C)(D)(E)	40 (A)(B)(C)(D)(E)

SECTION 4

1 Ⓐ Ⓑ Ⓒ Ⓓ Ⓔ	11 Ⓐ Ⓑ Ⓒ Ⓓ Ⓔ	21 Ⓐ Ⓑ Ⓒ Ⓓ Ⓔ	31 Ⓐ Ⓑ Ⓒ Ⓓ Ⓔ
2 Ⓐ Ⓑ Ⓒ Ⓓ Ⓔ	12 Ⓐ Ⓑ Ⓒ Ⓓ Ⓔ	22 Ⓐ Ⓑ Ⓒ Ⓓ Ⓔ	32 Ⓐ Ⓑ Ⓒ Ⓓ Ⓔ
3 Ⓐ Ⓑ Ⓒ Ⓓ Ⓔ	13 Ⓐ Ⓑ Ⓒ Ⓓ Ⓔ	23 Ⓐ Ⓑ Ⓒ Ⓓ Ⓔ	33 Ⓐ Ⓑ Ⓒ Ⓓ Ⓔ
4 Ⓐ Ⓑ Ⓒ Ⓓ Ⓔ	14 Ⓐ Ⓑ Ⓒ Ⓓ Ⓔ	24 Ⓐ Ⓑ Ⓒ Ⓓ Ⓔ	34 Ⓐ Ⓑ Ⓒ Ⓓ Ⓔ
5 Ⓐ Ⓑ Ⓒ Ⓓ Ⓔ	15 Ⓐ Ⓑ Ⓒ Ⓓ Ⓔ	25 Ⓐ Ⓑ Ⓒ Ⓓ Ⓔ	35 Ⓐ Ⓑ Ⓒ Ⓓ Ⓔ
6 Ⓐ Ⓑ Ⓒ Ⓓ Ⓔ	16 Ⓐ Ⓑ Ⓒ Ⓓ Ⓔ	26 Ⓐ Ⓑ Ⓒ Ⓓ Ⓔ	36 Ⓐ Ⓑ Ⓒ Ⓓ Ⓔ
7 Ⓐ Ⓑ Ⓒ Ⓓ Ⓔ	17 Ⓐ Ⓑ Ⓒ Ⓓ Ⓔ	27 Ⓐ Ⓑ Ⓒ Ⓓ Ⓔ	37 Ⓐ Ⓑ Ⓒ Ⓓ Ⓔ
8 Ⓐ Ⓑ Ⓒ Ⓓ Ⓔ	18 Ⓐ Ⓑ Ⓒ Ⓓ Ⓔ	28 Ⓐ Ⓑ Ⓒ Ⓓ Ⓔ	38 Ⓐ Ⓑ Ⓒ Ⓓ Ⓔ
9 Ⓐ Ⓑ Ⓒ Ⓓ Ⓔ	19 Ⓐ Ⓑ Ⓒ Ⓓ Ⓔ	29 Ⓐ Ⓑ Ⓒ Ⓓ Ⓔ	39 Ⓐ Ⓑ Ⓒ Ⓓ Ⓔ
10 Ⓐ Ⓑ Ⓒ Ⓓ Ⓔ	20 Ⓐ Ⓑ Ⓒ Ⓓ Ⓔ	30 Ⓐ Ⓑ Ⓒ Ⓓ Ⓔ	40 Ⓐ Ⓑ Ⓒ Ⓓ Ⓔ

SECTION 5

1 Ⓐ Ⓑ Ⓒ Ⓓ Ⓔ	11 Ⓐ Ⓑ Ⓒ Ⓓ Ⓔ	21 Ⓐ Ⓑ Ⓒ Ⓓ Ⓔ	31 Ⓐ Ⓑ Ⓒ Ⓓ Ⓔ
2 Ⓐ Ⓑ Ⓒ Ⓓ Ⓔ	12 Ⓐ Ⓑ Ⓒ Ⓓ Ⓔ	22 Ⓐ Ⓑ Ⓒ Ⓓ Ⓔ	32 Ⓐ Ⓑ Ⓒ Ⓓ Ⓔ
3 Ⓐ Ⓑ Ⓒ Ⓓ Ⓔ	13 Ⓐ Ⓑ Ⓒ Ⓓ Ⓔ	23 Ⓐ Ⓑ Ⓒ Ⓓ Ⓔ	33 Ⓐ Ⓑ Ⓒ Ⓓ Ⓔ
4 Ⓐ Ⓑ Ⓒ Ⓓ Ⓔ	14 Ⓐ Ⓑ Ⓒ Ⓓ Ⓔ	24 Ⓐ Ⓑ Ⓒ Ⓓ Ⓔ	34 Ⓐ Ⓑ Ⓒ Ⓓ Ⓔ
5 Ⓐ Ⓑ Ⓒ Ⓓ Ⓔ	15 Ⓐ Ⓑ Ⓒ Ⓓ Ⓔ	25 Ⓐ Ⓑ Ⓒ Ⓓ Ⓔ	35 Ⓐ Ⓑ Ⓒ Ⓓ Ⓔ
6 Ⓐ Ⓑ Ⓒ Ⓓ Ⓔ	16 Ⓐ Ⓑ Ⓒ Ⓓ Ⓔ	26 Ⓐ Ⓑ Ⓒ Ⓓ Ⓔ	36 Ⓐ Ⓑ Ⓒ Ⓓ Ⓔ
7 Ⓐ Ⓑ Ⓒ Ⓓ Ⓔ	17 Ⓐ Ⓑ Ⓒ Ⓓ Ⓔ	27 Ⓐ Ⓑ Ⓒ Ⓓ Ⓔ	37 Ⓐ Ⓑ Ⓒ Ⓓ Ⓔ
8 Ⓐ Ⓑ Ⓒ Ⓓ Ⓔ	18 Ⓐ Ⓑ Ⓒ Ⓓ Ⓔ	28 Ⓐ Ⓑ Ⓒ Ⓓ Ⓔ	38 Ⓐ Ⓑ Ⓒ Ⓓ Ⓔ
9 Ⓐ Ⓑ Ⓒ Ⓓ Ⓔ	19 Ⓐ Ⓑ Ⓒ Ⓓ Ⓔ	29 Ⓐ Ⓑ Ⓒ Ⓓ Ⓔ	39 Ⓐ Ⓑ Ⓒ Ⓓ Ⓔ
10 Ⓐ Ⓑ Ⓒ Ⓓ Ⓔ	20 Ⓐ Ⓑ Ⓒ Ⓓ Ⓔ	30 Ⓐ Ⓑ Ⓒ Ⓓ Ⓔ	40 Ⓐ Ⓑ Ⓒ Ⓓ Ⓔ

Only answers entered in the ovals in each grid area will be scored.

SECTION 4 STUDENT-PRODUCED RESPONSES

PRACTICE TEST

ANSWER KEY

Section 1 Critical Reading	Section 2 Math	Section 3 Critical Reading	Section 4 Math	Section 5 Writing Skills	
1. A	1. E	1. E	1. 1/5 or .2	1. B	25. E
2. B	2. D	2. B	2. 3	2. E	26. A
3. B	3. E	3. A	3. 7 or 37	3. B	27. D
4. D	4. D	4. C	4. 8	4. C	28. B
5. B	5. C	5. B	5. 34	5. D	29. B
6. A	6. D	6. A	6. 54 or 56	6. A	30. D
7. E	7. E	7. E	7. 2 or 3	7. C	31. D
8. E	8. A	8. B	8. 1	8. E	32. B
9. E	9. E	9. D	9. 2 or 3	9. D	33. A
10. E	10. D	10. D	10. 16	10. C	34. B
11. D	11. A	11. B	11. E	11. E	35. B
12. A	12. E	12. E	12. B	12. A	36. A
13. C	13. D	13. E	13. E	13. A	37. D
14. E	14. B	14. B	14. E	14. A	38. E
15. B	15. A	15. B	15. C	15. D	39. A
16. C	16. B	16. D	16. E	16. D	
17. E	17. C	17. D	17. B	17. C	
18. E	18. E	18. A	18. A	18. E	
19. D	19. E	19. C		19. A	
20. D	20. B	20. A		20. B	
21. D		21. D		21. A	
22. B		22. C		22. C	
23. E		23. E		23. E	
24. D		24. A		24. B	

DETAILED EXPLANATIONS

SECTION 1—VERBAL

1. (A) The correct answer is (A) because the word "frustrated" indicates that some sort of problem was faced by the scientist. Because of this problem, the scientist had to do something that he or she wouldn't normally do: end or "terminate" the experiment. Choice (B) "dangers" is possible, but under few circumstances would an experiment be "extended" because of the dangers; nor, would a scientist "reluctantly" end a dangerous situation. Choice (C) is not correct because a scientist would not be frustrated by "successes." Choice (D) makes no sense semantically. Choice (E) is not correct because, although the scientist might be frustrated by many "liabilities" or limitations of the experiment, he would enthusiastically, not "reluctantly," want to "study" where he went wrong.

2. (B) Although some knowledge of history might be helpful in answering this question, it was the "serfs" who toiled in "endless" jobs. Therefore the correct answer is (B). The "nobles" (A) might have had a more "enjoyable" existence, but they did not do so by working the land. The "monks" (C), while praying for "everlasting" salvation, did not work the land either. "Merchants" (D) and "knights" (E) did not work the land. Nor did nobles, monks, merchants, or knights comprise the majority of the population. Serfs were more numerous.

3. (B) There are two clues in this sentence: "monotonous" and "hourlong" describing the "speech." Anyone who has sat through a monotonous, long speech would know that this situation would be never-ending or "interminable," and that you would be "impatient" for it to end. Therefore, choice (B) is the correct answer. Choice (A) is not correct because a monotone delivery would not be "exciting." Although an hour-long speech might be "unbelievable" (C), the audience would not be "skeptical" or disbelieving while waiting for the conclusion. An hour-long speech is "long" (D), and although the audience might be "doubtful" if it would ever end, this is not the best choice. An hour-long speech delivered in a monotone is undoubtedly "uninteresting" (E), but surely the audience would not be excited about the ending, just excited that it ended at all.

4. (D) The key words here are "even though," which will indicate that a contradiction is being set up. Therefore, the verses would not be those that would "receive great acclaim." Choice (D) "inane" (silly, absurd) is the best answer. Absurd verses would not normally receive great acclaim. Choice (A) "grand" and choice (B) "impressive" are wrong for the same reasons. Verses which were grand or impressive would be worthy of acclaim, and if these answers were chosen, it means that "even though" was not acknowledged properly by the test taker. Choice (C) "musical" is an adjective that describes the verses in a neutral way. We are looking for an adjective that is negative to show why the verses did not deserve "great acclaim." Choice (E) "unlikely" is a possibility, but not the best choice. "Unlikely" (improbable) is a negative way to describe a poem, but is not as strong or as satisfactory as "inane."

5. **(B)** The context of the sentence implies that the actor was rejected for parts because "no one could be sure how he would behave." The best answer is (B) "mercurial" (unpredictably changeable). (A) "confident" (self-assured) is an incorrect choice because it doesn't address the sense of change and wide mood swings that would cause the problems for directors. (C) is incorrect because "pessimistic" (an inclination to take the worst possible view) is an inappropriate choice for the context of the sentence. (D) "overpowering" (overcome by superior force) has no contextual meaning for the sentence. (E) "Inhibited" (restrained in expression or functioning), although a possible answer, is not appropriate to the sentence context of "no one could be sure how he would behave." An inhibited person does not necessarily exhibit change of temperament.

6. **(A)** The key word here is "marathon," which indicates that we are looking for a word that connotes a task requiring fortitude. The best answer would be "Herculean" (of extraordinary power). "Leg cramps" indicate that the second word means that the runner has problems. "Debilitate" (impair the health or strength of) would be the best choice because the cramps interfere with the runner's ability to participate in the marathon. This interference (the debilitation of leg cramps) would make running the marathon more difficult than normal (a Herculean task). (B) "hard" is a possibility, but not the best choice because it only connotes moderate difficulty as compared to "Herculean." In addition, "impel" (to urge or drive forward) is an incorrect choice because it means the opposite of what the sentence implies. (C) "frustrating" is a possibility, but "spur" (urge forward, incite) is contrary to the meaning of the sentence. (D) "invigorating" (give life and energy) and (E) "thrilling" are incorrect choices because both imply that leg cramps are a positive experience for the runner.

7. **(E)** Choice (E) "curtail" (limit) and "penetrate" (to enter into, permeate) is the best choice. When substituted into the sentence, this combination of words makes the most sense. Scientists warn us that unless we "limit" the poisons in the air, global warming could happen as the sun's rays "enter into" the atmosphere. Choice (A) is incorrect because scientists would not want to "collect" the poisons. This would not prevent "global warming." Choice (B) is wrong because although "weaken" is a possibility, "combine" is incorrect. "Combining" the poisons would not prevent global warming. (C) "restrict" (limit) is a possibility, however, "expedite" (carry out promptly) is wrong because the word makes no sense when inserted into the sentence. (D) "aggravate" makes no sense in the context of this sentence.

8. **(E)** The author describes the Irish Parliament all through the 1700s as being corrupt in many respects. (E) is the best answer. Choice (A) cannot be chosen since the 1700s and the eighteenth century are the same time periods. The Parliament was not contrived for the benefit of the Catholic clergy; in fact, the Parliament worked against the Catholics, according to the author. (B) is not an appropriate answer. The passage implies corruption in both the Upper and the Lower Houses; (C) is an incorrect choice. The author in no way implies that the Irish Parliament was a model of decency; (D) should not be selected.

9. **(E)** The main idea of the passage is to (E) raise the sham of the Irish Parliament from the dark waters of the past. The author in no way is trying to point out a truly distinct and admirable system of government. (A) should not be chosen. The author has little respect for the way that the Irish Parliament was "stacked"; he was not trying to point out the sincerity and honesty of those who brought about the system. (B) is not an appropriate choice. The author was not seeking to stress again the model Irish Parliament, which many countries could use as a successful system of government (C) or to bring to the surface the forgotten system with its many attributes (D).

10. (E)   The writer tries to attribute the corruption to the borough system (E). The Catholic religion did not develop the corruption so (A) should not be selected. Mr. Lecky (B) is only quoted in the passage and is not the source of the corruption nor is the legend-haunted lake (C). A two-house system does not necessarily result in corruption; (D) should not be chosen.

11. (D)   The word "simulacrum" in line 4 can be best defined as (D) "a pretense." The test-taker who selected (A) "symmetry," or one side like that of the other, must have had the word "similar" in mind. "Simulacrum" has nothing to do with a ghost or haunting (B). As stated above the word means a pretense or a sham; it is not the name of a type of government (C) or a legislature or law-making body (D). Neither answer should be chosen.

12. (A)   To give credence to his writings, the author calls on the statements of Hely Hutchinson. (A) is the best answer. The writer does not use subliminal persuasion; (B) should not be selected. The writer gives opinions as well as facts and figures; (C) should not be chosen. The author does consult the voting records so (D) cannot be chosen. The author does not ignore the complicated method of corrupting both Houses. (E) is not the best choice.

13. (C)   The text bears out the economic factor early (line 10); the geographic influence becomes obvious at line 12. (A) is a strong distractor, but line 34 has "America . . . free from . . . exact imitation." (D) is a misreading of line 9; material dealing with Charleston does not confirm (B) or (E).

14. (E)   Line 35 bears out freedom of style, denying (A) (European/ British tradition) and (C), since log cabins are not indigenous to the Eastern Coast. Line 38 denies that brick predominated all American architecture (D).

15. (B)   Line 20 establishes the call to woodwork; wood is hardly "nonflammable" (D). (A) is unjustified by the text; (C) is a misreading of line 33. Clapboard is not a function of the Flemish (E); brick is.

16. (C)   Charleston has "a certain southern flavor" (line 42) "unlike any other colonial metropolis" (line 49), denying (B) and (A) (since the South is a regional factor). Both (D) and (E) are invalidated by their respective generalizations.

17. (E)   The author believes that the order of insects as fertilizers of native flowers in order of their importance is bees, Lepidoptera, flies (E). The passage states that bees come first, and that the second place is either the Lepidoptera (butterflies) or the flies. Choice (A) is inappropriate because it does not place bees as the number one insect for fertilizing native flowers. Choice (B) is inappropriate because it omits bees and it lists both butterflies and Lepidoptera which are one and the same. Choice (C) is not the best choice because it, too, lists Lepidoptera and butterflies as two separate divisions; it is better than choice (B), however, since it does include bees. (D) is not the best choice because bees come first—not Lepidoptera.

18. (E)   The only order which is fitted for taking honey from flowers in all its family is the Lepidoptera. This answer (E) is given in lines 8–11. Not all bees (A) are capable of doing this; this means that both choices (A) and (B) are inappropriate since they both include the bee. Since it has already been established that Lepidoptera and butterflies are the same, we can disqualify choices (C) and (D) on that point alone. Choices (C) and (D)

are also incorrect since they include bees also; choice (D) includes flies and bees (both of which are incorrect) and lists also Lepidoptera and butterflies which are one and the same. Again, the best answer is (E).

19. (D) The mouth of the butterfly can be best described as a long, thin, tube which can be rolled up into a small space and an upper lip and mandibles which are short (D). The mouth of the butterfly is definitely not simple (A). The long, thin tube on the butterfly does not extend in a stiff manner; (B) is not a good choice. Choice (C) is incomplete; the mouth does consist of a long, thin tube which can be rolled up into a small space, but it is more than that. Choice (E) is incorrect; the mouth cannot be accurately described as a pointed "stinger" for sucking up the pollen.

20. (D) The Lepidoptera, at the time of this writing, had been studied by too many scientists to list. (D) is the correct answer. Neither Müller only (A) nor Müller and his brother (B) are correct answers. Choice (C)— the two Müllers, Speyer, and MacLachlan—is an incomplete answer and should not be chosen. The study of the Lepidoptera is not inconsequential; choice (E) is false.

21. (D) The main purpose of this writing is to show the importance and development of the Lepidoptera. (D) is the best choice. The article is not just designed to emphasize the importance of the mouth parts of the bee. (A) is not the best choice. The article does show the importance of the bee in fertilization of native flowers, but that is not its primary purpose. (B) is not the best choice. The butterfly is NOT number one in fertilization of native flowers. Choice (C) is false and should not be chosen. Choice (E) is true; the Lepidoptera do seem to be the only insects which do not confine their visits to flowers to the daylight, but that is not the primary purpose of the article. (E) is not the best choice.

22. (B) The writer speculates that there are few nocturnal Lepidoptera in our climate because of the shortness of the period suitable for their flight. (B) is the best answer. The writer does not attribute the few nocturnal Lepidoptera to the pursuit of collectors during nocturnal hours. (A) is not the best choice. The Lepidoptera has swift movements (C) and violent movements (D) but this does not relate to the fact that there are few nocturnal Lepidoptera. There are nocturnal flowers in our climate so (E) is false. Choice (B) is clearly the best choice.

23. (E) Nocturnal flowers to be visited by the Lepidoptera usually are light-colored. (E) is the best answer. If the flowers are dark-colored (A), they would be less visible. (A) is a poor choice. Odor helps attract nocturnal insects; choice (B) which states that they are without odor is incorrect and should not be chosen. If flowers open early in the day and close at night, then they cannot be visited by nocturnal Lepidoptera. (C) is not an acceptable answer. If the flowers secrete their nectar early in the day, they would not be attractive to nocturnal insects. (D) is not the best choice.

24. (D) The context of the passage supports "incompletely formed" as the correct answer. The context clue is "which are not visible in my figure" indicates that the maxillary palps are not completely formed. Shortened (A), suggests that the maxillary palps were once complete, which is not supported by the material. Both imperfect (B) and mangled (C) suggest that the palps were damaged in some way. Obsolete (E) does not make sense; the author believes that Lepidoptera has adapted in a superior way.

DETAILED EXPLANATIONS

SECTION 2—MATH

1. **(E)** We know that $\frac{2}{5}$ of the French club were females. Thus, there were $\frac{2}{5} \times 40 = 16$ females in the French club. Since there were a total of 70 students, there were 30 students who are not in the French club. Of these, $\frac{1}{3}$, or 10, were male. Therefore, there were 20 females not in the French club. By adding the 16 females in the French club to the 20 not in the club, we arrive at the answer: 36.

2. **(D)** If we take this problem one step at a time, it will cause no problems. First of all, the problem asks us to find a number such that $\frac{1}{3}$ of that number will be the same as 40% of 75.

    The first computation is to find 40% of 75. We can do this by multiplying $.4 \times 75$, which equals 30. $(40\% = .4)$.

    Now we are asked to find a number (x) such that $\frac{1}{3}$ of x would equal 30. To do this we can set up the following equation:

    $\frac{1}{3} \times x = 30$

    Multiply both sides by 3 and you get $x = 90$

3. **(E)**

angle ADC is a right angle	all angles of a square are right angles
ADC is a right triangle	a triangle with a right angle is a right triangle
$AD = DC$	all sides of a square are equal
angle DAC = angle ACD	if 2 sides of a triangle are equal, then the corresponding angles are equal
angle $DAC = 45$ = angle ACD	if 2 sides of a right triangle are equal, the 2 corresponding angles are equal and the triangle is a 45-45-90 right triangle
$g = 8 = CD$	Remember the ratio of the lengths of the sides on a 45-45-90 triangle, since the hypotenuse is $8\sqrt{2}$, the legs must be 8.
area of $DEFC = 128$	area of rectangle = $l \times w$ (8×16)

4. (D) With a problem such as this, it is easier to test the answer choices than to do the algebra.

Because we are asked to find the greatest possible integer, we will test the greatest answer choice first.

If $y = 2$, then all three expressions are positive, and the result of multiplying them is positive.

If $y = 1$, then all three expressions are positive, and the result of multiplying them is positive.

If $y = 0$, then one of the expressions equals 0, and the result of multiplying them is 0.

If $y = -1$, then one of the expressions (y) is negative and the other two expressions ($y + 3$) and ($y + 5$) are positive, and the result of multiplying them is negative.

Because -1 is greater than -2, (D) is the correct answer.

5. (C) Because an average is the sum of the numbers divided by the number of numbers, if five numbers have an average of 8, their sum must be $8 \times 5 = 40$.

We now must find the largest possible integer in the group, if the other four integers are different positive integers. To get the largest integer we must make the other integers as small as possible.

The four smallest different positive integers are 1, 2, 3, and 4. Thus we can set up the following equation:

$$1 + 2 + 3 + 4 + x = 40$$
$$10 + x = 40$$
$$x = 30$$

6. (D) A triangle with angles of 45, 45, 90 is an isosceles right triangle. The area of any triangle is equal to $\frac{1}{2}$ the base times its height, but in the case of the isosceles right triangle the two non-hypotenuse sides do not only function as the base and height of the triangle, but they are also equal to each other. Thus we can set up the following equation:

$$\text{Area} = \frac{1}{2} \text{side} \times \text{side}$$
$$64 = \frac{1}{2}s^2$$
$$128 = s^2$$
$$\sqrt{128} = s$$
$$\sqrt{64 \times 2} = s$$
$$8\sqrt{2} = s$$

If the legs of an isosceles right triangle each equal $8\sqrt{2}$, then the hypotenuse must be $8\sqrt{2} \times \sqrt{2}$ (Remember the ratio of the lengths of the sides on a 45-45-90 triangle). So the perimeter of the triangle is $8\sqrt{2} + 8\sqrt{2} + 16 = 16\sqrt{2} + 16$.

7. **(E)** Cross multiply both equations

$$\frac{m}{g} = \frac{1}{y} = g = my \quad \text{and} \quad \frac{m}{d} = \frac{1}{(y+1)} = d = my + m$$

Substitute g for my in the second equation and you get

$$d = g + m$$

Subtract m from both sides of the equation to come up with the answer:

$$g = d - m$$

8. **(A)** Cross multiply to get $ab = 900$. Since a and b are the base and height of the square, you know its area must be 900, which means the triangle's area is also 900. The equation given for the triangle, $o^2 - m^2 = n^2$, looks similar to the Pythagorean theorem because it is. Add m^2 to both sides and you get $o^2 = m^2 + n^2$. This tells you that o is the hypotenuse and m and n are the perpendicular sides, which is the same as the base and height. Therefore, if the area of the triangle is 900, you can write out the equation

$$\tfrac{1}{2}mn = 900, \text{ and } mn = 1{,}800$$

9. **(E)** Substitute -6 in each of the choices.

$$-6^2 = 36$$

$$36 + 36 \neq 0$$

10. **(D)** To solve this problem, we can set up a single proportion.

$$\frac{1}{1{,}000} = \frac{4.8}{x}$$

$$x = 4.8 \times 1{,}000$$

$$x = 4{,}800$$

11. **(A)**
$$\angle ABD - \angle ABE = \angle EBD$$

$$80° - 30° = \angle EBD$$

$$50° = \angle EBD$$

Since there are 180° in a triangle, you know that $\angle BED$ (90°) + $\angle EBD$ (50°) + $\angle BDE$ ($x°$) = 180. Therefore $\angle BDE = 40°$. Since a straight line has 180°, $\angle BDE$ (40°) + $\angle BDC$ ($y°$) = 180°. Therefore $\angle BDC = 140°$. The sum of the two remaining angles ($\angle DBC$ and $\angle BCD$) in $\triangle BCD$ must add up to 40°.

12. **(E)** The key to doing this problem is to recognize that all the fractions equal $\tfrac{1}{3}$. Thus we have

$$\frac{1}{3} \times \frac{1}{3} \times \frac{1}{3} \times \frac{1}{3} \times \frac{1}{3} = \frac{1}{243}$$

When you get a problem such as this, where it appears as though a great many computations are involved, you should realize that there is usually a way to simplify the problem. In your studies, try to avoid doing problems the long way, and work instead at finding the more efficient way to do the problem.

13. **(D)** Because all parts of all the answer choices are expressed as whole numbers, we must express all parts of the recipe as whole numbers. Cashews and whole wheat flour are already expressed as whole numbers so we can turn our attention to the sunflower seeds. The recipe given calls for $\frac{1}{4}$ a cup of sunflower seeds.

To get from $\frac{1}{4}$ of a cup to a whole cup, we must multiply by 4:

$$\frac{1}{4} \times 4 = 1$$

If, however, we multiply the amount of sunflower seeds by 4, we must multiply the amount of cashews and whole wheat flour by 4. Cashews: 2 cups $\times$ 4 = 8 cups

Whole wheat flour: 6 cups $\times$ 4 = 24 cups

Thus, the ingredients could be expressed as 8:24:1.

14. **(B)** Because John walks at 90 feet per minute and Debbie walks at 65 feet per minute, John travels 25 feet more per minute than Debbie.

$$90 - 65 = 25$$

25 feet per minute $\times$ 120 minutes (the number of minutes in 2 hours) yields 3,000 feet.

15. **(A)** The key to this question is to recognize that $25a^4 - 36b^{18}$ can be factored into

$$(5a^2 - 6b^9)(5a^2 + 6b^9)$$

Thus if $25a^4 - 36b^{18} = 72$, then

$$4(5a^2 - 6b^9)(5a^2 + 6b^9)$$

must be equal to 4×72, which equals 288.

16. **(B)** To find the sum of the interior angles of a polygon, we can make use of the following formula: the sum of the interior angles of a polygon = $180 \times (n - 2)$, where n = the number of sides.

Because polygon $ABCDE$ has 5 sides, it has $180 (5 - 2)$ or 180×3 or $540°$. Thus,

$A + B + C + D + E = 540$	the whole equals the sum of its parts
$500 + E = 540$	substitute
$500 - 500 + E = 540 - 500$	equals minus equals are equal
$E = 40$	simplify
$F = 40$	vertical angles are equal

Because polygon $FGHI$ has four sides, it equals $180 (4 - 2) = 180 (2) = 360°$

$F + G + H + I = 360$	whole equals the sum of its parts
$40 + G + H + I = 360$	substitute
$40 - 40 + G + H + I = 360 - 40$	equals minus equals are equal
$G + H + I = 320$	simplify

17. **(C)** To change a mixed number to an improper fraction, multiply the whole number (4) by the denominator (6) of the fraction ($4 \times 6 = 24$). Add the numerator (5) to the product (24). Write the sum (29) over the denominator of the fraction, $\frac{29}{6}$.

18. **(E)** Because we are told $m + n$ is the longest side (hypotenuse) of the right triangle, we can set up the equation:

$$m^2 + (m - n)^2 = (m + n)^2$$

$$m^2 + m^2 - 2mn + n^2 = m^2 + 2mn + n^2$$

Simplify:

$$2m^2 - 2mn + n^2 = m^2 + 2mn + n^2$$

$$m^2 = 4mn$$

$$\frac{m^2}{4m} = \frac{4mn}{4m}$$

$$\frac{m}{4} = n$$

19. **(E)** If opposite sides of a quadrilateral are equal and parallel, the quadrilateral is a parallelogram. Thus, $ABCD$ is a parallelogram.

If $GM = \frac{3}{4}$ of AD, then we can let $GM = 3$ and $AD = 4$. If $MY = \frac{4}{5}$ of CE, then we can let $MY = 4$ and $CE = 5$.

If $GM = 3$ and $MY = 4$, because GMY is a right triangle, its area would be $\frac{1}{2}(3 \times 4) = 6$.

Because $ABCD$ is a parallelogram and CE is its altitude, its area would be $CE \times AD = 5 \times 4 = 20$.

Thus, the ratio of the area of GMY to $ABCD$ would be $\frac{6}{20} = 3:10$.

20. **(B)** The key to the problem is that they received the same amount of money per hour of work. Because Rosina earned \$225 while Mary only earned \$75, we know that Rosina worked longer than Mary did. Additionally, if we divide 225 by 75, we learn that Rosina worked 3 times as long as Mary did.

Thus, if g represents the amount of time Mary worked, then $3g$ would represent the amount of time Rosina worked. We can now set up an equation.

$$g + 3g = 16$$

$$4g = 16$$

$$g = 4$$

DETAILED EXPLANATIONS

SECTION 3—VERBAL

1. **(E)** In this sentence there is a contrast between city living ("highrises") and country living ("white picket fences and cupolas"). People usually view the city as "modern" and the country as old fashioned or "quaint"; therefore, (E) is the right answer. (A) is wrong because "aloof" (reserved) does not fit into the implied meaning of the sentence. (B) is also incorrect because "capricious" (changeable) would mean that country living is changeable as compared to city living, and that makes no sense. (C) "redundant" (repetitious) is wrong because the use of this word would make the sentence meaningless. The contrast between city and country living is not repetitious. The choice of (D) "ornate" (elaborate) is a possibility, because although cupolas are ornate, white picket fences are not. Cupolas and white picket fences may be considered more·"quaint" than "ornate."

2. **(B)** The best answer is (B) "incompatible" (disagreeing, disharmonious) because the sentence tells about two people who cannot agree on friends, books, movies, and sports. These people are definitely incompatible. Choice (A) "dispassionate" (lack of feeling, impartial) is a possible choice if the question only contained a sentence about two people getting a divorce. However, there are several sentences preceding that describe the situation where two people cannot agree. Choice (C) "arbitrary" (based on one's preference or whim) does not fit semantically. These people were not arbitrary about getting a divorce; they had reasons listed in several sentences in the question. Choice (D) "meticulous" (exacting, precise) is wrong because it is not a semantic equivalent of "not being able to agree," which was the context of this question. Choice (E) "nostalgic" (longing for the past; filled with bittersweet memories) is not semantically accurate. It does not fit into the implied meaning of the sentences.

3. **(A)** "Discern" (distinguish one thing from another), choice (A), is the correct answer because we are looking for a verb that tells us that since Marcia is an art expert (many years of art school) she could distinguish an authentic painting from its copy. Choice (B) "condone" means "to forgive" and would make no sense if it was inserted as the verb in the sentence. "Laud" (praise), choice (C), is an incorrect verb substitution because "laud" is not a comparison word. You would "laud" something directly. Choice (D) "emulate" (follow the example of) makes no sense semantically. Choice (E) "rationalize" (to offer reasons for) is wrong, because the word is commonly used as a way for people to account for something, not as a differentiating word.

4. **(C)** The best answer here is "torpid" and "lethargic" (lazy, passive). The sentence sets up the conditions: "hot summer sun and high humidity." Certainly, anyone who has knowledge of what the effects of heat and humidity can do would choose two adjectives that described lazy, passive reactions. Choice (A) "unruly" (disobedient) and

"urbane" (cultured, suave) is wrong because these words do not apply as adjectives for people who are faced with the kind of day described in the sentence. Choice (B) "pallid" (shallow, colorless) does not describe a feeling, and although people might be "vulnerable" (open to attack, unprotected) on a hot, humid day, this is not the correct answer because "pallid" is wrong. Choice (D) "immune" (protected, unthreatened by) is not semantically appropriate for the sentence; therefore, (D) is an incorrect choice. "Depleted" (to reduce, to empty) and "contrite" (regretful, sorrowful), choice (E), is incorrect because a hot summer day would not be considered sorrowful.

5. (B)   The contextual meaning of this sentence is that the author has to do something to the conclusion of his last chapter so that he doesn't miss his deadline. The next choice is (B) "execute" (carry to completion) because if he "executes" his last chapter, he won't miss his deadline. Choice (A) "expand" is incorrect because if he expands his chapter, he will be adding more information, and might miss the deadline. Choice (C) is incorrect because "exhaust" (tire, wear out) does not fit into the meaning of the sentence. Choice (D) "endorse" (support, approve of, recommend), when inserted into the sentence, makes the sentence meaningless. Choice (E) "extol" (praise) has no meaning in the sentence. Whether or not the author praised his last chapter would not help him meet his deadline.

6. (A)   The semantic implication of this sentence asks you to find an adjective that describes what type of belief would cause an environmental group to face "overwhelming forces." The best answer is (A) "adamant" (not yielding, firm), because only firm beliefs would stand up in the face of "overwhelming forces." Choice (B) "deliberate" (intentional) is a possibility, but not the best choice. Intentional beliefs are done with a purpose, but might back down in the face of adversity. Choice (C) "didactic" (instructive) is not correct because it is not semantically related to "overwhelming forces." Choice (D) "fallacious" (misleading) has no meaning when inserted into the sentence. Choice (E) "pragmatic" (practical, matter-of-fact) beliefs would back down in the face of overwhelming forces as a matter of protection.

7. (E)   In line 14 the word "embalmed" means preserved. (E) is the best answer. Embalming actually prevents decay; (A) is a poor choice. The word "embalmed" does not mean exaggerated; there is no hint given that the authors exaggerate in their writing. (B) should not be chosen. The writing of the authors mentioned is not referred to as boring (C) or that which omits the faults of (D); both answers should be avoided.

8. (B)   The writer's main objective in the writing of the passage is to present both a geographical and a literary description of the area to the reader. (B) is the best choice. The passage is not primarily geographical in nature; (A) is not accurate. Since the passage does not give a history of the area, choice (C)—to present both a geographical description and a historical description—is inaccurate. The "ramble" is not fictional so (D) is not a good choice. The main purpose is not to inform the reader of outstanding literary contributions; some literary contributions are mentioned, but the geography must not be overlooked! (E) should not be chosen.

9. (D)   The writer would attest that Irving was more influenced by the environment than other writers were influenced. (D) is the best answer. The author of this passage has written— at length—on the influence of the environment on a writer. (A) should not be chosen. The writer does not talk about blocking out the environment; he talks about how it can influence the writer consciously and subconsciously; (B) should not be selected. It was Irving—not Cooper—who was more influenced by the environment than other writers

were influenced. The author mentions the duel that was fought there; this murder shows that violence can occur even in this lonely spot. (Duels were, of course, legal at the time.)

10. (D) The passage describes Constitution Island as composed of rude masses of rock. (D) is the best answer. (A) is not the best answer since the island is not far from water. (B) is a reference to the Hudson River. It should not be selected. The heart of the Highlands refers to West Point, not Constitution Island. (C) should not be used. (E) is a reference to the Hudson. (E) is not an appropriate answer.

11. (B) The primary focus of the passage is on the lack of importance of the primary self of Eliot. (B) is the correct answer. The passage does not indicate that there is an impressive number of portraitures of men and women created by that great writer George Eliot. (A) is not the best choice. The writer indicates that Eliot has impartiality toward her characters. Choice (C) states that the evident bias of Eliot toward each of her characters is "needful to her own deepest life." (C) is false and should not be chosen. The author states that "when a work of art can be understood only by enjoying it, the art is of a high kind." The writer does not consider the writings of George Eliot to be inferior. (D) is not an appropriate choice since it states that the works of Eliot are inferior; choice (D) indicates that her works can be understood only by enjoying them and enjoyment is inferior to cognition. (D) should not be chosen. The author states that we cannot say with any truthfulness that Eliot projects herself into any of her writings. (E) is false since it suggests that projection of Eliot appears in her creations.

12. (E) The author refers to her writings primarily as works of art with a moral soul. (E) is the best choice. We cannot say with any confidence that Eliot's writings are a projection of herself. (A) should not be chosen since we do not know that they are painful personal recollections. The author indicates that many good things are detachable from Eliot's writings; they are not necessarily compositions which must be kept intact at all cost. (B) should not be chosen. The writer states emphatically that Eliot's works are not didactic treatises; (C) should not be chosen. The works are described as the "second self of George Eliot." We do not know that Eliot projects herself into her writings. (D), then, should not be chosen.

13. (E) In context the reference to Eliot's works as being "not didactic treatises" (line 24) suggests that they are pleasurable readings (E). The word "didactic" suggests instruction, particularly moral instruction. This means that moralistic compositions (A) and instructive writing (B) must not be selected. Eliot's writings are not dramatic revelations (C) or social criticisms (D); neither choice should be chosen.

14. (B) The passage indicates that the reader's correct response to Eliot's writing should be to enjoy the writings given us by the artist and detach from them what we can. (B) is the correct answer. Eliot's works are not designed to be analyzed completely; (A) should not be chosen. We do not know that Eliot places herself in her writings; one should not, then, search for the glimpses of George Eliot's real self which are hidden there. The writer states that one should not separate the moral soul of any complete work of hers from its artistic medium; (C) should not be chosen. Since the author states that we should not dissect nor separate the moral soul from her work, (D) should not be chosen. Eliot is objective toward her characters; we cannot easily search for Eliot's feelings toward each character. Her true feelings are not evident upon careful scrutiny. (E) should not be chosen.

15. (B) Eliot's characters can best be described as impartial presentations. (B) is the best answer. We have no evidence that the characters are projections of Eliot herself. (A) is not

the best choice. Eliot is said to condemn but not to hate; her characters do not live their own lives without any presence of the author; (C) is not the best choice. Eliot's writings are not instructive or didactic; (D) should not be chosen. Eliot's characters are complete since they live their own lives; "incomplete portraitures" (E) is not the best choice.

16. (D) The main idea of Passage 1 is (D). Carnegie suggests that active work (D) is superior to a college education. Carnegie does not promote a classical education. (A) should not be chosen. Carnegie does not promote the prejudice against educating the masses (B), but he does understand why it exists. (B) is not the correct answer. He does not advocate a study of mythology; (C) should not be chosen. Carnegie does not see the value of the liberal arts; (E) should not be chosen.

17. (D) The author of Passage 1 describes the college graduates of today as ignorant of Shakespeare. (D) is the correct answer. The college graduates have NOT received valuable instruction in his opinion. (A) is not the best answer. He sees a college education as having hurt, not bettered, their life. (B) is not a good choice. Carnegie states that the students are NOT educated for life in our world. (C) is not the best choice. Graduates are NOT filled with fire and energy, according to Carnegie; that has been stamped out of them. (E) should not be chosen.

18. (A) The main purpose of Passage 2 is to renounce the modern humanities. (A) should be chosen. The writer of Passage 2 does not view with pleasure the modern humanities. He believes the classical courses are most important. (B) should not be chosen since it states that the writer tries to present the modern humanities as important general culture. The writer of Passage 2 does not ridicule the traditional courses of study. The writer, rather, seems to endorse the traditional courses. (C) is not the best answer. The writer does not advocate the new so-called "special education." (D) should not be chosen. The writer opposes the total reorganization of secondary education. (E) should not be chosen.

19. (C) When the writer of Passage 2 states that "we are saved by adding Goethe's 'Faust' to Shakespeare's 'Hamlet,' instead of the 'Aeneid,' he is employing a tongue-in-cheek attitude. (C) is the best answer. The author does not use alliteration. Alliteration (A) is a repetition of sounds. (A) should not be chosen. A simile (B) uses the words *like* or *as*; (B) is not the best choice. The writer does not use denotation—saying exactly what you mean. (D) should not be selected. The writer is not using an understatement. (E) is not a good choice.

20. (A) The best meaning of being "asphyxiated by a rarefication of its environment" in line 96 of Passage 2 is (A), killed by purification. In this case "purifying the schools" with the new curriculum, the writer feels, will kill education. The writer is fearful of destroying learning, but not through vocational education; he is fearful the academic curriculum will destroy learning. (B) is not the best choice. The reference is not to Greek mythology; (C) is not the best choice. The writer is fearful that important content is being left out; he is not fearful of being smothered by important concepts (D) or being choked with the amount of material to be learned (E).

21. (D) The main point made by the writer of Passage 2 about "practical" courses, like bookkeeping, is that they can be taught at special classes; they are not to be a part of the school curriculum. (D) is the best answer. The writer of Passage 1 would not advocate the subordination of general culture to bookkeeping; (A) should not be selected. The writer believes just the opposite of (B); he believes that the courses should be provided

at special lessons—not by the schools. (B) should not be selected. The bookkeeping courses, in the mind of the writer of Passage 2, are NOT within the scope of the public schools; he believes they can be provided at special lessons. (C) should not be chosen. The writer does not believe that Latin should be given up for bookkeeping. (E) is an incorrect choice.

22. (C) The writer of Passage 1, when questioned about classical education, would point out its inadequacies. (C) is the best answer. Since the writer does not support classical education, he would not criticize those who say negative things about classical education. (A) should not be chosen. Since no research was done, the writer could NOT show the recent research to back up his beliefs. (B) is not a good choice. The writer does not advocate classical education; he does not feel the structure is adequate; he would not point out the quality of the structure which has survived for a long period of time. (D) should not be selected. Those who would dispense with the system do not have humility; rather, they feel their system is best. (E) should not be chosen.

23. (E) The writer's question as to which minds are insulted by Latin and English criticizes those who seek to change the curriculum. (E) is the best choice. The writer advocates the classics; he thinks the past should be used as a model for education. He would not likely bring out the mistakes made in the past. (A) should not be chosen. The writer advocates the program of the past; he does not think it needs to be changed. He would not likely indicate why the secondary education program had to be changed. (B) is not the best choice. Since the classics are in effect and since the writer wants to keep what is, he would not show what should be as opposed to what is. He would advocate keeping what is. (C) should not be chosen. What was IS the ideal to the writer; he would NOT highlight the distinction between the ideal and what was. (D) should not be chosen.

24. (A) The writer of Passage 2 would agree that modern humanities should not be employed by secondary education. (A) is the best choice. The writer of Passage 2 does not think the modern humanities include the important classical components, like Latin. (B) should not be chosen. The writer claims that the classics contain "all that is comprised in special instruction" and does prepare students for industrial, commercial, and agricultural life. (C) should not be selected. The writer believes the science component of the modern humanities is basically like the science component in classical education; he would not agree that the modern humanities have a superior science component which is evident when compared with the classical course of study. The writer of Passage 2 does not advocate the present improvements; (E) is not a suitable choice.

DETAILED EXPLANATIONS

SECTION 4—MATH

1. The correct response is: $\frac{1}{5}$ or .2

   The equation $4^{n+4} = 64$ is equivalent to $2^{2n+8} = 2^6$. This yields $n = -1$; hence, $5^n = \frac{1}{5}$ or 0.2.

2. The correct response is: 3

   The question gives you

   $$3A + 2B + 2C = 5$$

   and $A + B + C = 1$.

   As $C = 1$ these equations become

   $$3A + 2B + 2 = 5$$

   and $A + B + 1 = 1$

   Subtracting the second equation from the first equation you get

   $$2A + B + 1 = 4$$

   hence $2A + B = 3$.

3. The correct response is: 7 or 37

   Primes of the form $3K + 1$ less than 40 are 7, 13, 19, 31, and 37. Primes of the form $5K + 2$ less than 40 are 2, 7, 17, and 37. The two possible solutions are 7 and 37.

4. The correct response is: 8

   The area of the shaded region is

   $$(\tfrac{1}{2})(3x) = 15$$
   $$x = 10.$$

   The area of the whole figure is given by

   $$\tfrac{1}{2}3(x + y) = 27.$$

   Plugging in $x = 10$, we get

   $$(\tfrac{1}{2})3(10 + y) = 27$$
   $$10 + y = 18$$
   $$y = 8$$

5.   The correct response is: 34

30 × 30 = 900 and 40 × 40 = 1600, therefore two consecutive even numbers that yield a product of 1,224 must be somewhere in between 30 and 40.

32 × 34 = 1,088 which is less than 1,224. Try the next big even integer and you get:

34 × 36 = 1,244. The lesser of these two numbers is 34.

6.   The correct response is: 54 or 56

$$54 = 2 \times 27 = 2 \times 3^3 \text{ and}$$

$$56 = 8 \times 7 = 2^3 \times 7.$$

All other x such that $50 < x < 60$ factorize with prime greater than 10.

7.   The correct response is: 2 or 3

The largest possible value for x is 9; this will give rise to largest possible values for y. For $x = 9$ we have $6y < 3x = 6y < 27$; hence, $y = 1, 2, 3,$ or 4. For $y = 4$ we have $z < y = z < 4$; hence, the possible values for z are 1, 2, and 3. However, condition (d) states that $z > 1$. Therefore, the correct answers are 2 and 3.

8.   The correct response is: 1

Adding the first equation to the second we obtain

$$7x = 7$$

hence $x = 1$.

Plugging $x = 1$ into the second equation we have

$$4 + y = 5$$

thus $y = 1$.

9.   The correct response is: 2 or 3

As $xyz = 24$ the only possible value for x (a perfect square) is 4; this implies $yz = 6$. The possible values are $z = 2$ or $z = 3$.

10.   The correct response is: 16

The area of a triangle is $\frac{1}{2}$ base × height. The height is defined as $x = 2^3$, or $2 \times 2 \times 2$, which is the same as $x = 8$. Therefore, the height is 8, the base is 4, and the equation is:

$$\tfrac{1}{2}(8 \times 4) = 16$$

11. (E) Because the average of the nine is 16, their total must be $16 \times 9 = 144$. (Average = $\frac{\text{sum}}{\text{number}}$ therefore, sum = number × average.)

Thus, if x = the smallest number, we can set up the equation.

$$x + x + 1 + x + 2 + x + 3 + x + 4 + x + 5 + x + 6 + x + 7 + x + 8 = 144$$

$$9x + 36 = 144$$

$$9x + 36 - 36 = 144 - 36$$

$$\frac{9x}{9} = \frac{108}{9}$$

$$9x = 108$$

$$x = 12$$

If $x = 12$, the average of the four smallest numbers would be

$$\frac{12 + 13 + 14 + 15}{4} = \frac{54}{4} = 13.5$$

12. (B) The average is equal to the sum of the numbers divided by the number of numbers. In this case the number of numbers would be 60, the number of students who took the test.

The sum of the numbers would be the cumulative scores of all those who took the test. We were told to find the lowest average, and this would occur when the students scored the least number of points possible. We know that 40 of them had grades of at least 75 or better, so we assume they scored as few points as possible, which would be 75×40 or 3,000 points.

To find the lowest possible class average, we must assume that the remaining 20 students (60 – 40) each scored the lowest he or she possibly could, which means each scored a 0.

Thus, the lowest possible sum of all the points scored by the class would be

$$(40 \times 75) + (20 \times 0) = 3,000 + 0 = 3,000.$$

Thus, the lowest number of points scored by the class would be 3,000. And the lowest average would be $3,000 \div 60 = 50$.

13. (E) First we find the number of people who would not support the new stadium. To do this we subtract 700 from 10,000.

$$10,000 - 700 = 9,300$$

Now we must find out what percent 9,300 is of 10,000. To do this we set up the fraction $\frac{9,300}{10,000}$, and then we convert that fraction to a percent by dividing the numerator by the denominator. $9,300 \div 10,000 = .93$, which is the same as 93%.

14. (E) Area of square $= \left(\frac{3}{4}\right)^2 = \frac{9}{16}$

The perimeter of the square $= \frac{3}{4} \times 4 = 3$

Their difference is $3 - \frac{9}{16} = 2\frac{7}{16}$

15. (C) The two numbers are $5x$ and $3x$; their difference is 12.

$$5x - 3x = 12$$

$$2x = 12$$

$$x = 6$$

One number is $5(6) = 30$; the other is $3(6) = 18$.

16. (E) Try each of the choices. The only one that gives an answer between 3 and 4 is (E), $\frac{28}{9} = 3.\overline{111}$

17. **(B)** Square each answer and compare answer choices.

(A) $\sqrt{\dfrac{5}{8}}^{2} = \dfrac{5}{8}$

(B) $\sqrt{\dfrac{7}{10}}^{2} = \dfrac{7}{10}$

(C) $\sqrt{\dfrac{6}{13}}^{2} = \dfrac{6}{13}$

(D) $\sqrt{\dfrac{4}{9}}^{2} = \dfrac{4}{9}$

(E) $\left(\dfrac{1}{2}\right)^{2} = \dfrac{1}{4}$

Compare these fractions by dividing the numerator by the denominator. (B) is the largest.

18. **(A)** Find a common multiple of 3 and 5 and multiply both sides of the equation.

$$2F = 3G$$

$$5G = 7H$$

$$10F = 15G$$

$$15G = 21H$$

Therefore, $10F = 21H$ (divide by H)

$$\dfrac{10}{F} = 21 \text{ (divide by 10)}$$

$$\dfrac{F}{H} = \dfrac{21}{10}$$

DETAILED EXPLANATIONS

SECTION 5—WRITING SKILLS

1. **(B)** "Were praised" is a plural verb; since the subject is Chief Joseph, a singular proper noun, the verb should be "was praised." The intervening phrase of choice (A), "*together with* 250 warriors and 500 women and children," does not change the singular subject. Choice (C), "bravery," is the correct noun form, and choice (D), "for," is idiomatically correct in that phrase.

2. **(E)** Choice (A), "upon which," is a correct prepositional phrase. Choice (B), "is based," agrees with its subject, "society." In choice (C) "are" agrees with its subject, "ideals." "Derived from" in choice (D) is correct idiomatic usage.

3. **(B)** Two past actions are mentioned. The earlier of two past actions should be indicated by past perfect tense, so the answer is "had been." Choice (C) is correct. Choice (A) contains two adjectives as part of an appositive phrase modifying the subject, and choice (D), "upon the death," is idiomatically correct.

4. **(C)** Choice (C) should be "depend," not "had depended" because that use of past perfect would indicate prior past action. There is a series of events in this sentence: first, the legislature "had not finalized" the budget (B); then, Representative Wilson "pointed out" this failure (A). Choice (C), needs to be present tense as this situation still exists, and (D) is future action.

5. **(D)** In order to complete the parallelism, choice (D) should be "arrangements." Choice (A) is a noun used as an adjective. "To plan" (B) is an infinitive phrase followed by noun objects: "puppet shows and movies" and "garage sales." Choice (C), "used," is a participate modifying books.

6. **(A)** An infinitive, "to understand," should never be split by any adverbial modifier, "completely." Choice (B), "effects," is the noun form, and choice (D), "affected," is the adjective form. "One must," choice (C), is used in standard English.

7. **(C)** "More" is used to compare two things. Since the number of nations is not specified, "more" cannot be used in this sentence. Choice (A), "known," modifies "roads"; choice (B) is idiomatically correct; choice (D), "is," agrees in number with its subject, "transportation."

8. **(E)** Choice (A), "many a," should always be followed by the singular verb, "wishes," of choice (B). Choice (C) is idiomatically correct. In "someone else," (D), "else" is needed to indicate a person other than the student would pay the bills.

9. (D) Choice (D) should read, "became very irritated." "To aggravate" means "to make worse"; "to irritate" means "to excite to impatience or anger." A situation is "aggravated" and becomes worse, but one does not become "aggravated" with people. Choices (A), (B), and (C) are correctly-used idioms.

10. (C) The reference in choice (C) is vague because it sounds as if the bus made the two students late. Choice (A) is a correct subject pronoun; choice (B) is the correct adverb form to modify "dressed"; choice (D) is a correct object pronoun.

11. (E) Choice (A), "among," indicates choice involving more than two things. The prepositions in (B) and (C) are correct. "Are," (D), is a plural verb, agreeing in number with the compound subject "singing…dancing…cooking."

12. (A) One is "disappointed by" a person or action but "disappointed in" what is not satisfactory. "Inexpensive," (B), is the adjective form. Parallel with "to work," choice (C), "save," had the word "to" omitted. Choice (D) compares the two models, one "inexpensive" and one "more expensive."

13. (A) The verb should be plural, "are," in order to agree with the compound subject, "budget . . . plans." Choice (B) begins an infinitive phrase which includes a participle, "existing," (C). Choice (D) is idiomatically correct.

14. (A) The expression should be phrased, "as delicate as." Choice (B) uses a possessive before a gerund; choice (C) is correctly used; and choice (D) is a possessive pronoun of neuter gender which is appropriate to use in referring to a plant.

15. (D) "Because" is the correct word to use in the cause and effect relationship in this sentence. Choice (A), "being that"; choice (E), "than me"; and choice (D), "the more" are not grammatically correct. Choice (C), "is made by you," is in the passive voice and not as direct as (D).

16. (D) "After they have been" completes the proper time sequence. Choice (A), "when"; choice (B), "have been"; and choice (C), "will be," are the wrong time sequences. Choice (E), "should be," is an idea not contained in the original sentence.

17. (C) "Since the plane is late" shows correct time sequence and good reasoning. Choice (A), "seeing as how," and choice (D), "being as," are poor wording. Choices (B), "when," and (E), "while," are the wrong time, logically, to be on the observation deck.

18. (E) Since a sentence should not end with a preposition, choices (A) and (B) are eliminated. Choices (C), "living in this world," and (D),"world's living," introduce new concepts.

19. (A) The construction, "than those," clarifies the fact that more vegetables have been added. Choice (C), "your suggestion"; choice (D), "than what"; and choice (E), "which," do not contain the idea of adding more varieties of vegetables. Choice (B) ends with a preposition.

20. (B) The voice must be consistent with "I", so (B) is the only possible correct answer. All other choices have a noun or pronoun that is not consistent with "I"; choice (A), "you"; choice (C), "a person"; choice (D), "people"; and choice (E), "some."

21. (A) The correct answer has two concepts—pieces are missing and pieces will probably never be found. Choice (B) has a singular verb, "is." Choice (C) indicates the pieces "probably will be" missing, which is not the problem. Choice (D) and choice (E) both indicate the pieces are "probably" missing, which is illogical because the pieces either are or are not missing.

22. (C) General reference should be avoided. The pronoun "which" does not have a clear reference in choices (A) or (B). In (C) "which" clearly refers to "facts." The reference "proving" in choice (D) is too general. In choice (E) "a proof" is an incorrect number to refer to the two strengths of women.

23. (E) Choice (E) is clear and concise and shows the correct comparison of architecture. The antecedent of "those" in choice (A) is not clear. Choice (B) is comparing "characteristics," not just architecture. Choice (C) is awkward, and choice (D) incorrectly uses an idiom, "characteristic with."

24. (B) Choice (B) is clear and direct. Choices (A) and (E) are too wordy. Choice (C) has the wrong concept, "balancing games." Choice (D) "this as an example" is poorly worded.

25. (E) An opposing force "gives" scattered resistance; therefore, choice (A) is incorrect. Choices (B), (C), and (D) are poorly worded and do not have the correct meaning.

26. (A) Choice (A) produces a complete sentence: "rainfall" is the subject and "let up" is the verb. None of the other choices produces a complete sentence.

27. (D) This choice uses the correct tense, "will have," showing action in the future. All the other verbs listed do not show correct future verb construction.

28. (B) The correct choice has a compound verb: "comes" and "falls in love." The salesman comes to town first, then he meets and falls in love with the librarian. Choice (A), with its misplaced participial phrase, sounds as if either the town or Iowa is in love with the librarian. Choice (C) would produce a run-on sentence. Choices (D) and (E) have unclear tense.

29. (B) This question of appropriate verb tense requires the simple past tense verb "took" because the Civil War happened in a finite time period in the past. The other choices all fail that test. The original and choice (E) are present tense, and do not logically fit the facts. Choice (D) is the present perfect tense, which suggests a continuous action from the past to the present. Choice (C) is the past perfect tense, which suggests a continuing action from one time in the past to another in the more recent past.

30. (D) We can eliminate fairly quickly choices (C) and (E) as either inappropriate or awkward appositives to "ornithology," instead of "ornithologists." Neither is (A) the best choice even though some may consider it acceptable. Likewise, choice (B) tends to be limited to nonrestrictive clauses, unlike this one. Choice (D) then correctly uses a "personal" relative pronoun.

31. (D) Choices (A), (D), and (E) are the best candidates because they are more concise than the other two choices. Each does express the same idea, but (E) does not as strongly indicate the contrast between the two clauses in the sentence as do choices (A) and (D). Choice (D) clearly makes its point in fewer words and is the better choice.

32. (B) The phrase "as to" often is overblown and unclear, so it is best to eliminate it when there are other choices. Likewise, "expectability" does not exactly roll of your tongue. That leaves choices (B) and (D). Choice (D) adds a definite figure, unwarranted by the original sentence. It also is duller than (B), which does change the wording for the better and also indicates that the "actual amount" is to be announced, rather than that it is already known.

33. **(A)** Choices (C) and (E) introduce unnecessary absolute phrases beginning with "it," which makes the sentences wordy. They can be eliminated immediately. Choice (D) has an illogical comparison suggesting notes = instrument, so it, too, is not the best choice. Between (A) and (B) the difference boils down to the present tense vs. the past tense. Choice (A) uses past tenses, which seem better in sequence to follow the past tense verb "developed."

34. **(B)** Choices (A), (C), and (D) can be disqualified quickly because they are not parallel to the structure of the main clause. Choice (E) is ungainly and introduces a vague pronoun "its" (unclear antecedent). Choice (B) reads well and has the virtue of brevity.

35. **(B)** Choice (B) clears up the pronoun usage problem, eliminating the ambiguous reference of "he"; it is clear that Dickens is delighted. Choice (A) does not clearly identify the antecedent of "he." Choice (C) incorrectly identified the "delighted" person as the giver, not Dickens. Choices (D) and (E) both create fragments.

36. **(A)** Choice (A) combines all the elements correctly and uses parallel structure, creating a balanced sentence. Choice (B) is not exactly parallel, and the many commas create confusion. Choice (C) does not have parallel verbs: "wanted" and "being." Choices (D) and (E) incorrectly combine the two ideas, making it seem as if the children are blocking Grip's action.

37. **(D)** Choice (D) keeps the formal tone of the essay and avoids passive voice. Choice (A) and choice (E) both break the formal tone and use another voice: "you" and "I." Choice (B) is perhaps too formal and not straightforward. Choice (C) uses the passive voice.

38. **(E)** Choice (E) smoothly combines both major ideas as a cause-and-effect sequence. Choice (A) is the next best choice, but it is not as smoothly worded in the first half; also, this choice eliminates the idea of "use" in the second half. Choice (B) does not clarify the source of Poe's dissatisfaction. Choice (C) does not clearly present the idea that the prophetic use was Poe's, not Dickens'. Choice (D) has too many interruptions.

39. **(A)** Choice (A) is correct; the paragraph gives information on the origin of the bird. Although the paragraph gives one or two humorous incidents, choice (B) cannot be the main intention. Choice (C) is unlikely; the bird's biting is presented as more humorous than tragic. Choice (D) would be a more effective label for paragraph two. Choice (E) is partly correct, but the second paragraph returns to the Dickens' household.

INDEX

Averages
mean, 213, 254, 256
median, 254–255
mode, 255, 257–258
Regular Math questions on, 373–374

B

Bad/badly, use of, 486
Base
exponents, 250
trapezoid, 325
Basic Math Skills Review
algebra questions (*see* Algebra questions, Basic Math Skills Review)
arithmetic questions (*see* Arithmetic questions, Basic Math Skills Review)
briefly described, 6–7, 212
formulas, 213
geometry questions (*see* Geometry questions, Basic Math Skills Review)
reference table, 213
symbols and their meanings, 213
word problems (*see* Word questions, Basic Math Skills Review)
Basic Verbal Skills Review
briefly described, 6, 78–79
Critical Reading questions (*see* Critical Reading questions)
drills, 115–125
Sentence Completion questions (*see* Sentence Completion questions)
Vocabulary Enhancer, words and drills (*see* Vocabulary Enhancer, words and drills)
word parts, 104–114
prefixes, 105–107
roots, 108–113
suffixes, 113–114
Binomial, 262

C

Calculator, use of, 370, 379
Cartesian coordinate plane, 340
Central angle, circle, 332
Chord, circle, 332
Circle(s), 331–338
area of, 213
circumference of, 213
defined, 331
types of, 333
Circumference, computing, 213
Circumscribed circle, 333
Coefficient, 262
Colons, 496–498
Comma splices, 468–469

Commas, use of
in abbreviations after names, 492
in dates, 494
and direct address, 492
and geographical names and addresses, 492
with interjections, 492
with introductory phrases, 490–491
with nonrestrictive elements, 493
with parenthetical words and phrases, 493
to separate sentences with two main ideas, 491–492
in a series, 490
to set off contrasting elements, 494
to set off direct quotations, 494
with subordinate clauses, 494–495
in tag questions, 492
with transitional words and phrases, 493
and unusual word order, 493
Comparisons
faulty, adjectives and adverbs, 487–488
of numbers containing decimals, 235, 239–240
Complementary angles, 302
Completing the squares, quadratic equations, 284–285
Complex fractions, 225
Concentric circles, 333
Conciseness, 463
Conditional inequality, 291
Congruent angles, 302
Congruent circles, 333
Connotative word meanings, 462–463
Consecutive angles, parallelogram, 323
Consecutive integers, 214, 408–409
Constant, 262
Context clues, 130–131
Coordinate geometry, 340–344
Coordination, 469–470
Correlative conjunctions, parallelism, 466
Critical Reading questions
answering
key words, 168
order of, 168
practice in, 169–176
question stems, 168
briefly described, 5, 158–159
detailed explanations, 197–210
directions, 159
drill, 177–196
passages
briefly described, 5, 159
humanities, 159–160
narrative dealing with fictional materials, 163–166
natural science, 162–163
social science, 161
points to remember, 167
questions
types of, 159, 166–167
evaluation, 166

Right triangle, 316, 317–320
Roots
    quadratic equations, 283
    as word parts, 108–113
Run-on sentences, 468

S

Scalene triangle, 315
Scoring
    conversion table, 12
    overview, 7
    practice test, 7
    worksheet, 7–8
Scrolling, 139
Secant, circle, 331
Semicolons, 495–496
Sense, inequalities, 292
Sentence Completion questions
    answering
        context clues, 130–131
        etymology, 139–140
        scrolling, 139
        word values, 131–138
    answer key, 148
    briefly described, 5
    deductive reasoning, application of, 128
    detailed explanations, 149–156
    directions for, 128–129
    drill, 140–147
    one-word completions, 129
    questions, types of, 129
    points to remember, 129–130
    two-word completions, 129
    vocabulary, importance of, 128
Sentences
    identifying errors in, 6, 439–442
    improving, 443–449
Sentence structure skills
    comma splices, 468–469
    drills, 470–471
    fragments, 468
    misplaced and dangling modifiers, 466–467
    parallelism, 465–466
    run-on/fused sentences, 468
    subordination, coordination, and predication, 469–470
Set
    defined, 358
    in word problems, 358–359
Similar triangles, 317, 321–322
Simple interest
    defined, 213
    in word problems, 353–355
Simplification
    arithmetic expressions, 403
    exponents, 253–254

    fractions, 225, 399–400
Single quotation marks, 500
Slang, 500
Solids
    cube, 213
    rectangular, 338–339
Solution
    equations in general, 271
    quadratic equations, 283
Sort of/kind of, use of, 486
Split infinitives, 467
Square
    area of, 213, 325
    defined, 325
    perimeter of, 213
Square root, 246
Squinting modifier, 467
Straight angle, 301
Student-Produced Response questions
    algebra questions, 404–409
    answering, 417
    arithmetic questions, 398–403
    briefly described, 5, 396
    detailed explanations, 429–435
    directions for, 396–398
    drill, 418–424
    drill answer key, 425–428
    geometry questions, 409–416
    points to remember, 416
    questions, types of, 398
Student Search Service (SSS), 3, 12
Studying for the test, 4, 8–9
Subject-verb agreement, 473–476
Subjunctive mood, 472
Subordination, 469–470
Substitution, for solving linear equations with two
        unknown variables, 276
Subtraction
    equations, 271, 276
    fractions, 224, 228, 231
    linear equations with two unknown variables, 276
    numbers containing decimals, 235, 237–238
    polynomials, 262, 265
    positive and negative numbers, 217
    radicals, 247, 250
Suffixes, 113–114
Supplementary angles, 302
Synonyms, 131
Synthesis/analysis questions, 166

T

Taking the test, 3–4, 8–9
Tense, verbs, 471–472
Term, 262
Terminating decimal, 233